FURTHER ON, NOTHING

D1603072

FURTHER ON, NOTHING

Tadeusz Kantor's Theatre

MICHAL KOBIALKA

University of Minnesota Press

Minneapolis

London

The University of Minnesota Press gratefully acknowledges financial assistance provided by the Kosciuszko Foundation, Inc., New York, NY, for the publication of
this book.

"My Work—My Journey," "Reality of the Lowest Rank," "The Informel: Terms
and Definitions," "The Emballage," "The Impossible Theatre," "Silent Night," and
"From the Beginning My Credo Was . . ." were previously published in Tadeusz Kan-
tor's A Journey through Other Spaces, 1944–1990, and appears here courtesy of University of California Press. "Memory" was previously published in Soviet and East
European Performance 11, no. 1 (Spring 1991): 19–28, and appear here courtesy of
SEEP. "To Save from Oblivion" and "The Real 'I'" appeared in PAJ: A Journal of
Performance Art 38 (1991). "My Meetings with Death" and "A Short History of My
Life" appeared in PAJ: A Journal of Performance Art 47 (1994). "The Informel Theatre," "The Zero Theatre," "A Room. Maybe a New Phase," "Prison," "The Au-
tonomous Theatre," and "Reflection" appeared in The Drama Review 111 (1986).
"My Room" and "A Painting" appeared in "Spatial Representations: Tadeusz Kan-
tor's Theatre of Found Reality," Theatre Journal 44 (1992): 329–56.

Published by the University of Minnesota Press
111 Third Avenue South, Suite 290
Minneapolis, MN 55401-2520
http://www.upress.umn.edu

Library of Congress Cataloging-in-Publication Data

Kobialka, Michal.
  Further on, nothing : Tadeusz Kantor's theatre / Michal Kobialka.
    p. cm.
  Includes bibliographical references. ISBN 978-0-8166-5480-2 (hc : alk. paper)—
ISBN 978-0-8166-5481-9 (pb : alk. paper)
    1. Kantor, Tadeusz, 1915–1990. 2. Theatrical producers and directors—Poland—
Biography. 3. Experimental theater—Poland. I. Title.
  PN2859.P66K3665 2009
  792.02'33092—dc22
  [B]   2009005236

Printed in the United States of America on acid-free paper

The University of Minnesota is an equal-opportunity educator and employer.

15 14 13 12 11 10 09   10 9 8 7 6 5 4 3 2 1

Contents

Preface

FORGET KANTOR

I thought that the obsessive nature of my real and imaginary encounters with Tadeusz Kantor (1915–1990), Polish visual artist, theatre director, designer, writer, and theoretician, would come to a halt with the publication of my book on Kantor's theatre, *A Journey through Other Spaces* (1993), and my essay, "Forget Kantor" (1994), which were an attempt to close that chapter of my academic life.[1] By the end of the essay, however, it became clear to me that forgetting, like Kantor's Emballage, could only shelter, protect, and preserve—thus restore—his material and immaterial contours, which would always escape me and the passage of time.[2]

Many impulses led to the writing of this book. Among them, the conflation of several anniversaries connected with Tadeusz Kantor may be the most relevant. The fiftieth anniversary of the founding of Cricot 2 Theatre took place in 2005, as did the thirtieth anniversary of *The Dead Class*, the twenty-fifth anniversary of *Wielopole, Wielopole*, the twentieth anniversary of *Let the Artists Die*, and the fifteenth anniversary of Tadeusz Kantor's death. Thinking about these events as well as a quickly approaching twentieth anniversary of Kantor's death in 2010 prompted me not only to revisit Kantor's writings and his productions with Cricot 2 Theatre but also to revise and reevaluate my own thinking about the theatrical phenomenon I had been writing and talking about for over twenty years.

Today, there is also another reason why a book about Kantor's theatre practice should be written. We are living in a time of global (cultural and political) wars. The existing conditions call for political theatre that will challenge globalization of the image in service of capital and culture industry, a belief that modern technological society based on a narrative of progress will create a bright future, or a rationalization justifying violence as indispensable in the mission of bringing liberty and democracy to the non-Western world. The modernist models for political theatre that we have and refer to—Erwin Piscator's political theatre (1920), Bertolt Brecht's epic theatre (1930), or Augusto Boal's theatre of the oppressed (1972), for example—have outlived their promise to give us an alternative representational praxis that could challenge the existing cultural or political regimes. They did so because the revolutions Piscator, Brecht, and Boal supported, or desired to start, had long lost their immanent presence and their words had long lost their radical attributes. In this age of global wars and globalization by liberal capitalism, it is necessary to revitalize the debate on the nature of political theatre. Kantor, in an uncanny way and, let me suggest, in an idiosyncratic manner, put forward proposals and a theatre praxis that could assist us both directly and indirectly in this evaluation of the utopian project of modernity—that project, which is today grounded in the ever-changing and chaotic reality, at once harmonious and conflicting, shaped by individual desires and geopolitical dynamics. Indeed, Kantor created a praxis that was not lodged on a smooth surface of the shown or the seen, or in the consensual or the salvific function of theatre to express oneself, but a praxis that went beyond the "ordinary" realm of established interests and differences, beyond the "ordinary" realm of approved knowledge, beyond the "ordinary" realm of the desire for the *jouissance* of prelapserian times, and beyond the "ordinary" realm of theoretical innovations that persist only through the proclamations of those who position themselves as the subjects of a marketable truth. No matter how hard we try to gloss this praxis over with words of nostalgia or neoliberal imaginary, even today, almost twenty years after his death, it carries this promise and radical potential for giving shape to the not-yet imagined realm—the promise of a theatre that is an answer to reality rather than a representation of its utopian alternative. His theatre, as I will argue, is *in* reality, but not *of* it—a phrase used by Alain Badiou to define the ethics of a radical event.[3] Kantor's is a theatre that opens up the potential for a radical repositioning of both the dominant representational practices as well as the idea of political theatre by exposing history and politics caught in the act of inventing forms of presentation of the events:

1 9 1 4

World War I.
Millions of corpses
in the absurd hecatomb.
After the War:
old powers were abolished;
generals' ranks, medals, and epaulets
monarchs' crowns
were thrown into the garbage cans;
Fatherlands went bankrupt;
nationalism turned out to be nothing more than a base primitive instinct.
In the context of such a colossal ignominy in the world, which up till that time
forced us to acknowledge its existence as the only judicially permissible one, the
attitude of the Dadaists was a healthy action and reaction:
DERISION,
DISREGARD,
MUTINY,
PROTEST,
NEGATION,
BLASPHEMY,
SACRILEGE of all the SHRINES,
QUESTIONING of all social values. . . .
A quarter of a century passed.
World War II.

Genocide,
Concentration Camps,
Crematories,
Human Beasts,
Death,
Tortures,
Human kind turned into mud, soap, and ashes,
Debasement,
The time of contempt. . . .
And this is my (and our) answer:
THERE IS NO WORK OF ART . . .
THERE IS NO "HOLY" ILLUSION,
THERE IS NO "HOLY" PERFORMANCE.
THERE IS ONLY AN OBJECT WHICH IS TORN OUT OF
LIFE AND REALITY . . .
THERE IS NO ARTISTIC PLACE . . .
THERE IS ONLY REAL PLACE . . .
ARTISTIC ATTITUDE IS DESCRIBED BY:
PROTEST,
MUTINY,
BLASPHEMY AND SACRILEGE OF SANCTIONED
SHRINES.[4]

This passage is as a summary par excellence of Kantor's attitude toward the events that surrounded him or his commitment to being *in* reality but not *of* it. To express this, Kantor created a theatre where he renounced the conventional categories of illusion and representation. In their place, he offered an object wrenched from the dominant representational practices; real, rather than a theatrical, performance place; and the annexed reality, where he "staged" his theatre experiments between 1944 and 1973 as well as talked about the need for ethical self-examination, or, to use Kantor's expression, where he "presented" his theatre of personal confessions: *The Dead Class*; *Wielopole, Wielopole*; *Let the Artists Die*; *I Shall Never Return*; and *Today Is My Birthday*. In all of these, political narrative address and current historical events coalesce to show the fissures in a traditional construction of meanings and symbols associated with national life.

Furthermore, looking back at Kantor's theatre practice and his writings, I want to explore further his relationship to what we call today postmodern practice or theory, which has had an impact on academe and the culture industry for the last four decades. Even though Hans-Thies Lehmann seems to address this issue by discussing Kantor's works in his recent *Postdramatic Theatre* in terms of a "theatre of states" and "scenically dynamic formations," these postdramatic categories locate Kantor's practice within traditional dramatic theatre conditions—that is to say, a theatre grounded in representational practices that evoke Greek tragedy (a theatre marked by the terror of past occurrences and their ghostly returns), or a theatre "after" a catastrophe, or a ceremony of the dead, or a feeling of failure and defeat.[5] I wish to argue, however, that Kantor's theatre was a radical departure from, or rupture within, the normative representational theatrical categories or structures. Kantor's theatre created a possibility of seeing what cannot really be grasped or understood because in its most concrete stage form it shows "nothing" or, at best, nostalgia for the impossible. Could it be that Kantor's theatre with its components, such as a poor or real object, reality of the lowest rank, an autonomous work of art, zero zones, the impossible condition, the complex mnemotechnics, and an Emballage, which were given different shapes and meanings depending on the pressures of the historical, cultural, and ideological networks of relations within which Kantor found himself positioned, elaborated an initial forgetting, that forgetting which was so poignantly described by Jean-François Lyotard on the pages of *The Postmodern Explained*?[6] Could it be that Kantor shed light on marginalized objects and everyday practices that were pushed aside by reality that was given meaning and right to exist by representation affirming life and its triad of *spatial practice* (perceived), which embraces the production and reproduction of each social formation; *representation of space* (conceived), which are linked to knowledge production; and *representational spaces* (lived), which form all senses and all bodies?[7]

The more I think and write about Kantor's theatre, the more I am intrigued by a proposition that Kantor, the high modernist by birth and practice, gave material form to a praxis that indeed perturbed the existing order of things— to a praxis that defined the very mode of postmodern operation and many of its theoretical notions still in circulation: an *anamnesis* that elaborates an initial forgetting induced by the languages of intelligibility; a *heterotopia* that is a countersite to the real site in which the rules of the real site are recognized, contested, and reversed; a *cairological* time that liberates a human being from servitude to continuous linear time and allows him or her, by his or her initiative, to grasp favorable opportunity; and a process of *deterritorializing* representation that challenges official art or mass culture.

Kantor's theatre was a testimony to his heterology: a practice of enunciating his own historicity in the encounter with the Other, defined not as a subject or an object but as a historically and ideologically structured field of perception. Kantor's theatre was, on the one hand, a tactical maneuver within a stable field of recognized forms and practices:

> The 1940s . . . 50s . . . 60s . . . 70s . . . have passed.
> Artistic ideas have been breaking the surface,
> however, all the time, as if from far beyond, maybe, it was my inner voice, I have been perceiving warning signals that ordered me and dictated that I choose one action over the other—
> PROTEST,
> REVOLT
> AGAINST THE OFFICIALLY RECOGNIZED SACRED SITES,
> AGAINST EVERYTHING THAT HAD A STAMP OF "APPROVAL,"
> FOR REALNESS,
> FOR "POVERTY. . . ."[8]

On the other hand, Kantor's theatre ruptured the modernist discourse, of which it was a part, in order to repoliticize its radical agenda at the time when

radical metanarratives were turned into failing ideologies (bureaucratic socialism, for example) and when late capitalism was situated as a desired option for
the development of civil society based on free market, highly developed technologies, and democratic institutions.

To substantiate this last point, consider briefly Fredric Jameson's *A Singular
Modernity*, which posits "modernity" as a social ideal and reconstructs that historical situation of "modernity" in which artistic modernism can be grasped as
an intelligible social process, rather than the stereotypical picture that features
the modern artist as outsider and rebel or marginal and renegade.[9] In this intelligible social process, it is the economy itself that determines the recognizable
tropes of modernity: a concrete autonomization of the aesthetics and language,
the loss of representational reality, and depersonalization or desubjectification.
What is important for Jameson is a distinction between those modernist artists
who functioned within the emerging framework of industrialization, immense
new social forces, political suffrage, and anarchist forces and who might have
either occupied the same space as these forces or reviewed them from a distance,
on the one hand, and, on the other, those modernist artists who could theorize
about the modernist transformation and its basic political and social program
in the form of aesthetics codified as an ideology of modernism.

If such a distinction is tangible, Kantor would belong to both of these categories at the same time, and his theatre practice would be an example par
excellence of the tropes of modernity. Chapter 1, "Topography of Representation," will discuss Kantor's playing with these tropes while drawing attention
to his stagings of the plays of Stanisław Ignacy Witkiewicz (Witkacy), which
culminated in the restaging of *The Water-Hen* as Theatre-Happening and the
production of *Dainty Shapes and Hairy Apes* as the Impossible Theatre, the last
transformation in Kantor's theory of the "Reality of the Lowest Rank," as well
as Kantor's experiments with the Autonomous, Informel, and Zero theatres.
Each one of them was a concrete autonomization of the aesthetics and language, a *punctum* in representational reality, and brought forth depersonalization or desubjectification. Ultimately, Kantor's rip across the traditional idea of
representation and interpretation not only denatured theatre, as we still know
it today, but also insisted that it be a place

> like a *catastrophe* happening unexpectedly to the canvas, inside figurative or
> probabilistic data. It is like the emergence of another world. For these marks
> or brushstrokes are irrational, involuntary, accidental, free, and random. They
> are nonrepresentative, nonillustrative, and nonnarrative. No longer are they
> significant or signifying: they are asignifying features. They are features of
> sensation, but of confused sensation. And above all they are manual features. . . .
> These almost blind, manual marks reveal the intrusion of another world into the
> visual world of figuration.[10]

This catastrophe, in Kantor's vocabulary, was the process of annexing reality—
that reality that could no longer be appropriated by a hegemonic constellation.
Within this reality, he sought his places of the lowest rank—a bombed room,
a café, a wardrobe, a poorhouse, a cloakroom—which depreciated the value

of reality through exploring degraded objects, matter, marginalized objects, everyday realness, or self-enclosed actions.

In the process of dismantling illusion and traditional theatrical conventions, Kantor created his own theatrical space that produced its own commentary and referential body in the process of folding back upon itself. Thus, in the process, which was so aptly described by Artaud in *Theatre and Its Double*, of destroying the organs without killing the body, Kantor did indeed deterritorialize representation.[11] But repetition is a presence born to itself. Despite his desire to sustain a creative act as dynamic endgame of materializing theatre from whatever it is not, the organs created their own body. Kantor, who frequently admonished the avant-garde for selling out to the museum market and the gallery markets, was acutely aware of the possibility of falling into the trap of culture industry. Hoping to circumvent it, he often altered the terms and conditions of his practice:

FURTHER ON, NOTHING!

I left all the road signs
behind me.
I felt anger against
history,
trends,
stages,
theories.[12]

This cry, "Further on, Nothing," repeated many times in Kantor's life, expressed his need and desire not to fall into the trap of the "official" history or "accepted" artistic trends critiqued by him in Lesson 12 of *The Milano Lessons*.[13] This cry, almost a slogan, can also explain the shifts and transformations both in the style of his visual works and in the production of Cricot 2 Theatre that took place when Kantor believed that their radical or transformative potential was lost or in the process of being diminished. The entropic quality of this praxis, which, while it lasted was a powerful means of an answer to, rather than representation of, reality, was one of the reasons why Kantor abandoned this project for the Theatre of Intimate Commentaries—*The Dead Class, Wielopole, Wielopole, Let the Artists Die, I Shall Never Return*, and *Today Is My Birthday*—materializing not only theatre from whatever it is not, but also, and maybe more important, the anguish of perceivedness and verbal hallucinations filling the sight by force. This anguish of perceivedness and verbal hallucinations is the subject of chapters 2 ("Spatial Historiography: *The Dead Class*"), 3 ("Theatre of Similitude"), 4 ("Spatial Historiography: Silent Night"), and 5 ("The Space of Khora").

These productions could indeed support Jameson's tropes of singular modernity if it were not for the fact that Kantor's theatre was never stable in its dramaturgical or representational designs as evidenced by the subsequent shifts in the history of Cricot 2 punctuated by the manifestos of the Autonomous Theatre, the Zero Theatre, the Informel Theatre, the Theatre-Happening, the Impossible Theatre, The Theatre of Death, and of the Theatre of Intimate Commentaries. The productions themselves were also always in flux due to Kantor's presence onstage during the performance. Going beyond the apocryphal stories about Kantor changing the order of scenes while a production was in progress, it is worth remembering that these shifts and transformations were due to his understanding of theatre as a space that was not a passive receptacle (Kazimir Malevich) but a network of specifiable and differential relationships (Michel Foucault; Henri Lefebvre). If theatre is a network of specifiable and differential relationships, thus, Kantor's presence onstage as well as his interaction with the actors in, for example, *I Shall Never Return* (1988), can be seen as a practice that gave visibility and materiality to the invisible thought, to the inside of the unrepresentable outside, and to the fold through which the outside comes into being to disrupt the history of forms.

Taking a cue from Gilles Deleuze, it can be said that Kantor visualized onstage what postmodern theory included in its narrative: a tactic of exposing the dominant representational practices that desire to freeze the gesture of thinking in order to communicate what escapes us in the commemorative procedures of history. Kantor constructed a field in which objects (both mythical and histori-cal) were wrestled from the "proper" meanings assigned to them by tradition and ideology. Once the performance space was separated from the auditorium by a rope in *The Dead Class*, the spectator could no longer see his or her image reflected in three-dimensional theatrical space or *construzione legittima*, but found himself or herself in the presence of what could not be organized into an epistemological unit by a historical or religious reference code. Try to imagine the movement of Kantor's thought that is materialized onstage. Rather than crossing the line of force to stage an attack, it bends the force and makes it im-pinge on itself once it encounters the "impassable barrier" Kantor presented us with in *The Dead Class*. The movement of Kantor's thought visualized onstage expressed a mode of intensity that, with the help of the object onstage, thinks its own "history (the past), but [it does so] in order to free itself from what it thinks (the present) and be able finally to think otherwise (the future)."[14]

Maybe, to paraphrase Kantor, this repetition will force us to abandon our pious vision of the events that protect our consciousness from doubt. Maybe this repetition is a procedure of anamnesis that elaborates an initial forgetting, prompted by the words delimiting the contours of silence. Maybe, while writing about theatre or performance, we will be able to acknowledge the presence of the Other who makes us enunciate our historicity in the moment of utterance.

Thus, since Kantor's productions never adhered to a linear progression of dramaturgical time but, through the use of repetition and echo, warped linear time, it could be suggested that Kantor presented us with cairological time, dis-rupting a smooth mimetic surface and liberating a human to think a thought anew as if in relation not to the preestablished conventions and categories but in relation to other objects in the field of perception. This differential specificity, in which a thought is rearticulated, perturbs the order and the regime of truth in his-tory or in culture industry. Examples of this practice abound in many of Kantor's productions from *The Return of Odysseus* (1944), the Happenings (1965–69), and the theatre of memory (1975–90) to the *Silent Night* cricotage (1990).

Kantor defined theatre as an activity that occurs if life is pushed to its final limits, where all categories and concepts lose their meaning and right to exist. Maybe such a definition and a description of the function of theatre will return us to the radical project and design for the fine arts as envisioned by both modernist and postmodern thinkers. Kantor's theatre practice revealed what had been initially forgotten or glossed over, named this void that comes into being as a sign of a radical innovation, and was a visual elaboration as well as materialization of a belief that "it is a part of morality not to be at home at one's home," shared by the modernists and postmodernists.[15]

"It is a part of morality not to be at home in one's home" is a reminder that each of us has an ethical responsibility to evaluate the structures of belonging grounding us in our "home." Kantor accomplished this moving through the aporias of his time and space. His theatre praxis opened up the potential for a radical repositioning of both a thought and a "home." My encounter with Kantor here registers my movement through the aporias of this time and this space.

This is why this book should not be read as an archival gesture or as a site to be "mined" for information about Kantor and his theatre. Rather, its every chapter is my attempt to align and realign myself and my thinking with Kantor's theatre, postmodern theory, and politics in order to remain faithful to the "further on, nothing" principle. This current singular restaging of Kantor in the twenty-first century, followed by old and new translations of Kantor's theoretical writings, are an exploration of the issues of visibility and visualism as well as of the utopian project and the struggle to negotiate with the deconstruction of memory, politics, and the cultural imaginary. When this strategy is coupled with philosophy of historiography, the resultant work, challenging a disciplinary divide, is a response to the current debates about the contested nature of representation, memory, and history. It is my hope that this book will be seen as a performance of the complex palimpsest of Kantor's work and my encounter with this work. This performance is the other discourse, or the other space, which does not belong to the holder of discourse or the holder of its representation; that is, it belongs neither to Kantor and the objects of his creation nor to my framed narratives. This other discourse, containing it all, makes the formation of thinking otherwise possible and turns attention to the mode of historicity, which exposes preestablished rules and categories that simulate presence or materiality. The task is to go beyond the ontologies of the present, which demand archaeologies of the future, as Jameson would have it, and attend to the now—an ethical gesture based upon a provisional and positional maneuver that will always be in reality but not of it.

And one more thing:

In front of us,
in this poor and dusky room,
behind the doors,
a storm and a inferno rage,
and the waters of the flood rise.
The weak walls of our ROOM;
of our everyday or
linear time
will not save us. . . .
Important events stand behind the doors
it is enough to open them. . . .[16]

Acknowledgments

"Further on, Nothing," as Tadeusz Kantor noted in one of his essays, was a phrase that accompanied him at various crossroads, and, no matter how seductive was its tone to abandon the journey, it also pointed to new thoughts, new directions, new people, and new theatre practices. Beyond and above its significance for Kantor, this phrase has haunted me over the last twenty years during my encounters with his writings, his productions, and the people with whom he was closely associated.

I would like to express my gratitude to all those people who offered their individual support to this project.

I would like to thank Maria Stangret-Kantor and Dorota Krakowska for their generous permission to use Kantor's writings and visual art and Anna Halczak from the Cricoteka Archives for her patience and continuous assistance. Special words of recognition should go to the photographers, or their representatives, who agreed to have their works published in this volume: Jacquie Bablet, Caroline Rose, Wojciech Plewiński, Jacek Stokłosa, Romano Martinis, Maciej Sochor, Leszek Dziedzic, Bruno Wagner, Wiesław Borowski, Teresa Chrzanowska, Tomisław Piotr Wasilewicz, and Jaromir Jedliński from the Galeria Foksal, and Natalia Zarzecka from the Cricoteka Archives. Also, I would like to thank the editorial staff of the University of Minnesota Press, headed by Jason Weidemann, for bringing this project to fruition and Henry Whitney from Scribe for a careful reading of the manuscript.

My thinking about Kantor's theatre could develop and take its shape thanks to Richard Gough, Bonnie Marranca, Marcia de Barros, and Hamed Taheri as well as Kathy Biddick and Daniel Watt, who, each in his or her own way, created for me a space, either physical or intellectual, where I could explore the ephemeral contours of Kantor's theatre "pushed to its final limits, where all categories and concepts lose their meaning and right to exist."

In my quest to find a form, which would best describe Tadeusz Kantor's nuanced understanding of theatre, I am particularly indebted to Herbert Blau, who taught me over the years how to avoid the vanities of theatre deceiving us with its ambitions and promises to represent what it is not; to Charles Nolte for his relentless passion for theatre and his courage to support what perturbs the known, the seen, and the accepted; and to Rosemarie Bank, Aleksandra Wolska, and Michael Lupu, who accompanied me on this journey through other spaces, for their perceptive criticism of my writings, editorial suggestions, and their insightful comments.

Dorit Cypis, Joanie Smith, Lynne Kirby, Neil Sieling, Keya Ganguly, Tim Brennan, Joanna and Andrzej Piotrowski, Beata Chmielewska, and Marek Kobiałka encouraged me to pursue this project at its precipitous crossroads—I am grateful to them for their support. I thank my parents, Wanda and Wiesław Kobiałka, for the early lesson in perseverance.

It was my good fortune that I had the opportunity to spend time while working on this book project with Ludmiła Ryba, who is among a select few keeping the traces of Tadeusz Kantor's memory alive, and Tim Heitman, whose unfailing patience and words let me proceed further and further on.

My Work—My Journey
(1988)

It is not easy for me to explain today that strange and remarkable time
after the war, that time still full of painful war memories, and yet one
in which I felt as though reborn. Today, it seems to me that the sun was
shining day and night during all those years of my, as it were, second
childhood.
My whole life was still ahead of me.
Standing at the threshold of my future, I was faced with its "infinity";
its e n d l e s s n e s s !
I rushed into this future with my eyes wide open and with the feeling
of "greatness" in my knapsack. If, on the next pages, you see a huge
rucksack on the shoulders of a poor individual, it will be my rucksack
with my greatness in it; the individual will be me.
I did not "retouch" my "Self-portrait" hurriedly as others did; nor did I
engrave my "image" in stone.
I felt already then that individuality was grounded neither in form nor in
stylistic gesture.
I did not "retouch" my facial features, so my portrait could later be
carried via proper channels straight into a museum.
I felt that this would be too simple and too false.
I knew that my "individuality" and my truth were to be found farther off,
that it would take me a long time to reach them, that *this journey and its
unforeseen obstacles*, rather than form, would ultimately shape me and
my "image."
In this period, in this pre-history of mine, I want to rediscover the
symptoms, *which like signs*, pointed me in the direction of the R O A D I
would travel on my JOURNEY, which was about to begin.

MY EARLY PAINTINGS

What I was painting then seemed to be close to a fairly safe kind of
painting. But this resemblance was illusory. More important was what I
"could not" do. For example, when I was painting "People Seated at a
Table," I could never have put a tablecloth or a basket with fruit on the
table. Flowers were out of the question, too. It was not a feast. The tables
were empty. Under the increasing number of layers of paint, the figures

1

began to resemble cardboard models. The colors faded. There was no illusion of air, but a hard, dry MATTER in which everything was slowly submerged. There was no "life's happiness." Nor was there any support from or in abstract speculations. I thought that I lacked the skill. I was suffering. However, I think that this experience was "necessary"; that this dry MATTER expressed something that refused to be perceived as purity of abstraction, or as sensuality of color. I could not discard the human figure, however. Its presence was important and indispensable. I must have seen beyond it a territory and reality, which I wanted to reach. I felt the need for a sphere which would expand beyond the boundaries of form and beyond the material surface of painting.

WORK

In 1946 and 1947, my paintings represented different types of work. Physical work done by women. "Washer-women," "Ironing-Women." Subtlety and physical brutality. Subtlety, even though those women were hardly subtle—being exhausted by work.
I had not expected that this subject-matter would soon become the officially legitimized subject. I managed to escape this appropriation. However, how can one explain an interest in this subject-matter shown by an individual with rather poor health, whose imagination had successfully "detached" him from mundane everyday concerns?
I can probably find an explanation . . . in the Gospels. "By the sweat of your brow." Both art and the Gospels have their roots in deep layers of existence.
EXISTENCE. At last, I have found the key-word,
which will explain a lot about my later JOURNEY.
And one more thing:
a word, WORK, sounds like one of the s i g n s, which I have just mentioned.
WORK and POVERTY. Inseparable.
Later on my ROAD, I will encounter the POOR theatre,
and "an object which was deprived of its function and purpose in life," whose "poverty" would allow it to become a "work of art."
AN OBJECT SUSPENDED "BETWEEN GARBAGE AND ETERNITY."
But this will come later, much later. . . .

METAMORPHOSES

1947.
A crucial year.
A year of radical decisions.
The image of a human being, which up till then was regarded as the only truth-telling representation, disappears.
Instead, there gradually emerge biological forms of a lower kind, almost animals, with few remaining traces of their past "humanity," or perhaps,

a few traces foreshadowing their humanity.
Let there begin a new cycle of creation.
Maybe, it will be successful this time!
Mine was not a manifestation of an avant-garde rebellion against the
traditional image of the human being.
The act of deforming classical beauty, for me,
did not take place in the territory of aesthetic categories.
The time of war and the time of the "lords of the world" made me lose
my trust in the old image, which had been perfectly formed,
raised above all other, apparently lower, species.
It was a discovery! Behind the sacred icon, a b e a s t was hiding.
This is an explanation I can offer today.
This was the explanation I offered in the post-war period.
I still remember the dislike and indifference I felt toward all those human
images that populated museum walls, staring at me innocently, as if
nothing had happened, while they were playing, dancing, feasting, and
posing. I was searching feverishly for another world and another space.
I was proud of myself to have seen "d i f f e r e n t l y" those dogmatic,
biblical days of "Genesis."
A distrust of the allegedly "higher forms" of the human species and
civilization was steadily growing in me.
So was an inner imperative to descend into
the deeper and lower layers of nature;
of nature and of the human condition.

If the truth be told,
it was not easy.
I needed to overcome
multiple obstacles.
The biggest of these was the
consciousness which
had been formed by many years of practice.
The down side of this otherwise valued virtue
is its inclination toward orthodoxy.
Because I have decided
not to hide anything,
I have to admit that there were
moments when I lost my
faith in the things to come.
FURTHER ON, NOTHING!
This cry will be
repeated many a time
in my life.
Moments of doubt.
But the act of repeating this
"nihilistic" cry,
gives me strength.

Despair always changes for me into
enormous strength.
One must not give up!

INFERNO

As early as 1947, I had anticipated my "descent" into the Inferno,
my crossing of the River Styx. The Land of the Dead.
In 1947, I stopped at the threshold, as if I were afraid to lose this precious
image of a human being, which I had just gained.
And the moment did arrive, when I decided to go over the threshold.
Going through this unknown passage, I tried to keep the memory of the
shape of a human body. And then everything was but MOTION and
MATTER.
Inferno. It was my "I N T E R I O R,"
where all passions, desires, emotions, despair, ecstasy, regrets, nostalgia,
memory, and flying thoughts kept swirling and crashing into each other.
This place was both a volcano, a battlefield, and an eremitical cell filled
with fervent prayers.
So far, I have only talked about an IMAGE, that image, which was the
secretion of my INTERIOR,
an image, rather than a "r e p r e s e n t a t i o n," almost a biological
substance of my organism.
I can no longer see the shape of the human body. I can no longer see the
external shape, which has always been identified with l i f e.
Life itself has become suspect; all too often its essence has been
oversimplified or reduced to a banal slogan.
I can feel the breath of death, the Belle Dame, as Gordon Craig referred to
her. Is it not She perhaps who rules art. . . .
The lack of life—life which was oversimplified by Naturalism [realism]
and materialism—the lack of "commands" sent by our brain, that part of
us which produces "rational" actions.
This "lack," which at first seemed blasphemous, has become the principle
article of faith.
I have experienced forces "from the other side" which roiled the
"smooth" surface of my IMAGE.
I began to feel that MATTER and "ASHES," scattered around by the
winds of COINCIDENCE, are the LAST SHAPE OF A HUMAN BEING,
his infernal image.
Before everything disintegrates, let me talk about the last trace:
CONSTRUCTION,
a sacred principle upon which, as until then I used to believe, the whole
world rested;
A rational, and even worse than that, practical process;
a device used to hold a creation together;
a warranty of its "s o l i d   e x i s t e n c e";
a guarantee of "solidness"; an almost industrial product.

And one more thing:
[Construction] produced works of art the value and success of which were
determined by the LOOK of the END-PRODUCT.
After that they could only be CONSUMED.
How totally insignificant this practice seemed to me in comparison
with the elements of the INFERNO-INTERIOR, with THE ACT OF
CREATION which is INFINITE!
INFERNO—a constant MOTION, out of which there emerges life in its
pure form, life which is pulsating, erupting, and bereft of any practical
purpose,
life, which is subject to a never ending process of
d e s t r u c t i o n and rebirth.
How indifferent I was, in this period of my bold discoveries, when I was
passing all those magnificent museum canvases which enclosed themselves
in their framed perfection.
How many defeats did I suffer, when my paintings, which had been born
out of this irrational idea, enclosed themselves in their frames only to
d i e.
I should have destroyed and buried those "dead corpses" of my works,
or hung them as funeral banners. I did not do that. Was I not radical
enough? I do not know. It was enough that I was left with a "message"
from "the other side of Styx" and an awareness of an imperishable
reminder.
DEATH would always appear in moments like this. She would try to give
me some warning signs. She would advise me against hasty decisions and
"temporary" solutions.
As she would say, I was destined for more shattering experiences
with her at my side.
I felt it was necessary to "salvage" the image. It may still be used.
The journey was becoming
a serious enterprise.
Something had to be done.
A decision had to be made.
I felt lonely.
I heard myself say:
FURTHER ON, NOTHING!
I left all the road signs
behind me.
I felt anger against
history,
trends,
stages,
theories.
My journey acquired dimensions
which were less and less material.
The final frontier of the space
started to recede and embraced

a new, unknown dimension:
imagination.
Pure Imagination.
FURTHER ON, NOTHING!
We will see!

CROSSROADS

It was a turbulent time, full of inner doubts.
It was as if I stood at the crossroads and could not make up my mind;
nor could I chose the path.
But this is always the case in any true journey.
From the very beginning, I knew that my JOURNEY would not be
simple.
The questions kept multiplying.
It was necessary to find some answers.
More than that—it was necessary to travel many roads at once.
Each one of them seemed to be important,
imperative, and needed.
Naïve was a strictly observed the dogma of
a single d i r e c t i o n and the belief of the "constructivists" that,
in any development, there matters only this path
that leads directly from one stage to another,
that leads into infinity, which is more and more perfect.
The problem is that all these dogmatic and highly-charged
truths never came true.
I quickly realized that this theory of theirs
was an evident counterfeit.
I was not afraid to travel many roads at once.
I was not ashamed to do so. I thought that this was
a sign of freedom and imagination.
I did believe in the righteousness of my i n s t i n c t .
Today, I want to travel those roads once again.

PEOPLE-FAÇADES

I entered the "Inferno-Interior."
The painting was the image of its "secretion"; of the matter of my own
organism;
of life's pure essence which flows
through this matter.
Only flows.
I must find the BEINGS who will l e t themselves be carried
f r e e l y by this flow.
(Always this human image.)
And I did find them:
FAÇADES. HUMAN FAÇADES.

I found them in my theatre,
in my poor Fairground Booth.
An important explanation must be given here:
How did THEATRE enter this discourse?
I am still looking for the answer; so are many others.
Will it do painting any good to have its problems solved by another
discipline? Many questioned my judgment and had doubts about my
commitment to painting. Am I a "genuine" painter?
It was the time, when, as it seems to me, I made an important
"discovery." I realized that the conventional thinking about art needs to
be corrected; that the rigid boundaries between the arts must be erased;
that the act of TRANSGRESSION is not only permitted, but sometimes
also desperately needed.
Any boundary will always limit and restrict THOUGHT, and its
capricious and "unpredictable" course.
The surface of a painting is thus too restrictive, too "orthodox," to
contain in itself the thought, which transcends all the laws governing the
painting's structure.

THE ANTI-EXHIBITION, OR THE POPULAR EXHIBITION
I keep stubbornly returning to my Inferno to cast a departing glance at
that "battlefield" of mine.
If the final brush stroke signified defeat, if each and every of my creative
endeavors ended in stasis, enclosed in a "finite" and dead form, could it
not be recommended that I LEAVE THE PICTURE
OR DISCARD ALL THOSE PROCESSES THAT GIVE BIRTH TO
DEAD FORMS
in order to create something that would not be a material competitor to
the painting.
VOID . . .
ZERO . . .
DEATH . . .
I take out a faded sheet of paper from my "wardrobe of memory":
THE ANTI-EXHIBITION MANIFESTO. 1963
A WORK OF ART,
AN ISOLATED COMPOSITION,
WHICH IS IMMOBILIZED BY,
AND ENCLOSED IN,
ITS OWN STRUCTURE AND SYSTEM,
WHICH IS UNABLE EITHER TO CHANGE OR LIVE,
WHICH IS AN ILLUSION OF A CREATIVE PROCESS.
A TRUE CREATIVE PROCESS IS CHARACTERIZED BY
ITS STATE OF FLUIDITY,
CHANGE,
IMPERMANENCE,
EPHEMERALITY—
THE CONDITION OF LIFE ITSELF.

ONE SHOULD BESTOW THE STATUS OF A CREATIVE ACTIVITY
UPON ALL THOSE THINGS THAT HAVE NOT YET BECOME
WORKS OF ART,
THAT HAVE NOT YET BEEN IMMOBILIZED,
THAT STILL CONTAIN THE PURE IMPULSES OF LIFE,
THAT ARE NOT YET "READY" [to be consumed]
"APPROPRIATED":
THAT IS, URGENT PROBLEMS,
IDEAS,
DISCOVERIES,
PLANS,
PROJECTS,
DESIGNS,
WORKING SCRIPTS,
MATERIALS,
AUXILIARY ACTIONS,
ALL THAT IS MIXED TOGETHER WITH
(EVEN THOUGH IT IS STILL FREQUENTLY ARTIFICIALLY
SEGREGATED FROM)
THE MATTER OF LIFE:
FACTS,
INCIDENTS,
PEOPLE,
LETTERS, NEWSPAPERS, CALENDARS,
ADDRESSES, DATES,
MAPS, TICKETS,
MEETINGS. . . .
It seems as if I wrote this today!

For the first time,
I fully realized the meaning
of the concept of:
Nothingness.
Suddenly, the immeasurable reality of life
was filled with innumerable phenomena
which could become
works of art.
I felt that I owned
this land claimed by N O O N E.
FURTHER ON, NOTHING!

EMBALLAGES

The time of the Informel art, our century's big adventure, was coming to
a close.
Many of its painters, using the remaining shreds of its glory, tried to
extend its life by continuing the nostalgic life of dreams about forgotten
landscapes and human figures, who, like ghosts, kept returning from the

past immemorial.
I did not want to live in the world of memories.
It was not yet my time to start my journey into the past; to weave out of
the poor shreds of the nostalgic past a "tragic" image of the present.
At that time, I did not yet know about the relativity of time and its
ultimatum.
I asked myself if the return of Orpheus from the Inferno was possible.
There, in my "Inferno,"
I felt for the first time the touch of
Grand Dame-Death and the power she has over art.
There was nothing more marvelous and grandiose.
Some years later I was supposed to
face Her, in Her "t h e a t r u m."
The possibility of return to the "external" world
seemed contemptible. It was too easy.
This was a strange time in my life. As if I lived in vacuum,
where something happened that was difficult to explain. There, in my
Inferno, the word "nothing" acquired a new, uncommon, and deep
meaning.
This banal word, which is empted out of meaning in everyday life,
down there put forth its victorious ultimatum.
UNIMAGINABLE. The characteristic features of the i m a g e,
which demanded that its features be remembered, started to fade away.
A rationalist in me, wishing to avoid
the CARNAGE of the "nothing," replaced it with
a different one: THE ZERO ZONES.
I called my theatre of that time, the Zero Theatre.
As if I was afraid to say that other word,
which stands behind NOTHING—the word "DEATH."
This is when I executed my first E M B A L L A G E.
When made a GESTURE, which, later, will be some well known to me,
of putting the shreds of crumpled paper (and something else, too)
into a poor paper bag,
I must have been ready inside not to return,
like a Prodigial Son, back to the abandoned HOUSE
filled with its "i m a g e"—
the IMAGE of:
the Mother, the Father, the Children, the Dogs, the Farm Animals, the
Horses, the Sky outside the Window, the Woods, the Hills, the Roads, the
Paths, the Clouds. . . .
All of this, which is so beautiful and precious in "life,"
as an "image" lost its truth for me.
I remember well that moment, that crumpled paper, and that something
else.
An O B J E C T
that exists outside of me.
I could draw it.
I could draw its IMAGE.

I can almost see it on the crumpled paper.
But, at that time, this was no longer sufficient.
It was no longer the IMAGE that mattered.

D e s t r o y it?
Only to feel superior to it for a split second.
Eat it?
So that it would be a part of my organism.
This was too simple and too much of a desperate act.
Call it an "a r t o b j e c t," "*l'objet prêt*"?
In the post-World War II world, I suddenly remembered this term
from the time of World War I and the Cabaret Voltaire.
It also came to me that I knew nothing about it [l'objet prêt] at the time
of World War II when I discovered it too in my Underground Theatre.
But in my case however this was not a simple, rational act,
which would find its essence in esthetics,
as it happened in Zurich, in the Cabaret, named, not without reason,
after Voltaire.
This was the time of the war. We played with death not in the Cabaret,
but
in the everyday, day and night.
This was also Slavonic lyricism mixed with tragic Fate
and some religious premonition of Transgression, Sin, and Guilt.
This was a transgression of the holy laws of creation, which demand a
strict
and m a t e r i a l observance of an artist's intervention.
As well as a "scornful" a b u s e of
the READY-MADE REALITY,
which, up till now, had been untouchable and a holy
MODEL, like the one in the tabernacle,
which demands reverence, prayers, and, finally,
an interpretation, which is always a dubious act.
Even though this description may sound too ornate today,
I wish to draw attention to this moment in 1944
when, from life's reality, I "pulled out" an OBJECT
I gave it the rank of a work of art.
A CART-WHEEL SMEARED WITH MUD
and A DECAYED WOODEN FLOOR-BOARD.

Somewhere in the deep recesses of that time of my "religious" childhood,
a feeling of guilt was born.
At the same time, the "heretic" in me had a magnificent
material for action.

And one more digression.
At that time, in 1944, my OBJECT had a singular characteristic. It was
given to it by

me: it was a P O O R [object]. POVERTY. This had nothing to do with esthetics.

Later, in 1963, I called it: "at the threshold of garbage. . . .

"at the threshold between eternity and garbage . . ."

If it had not been for that P O V E R T Y, there would have been nothing more

than an ordinary ennobling of the object to the status of an artistic monument.

An artistic monument . . . I held it in contempt at the time of that despicable war.

It was important to protect this P O V E R T Y.

It was important to make it stay.

P O V E R T Y was to become for a long time, and maybe even until the very end,

the subject of my art.

Let me return to my story of the OBJECT,

to that moment when I was holding a poor bag in my hand,

not really knowing what to do with it.

And I was supposed to put my future into it.

All I knew was that I could not repeat my gesture

from 1944, even though

realness and object

still mattered and had a big chance

to stay with me for a long time.

I was aware of the fact that this which was created during the war

against all esthetic, in 1963, was nothing more than

a refined gesture and . . . esthetics.

It was at that time that I did something that would decide about my future: quickly and somehow "noiselessly,"

I h i d that OBJECT.

I am very much attached to this period of my life and my artistic work, which

I called "Emballage."

I value it very much. I do not want to leave it open or vulnerable to dubious

interpretations and naïve analyses.

Remain patient with me just a bit longer.

Today, from the distance of time, I want to o r g a n i z e

logically (today, I can afford to use this word)

that which, at that time, was a stormy eruption and a quest in darkness.

It will be my "table of contents."

So:

. . . The period of the "informel" art, as I have already mentioned, I called "the descend to hell," to the "inferno."

The external world disappeared; so did the world of objects;
a new world opened up in front of me.
This "inferno" however had nothing to do with antiquity.
It belonged to our century, where our i n t e r i o r
was our hell.
A painting was simply a secretion of my interior.

. . . After a few years I had enough of . . . myself and
I started to think about my return.
I asked then if the return of Orpheus was possible.
A return to "our" world.
But, there are no returns.
This is the tragic fate of a human.

. . . Instead, something else returned—the time of the o b j e c t;
of that "something" that exists at the opposite pole of my consciousness,
of "me"—
unreachable;
of the centuries-old desire to "t o u c h" it at any price.
The object, which has been deep inside of me,
now started to call my name obtrusively and enticingly.

. . . I had to do something about it.
I was aware of the fact that its traditional representation, its "image,"
could not return,
because it was merely a reflection,
just like the moonlight,
a dead surface.
But the object is alive.

. . . I also knew that all its "interpretations" were bankrupt. Gone were
the times, when it was enough to transform, deform, and stylize the
object, and, at the same time, to be convinced of the demiurge's activity.
Such a maneuver was too simple.
The object still existed
u n t o u c h e d.

. . . The Moon
and its
i n v i s i b l e side!
Can one see what is on the invisible side?
Is there such a side?
Invisible.
Invisibility!
To make invisible!
To hide!
To wrap up!

. . . and it is here that my old idea that the "artistic" activity be derived
from mundane everyday life, from this reality which by comparison to
"rich" i m a g i n a t i o n remains
POOR, played an important part.

I carried carefully this gesture of WRAPPING,
which was performed in the most mundane reality of everyday life,
over onto my creative work.
A work of art.
I was excited by the uncertainty whether or not the work of art itself
would survive this hazardous maneuver.
I do remember that, for a long time, I could not reconcile
the mundane sound of the word "wrapping" with the stately sounds of
the notion of "creativity" in my consciousness.
W R A P P I N G. . . . The word was heard everywhere:
on the streets, in the shops, when people discussed buying or selling.

The action gradually acquired the dimension of a ritual.
It became a symbolic act;
somewhere at the threshold between
miserable reality,
scorn,
contempt,
and
ridicule
there emerged suddenly
a growing shadow of pathos.
Instinctively, I sensed,
and to be more precise I still do,
an imminent threat to the highest
spiritual human value.
It was, and still is, necessary to
p r o t e c t it
from destruction,
from time,
from the primitive decrees of the authorities,
from the questioning by the official and slow-minded judges.
And thus the decision
to w r a p   i t   u p!
To preserve it!
IT WAS THIS VERY ACTION, WHICH HAD ITS EXISTENTIAL
JUSTIFICATION, THAT DISTINGUISHED MY WORK
from all those other works that seemed to belong to the same category.
However, they only seemed to belong together.
Theirs were purely aesthetic practices,
or simply, plagiarism.

My activity during that time (1958–60–63)
was to a great degree driven by my instinct,
by a necessity, whose pressure, at that time,
was not fully realized by me.
This is often the case.
It is only later that we realize that our
"spontaneous" and "individual"
creative act was driven
by a higher Power,
by NECESSITY—
and I want to talk about it now.

There is a human characteristic which is exceedingly moving:
the human being
is a species
which was raised above all other creations of nature,
which was given consciousness by the malicious gods,
that is both his blessing and his curse.
A human being, who is amazingly fragile and delicate,
who is unable to deal with
his own Self,
H I D E S in himself
certain things,
which I will call sacred.

A human being does not want to
REVEAL,
at any price,
that which is hidden,
because the act of revealing will always signify its
R E D U C T I O N and
W E A K E N I N G .

A human being wants to conceal
all that contains the essence of life
the strength of survival,
the past, whose memory is always the most costly,
the memories of close people,
God. . . .
It is a human characteristic
which resists everybody
and everything;
a desperate act of
heroism,
invincible;
which will not even be surrendered
in the hour of D E A T H.

Having first created the idea of resurrection,
it buries the dead body
in coffins and graves.
The *image* of Death,
the most powerful
enemy of life,
is "constructed" by human imagination
from b o n e s,
the most durable parts
of the human body, which have the best chance
to s u r v i v e .
Human flesh is but
a fragile and "poetic"
Emballage of
the skeleton, of death,
and of hope that it will last
until Doomsday.

And let me finish—
there is a pure notion of
an interior
in this ur-instinct.
An invisible interior.
Threatened by the external,
hostile world.

For many years, I had been discovering the lands, where the word
EMBALLAGE had a deeper meaning.
The way a spell does.
I keep encountering it in the remotest corners of my past.
It and its contents.
It is as if some HAND had written the book of my life there.
And I can only slowly turn over its pages.

1944   I turned Odysseus, a Homeric hero, into
        "something,"
        that was bundled up, wrapped in poor, dirty rags of a military
        overcoat.
        It was difficult to recognize a great human being in that bundle.
        Somewhere, in the upper part of this "something," a mouth
        suddenly opened and a few words were heard: "I have returned
        from Troy . . ."

1957   I hid the figures of actors, their bodies and movements, all their
        psychological
        states and conditions—
        this most significant essence of stage acting—

in a huge, black
s a c k;
its jerky and sudden movements
were to express human emotions, passions, and conflicts. . . .
It was an act that required a big dose of determination and faith
that the actors can imbue dead objects with life.

1962   I nailed brutally poor crumpled paper
b a g s,
taken out of the garbage—
as if they were rare species of butterflies—
onto the pure, white canvases of my paintings.
Their mechanical foldings became a substitute for the refined
abstract g r i d s.
Now, they had much more value to me than those other ones
which were proud and "avant-garde."
Tortured bags; crucified bags;
I m p r i s o n e d bags.

1963   I kept placing and immobilizing
the e n v e l o p e s-p a c k e t s,
which were addressed to my friends,
and which they will never receive,
on the canvas.
They had post marks on them, like the suns shining over the
landscapes of their journeys and the unknown destinations.
A canvas was becoming
the POST-OFFICE—
this strange place of emptiness and nothingness,
in-between an addressee and addressors,
in-between a beginning and a final destiny.

1965   I discovered a new possible site for the art exhibitions:
the POST-OFFICE.
It was only because of mundane difficulties an exhibition never
materialized there.

1967   But the POST-OFFICE
returned.
A procession of the seven "real" retired POSTMEN
carrying a gigantic 14 meter-long LETTER
started at the "real" Warsaw POST-OFFICE
and continued along the streets in Warsaw until it reached the
Foksal Gallery
where a crowd of people, who had continuously been informed
about the progress of the procession, shred it spontaneously to
pieces.

Later, there were:
PACKETS
laboriously tied together with a string
revealing a complex and infinite permutation of knots
guarding some nameless secret,
and an old
SUITCASE
filled with shreds and pieces
that could have easily belonged to a mad person
    and
INDUSTRIAL BAGS
with a discredited aesthetic value, with mysterious labels,
which were completely incomprehensible to a lay person.
Then, there came the time when I decided to w r a p
the PEOPLE,
living people.
In a Warsaw café, I wrapped a human being with
toilet paper.
A strap of paper, unfolding almost into infinity, wrapping around
a human body
was almost like an act of a good Samaritan.
I repeated it in an old grain elevator in Basel.
Finally, there was that something, which I called
"a little revenge on Hitler,"
which took place in the middle of the massive ruins of
Hitlerjugendparadengelände.
It was almost like a Mass for a Human Emballage.

1962   One day I met a rhinoceros.
It was almost like meeting it in a wild jungle, face to face,
alone.
It did not matter that the Rhinoceros lived inside of Dürer's
drawing.
I must have been that I was waiting for it.
I suspected that this meeting may have been important.
The Rhinoceros had a lot to say to me.
I was convinced that I heard him say:
"My skin, hmmmm, look carefully at these
arabesques,
ornamentations,
lumps,
this most interesting composition,
this matter, possibly destined to be eternal,
this is an impressive—it did not know what word to use; neither
did I since I did not yet
discover the word—
Emballage.
The Rhinoceros kept bragging—

my skin,
a work of art,
a masterpiece,
I could easily be exhibited in the Louvre. . . .
What about that which is inside?
That does not matter.
It dismissed my question.
Or maybe it did not want to admit that the inside is like
everybody else's. . . .
Was it pride?
Disinterested.
A work of art.
This helped me a lot
a year later, when
I was holding a poor, paper bag
to put in it . . .
it does not matter what.

1964   A year, or maybe two years later, there was my second meeting
with the Rhinoceros.
In Nürnberg.
In a film, "Kantor is da."
In a café-restaurant.
I was sitting at the table, wearing black as always, black scarf, etc.
Coffee, cigarettes, I was not aware of what was going to happen.
Suddenly, someone, or "something" (like Odysseus during World
War II)
comes in.
A dirty, gray, bundled-in-rags being, wearing an overcoat,
appearing as if it were a formless mass—
not much of a human being.
It is carrying a monstrous knapsack, like a growth on its back.
It sits down unceremoniously at, of course, my table.
And I, all in black, elegant, black patent shoes, a scarf, a hat with
a wide brim, and all the rest that for others spells out an artistic
poser.
But this is beyond the point here.
I order a big schnitzel and something else.
The "Rhinoceros" throws itself on the food
and devours it.
I am waiting for it to finish and then pose a series of unobtrusive
questions:
Where is it coming from?
How long has it been traveling?
Is it tired?
What is it doing here?
The Rhinoceros answers my questions mumbling through the
layers of the devoured meat.

Then I go beyond the polite questions and ask about more
substantive things—
its lifestyle?
does it live alone?
a philosopher?
maybe an artist?
The Rhinoceros has finished eating.
It responds to my last question with one word—
"merde"!
This formless mass gets up from the table destroying everything in
sight
and moves towards the exit.
At this very moment, the police, called in by
the offended patrons.
The owner assumes the responsibility for all that happened.
I am slowly drinking up my coffee. . . .

Later, the clothing was enough for me.
But I continued to hear the stamping of the running rhinoceros.
Clothing.
This strange "addition" to a human being.
To his body,
His naked body.
An "addition" which in its very matter has nothing in common
with a human body, with a h u m a n   b e i n g.
Foreign to us.
It tries to deceive us.
It is a liar.
This is why it is necessary to investigate its actions,
its pseudo autonomy,
expose it "from the inside."
The condition is very dramatic.
Different parts of the body as if trying to save themselves,
escape from their prison.
Give a sign of life.
I used this condition to show the human being anew,
and his fate, which, for centuries, has been given to him as toil by
this civilization.

Theatre, of course, came to the rescue.
A perfect site for this showing.
What an excellent suspension of disbelief,
what posturing and posing,
false pretence,
perfect illusion
and . . .
emptiness,
the site so much cherished by me.

There follows a parade of characters who traveled through my
theatre and my paintings:

A GREAT GYMNAST with a Knapsack from *The Water-Hen*,

A MAN WITH SUITCASES (from *The Water-Hen*),

A WANDERING JEW with the Trumpet of the Last Judgment
tightly wrapped in a black mournful emballage;
decked out with pillows, the same pillows that the old Jewish women left
in the windows to air in Wielopole. In red pillow cases.
The Wandering Jew performed his "de-emballage"
while he was ripping the pillows and letting the feathers cover the
audience,

TWO HASIDIC JEWS with the Plank of the Last Resort
in a black "ritual" emballage,

A MADWOMAN carrying a heavy sack with suspicious contents,

A MADMAN wearing a costume made out of little black sacks,

A GIRL FROM A GOOD FAMILY dressed like a prostitute,

and

A TRAVELING EMBALLAGE,
a huge knapsack traveling on a bicycle wheel.

I made a decision to "wrap" museum figures.
Here are Velàzquez's "Infantas." Almost like relics or Madonnas,
wearing ornate dresses, making forced gestures, with emptiness filling
their eyes,
they continue to exist defenseless. . . .
The famous dress of the Infanta, looking like a chasuble, I replaced with
an old, used postman's bag.
Castaway, small pieces of wood, corroded by sea salt, are
the only allusion to an interior skeleton construction. . . .
I had the courage to touch the emballage of "the national pride"—The
Teutonic Order Oath of Allegiance—by Matejko. The proud figures
of the royal court, the knights, the bishops were "wrapped" up with
desperation, fear, and solemnity—
for eternity.
The only figure which remained alive was the King's Fool—
Stańczyk.

Using this method of wrapping, I created a portrait of
a person, who is most dear to me, my Mother.

From youth to the grave.
Finally, there came my turn.
My Self-portrait.
I placed my images from the time I was a baby until now on the black
boxes from the department store.
Some 70 years.
Many things to look at!
All is thrown carelessly into something that can look like
an open . . . grave,
as if waiting for the Last Portrait.

AN UMBRELLA

Where did the umbrella
come from,
into my
Poor Room of Imagination. . . .
Sometime around 1965,
their hoards started to rain down
from above.
They mixed together
with other object and people
inhabiting my Room.
One day, not knowing what to do,
I hung an umbrella
on the frame of the painting.
I had a lot of fun with these,
with their multiple meanings and ambiguities;
they aided me perfectly
in discussing many matters,
which I had problems discussing until now.
Simply, they spoke for me.
I called them
Poetic Emballages.
In order not to forget anything,
I need to say, that they did not really rain down from "above."
Right after the war,
I used to collect old umbrellas.
Space, this scientific term,
I called the "umbrellic space."
Of course, it only existed in my ROOM.
In real life, personally, I cannot stand the umbrellas.

IT WAS THAT ONE NIGHT . . .
It was that one night,
that the reality of life,
a heroine of the un-divine
comedy,

whose performance we followed
with a waning interest,
unveiled her face. . . .
Frightened, I shut
the doors to my poor
room of Imagination.
I could not erase from my memory
that image,
which was as empty as
the hollow pit of a grave.
No trace of life.
Now, really:
FURTHER ON, NOTHING!
It was not that
splendid La Belle Dame—
Death.
What I saw was
a rite
of her official
priests.

Today, I can recall
a similar scene that
I witnessed a few years later:
"From a nylon bag,
he took something dark
and earth-colored.
Black soil was stuck to
the skull. And there were also some rotten shreds
of a dress.
That was my Mother.
Her skull. That magnificent
creation of nature and
humanism—now,
rust-eaten
clotted with earth and mud.
I shut myself in
my Poor
Room of Imagination.
I kept repeating with despair,
FURTHER ON, NOTHING. . . .
I knew that I needed to
destroy that gaping hole. . . .
I began to cover it up,
wrap it up, gag it,
board it up . . .
with despair,

anger
and with great love
for the image of
a human being.

PEOPLE

When I think about the past,
I realize, to my surprise, that I have never painted
not a single landscape or a "still life" in my life.
I have never painted a world in which a human being was absent.
When I traveled through abstract thoughts, I had always encountered there
a figure and an image of a human being.
A human figure.
Strange is the human nature of an artist.
Everything is mixed there together:
good and bad
truth and lies
sacred and profane,
ethos and curse,
purity and filth,
progress, radical thinking and nostalgic desire for the past, for going back,
avant-garde and tradition. . . .

Having said this litany of contradictions, I can now admit
that, despite all my provocations and protests—
somewhere in the corner of my Poor Room of Imagination,
"on the side," as if
only for myself,
I have always drawn and painted . . . human figures bereft of any
desire to lay claims to theory or refinement of form.
Only for myself.
Today, I understand the meaning of this simple statement.
Only for myself!

In those intimate moments, without paying attention
to the things happening around me, I talked with myself.
With myself. The way I did when I was a child.
A madman, eccentric, self-centered, asocial, an enemy of the people.
I do recall other names I was called.
Today, I know for certain, at those times,
I p r o t e s t e d
against the world,
against its proudly-manifested civilization of herd mentality,
against its ideology of the masses,
against its theories of art for the masses,

against its brutal demand for a sacrifice, which I was supposed to
willingly make out of my inner and private life.
Out of my tragedies,
my pain, suffering,
my weaknesses,
my fears. . . .
Today, I know for certain, that those paintings, painted for "myself"
belonged really to "me."
I also know that this was my biggest revolt and protest.

The figures have multiplied,
the whole parade of figures:
Wanderers and their luggage
Boys from the time of my happy childhood,
Old People who return to the Dead Classroom,
Children imprisoned in their school desks,
Homeless, Wandering Jews,
People and their objects,
tables,
chairs,
doors,
windows,
Death,
their lovers.
Rejects, hanged-men, hangmen, prostitutes, the whole cortege of my Saint
François Villon,
Soldiers marching to the front,
my family, my mother, my father, my cousins. . . .
Sometimes, when I was angry, I assumed the function of a hanging Judge.
I crucified them, bound them, replaced their real arms with wooden arms,
contorted their faces, rolled them like "pancakes,"
drained them of thoughts and emotions.
I revenged myself.
It was my indictment, too.

FURTHER ON, NOTHING

Ever since that time,
l i f e
has invaded
my Poor
Room of Imagination.
It attempted to gain control over it,
as if it tried to avenge itself for
my impudence to
make use of
its refuse,

cast-off ends and odds,
rather than of its
majestic glory.
It prepared for me
defeats and failures
in life.
In despair, I sought
shelter in the corners of
my Poor
Room.
FURTHER ON, NOTHING!
I screamed.
I cursed
the P A I N T I N G
I had been faithful to for a long time.
I made a mad decision
to leave its space.
Never to return.
I was not an escape,
rather a dignified
withdrawal from
a privileged site;
an acknowledgement of my
failure.
I was fascinated by the idea of
playing the clown.
I have always been.
My Theatre, that Fairground Booth,
can testify.
The performance is over.
The audience has left.
At the doors, Old Pierrot
with tears smeared all over his face
is waiting for his Columbine
who left for her poor hotel
a long time ago.
FURTHER ON, NOTHING!
And to end this
THEATRE OF LIFE:
the epilogue,
the last painting.
In this painting
"I SHALL ALWAYS REMAIN."
The painting must be
victorious.

Topography of Representation

I

The question of what it means to represent has haunted Western academic and nonacademic culture ever since Plato and Aristotle defined the concept of representation some twenty-four centuries ago. According to Plato, representation is a process of doubling of the one that becomes two: "Whenever you see one, you conceive the other," avers a statement in *Phaedo*.[1] Thus, an object, which has been perceived, or a thought, which has been conceived, is doubled and finds its material representation somewhere else than in its originary location. Aristotle in *Physics* suggests a different process; that is, a process of transferring an object or a thought from one space to another: from real space to constructed space. Thus, whatever is seen onstage (art) imitates what exists in nature. However, this is not necessarily a process of creating an exact copy of the original, as was the case with Plato, but a different one in which exactitude is not necessarily at premium. Thus, according to Aristotle, art has a potential to carry to its end what nature is incapable of effecting. For this very reason, art will always be marked by some form of utopian performative dream or a dystopian performative nightmare.[2]

Whether it is understood as a process of doubling or transfer, representation, even when modified by the rules of perspective by Alberti in 1435, is by its very nature a restricted form exposing a complex relationship between the original and the copy, between what is and what is not, between what is given and what is desired, between what is real and what is made real, between the subject (the locus and the vehicle of representation) and the object (coming to be only as it is known or represented), and, finally, between the social and visual ordering—a relationship that could offer all the members of the community a possibility of identifying their place. To quote Jean-François Lyotard,

[Representation] was given almost princely right during the Quattrociento.
Since then and for centuries, it made its contribution to the fulfillment of the
metaphysical and the political programme for the organization of the visual
and the social. Optical geometry, the ordering of values and colours in line
with a Neoplatonically inspired hierarchism, the rules for fixing the high points
of religious or historical legend, helped to encourage the identification of new
political communities: the city, the State, the nation, by giving them the destiny
of seeing everything and of making the world transparent (clear and distinct) to

monocular vision. Once placed on the perspectivist stage, the various components of the communities—narrative, urbanistic, architectural, religious, ethical—were put in order under the eye of the painter, thanks to *construzione legittima*. And in turn the eye of the monarch, positioned as indicated by the vanishing-point, receives this universe thus placed in order. When they are exhibited in the palace rooms of the lords or the people, and in the churches, these representations offer all the members of the community the same possibility of identifying their belonging to this universe, as though they were the monarch or the painter. The modern notion of culture is born in the public access to the signs of historico-political identity and their collective deciphering.[3]

Even though this modern notion of culture and representation drives the common understanding of the function of the arts in general and theatre in particular in Western civilization—from the "Broadway" stages to theatres in the basement worldwide—it does not mean that the concept of representation has not been championed. Even if new and renegade practices may not last for a long time or do not displace the existing stage conventions, they are often absorbed, or appropriated, by mainstream theatres and become part of the accepted practice. To substantiate this point, I would like to locate Kantor's theatre practice within a framework of other practices that challenged the his-toricopolitical identity of representation and its signs. These practices, which are scattered around, create a network of relations, references, and dependencies. To investigate them, I am using the notion of topography of representation, which signifies an open space wherein different representational practices can be positioned simultaneously. What is of interest to me is how some of these practices, which were prompted by (a) the changes in the understanding of space and time, (b) the events of World War II, and (c) the desire to liberate theatre from the constraints of dominant conventions, resonate with or create tensions between them and Kantor's thinking about the function of theatre and the nature of a creative process.

The idea that art was "an essentially *concrete* art and [could] only con-sist of the representation of *real* and *existing* things" and visible objects, was challenged by philosophers, physicists, and artists in the second half of the nineteenth and the first decades of the twentieth century.[4] Among the changes introduced, those in the perception of time and space were the most asser-tive. The realm of Newtonian absolute time and space, which had dominated Western epistemology since the publication of *Principia* in 1687, was infiltrated by Nicolai Lobachevsky's and János Bolyai's systems of non-Euclidean geom-etry, Bernhard Riemann's *n*-dimensional geometry, Henri Poincaré's assump-tions concerning the inability to measure space itself, Clerk Maxwell's field theory, Ernst Mach's idea of relative spaces, Hendrik Lorentz's experiments with objects moving through motionless ether, Hermann Minkowski's space-time manifold, Hermann Weyl's four-dimensional continuum, Albert Einstein's special theory of relativity, and Werner Heisenberg's indeterminacy principle. They provided support for Einstein's famous dictum that "time and space are modes by which we think and not conditions in which we live."[5] If, indeed, time and space are no longer absolute—that is, the linear movement of time from the past via the present and into the future is broken and space is not an empty receptacle—the artistic expression, rather than being a representation of *real* and *existing* things, focused on the theatricalization of the unseen forces that control human destiny, on the invisible world hidden behind the façade of everyday reality and its practices, and on the construction of new time and new space, which existed parallel to the three-dimensional traditional space. In this new space, which invalidated the linear perspective, the artist and the spectator could observe not what can be seen but what can be thought or contained in a heightened state of consciousness. As they moved away from traditional concepts of matter, time, and space, Symbolist writers and painters recognized the unthought, the hidden, and the invisible as a legitimate part of human experience. Their dramas and paintings brought forth a space that would not be disciplined by the external order of things but would allow the subjective "I," the Self, to travel through a multidimensional space (mode of thinking) in a direction not contained in the knowledge of the Self in a three-dimensional universe of social and political order.[6]

This growing belief that time and space are modes by which we think and not the conditions by which we live allowed some of the artists and thinkers to envision not only a universe in which a creative act is not a process of representation of some material "real" but a process that constructs an entirely new universe of things and objects. Vasilii Kandinsky noted in 1912,

> A scientific event removed one of the most important obstacles from my path. This was the further division of the atom. The collapse of the atom was equated in my soul with the collapse of the whole world. Suddenly, the stoutest walls crumbled. Everything became uncertain, precarious and insubstantial. I would not have been surprised had a stone dissolved into thin air before my eyes and become invisible. Science seemed destroyed: its most important basis was only an illusion, an error of the learned, who were not building their divine edifice stone by stone with steady hands, by transfigured light, but were groping at random for truth in the darkness and blindly mistaking one object for another.[7]

Thus, perception grounded in some kind of an external (real, imaginary, or political) referent was questioned and ultimately seen as an error of the learned, who were now "groping at random for truth in darkness and blindly mistaking one object for another." This rejection of the traditional tools of artistic expression created new possibilities. In the fine arts, experiments with space-time, and specifically with its speed, direction, shape, rhythm, and density, were the most revolutionary formal devices in Cubism, futurism, Dada, surrealism, and constructivism.[8] Collage, montage, nondevelopmental dialogue, compressions of time and space, and phonic exercises were frequently random combinations of a certain number of elements from other works, objects, and preexisting messages, which were put together to constitute a new creation. This new creation was the work of a modernist artist who, unlike his or her past stereotypical images of a rebel or an alienated outsider, was participating in an intelligible social process challenging the emerging framework of industrialization and supporting new social constellations, such as the Russian Revolution. The new work of art was now believed to be "real" in itself, an autonomous reality that existed nowhere else, as exemplified by Georges Braque's paintings animating the discrepancies between vision and cognition; Luigi Russolo's dynamic paintings of color zones and the objects positioned within them; Marcel Duchamp's experiments with the *l'objet prêt*, found objects such as an umbrella, a bottle rack, or a urinal, which replaced the conventionally defined "artistic objects" in a museum; or Kurt Schwitter's *Mertz* construction.

The events of World War II cleaved the Western subject into frequently irreconcilable fragments stigmatized forever by negative ontology. As the existence of concentration camps or, for that matter, recent political events in Europe, the Middle East, and Africa make painfully obvious, human life is a fatality—a condition that proclaims that men and women are "unwanted intruders on creation, as being destined to undergo unmerited, incomprehensible, arbitrary suffering and defeat." "Pues el delito mayor / Del hombre es haber nacido"—Calderon's sin of having been born has acquired a tangible enactment for human being's presence and identity are transgressions. "During the Holocaust, the Gypsy or the Jew had very precisely *committed the crime of being*. That crime attached by definition to the fact of birth. Thus even the unborn had to be hounded to extinction. To come into the world was to come into torture and death."[9] Theodor Adorno's "Commitment" (1962) drew attention to the need for a fitful process of reckoning with the past, redefining and reevaluating all the phrases both secular and theological that lost their right to exist after Auschwitz, unless it was acceptable that genocide become a part of the culture that had legitimized murder.[10] More importantly, how could suffering find its voice without being appropriated or assimilated by bourgeois subjectivity and its systems of power, without which there could have no been Auschwitz? How can suffering find its voice in art without immediately being betrayed by its conventions or culture industry that defames the uncompromising radicalism of the artists showing suffering as formalism? As he remarks,

> There is something painful in Schönberg's compositions—not what arouses anger
> in Germany, the fact that they prevent people from repressing from memory
> what they at all cost want to repress. It is rather the way in which, by turning
> suffering into images, despite their hard implacability, they wound our shame
> before the victims. For these are used to create something, works of art, that
> are thrown to the consumption of a world which destroyed them. The so-called
> artistic representation of the sheer physical pain of people beaten to the ground
> by rifle butts contains, however remotely, the power to elicit enjoyment out of it.
> The moral of this art, not to forget for a single instant, slithers into the abyss of
> its opposite. . . . Works of less than highest rank are even willingly absorbed, as
> contributions to clearing up the past. When genocide becomes part of the cultural
> heritage in the themes of committed literature, it becomes easier to continue to
> play along with the culture which gave birth to murder.[11]

These statements may explain why Adorno, aware of the practice of using art as a kind of proxy allowing postwar generations not to approach a difficult history, perceived art not as a weapon in class struggle, as did the constructivists,

Bertolt Brecht, or Erwin Piscator in the early decades of the twentieth century, but as a mode of cognition. Adorno, for example, rejected any esthetic potential of "socialist realism" or "committed literature" in societies that had thoroughly been integrated by the "culture industry," a term Adorno coined. The culture industry, according to him, eliminates art that could be a trial arena for alternatives. What remains is fetishized art that protects society from social revolution and transformation. This is why Adorno calls for the autonomization of art—the autonomization of representation and the concomitant desubjectivization of artistic language: "The principle that governs autonomous works of art is not the totality of their effects, but their own inherent structure. They are knowledge as nonconceptual objects. This is the source of their greatness. It is not something of which they have to persuade men, because it should be given to them."[12] In was only an autonomous work of art that, according to Adorno, could represent suffering in the post-Auschwitz reality wherein a mass culture was produced and manipulated by culture industries realigned with an ideology that had given birth to murder.[13]

When expressed in art, these experiences had to abandon the tradition that defined art in terms of representation affirming the external order of things. Beckett's dramaturgy or the Art Informel of Wols, Jean Fautrier, Georges Mathieu, and Jackson Pollock's action paintings manifested forms that were freed from the strict laws of construction of prewar representational art and were instead always changing and fluid, negating, decomposing, dissolving, deconstructing, or destroying any promise of representation. All these works are stark examples of representational practices that challenged traditional representation by exposing the fissures in its surface and the crisis of its referential systems. There is no linear progression toward some resolution waiting at the end. Contemplation of the post-Auschwitz, post-Hiroshima world needs to happen in a place where mind can go without the fear of degrading itself. As nonconceptual objects, these works of art destabilize the constancy of distance between the points of reference, show "nothing" that screams in the presence of the invisible, turn against our instincts, and force us to renounce our experience.

The displacement of the temporal and spatial boundaries that define representation, the reevaluation of the nature of the speaking subject, and the new mode of functioning of the subject have reconstituted the concept of representation. They did not, however, penetrate the very foundations of representation increasingly geared to the demands of politics and defining access to the signs of historicopolitical identity, no matter how problematized by cultural or political events and transformations.

Antonin Artaud's theatre of cruelty is an example par excellence of how this penetrative process can be accomplished. In "The Theatre of Cruelty and the Closure of Representation," Jacques Derrida provides an insightful reading of Artaud's statement that theatre has not yet begun to exist.[14] It still needs to be born, because its "proper body, the property and propriety of [its] body, had been stolen from [it] by the thieving god who was born in order to 'pass himself off' as [it]."[15] According to Artaud, "Western theatre has been separated from the force of its essence, removed from its *affirmative* essence, its *vis affirmative*" by a thieving god—by representation in which life "lets itself be doubled and emptied by negation."[16] One of the ineluctable consequences of this separation is that theatre accepted the functions that have been imposed upon it by the external order of things and successive models of representation. Representation imprints the culture within which it is positioned, and all attempts at dissolving or destroying representation by the avant-garde rarely modify cultural apparatuses. At best, aesthetic revolts serve as dialectical oppositions until, as was the case with constructivism, futurism, surrealism, Art Informel, and the Happenings, the dominant structure absorbs their techniques of representation and nullifies their revolutionary content.

Artaud opposes theatre of cruelty to these practices, viewing it as a site where a complete destruction of representation is possible through the destruction of the structures of belonging. "The theatre of cruelty is to be born by separating death from birth and by erasing the name of man. The theatre has always been made to do that for which it was not made."[17] This is one of the reasons why, for Artaud, the theatre of cruelty is not a representation: "It is life itself, in the extent to which life is unrepresentable."[18] This life is unrepresentable because it is the imitation of a transcendental principle that art puts us into communication with. Thus, Artaud rejects the imitative concept of art and its Aristotelian aesthetics of representation affirming life by pointing out that theatre should be a privileged site of the destruction of imitation and the structures of belonging, delimiting the very foundations of Western theatre engendered by bourgeois religion, philosophy, politics, and culture. As long as theatrical revolutions remain on the level that questions the technical or metatechnical aspects of this construction, they will belong to theatre history narratives and to the stage only.

"The theatre of cruelty expulses God from stage. It does not put a new atheist discourse on stage, or give atheism a platform, or give over theatrical space to a philosophizing logic that would once more, to our greater lassitude, proclaim the death of God. The theatrical practice of cruelty, in its action and structure, inhabits or rather *produces* a nontheological space."[19] This nontheological space is independent and autonomous and "must, in order to revive or simply to live, realize what differentiates it from text, pure speech, literature, and all other fixed and written means."[20] Theological space, for Artaud, is the stage dominated by speech or logos, which does not belong to the theatrical site and governs it from a distance, and by an author-creator who, "absent and from afar, is armed with a text and keeps watch over, assembles, regulates the time or the meaning of representation, letting this latter *represent* him through representatives, director or actors, enslaved interpreters who represent characters, who primarily through what they say, more or less directly represent the thought of the 'creator.'"[21]

Released from these constraints, the theatre of cruelty will no longer represent a known present but will produce a space and commentary of its own that no external authority or systems of conventions could comprehend or appropriate. The constitution of a closed space of representation, that is, "a space produced within itself and no longer organized from the vantage of an other absent site, an illocality, an alibi or invisible utopia,"[22] will allow for the experience of the elements positioned within it. If the stage signifies an experience that produces its own space that no speech could condense or comprehend, this *spacing* aligns itself with the new notions of space and time that had dominated the early decades of the twentieth century. For Artaud, this *spacing* signifies the closure of classical representation and the creation of autopresentation, whose elements fold back upon themselves rather than refer to some external structures of belonging. This is why Artaud rejects all nonsacred theatre, all theatre that privileges speech, all abstract theatre that excludes something from the totality of art, all theatre of alienation that remains the prisoner of a classical ideal of art that "attempts to cast the mind into an attitude distinct from force but addicted to exaltation," all ideological theatre, and all cultural theatre or interpretative theatre seeking to transmit a content or deliver a message or a concept of a politicomoral vision of the world.[23]

Artaud's theatre of cruelty, his idea of a theatre without representation, or the idea of the possibility or impossibility of the experience that produces its own space, is both the closure of classical representation and the limit of a theatrical possibility. Artaud wanted to annihilate the stage organized by the structures of belonging or by the tyranny of the theological stage and to produce the stage of pure visibility and mise-en-scène. The gesture of annihilation and production kept him at the very limit that allowed him to think a thought that eludes itself in its presence, that is born to itself:

> And now I am going to say something which, perhaps,
> is going to stupefy many people.
> I am the enemy
> of theatre.
> I have always been.
> As much as I love theatre,
> I am, for this very reason, equally its enemy.[24]

These three fragments, which bring focus to philosophical, historical, sociological, and aesthetic concerns rupturing the solidity of *construzione legittima*, are the referent points in the topography of this dynamic, rather than fixed or singular, space of representation. In the course of this book they will be many more fragments and practices that will come into being and take shape while rupturing the traditional notion of representation. These fragments, and to be more specific, these fragments in Tadeusz Kantor's theatre, will draw attention to the authorities that control the flow of representation, question the ever-shifting claims to reality, and focus on the manner in which the subjects and objects are or can be thought, identified, and enunciated. Finally, these fragments will address the notion of differential specificity in which a medium itself (a theatre practice) is reinvented and rearticulated so that the object (the actor and the object), which is dissociated from its original function, can enunciate its new possibilities or relationships while encountering other objects in the field.

Kantor's practice of challenging, or to borrow a phrase from Gilles Deleuze, of deterritorializing representation in the period between 1944 and 1973 by surrounding himself with the objects that can no longer be or are not yet appropriated by the artistic convention or commodified into an assigned use-value, was deeply grounded in his experience of World War II, his need to revise the by now compromised ideological agenda of high modernist avant-gardes, and in his credo that the function of art is to be an answer to, rather than a representation of reality. In an important sense, Kantor belongs to the category of artists whose work is marked by one major task. This task was described poignantly by C. Wright Mills: "The independent artist and intellectual are among the few remaining personalities equipped to resist and to fight the stereotyping and consequent death of genuinely living things. Fresh perception now involves the capacity to continually unmask and to smash the stereotypes of vision and intellect with modern communications swamp us."[25]

Let this thought guide us through the topography of Kantor's theatre.

II

Kantor's experiments in the visual arts and theatre in the period bracketed by his activities in the underground Independent Theatre (1942) and in the Impossible Theatre (1973) can be seen as signposts marking different directions, shifts, and transformations that do not, however, create a coherent whole but, on the contrary, lead onto the paths that fork, establish parallel tracks, or abruptly end. Moving through the topography of Kantor's theatre and representational practices is to realize that they eroded the utopian dream that history is a narrative of progress shaped by human will as well as deconstructed the remnants of metaphysics of the past century by a continuous, unrelentless, and never-ending

DERISION,
DISREGARD
MUTINY,
PROTEST
NEGATION,
BLASPHEMY,
SACRILEGE of all the SHRINES,
QUESTIONING of all social values.[26]

The question that comes to mind is whether or not such a challenge could indeed have any value in a world where everything seems to be immediately appropriated by a dominant ideology, be it the Nazi regime during World War II or bureaucratic socialism in postwar Poland. More important, could such a challenge materialize as a performance or a painting, escape the stabilizing procedures, and maintain its quality of a dynamic work of art deriding or negating the existing forms and conditions? Finally, was Kantor's challenge yet another illusionary act that tried to make us believe, as did the manifestos of the avant-gardes of the early twentieth century, that it was possible to provide a model for an oppositional representational praxis that would escape the gallery or museum markets?

I will address these questions in this chapter while describing Kantor's theatre practices, which, for him, were synonymous with a process of annexing reality.

The concept of annexing reality emerged and was realized in the production of Stanisław Wyspiański's *The Return of Odysseus* (1944):

> It was the time of war; the time when one's awareness could be altered in a split second and one's instincts had to be infallible and ahead of their time. The idea of the process of annexing reality proclaimed the necessity of questioning art's sacred dictum of being allowed only to present, in a work of art, a fictitious reality, a reflection of reality, a r e p r e s e n t a t i o n of reality (simply, a "false-pretense"); a dictum which barred reality from being a part of the work of art.[27]

The need to interrogate representation, which barred reality from being a part of a work of art and was used to affirm the original or reality or life, was of great importance. However, is it possible to do this without falling into the trap of a dominant convention defining what is to be seen, where it is to be seen, how it is to be seen, and who is going to see it?

Kantor, who left behind his notes, theoretical writings, and manifestos, provided us with a road map that both registered the process of putting together *The Return of Odysseus* and marked the changes in his thinking about representation and the process of annexing reality. Here are some of them:

THE RETURN OF ODYSSEUS I—SOME THOUGHTS

For a long time, I was trying to figure out if Wyspiański's Odysseus is a villain. What do his actions amount to, once all these psychological moments, used to explain them, veiling them in mysticism, or glossing over their true value are removed? The Trojan War was a Greek invasion. Sanctioned by the imaginary ritual slogan, Odysseus' "heroic" actions belong to the category of common murders.

Once the problem of destiny is removed, the return of Odysseus is nothing more than an ordinary assault: Odysseus returns with his gang to ransack and burn down his home and to kill his own father. One can find a justification for the fact that Odysseus kills like flies the lovers of his wife; but his plans to murder his father without having a clear cause except for some vague justification that he is driven by some fatal force, destiny, or curse does not convince me. I am much more captivated by unmasking this mythological hero.

THE RETURN OF ODYSSEUS II

There were many. Many inglorious returns from Troy. All are marked with the imprints of human unhappiness, inhuman crimes committed in the name of religious slogans.

The returns which are veiled in the tattered false military banners.

The returns—escapes from justice.

Charon's boat does not stop for Odysseus lost in the night of his epilogue.

The epilogue is not his epilogue.

Odysseus walks into the space of history.

He becomes its tragic actor.

The realness of *The Return of Odysseus* becomes more real every day.

The German retreat was in full swing.

The newspapers announced the invasion of allied forces on the opening night. It was necessary to leave aesthetic, ornamental, and abstract constructions aside. The space, which was delineated perfectly by the art's parameters, was invaded brutally by a "real object."
It is necessary to bring a work of art in theatre
to such a point of intensity where only one step
separates drama from life,
performer from audience.

THE RETURN OF ODYSSEUS III

Odysseus must REALLY return.
It would be dishonest to create for this purpose a false illusion of Ithaca.
Everything that surrounds him must be grand; everything that is spoken must be true and honest.
It would be a wicked pettiness to create *papier-mâché* columns and waves
for Odysseus's tragic return. I want to place actors among simple parcels,
ladders, and chairs—take their costumes away from them—discard all aesthetic values—introduce
c o i n c i d e n c e and even chaos—so this return would be real. Odysseus returns onto the s t a g e, and, it is onstage that he recreates laboriously the illusion of his Ithaca.
Theatre is a site where the laws of art clash with life's uncertainty and fortuity to give rise to the most powerful tensions and conflicts.[28]

This clash between the laws of art and life's uncertainty, which gave rise to tensions and conflicts in Kantor, who was captivated both by unmasking the mythological hero and his many inglorious returns from Troy and by the demand to bring a work of art in theatre to such a point of intensity where only one step separated drama from life or a performer from the audience, were made also visible in his descriptions of the set design for the production:

THE FIRST DESIGN VARIANT

The performance area is framed by the wings.
The wings are made of boards, planks, slats, plain canvas, all of which are covered with numbers and letters.
In the middle of the stage, there is a huge cube—a delphic thymele.
*BEHIND IT, AN UNREALISTIC, MOBILE SURFACE, WHICH IS
FILLED WITH SOUNDS, KEEPS FLOATING CONTINUOUSLY AND
INTERMINABLY.*
It is a measure of a different time and a different space.
THIS CAN BE NAMED ABSTRACTION, ABSOLUTE, OR DEATH.
The events onstage take place despite and independently of this abstract object, which is clearly separated from reality and the realness of the stage action.
Every so often, the actors freeze and become indifferent, as if they were compelled to do so by some inner force, or as if they forgot their lines.
The pauses are filled with the presence, motion, and sound from this mysterious floating surface.

The actors resume their parts.

The scene of the killing of Penelope's lovers is syncopated with similar pauses, which now, however, are filled with a different reality.

The pauses are getting longer.

The figures and events dissipate; there is only a surrealistic object.

Odysseus and a black cube—in act III,

this audio-mobile element becomes his stage partner.

THE SECOND DESIGN VARIANT

Real objects are substituted for illusionary objects.

Act I depicts the surroundings of Odysseus's home—

a rock, a fence, a house, all very simple, as if designed by a poorly educated human being, who also made them, covered them with canvas when necessary, etc. To use a language of poetic devices, an arrangement and a convincing illusion of i m a g i n a r y reality have been created.

Act II brings complications, even though a rock, a fence, and a house stay the same, because they lose their power to create

i l l u s i o n. A spotlight stands in the middle of the stage; the wings are turned around; a ladder leans over one of the wings; Melantho dances in between the electric cables; Penelope sits on a simple kitchen chair; the lovers are on the ladders; a rock, a house, a fence are nothing more than facades from Act I which are pushed aside by utilitarian and technical objects. This new reality, which is pushing aside the reality of Act I, is a stage equivalent of a new situation—having killed the lovers, Odysseus, who is entrapped in this alien and ruthless world, leaves his dreams and illusions of his childhood Ithaca never to return to them.

Act III—when they all leave,

only a rock, a fence, a wall of a house, and a s p o t l i g h t will be left. The light will turn them into lifeless facades. In vain will Odysseus try to recognize his Ithaca in them.

THE THIRD DESIGN VARIANT

Act I is grounded and takes place on a neutral stage which is stripped of its illusion.

At the same time, this o t h e r reality, which will be illusionary and imagined and is, for the time being, suppressed by the "raw" matter of the stage, begins to be perceived. Even though the crude stage reality and its ladders, wings badly put together, rostrum made of simple boards, still dominate, a white Greek sculpture of the head of a singer introduces a tension.

The actors, who still rehearse and repeat their parts, belong to the reality of the stage.

In Act II, i l l u s i o n begins to conquer the stage gradually. There appear well-s t r u c t u r e d and

i l l u s i o n a r y fragments.

The lovers put on the white masks, which are exact copies of faces from classical monuments.

Femios will stand next to a sculpture of a head and will sing a song; the same song which was sung by the spotlight operator in Act I.

Odysseus enters this deceptive space of illusion; this world which is alien and ominous to him.

Act III is a ruthless and a cruel amplification of the atmosphere of Act I.[29]

These three variants of the set design for *The Return of Odysseus* could be seen as Kantor's gesture toward the revolutionary pre–World War II avant-gardes who had explored the relationship between reality and art (cubism, Dada, formalism), the function of art in the post-1917 political order (constructivism), and the coexistence between the world of reality and abstraction (Oscar Schlemmer and Kazimir Malevich). According to the avant-garde thinking about developing a theatre practice, each one of these three variants could unfold in a specific direction. However, no matter what design was chosen, as Kantor observed, a theatre piece was built around just one form or one element. Its discovery would "blow up the structure of drama and to reveal its pulsating and vibrant interior."[30] This one form would draw to itself other compositional forms, all of which can be explained through it, arrange themselves around it, and be allowed to comment on other forms. Moreover,

Theatrical forms pulsate in any dramatic texts. All that should be done is to feel and express their pulse.

The network of relationships between the forms is built by contrasts and conflicts. It is the contrasts, unable to co-exist peacefully and brought together by force, which create new values and the totality indispensable for the existence of the work of art. In theatre, this totality is achieved via the process of balancing the contrasts between diverse scenic elements, such as, motion and sound, visual forms and motion, space and voice, word and motion of forms, etc. As far as the cognitive aspect of theatre is concerned, these contrasts must have sharp edges, come as surprise, shock, and lead to the creation of tension between two separate and incompatible realities or objects. A reality "will be created" by placing the other reality next to it, or by grounding it in the other reality existing in a different dimension.

Contrast should not, and ought not, be positioned in one dimension and within one category only.

A square should not only be contrasted with a circle, but also with a sinuous line, a voice, or a wheel.

THE PROCESS OF CREATING "STAGE FORMS" IS EQUAL TO THE PROCESS OF THE "SHOWING" OF DRAMA ONSTAGE.[31]

In an important sense, this last statement encapsulates one of the most significant characteristics of Kantor's creative process as well as understanding of the function of theatre. It posits that the process of staging a drama did not signify for him the process of interpreting the text or finding its stage equivalent. On the contrary, it was a process of the discovery of theatrical forms as well as creating conflicts and tensions between these forms, rather than scrutinizing the psychology of characters. The conflicts and tensions produced a reality of the work of art, whose totality could only be achieved by balancing the contrasts

Tadeusz Kantor's drawing for
Balladyna (1942; the drawing
was executed at a later date).
Collection "A." Photo courtesy
of the Kantor Estate.

between motion and sound, space and voice, words and objects. This technique placed Kantor's creative process outside of the traditional mainstream theatre—in an autonomous space that, as Artaud would have it, "must, in order to revive or simply to live, realize what differentiates it from text, pure speech, literature, and all other fixed and written means."[32]

In Juliusz Słowacki's *Balladyna*, staged by Kantor with the Independent Theatre on May 22–25, 1943, the abstract forms invaded the stage.[33] For Kantor, this romantic ballad was perfect for exploring the tension between the avant-garde traditions and Polish national myths at the time when Poland was under the Nazi occupation. As he noted, "The reality was so absurd that most of us turned toward abstract painting, and our first spectacle, that is *Balladyna*, was an abstraction. It was a translation of Słowacki's romanticism into abstract concepts of the Bauhaus. In the production, I used geometric forms, such as a circle, a square, an angle and materials such as sheet metal, tar paper, and woolen cloth."[34]

As in the works of Schlemmer, Malevich, and Kandinsky, the geometric and abstract forms used by Kantor were the instruments of universal knowledge—universal knowledge that would obliterate or transcend the war experience. For example, Malevich believed that painting could be used to attain universal knowledge and, therefore, sought in abstract art the same mysticism that Kandinsky pursued in his paintings and in "On the Spiritual in Art." Both Malevich and Kandinsky attempted to substitute subjective abstract art for the objective concrete artistic language of naturalism. Malevich's supremacist "A Black Square on a White Ground" could serve here as an example of this philosophy. In the painting, a black square is used as a visible unit of sensation in an objectless consciousness. It functions not as an image of a physical reality but as a living, dynamic, and autonomous form. The act of creating a work of art was thus a process during which a form that did not exist in nature arose out of a painted mass without repeating or altering the primary forms of objects in nature.[35]

Balladyna (1942). Photo by
Witold Witaliński courtesy of
the Cricoteka Archives.

The Return of Odysseus did not, however, follow the thought pattern presented in *Balladyna*. In *The Return of Odysseus*, it was not the abstract forms but reality itself that invaded and clashed with the illusionary scenic forms.[36] Why this shift? And what might be the consequences of such a maneuver?

While thinking about Wyspiański's Odysseus—a war criminal, cursed and pursued by the furies—Kantor remarked,

> His [Wyspiański's] *The Return of Odysseus* became my "war" theme. . . . The war turned the world into a "tabula rasa." The world was one step closer to death— and metaphorically—to poetry. At least this is what I thought. Everything could happen. . . . Time as if it had stopped.
>
> Easily, I had moved to Ithaca. I placed there a white rock, a wall, which surrounded the palace yard, a column, stairs leading into some depth, sea waves, a sky made of blue papier-mâché. . . . I felt at home there. I watched carefully Odysseus' every passage. . . .
>
> Odysseus' image has gradually changed. It became more and more vivid. I was convinced that, one day, he would appear in my tiny and crowded room. I was waiting for him. This feverish condition had nothing to do with a dream; it was real. Odysseus would appear to me more and more often; however, I noticed that he would stop at the threshold of my tiny room. I would see him disappear around the corner, or in a dark lobby, where, with his back to me, he would pretend to be extremely preoccupied with something, even though I felt that he knew perfectly well that I was looking for him . . .
>
> at the station, where I would see him get off the train and then quickly disappear into the crowd. . . .

These half-dreams, half-mystifications, convinced me that Odysseus refused
categorically to be only an i m a g e.
I had to think about it.
In times of madness created by men, in times of war, death and its frightening
troupes, which refused to be shackled by Reason and Human Senses,
burst into and merged with the sphere of life.[37]

The pathos of drama and its mythological character were thus thrown into
and merged with the sphere of life; that is, in the time of war, the play was
staged not in a theatre building but in a room that was destroyed:

There was war and there were thousands of such rooms. They all looked alike:
bare bricks stared from behind a coat of paint, plaster was hanging from the
ceiling, boards were missing in the floor, abandoned parcels were covered with
dust (they would be used as the auditorium), debris was scattered around; a
plain platform reminiscent of the deck of a ship, were discarded at the horizon
of this decayed decor; a gun barrel was resting on a heap of iron scrap; a military
loudspeaker was hanging from a rusty metal rope. The bent figure of a helmeted
soldier wearing a faded overcoat stood against the wall. On this day, June 6, 1944,
he became a part of this room. ("Theatrical Place")

In Kantor's theatre, Odysseus was not an image but was to become a German soldier returning from the battle of Stalingrad (the Soviet Union). The production opened to the sounds of a German *Paradenmarsch*. Phemius' song was
accompanied by the Nazi war announcement coming from a loudspeaker. When
Odysseus directed his bow against the lovers, a sound of a machine gun filled
the space.

This act of transgression, from the world "on the other side" (drama) into
the world of reality, as manifested by the entrance of the mythical figure of

Tadeusz Kantor's drawing for
Return of Odysseus (1944; the
drawing was executed in 1984–
1985). Collection "A." Photo
courtesy of the Kantor Estate.

Odysseus into the room destroyed by war, led to the absorbing of the fictitious world by the reality of life. The events and characters seen by the audience were thus necessarily molded by the real place and its characteristics rather than by the illusionary world of the text, just as the behavior of the audience in the room was necessarily shaped by war conditions rather than by the characteristics of a traditional theatre auditorium. Accordingly, the demarcation line between audience and actors had to disappear, since the space of the action of the play was also the space of the audience. Kantor's description of the opening scene from *The Return of Odysseus* showing the original playtext and the actual stage action is illuminating in its elucidation of this process:[38]

PLAYTEXT	STAGE ACTION
A shepherd and Odysseus disguised as a beggar enter. The shepherd is talkative. He describes in detail all the feasts and orgies that took place in the Odysseus' absence.	The silence of the room is broken by the sharp and rhythmical tones of Paradenmarsch. One can almost see soldiers' feet high in the air, hear their steps on the streets, or palace during the sound of the noisy orchestra's drums and trumpets.
Beggar allows himself to be recognized by the shepherd. Odysseus unfolds his story, i.e., the story of a war criminal cursed by the goods, the story of a man who is afraid to return home and bring the curse with him.	Helmeted Odysseus wearing a faded overcoat, like a ghost, enters through the doors. He wanders among the audience. The sounds of the triumphant march are heard. Odysseus sits down on a gun barrel.
The shepherd leaves to fetch water.	His bent figure creates a formless mass resembling nothing.
	The actor playing the part of the shepherd is sitting in the corner among the audience members. He slowly gets up as if to say his lines. He is just about to speak when, suddenly, he perceives the bent figure sitting on a gun barrel. Surprised, he forgets that he was supposed to say his opening lines. Instead, he inspects the figure carefully and shouts: "beggar.". . . . The scream should be a testimony to the authenticity of the action.
	Such a device will help to maintain the meeting and dialogue between Odysseus and the shepherd at the

threshold between the reality of the audience and the illusion of the text. . . . Bent Odysseus, with his back to the audience, constitutes a formless mass which merges with other objects in the room. The shepherd's talk to this "something" is in vain. . . . The lack of an answer creates a dreadful silence. Suddenly, when the word "Troy" is heard, a human face appears out of the formless mass.

The discrepancies between the play text and the stage action not only epitomized the act of transgression, from the world "on the other side" into the world of reality but also drew attention to Kantor's departure from the practices of the pre–World War II avant-gardes. Kantor noted in "Lesson 1" of *The Milano Lessons,*

Return of Odysseus (1944).
Photo by Zbigniew Brzozowski
courtesy of the Cricoteka
Archives.

1944. KRAKÓW. CLANDESTINE THEATRE. THE RETURN OF
ODYSSEUS FROM THE SIEGE OF STALINGRAD.

Abstraction, which existed in Poland until the outbreak of World War II,
disappeared in the period of mass genocide. This is a common phenomenon.
Bestiality, brought to the fore by this war, was too alien to this pure idea. . . .
Realness was stronger.
Also, any attempt to go beyond it came to naught.
The work of art lost its power.
Aesthetic re-production lost its power.
The anger of a human being trapped by other human beasts cursed A R T. We had
only the strength to grab the nearest thing,
THE REAL OBJECT
and to call it a work of art!
Yet,
it was a P O O R object, unable to perform any function in life, an object about
to be discarded.
An object which was bereft of a life function that would save it.
An object which was stripped, functionless, a r t i s t i c!
An object which would make one feel for it pity and affection.
This was the object that was completely different from that other [earlier] object:
A cart wheel smeared with mud;
A decayed wooden board;
A scaffold spattered with plaster;
A decrepit loud-speaker rending the air with screeching war announcements;
A kitchen chair. . . .[39]

This explanation given in 1988 is the clearest statement regarding Kantor's
practice of annexing reality. In its most obvious form, this reality was parallel
to, outside of, or an answer to the existing order—here, to the existing historical order. Kraków was under the Nazi occupation in 1944. Any artistic activity
was punished by death—thus, indeed, as Kantor noted in 1944, the audience
took the full responsibility for entering the performance space.[40]
    What was and where was this performance space? *The Return of Odysseus*
could not be staged in a traditional theatre, not only because Kantor perceived
traditional theatre as mind-deranging,[41] but also, and more important, because
such an act would be a betrayal of his nonconformity in the face of bestiality
brought by the war. "The anger of a human being trapped by other human
beasts cursed A R T." Thus, the artistic creation—the act of grabbing the nearest things, the real object, and calling it a work of art—took place in a space
outside of the prevailing order of things, a Nazi occupation of Kraków. This
site was marked by the pressures of the "state of emergency" in which he lived
and which defined the urgency of the struggle against Fascism.[42] *The Return of
Odysseus* was staged in a room that had been destroyed by war. It was a useless
room, a useless object, that could no longer perform its function as an inhabit-
able space assigned to it by a cultural norm, a convention, or an architectural
design. Bereft of its use-value, destroyed by the very culture and civilization

that had assigned its value to it, this room signified, for Kantor, a reality of the lowest rank. It was "ANTITHETICAL to life, and that is why [it was] *scandalous* and shocking when defined in terms of its categories."[43] Into this room the performers brought different objects found in the war zone: a cart wheel smeared with mud, a decayed wooden board, a scaffold spattered with plaster, a decrepit loudspeaker rending the air with screeching war announcements, and a kitchen chair. These were poor objects, that is, like the room to which they were brought in, functionless, discarded, and useless. They were wrenched from the war reality and placed in a space wherein the object's objectness could only be established in its relationship to other objects or people in space. Thus, the object's function was not assigned by a convention that had been compromised by the bestiality of the war, by a performative process outside of the normative categories. Consider, for example, how Kantor viewed the relationship between an actor or character and an object:

> This object was empty.
> It had to justify its being to itself rather than to the surroundings which were foreign to it.
> [By so doing, the object] revealed its own existence.
> And when its function was imposed upon it, this act was seen as if it were happening for the first time since the moment of creation.
> In *The Return of Odysseus*, Penelope, sitting on a kitchen chair, performed the act of being "seated" as a human act happening for the first time. The [physical] object acquired its historical, philosophical, and a r t i s t i c function![44]

This simple example draws attention to a process during which a useless object—an object destroyed by war or wrestled away from the conditions that provided it with a use-value—came into being through setting up a relationship with other objects or people in that space. This is why, when Penelope was sitting on a kitchen chair, the act of being seated was an act happening as if for the first time. This act was the act of naming what did not exist before or what did not yet have a name assigned to it. In other words, this act was the act of naming the void. The event itself was momentous—it was only grasped as living present in bodies and objects that acted and were acted upon or engendered and were engendered. In other words, the event, the staging of *The Return of Odysseus*, and the bodies as well as objects shaping it took place *in* the war reality. However, the event and the bodies as well as object were not *of* that reality. Bereft of their preassigned identities, these useless objects—a cart wheel smeared with mud, a decayed wooden board, a scaffold spattered with plaster, a decrepit loudspeaker rending the air with screeching war announcements, or a kitchen chair—needed now to name themselves in the act happening as if for the first time:

> The bent figure of a helmeted soldier wearing a faded overcoat stood against the wall. On this day, June 6, 1944, he became a part of this room. He came there and sat down to rest. Despite his poor condition, he carried a menacing air. When everything returned to normal after the intrusion from the outside, when the

date was established, and when all the elements of the room seemed to become indispensable elements of this composition, the soldier turned his head to the audience and said this one sentence: "I am Odysseus, I have returned from Troy." This everyday REALNESS, which was firmly rooted in both place and time, immediately permitted the audience to perceive this mysterious current flowing from the depth of time when the soldier, whose presence could not have been questioned, called himself by the name of the man who had died centuries ago. A split second was needed to see this return, but the emotion raised by it stayed much longer . . . in memory! ("Theatrical Place")

"I am Odysseus. I have returned from Troy," said a bent figure seated on an abandoned gun barrel. A split second was needed to see this return. A split second was needed to rupture continuous linear time with the emotion that remains with us much longer. Is it possible that this complex, though infamous, transition from one world to another, rather than affirming the dominant ideology or life, liberated the audience from the servitude to linear time and provided them with the opportunity to witness how the objects and people contest the House of History? The time of history and the *cairós*, the abrupt and sudden conjunction where decision grasps opportunity and life is fulfilled in the moment, marked a missing articulation between the continuous time and the cairological time when the events *in* reality absorbed the events *of* reality.[45]

The staging of *The Return of Odysseus*, at the time when artistic activities were forbidden and punished, when "human kind [was] turned into mud, soap, and ashes" some forty miles from Kraków, ruptured and froze "historical relations which nowhere seem ready to melt [so that] mind [could] go where it need not degrade itself."[46] This was also the place of the event staging a strike in the House of History, halting time and interrupting its linear movement, so that the audience bereft of the veil of the progressive unfolding of history and of stage illusion would finally see

> many inglorious returns from Troy. All are marked with the imprints of human unhappiness, inhuman crimes committed in the name of religious slogans.
> The returns which are veiled in the tattered false military banners.
> The returns—escapes from justice.
> Charon's boat does not stop for Odysseus lost in the night of his epilogue.
> The epilogue is not his epilogue.
> Odysseus walks into the space of history. ("Independent Theatre")

To use Kantor's vocabulary: real place and poor object-actors, as well as the transgression of the text by the world "on the other side," destroyed all attempts at representation. Theatre ceased to function as a mechanism reproducing the external order of things. Theatre was an answer to reality the same way as Kantor's poor objects were an answer to artistic objects. When, as was the case with *The Return of Odysseus*, the external reality, whose value was depreciated by the war, was refused the right to control the stage action, a different process was created. Now, theatre itself was a reality and the stage a real place, a room destroyed by war, no longer able to perform its traditional function.

As Kantor noted in an essay about the Cricot 2 Theatre, the rejection of the artistic theatrical object, which contained in itself the notions of representation, performance, and illusion, led to the elimination of a stage prop, which was replaced by the real object; of a set design, which was replaced by the real place; of a costume, whose design was controlled by dramatic fiction, the spatial organization of a stage, the lights, the blocking; and, finally, of the stage action itself, whose sequencing was replaced by the actions associated with the real place.[47] This "theatre" was the real site where the artistic process took place. It was an autonomous space where modes of thinking and seeing were entangled in an intricate interplay between the objects found or brought into the real space and human figures moving through that space.

III

In 1947, Kantor wrote,

> While I was in Warsaw, I saw a piece of an iron bridge, which must have been hit by a bomb.
> I was struck by the sight of this incredible
> c o m p r e s s i o n .
> [I had] a shocking sensation of the force, which had done it;
> unimaginable as a human force.
> This intense sensation was almost "artistic,"
> because it was bereft of human, unpredictable emotions, which would have been caused by the explosion itself; [it was similar to] the sensation of watching the "natural forms" of the victims in Pompeii.
> A thought crossed my mind that if someone, a joker, placed this piece of iron as a monument on a public square,
> in the future, the historians would, in its entangled form,
> decipher the f o r c e s which governed our time.
> I also had a thought that this incredibly c o m p r e s s e d form could herald the artistic c o n v e n t i o n s of the postwar a e s t h e t i c s.[48]

This piece of an iron bridge, which was destroyed by the war, not only heralded the postwar artistic convention but also, as chronicled by Kantor, was a metaphor for the changing artistic conditions. On the one hand, this piece of an iron bridge was a concrete and material reminder of the recent war events and of the forces that had destroyed it. On the other hand, this piece of a useless iron bridge, as *The Return of Odysseus* made clear, could now acquire its autonomous artistic function because it was bereft of its signifying features. Could this incredibly compressed form herald the new artistic convention in the changing political conditions of postwar Poland?

Poland, which had been a capitalist state prior to World War II, found itself in a new socialist reality. Prior to solidifying the rules of socialist realism in 1949, the Polish government allowed artists to explore freely diverse artistic conventions. This strategy was similar to that employed by the Russian revolutionary government, which some thirty years earlier allowed Vladimir Mayakovsky,

Vladimir Tatlin, Alexander Rodchenko, Lyubov Popova, Vsevelod Meyerhold, and many other artists to develop the avant-garde practice and art in a new post-1917 socialist reality—autonomous art freed from the prerevolutionary bourgeois aesthetic. Since the revolution established a break with tsarist Russia and its culture, new art forms and new criticism needed to be created in order to express the new reality. Initially, the artists welcomed the Revolution. They perceived themselves as agitators, transmitters of the socialist ideas and ideals, thus, creators of the new radical socialist reality. Tatlin headed the Department of Museums and Conservation of Antiquities, Popova designed the decoration of the Moscow Soviet building for May Day celebrations, Rodchenko designed posters for the Red Army, Mayakovsky designed posters for the Russian Telegraphic Agency and wrote short plays that dealt with the most pressing issues of the new society, and Meyerhold's constructivist productions celebrated the age of the machine and new political order. The art, like Tatlin's Monument to the Third International, corresponded to "all invented artistic forms of the present time. In the present position of art these forms will obviously be cubes, cylinders, spheres, cones, segments, spherical surfaces, pieces of these."[49]

Similarly, in a new post–World War II Polish reality, Kantor actively participated in the artistic life in Kraków. As a member of the Group of Young Visual Artists, he presented his paintings at the exhibition, which opened at the Writers' Club on June 24, 1945. As noted by an art critic, these young painters, who during the war had been associated with Kantor's experimental theatre, created works that drew on the most radical examples of formalist, uncompromising, and constructivist art of the 1920s.[50] The exhibition was opened to the general public on October 12, 1946. At the same time, Kantor and Mieczysław Porębski, an art critic, published in a Polish literary magazine, *Twórczość* (*Creativity*), a manifesto of the Group of Young Visual Artists. In it, they attempted to describe their position and place not only vis-à-vis other artistic groups and individual painters but also vis-à-vis Polish postwar reality.[51] The manifesto emphasized their relationship to other avant-garde traditions and to the dialectical approach to the arts—that is, the value of art was found in its attempt to establish a dynamic relationship with reality, which was believed to be changing and fluid. This may explain why Kantor and Porębski were against naturalism in painting. According to them, the object in this painterly tradition was fixed and could only be repeated, imitated, or represented as a copy rather than express and interact with the changing environment. They, however, extolled Pablo Picasso, Marcel Gromaire, and Paul Klee as well as their uncompromising visual vivisections aimed at liberating the object from its schematic cultural or ideological placement.

In order to address this new Polish reality, Kantor and Porębski introduced the notion of *intensified reality*. This intensified reality signified the process of enclosing and strengthening that reality in an artistic form so that it could be investigated in detail. This process was supposed to be dynamic, revealing the object in its singularity, as well as articulating and rearticulating its presence in its relationship to other objects. The concept of intensified reality in painting was an elaboration of the practices that Kantor had discussed while working on *The Return of Odysseus*. (Recall, for example, Penelope sitting on a kitchen chair, which had been brought to a destroyed room—a found performance space.) Maybe this is the reason why, when the socialist government appropriated this concept for socialist realism, Kantor abandoned the term, since it was now an officially sanctioned fixed reference point against which the works promoting the proletarian esthetics were to be measured. Even though the term intensified reality disappeared from Kantor's artistic vocabulary, the very practice of playing with reality would always remain present in his artistic endeavors.

In 1947, Kantor received a stipend for a trip to Paris:

I knew then that French Art was grand art. But there was no French art in Poland. I had to learn about it from books and reproductions.

But my own learning process was not scholarly: [my teachers were] Imagination and its free will.

I saw French art only after the war in 1947.

It is hard to tell whether this physical act of seeing, or the act of seeing through my mind's eye, was more significant. [The physical act] was different, concrete; it was a [material] verification.[52]

Kantor spent his time at the Louvre, Jeu de Pomme, the galleries in the Beaux Arts district on the Left Bank. He saw both the abstract and mystical modernist works of Kandinsky, Picasso, Klee, Max Ernst, and Jean Mirò, and the new canvases of heavy texture and intense energy by Yves Tanguy and Hans Hartung. His interview with André Fougeron, a representative of the new French style in painting, was published in Poland in 1947. Accidentally, Kantor stumbled upon the Palais de la Découverte where he found new type of paintings—paintings resembling "cross-sections of metals, cells, genes, molecules, structures, a completely different morphology, the concept of Nature embracing Eternity and the Unimaginable."[53] Kantor's fascination with this new image finding its roots and inspiration in a scientific knowledge of the world was grounded for him in

a completely different concept of space. The model of space we are used to—all solid mass and figures that pull and push against each other, move towards each other, move suddenly forward, bump into each other, cross each other, pulsate, grow, are pushed into the frames; into an enclosed field; all this slowly built and transformed by evolution model of space—suddenly collapsed for me. As if driven by the euphoria of discovering new lands, I wrote in my notebook, "This is nothing but a cemetery of illusion and useless props." In these stormy times of things losing meaning and value, in the times when the past signaled its presence through intuition rather than a well-formed consciousness, all this slowly started to come together; I became aware that a painting is conditioned first and foremost by a particular model of space. I used to believe that, in different periods, different concepts of space were established, because of cultural, social, scientific pressures; and it is only later that these concepts informed an artistic process. Space became for me an object of artistic investigation.[54]

This fascination with space was an ineluctable consequence of Kantor's war experiences, when the idea of reality and its representation in art were disjoined. As Kantor asserted,

> The act of deforming classical beauty, for me,
> did not take place in the territory of aesthetic categories.
> The time of war and the time of the "lords of the world" made me lose my trust in
> the old image, which had been perfectly formed,
> raised above all other, apparently lower, species.
> It was a discovery! Behind the sacred icon, a b e a s t was hiding. ("My
> Work—My Journey")

Kantor abandoned the "sacred icon":

> And the moment did arrive, when I decided to go over the threshold. Going
> through this unknown passage, I tried to keep the memory of the shape of a
> human body. And then everything was but MOTION and MATTER.
> Inferno. It was my "I N T E R I O R." ("My Work—My Journey")

Because of the works he saw at the Palais de la Découverte, Kantor made a double shift at that time. Not only did he discard a memorable image of the 1944 Odysseus for the Inferno of cross-sections of metals, cells, genes, molecules, and structures, but he also questioned the traditional and his own understanding of the attributes of space, which had been grounded in cubism, constructivism, and geometric abstraction. He rejected their notion of space defined as "a receptacle without dimension into which the intellect puts its creation."[55] In its place, he put forth the notion of space that

> does not have an exit, or a boundary;
> [space] which is receding, disappearing,
> or approaching omni-directionally with changing velocity;
> it is dispersed in all directions: to the sides, to the middle;
> it ascends, caves in,
> spins on the vertical, horizontal, diagonal axis. . . .
> It is not afraid to burst into an enclosed shape,
> defuse it with its sudden jerking movement,
> deform its shape. . . .
> Figures and objects become the function of space
> and its mutability. . . .
> Space is not a passive r e c e p t a c l e
> in which objects and forms are posited. . . .
> SPACE itself is an OBJECT [of creation].
> And the main one!
> SPACE is charged with E N E R G Y.
> Space shrinks and e x p a n d s.
> And these motions mould forms and objects.
> It is space which G I V E S   B I R T H to forms!

It is space that conditions the network of relations and tensions between the objects.
TENSION is the principal actor of space.
A MULTI-SPACE. . . .
The process of reaching it is childishly simple.
It requires however an intervention of omni-present and impulsive free will.
SPACE is compressed into a flat surface.
This surface is put into various types of motion.
CIRCULAR MOTION,
around an axis posited vertically, horizontally, diagonally
in relation to the surface of the image. . . .
This motion requires a constant COUNTER-MOTION.
PENDULUM MOTION,
whose s w i n g i n g—
losing
and regaining of momentum—
conditions expansion
and GROWTH of space.
MOTIONS OF MOVING [surfaces]
of *PUSHING* them together,
of *PULLING* them apart,
of c o v e r i n g and u n-c o v e r i n g.
MOTIONS OF DESCENDING and ASCENDING.
MOTION OF MOVING [surfaces] apart until they disappear.
MOTIONS OF DRAWING them NEAR and PUSHING them AWAY.
SUDDENNESS and VELOCITY of these motions
create new aspects:
TENSION
and a change of SCALE.[56]

This transformation in Kantor's thinking about space manifested itself in the paintings he created upon his return from Paris in July 1947. His paintings from this period, on the one hand, were single objects molded by dynamic forces of space, that is, paintings showing how the shape of an object was defused by space "approaching" the object simultaneously from many directions. Thus, for example, a cone ceased to be a perfect geometrical figure located in an empty space and became condensed or expanded depending on where and how space burst into this enclosed shape.[57] On the other hand, his 1948 "umbrella" compositions explored the relations and tensions between an object and multi-dimensional space. According to Kantor, an umbrella "opened" and "closed" space. The tension between the object and space was contained in a metal skeleton of the umbrella. This tension was so powerful that it could destroy the structure of an umbrella and give birth to a new form.[58] Kantor, thus, abandoned visual sovereignty of the eye producing the representational image in a classical, three-dimensional, pictorial space for the process in which the eye did not perform a visual or ordering function but followed the contours of what organized its field of perception.

The dynamic powers of physical space were further explored and redefined by Kantor in his metaphoric paintings, which were filled with a variety of biological and mechanic organisms, Art Informel, set designs, and in his theatre experiments starting in 1955—after a five year hiatus in Kantor's public activities. His disappearance from an active public engagement was his protest against the imposition of the rules of socialist realism in 1949, which started to have an impact on what was being created and how works of art were evaluated by the critics.

The first signs of the changes in the Polish government's cultural policy were felt at the First Exhibition of Modern Art in Kraków in 1948, where Kantor presented one of his geometric-technical or metaphoric forms, as well as at the meeting of Polish visual artist in Nieborów (February 12–13, 1949) and in Katowice (June 27–29, 1949). These three events were a site of the encounter between the radical avant-garde and the new type of art that was promoted by the State.[59] At the two meetings, the representatives of the state defined the artistic creation in terms of Marxist ideology and its function in terms of representing the new social reality. Kantor participated in both meetings. He and his friends, including Maria Jarema, with whom he would create Cricot 2 Theatre in 1955, defended freedom of art. Until the very end, they remained faithful to their ideals—they spoke against reducing art to being an overdetermined superstructure defined by the rules of socialist realism and the destruction of the many autonomous trends and movements in postwar Polish art. Kantor defended avant-garde art against those who wanted to criticize its nonconceptual aspect. It was only because it presented reality as nonconceptual, that is, in the form of the tension between its elements and other dynamic forms, that avant-garde art could fully express the complexity of the postwar reality. No matter how powerful his arguments were in support of the autonomy of the creative process and the condition of the artist, Kantor's statements did not delay the arrival of the officially sponsored and recognized art. In December 1949, Kantor gave the last lecture, "About Art (About Dreaming)," at the Academy of Fine Arts in Kraków, which summarized his attitude toward avant-garde art and its radical possibilities for opening up the field and the substance of history:

> To dream. . . .
> I place such an emphasis on this phrase, because this condition [of being able
> to dream] has recently become suspicious. Some pseudo-artists, whose organ of
> imagination has ceased to function, perceive it as too esoteric. I dare to disagree.
> To dream is a condition that was ridiculed by the bourgeois mentality in the most
> idiotic and philistine manner; it was turned into something banal; it was forced to
> sit down at the table overflowing with food and pushed into a stuffy bedroom. . . .
> To dream is to separate oneself from reality, which we continuously inhabit; and
> which, because we are continuously in it, becomes invisible.
> To dream is to separate oneself from reality, which is far from being a nirvana;
> on the contrary, it is a transition into different ways of thinking and imagining
> things—into the domains which are freer and faster, which will help us perceive
> this reality and its fabric in a sharper and more intensive manner.

To dream is to experience an intensified functioning of imagination.
It is only through imagination that we can see and observe reality and its object in the space of art.
And what is more interesting, we can accomplish this thanks to imagination which moves in a direction which is opposite to this of reality.
It happens sometimes that, when after an intense encounter or emotion, in which our imagination moves through the regions severed from reality, we return to the normal condition, the objects reveal to us their new aspects as if we saw them for the first time. . . .
I am reminded about Mayakovsky's suggestive statements—if you want to write a poem about love, take a tram, not an empty one, but one which is full of people—under these conditions, squeezed and uncomfortable, begin to think intensely about the person for whom you are writing a poem—s/he will appear in your imagination sharper and filled with all kinds of emotions.
When he was to write a poem about Jesienin's death, he took a train, stayed in little towns, slept in small hotels, and came back with nothing. It is only at home that he realized that he stayed in gloomy hotel rooms similar to the one where Jesienin had hanged himself.
If you want to describe a reality—writes Mayakovsky—sever your links with it and travel to a different one—it is where imagination and dreams will give this reality of yours its fullness and depth. . . .
Forgive me this sermon.
I am saying it as much to you as to myself. . . .[60]

Kantor was demoted at the end of the academic year in June 1950. The reason for dismissal given by the university was his socially and academically unacceptable teaching strategies. For the next five years, Kantor, who refused to accept the rules that framed art in terms of officially sanctioned socialist realism, and, consequently, could not exhibit his paintings, worked as a set designer, continuing his experiments with abstract art in a traditional theatrical space.[61]

IV

The so-called thaw that followed Stalin's death began in 1955. In real terms, the thaw signified a brief moment in the history of Poland when the rules of socialist realism were less strict and the people who had been in power between 1945 and 1955 were often demoted from their official positions. Nineteen fifty-five was a transformative year for Kantor. While still working as a scenic designer for the Stary Teatr (the Old Theatre) in Kraków, he published an essay "The Artistic Theatre" in *Życie Literackie*.[62] In it, Kantor explored the idea of the artistic theatre—that is, theatre whose artistic process would not be controlled by administration and bureaucracy. Neither would its technical aspect be allowed to reduce the creative process to a craft. Artistic theatre, unlike bureaucratic theatre or a theatre temple, would reject conventions that had established the contours of the existing theatre practices and the cultural status quo, which was defined by its mission statement or institutional character. Artistic theatre, unlike bureaucratic theatre or a theatre temple, would challenge the accepted categories as well as transgress the boundaries in its quest for new means of artistic expression. Artistic theatre, according to Kantor, had to be revolutionary in terms of its social function and artistic endeavors, the way Piscator's theatre practice was. In his commitment to political theatre, continued Kantor, Piscator rejected illusion because the existence of illusion in theatre questioned the realness of the audience and participants as well as diminished the gravity of the issues discussed.

Kantor returned to his thinking about the creative process, which he had started to explore while working on *The Return of Odysseus* as well as in his postwar experiments with space:

> I am bored being an interior designer, placing furniture on stage; an architect constructing useless buildings; a set designer seeking a director's approval; I am bored with a theatre in which I could perform all these functions. I am not bored with an actor, whose fate and metamorphoses are visually shaped by me; I am not bored with the stage space, the most suggestive of all the universes, where the fate of the actor is fulfilled; where all the forces of pulling and pushing away, all tragic conflicts and comic tensions, the last farewells and dramatic returns, all emotions, exultation and enthusiasm, fears and happiness, and the life itself are fulfilled.[63]

In the summer of 1955, Kantor traveled to Paris with the Stary Theatre. While in Paris, he saw the works of Wols, Fautrier, Mathieu, and Pollock that experimented with a new style called Art Informel. Art Informel was a spatial improvisation examining the texture of compositions. Wols's semiorganic forms were disclosed in colors and light, Fautrier's images were created by paste applied to prepared paper that in turn was glued to the canvas, Mathieu's and Pollock's action-paintings employed dripping, spraying, imposing paint on the canvas surface with a brush or gestures of the body. Kantor noted that Art Informel manifested to him the process of discovering the forms that were freed from the laws of construction, always changing and fluid, and negated the concept of a finished work.[64] Art Informel was synonymous with spontaneity of action and movement during which forms and their matter or essence were revealed by the process of demolition, decomposition, dissolution, disintegration, deconstruction, and destruction. His 1956 painting "Two Figures" was created by mixing on the canvas two liquids, water and turpentine, which decomposed each other and created an illusion of fluid forms dissolving in an infinite spatial depth. Once that was achieved, thin films of paint were squeezed upon this background. A complex network of linear structures and contrasts slowly emerged. When the process of a composition was completed, "there emerged life in its pure form, life which [was] pulsating, erupting, and bereft of any practical purpose, which [was] subject to a never ending process of destruction and rebirth" ("My Work—My Journey"). This process received a full and detailed treatment in Kantor's paintings exhibited in 1956 and in his writings from the period as well as later commentaries:

I entered the "Inferno-Interior."
The painting was the image of its "secretion"; of the matter of my own organism;
of life's pure essence which flows
through this matter.
Only flows. ("My Work—My Journey")

Nineteen fifty-five was also the year when Cricot 2 Theatre was founded. Together with a Polish avant-garde artist, Maria Jarema, Kantor, as he would later assert in his "The Conditions for the Autonomous Theatre," gathered a group of radical artists—actors, painters, poets, and musicians who in their individual disciplines were searching for new means of artistic expression—who were interested in new modes of expression in the arts in general and theatre in particular.[65] As Kantor noted, this new concept of theatre did make use of certain elements out of which a traditional theatre piece was created—an actor, a costume, a text, and an auditorium. However, these elements were not assembled or arranged in a particular fashion in order to present the audience with a coherent interpretation of a text or an exploration of the psychology of a character but were used to construct tensions and new relations between them. Each of these elements was, for Kantor, real and autonomous. Each one of them was a complete and enclosed form that was created outside of the performance or a production. It was the reality or realness of this element, and not how it could be shaped or molded for the purpose of a production, that Kantor was interested in exploring in his new theatre. Thus, Cricot 2 Theatre from its founding moment in 1955 was a theatre that claimed that it was impossible to transfer a written play—a literary text conceived in immaterial imagination—onto the stage—a physical domain defined by temporal and spatial dimensions.

A different process was needed. The text to be used in a production was viewed as a ready-made reality that had been created somewhere else and at a different time. This reality was to be accepted. It could never, however, become a theatrical reality, because a creation of a theatrical reality modeled after a textual reality was nothing more than an illustration and interpretation. Consequently, the text, like an actor and an object, was one of the autonomous elements that clashed with other elements, entered into a conflict with them, and generated a tension between them.[66] This process signified

a rejection of a method of "illustrating," reporting, representing the plot of the play through a stage action and a need to employ a new method. This new method is the process of creating p a r a l l e l   t r a c k s which do not illustrate, explain, or interpret each other, but "correspond" to one another through pointed dynamic tensions. One of these tracks is a t e x t, which was bereft of a surface plot structure; the other is a parallel TRACK OF THE AUTONOMOUS STAGE ACTION, pure element, pure theatrical matter.[67]

Cricot 2 Theatre claimed to reveal the very matter and energy of theatre by excising its traditional representational function in a long process of exploration. The opening night was both the culmination of this process and the beginning of the next stage—the stage of a slow and gradual process during which the individual elements of the production would continue to evolve and change. Some of these elements would lose their power or depth, empty themselves out, and need to be abandoned or replaced in order for the production to remain faithful to Kantor's call for a dynamic creative process. When this process reached its final limit—that is, when its constitutive elements lost their dynamism and inner energy—a new creative process would be initiated. This method of work may explain why there were only some ten productions in the history of Cricot 2 Theatre, which spanned over fifty years. Each production marked a transformation in a theatrical practice, known as the Autonomous Theatre, the Zero Theatre, the Informel Theatre, the Theatre-Happening, the Theatre of Death, and the Theatre of Intimate Commentaries.

The first production of Cricot 2 Theatre, *The Cuttlefish*, by Stanisław Ignacy Witkiewicz (Witkacy), was presented to the public on May 12, 1956, at 10 PM. The 10 PM curtain was due to the fact that some of the company members were also performing in regular theatres.[68] Since traditional theatre (that is, a building, a stage, and an auditorium), was, for Kantor, the least appropriate place for a creative process because it had been anesthetized by the century-old conventions and practices, theatre (that is, a play, a playtext, and a production) could only come into being in a place that was not designed for it. During World War II, a bombed room was such a place. Now, in 1956, it was a building housing the organization of the visual artists (Dom Plastyków). As Kantor observed, "The stage, bereft of all illusion, was simply a floor made of wooden planks which was thrust into the middle of the auditorium. The auditorium was what really mattered. The auditorium was a café and the audience seated by the tables behaved the way one did in a café. This café was created not to function as a cabaret space, but so that the auditorium was a site where people might gather naturally or accidentally and not specifically to watch a performance."[69]

When a jazz group finished playing, a performance began. During the intermission and after the show, the audience danced on the stage floor. During the opening night, this spontaneous and accidental character of the performance site encouraged two young poets, Andrzej Bursa and Ireneusz Iredyński, to interrupt the stage action and read their own radical poetry to the audience from the pulpit reserved for the character of Pope Julius II.[70] Thus, indeed, the auditorium was a café, where many things happened simultaneously and accidentally, despite the fact that *The Cuttlefish* was supposed to be presented there. The staging of the play was on equal footing with other, equally accidental, events taking place there that evening.

Witkacy's play is about a conflict between art and the institution, art and bureaucracy, or art and the government. An artist, Rockoffer, stages a fight for the people's souls with the despotic ruler, the King of Hyrcania, Hyrcan IV, who believes that art has come to an end and nothing will ever revive it. Rockoffer and Hyrcan IV, who are joined by Pope Julius II, an art patron who commissioned Michelangelo to paint the ceiling of the Sistine Chapel, dressed as in the portrait by Titian, exchange their view on the function of art.[71] Kantor's choice of Witkacy, who had been banned during socialist realism, or of Witkacy's topical play would probably be sufficient to draw attention to Cricot 2 Theatre in a new political situation. As Polish poet Zbigniew Herbert wrote, "For the audience member who saw *The Cuttlefish* in May 1956, Hyrcania, that is, a country where a few infallible and unerring partake in the orgy of power and control over a society—'a flock of lost sheep'—was neither an abstraction nor, unfortunately, a utopia. When the words of the syndicate of the hand-made kitsch, which destroyed the paintings of the play's hero, were heard from the stage, the banned artists seated in the auditorium looked at each other with understanding."[72]

Such a reading of *The Cuttlefish* could have been prompted by Witkacy's play. Kantor, however, was not interested in staging a politically charged text in the post-Stalinist era as a representation of the new political situation or as theatre therapy, achieved by exploring textual ambiguities that would be immediately recognized by the audience. Actually, as he asserted, the Polish critics were divided—they either approved the staging that brought forth what they had deciphered as a political commentary or were puzzled by the incomprehensible staging of what, for many, was an incomprehensible play to begin with. Neither of the two groups, said Kantor, had the language to describe his attempt at creating an autonomous theatre. Consequently, the critics trained in recognizing political innuendos or in traditional representational practices could only evaluate the production in terms of the relationship between the stage presentation and Witkacy's playtext: Did the director render the text successfully or not? Was the interpretation of the text adequate? The lack of correspondence between the playtext and its stage equivalent was seen either as a failure or, at best, a departure from convention. Whereas the critics saw *The Cuttlefish* only as the extension of the existing representational practice in theatre or in terms of a shift in the existing political conditions, Kantor, faithful to his notion and practice of autonomous theatre and annexed reality, kept drawing attention to what these critics could not see while seeing, that is, the forms pulsating in a dramatic text.

In "The Production's Reality," Kantor reiterated this process: *The Cuttlefish* was built around three principle forms or elements: the environment, objects, and actors. Positioned within the boundaries of a space where any definition of their "essences" was possible, they engaged in an intricate and complex process of constituting diverse spatial formations. The opening sequence illustrated this process:

> The stage is bereft of its illusion.
> The a u d i t o r i u m is the only space that matters.
> The auditorium is a café.
> The spectators are sitting at the tables.
> They behave the way one does in a café.
> A wooden floor, wedged aggressively into the middle of the café floor,
> is the stage.
> 1 sequence:
> The hero of the play, Rockoffer,
> a decadent, probably even a great, artist,
> is sitting, on an iron stool,
> chained to a c o l u m n.

It is a classical column,
reminiscent of those at tombstones,
whose top is cut off.
A second actor, the hero's double,
is inside the column.
Only his head can be seen emerging from the top of the column.
It gives the impression that it rests on a plinth.
The hero's head on a plinth,
one may argue,
looks as if ex cathedra or from Olympus;
this does not mean, however,
that it is unable to express human reactions.
It cannot be read as a symbol,
because it would lose its sense of humor.
The hero must behave the way any
normal, intelligent being would
in a situation when someone, as a joke,
put him in this humiliating situation;
and, to add insult to injury, invited the audience to look at him.
He is embarrassed,
he is trying to find excuses;
then, since there is nothing that can be done,
he begins to talk to his head on a plinth;
finally, he begins to speak his lines,
as it was earlier agreed upon. . . .
A swift exchange of thoughts,
agreements,
conflicts,
tensions,
glances,
smiles,
whispers
between Rockoffer and his head on a pedestal takes place.
This situation, or rather
"i n s t a l l a t i o n,"
makes it impossible for the hero
to *realign himself in an expected manner*
with the situations unfolding in the play;
rather, it functions as a *barrier* between him and the plot of the play.
His actions, which are limited by it,
are not logically connected with
the o t h e r   e l e m e n t s.
This is how the individual elements and the totality
become a u t o n o m o u s.
Next to him, on an *operating table,*
like a sphinx,
is Alice d'Or,

who is bold,
with her breasts uncovered,
wearing a tight cinnabar costume,
exuding overintellectualized eroticism,
cynicism, sex, perversion, wallowing in the
fall of her lovers, a decadent, a prostitute
a walking image of egotism and the hero's suffering.
A sterilized operating table turns this
erotic operating table
into something even more scandalous.
2 sequence:
Pope Julius II
appears at the pulpit, which is
located among the audience members.
Actually, he is not a pope but a clown. . . .
From the pulpit, he preaches about art, eternal life, art support. . . .
All these elements . . .
create separate situations and events that
increase the general tension and
"temperature"
by clashing with each other
and a shocking lack of any logical explanation.[73]

The same sequence in Witkiewicz's play opens with a conversation between Paul Rockoffer, an artist, and Alice d'Or, a statue, about the meaning of existence and the crisis of modern art. The exchange takes place in front of a black wall with a blood-red window that lights up at irregular intervals marking the disappearance of the light of Eternal Mystery. Pope Julius II joins the conversation and expresses his views on art, philosophy, and life.[74]

The discrepancies between the stage action and the playtext are addressed in Kantor's manifesto of the Autonomous Theatre:

The theatre which I call **autonomous**
is the theatre which is not
a reproductive mechanism,
i.e., a mechanism whose aim is to
present an interpretation of a piece of literature
on stage,
but a mechanism which
has its own **independent**
existence.
Due to the notion of **unity**
which is an inherent part of
a true work of art,
this concept,
which is as complex as the nature of theatre
and the creative process,

cannot be fully explained
unless all its germinal parts are defined.
At least, all the theatrical elements
must be integrated to a degree and
create a composite unit.
Because the term
the "highest"
(degree of integration)
does not mean anything
and thus leaves room for misunderstandings
let us label it
the **zero** (degree).
I do not apply the concept of
the autonomous theatre
to **explain**

the dramatic text,   The relationship between
to **translate** it   theatre and drama

into the language of theatre,
to **interpret** it
or **find** its new meanings.
The concept of the
autonomous theatre
is not the tool to
excavate the so-called
"stage equivalent"
which could be perceived
as a second parallel "action"
that is mistakenly called
autonomous.
I consider such interpretations
as naive stylizations.
I create such
reality,
such plots of events
which have neither
logical,
analogical,
parallel,
nor *juxtaposed*
relationship with the drama;
and such forces
that could **crush**
the **impregnable shell** of
drama. ("The Autonomous Theatre")

Thus, the function of theatre, as *The Return of Odysseus* had already sig-naled, was not to explain, translate, or interpret a play. Rather, its aim was to "crush the impregnable shell of drama" to expose the inadequacies of a literary text in the intimate process of creating art. Unlike Odysseus's actions, Rockof-fer's actions were not logically connected either with any other elements onstage nor did they belong to the text of the play itself. They were in sharp contrast to what the play required, not analogical, parallel, or juxtaposed but shocking and scandalous. By blocking the transfer of the text, Kantor turned the performance into "a mill grinding the text. Does the mill," he asked "'interpret' the product which it grinds?" ("The Autonomous Theatre").

Shocks, scandals, tensions between the environment, objects, and actors were used to unblock imagination, sever logical life or dramaturgical connec-tions, and draw attention to the autonomous field of action in the production. This autonomous field of action was real in itself; however, this reality, when compared to the physical reality or text's reality, was nonrepresentative (they were not engaged in the process of doubling or transfer from a "real" to an "il-lusionary" site), nonillustrative (they did not illustrate some "real" object exist-ing elsewhere), and nonnarrative (they did not present a stage equivalent of a playtext); rather, it was grounded in the complex network of relations created in order to disclose a falsehood of illusion as well as traditional representational theatre techniques.

In its relationship with life or text, theatrical performance functioned, therefore, as a simultaneous and parallel, rather than reflective, structure. The parallel and simultaneous coexistence of drama and theatrical action received particular attention in Kantor's and Cricot 2's productions between 1961 and 1973. All of these experiments centered on the processes of dismantling tra-ditional representation by exposing the bankruptcy of its techniques. Kantor defined this experience as the "Theatre of the Lowest Rank," which was his answer to the commercial aspect of theatre organization:

> The theatre is probably one of the most anomalous of institutions. The actual auditorium made of balconies, loges, and stalls—filled with seats—finds its parallel in a completely different space. This "s e c o n d" "lurking" space is the space in which everything that happens is FICTION, illusion,
> artificial, and produced only to m i s l e a d or "c h e a t" a spectator.
> All the devices which are used to achieve this deception are skillfully hidden and imperceptible to the spectator.
> What he sees are only mirages of landscapes, streets, houses, and interiors.
> They are mirages because this world, when seen from backstage, is artificial, cheap, disposable, and of "*papier-mâché.*" ("Theatrical Place")

In its stead, Kantor suggested autonomous spaces, that is, physical sites, such as galleries, warehouses, gyms, and altered theatres, which had nothing to do with the space of FICTION, that is, the space of drama. It was not enough, however, to abandon a theatre building, since, though drama did not belong to those places, it still could appropriate them once brought inside. In order to prevent this, Kantor introduced a process in which the world of FICTION was disrupted by his experiments with autonomous theatre breaking "the impreg-nable shell of drama," in his case the dramas of Witkacy, and the process of de-preciating the value of reality by exploring its unknown, glossed-over, hidden, or everyday aspect. The different stages of Cricot 2 Theatre—the Informel The-atre, the Zero Theatre, the Happenings and the Theatre-Happening, and finally the Impossible Theatre—were the sites of this battle, the battle for matter, mar-ginalized objects, degraded objects, everyday realness, and the "impossible."

V

In December 1957, Kantor published an essay, "Abstraction is Dead. Long Live Abstraction," which followed the exhibition of his Informel paintings at the Zachęta Gallery in Warszawa. The paintings at the exhibition were no lon-ger exploring metaphoric constructions, space, motion, or time, but a new ele-ment—matter: "We are on the threshold of being able to understand the enor-mous inspirational force that is contained in this one word. Matter—the ele-ment and impulsiveness, continuity and eternity, viscidity and slowness, fluidity and volatility, lightness and weightlessness. Burning matter, which is exploding, emitting light, lifeless, and pacified. Congealed matter, in which all traces of life are imprinted. Bereft of any type of construction; only consistency and struc-ture. A different kind of space—a different kind of movement. How is it pos-sible to frame or conquer matter, which is life itself?"[75]

Kantor believed that Informel paintings were an extension of life or reality itself, which was engaged in the process of exposing the weaknesses and fis-sures in the traditional artistic process of imitating or representing an object. Informel painting was, for Kantor, a manifestation of his desire to "create a painting, which in itself would be a living organism, as dynamic as an ant-hill, a consequence of movement, which would transgress all the accepted laws of a work of art—a painting would appear in front of us almost like an incarnation of MOVEMENT."[76]

Kantor's paintings, "Oahu," "Ramamaganga," "A Painting," "Alalaha," and "Pasakas," were formless and colorful inferno, "secretion" of the matter of his own organism created by pouring paint directly onto the canvas or by using techniques of nonpainterly actions similar to those employed by Pollock bereft of what Kantor would call a decorative element.[77] "A painting is a manifesta-tion of life. To ask me why I paint is like asking me why I am alive"[78]

Maybe this last statement could be used as a manifesto of Kantor's ceaseless need to explore the eroded fabric of reality in which he found himself—World War II, Stalinist Poland, or the postwar questioning of the remnants of the struc-tures that made him abandon the revered image of a human being. His theatre experiments and his Informel paintings—the notion of a parallel action, of re-ality that is nonrepresentative, nonillustrative, and nonnarrative since the times of *The Return of Odysseus*, or of the explorations of matter—were examples of "'close-range' vision, as distinguished from long-stance vision; 'tactile,' or rather 'haptic' space, as distinguished from optical space."[79]

Imagine standing in front of Kantor's inferno of lines and blotches or spots and congealed lava of matter. If looked at from a distance, the frame of the painting delimits the optical field of vision. The eye, or the "I," striates the space within the frames, establishing constancy of orientation and a central reference point according to which the milieu is epistemologically organized. If, however, the Informel painting is an extension of life or life itself, a long-distance vision fails, since the painting is no longer a representation of a real object that is transferred from real site to a canvas. I find myself in the painting, within its frames, not being able to see what delimits the field of vision. Close-range vision replaces long-distance vision. The tactile experience of tracing the lines and matter replaces the smooth surface. The eye, or the "I," performs a nonoptical function. The lines move forward, curve, cross, stop, and move again, fall into a vortex of other lines; matter

> is freed from abiding by the laws of construction, is always changing and fluid, infinite, negates the concept of form that is limited and finite, unchangeable and stable, [and its] essence is revealed by processes such as:
> DEMOLITION,
> DECOMPOSITION,
> DISSOLUTION,
> DISINTEGRATION,
> DESTRUCTION. ("The Informel")

Ultimately, Informel paintings seen as haptic space allow the observer to experience a condition where "no line separates earth from sky, which are of the same substance; there is neither horizon nor background nor perspective nor limit not outline or form nor center."[80] "A new image of a human being is born: 'an inner landscape.' Its condition—human: FREEDOM, nostalgia, anxiety, passions and desires. . . ."[81]

This idea of Art Informel in theatre was realized in the 1961 production of Witkacy's *The Country House*.[82] *The Country House*, a comedy with corpses, is Witkacy's counterplay that constitutes his criticism of the fin-de-siècle hysteria and the conventions of realism. In act 1, at a séance conducted by two daughters, Anastasia Nearly, the dead wife of a provincial gentleman farmer, is revived. She joins the inhabitants of the country house, including Diahant Nearly, his two daughters, cousins, bailiffs, a cook, and a scullery boy, and resumes her former life. In act 2, the ghost argues with her husband and her two lovers, Wendell Pundwood, one of the bailiffs, and Jibbery Penbroke, her cousin, about the circumstances of her death. In act 3, to put an end to the conflicting claims regarding her death, Anastasia's diaries are read by the two lovers, who discover the truth about the relationship she had with them. The play ends with Nearly discovering the corpses of his two daughters, who, following their dead mother's instruction at the end of act 2, died having drunk the contents of a little bottle of brown liquid stored in their mother's pharmacy. The gloomy atmosphere is interrupted by the cook, who announces that supper is served.[83]

The performance space for the 1961 production was filled with stools, parcels, and benches placed at random; there stood a wardrobe on a rostrum at the wall:

1.   A POOR, MOLDING W A R D R O B E BROUGHT DOWN FROM
     THE ATTIC and its tiny interior, rather than a magical s t a g e on which
     a sacred mystery of illusion was celebrated, had to be a sufficient space for
     the actors.
     A W A R D R O B E had to replace the nostalgic country house
     demanded by the playwright. ("The Reality of the Lowest Rank")

Its doors, like stage doors, open suddenly to
the deeper and deeper regions of what might otherwise be seen as a domestic
Interior.
Inside, in a suffocating and humid atmosphere, the dreams are unfolded, the
nightmares are born,
behaviors which hate the light of day, are practiced. . . .
It was enough to open the doors of the wardrobe.[84]

Once the doors of the wardrobe were opened, the mother, covered with a
dust-sheet like a piece of furniture, appeared and disappeared, the barking and
howling of dogs were heard, and innumerable numbers of bags mixed together
with the bodies of actors dropped out of the wardrobe. The wardrobe was, for
Kantor, a reproductive organ of all human matters and secrets that materialized
as well as evaporated within its boundaries.[85]

A description of a stage action from act 3 of *The Country House* translates
this concept into theatrical terms:

Tadeusz Kantor's object or
installation, "Wardrobe—
Interior of Imagination." Photo
by Tim Heitman courtesy of the
Kantor Estate.

The wardrobe is open.
The husband and two lovers, the Steward of the estate and the Poet, of the deceased wife
are hanging in the wardrobe like clothes on hangers.
They are swinging, losing balance,
and bouncing into each other.
They are reading the diaries of the Deceased.
The revealed information, the most intimate details
make the three rivals
euphoric,
satisfied, desperate,
and furious.
These emotions are manifested
openly
with an increasing excitement.
The lovers, who are imprisoned in the wardrobe,
hanging on the hangers, are
spinning around,
bumping into each other,
and hanging motionless.[86]

The molding wardrobe and the actors hanging on hangers like pieces of clothing while having a conversation were not the only attribute of the Informel Theatre. Kantor enumerated some other elements that contributed to the exploration of reality—that dramatic reality that elaborated an initial forgetting prompted by the theatrical conventions or other representational practices:

2. A GARBAGE CAN, a gloomy chariot of the Sanitation Unit, was used as a pram for the children.

3. A FUNERAL MACHINE, a MONSTROUS GRINDER WITH UNSPECIFIED GRINDING PROCEDURES—covered with a thick dirty cover, from under which an immense bolt and handle were protruding—was a substitute for a family tomb.

4. SACKS and SACKCLOTH BAGS filled with grain (artificial grain, of course), rather than the charming atmosphere of a country house, filled the space.

5. The individual actors' performances, which were threatened and limited by the absurdly small space in the wardrobe and the motionless state of the inanimate objects (sacks), were lost in this totally "f o r m l e s s" matter, in the limited possibilities of the process of COMPRESSION, CRUMPLING, CRUSHING, COMIXING, and DEGRADATION.

6. Instead of classical linguistic forms, THE COARSE "BRUTE" MATTER OF LANGUAGE, which is formed by emotions, feverish states, the conditions of the Lowest Rank, INARTICULATE SOUNDS and PHONEMES, emerges. ("The Reality of the Lowest Rank")

Tadeusz Kantor's drawing to
The Country House (1961).
Galerie de France. Photo by
Michal Kobialka courtesy of the
Kantor Estate.

A funeral machine was used to bury the Mother, who, as was often the case in Witkacy's drama, would come back to life. Her funeral was staged in the following manner: a gravedigger pulled the Mother onto the machine and pushed her through the grinder while he was turning the handle. Once this was finished, he pulled out a drawer that revealed the decomposed, compressed corpse of the Mother. The drawer, which was on wheels, became a movable stage, since the small space in the wardrobe was already occupied by the lovers. According to Kantor, when *The Country House* was shown in München, Germany, in 1966, the audience reacted strongly to the funeral sequence: "I was asked if the audience had ever witnessed grinding of bodies. I answered—yes, the Nazis did it during World War II."[87]

The passages quoted here and "The Informel Theatre" manifesto (1961) reveal that Kantor used space, here a "molded" wardrobe, not only to show the tension between the dramatic text and a parallel action or between the mildewed wardrobe—the surplus of the knowable—and what was forgotten, but also to discover

an unknown aspect of
REALITY or of its elementary state: MATTER.
Matter which is freed from abiding by the laws of construction,
always changing and fluid;
which escapes the bondage of rational definitions;
makes all attempts to compress it into a solid form
ridiculous, helpless, and vain;
which is perennially destructive to all forms,
and nothing more than a manifestation;
which is accessible only through
the forces of destruction,
by whim and risk of a c o i n c i d e n c e,
by fast and violent a c t i o n. ("The Informel Theatre")

As in his Informel paintings, the introduction of the concept of matter into drama and theatre altered Kantor's discourse on representation. The manifesto's primary focus was on the elementary state of reality, matter. Matter, always changing and fluid, contains in itself all possible past, present, and future. Matter inhabits its own world, which does not have horizons limited by external referents. In writing a play, however, matter is altered by a convention that gives it a shape and turns it into a specific solid object. This object, here a play, derives its meanings from historical, social, and political formations. The interpretation of a text onstage solidifies even further its structure by privileging one reading over the other or by approximating its "thought."

In the Informel Theatre, by defying all conventions, by rejecting psychological processes, states, or situations, and by leaving them without resolutions, Kantor introduced a strategy for dissecting the textual fabric of the play to reveal the traces of matter that had been silenced by the traditional stage interpretation of the playtext. Cricot 2's *The Country House* helped the spectator to envision this different dimension in the process of opening and closing the space and allowing it to burst into the objects "by whim and risk of COINCIDENCE" in order to reshape them. "The remnants of objects, relics, 'what has remained of them' will thus have a chance to become the form" ("The Informel Theatre").

One may ask: is this Kantor's materialization of theatre from whatever it is it is not? In "Music, Mutic," Lyotard observes the following: "But what there is that is art in works of art is independent of these contexts [observable phenomena of historical reality, like political events, demographical mutations, and economic changes], even if art shows itself only within those contexts and on their occasion. The art of the work of art is always a gesture of space-time-matter, the art of the musical score, a gesture of space-time-sound."[88]

What is art in works of art is always a gesture of space-time-matter. This gesture is not a semantic or ethnographic sign operating within a particular culture or as an emphatic movement of the body. Neither is it a Brechtian *gestus* conveying particular social attitudes adopted by the speaker toward other people.[89] This gesture is the exploration of the attributes of the object—the exploration of the object's objectness, to use Kantor's phrase. "The remnants of objects, relics, 'what has remained of them,' will thus have a chance to become the form." This form is the matter that is located in space and in time. However, space and time are no longer Newtonian absolute categories but modes of thinking. The emotive power of objects is established not in terms of absolute categories but in terms of their relation to other objects in the space of representation, which is delimited by the observable phenomena of a specifiable historical reality. They are *in* it but not necessarily *of* it. They are located within the observable and sonorous space, but, as was the case with the objects brought into a performance space in *The Return of Odysseus*; they are not defined by the use-value assigned to them by a convention. As their relationship to other objects in the field is established, the use-value is questioned in the process of revealing the traces of matter that were glossed over by an initial forgetting prompted by a convention naming the object so that it becomes visible as a cultural product. Thus, Kantor's objects, a gesture of space-time-matter, labored to release what was rendered invisible or inaudible in them so that, indeed, they could become visible and intelligible.

To continue this thought: Kantor's experiments with abstraction in general and with the Informel Theatre and paintings in particular expressed his deep belief that art was a space of haptic tensions—the tensions between objects and space or between different textures. In order to remain faithful to his own dictum, Kantor had to break the solidity of Art Informel, since the function of an artist was to abort the birth of a form by erasing and contradicting a previous action that would give it fixed contours. Art Informel was the process of destruction of what might become an accomplished and finished work or art. The processes of negating of the previous action and of recording the whole series of negations and erasures was to destabilize traditional representation. If Art Informel, however, was to register spontaneity of action, motion, demolition, decomposition, destruction, and coincidence, how could this process be reconciled with the fact that Art Informel had become a museum object? According to Kantor, the moment the avant-garde work of art was recognized by a convention or the culture industry, the creative process was stopped. As the works of Mathieu, Iaroslav Serpan, Jimmy Mannasier, and Pierre Soulages appeared on the commercial markets, their Art Informel ceased to be the expression of existentialist critique of the pre- and postwar conditions and became a new painterly technique or a style. Kantor, whose own work had acquired commercial value, tried to find a way out of the impasse that had threatened his belief in the autonomous works of art—works of art governed not by the totality of their effects but their own inherent structure—works of art viewed as nonconceptual objects. In his 1961 essay "Is the Return of Orpheus Possible," Kantor questioned whether Orpheus could return from his Inferno; that is, whether having gone through the "matter" of Informel and Informel's process of deforming the object to reach the regions of "Death, Nothingness, and Existence,"[90] he could return into the world of visible objects:

> But, there are no returns.
> This is the tragic fate of a human.

. . . Instead, something else returned—the time of the o b j e c t;
of that "something" that exists at the opposite pole of my consciousness, of "me"—
unreachable;
of the centuries-old desire to "t o u c h" it at any price.
The object, which has been deep inside of me,
now started to call my name obtrusively and enticingly.

. . . I had to do something about it.
I was aware of the fact that its traditional representation, its "image," could not return,
because it was merely a reflection,
just like the moonlight,
a dead surface.
But the object is alive. ("My Work—My Journey")

VI

The return of the object marked Kantor's desire to destabilize Informel's creative process, which, despite its call for coincidence and active engagement, had ended up perpetuating and multiplying Informel conventions. Kantor abandoned Informel and embarked on yet another quest: "Instinctively, my attention, which would soon be a driving force for my passion, was turned onto the objects 'of the lowest rank'; the objects that nobody pays attention to, are dismissed, forgotten, and just about to be thrown away. I started to collect my notes, drawings, pieces of paper, impatiently scribbled notes about important matters, the first discoveries, the initial thoughts where nothing is yet certain, when nothing is yet 'official,' when nothings is yet ready for consumption."[91]

While collecting the objects, which were just about to be discarded as trash into garbage bins, Kantor rethought his notion of a work of art. He found it absurd and outmoded that it was only a finished product or an action painting that could provide these objects with identity. The work of art, believed Kantor, could not be reduced only to the presentation of the visible, which was the last stage of the creative process, but should include all those other elements that, traditionally, were "merely a reflection, just like the moonlight, a dead surface."

In 1963, Kantor opened an exhibition called The Anti-Exhibition or The Popular Exhibition at the Galeria Krzysztofory (Krzysztofory Gallery) in Kraków. "The Anti-Exhibition" was an environmental assemblage of 937 relics of Kantor's artistic creativity—that is, letters, newspaper clippings, calendars, address books, maps, tickets, photographs, drawings, sketches, theatrical costumes, recipes, etc.—which were thrown into the space without any consideration for composition, arrangement, or form. All of them were objects that, in one way or the other, were associated with the process of creating a work of art. They were records of events, thinking processes, and struggles that would inform the shape and the texture of Kantor's paintings. When finished, however, a painting, which was enclosed in its own static structure, would marginalize, cover up, or dissolve all those objects and records of a creative process. Consequently,

A WORK OF ART,
AN ISOLATED COMPOSITION,
WHICH IS IMMOBILIZED BY,
AND ENCLOSED IN
ITS OWN STRUCTURE AND SYSTEM,
WHICH IS UNABLE EITHER TO CHANGE OR LIVE,
WHICH IS AN ILLUSION OF A CREATIVE PROCESS.
A TRUE CREATIVE PROCESS IS CHARACTERIZED BY
ITS STATE OF FLUIDITY,
CHANGE,
IMPERMANENCE,
EPHEMERALITY—
THE CONDITION OF LIFE ITSELF.
ONE SHOULD BESTOW THE STATUS OF A CREATIVE ACTIVITY UPON
ALL THOSE THINGS THAT HAVE NOT YET BECOME WORKS OF ART,
THAT HAVE NOT YET BEEN IMMOBILIZED,
THAT STILL CONTAIN THE PURE IMPULSES OF LIFE,
THAT ARE NOT YET "READY" [to be consumed]
"APPROPRIATED." ("My Work—My Journey")

The process of reclaiming the "things that have not yet become works of art" provided the answer to Kantor's Informel question. But how is it possible to maintain the condition of the object that is not yet appropriated by the prevailing convention or whose use-value is not yet assigned? On the other hand, can such an object exist at all, or is it just a naïve dream that promotes a utopian vision?

Even though there is no single answer to these questions, Kantor's theatre practice since *The Return of Odysseus* visualized the processes of revealing the object's objectness once the object itself was bereft of its function. The by-now-famous act of Penelope sitting on a broken chair in a bombed room is one such example. In postwar Poland, the idea of reclaiming the object was visualized as the process of crossing the threshold of the material world into the domain of motion and matter. Recall, for example, the description of the opening sequence in *The Cuttlefish* or of the third act in *The Country House*. This desire to transform, deform, and stylize the object was initially successful, though, as Kantor noted, it ended in the stultification of the creative process. Thus, the process, which was supposed to reveal the object's objectness, ended up being a process that engendered its own space of production of the identity of the object. That is to say, Kantor's artistic process produced its own convention, commentary, and referential object in the process of folding back upon itself. In his critique of Art Informel, Kantor made clear that he was aware of this fatal strategy, and this might be why he returned to the reality of the lowest rank. In 1963, use-less, functionless objects just about to be discarded were gathered to be shown on equal footing with a completed work of art. They constituted the invisible

Anti-Exhibition (1961).
Photo courtesy of Tadeusz
Chrzanowski.

side of a work of art. As such, they needed to be protected. In order to accomplish this, Kantor introduced the idea of *emballage*—from the French *emballer*, which means *to wrap*:

> W R A P P I N G. . . . The word was heard everywhere:
> on the streets, in the shops, when people discussed buying or selling.
>
> The action gradually acquired the dimension of a ritual.
> It became a symbolic act;
> Somewhere at the threshold between
> miserable reality,
> scorn,
> contempt
> and
> ridicule
> there emerged suddenly
> a growing shadow of pathos.
> Instinctively, I sensed,
> and to be more precise I still do,
> an imminent threat to the highest

spiritual human value.
It was, and still is, necessary to
p r o t e c t it
from destruction,
from time,
from the primitive decrees of the authorities,
from the questioning by the official and slow-minded judges.
And thus the decision
t o w r a p i t u p!
To preserve it! ("My Work—My Journey")

Emballages were objects, such as a bag, an umbrella, an envelope, and a piece of clothing, that performed a double function in life. They protected their contents from destruction or view. Once the content was removed, however, they were cast aside or, to use Kantor's vocabulary, they were relegated to the status of objects of the lowest rank. Kantor was interested in isolating those objects because of the function they performed in life rather than because of their form or physical characteristics. Unlike Cesar Baldaccini's controlled compressions of automobile sculptures made with baling machines working in scrapyards, or Mimo Rotella's double *décollages*, created by first gluing photographic

Human Emballage (1968).
Photo by Rudolf Hortig courtesy
of the Cricoteka Archives.

materials torn from walls onto a canvas and then tearing them off, or Christo's *empaquettages*, which both concealed and revealed the shapes of forms covered by fabric and plastic materials, Kantor's Emballages emphasized the relationship between a discarded object and reality:

> The first umbrella ever fastened to the canvas.
> The very choice of the object was, for me, a momentous discovery; the very decision of using such an utilitarian object and of substituting it for the sacred object of artistic practices was, for me, a day of liberation through blasphemy. It was more liberating than the day when the first newspaper, the first piece of string, or the first box was glued to a canvas.
> I was not looking for a new object for a collage; rather, I was looking for an interesting "emballage."
> An Umbrella in-itself is a particularly metaphoric Emballage; it is a "wrapping" over many human affairs; it shelters poetry, uselessness, helplessness, defenselessness, disinterestedness, hope, ridiculousness. Its diverse "content" has always been defined by commentaries provided by first "Informel" and then figurative art. ("The Emballage")

The metaphoric aspect of an Emballage draws attention to a process that Kantor explored both in his visual art and in Cricot 2 Theatre. An umbrella protects when it is raining. When it does not rain, an umbrella is useless and "a pitiful sign of its past glory and importance."[92] By fastening a functionless umbrella onto a canvas, Kantor himself ascended into the regions of the degraded object. By so doing, he was able to "get into" the object's essence as yet not modified by a function imposed upon it. The object (an envelope, an umbrella, a piece of clothing) could reveal its own physical features (to protect, to preserve, to reveal the shape of a human body) and emotional attributes (promise, hope, premonition, temptation):

> Human flesh is but
> a fragile and "poetic"
> Emballage of
> the skeleton, of death,
> and of hope that it will last
> until Doomsday. ("My Work—My Journey")

At the same time, the Emballages challenged the systems of significations operating within a society. Kantor's function was not to elevate a "ready-made" to the level of an art object or to impose new meanings upon it, as Duchamp or Schwitters did in their works, but to articulate its existence and to access its existence "between eternity and garbage."[93] In other words, Emballage, for Kantor, articulated a zero condition. The zero condition of the Emballage was, for example, manifested by the wanderers, people who are "outside of a society, continuously on the move, aimlessly walking, unhoused, molded by their own madness and their own desire to wrap their bodies in overcoats, blankets; lost in the complex anatomy of their own clothing; in the deep secrets of their packages, bags, parcels, straps, strings; protecting their bodies against the sun, the rain, and the cold."[94]

The zero condition was explored in the 1963 production of Witkacy's *The Madman and the Nun*, which was accompanied by the "Zero Theatre" manifesto.[95] The Zero Theatre was, for Kantor, a process of radically repositioning the representation of actors' emotional states and their relationship with a dramatic text—that is, all the elements in traditional theatre, which developed during the course of a play: tragic emotions, passions, and desires, or battles, wars, and conflicts in general, were brought down to the zero condition where they appeared stripped of human pathos and were left to exist in a gray zone of a plateau where the beginning, middle, or end signified nothing:

> The traditional techniques of plot development made use of human life as a springboard for movement upwards toward the realm of growing and intensified passions, heroism, conflicts, and violent reactions.
>
> When it first emerged, this idea of "growth" signified man's tragic expansion, or a heroic struggle to transcend human dimensions and destinies. With the passing of time, it turned into a mere show, requiring powerful elements of a spectacle, and the acceptance of violent and irresponsible illusion, convincing shapes, and a thoughtless procreation of forms.
>
> This pushy, morbidly inflamed, and pretentious form pushed aside the object and thus what was "real." The entire process has ended up in pathetic pomposity.
>
> The movement in the opposite direction: d o w n w a r d s into the realm
> b e l o w, THE ACCEPTED WAY OF LIFE,
> which is possible by elimination,
> destruction,
> misshaping,
> reduction of energy,
> cooling;
> [the movement] in the direction of e m p t i n e s s,
> DEFORMITY,
> non-form
> is an ILLUSION-CRUSHING process
> and the only chance to t o u c h   u p o n   r e a l i t y! ("The Zero Theatre")

Kantor's illusion-crushing process forced actors to discard the emotions assigned to them by the text. In this system, they needed to eliminate dependence on the arrangement that existed outside of them (the text) and to gain autonomy by exposing only themselves rather than their characters:

> [They] would create [their] his own chain of events, states, situations which would either clash with those in the play or be somehow completely isolated from them. This seems impossible to achieve.
> However, those attempts to cross over this borderline of IMPOSSIBILITY are fascinating.

On the one hand, there is the reality of the text,
on the other hand, the actor and his behavior.
Two parallel systems which
are neither dependent
nor reflect each other.
The actor's "behavior" should
"p a r a l y z e" the reality of the text,
be juxtaposed to it.
If this happens:
the reality of the text will be
relieved of its questionable ally, the actor (questionable because it is rendered only
through him) and become independent, (also) autonomous,
and concrete. ("The Zero Theatre")

In order to achieve actors' autonomy, Kantor used a construction made of folding chairs, "The Annihilation Machine." When the machine was operating, its robotlike movements and annoying sounds destroyed any possibility of executing Witkacy's dramatic action onstage.[96] The actors, trying to avoid the machine, were pushed aside, had to fight for the acting space, and struggle not to be thrown off the stage. The presentation of the text was thus dismembered by the actions of the machine and of the actors. Rather than presenting the emotions demanded by the text, the actors presented "that 'something' that exists at the opposite pole," that is, emotions, such as apathy, melancholy, exhaustion, dissociation, neurosis, depression, frustration, and boredom, that described their fight against the machine, their sluggish resistance so that they were not to be annihilated by it.[97] Consequently, the events onstage did not illustrate the plot but referenced the most immediate actions. Both the negative emotions and these actions performed as if in spite and relegated to an almost outlaw status rendered the reproductive mechanism fictitious and nullified or erased the illusionary emotions—"Excitement, agitation, anxiety, fury, rage, frenzy. Suddenly, they cave in, disappear, as if sucked in, and only empty gestures remain."[98] These negative emotions brought the actors into Kantor's "zero zones," that is, zones where the actors could not create the illusion of other characters because they were constantly escaping the machine, deconstructing the performance space. The machine was, however, only a visual trope for the processes of eliminating the possibility that the actor could represent a play's character through the actions onstage. In the traditional staging of the play, the actor would interiorize the character's psychology, physical traits, and emotions in order to exteriorize his or her personality during a performance onstage. This process of interiorization and exteriorization was aborted by Kantor. It was replaced by the actions of the actors, who, while escaping the Annihilation Machine, could only create their own chain of events, states, and situations hastily and without much attention to detail. Their own chain of events would either clash with those in the play or be entirely separated from them. The actors often ended up repeating the same lines and dissecting the meaning of words:

Reduce meanings
to merely phonetic values,

juggle with words
to bring up their other meanings,
"dissolve" their content,
loosen their logical bonds,
repeat. ("The Zero Theatre")

While onstage, the actors tried to adjust to the performance conditions by economizing on their vital powers, by not showing their own emotions, and by reducing their actions to a minimum. The machine, however, kept forcing them to respond and to act.

The Zero Theatre helped Kantor identify those traces, both physical and emotional, that would disappear in a traditional theatre space in the process of interpreting a text. They were brought onto the surface by dismantling the traditional techniques of plot development. This was accomplished by the processes triggered by the Annihilation Machine, which prompted antiactivity, nonacting, surreptitious acting, acting under duress, erasing, internalization of expressions, economy of movement and emotions, reduction of meaning, elimination by force, and automation. By positioning the spectators in his theatre of "negative" emotions and zero zones, Kantor not only forced them to question the tradition that had dazzled them with "violent and irresponsible illusion, convincing shapes, and a thoughtless procreation of forms," but more importantly, refused to provide them with tools that would allow them to produce meanings. His Zero Theatre was thus a detour from instant gratification, exposing the audience to the lack of synchronization between the text and the stage action, or between expected emotions and the actors' expression in the zero zones.

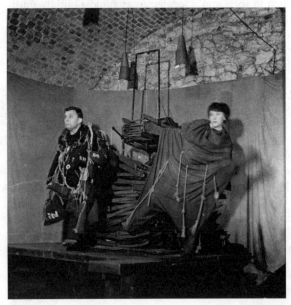

**The Madman and the Nun
(1963). Photo by Aleksander
Wasilewicz courtesy of
Tomisław Piotr Wasilewicz.**

As Kantor observed in the 1963 essay, "Annexed Reality," the Informel, the Zero Theatre, and the Emballage expressed his need to confront a convention that allowed only a presentation of a fictitious reality and that barred reality from being part of a work of art.[99] His rejection of the canons of representational paintings led, consequently, to a rejection of their technical devices and to fascination with "raw" reality that was not yet altered by any artistic modes of representation. Informel paintings (1956), *The Cuttlefish, The Country House* (1961), *The Madman and the Nun* (1963), The Anti-Exhibition, or the Popular Exhibition (1963), and the Emballages manifested different stages in Kantor's closure of representation: real space, reality of the lowest rank, environments; real objects, matter, marginalized and degraded objects, and the Emballage; the Autonomous Theatre, the Informel Theatre, and the Zero Theatre.

VII

His incessant probing into the ever-present traditional representational practices and their aesthetic of the sublime, which "allows the unpresentable to be invoked only as absent content, while form, thanks to its recognizable consistency, continuous to offer the reader or the spectator material for consolation and pleasure,"[100] led Kantor to the invisible side—the untouched side—of the object. The Autonomous Theatre, the Informel Theatre, and the Zero Theatre provided some answers to how one could show something that could not be seen. As Kantor noted, however, these experiments emptied themselves out and needed to be discarded.

It is exactly against this backdrop that Kantor attempted to liberate "things from the bondage of utility" so the object, which was dissociated from all its original functions, could "enter into the closest possible relationship with its equivalents."[101] The work of art was a gesture that accomplished this.

If indeed a work of art is a gesture, this gesture, let me reiterate here, should not be confused with a process of representing an object or with a means of addressing a goal or a purpose of an action. Neither should it be viewed in terms of aesthetics. "The gesture," as Giorgio Agamben notes, "is the exhibition of mediality: it is a process of making a means visible as such."[102] When faced with such diverse works as those of Hanna Hoch, Elaine de Kooning, Willem de Kooning, Franz Kline, Lee Krastner, Agnes Martin, Jackson Pollock, Josef Albers, Barnett Newman, Ad Reinhardt, Mark Rothko, Jean Dubuffet, Jean Fautrier, Georges Mathieu, Henri Michaux, Antoni Tàpies, Hans Hartung, Wols, Alberto Burri, Lucio Fontana, Yves Klein, Piero Manzoni, Robert Rauschenberg, Frank Stella, Donald Judd, Robert Smithson, or Jasper Jones, one experiences the tension between the inherent structure of a work of art and a social striation, between the unpresentable and the need for correct forms, between what cannot be grasped, because in the most concrete form is shows nothing, and the process of turning these works into cultural products that are positioned within the observable phenomena of historical reality, social mutations, economic changes, and academic disputes over race, gender, ethnicity, or sexuality, and, finally, to paraphrase Agamben, between the emergence of a being-in-a-medium of beings, which opens the ethical dimension in the understanding of presence or being, and commodification, which erases the uniqueness as well as the specificity of the medium.

Kantor's Happenings in the period between 1965 and 1969—*Cricotage* (December 12, 1965), *A Demarcation Line* (December 18, 1965), *A Grand Emballage* (October 20–November 1, 1966), *A Letter* (January 12, 1967), *A Panoramic Sea-Happening* (August 23–27, 1967), *Hommage à Maria Jarema* (October 30, 1968), *A Winter Assemblage* (January 18, 1969), and *Anatomy Lesson According to Rembrandt* (January 24, 1969)—were an extension of this mode of thinking. Although linked conceptually to the Happenings in the West, Kantor's Happenings were grounded in his understanding of the reality of the lowest rank, an object and objectness, matter, space, avant-garde movements of the twentieth century (especially Dada and surrealism), and his notion of the autonomous work of art, rather than in "the dominant cultural logic of their time, as advertised by Madison Avenue and promoted by industry, promoted by the new, the exciting, the spontaneous—and the systematic forgetting of self, community, and history."[103] It may be argued that, in the West, the Happening, at least in Europe, was a consequence of a rebellion against the consumer society and figurative representation of reality, both of which shaped the new urban culture and cityscape. Thus, New Realism found and processed fragments of reality and materials not commonly associated with high art (Pierre Restany, Yves Klein, Mimo Rotella, Raymond Hains, Arman, Niki de Saint-Phalle, Christo); Informel paintings abandoned representation to the delirium and the jubilation of materials (Michel Tapiés, Piero Manzoni); the Zero Group in Düsseldorf (1957; Otto Piene, Heinz Mack, Günter Vecker) explored the words indicating a zone of silence and of pure possibilities in Zero Happenings; Wolf Vostell's décollage (1964–66) and open-air Happenings (No-nine dé-coll/age, September 14, 1963, for example) became the events of change or decomposition of life principles that surround us; Joseph Beuys's FLUXUS experiments; Bazon Brock's Railway Poems and Agit-Pop (1959–62) were fragments of everyday reality that were framed or slightly altered or collaged to create an alienating effect to confront the problem of the evolving mass consumer society; Jean-Jacques Lebel's Festivals of Free Expression challenged the existing standards and modes of operation.[104]

In April 1965, Kantor and his wife, Maria Stangret, arrived in the United States. During a half-year stay, sponsored by the Ford Foundation, Kantor visited museums and galleries in New York and California, where he encountered the works of Robert Rauschenberg and John Cage and met with Roy Lichtenstein, Claes Oldenburg, Mark Rothko, George Segal, and Alan Kaprow. Upon his return to Poland, Kantor shared his observations about American minimal art, pop art, the Happenings, and the Assemblage with the artists in Warszawa and Kraków. Wiesław Borowski, the director of the newly opened Galeria Foksal (Foksal Gallery) exhibiting "experimental" artists in Warszawa, invited Kantor to organize a Happening in the gallery. On December 10, 1965, Kantor organized his first Happening, called *Cricotage*, in the café of the Society of the Friends of the Fine Arts (Towarzystwo Przyjaciół Sztuk Pięknych).[105]

In its form, the *Cricotage* demonstrated a tension that existed between Kantor's theatre practices and his newly gained knowledge about the American

Happenings. "Fourteen everyday actions: sitting, eating, shaving, talking on the phone, carrying buckets with coal for heating, moving objects, etc., bereft of the cause-and-effect pattern of development, enclosed upon themselves, sentenced to developing in isolation and taking place simultaneously, gained their own autonomy and realness in 45 minutes."[106] Here are some of these actions:

The café is full. The people are crowding all around.

1. a woman is sitting on a chair in the middle of the room; she keeps repeating "I am sitting" using different voices, tone, etc.; this repetitive action leads to a maddening crescendo of the unlimited possibilities for describing this event;
2. in a corner, a naked body of a girl is on the table; her body is slowly but meticulously covered with coal dust;
3. three well-dressed men are sitting at one of the tables; they begin to shave and to undress (individual actions); they lather their faces, but, then, the action is extended to other parts of their body, the objects on the table, the floor, and the people who are standing or sitting in the vicinity;
4. two men are sitting in front of a suitcase at another table; they open it and begin to eat spaghetti which is inside; spaghetti becomes matter. . . .
5. a woman is making telephone calls;
6. a woman standing in the crowd begins to repeat a sentence; in time, this repetition attracts the attention;
7. men carrying heavy objects keep moving through the crowd;
8. a man is trying to say something about a work of art; he seems to be quoting obvious, officially recognized and sanctioned, ambiguous, meaningless statements regarding the piece;
9. a man begins to cover up the body of a woman with a white tape.[107]

The everyday and actions presented in this Happening constituted its fabric. In life and in traditional art, these actions were relegated to secondary status and made invisible. So were the emotions that accompanied them. As in

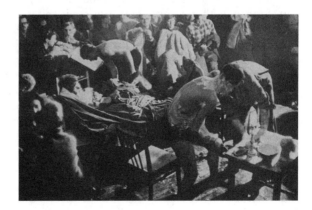

Happening—Daily Practices (1966). Photo courtesy of Wojciech Plewiński.

the case of the Zero Theatre, Kantor was interested in abandoning the pathos of traditional plot development and, by focusing on the immediate events happening in the café, drawing attention to the apathy, melancholy, exhaustion, amnesia, neurosis, depression, frustration, boredom, and misery that nullified the illusionary emotions and brought the participants into the "zero zones." It was there that both the emotions and the actions were dismantled and able to reveal the unthought or the unpredictable elements of a particular emotion or action. More importantly,

> The movement in the opposite direction: d o w n w a r d s into the realm
> b e l o w, THE ACCEPTED WAY OF LIFE,
> which is possible by elimination,
> destruction,
> misshaping,
> reduction of energy,
> cooling;
> [the movement] in the direction of e m p t i n e s s,
> DEFORMITY,
> non-form
> is an ILLUSION-CRUSHING process
> and the only chance to t o u c h   u p o n   r e a l i t y! ("The Zero Theatre")

Thus, for Kantor, the Happening was "the site of the complete disintegration of disciplines" as well as a practice that "signifies the highest risk possible due to transgressing the accepted and recognized art forms."[108] This is one of the reasons why Kantor was fascinated by the potential, which the Happening created, for exploring the objectness of the action in its relation to the other objects in the site. Here, the fourteen everyday actions did not lead to the creation of a closed work of art, but, being significant in themselves, troubled the recognized reality by bringing to the fore its unknown or illegitimate aspect. Kantor by no means transformed reality, the real, or the everyday. He simply took it and brought it into a higher pitch. Could it be that this idea of bringing these actions to a higher pitch was reminiscent of the concept of "intensified reality," which Kantor worked with 1946? If indeed reality was taken up, rather than transformed, both it and its content were viewed as ready-mades, which were defined by the whole system of values connected with its ideology. What Jean Baudrillard calls "the murder of the real" Kantor labeled annexing reality in order to dislocate the existing configurations.[109] These existing configurations were disfigured by subjecting both actions and objects to the disinterested and repetitive operations, to liberating them from "the bondage of [moral or aesthetic] utility," and constructing new relationships between them in order to exhibit their mediality. Existing-in-a-medium consumed the energy necessary for creating an object in the image of the object with an assigned use-value so it could become a subject of an artistic exchange. Bereft of this energy, an object or an action, existing-in-a-medium, was autonomous or a nonconceptual object or action that, like an Emballage, needed to be protected from "trespassing, ignorance, and vulgarity."[110] These notions would receive a full treatment in Kantor's 1967 production of Witkacy's *The Water-Hen*:[111]

In my treatment of *The Water-Hen*, I have tried to avoid an unnecessary construction of elements. I have introduced into it not only objects but also their characteristics, and READY-MADE events which were already molded. Thus, my intervention was dispensable. An object ought to be won over and possessed rather than depicted or shown. What a marvelous difference! Important and unimportant, mundane, boring, conventional events and situations constitute the heart of reality. I derail them from the track of realness (*The Zero Theatre Manifesto*, 1963), give them autonomy, which, in life, is called aimlessness, and deprive them of any motivation and effects. I keep turning them around, re-create them indefinitely, until they begin to have a life of their own; until they begin to fascinate us.[112]

A few days later, on December 18, 1965, Kantor organized a new Happening, *A Demarcation Line*, at the Society of Art Historians (Stowarzyszenie Historyków Sztuki) in Kraków. Even though it can be seen as a repetition of the *Cricotage*, *A Demarcation Line* had a strong anti-institutional character. Thus, the repetitive actions from the Happening of December 10 were accompanied by a new action—the entrance door was walled up. Kantor, who was overseeing the actions, read the following text:

One needs to draw the demarcation line everywhere and at all times,
quickly and forcefully,
because, even without our participation or willingness,
it will be drawn automatically and mercilessly
leaving us either on this or the other side.
If drawn by us, even if we find ourselves in a situation which is worse than before,
it will give us a sense of the freedom of choice
or the awareness of the need.
The demarcation line is drawn everywhere and at all times,
it fulfills all possible roles,
it assumes all possible shapes,
it is eternal and immoral.[113]

Today, and I would venture to say in 1965 as well, the ambiguity coded into the language was transparent. The act of repeating the everyday actions, giving life to the ready-made, annexing the reality, drawing the line by walling up the entrance-exit, and the text of the manifesto create a material, multidimensional Emballage in space protecting poor objects, marginalized actions, and degraded individuality from extermination by the system of values connected with the outside, historical reality. If the Real as such implied the existence of the artistic institutions (the Society of Art Historians in Kraków) and recognized artistic, not to mention individual, processes, the Emballage created in the annexed reality signified a possibility that "space is the object's true freedom."[114]

Figures and objects become the function of space
and its mutability. . . .
Space is not a passive r e c e p t a c l e
in which objects and forms are posited. . . .
SPACE itself is an OBJECT [of creation].

And the main one!
SPACE is charged with E N E R G Y.
Space shrinks and e x p a n d s.
And these motions mould forms and objects.
It is space which G I V E S   B I R T H to forms!
It is space which conditions the network of relations and tensions between the objects
TENSION is the principal actor of space.
A MULTI-SPACE.[115]

It also signified a possibility that the diagram "is like a *catastrophe* happening unexpectedly to the canvas, inside figurative or probabilistic data. It is like the emergence of another world. For these marks or brushstrokes are irrational, involuntary, accidental, free, and random. They are nonrepresentative, nonillustrative, and nonnarrative. No longer are they significative or signifying: they are asignifying features. They are features of sensation, but of confused sensation. And above all they are manual features. . . . These almost blind, manual marks reveal the intrusion of another world into the visual world of figuration."[116]

At the same time, space, the object, and a diagram constitute the necessary components of creating a tension between them and reality. For Kantor, space, the object, or a diagram existed as a nonconceptual mediality whose asignifying features were made visible in the network of relationship into which it entered. This is the reason why, as such, space, the object, and a diagram were nonrepresentative, nonillustrative, and nonnarrative. Therefore, space, the object, or a diagram would always place the reality, a concept in itself that attempted to striate them with the whole system of values connected with it, in an unreal condition.

Happening—The Letter (1967).
Photo by Zygmunt Targowski
courtesy of Galeria Foksal.

This particular thought was materialized in Kantor's Happening, *A Letter*, which was presented in Warszawa on January 21, 1967.[117] A letter that was some forty-four feet long and six feet high was carried by seven postmen from the post office in Ordynacka Street to Galeria Foksal. Some 150 people gathered at the gallery were listening to four commentators, who provided the information (prerecorded) about the whereabouts of the letter. When the letter arrived at the gallery, the postmen threw it into the crowd. The people began to read their own private letters. This was followed by a monologue of an unknown recipient of the letter. Once this was accomplished, the letter was destroyed.[118]

In his commentary about this Happening, Kantor insisted that the change of the scale of the object, here a letter, was not a form of expression linked to the process of deforming or disfiguring the object. The function of the object remained the same. "Simply there needed to be a big object if it were to be carried by seven postmen. More important, they brought in a letter, which was expected by 150 people. . . . I did not change the scale of the objects to decrease their realness. I am not interested in destabilizing the practices or relations existing in the everyday life. I am interested in exposing them."[119]

A Panoramic Sea-Happening, possibly the best known of Kantor's Happenings because of the now-famous black-and-white photograph of a music conductor, wearing a tail coat, standing in water and conducting the sea while the beachgoers in deck chairs observe his actions,[120] had many elements that surfaced in previous Happenings but also treated the Happening itself as a ready-made, or a convention that already had its own history and tradition linked onto it.

A Panoramic Sea-Happening, watched by over two thousand beachgoers, accidental tourists, and invited guests wearing either bathing suits or formal attire, consisted of four parts:

Part I: A Sea Concert. A few hundred deck chairs were placed on the beach in rows facing the Baltic Sea. The people took the seats. The first few rows were continuously hit by the waves. About thirty feet from the first row, a dais was placed in the sea for a conductor. A motorboat brought the conductor, who climbed the dais submerged in water and began the sea concert. Upon a sign given by the conductor, a group of bikers drove toward the "auditorium" at high speed; a rescue boat approached the beach with the alarm signal piercing the air; a man on a white horse galloped in between the rows of deck chairs. The conductor turned around to face the audience and threw dead fish at them. Having completed this action, he covered his face with the tails of his coat.

Part II: "The Raft of the Medusa." A few hundred copies of Théodore Gérocault's painting *The Raft of the Medusa* were distributed among the participants, who were gathered around a table covered with white cloth, where the critics and the specialists were seated. The audience members were invited to participate in the reconstruction of this romantic painting of the shipwrecks on the raft who survived the sinking of the *Medusa*. The reconstruction was monitored by the jury seated at the table. Long discussions between the art critics and historians regarding the nature of the conflicts between the classics and the romantics were heard. Finally, a group on a raft began to resemble the group in Gérocault's painting despite the fact that today's shipwrecks were wearing bathing suits and trunks and were surrounded by life preservers and beach equipment.

The Panoramic Sea-Happening (1967). Photo by Józef Piątkowski courtesy of Galeria Foksal.

Part III: Erotic Barbouillage. A group of young women wallowed in a ditch filled with tomato sauce, being transformed into amorphous matter that dematerialized their human shapes into a total assemblage. Suddenly, the women stopped, got up, and disappeared among the participants.

Part IV: Agri Cultura on a Beach. The organizers distributed pieces of paper, which were carefully planted in the sand by the participants. While these actions were taking place, there was yet another group on the beach, which was engaged in the process of wrapping a big trunk with paper and cloth. They seemed to be in a hurry. The trunk was sealed and labeled "Galeria Foksal, Warszawa, ul. Foksal 1/4." A rumor was spread that the trunk contained important and valuable documents about the gallery. While the people gathered around the trunk, it was carried onto the boat. The boat left. The safety signal was shot. The trunk was thrown into the sea.[121]

The four parts presented here contained the elements, such as compartmented structure, fragmented nonlinear narratives, nonmatrixed performing and improvisation, active audience participation, the erasure of the demarcation line between art and life, and the ephemerality of action that are what defines the Happening as a performative act.[122] There is no question that Kantor positioned himself within this tradition; however, as was the case with his staging of the plays by Witkacy, he did not interpret, explain, or translate these actions into the language of theatre but created a tension between them and his reality in order to reveal what he referred to as the objectness of the object. *A Panoramic Sea-Happening* was a complex system of folds—a mode of thinking that begins with something existing in the exteriority, but then it makes a gesture that seems to surpass the visible or the standard and turns back upon itself in order to explore its own mode of effectivity and historicity in the process of the realignment of thought. Thus, part I was Kantor's attempt at folding one (ready-made) reality (that is, the beach, the sea) into another, alien reality (a concert hall, a conductor, an auditorium), plus an acoustic reality (the sound of the bikers, speed boats), in order to liberate both realities. Part II was Kantor's attempt at using the ready-made or existing reality, Gérocault's *The Raft of the Medusa*, to explore the consequences of folding three realities into one: the event in 1822, the artistic rendering (the notes and the painting viewed already as a museum piece), and the banal, everyday reality (beach, sea, tourists, etc.) in order to disclose its hitherto hidden aspect glossed over either by a convention or a historical significance assigned to it. In parts III and IV, Kantor consciously created situations in which the participants and their behavior were incorporated into the events as the ready-mades. As Kantor asserted in his notes,

> Happening is for me an attempt at infiltrating the object in order to disclose or to find out its elements, mistakes, crimes, adventures, or hidden and covered-up details. . . . A dream—a beach: the inexhaustible volume of both the sea and the air are too much for a human being standing on the shore, especially since this "standing" on the shore is closer to "being imprisoned" than to being able to embrace this something beyond. It is as if we found ourselves at the edge of a dream. The beach is this edge of this dream. Rather than saying a dream, one should say an "impossible."[123]

This "impossible," whose sense and meaning were revealed only in the process of folding and exploring the tensions between the different realities, was to bring us to the edge where liberation from the conventions of our historical environment was possible. In an important sense, a beach, according to Kantor, can become a reality that, under certain conditions, was freed from the existing rules. More important, it could become a reality that because of its heterotopic nature could only perturb rather than exist as a permanent form. It rearticulated and exposed the ready-made convention: "If one attempts to transfer this reality into a different location, its laws and regulations will not be understood or accepted. A reality of leisure can also construct its own conventions that are as ruthless as those existing in the practices of every day life. . . . The Happening exposed this possibility."[124]

What sounded only like a threat here became one of the elements that made Kantor abandon the Happenings altogether. His "Theatre-Happening" realized in the 1967 production of *The Water-Hen* was both the closure and the opening in his artistic journey. *The Water-Hen*, yet another of Witkacy's plays that was realized in Kantor's Cricot 2 Theatre, made it clear that theatre could not be equated with a Happening and a Happening could never be equated with theatre. What could happen was a possibility of bringing these two notions as close to each other as possible. In Witkacy's play, the main characters are a duchess, businessmen, and the servants of the duchess' household. The play opens as the hero Edgar, in an eighteenth-century costume, shoots a woman named Water-Hen, who is standing under a gas street lamp before an open field by the seashore. Gradually, the open space is enclosed and peopled. Burdened with a father, a wife, and a son (who keeps waking up from a dream throughout the play), Edgar finds it difficult to define himself in a world gone awry. Finally, as revolution breaks out into the streets, Edgar shoots the Water-Hen, who has returned to life, and then kills himself. As the old world is coming to naught, four old gentlemen begin to play cards. The play ends with the revolutionaries entering the room, in which only "Pass" spoken by one of the players reverberates in the air.[125] Kantor's world was populated by characters who, for Kantor, existed on the margins of any society—here they were shown as poor people, street bums, and wanderers traveling with their suitcases and a big knapsack. They did not act out the parts or attempted to create the characters from Witkacy's play. They only spoke the text that was assigned to them.

Kraków's Galeria Krzysztofory was filled with mattresses, old packets, ladders, wooden partitions, stools, and chairs. A wandering group of travelers with their bags entered. Kantor observed, "For the time being, the actors do not have names." Once inside, they engaged in banal, everyday activities:

1.   A man with suitcases looks around the room and says to one of the audience members, "I must have seen you somewhere." He begins to run, pulling his suitcases behind him. He stops, arranges the suitcases, rearranges them, counts them, etc.

2.   Someone demands a cup of coffee.

3.   A girl with a paper bag full of receipts . . . turns around and, without any interest in her voice asks: "What time is it?"

. . .

10.   A man with a bucket full of water runs across the room.

. . .

12.   Someone is making a telephone call.

13.   The waiters serve the customers.

. . .

19.   A woman counting tea-spoons screams hysterically, "One spoon is missing," and throws all the spoons on the floor.

20.   Someone asks, "Do you have a problem?"

21.   Someone else asks, "Has it started yet?"

29.   Someone pours hot water into a bathtub.[126]

All these activities at one moment were mixed with a dramatic text. Thus, while the waiters were still serving the customers, and the dubious customers were furiously fighting and crowding around the tables with their suitcases and packets, the opening dialogue between Edgar and Water-Hen seeped into "the reality of the theatrical space bordering on life," or the modified Happening. The actors kept pulling the accidental lines or words out of Witkacy's opening scene and repeating them as slogans or meaningless phrases that acquired meaning in the process of assigning to them different intonation, rhythm, or grammatical patterns:

1.   Be brave! Only for a moment.

2.   This is humiliating.

3.   Death means nothing to me.

4.   Something has snapped inside me.

5.   That is my only joy in life.

6.   Honestly, absolutely.

7.   Life for life's sake.

8.   Anything that lives is unique.

9.   I accept the inevitable.

10.   Oh, how splendid!

The Water-Hen (1967). Photo
courtesy of Jacek Stokłosa.

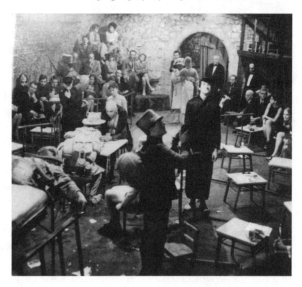

The actors conjugate the verbs:

1.   Water-Hen: "Later, you will think it over. . . ."
one of the actors: I will think it over, you will think it over, he will think it over,
she will think it over, etc.
2.   Water-Hen: "Indeed, there are some possibilities."
one of the actors: she is thinking—
are there any possibilities?
suddenly, with fear in her voice:
are there any possibilities?!
she turns to one of the audience members and says secretly:
are there any possibilities?
. . .
Edgar aims at Water-Hen.

15.   A shot is fired—Water-Hen falls down.
16.   The angry waiters were only waiting for this moment. They seize Water-Hen,
drag her, and throw her into a bath-tub in her coat, hat, and shoes.
17.   Someone pours a bucket of hot water into the bath-tub.
18.   The actors run into the bath-tub, pull out the soaking wet body of Water-
Hen, toss her into the air, and throw her back into the bath-tub. The agony of
Water-Hen happens simultaneously with the conversation between Edgar and his
illegitimate son. A naked child sitting on a stool suspended from a ceiling, as if
he were imprisoned there, pronounces statements about life and the mystery of
essence as though in a somnambulistic dream. Edgar is undecided between his
creation and a bath-tub, in which, finally, Water-Hen dies.[127]

As these two passages show, the text of the play was no longer material that would be formed and molded by a director or by space. Rather, the text of *The Water-Hen* was a ready-made reality. In Kantor's view, this preexisting reality ought to be isolated from the reality of a space wherein it emerged. The ready-made reality of the text and the reality of a space should not be complementary; rather, they should coexist. The ready-made text and the troupe of wanderers constituted two independent and self-consistent spaces within the space of a "poorhouse" on the margins of a society. During the production, they merged and created a cluster that, like an alloy made of two metals having different burning temperatures, would respond differently to the artistic process instigated and sustained by Kantor's constant presence in the performance space. As he did in the 1965 Happening Cricotage, Kantor created the identity of the wanderers by forcing them to keep repeating everyday actions and situations. Once that was achieved, he brought the text of the play into the space of the poorhouse. The group of travelers did not begin to act out the parts of characters from the play. Instead, they spoke the lines of the characters with different intonation and rhythm. By so doing, they escaped the functions or character's personality traits that otherwise would have been imposed upon them by the ready-made text. As already noted in the Zero Theatre, the group of the wanderers, the actors, maintained their own individuality by "communicating" those functions. The wanderer and the character remained in their separate spaces.

The Theatre-Happening, as Kantor observed, was in the end a process of sublimating the Happening's physical reality, that is, the performance space. In its action of depicting reality via reality, the Theatre-Happening affirmed and accomplished its task of dismantling representation and its all-powerful illusion. By so doing, the event, however, created its own commentary and its own representation in a space it produced for itself—it thus fell into the trap of the bondage of artistic utility. Kantor commented on this phenomenon in the essay "Crisis of the Real Place," where he noted that the idea of the real place became too restrictive to him once it acquired the recognizable features of a convention.

The Water-Hen (1967). Photo courtesy of Jacek Stokłosa.

The Happenings and the Theatre-Happening became a convention not because they failed to secure the realness of the place, environment, or objects or because the actors, who were supposed to perform the functions determined by this place, could no longer successfully accomplish this, but because the Happenings and Theatre-Happening deprived the audience of the privilege and the condition of being an audience member. The audience in a launderette, argued Kantor, was or was not accidental. No matter what status was assigned to them, they were forced to experience the actions presented there. They were bereft of the privileged position of the audience member, which would allow them to maintain a distance, draw conclusions, or pass judgments about the events unfolding in front of and around them. They were, according to Kantor, bereft of the possibility of experiencing "art." Rather,

> They were lured into and abandoned in this REAL PLACE without defenses and safety which ILLUSION AND DISTANCE provide.
> They were thrown into situations in which they were forced to deal with raw and rough matter of life that—according to the sacred laws of aesthetics—had nothing to do with a work of art.
> Bereft of the privileges, they had the same status as the PLACE and its FUNCTIONS; they were unceremoniously stirred into the matter of life; they were expected even to participate in the actions taking place around them. Their response at first was this of disappointment and indignation—until they got used to their new roles.
> After some time, this violent encounter between ILLUSION and the rough matter of real life was reduced to a sanctioned practice, a convention, and, finally, a pretentious f a d.
> The feeling of a constant threat, even surprise, or danger gave birth to some kind of masochism, which became more and more intolerable, especially since this new kind of pleasure, which had in it the thrill of something forbidden and risky, was false, more and more driven by experience that this constant threat was nothing more than fiction and the danger was staged and fake.[128]

The initial raw encounter with this new reality was thus replaced by the audience's experience of the events, which, by now, had become the tropes of an artistic style or a performance convention. Dissatisfied with the Happening, Kantor abandoned the project for a new theoretical and practical discourse, the Impossible Theatre. He pointed out in the "Impossible Theatre" manifesto (1973) that the "impossible" is the main component of the play perception:

> What I regard as important here is the integration of a
> great m u l t i t u d e of
> s u g g e s t i o n s
> so structured that they create in the audience
> the i m p r e s s i o n of
> the i m p o s s i b i l i t y of
> g r a s p i n g
> and i n t e r p r e t i n g the whole
> from the audience's position. ("The Impossible Theatre")

VIII

The idea of the "impossible" emerged in Kantor's work around 1972. At that time, he played with the idea of the "impossible" in a work of art—a folding chair fourteen meters high, for example. It was to be an exact copy of folding chairs that he had used in his productions and in everyday life. The fourteen-meter-high chair showed nothing; it simply was an absurd object that, according to Kantor, would place the surrounding reality in which it finds itself positioned under question, draw attention to its unreal condition, and point to the illusionary aspect of the surrounding reality and the world at large.

His Impossible Art made use of the ready-made reality. A glass, a spoon, a hanger, an electric bulb, and a chair were all ready-mades. This ready-made reality in confrontation with everyday reality questioned its realness as well as the realness of the objects and people in it. As Kantor argued, "If, while I was shaving, I saw it and believed in what I was seeing, this huge chair made of concrete would query everything around it. It would test the realness of stones, people walking by, and activities taking place around it."[129]

This notion of the "impossible" was used in a production, loosely based on the scenes from Witkacy's *The Country House*, which was produced in Yugoslavia over the period of three months in 1969. This *Country House* contained the elements or objects and modes of thinking that informed the productions associated with the 1961 Informel Theatre, the 1963 Zero Theatre, and the 1967 Theatre-Happening. Until now, argued Kantor, he had used alternative sites, such as a bombed room, a café, a wardrobe, a gallery, or found spaces, for example, to conquer or to reveal the fissures in a traditional understanding of the function of the stage in a theatre; now, he decided to get rid of it altogether—that is, to get rid of the site that remained intimately connected to the audience. In 1969, the select scenes from *The Country House* were presented, or rather thrown into, reality. They were presented at a small train station in the middle of nowhere, where the characters from the play, crowded together with their luggage, were waiting for a coming train; in a well-appointed room in Tito's summer house, where the actions of the characters of the play were suddenly interrupted by a flock of frightened sheep; in a casino in Bled, where the characters from the play mixed freely with the guests playing at the roulette table, which was filled with hay; on a glacier, where a molding wardrobe, inside of which the characters of the plays had been hanging on hangers in 1961, was dropped from a helicopter; on a beach, where the characters of the play found themselves again crowded in a wardrobe before they fell out and started to walk slowly toward the sea until the waves covered them completely.[130]

Each individual scene contained in itself the condition of the "impossible":

a wardrobe
dropped from 6000 feet
in the wild mountains,
a luxurious gambling casino,
filled with
hay,
a frightened flock of sheep

Tadeusz Kantor's drawing, "The Chair Monument on the Main Square in Kraków" (1970). Photo by Michal Kobialka courtesy of the Kantor Estate.

in a drawing-room
had nothing in common
with the old trick of "shocking" [the audience].
They were
an unusual
"*measure*" of
imagination
with the help of which
the ordinary
the "everyday"
reality
was "measured." ("The 'i' Theatre")

A similar technique was employed in the Impossible Theatre. The 1973 production of Witkacy's *Dainty Shapes and Hairy Apes* was presented in a space that resembled a theatre cloakroom—"a huge iron cage with hooks and hangers

similar to those in a slaughter-house, where they are used for pieces of meat."[131]
The audience entering the performance space found itself in this cloakroom/
iron cage/slaughterhouse, where they were forced to leave their coats before
they could sit down, having a wall with a door, the entrance to the "theatre"
on the other side:

> If one were to think about it,
> a cloakroom is shameless
> in its invasion of one's privacy:
> we are forced to leave there
> an intimate part of us.
> It is a terrorist act.
> We could push this metaphor even further and say that
> during a production
> parts of us are hanging there mixed together
> with people we do not know;
> we are hanging motionlessly
> marked by numbers,
> violated,
> punished,
> and so on . . .
> . . . this infamous institution has
> dominated theatre,
> it stands there like a punishing, soulless death squad
> led by a group of thugs.
> A cloakroom, moving in no direction,
> is constantly, aimlessly there,
> for its own sake
> like art for art's sake.
> Cloakroom for cloakroom's sake. . . .
> A cloakroom works,
> expands,
> devours more and more spheres of the imagination.
> It is continuously working. . . .
> It rejects the actors and their rights,
> it throws them ruthlessly beyond the boundaries,
> or it appropriates, belittles,
> deforms,
> sterilizes,
> tarnishes,
> ruthlessly breaks,
> and gives false testimonies
> to their attempts to "smuggle" in their artistic
> activities. ("The Impossible Theatre")

The actors tried to "smuggle in" Witkacy's characters. In the play, the adolescent Tarquinius Filtrius-Umbilicus is about to be initiated into the higher
mysteries of life by his decadent friend Pandeus Clavercourse when the latter's

former wife, the demonic Princess Sophia, arrives, whip in hand, followed by her admirers, including an English biochemist (Sir Grant Blaguewell-Padlock), a Jew (Goldmann Baruch Teerbroom), an American billionaire (Oliphant Beedle), a Spanish cardinal (Dr. Don Nino de Gevach), and a Russian count (Andre Vladimirovich Tchurnin-Koketayev), as well as forty characters named Mandelbaum, representing masculinity. Havoc erupts. Tarquinius is killed by Sophia in a duel, the lovers all take a deadly green pill that gives infinite sexual desire but kills within hours, and Sophia is devoured by the forty Mandelbaums.[132]

The cloakroom, a place of the lowest rank in theatre, however, imposed its prosaic and banal characteristics on a creative. Thus, Princess Sophia did not live in a palace but in a henhouse-cage, which must have been left behind by the audience members; her admirers were turned into a man with two bicycle wheels grown into his legs, a man with a wooden board on his back, a man with two heads, a man carrying the doors, and a man with two additional legs—the objects grown into their bodies made it impossible to create a coherent image of a character; Tarquinius Filtrius-Umbilicus, the hero, was killed by an immense mouse-trap in a duel; the forty Mandelbaums, played by audience members vested in black costumes, "driven by their desire and jealousy, TRAMPLE THE PRINCESS TO DEATH and join in the dance of the living and the dead," the last scene.[133]

The cloakroom was supposed to be a device that, like a fourteen-meter-high chair, the hanger, the characters invading a casino, or a room in Tito's summer house, would question the surrounding reality, here a performance or theatre space, of which it was a part. It would accomplish this by drawing attention to theatre's illusionary aspect, that is, by being the "stage" for actions and events that ordinarily should be onstage and not in the cloakroom.

The Impossible Theatre was the last transformation in Kantor's theory of the reality of the lowest rank, which challenged representation affirming life. His experiments with the Autonomous, Informel, Zero, Happening, and Impossible theatres, each in its own way, questioned the traditional idea of representation and interpretation by insisting that theatre be a place "like a *catastrophe* happening unexpectedly . . . like the emergence of another world."[134]

Dainty Shapes and Hairy Apes
(1975). Photo courtesy of
Romano Martinis.

Dainty Shapes and Hairy Apes
(1975). Photo courtesy of
Romano Martinis.

This catastrophe, in Kantor's vocabulary, was the process of annexing reality. The consequences of this process, which materialized in performance space, were Kantor's contribution to the question of what it means to represent. Kantor's notion of representation had nothing to do with a process of doubling or transfer modified by the rules of perspective. Nor was it connected with the exploration of the relationship between the original and the copy or between the "real" and what is made "real." Like the three fragments mentioned at the beginning of this chapter—the changes in the perception of time and space in the last century, the events of World War II, and the penetration of the very foundations of representation and the solidity of *construzione legittima*—the process of annexing reality was Kantor's attempt at unmasking both the authorities and their practices, which control the flow of representation and make claims to reality and the manner in which the objects of this reality can be identified and shown. Within this annexed reality, Kantor sought the places of the lowest rank—a bombed room, a café, a wardrobe, a poorhouse, and a cloakroom, which, as exemplified by the Autonomous, Informel, Zero, Happening, and the Impossible theatres, depreciated the value of reality through exploring its unknown, thus far hidden or everyday, aspect of life: degraded objects, matter, marginalized objects, everyday realness, or self-enclosed actions.

In the process of dismantling illusion and traditional theatrical conventions, Kantor created a space that produced its own language and commentary in the process of folding back upon itself. This praxis, while it lasted, was a powerful answer to political, social, and cultural reality and indeed liberated matter, objects, and everyday realness from the bondage of utility. However, it became an enchanted simulation and Kantor, aware of falling into the trap of this fatal strategy, abandoned it for an entirely different project—the theatre of intimate and personal commentaries.

Independent Theatre: Theoretical Essays
(1942–1944)

One does not look at the work of art in theatre
the way one looks at a painting,
to discover its aesthetic values,
but to experience it in a concrete way.
I do not follow any superficial artistic dogmas.
I do not feel that I am linked to any epoch in the past;
they will remain unknown to me; nor do they interest me.
I do feel a strong commitment to the time
I live in, and to the people around me.
I do believe that my time and these people can accommodate totality—
both barbarity
and the sublime, tragedy and robust laughter—
that this totality is created by contrasts; the bigger the contrast,
the more real, more concrete, and more vibrant the totality.

THERE, WHERE DRAMA COMES TO LIFE

It is only in a place and at a time where we do not expect anything to
happen, that something we will unquestionably believe in, can h a p p e n.
This is the reason why the theatre, which has been completely sterilized
and neutralized by centuries-old practices, is the least appropriate site for
drama to be
m a t e r i a l i z e d.
Today's theatre is artificial, in its form, and unacceptable, in its pretence.
I am standing in front of a useless public building, which, like an inflated
balloon, sticks out in living concrete reality. Before I show up, it is empty
and silent. When I enter, it pretends it can be functional. This is why I
always feel embarrassed when I am sitting in a theatre seat.

ACTION

Dramatic action must exist parallel to stage action.
Stage action must be conceived as being parallel to dramatic action.
Dramatic action is always ready to be used and finished.

Once it enters the stage, it can assume unexpected forms and shapes.
This is why I never know anything about the epilogue scene.

Everything is ready:
a column supporting an architrave;
a green rock, behind which a solitary mast is visible; a fragment of a
fence, where Odysseus will stop, a bow, behind which Penelope will
stand.
Everything has been prepared, because it existed earlier in a drama.
In a moment, the actors will enter.
From this moment on, the drama will be nothing more than reminiscence.

THE MIND-DERANGING FUNCTION OF THEATRE

Everything is responsible for it. The seats are all turned in one direction.
The stage whose raised curtain will mark the beginning of the gaping
ritual of the faithful.
A force of habit becomes a nervous tic; it dulls one's senses.
I want to create such theatre which will have *a primordial power of shock
and action.*

CONCRETENESS

I want to create such atmosphere and circumstances which will make the
illusory dramatic reality positioned in it
believable and c o n c r e t e.
I do not want my Odysseus to move around within an illusionary
dimension, but within and without our reality, our objects—that is,
objects that have certain specific value to us today—and real people—that
is, people who are in the "auditorium."
It is already late night. I am sitting in a room that could be a waiting
room, or a room in a hostel. Wooden benches, on which people with dull
faces are resting waiting for their trains or dawn, are around me. I might
as well be waiting for the return of Odysseus.
In a corner, there is a table with a dark lamp on it. Bent figures of
accidentally met people are looming over the table.
Maybe, they are playing cards, or maybe,
they are bent over the dead body of the Shepherd
killed by Telemachus.

EXTERIORITY OR E X T E R N A L   R E A L I S M

One must treat the s u r f a c e structure of the events pointedly and
with all due respect. One must remain on their surfaces, and only on the
surfaces, rather than go inside them, toward inner interpretations and
commentaries.

This will be looking at surfaces as if "from the side," an almost cynical realism which will be voided of all analyses and explanations, a new type of realism,
which I would call external realism.
Odysseus sits on a chair in the centre of the stage. The very act of sitting is a physical act
which has its own significance. Is it not that the very act of sitting, which must be precisely outlined, highlighted, and assigned a specific import, has the most concrete and real value—the external value (exteriority should not be confused with "superficiality"). Suddenly the events on stage are "timeless." Eumaios is not killed but
f a l l s down. From a distance, a figure of a human being falling down is more powerful than a face contorted with pain.

NOTES FROM THE REHEARSALS OF *THE RETURN OF ODYSSEUS*

Sometimes during a rehearsal, an atmosphere is created which allows one to see this artificial entity onstage as something that is as r e a l as our own existence, even though, one might suggest, that everything around should promote distancing. Later, when the opening night machinery—when the "real" props are substituted for the rehearsal props, when the fake nature of stage decorations and costumes is covered up; and when a demarcation line between the stage and the auditorium is applied—this something disappears irrevocably.
. . . In a tiny room, pieces of furniture are pushed aside, those, who have come to watch, sit wherever they can, a spotlight brings to life a piece of yellow floor, some of the actors are seated on dusty parcels, others on the floor. Odysseus sits on a chair. The Shepherd stands next to him. They have a conversation. The rest of the actors listen and observe attentively. The Shepherd makes a mistake. He repeats his part. The actors are heard commenting. Then, Odysseus kills the Shepherd. Wrong. He kills him again.
The text becomes almost a concrete object. I can feel that it will brush against me in a second. When Odysseus says: "I am Odysseus. I have returned from Troy," I do believe him, even though he w e a r s a d i r t y r a g o n h i s b a c k.
One must capture the weight of this moment by s t r e n g t h e n i n g the imprints of this accidental transgression from the reality of life; by inserting the r e a l i t y o f
f i c t i o n in the r e a l i t y o f l i f e.

ILLUSION AND CONCRETE REALITY

Drama is reality. All that happens in drama is real and true.
THEATRE, the moment drama is presented on stage, uses all the means at its disposal, in order to create the illusion of that true reality: a curtain, a backstage, a stage design of all kinds ("topographic," "geographical,"

historical, symbolic, explanatory—all of which however can only be a mere reflection of the original), and costumes (bringing to life all types of heroes). All those elements make the audience perceive theatre as nothing more than a s p e c t a c l e which can be l o o k e d at with impunity or moral consequences.

Certain amounts of aesthetic or emotional experiences and moral reflections are perceived; however, they are perceived from the comfortable position of an objective spectator who can always show his lack of interest if he is challenged.

A work of art in theatre should not be "l o o k e d a t!"

One must take a full responsibility for entering the theatre. One must not leave unexpectedly. One must experience all that awaits him there.

Theatre should not create the illusion of reality, which is contained in the drama. This reality of drama must become the reality on stage. The stage "matter" (I call the stage matter the stage and its fascinating atmosphere, which is not yet spoiled by illusion of drama, and the "readiness" of an actor, who carries with him the potential to perform any part and all characters) must not be glossed over nor covered up with illusion. It must remain crude and raw. It must be ready to face and clash with a new reality, that of the drama.

The ultimate goal is the creation on stage not of illusion (which makes the audience feel safe), but of REALITY, WHICH IS AS CONCRETE AS THE AUDITORIUM.

The drama on stage must "become," rather than "take place," In front of the audience. The d r a m a i s b e c o m i n g.

The plot development should be spontaneous and unpredictable.

A spectator must not feel the presence of the machinery which has always been a part of the theatre.

Therefore, one should avoid situations which might bring back this feeling, but one should add the situation that might expose a spontaneous g r o w t h of drama.

This act of drama's "b e c o m i n g" cannot be hidden in the wings. One must not allow drama to sneak, using the side door, into the secret domain of the stage manager or the backstage machinery.

The reality of the auditorium is inserted into the process of drama's becoming and vice versa.

Before you create a new stage, you must create a new audience. The performance should be the act by which the new audience is brought into being.

THE ACTORS' PLAYING

The actors are not involved emotionally.
In their first phase of being on stage they almost belong to
the r e a l i t y o f t h e a u d i t o r i u m
(in other words, they are almost the audience members.)
From this moment on, their autonomy,

difference,
otherness
will be made visible.
Slowly, they make visible
the i l l u s i o n of their stage characters.
They will always however remain the FORMS, which were
CONSTRUCTED,
that MAKE USE OF MOVEMENT AND SOUND.

The body and the movement of the actors
should e x p l a i n each surface
each form and object and each action development in a scene.
Each movement leads to another, is transferred from one actor
to another. This is how an abstract axis
of movement is created.
One must not be afraid of m o n o t o n y or m e c h a n i c a l actions
replacing
expressive and spontaneous actions.
One must avoid at all cost parallel expression (movement, sound, speech,
shape), which is nothing more than a banal realistic representation.
If one believes that c o n t r a s t is creative, then, even when it clashes
with life's common sense, it should be maintained.

THE DEFORMATION OF ACTION

Deformation in the visual arts is the excess within a form, which, thanks
to it, becomes more dynamic and mobile.
An equivalent in theatre will be the excess of stage action, which is
achieved by either slowing down or accelerating the pace; of psychology,
which is achieved by giving importance to unimportant events, by a
pedantic "registering" of every movement, every thought, and every
expression, by elongating every action until b o r e d o m and
e x h a u s t i o n strike.

The e x p a n s i o n and i n t e n s i f i c a t i o n of illusion can be
achieved gradually—from simply noticing it, marking its presence as
if in spite, taking a step away from it to complete metamorphoses and
complete involvement—thus total i l l u s i o n.

ILLUSION AND REALITY

A contrast to the reality of illusion can be achieved not only with the help
of everyday objects but also people—for example, stage hands or people
who cross the stage with no apparent reason, indifferently, the way people
who unexpectedly show up in dreams and have no connection whatsoever
to the unfolding events cross the dreams' backstage with an impenetrable
smile.

THE INNER CONNECTION BETWEEN THE AUDIENCE AND THE STAGE

Even though, according to Wyspiański's text, Odysseus enters with the Shepherd, I do not "see" him. For the time being, he is a nameless beggar. He will reveal himself later.

This is why Odysseus cannot enter the stage. From the very beginning, what is there that exists on stage is a pile of f o r m l e s s rags. Nobody knows what "that" is.

He is with his back to the audience, bent, "mixed" together with other objects on stage. The moment he turns around to face the audience, reveals his face—must be shocking.

Odysseus reveals himself to the Shepherd first and only then to the audience.

This is what I call the inner connection between the audience and the stage.

TWO REALITIES

Odysseus is our contemporary—a man who is driven by angst, full of anxieties, and who moves the way we do (one needs to find gestures and movements which are of our time and can be derived from how we live, dress, etc.). The rest—that is, the manner of speech is how we imagine the Greek form of delivery should be. That "rest" is
i l l u s i o n. . . .

PATHOS (SOME COMMENTS ABOUT "THE RETURN OF ODYSSEUS")

When everyday events become symbols, they inadvertently acquire the markings of pathos (though, this is not the only way of turning reality to pathos). Pathos in itself is an unbearable trait. Wyspiański not only infuses the text with symbolism and pathos, but also the very manner with which the text is expressed (Odysseus and Telemachus use a heightened language).

If a director, with no sense of humor, adds to these two elements a third one: voice and intonation, a fourth one: movement and gestures, a fifth one: costume and stage design, and the sixth one: music—all filled with pathos to the brim—we will certainly end up watching a perfectly boring production of a Greek mythos.

THE RETURN OF ODYSSEUS I—SOME THOUGHTS

For a long time, I was trying to figure out if Wyspiański's Odysseus is a villain.

What do his actions amount to, once all these psychological moments, used to explain them, veiling them in mysticism, or glossing over their true value are removed? The Trojan War was a Greek invasion. Sanctioned by the imaginary ritual slogan, Odysseus' "heroic" actions belong to the category of common murders.

Once the problem of destiny is removed, the return of Odysseus is nothing more than an ordinary assault: Odysseus returns with his gang to ransack and burn down his home and to kill his own father. One can find a justification for the fact that Odysseus kills like flies the lovers of his wife; but his plans to murder his father without having a clear cause except for some vague justification that he is driven by some fatal force, destiny, or curse does not convince me. I am much more captivated by unmasking this mythological hero.

THE RETURN OF ODYSSEUS II

There were many. Many inglorious returns from Troy. All are marked with the imprints of human unhappiness, inhuman crimes committed in the name of religious slogans.
The returns which are veiled in the tattered false military banners.
The returns—escapes from justice.
Charon's boat does not stop for Odysseus lost in the night of his epilogue.
The epilogue is not his epilogue.
Odysseus walks into the space of history.
He becomes its tragic actor.
The realness of *The Return of Odysseus* becomes more real every day.
The German retreat was in full swing.
The newspapers announced the invasion of allied forces on the opening night. It was necessary to leave aesthetic, ornamental, and abstract constructions aside. The space, which was delineated perfectly by the art's parameters, was invaded brutally by a "real object."
I t   i s   n e c e s s a r y   t o   b r i n g   a   w o r k   o f   a r t   i n t h e a t r e   t o   s u c h   a   p o i n t   o f   i n t e n s i t y   w h e r e o n l y   o n e   s t e p   s e p a r a t e s   d r a m a   f r o m   l i f e, p e r f o r m e r   f r o m   a u d i e n c e.

THE RETURN OF ODYSSEUS III

Odysseus must REALLY return.
It would be dishonest to create for this purpose a false illusion of Ithaca. Everything that surrounds him must be grand; everything that is spoken must be true and honest.
It would be a wicked pettiness to create *papier-mâché* columns and waves for Odysseus's tragic return. I want to place actors among simple parcels, ladders, and chairs—take their costumes away from them—discard all aesthetic values—introduce
c o i n c i d e n c e and even chaos—so this return would be real.
Odysseus returns onto the s t a g e, and, it is onstage that he recreates laboriously the illusion of his Ithaca.
Theatre is a site where the laws of art clash with life's uncertainty and fortuity to give rise to the most powerful tensions and conflicts.

THE FIRST DESIGN VARIANT

The performance area is framed by the wings.

The wings are made of boards, planks, slats, plain canvas, all of which are covered with numbers and letters.

In the middle of the stage, there is a huge cube—a delphic thymele. BEHIND IT, AN UNREALISTIC, MOBILE SURFACE, WHICH IS FILLED WITH SOUNDS, KEEPS FLOATING CONTINUOUSLY AND INTERMINABLY.

It is a measure of a different time and a different space.

THIS CAN BE NAMED ABSTRACTION, ABSOLUTE, OR DEATH.

The events onstage take place despite and independently of this abstract object, which is clearly separated from reality and the realness of the stage action.

Every so often, the actors freeze and become indifferent, as if they were compelled to do so by some inner force, or as if they forgot their lines. The pauses are filled with the presence, motion, and sound from this mysterious floating surface.

The actors resume their parts.

The scene of the killing of Penelope's lovers is syncopated with similar pauses, which now, however, are filled with a different reality.

The pauses are getting longer.

The figures and events dissipate; there is only a surrealistic object.

Odysseus and a black cube—in act III,

this audio-mobile element becomes his stage partner.

THE SECOND DESIGN VARIANT

Real objects are substituted for illusionary objects.

Act I depicts the surroundings of Odysseus's home—

a rock, a fence, a house, all very simple, as if designed by a poorly educated human being, who also made them, covered them with canvas when necessary, etc. To use a language of poetic devices, an arrangement and a convincing illusion of

i m a g i n a r y reality have been created.

Act II brings complications, even though a rock, a fence, and a house stay the same, because they lose their power to create

i l l u s i o n. A spotlight stands in the middle of the stage; the wings are turned around; a ladder leans over one of the wings; Melantho dances in between the electric cables; Penelope sits on a simple kitchen chair; the lovers are on the ladders; a rock, a house, a fence are nothing more than facades from Act I which are pushed aside by utilitarian and technical objects. This new reality, which is pushing aside the reality of Act I, is a stage equivalent of a new situation—having killed the lovers, Odysseus, who is entrapped in this alien and ruthless world, leaves his dreams and illusions of his childhood Ithaca never to return to them.

Act III—when they all leave,

only a rock, a fence, a wall of a house, and a s p o t l i g h t will be left. The light will turn them into lifeless facades. In vain will Odysseus try to recognize his Ithaca in them.

THE THIRD DESIGN VARIANT

Act I is grounded and takes place on a neutral stage which is stripped of its illusion.

At the same time, this o t h e r reality, which will be illusionary and imagined and is, for the time being, suppressed by the "raw" matter of the stage, begins to be perceived. Even though the crude stage reality and its ladders, wings badly put together, rostrum made of simple boards, still dominate, a white Greek sculpture of the head of a singer introduces a tension.

The actors, who still rehearse and repeat their parts, belong to the reality of the stage.

In Act II, i l l u s i o n begins to conquer the stage gradually. There appear

well-s t r u c t u r e d and

i l l u s i o n a r y fragments.

The lovers put on the white masks, which are exact copies of faces from classical monuments.

Femios will stand next to a sculpture of a head and will sing a song; the same song which was sung by the spotlight operator in Act I.

Odysseus enters this deceptive space of illusion; this world which is alien and ominous to him.

Act III is a ruthless and a cruel amplification of the atmosphere of Act I.

ITHACA

The walls of the room are around us. Empty, barren, and cold. One of the walls with falling plaster gives the impression of a huge nightmarish, white void.

Above, there hangs a molding wooden beam.

On the floor, there is a scaffold made of yellow floorboards.

A metal rope cruelly cuts through the empty space.

A decrepit and warped spotlight, like our civilization, is washed ashore of this decaying reality.

"The Audience Members" are crowded together here and there.

A lifeless, huge gun barrel is in the middle of the room.

Above it, there is a loudspeaker.

A wooden cart wheel smeared with mud leans against the wall.

ODYSSEUS

A sharp and loud noise of a marching song.

A goose step of soldiers marching in a parade is heard from a loudspeaker.

Odysseus, wearing an old and tattered military coat with a helmet down
his eyes walks very slowly from the doors.
He is tired and withered.
He stops in the middle.
He sits on the gun barrel.
With his back to the audience, he looks like a formless mass.
It is only when the word "Troy" is heard—he will get up slowly and with
difficulty, reveal his face, and spit out the words: "I am Odysseus. I have
returned from Troy."

RÉSUMÉ

These [three] variants of *The Return of Odysseus* are pointed in a specific
direction. The interpretative surface extends beyond these variants.
A theatre piece is built AROUND JUST ONE FORM. F i n d i n g   i t,
or its shape, i s   a   t r u e   r e v e l a t i o n. Maybe, this form is a
pure idea or a key-concept in the process of deciphering drama. Its inner
strength has the power to explode the structure of drama and to reveal its
pulsating and vibrant interior—all its nerves and cells.
It also attracts other compositional forms.
Its adequacy is measured in terms of the number of situations that can be
explained via its structure.

Theatrical forms pulsate in any dramatic texts. All that should be done is
to feel and express their pulse.
The network of relationships between the forms is built by contrasts and
conflicts.
It is the contrasts, unable to co-exist peacefully and brought together
by force, which create new values and the totality indispensable for
the existence of the work of art. In theatre, this totality is achieved via
the process of balancing the contrasts between diverse scenic elements,
such as, motion and sound, visual forms and motion, space and voice,
word and motion of forms, etc. As far as the cognitive aspect of theatre
is concerned, these contrasts must have sharp edges, come as surprise,
shock, and lead to the creation of tension between two separate and
incompatible realities or objects. A reality "will be created" by placing the
other reality next to it, or by grounding it in the other reality existing in a
different dimension.
Contrast should not, and ought not, be positioned in one dimension and
within one category only.
A square should not only be contrasted with a circle, but also with a
sinuous line, a voice, or a wheel.

THE PROCESS OF CREATING "STAGE FORMS" IS EQUAL TO THE PROCESS OF THE "SHOWING" OF DRAMA ONSTAGE.

The "Trial" scene in *Balladyna* (a play) is crowded with people till the very end. The inner "pulse" of this scene, however, suggests the number of people is decreasing; a continuous disappearance of the people until the heroine is left alone onstage.

There emerges a major difference between my staging of *Balladyna* and *The Return of Odysseus*. This difference is created by the development, building, and construction of a theatrical problem.

Balladyna was an example of an interpretation in which abstract form burst into the reality of drama and stage.

In *The Return of Odysseus*, real life had the strength to explode and clash with the illusionary stage forms, which were being formed.

Will real life win this conflict?

I think so.

It would put us on the road toward external realism.

After the War: A Night Notebook or Metamorphoses
(1947–1948)

I am starting to rebuild my world. I need to establish the rules. New rules.
The old ones died away. What remained are emptiness and space. It is
space which will rule now. Rule and regulate. Dynamic, commanding.
It will give birth to a new life, objects, organisms, and figures. At the
beginning of the world, one must write a book. I am writing it right now,
alone, almost in secrecy. I call it a n i g h t notebook. Almost in secrecy.
December 1947.

SPACE

. . . I am drawing a lot. . . . I am fascinated by space. . . .
space is quickly becoming the main subject of my n o t e b o o k. I call
it a n i g h t notebook. I am drawing during the night. But this is not
the reason why I call it so. Until now, I have been drawing (and painting)
figures and objects.
Now, I am "drawing" space. New space!
I call it m u l t i – s p a c e.
I get lost in it as in a labyrinth (here comes mythology).
Maybe this form of a labyrinth is one of its attributes.
I am trying to discover its secrets and its directions.
Lost in it. Horizons and borders.
At first, I saw these multiple drawings as the necessary practice and
analytical exercises that would prepare me for the right and "serious"
activity such as a painting. I thought that these first attempts should
remain in hiding. The night is the best time for that.
Later, I noticed that this "experience" of space was not at all a tryout.
That, in itself, it was an essential activity and the end product;
that it CONDITIONS THE BEING OF THE IMAGE;
that it is naïve to follow a train of thought that separates an act of
forming space from the act of placing in it the figures, objects, or forms,
which are said to originate or be born in imagination.
THEY ARE BORN IN THIS SPACE! THEY ARE GIVEN BIRTH AT
THE SAME TIME!
I am fascinated by a mystical or utopian idea and a supposition that in
every work of art, there exists, independent of an artist, some

UR-MATTER that shapes itself, and that grounds all possible, infinite variants of life.

By no means, this UR-MATTER [and its ability to shape itself] belittles the artist's function in the creative process; nor does it detract from the power of his imagination. On the contrary! It only shifts his abilities in a proper direction. And a desired one!

It seems that the autonomy of the image is born in this remote layer of the creative process.

I believe in this SIMULTANEITY of and this EQUALITY between my individual actions and the action of this Primordial Matter.

This *"unité"* will always stay an unfathomable mystery of creation.

This UR-MATTER is space!

I can feel its pulsating rhythm.

Shapes, volume, figures, and objects are not a reflection of some "v i s i o n" of mine.

I am not a prophet. Actually, I am very suspicious of the people who claim to have them.

THE EXISTENCE OF A VISION REDUCES ITS BEING TO THE ACT OF REPRESENTATION!

It is a naïve method counting on its sentimental reception by the naïve.

Well-known are its pretentious posing, stylized dandyism showing off its obsessions and psychological deviancy.

A work of art must show a sufficient degree of objectification of an artist's private emotions and feelings.

A painting is an object, after all. One needs to recognize

its material surface,

its inner structure, unfathomable, but demanding

a logical formation,

its condensed space, whose inner pressure is much higher than that of the reality outside of it, causing the image to maintain its autonomy.

MAY 1948

Space,

which does not have an exit, or a boundary;

which is receding, disappearing,

or approaching omni-directionally with changing velocity;

it is dispersed in all directions: to the sides, to the middle;

it ascends, caves in,

spins on the vertical, horizontal, diagonal axis. . . .

It is not afraid to burst into an enclosed shape,

defuse it with its sudden jerking movement,

deform its shape. . . .

Figures and objects become the function of space

and its mutability. . . .

JUNE 1948

Space is not a passive r e c e p t a c l e
in which objects and forms are posited. . . .
SPACE itself is an OBJECT (of creation).
And the main one!
SPACE is charged with E N E R G Y.
Space shrinks and e x p a n d s.
And these motions mould forms and objects.
It is space which G I V E S   B I R T H to forms!
It is space which conditions the network of relations and T E N S I O N S
between the objects
TENSION is the principal actor of space.
A MULTI-SPACE. . . .
The process of reaching it is childishly simple.
It requires however an intervention of omni-present and impulsive free
will.
SPACE is compressed into a flat surface.
This surface is put into various types of motion.
CIRCULAR MOTION,
around an axis posited vertically, horizontally, diagonally
in relation to the surface of the image. . . .
This motion requires a constant COUNTER-MOTION.
PENDULUM MOTION,
whose s w i n g i n g—
losing
and regaining of momentum—
conditions expansion
and GROWTH of space.
MOTIONS OF MOVING [surfaces]
of PUSHING them together,
of PULLING them apart,
of c o v e r i n g   and u n - c o v e r i n g.
MOTIONS OF DESCENDING and ASCENDING.
MOTION OF MOVING [surfaces] apart until they disappear.
MOTIONS OF DRAWING them NEAR and PUSHING them AWAY.
SUDDENNESS and VELOCITY of these motions
create new aspects:
TENSION
and
a change of SCALE.

SEPTEMBER 1948

. . . bringing the forms out from SPACE
precludes a process, which creates them out of OBSESSION
DEFORMATION

empty STYLIZATION,
aggressive expressionism,
dubious sign of individualism.
. . . SPACE frees IMAGINATION,
disclosing its INFINITY, its secrets
and its METAPHYSICS.

1948

. . . SPACE
more dynamic
than the one we live in.
Alive,
autonomous and . . .
more cruel.
Space, which convulsively shrinks
and expands to infinity.
[Space] gives birth to objects,
conditions their shapes,
deforms them capriciously,
where everything is possible,
or rather, where the IMPOSSIBLE
finds its rationale and right to exist.
A figure of a human being is formed at the threshold between
a living, suffering organism and
a mechanism,
which functions automatically and absurdly.
It is governed by the laws of M E T A M O R P H O S I S.
A figure of a human being is subject to
transformations,
expansions,
transplants
and interbreeding.

METAMORPHOSES.
One more mythological action.
This magic word will free me from theoretical
discussion and conflicts,
will loosen the canon with f r e e d o m of POETRY.
And, then, it will all be clear!

Cricot 2 Theatre
(about 1963)

Once the theatre avant-garde of the 1920 and 1930s was gagged (an act that received full support of world conformism), there appeared a reactionary proposition that, in theatre, an institution of mass perception and of complex interdependencies, an avant-garde, which has a very narrow scope and no outreach, is an ephemeral and artificial phenomenon. This conviction persisted for a quarter of a century before and after the war.
Theatre, despite its official support and recognition, started to slide into a place where the laws of art and its development ceased to be binding. Cricot 2 Theatre, founded in 1955, and its productions gave an "infectious" testimony of a successful avant-garde operation.

It exposed an artistic emptiness in the official theatres;
having located the idea of the function of art
outside of them,
it took their theatre "monopoly" away from them.

It exposed an erroneous and false opinion that the structure of theatre is "unchangeable" and not susceptible to the avant-garde thought.

It gave hope, because of its successful productions, that radical action in theatre is possible.
It showed that radical avant-garde thought could not be ignored in theatre, if theatre is to exist and develop.
It created the "need" (and the snobs, too) for avant-garde in theatre.

The first production of Cricot 2 Theatre was the founding manifesto of its new concept of theatre.

The amount of ink that Polish press devoted to Cricot 2 Theatre at the time is proof of the singular significance of the event.

The year that Cricot 2 Theatre was founded—1955—the fact that it was a continuation of the work of the Experimental Underground Theatre (1942 and 1944), as well as 20 years of Cricot 2 activities, will be helpful in reviewing the chronology of its theatrical events after the war, the 1950s, the 1960s until now.

THE STRUCTURE OF CRICOT 2 THEATRE

During the 20 year of its existence, Cricot 2 Theatre had developed its own style of work, which, in turn, had an impact on a specific structure of this theatre. Its structure is as follows:
Cricot 2 Theatre does not function on regular basis.
The path of the development of Cricot 2 Theatre is not shaped by the continuous opening of new productions, but by stages, whose content is molded by a slow, though continuous, movement of thoughts and ideas. Consequently, these stages are formed gradually.
The infrequent nature of the new productions of Cricot 2 Theatre is not due to some external problems or a weakening of creative energy.
It is a natural condition.

The need to put a production together is dictated by an urgency to express an idea, which is processed for a long time, then slowly matures, and, finally, demands and is ready to be m a t e r i a l i z e d.
Each time this happens, it has a form of a creative explosion.
This is why this does not happen often.

ANNEXED REALITY—1944

The process of annexing reality, defined as a strategy and a method, has been Cricot 2's ideological foundation since 1955.
It was discovered, however, while I was working with the Experimental Underground Theatre in 1944.
It first emerged and was fully realized in the production of Stanisław Wyspiański's *The Return of Odysseus.*
It was the time of war; the time when one's awareness could be altered in a split second and one's instincts had to be infallible and ahead of their time. The idea of the process of annexing reality proclaimed the necessity of questioning art's sacred dictum of being allowed only to present, in a work of art, a fictitious reality, a reflection of reality,
a r e p r e s e n t a t i o n of reality (simply, a "false-pretense"); a dictum which barred reality from being a part of the work of art.
[Art's] Depreciation of Reality
and its privileging of
imitation,
illusion,
fiction,
representation
led me, consequently, to a radical rejection of these devices, and to my fascination with
"raw" reality

that was not altered by any "artistic modes,"
and with a R E A L   O B J E C T
that took the place of
an "Artistic object."

OBJECT 1944

An object became for me a sign for the problem of boundaries in art.
The substitution of the "real" object for the "artistic" object was not a
manifestation of anti-art attitude.
An object—alien and undefinable by our minds—is fascinating.
The desire to possess it, as well as all attempts to imitate it, or
r e p r e s e n t it are futile and vain.
It must be "touched" in a different manner.
This process (this r i t u a l) is childishly simple: the object must be
wrenched from its life's conditions and functions, left alone without their
c o m m e n t a r y, which would give it a meaning; [the object] must be
left a l o n e.
Such a procedure is almost unthinkable in everyday practice.
In theatre /1944!/: the object ceased to be a prop, used by the actor in his
act.
Simply
[the object] WAS, EXISTED—on an equal footing with the actor.
[the object] WAS THE ACTOR! The Object-Actor!!

(In *The Return of Odysseus*, the above-mentioned strategy described a
very specific
R I T U A L resembling a "representation" of a cultural fetish. The
major difference was, however, that the object was not exhibited to be
"venerated," but to be scorned and laughed at. Similar practices emerged
in the French New Realism and in Fluxus + Happening in the 1960s.)

THE OBJECTS USED IN *THE RETURN OF ODYSSEUS* (1944):

A CART WHEEL—simple, primitive, smeared with mud
A BOARD—old, rotten, with marks after nails and rust
A CHAIR—simple, kitchen chair, well-worn
A GUN BARREL—iron, rust-eaten, big, and heavy; not on wheels, but
resting on A TRESTLE smeared with mud, cement, lime
A METAL ROPE—thick and rusty
A LOUDSPEAKER—military, imperfect, hanging on a metal rope
PARCELS—covered with dust, lime, the audience "members" sit on them
WALLS—of the room where the performance takes place, bombed, full of
holes, bare bricks, coats of paint on the floor
A FLOOR—missing floorboards, debris scattered all over.

THE POOR OBJECT

The real object wrenched from reality, a substitute for an "artistic object,"
was not just any "neutral" object.
It was the object which was
the simplest,
the most primitive,
old,
marked by time,
worn out by the fact of being used,
P O O R.
This condition of being "poor," disclosed the object's deeply hidden
objectness. Bereft of its externalities, the object revealed its "essence," its
primordial function.
All these processes marked a radical departure from the ideas of
constructivism—the process of seeing the development of modern theatre
in terms of technology and mechanics collapsed definitely and irrevocably
for me in 1944. In Witkiewicz's *The Cuttlefish* (1956), real, poor, and
primitive objects performed the function of g r o u n d i n g pathetic
situations, sublime conditions, and venerable characters. For example,
a simple iron stand, rather than an ornamented pulpit, was used for the
Pope's speeches; a hospital stretcher, rather than a comfortable couch, was
used by Alice d'Or. . . .
Poor object (1944) was a portent of the idea of the "Reality of the Lowest
Rank," which was fully defined in the production of Witkiewicz's *The
Country House* ("The Informel Theatre") in 1961.

ELIMINATION OF THE CONVENTIONAL ELEMENTS OF THEATRE

The rejection of an "artistic object," which contained in itself both
imitation and representation of the fiction of reality, led, in theatre, to
the rejection of all of those elements associated with an "artistic object."
Among them were:
—the p r o p—whose place was taken by a r e a l o b j e c t which
revealed its essence once outside the functions ascribed to him by life (AN
OBJECT-ACTOR).
—the d e s i g n—whose place was taken by a r e a l p l a c e, whose
characteristics (for example, a launderette, a cloakroom, a railway station,
a storeroom, bombed rooms) imposed behaviors, actions, emotions, lines,
that would reflect the reality of the space, upon the actors, and made the
audience a part of the general atmosphere.
—c o s t u m e formed by fiction
—all aesthetic arrangements
—the s p a t i a l o r g a n i z a t i o n of the stage
—the l i g h t i n g, b l o c k i n g

—finally, the p l o t of a play, whose sequences were rejected for the actions and situations
g e n e r a t e d and imposed by the reality of the p l a c e.

THE QUESTIONING OF THE "ARTISTIC" PLACE RESERVED FOR THEATRE

Theatre "is being created" in the midst of reality and life.
The following are the excerpts from 1943:
. . . theatre (a building, a stage, and an auditorium), a site of centuries-old practices, indifferent and anaesthetized, is the least suitable place for the m a t e r i a l i z a t i o n of drama. . . . Theatre, drama, art, and spectacle, which are supposed to be b e l i e v a b l e, can only appear in a place that is not legally sanctioned or reserved for them.
Having rejected an "artistic object" and its fiction of reality, consequently, I had to reject the notion of a place that was reserved for the theatre. In its stead, I called for a real place which was a part of reality. It was a "poor" place that was on the margin of the life's practice.
Those places were:
rooms destroyed by the war,
abandoned railway stations,
launderettes,
cloakrooms,
waiting-rooms, storage-rooms. . . .

THE IDEA OF THE AUTONOMOUS THEATRE

Cricot 2 Theatre brought back the idea of the autonomous theatre, which after the downfall of the avant-gardes of the 1920s and 1930s was believed to be a fiction and pure formalism. In the 1950s, when the emergence of the phenomenal texts of the avant-garde artists was equated with the emergence of a new theatre, Cricot 2 Theatre put forth the idea of the avant-garde theatre, which was not circumscribed by the staging of the avant-garde literature (usually this was done with the help of traditional stage means). The possibility of resurrecting the avant-garde, Cricot 2 Theatre practiced in a purely theatrical domain, in separating the theatrical work of art (a production) from its slavish representation of a literary text.
In a theatre practice this signified a rejection of a method of "illustrating," reporting, representing the plot of the play through a stage action, and a need to employ a new method. This new method is the process of creating p a r a l l e l   t r a c k s which do not illustrate, explain, or interpret each other, but "correspond" to one another through pointed dynamic tensions. One of these tracks is a t e x t that was bereft of a surface plot structure; the other is a parallel TRACK OF THE AUTONOMOUS STAGE ACTION, pure element, pure theatrical matter.

REALNESS OF A THEATRICAL ACTION

A theatrical work of art (a production) is not a structure which is purely aesthetic (illusion). Its realness is of the same degree and intensity as the reality of the place which comprises the stage and the auditorium.

The plot (fiction) is brought into the conditions of the place (and the auditorium). In the process, a parallel action is born in the form of real action of the production and the CHARACTERS who are defined by the attributes of the place (a cloakroom, for example), or a specific idea (the idea of a journey, for example).

The elements of this real action are as if anchored somewhere in the past (in the fiction of the dramatic text), as if the past repeated itself but in a strangely different form.

The time and space of the plot unfolding in the production equals (and is) the time and the space of the audience.

The process of deriving the realness of the production/stage/actor from the reality of the auditorium, provides the audience members a feeling of belonging to the reality of the stage and the production, which are of the same kind and degree as the auditorium in a theatre.

This is something more than just a superficial, mechanical participation of the audience members achieved by "thrusting" a stage into the auditorium. This was an essential discovery made by Cricot 2 Theatre, which became a main motif and subject of its artistic work.

THE ZERO THEATRE

Excerpts from my essays from 1963:

. . . theatre that I call the z e r o theatre does not refer to "zero" zones, that is, it is not a complete rejection of the materialization of a work of art. . . .

. . . the traditional techniques of plot development made use of human life as a springboard for movement "UPWARDS" towards the realm of growing and intensified action and reaction "IN PLUS"—they became a naïve fiction. . . .

. . . the movement in the opposite direction: "DOWNWARDS" into the realm below the normal, accepted way of life, which is possible by eliminating excessive emotions, "cooling" of temperature—is a process of DE-ILLUSION and the only chance to touch upon REALITY. . . .

Reality of the Lowest Rank

(1980)

1960

FOR A FEW YEARS, A GRAND WAVE OF THE "I N F O R M E L"
ART HAS BEEN MOVING THROUGHOUT THE WORLD.
Since the very beginning, I and my painting have been a part of the
movement.
1950s . . . 1960s.
A discovery of a new unknown aspect of reality, of its elementary state.
This state is:
MATTER
which is freed from abiding by the laws of construction, which is always
fluid, which is infinite, which negates the concept of form,
which is FORMLESS, INFORMELLE
which is discovered in
the EXPLOSIONS OF THE FOUR ELEMENTS,
in the BIOLOGICAL PROCESS OF DECAY,
which is transformed by TIME,
DESTRUCTION and
COINCIDENCE.

MATTER,
which is revealed in such activities as:
COMPRESSION, TEARING, BURNING, SMEARING;
which is represented by:
MUD, EARTH, CLAY, DEBRIS, MILDEW, ASHES.

The following are the objects which are at the threshold of becoming
matter:
RAGS, TATTERS, GARBAGE, REFUSE, MUSTY BOOKS, MOLDERED
PLANKS,
W A S T E.
The emotional states which correspond to matter are:

EXCITEMENT, FEVERISHNESS, HALLUCINATION,
CONVULSIONS, AGONY, MADNESS.

The essence of the "Informel" art was a complete fulfillment of my inner
inclinations and desires regarding art as well as
a c o n f i r m a t i o n
of the D I S C O V E R Y, which I had made
ten years earlier in 1944
during a time of genocide
and which I revindicated stubbornly.
This discovery was the need to
ACCEPT THAT REALITY, WHICH WAS WRENCHED AND
SEPARATED FROM THE EVERYDAY, AS THE FIRST ELEMENT OF
THE CREATIVE PROCESS;
SUBSTITUTE A REAL OBJECT FOR AN ARTISTIC OBJECT;
AN OBSERVATION THAT
A DISCARDED OBJECT, WHICH IS AT THE THRESHOLD OF
BEING THROWN OUT, WHICH IS USELESS, GARBAGE,
HAS THE BIGGEST CHANCE TO BECOME THE OBJECT OF ART
AND THE WORK OF ART. I CALLED IT THEN
A P O O R O B J E C T.
TEN YEARS LATER, THE ADJECTIVE POOR WAS EXPANDED AND
TRANSFORMED INTO A NEW AND SHARPER PHRASE:
THE REALITY OF THE LOWEST RANK.
MY ARTISTIC PROCESS HAS ALWAYS BEEN FAITHFUL TO THIS
NEW DEFINITION AND ITS SCANDALOUS CONSEQUENCES.

THE IDEA OF THE REALITY OF THE LOWEST RANK
THE EXPOSITORY STRATEGY OF "CRICOTEKA"

In my discussion of this strategy, I will not provide chronological divisions
delineated by a succession of the stages of development. I will attempt to
bring to the fore those IDEAS, which emerged and materialized at a given
STAGE and in a particular production. These did not disappear, however,
when they were presented onstage; they would exert an impact on all
future stages of the development of my theatre—they would reemerge at
a different stage and realize themselves according to the principles of this
other stage.
It is these ideas, which appeared and disappeared throughout, that
contribute to the shape and character of the phenomenon known as the
Cricot 2 Theatre.
This particular strategy, revealing the CONSEQUENCES OF THE
ARTISTIC ACTIONS and their INDIVIDUAL character, separates the
Cricot 2 Theatre from all those other pseudo-avantgarde theatres and
their activities which were either plagiarisms or made use of external

effects that had nothing in common with the concepts of IDEA and DEVELOPMENT.

"POOR" REALITY
THE REALITY OF THE LOWEST RANK

One of these ideas is the idea of a "POOR" OBJECT which emerged in the UNDERGROUND Theatre in 1944, and which acquired the name of THE REALITY OF THE LOWEST RANK in the "INFORMEL" THEATRE in 1960 [1961—MK].
In Cricoteka, in my expository strategy, I will try to document carefully and meticulously all these ideas in terms of:
A/ a visual system of
1.   objects, props
2.   big drawings, or, even possibly, their enlargements
3.   definitions, slogans, instructions, directions represented by INDI-CATORS (INDICATORE STRADALE): ROAD SIGNS
                                        FREEWAY SIGNS,
                                        SUBWAY SIGNS, RAILWAY
                                        STATION SIGNS.
4.   miniature models
5.   texts presented in a slightly enlarged form
6.   models presented as a painting, or a relief
7.   short FILMS with a corresponding ACTION.
B/ an audio system of:
recordings of sounds reproducing different linguistic modes, sounds of expressions which were used in the "INFORMEL" Theatre.

Because the IDEA OF THE "POOR" REALITY
(it is important that the year of its discovery be remembered: 1944)
is a fundamental idea for the development of the Cricot Theatre, and one which has frequently been appropriated by other theatres for its external value and effect, I find it necessary to illustrate it via the practices of CRICOT 2.
The below-mentioned key-words
will be strategic points, something like a roadmap, or a list of road-signs or indicators, in our journey and will refer to specific OBJECTS,
                                        PROPS,
                                        MODELS,
                                        MINIATURE
                                        MODELS
or to THEORETICAL TEXTS.

I.   1944. Underground Theatre. *The Return of Odysseus*

1.   The ROOM
        was destroyed by the war activity of 1944.
        Odysseus returned to this room, rather than to a mythological Ithaca.

The ROOM was not the auditorium,
the ROOM was not a part of the "stage design,"
the ROOM was a real site,
which was as real as the events surrounding the audience.
The ROOM was thus an integral part of a work of art: a production.
The audience was *inside* the work of art.
It was the first environmental art.
The ROOM—OBJECT
"POOR" OBJECT.

2.   The naked and poor WALLS, marked by gun shells, were a substitute
for a Greek horizon and its blue and sunny skies.

3.   A WHEEL smeared with mud,
A ROTTEN BOARD hanging from the ceiling,
A rust-eaten GUN BARREL, resting not on wheels, but on a
TRESTLE smeared with mud and cement,
DEBRIS,
EARTH
were used instead of
a palace interior,
marble,
columns. . . .

4.   The WAR ANNOUNCEMENT was played through a street loudspeaker, instead of the heroic song of a Homeric bard.

II.   1955. The Founding of the Cricot 2 Theatre. *The Cuttlefish*

1.   A HOSPITAL STRETCHER is used by Alice d'Or as a comfortable
couch.

2.   AN IRON, INDUSTRIAL STAND is used by Pope Julius II as a
church pulpit.

3.   A MUSTY COFFIN is used as a conference table at the meeting of
high-ranking
officials who gathered together to decide the fates of art and culture.

4.   A THUG in a costume adorned with iron and poor quality utensils
becomes a dictator.

5.   A CLOWN, A PITIFUL MUMMY COVERED WITH BANDAGES,
A POOR RELIC OF POWER
IN A STATE OF CEMETERY DECAY,
dares to assume the power of Pope Julius II the Great.

III.   1961. The Informel Theatre. *The Country House.*

1.   A POOR, MOLDING W A R D R O B E BROUGHT DOWN
FROM THE ATTIC and its tiny interior, rather than a magical
s t a g e on which a sacred mystery of illusion was celebrated, had to
be a sufficient space for the actors.
A W A R D R O B E had to replace the nostalgic country house
demanded by the playwright.

2.   A GARBAGE CAN, a gloomy chariot of the Sanitation Unit, was used as a pram for the children.

3.   A FUNERAL MACHINE, a MONSTROUS GRINDER WITH UNSPECIFIED GRINDING PROCEDURES—covered with a thick dirty cover, from under which an immense bolt and handle were protruding—was a substitute for a family tomb.

4.   SACKS and SACKCLOTH BAGS filled with grain (artificial grain, of course), rather than the charming atmosphere of a country house, filled the space.

5.   The individual actors' performances, which were threatened and limited by the absurdly small space in the wardrobe and the motionless state of the inanimate objects (sacks), were lost in this totally
"f o r m l e s s" matter, in the limited possibilities of the process of COMPRESSION, CRUMPLING, CRUSHING, COMMIXING, and DEGRADATION.

6.   Instead of classical linguistic forms, THE COARSE "BRUTE" MATTER OF LANGUAGE, which is formed by emotions, feverish states, the conditions of the Lowest Rank, INARTICULATE SOUNDS and PHONEMES, emerges.

7.   AN OBJECT WRENCHED OUT OF THE EVERYDAY REALITY is a substitute for an artistic object, or an object artistically formed. THE "POOR" OBJECT is a substitute for "the work of art."

8.   AUTONOMOUS ACTIONS or INDEPENDENT ACTIONS are a substitute for the process of "building" or the constructive and "positive" process. Those actions are clearly demonstrated in COSTUMES. A costume is created via such processes as:
TEARING APART,
PULLING APART,
SEWING,
MENDING,
BURNING,
BLEACHING,
SOILING,
SMEARING,
WEARING OUT,
FADING. . . .

IV.   1963. The "Zero" Theatre

1.   A monstrous, apocalyptic DESTRUCTION MACHINE, which brings mental devastation into our glorious world of technology and science, this "Deus ex Machina" is made of old, decrepit, poor FOLDING CHAIRS in Witkiewicz's *The Madman and the Nun.*

2.   ACTING: a sacred dramatic convention demanding "positive" techniques of "growth" in
EMOTIONS,

EXPRESSIONS,
REACTIONS
is rejected for the movement in the opposite direction into the sphere
below ("in minus") of reduction of
ENERGY,
EXPRESSION,
COOLING
in the direction of "zero," EMPTINESS. . . .

3.   A COSTUME ceases to be used to demonstrate its own splendor and
     charming landscapes; instead it becomes
     a poor, AUTONOMOUS MODEL of clothing
     bereft of its external "decorative" function,
     but exposing its arteries, veins, organs, and diseases . . .

V.   1967. Theatre-Happening

1.   Poor WANDERERS, TRAVELERS, carrying weathered luggage
     with them, VAGRANTS play the parts of princes, dukes, barons,
     courtesans, decadent artists, and cardinals.
     POOR, ETERNAL WANDERERS subscribing to the philosophy of
     "omnia mea mecum porto."

2.   Sensational and sublimated situations and activities are replaced
     with THE SIMPLEST, EVERYDAY, PROSAIC ACTIVITIES, AND
     THE RAW REAL MATTER OF LIFE (NOT TRANSFORMED BY
     "ARTISTIC" MODES).

3.   Instead of the auditorium with seats, loges, and balconies designed for
     the comfortable consumption of art,
     A POOR-HOUSE
     with mattresses,
     bunk-beds,
     old parcels,
     and ladders,
     is the performance site.
     The matter of the stage is the matter of the auditorium, the audience
     and the actors experience the same problems and emotions.

VI.   1972. The Impossible Theatre

1.   It is not the STAGE with its mirages, a "s a c r e d" site in the temple
     of art, but a CLOAKROOM, the place of the LOWEST RANK in
     theatre, which becomes a performance space, a space which imposes
     its prosaic characteristics upon both art and the actors.

2.   The PRINCESS, a descendent of the old family of Abencerag, lives in
     a HEN-HOUSE rather than in a palace.

3.   The Cardinal is a simple porter who carries the "poor" DOORS.

4.   A monstrous MOUSE-TRAP is used as a weapon in a pretentious
     aristocratic duel!

VII. 1975. The Theatre of Death

1.   The mystery of death, a medieval "dance macabre," is executed in a CLASSROOM.
     The decrepit and old-fashioned school DESKS become the ALTAR in this ritual of death.
2.   A symbol of death is a symbol of life, a CRADLE is a COFFIN.
     Instead of a new-born baby, two wooden, dead balls are used. Instead of the child's whining, the dry rattle of the balls is heard.
3.   The act of giving birth takes place in a primitive FAMILY MACHINE.
4.   THE OLD PEOPLE AT THEIR GRAVES, dressed in funeral clothes, rather than the noble heroes of Proust's novel, are on the quest for the lost time.

An extremely important REMARK:
   All these figures, objects, and situations of
   the LOWEST RANK
   are not a manifestation of a PROGRAMMATIC (PLANNED) CYNICISM.
   They are shielded from this old fashioned and easily available idea by POETRY and LYRICISM. In the domain of the lowest reality,
   THE ESSENCE OF LIFE, bereft of
   STYLIZATION, GLITTER, false PATHOS, or ACADEMIC BEAUTY,
   is to be found.

The Autonomous Theatre
(1956/1963)

1. The Autonomous Theatre:

I applied
the concept of the **Autonomous Theatre**
to two productions of
the Underground Experimental Theatre,
which were staged in
1942
and
1944,
as well as to the post-war productions
of the Cricot 2 Theatre
in 1956, 1957, and 1960.

The theatre which I call **autonomous**
is the theatre which is not
a reproductive mechanism,
i.e., a mechanism whose aim is to
present an interpretation of a piece of literature
on stage,
but a mechanism which
has its own **independent**
existence.
Due to the notion of **unity**
which is an inherent part of
a true work of art,
this concept,
which is as complex as the nature of theatre
and the creative process,
cannot be fully explained
unless all its germinal parts are defined.
At least, all the theatrical elements
must be integrated to a degree and
create a composite unit.
Because the term

the "highest"
(degree of integration)
does not mean anything
and thus leaves room for misunderstandings
let us label it
the **zero** (degree).
I do not apply the concept of
the autonomous theatre
to **explain**

the dramatic text,   The relationship between
to **translate** it   theatre and drama

into the language of theatre,
to **interpret** it
or **find** its new meanings.
The concept of the
autonomous theatre
is not the tool to
excavate the so-called
"stage equivalent"
which could be perceived
as a second parallel "action"
that is mistakenly called
autonomous.
I consider such interpretations
as naive stylizations.
I create such
reality,
such plots of events
which have neither
logical,
analogical,
parallel,
nor *juxtaposed*
relationship with the drama;
and such forces
that could **crush**
the **impregnable shell** of
drama.
This can be achieved by
implementing **shocks**   The meaning of a shock
and **scandals.**
Shock which is used in art
is not a means of
calming down the senses.

On the contrary:
it is a physical device to
break through
petty,
universal,
practical philosophy of life of
modern man;
a device to **unblock**
the channels of his subdued
sphere of imagination;
to transfer **"different"** messages   Different message
which are guarded off by his
pragmatism
and deliberation.
All celebrations
and "strange" actions of modern man
are nothing more than
empty and
pretentious
phraseology
piloting modern man
safely aground.
Modern theatre,   Passéist theatre
in spite of new talents
appearing sporadically;
in spite of the false seriousness of its
official representatives,
is dead,
academic,
and, at its best, entertainment
when it makes use of different
means that trigger excitement.
However, those means
push the theatre, even further, towards the
ridiculous,
past styles and techniques;
the deserted plane;
and finally, turn it into the prey of
private interest groups.
This theatre lacks
any ambition of
being **"different";**
the desire to
discover its definition and shape
in the analysis of the generations to come.
This theatre is sentenced to be erased from the memory.

2.   The stage description:

A space which is   Bankruptcy of
small in size   theatre techniques
constitutes the stage.
Almost all of it is taken by
a huge pile of
deck-chairs which are
similar;
weathered by wind and rain;
worn out;
useless;
randomly connected with a wire;
and put into motion;
Their movement could be described in terms of human **psychology:**
it is sudden,
furious,
nervous,
convulsive,
dying out,
uncoordinated,
ridiculous,
monotonous,
threatening.
It emits a
dull death rattle.
This huge object
has many functions:
to eliminate,
to push aside,
to work eternally
without any pattern and thought;
to perturb,
to look ridiculously funny and immensely tragic;
to fascinate; to draw us to it, and to push us aside.
I created an object   Object
whose utilitarian character
stands in opposition to its
new function that creates this
oppressive and brutal
reality.
I assigned to it
a movement and function
which are absurd when compared with its original ones.
Having done so, I elevated it
to the plane of
ambiguous meanings and

disinterested functions,
that is, to the plane of
poetry.
The space which is left   Against the space
to the performers
has nothing in common
with the space
which has fascinated theatre
for centuries.
This space nearly ceases to exist.
Its size could be equated with "zero."
It is so small and infinitesimal that
actors have to
fight from being
pushed aside.
Circus is   Circus
at the roots of this theatre.
Its comical,
sharp,
clownish
character, which
stretch beyond accepted life conventions,
is like a filter
through which human actions are
used to remove
the particles that blur their perception and sharpness.
The actor in this uncompromising   The Actor
arrangement
must reveal and relinquish his
clumsiness,
poverty,
and dignity
to the spectator.
He must appear
defenseless,
without safety,
shields
in front of the audience.

This realization of the "impossible"   From the "impossible"
is the strongest fascination   to the real
and the deepest secret
of art.
This realization is an act of our imagination
and of a sudden, spontaneous,
desperate decision to cling to
unprecedented,

absurd,
ridiculous,
possibilities which are beyond our imagination
rather than to the process.
In order to create the magnetic field to
pull the "impossible" into it,
one must lack experience,
be a rebel, be insatiable,
defy all the laws,
be in a state of
an absolute emptiness.
Needless to say
one has to be in the grip of
the feeling of the "impossible."
Without this phenomenon
which escapes beyond the confines of common sense,
there would not be
any development.
The **reproductive technique**
of acting and
directing
is so strong a convention
that it is perceived as
the only one that is
true and in agreement
with the text.
In my last production [*The Madman and the Nun*—MK]
a dramatic text   The text
is not **presented** but
discussed,
commented upon;
the actors speak the lines,
reject them,
return to them,
and repeat them;
the parts are not assigned
thus, **the actors do not identify with the text.**
The performance turns into
a mill grinding the text—
Does the mill "interpret" the product which it grinds?
However, this sort of questions and problems,
which are difficult and uneasy in terms of the old convention,
are pointless in the arrangement I am suggesting.
All we have to do is to "construct the mill."
"Action" in the old naturalistic theatre
is always connected with
the progression of events of
the dramatic text.

The Elements of theatre:
"action"
and acting
rage blindly
through a narrow passage.
How naive and
poor
is this method.
All we have to do is to be able to see
in order to get to the heart of
the stage "action" of the
theatre elements.   The text and action
In order not to destroy the text
during this process,
the text and the action must be exposed.
This seems to be impossible to achieve
from the perspective of life's practical requirements.
In art—and in this case
in theatre,
as a result of our action,
we will create reality
whose elements will be loosely connected;
which will be easy to mould.
This act of **nullification** of actions,
of placing them in the state of weightlessness,
of juggling with them
allows us to intertwine them with
pure theatrical activities
which are the part of theatre elements.
The concept of the Zero Theatre
which, in preparation of the spectacle,
fascinated me by its unlimited potentials,
is a manifestation
rather than a method.
Radical, even one-time changes   The significance of
have a crucial significance   radical actions in art
in its development:
they cleanse the atmosphere
from the false myths,
imaginary alternatives,
unresolved disputes,
and thus from the whole spectrum of speculations
that offer many solutions.
The concept of the zero theatre
embraces all elements of this rite of cleansing
and puts them
together under one headline.

Modern theatre offers many
of those stylish nuances:
pseudo-naturalistic theatre
stems from laziness
and idleness
(in the times of Zola,
naturalism was exposed to
the scathing criticism);
pseudo-expressionist theatre,
which, after the authentic
deformation of expressionism,
was left with nothing more than
a stylized, dead
grimace;
pseudo-surrealistic theatre
which makes use of deplorable
surrealist ornamentations that
resemble the taste of shop window designers;
theatre which does not want to take risks
and, having nothing, to say employs
moderate cultural policy that
is dressed up in eclectic elegance;
pseudo-modern theatre, which makes use
of various gimmicks taken out of different
fields of modern art.
In real life, reaching the zero state
means negation and destruction.
In art, the same process might give
totally different results.
Reaching zero, destruction,
annihilation of phenomena, elements,
events,
relieves them of the
burden of leading
practical life
and allows them
to turn into the stage matter
which is molded independently.
Here are some examples of
annihilation
used in
The Madman and the Nun:
indifference to situations,
events,
conflicts,
and to psychological states,
as they are defined by their conventional

The image
of modern
theatre

"appearances";
monotony,
manipulating the condition of
being bored, boredom,
the **elimination** of action
    movement
    speech
the **economy** of disclosing
    the emotions
    bordering on being in a vegetative state
"**surreptitious**" acting
juggling
    with the **void**
    "with **anything**"
    with the **insignificant**
with all that is
"u n w o r t h y"
    of being shown on **stage.**

The Litany of the Informel Art
(1955)

The discovery of the u n k n o w n side of r e a l i t y:
of its elementary state:
MATTER.
And this is how the c o n q u e s t of this mysterious continent begins.
A feverish exploration of the unknown lands.
A New Epoch.
Human sensitivity absorbs all its
attributes and characteristics
which, until now, have not been noticed,
deemed significant,
viewed as suspicious,
warned against,
perceived as abnormal, as deviations,
and as exaggeration. . . .

Below is its index-litany:
matter
fluid and changing
capricious
and dynamic,
unimpeded
and unpredictable,
irreverent of
all Holy Laws
of Rational
Construction
and Logic;
e x p o s i n g t h e i r m i s a p p r o p r i a t i o n s,
r i d i c u l i n g t h e i r m e c h a n i s m s
o f R i g i d i t y,
and q u e s t i o n i n g t h e i r r i g h t to
P o w e r. . . .

Matter
without frontiers,

without a beginning, middle and end,
frivolously spilling over the f r a m e s of a work of art. . . .
The frames, which are believed to be a safety b a r r i e r
protecting against the outlawed symptoms of disorder,
which function as a security g u a r d. . . .
A work of art is e n c l o s e d!
The art historians use a word:
"completed."
Or maybe:
imprisoned. . . .

Matter
allowing itself to cross the boundaries,
spreading in all directions,
expanding beyond an accepted norm,
immeasurably,
"without measure,"
without the frontiers, without the frames, without the "square,"
w i t h o u t a f o r m
f o r m l e s s!

S p a c e annexing
(unselfishly!)
life;
bursting into l i f e. . . .

and finally—something that is most amazing—
finding its own r e f l e c t i o n
in a h u m a n being
in his interior—
where its equivalents are born,
ferment,
grow,
expand;
tragic,
heretical,
and sinful against Nature and God,
dissenting. . . .

A n e w i m a g e o f a h u m a n b e i n g is born:
"an inner landscape"
Its condition—human:
FREEDOM,
nostalgia,
a n x i e t y,
passions and desires. . . .

Emotional states:
suffering,
pain,
lunacy,
madness,
feverishness,
delirium,
hallucination,
delusion,
spasm,
ecstasy,
agony,
a desire to d e s t r o y,
shadowy realms of shameful practices,
forbidden acts,
debauchery,
cruelty,
f e a r
and s h a m e. . . .

Matter
and its irreversible end:
disintegration,
d e c o m p o s i t i o n,
decay,
molding. . . .
wood dust,
earth,
poor remnants,
pitiful traces. . . .

Pitiful practices surrounding this inferno:
kneading,
imprinting,
crushing,
compressing,
splashing,
smearing,
pulling,
tearing,
burning,
splashing. . . .

and all other shameful activities:
crying,
sobbing,
howling,

stuttering,
gibberish,
cursing,
shrieks,
screams,
an ungrammatical language with no articulation,
a raw matter of language,
phonemes. . . .

P o o r objects,
used,
at the threshold between destruction and garbage,
s h r e d s,
rags,
tatters,
moldered planks,
refuse,
worm-eaten wood,
a nightmarish overcrowding,
a business of an anthill. . . .

MATTER
AND ITS FAITHFUL COMPANION:
COINCIDENCE,
THE ILLEGITIMATE CHILD OF REALITY!

THE INFORMEL THEATRE
The stages of the development of Cricot 2 Theatre: 1960, 1961, 1962.

The "informel" art
was the second trend (CONSTRUCTIVISM in the 1920s was the first one)
which exerted a significant impact on the fine arts of the twentieth century.
The most productive and expansive period of the informel art was the period from 1955 until 1965.

CONSTRUCTIVISM, which emerged first in paintings and sculpture, left a significant mark on poetry and theatre.
In theatre, it created an extremely important movement which embraced all spheres of theatrical activities.
It opposed Naturalism, Expressionism, and Symbolism.
The ideas of constructivism found their equivalent in social revolution and technological development.

In the post-war PERIOD (after World War II), "INFORMEL" art was the next wave of the avant-garde that followed CONSTRUCTIVISM.

In the 1960s, CRICOT 2 THEATRE created the first and most complete manifestation of Informel in theatre, which was as radical as informel paintings.
The ideas of "INFORMEL" had a profound impact on a further development of Cricot 2 Theatre. The last two productions, *The Dead Class* and *Wielopole, Wielopole*, exemplified and encapsulated them.

The INFORMEL theatre integrated the ideas of INFORMEL art and theatre.

This is the reason why I find it imperative that this period be treated comprehensively for the archives of the Cricot 2 Theatre.

The Concepts, Definitions, Ideas of the "Informel" Art

> [The Informel art signifies] A discovery of a new, unknown aspect of reality, of its elementary state. This state is:

MATTER

Matter which is freed from abiding by the laws of construction, which is always changing and fluid, infinite, which negates the concept of form that is limited and finite, unchangeable and stable; the concept that describes these states is:

FORMLESSNESS;

Matter which absorbs and is defined by speed and rhythm of action, that is

SPONTANEITY of action;

Matter which is always in motion. This is the reason why

ACTION, MOVEMENT

are its only equivalent and a means to contain it.

> Matter, whose essence is revealed by processes such as:

DEMOLITION,
DECOMPOSITION,
DISSOLUTION,
DISINTEGRATION,
DESTRUCTION.

Matter, whose the most effective ally is

COINCIDENCE

that has thus far been eliminated from the domain of art.
Various different manifestations of human life correspond to these characteristics and attributes of matter.

WAYS OF TREATING MATTER/PHYSICAL ACTIONS WITHIN AND WITHOUT MATTER:

COMPRESSION,
CRUMPLING,
CRUSHING,

CONTRACTION,
COMINGLING,
KNEADING (as one does with dough),
POURING/LEAKING/FLOATING/SWIMMING,
BRANDING,
THROWING,
SPLASHING,
DABBING,
TEARING,
BURNING,
RAVAGING,
ANNIHILATING,
STITCHING,
BLEACHING,
DIRTYING,
SMEARING.

DIFFERENT KINDS OF MATTER:

EARTH,
MUD,
CLAY,
DEBRIS,
MILDEW,
ASH,
DOUGH,
WATER,
SMOKE,
FIRE.

MATERIALS AND OBJECTS AT THE THRESHOLD OF BECOMING MATTER:

RAGS,
TATTERS,
SACKCLOTHS,
SACKS,
SHREDS,
JUNK,
MUSTY BOOKS,
MOLDERED PLANKS,
COMPRESSED BOXES,
GARBAGE
REFUSE,
WASTE,
WORM-EATEN WOOD,
ANT-HILLS (their business),

HEAP OF SPLINTERS.

<u>EMOTIONAL (PATHOLOGICAL) STATES:</u>

EXCITEMENT,
EXAGGERATION,
HALLUCINATION,
FEVERISHNESS,
DELIRIUM,
CONVULSIONS,
AGONY,
SPASMS,
ECSTASY,
SUFFERING,
PAIN,
MARTYRDOM,
ANGER,
RAGE,
FURY,
MADNESS.

<u>CUSTOMS, BEHAVIORS:</u>

DEBAUCHERY,
IMPUDENCE,
INDECENCY,
IMMODESTY,
DEMORALIZATION,
LAWLESSNESS,
SINFUL PRACTICES,
SCANDALOUS ACTIVITIES,
DISGRACEFUL ACTS,
    POOR
    BANAL,
    PROSAIC ACTIVITIES,
SADISM,
CRUELTY,
FEAR,
SHAME.

<u>LANGUAGE. THE RAW MATTER OF SPEECH:</u>

INARTICULATE SOUNDS,
MURMUR,
STUTTER,
DRAWL,
WHISPER,

CROAK,
WHINING,
SOBBING,
SCREAMING,
SPITTING,
PHONEMES,
OBSCENE LANGUAGE,
SYNTAX-FREE LANGUAGE.

—n.d.

The Informel Theatre
(1961)

The opening of Witkiewicz's *The Country House* in Cricot 2 Theatre.
The first full realization of the Informel Theatre.
The concept, which invaded deeply my past autonomous activities that had been derived from my acceptance of coincidence, the process of destruction, spontaneous movement, and the dynamic aspect of matter, has penetrated the theatrical terrain.
It was the burning time of the spiritual revolution, which transferred the artist's commitment from the "visible" plane into the interior.
There is a lot of confusion linked onto this transfer. It is often superficially linked to the practices of the surrealists (in theatre—to the activities of Antonin Artaud). On the other hand, it is simplistically interpreted in a manner that brings to mind the imprecise and anti-intellectual practices of delayed expressionism.
This is why it is necessary to describe the essential meaning of Informel art.
Informel art is a process of exploration of neither the unconscious nor of one's obsessions.
Something more important is at stake here! Something NEW!
It is a discovery of an unknown aspect of
REALITY or of its elementary state: MATTER.
Matter which is freed from abiding by the laws of construction,
always changing and fluid;
which escapes the bondage of rational definitions;
makes all attempts to compress it into a solid form
ridiculous, helpless, and vain;
which is perennially destructive to all forms,
and nothing more than a manifestation;
which is accessible only through
the forces of destruction,
by whim and risk of a c o i n c i d e n c e,
by fast and violent a c t i o n.

Creating a method out of those speculations and applying it in theatre would be nothing but a naive camouflage of the creative process by pseudo-scientific "laboratory experiments."

141

The theatre and art have to be born out of themselves as a spontaneous
act of creation.

Gradually, the new, homogenous
"i n f o r m e l" structure has surfaced.
Even though, the end result might appear to be similar, I have always
insisted on keeping it separated from surrealist or expressionist
experiments and their obsessions or exhibitionism.
This relentless elimination of these undesirable influences was achieved
by rejecting shrewdly those arranged psychological processes, states
and situations, even the shocking ones, by leaving them without any
significance or importance—
it was done so to have them become helpless and ineffectual
façades.
I did this because I came to the conclusion that, in art, reality has
unexpectedly become nothing more than a façade. And it was this very
r e a l i t y that I was interested in. It was this reality that was supposed
to rescue me from all false retreats. Besides, I have always suspected that
realness of art was a cover for pretentious conceit. The experiments lasted
for a long time. The completely unexplored territory was, I might say,
"won" step by step. Normal emotional states change imperceptibly into
excessive conditions marked by
cruelty,
sadism,
spasm,
lust,
feverish ravings,
agonies. . . .
These b i o l o g i c a l states,
which are extraordinarily intense,
lose touch with the sphere of everyday life
and become the matter of art.
In s p e e c h,
one touches upon the *matière brute*,
which is primordial and crude,
defies all classical conventions:
both those which are deformed by daily usage of words
and those which are reserved for the moments when the emotional states
attain feverish excitement; when words are mixed up and their meaning is
blurred; when the words defy the rules of classical syntax.
Human articulation collides with the remotest
and the wildest forms (howling of the pack of dogs),
and the cruelest sounds (cracking of bones).

The Actors are c r o w d e d into an absurdly small
space of a w a r d r o b e;

they are squeezed in between and mixed with dead objects (sacks, a mass
of sacks);
degraded, without dignity;
they are hanging motionless like c l o t h e s;
they are identified with the heavy mass of sacks
(sacks—emballages rank the lowest in the hierarchy of objects and as such
they easily become
o b j e c t l e s s matter).
"C o n s t r u c t i n g,"
the process of "designing and putting the project to life" is avoided.
The process [of constructing] is ridiculous!
Instead, ideal becomes the tendency to have, for example the form of a
costume
be shaped by ITSELF; by
wearing, wearing out, destruction.
The r e m n a n t s of objects,
relics,
"what has remained of them"
will thus have a chance to
b e c o m e t h e f o r m!

The Zero Theatre

(1963)

THE ZERO THEATRE

(Fully) autonomous artistic endeavor (in theatre, I mean) does not exist according to the principles or norms of everyday life. For this very reason neither any positive nor negative value judgments can be applied to appraise it.

The traditional techniques of plot development made use of human life as a springboard for movement upwards toward the realm of growing and intensified passions, heroism, conflicts, and violent reactions.

When it first emerged, this idea of "growth" signified man's tragic expansion, or a heroic struggle to transcend human dimensions and destinies. With the passing of time, it turned into a mere show, requiring powerful elements of a spectacle, and the acceptance of violent and irresponsible illusion, convincing shapes, and a thoughtless procreation of forms.

This pushy, morbidly inflamed, and pretentious form pushed aside the object and thus what was "real." The entire process has ended up in pathetic pomposity.

The movement in the opposite direction: d o w n w a r d s into the realm
b e l o w, THE ACCEPTED WAY OF LIFE,
which is possible by elimination,
destruction,
misshaping,
reduction of energy,
cooling;
[the movement] in the direction of e m p t i n e s s,
DEFORMITY,
non-form
is an ILLUSION-CRUSHING process
and the only chance to t o u c h u p o n r e a l i t y!
The symptoms of this process are momentous:

Pragmatic forms of life cease to be binding,
a creative process loses its sacred status and allegedly its only function—to
create—which has become nothing more than a burden.
An object loses its meanings which were thoughtlessly assigned to it,
its symbolism—
and reveals its
autonomous
empty (according to standard opinions) existence.
The creative process becomes
the realization of the impossible.

Theatre, which I have called the "Zero" Theatre, does not refer to
a ready-made "zero" situation. Its essence lies in the process leading
TOWARDS THE EMPTINESS AND "ZERO ZONES."
This process means
dismembering of logical plot structures,
building up scenes not by textual reference but
by reference to
associations triggered by them,
juggling with CHANCE or
junk,
ridiculously trivial matters,
which are embarrassingly shameful,
devoid of any meaning
and consequence;
by showing indifference towards
the importance of matters,
the meaning of facts,
emotions;
by invalidation;
elimination of stimuli and portents of livelier activity;
"diffusion,"
"discharge" of energy;
by cooling of temperature and expression,
use of awkward silences and inaction,
the dilution of
setting structures,
universal decomposition of
forms;
by cracking of mechanism,
"jamming,"
slowing of pace,
loss of rhythm,
repetition,
elimination through noise,
stupidity,
clichés,

automatic action,
terror;
by disinformation,
withholding of information,
dissection of plot,
decomposition of acting;
by acting poorly,
acting "on the sly,"
acting "non-acting!"
These actions
are accompanied by
specific mental states—
on the condition that these actions are neither independent of nor
triggered by these states.
These actions are appearances of specific mental states rather than the
symptoms of cause and effect.
These mental states are
isolated, groundless, autonomous.
And as such they can be perceived as the factors influencing artistic
creation.
Here are some of them:
apathy,
melancholy,
exhaustion,
amnesia,
dissociation,
neurosis,
depression,
unresponsiveness,
frustration,
minimalization,
distraction,
boredom,
impotence,
sluggishness,
tearfulness,
senility,
sclerotic or
maniacal states,
schizophrenia,
misery . . .

NOTES ON THE ZERO THEATRE

Let us try to list some of the life conditions which are charged with
intense emotion and deep meaning . . .
LOVE, JEALOUSY, LUST, PASSION, GREED, CUNNING,
COWARDICE, REVENGE, MURDER,

SUICIDE, WAR, HEROISM, FEAR, SUFFERING . . .
For a long time, this "highly inflammable" material has served theatre
and art as a primary source for literary plots, dramatic action, peripeteias,
conflicts, and sensational dénouements.
Its inherent characteristics to *expand* and *defuse* [plots] have determined
the choice of formal means of expression, which of course were of a
similar nature and effect:
e x p r e s s i o n,
m o l d i n g,
f o r m,
i l l u s i o n,
n a t u r a l i s t i c   a p p r o a c h t o l i f e,
"f i g u r a t i v e n e s s . . ."

This system of expansion, its values and flaws are well known to us.
What happens if its means of expression, which almost universally are
identified with the nature and essence of art or which have been perceived
as the highest and mandatory formulas, become bereft of vitality? As
a corollary of this newly achieved passive state, the whole impressive
compilation or index of signs of life will change into an empty prop room.
The moment we reject the formal means which are impotent now;
the moment we reject illusion,
the automatic reproductive apparatus,
fictitious plots representing life,
and raise questions concerning the concept of
form and molding,
all this baggage of old meaning and depth,
—"above zero"—
proves useless.
All our sensitivity then is directed to such states as:
reluctance,
unwillingness,
apathy,
monotony,
indifference,
minimalization,
ridicule,
banality,
ordinariness,
emptiness. . . .
These states are the states of disinterestedness.
And this is what we want to achieve.

NON-ACTING

Is the state of
non-acting possible?
(that is, if we take for granted the existence of stage

and a play, *la pièce, das Stück*).
Is this state of non-acting possible,
even though the stage automatically imposes upon us its identification as a
place to act and
a play as a genre which is meant to be acted?
This obtrusive question
has long been associated in my work
with the wish (which might seem to be the portent of
maniacal eccentricity,
or stubborn pedantry)
to achieve
full autonomy of the theatre;
so that everything that happens on stage
would become an event—
perhaps a different one from
those that occur in the audience's spatial and temporal reality of life—
but still an event with
its own life and consequences rather than an artificial one.
I wish for a situation
in which one could discard so-called "acting"
(supposedly the only way for an actor to behave "on stage"),
which is nothing more than
naive pretence,
exulted mannerism,
irresponsible illusion!

This wish could be fulfilled by an actor who rejects illusion as a point
of reference to the text and stays on the plane of his own "Self"; his
INDIVIDUALITY does not extend beyond it in order to create the
illusion of being another character. Having done so, he would eliminate
dependence on the arrangement which exists outside of him, gain
autonomy and expose only himself, and his own character which is the
only reality on stage.

He would create his own chain of events, states, situations which would
either clash with those in the play or be somehow completely isolated
from them.
This seems impossible to achieve.
However, those attempts to cross over this borderline of IMPOSSIBILITY
are fascinating.
On the one hand, there is the reality of the text,
on the other hand, the actor and his behavior.
Two parallel systems which
are neither dependent
nor reflect each other.
The actor's "behavior" should
"p a r a l y z e" the reality of the text,

be juxtaposed to it.
If this happens:
the reality of the text will be
relieved of its questionable ally, the actor (questionable because it is
rendered only through him) and become independent, (also) autonomous,
and concrete.

ANTI-ACTIVITY

Actors become deeply
d i s c o u r a g e d.
They show a sudden
"u n w i l l i n g n e s s" to act
and an embarrassing "interest in the audience."
They alter the function of and the relationship between actors and
audiences in an unnatural and contemptuous way. The audience, which
has been a forbidden object of interest and attention, triggers in them
responses of infinite variety and nuance which include:
n o n c h a l a n c e,
c o n t e m p t and
d i s g u s t.
Then they return to the text, but they deal with it in a way which is also
f o r b i d d e n:
they repeat some lines,
dissect the meaning of words, analyze and appraise them critically,
with suspicion,
with doubt,
disapprove of them,
mock and
RIDICULE them,
or they DON'T UNDERSTAND the text
treat it as an ALIEN entity,
try to fathom its meaning
to put it together,
fit its elements together, compare it, analyze it linguistically,
but, finally, when they realize the futility of their actions,
they d i s c a r d it
and s u d d e n l y f o r g e t about it.
They g i v e u p.
And then submerge in the feeling of
a p a t h y,
m e l a n c h o l y,
d e p r e s s i o n.
They are absorbed in
t h o u g h t.
N u m b n e s s engulfs them.
But this reverie can either be due to exercising the intellect

or, it might be caused by their dullness and complete vanity.
They behave as if they were in private.
An e m b a r r a s s i n g   d i s r e g a r d for the audience.
"An empty stare" into the space.
A s u d d e n   r e c o l l e c t i o n of something.
A sudden interest in inconsequential details, or trivial matters.
(The rubbing of a non-existent spot.)
A careful examination of a piece of string or something insignificant.
And then again d e l i b e r a t i o n.
A desperate attempt to recapture a lost theme.
Resignation.
And so on, indefinitely
until boredom and
insanity strike. . . .

SURREPTITIOUS ACTING

Counteract "open" acting
which has become completely ineffective and almost shameless by its
universal acceptance
with acting "on the sly."
Actors perform in the place
which is the least suitable!
They are hidden behind
noisy, conventional, and stupid events
which are brought to the fore.
Actors are humiliated by
the act of pushing them "behind."
They perform as if "in spite."
They are relegated to outlaw status.
Actors, who are being extirpated by the events which are "official" and
featured,
give way and leave
to look for the last ray of hope,
the last patch of land
where they try to "make a statement"
quickly, as quickly as possible,
before the final extermination.

ERASING

Erasing is a method which
is often used in art.
The old Masters knew it well.
I am thinking about paintings. I am thinking about situations in which
erasing is visible
and meaningful.
I passionately used this method in Informel Art.

When too many distracting densities of forms were squeezed into
some part of a painting, I could erase them in one move—
to the naught,
to nothingness which devoured those protruding parts.
One could say that this movement of the hand was cruel,
that it condemned, wrought destruction and eliminated those forms
from the face of the earth.
But those areas of nothingness and silence have jealously guarded the
secrets of the past epochs.
The act of erasing could also be equated with the simple act of
c l e a n i n g   u p,
of leaving the centre of the room cleanly swept by pushing litter and other
rubbish against the walls or into the corners and thus depriving them
of any meaning. We are just a step away from the time when this act of
e r a s i n g   could be transferred onto the stage. . . .

INTERNALIZATION OF EXPRESSION

"Expressive" states appear
suddenly, caused by
some "scratches."
They build up.
Excitement, agitation, anxiety,
fury, rage, frenzy.
Suddenly, they cave in, disappear
as if sucked in
and only empty gestures remain.

MINIMALIZATION. ECONOMY OF MOVEMENT AND EMOTION

Inertness as defense.
Actors try to
adjust to minimal
living conditions
by economizing on their vital powers,
by limiting their movements to the minimum,
by not showing their emotions,
(as does a mountaineer
who holds onto the rock on a narrow path).
A ridiculous economy of movement.
Caution.
Every response is calculated and
measured out.
Intense concentration and
awareness that each additional violent sign of life
might lead to instant death.

REDUCTION OF MEANINGS TO THE ZERO STATE

Reduce meanings
to merely phonetic values,
juggle with words
to bring up their other meanings,
"dissolve" their content,
loosen their logical bonds,
repeat.

ELIMINATION BY FORCE

The Annihilation Machine
(a shapeless construct made out of decrepit chairs)
shoves the actors aside, throws them "out,"
exterminates
by its sudden, robot-like movements.
There remains a ridiculously small space for
acting and living. Actors resist
being pushed aside,
try to keep their balance and cling to the surface
as does a drowning man; wage a hopeless struggle
but fall off.

EMBARASSING SITUATIONS

Replace a shock with an embarrassing
situation.
An embarrassing situation is something more
than a shock.
To do so, one requires much
courage,
courage to take risks,
the ability to make decisions.
An embarrassing situation destroys the audience's
life experience, its conventionally validated existence,
and puts it "down"
much more effectively than a shock.

AUTOMATION

The nature of an automatic activity
is defined by its constant repetition.
After some time, this repetition completely deprives
both the activity and the object of their meaning.
Their "life" meaning, of course.
Now they can easily be manipulated.

ACTING UNDER DURESS

Actors are forced,
flattered,
admonished,
scolded,
tormented,
terrorized to act.
This duress is inflicted upon them by
two "additional" characters,
unquestionable villains,
who are dumb and stupid,
sad clowns,
who are half-janitor and half-thug,
cruel persecutors
brutal and blunt tools,
thoughtless automatons
who change easily, if required,
into devout moralists, strict
mentors,
dumb interpreters,
pimps,
soul collectors,
and sadists.

EMBALLAGE

A huge, black "emballage"
is the final and radical
tool of complete
extermination.

The Emballage
(1957–1965)

1956: the first production at the Cricot 2 Theatre.

I was looking for systems that were artificial, that is, such systems which had a chance to become autonomous.

Walking is probably most naturalistic among all other elements onstage. It is so natural that it hurts. Sometimes, I would see only legs in theatre. Expressionless.

One needs to eliminate certain parts of an object; "erase" and make them invisible in order to be aware and to be conscious of them (these principles were well known to the Old Masters).

The space of the stage was filled out with an immense black sack. All the actors and a few supernumeraries were inside of it. Only their heads and hands were visible through the narrow openings in the sack. The heads would come closer and then move apart. The hands moved and "lived" independently of the actors—they were autonomous.

. . . In a different play, the actors were not visible at all—they were enclosed inside the sack. All the conflicts taking place inside would be transmitted through and intensified by subtle movements and different tensions in the external surface of that emballage.

(1957)
THE EMBALLAGE MANIFESTO

Emballage—
One ought to
categorize first
some of attributes
which define it.
It would not however
be wise to generalize,
or to create ready-made formulas.
Anyway, it would almost be impossible to do so—
Emballage, Emballage—
Since a discussed phenomenon

has many meanings;
worse than that,
it is ambiguous.
It should be stated at the very beginning that
emballage actually exists
beyond the boundaries of reality.
It could thus be discussed—
Emballage, Emballage, Emballage—
in terms of metaphysics.
On the other hand,
it performs a function which is
so prosaic,
so utilitarian,
and so basic;
it is enslaved to its
precious contents
to such a degree that
when the contents are removed,
it is functionless,
no longer needed,
a pitiful sign of
its past glory
and importance—
Emballage, Emballage—
Branded
and accused of
the lack of any content,
it is bereft of its
glamour and
expression—
Emballage, Emballage—
It must be objectively noted here
that it is a victim of
the fates' injustice.
First, an extremely high honor
is bestowed upon it,
since one's success depends on its
looks,
opacity,
ability to convey,
expressiveness,
precision.
Then,
it is ruthlessly cast aside,
exposed to ridicule,
doomed to oblivion,
and banished.

Such an ambiguous behavior toward it
leads to further
misunderstandings,
and contradictions;
prevents any serious, legitimate
attempt to classify it—
Emballage—
As a described phenomenon, it
balances at the threshold—
Emballage, Emballage—
between eternity
and
garbage.
We are witnesses of
a clown-like tom-foolery
juggling
pathos and pitiful
destruction—
Emballage, Emballage, Emballage—
Its potential is limitless—
E m b a l l a g e—
any extra activity connected with it
must be
a completely disinterested service,
since it should be remembered that
it is performed with a full awareness of
the fatal end.
Let us discuss some of
the stages of this ritual:
f o l d i n g,
whose complicated strategies
requiring some mysterious initiation
and a surprising end effect,
bring to mind magic
and a child's play;
t y i n g   u p,
the knowledge of various types of knots
touches almost upon
a domain of sacred knowledge;
s e a l i n g,
always full of dignity
and complete concentration;
this gradation of actions,
this adding of
surprising effects,
as well as human need
and desire to

store,
isolate,
hide,
transfer—
becomes an almost
autonomous process.
This is our chance.
We must not overlook
its emotional possibilities.
There are many such possibilities inside it:
promise,
hope,
premonition,
temptation,
desire for the unknown
and secretive—
Emballage—
Marked
with the symbols of fragility,
of urgency,
of hierarchy,
of degrees of importance;
with the digits of its own time,
of its own language—
Emballage—
with the address of a receiver,
with the symbols of power,
with promises of
effectiveness,
durability,
and perfection.
It shows up in
special,
mundane,
funny,
grand,
and final
circumstances of
our everyday life—
Emballage—
when we want to send
something important,
something significant,
and something private—
Emballage—
when we want to shelter
and protect;

to preserve,
to escape the passage of time—
Emballage—
When we want to
hide something
deeply—
EMBALLAGE—
Must be isolated,
protected from trespassing,
ignorance,
and vulgarity.
Emballage.
Emballage.
Emballage.

(1964)
AN UMBRELLA

The first umbrella ever fastened to the canvas.
The very choice of the object was, for me, a momentous discovery; the very decision of using such an utilitarian object and of substituting it for the sacred object of artistic practices was, for me, a day of liberation through blasphemy. It was more liberating than the day when the first newspaper, the first piece of string, or the first box was glued to a canvas. I was not looking for a new object for a collage; rather, I was looking for an interesting "emballage."
An Umbrella in-itself is a particularly metaphoric Emballage; it is a "wrapping" over many human affairs; it shelters poetry, uselessness, helplessness, defenselessness, disinterestedness, hope, ridiculousness. Its diverse "content" has always been defined by commentaries provided by first "Informel" and then figurative art.
I was not aware of the fact that, already in 1946, 1947, 1948, an umbrella had been my fetish. I was collecting umbrellas; I was obsessed by umbrellas. Umbrellas informed my surrealistic landscapes. Their construction was instrumental in the creation of my concept of "umbrellic space."
An umbrella means also circus, theatre.
The actors in Mikulski's play *A Circus* [Cricot 2, 1957—MK] used umbrellas as shields for their poor and deranged lives, as well as for what was left of scraps of hope and poetry.

(1964)
THE POST-OFFICE

is a very special place
where the laws of
u t i l i z a t i o n

are suspended—
objects—letters, packages,
packets, bags, envelopes
and all their contents
exist, for some time,
independently,
without an addressee,
without a place of destination,
without a function,
almost as if in a vacuum,
in-between a sender and a receiver,
where both are powerless,
with no meaning,
bereft of their authority.
It is a rare moment when
an object escapes its destiny.

The "i" Theatre
(about 1969)

EXPLANATIONS
. . . for a long time (since 1957)
(Kazimierz Mikulski's *Circus* with Cricot 2)

A w a r d r o b e   a wardrobe
played in my theatre
an important part.
As in a circus,
or a surrealistic piece
a wardrobe
was
a catalyst
for human affairs
human fate,
its mystery.
A ludicrously tiny space of
the wardrobe's interior
easily deprived
the actor of
his dignity
personal prestige,
turned him into
matter,
almost a piece of clothing.

S a c k s   were similarly
moldable
(The Country House
or *The Wardrobe* as it was called
in Baden-Baden in 1966)
sacks
belong
to the category of the objects
of the lowest rank
and as such

they become
or may become
　　　an almost
objectless matter.

"I n f o r m e l"
Theatre　　. . . in my production of
Witkiewicz's play
　　　　The Country House
in 1961
　　　in Kraków,
I decided to use
　　　the method of
　　　"Informel."
I made use of stage devices,
which were an equivalent of
the idea of
"formless matter"
and all the adjectives linked to it:
　　　accidental
　　　spontaneous
　　　abrupt
　　　burning
　　　fluid
　　　elemental
　　　hallucinatory
　　　spasmodic
　　　obsessive
　　　ecstatic
　　　frenetic
　　　depraved
　　　unexpected
　　　infernal
the production
in Bled . . .　the production in Bled
　　　　in 1969,
　　　　contained
　　　in its "Informel" matter
　　　the elements from my Kraków
　　　　production in 1961,
　　as well as the experiences
　　of the "zero theatre," 1963,
　　and the "theatre-happening" (1967).

I l l u s i o n . . .　　Despite all
　　　　radical
　　　　actions,

there appeared at the end
the illusion,
illusionary, fictitious reality,
                a closed system,
"facing"
                the audience.
                What I did
                        later
could be described as follows:

The rejection   until now, I had tried to
of   conquer the stage,
the stage   now, I decided to reject
                       the stage altogether,
                       that is,
                       this space
         which remains in a particular
                relationship to the audience;
         a relationship which is not perturbed
         by any of life's activity.
                Having abandoned the stage,
         f o r   t h e   q u e s t   f o r   a   n e w   p l a c e,
         I had at my disposal,
                theoretically,
         the entire realness of life.
         This did not mean
         a successful completion
                of the quest.
         From the very beginning,
         it must be noted in a footnote
         to this new adventure,
                that
         i t   i s   p r e c i s e l y   h e r e
         a n d   n o w
         (a n d   n o t   l a t e r)
         t h a t   w e   f o u n d   o u r s e l v e s
         i n   t h e   c o r e   o f   t h e
         c r e a t i v e   p r o c e s s:
         t h e   n e e d   t o   m a k e   a   c h o i c e!

A c h o i c e   A choice
         is an activity of
         daring imagination,
         which is prepared to
         accept the possibility of "impossibility."
                A choice
         in this case

has nothing to do with
the capricious possibility
of having multiple perspectives.
It is rather like
    a single, but perfect,
    shot.
Those who cannot understand this
are hit by its
    otherness,
absurdity,
and its risk factor.
It always strikes
that reality
which is thick with substance.

The use of
the formed   I wish to explain
illusion   why I did not abandon altogether
            the formed stage illusion itself
(I have in mind the production of
Witkiewicz's play in Bled).

The function of
the formed   Those elements, which had already been formed,
illusion   were necessary;
        in this creative process
        they functioned as
            the barriers,
which conditioned
the moment of the "i m p o s s i b l e";
it is only because of this formed
        illusion
certain peculiar situations
        could reach
        the impossible!
An example of this could be
a scene, which was executed
in the Alps,
in the high mountains, in the wilderness,
on a glacier.
The mountains themselves do not constitute
the reality of the impossible.
They can easily be conquered by
the climbers.
This illusion,
which had earlier been formed,
together with its stage action, unfolding of the plot,
    and characters,

was freely used by me;
they were the pieces,
            and even less, the shreds,
which gave the impression that
they belonged to
            a past
but also contained a possible future.
In this activity,
where the ordering
of a theatrical action
            was ignored,
the extreme choice
of that "impossible"
            reality,
or of that condition of life
and its fulfillment
and its consequences
become
the extraordinary
and uncommon adventure.

the meaning of the
new   For the participants
arrangement and accidental spectators
            the unexpected meaning of
                    this
                    adventure
                    was in
            the encounter with an arrangement
                    which
            was positioned in the reality
                    of life
            and, at the same time,
            beyond and outside of it!
            Something which is difficult to comprehend.

a new   In this arrangement
element   I would like to describe
                    one more element,
                            without which
                    this arrangement
            would be nothing more than a banal confrontation
                    between two realities:
                            illusion
                    and reality.
            The function of this element
                    is quite mysterious

and this should be given to it.
                    A wardrobe
dropped from 6000 feet
in the wild mountains,
a luxurious gambling casino
filled with
                    hay,
a frightened flock of sheep
                    in a drawing-room
have nothing in common
with the old trick of "shocking" [the audience].
                    They were
an unusual
          "m e a s u r e" of
"imagination"
"with the help of which"
"the ordinary"
"the "everyday"
"reality"
"was "measured."

Procida 9/14/1969

executed in Bled on
August 6, 1969

A TRAIN STATION

A small, abandoned and forgotten train station,
a platform, railways tracks, the signaling lights,
a train-station chief.
A group of actors is standing on the platform,
     they are crowding together
mixed with suitcases.
Diahant Nearly, a pathological sadist,
who is wearing a tuxedo, a top hat,
and white socks,
is laughing appallingly.
A Music Teacher,
in a ragged-looking wedding dress,
madness in her eyes,
with a huge hairdo on her head;
A Servant, in a ceremonial
tuxedo over his naked chest and a top hat,
holds a black open umbrella;
Two children in sacks
looking like packages to be shipped;

Anastasia Nearly, almost naked
is dripping with dough;
Kozdron [Scullery Boy], barefoot, half-naked,
bent under the heavy weight of the sacks,
the whole pile of sacks, suitcases,
packages,
everything wrapped in dust-sheets;
hordes of dogs;
actors are wearing socks.
All of this gives the impression of
a compressed mass of people, bodies, suitcases,
packages, dogs.
Everyone is focused,
they are all waiting,
looking in one direction,
looking harder,
they become more and more anxious.
Suddenly, someone runs forward,
pulling behind many suitcases;
he runs to a new place;
and, suddenly, everyone else,
in panic, falling down,
pulling behind the packages,
creating a complete mess,
calling and making gestures to each other,
runs after him.
Everything comes back to normal and again
they are all waiting,
looking in one direction,
the children in sacks are laid down on the tracks;
Diahant Nearly—is laughing appallingly.
The Mother, Anastasia Nearly—the deceased—
dripping with dough,
burst out in a hysterical laughter;
a suddenly, a piercing whistle of a locomotive is heard;
a train is approaching,
puffs of black smoke. . . .

executed on
August 13, 1969
Yugoslavia

A DRAWING-ROOM

Wallpaper
portraits
fringes

palm trees
carpets
mirrors
golden frames
screens
chandeliers
candelabras
candles
armchairs
sofas
a piano
busts
stuccos
the twins
in white sacks
standing by a pulpit
are singing.
A Servant
wearing a top hat
is standing upright
under an open black umbrella;
it is raining heavily;
the sheets of rain are hitting the umbrella;
The deceased—Anastasia Nearly,
naked,
is lying on a sofa,
covered with sticky dough,
which is slowly dripping onto the carpet.
In the corner, under the palm tree,
Diahant Nearly in black
is tormenting horrifically
a Music Teacher.
The Poet leaning onto the column
is reading
his gibberish poem;
in the doors, under the porticos,
a crowded group of
yodeling highlanders;
a flock of sheep
squeezes through the doors;
elderly gentleman, in old-fashioned clothes,
all in black, with top hats on their heads,
are sleeping on the floor;
they are lying down on sheets and cushions
one by one,
in a deep sleep.
The man of the household is still tormenting a Music Teacher.
The deceased is still pouring the dough.

The sheets of rain
drench the carpets and extinguish the candelabras;
the old-fashioned gentlemen remain asleep;
the wild highlanders are still yodeling
in a complete frenzy.
Palm trees,
carpets
mirrors,
chandeliers,
burning candles,
defenseless, packaged children.
The Father—the sadist torments inhumanly;
the Mother—the deceased is in a complete
        dough decay;
a frightened flock of sheep
bleats hideously;
the old gentlemen sleep peacefully;
the poet, leaning against the column, recites;
the sheets of rain. . . .

THE CASINO

All is
monumental,
and ostentatious—
marble floors,
massive chandeliers,
heavy, solid-looking candelabras,
purple curtains,
lights,
croupiers in the tuxedos,
a green-covered table,
a golden roulette,
guests,
gentlemen in dinner jackets,
ladies in evening gowns,
hairdos,
pearls,
décolletages,
gold,
diamonds,
everyone is by the tables,
fans,
suddenly,
a half-dressed, barefoot factotum,
charged into the casino room

pulling behind him piles of hay;
he is pulling
and pushing them;
he is industriously filling
the room with hay;
more and more hay;
a massive pile of hay;
the whole room is drowning in hay;
the factotum keeps
pulling endlessly
more and more; boundless piles of hay;
he fills the room;
he levels the hay;
the guests are focused on the game,
the croupiers perform
their actions with precision;
the savage factotum
lets in the chickens;
the frenzied chickens
cackle,
fly in the air,
disappear in hay;
the factotum is after the chickens,
the cackle of the chickens;
the shouts of the factotum;
the chickens fly in frenzy;
the guests suddenly get up from the table;
they stop playing roulette;
they begin to chase after the chickens;
croupiers try to
protect the roulette table
from the invasion of the chickens
and against general rage and fury;
in this growing euphoria,
the chase
turns
into an apocalyptic
and frantic
psychosis.
Exhausted,
the guests
return to the roulette table
one by one;
everything returns to normal.
Nobody pays any attention to
Diahant Nearly (a character from Witkiewicz's play),
who begins to torment

a Music Teacher sitting next to him—
he suffocates her;
squeezes
sadistically,
with passion only known to him,
he plays out some part from
his own life;
at the other end of the table,
someone begins suddenly
to undress completely;
the people sitting next to him, as if infected,
begin to follow his suit automatically;
the game continues
uninterrupted by
the embarrassing turn of the events.
The Poet (a character from Witkiewicz's play)
begins to read
his poem,
which is becoming more and more
sentimental,
which turns from bad to worse;
the Poet,
calls for tears,
everyone is in tears;
the Poet continues to read the poem;
the deceased Anastasia Nearly
(a character in Witkiewicz's play),
who, until now, was fervently involved in roulette,
suddenly pours
dough all over herself;
the dough, slowly,
drips on the roulette table,
the carpets,
the marble floor,
and, of course,
everything is covered with hay;
the chickens are on the roulette table.

executed in Bled
on August 7, 1969

THE MOUNTAINS

As if from the heavens
(from a helicopter),
in high Alps,
some 6000 feet of open-face rocks,

a wardrobe
falls down.
A wardrobe
falls down
into a precipice;
hits the glacier
and falls into pieces,
in this rocky desert.
On the black square
of velvet
there are the wardrobe's remains
and the body of the deceased
Anastasia Nearly.
In the snow,
there is an armchair, in the Biedermeier style,
where the Poet, Jibbery Penbroke,
in a straw hat
    and a soft flannel suit,
    a copy of Manet's,
is sitting.
The children—orphans—as always
    wrapped in white sacks.
The Deceased keeps
    repeating
    the story of
    her lovers,
    passions,
    her illnesses,
the illnesses especially excite her
    enormously
    snow
    and ice
    abound around.
The Poet in vain tries to discover
    a meaning and continuity in
    his poem.
The children—orphans understand
    nothing
A group of accidental skiers
    is looking at
    this free
    catastrophe
    with indifference.

> executed on August 21, 1967
> in Portoroz, Yugoslavia

THE BEACH. BY THE SEA

On a pebble beach, bathed in the sun,
there stands an old-fashion wardrobe,
    unknown,
    close to the water;
inside the wardrobe, three men are squeezed,
Diahant Nearly in black suit,
a Bailiff, half naked and barefoot,
a Poet in a straw hat;
a colorful, big,
Persian carpet
is spread on the sand;
in another spot,
a golden, suede-covered armchair, Biedemeier style,
is half-buried in sand and pebbles;
a second, similar armchair, is half-submerged in the sea;
two huge black candelabras with burning candles
rise from the sea;
    the men
squeezed into a tiny space of a wardrobe,
with great effort,
    desperately
      try to move around;
      bump into each other;
      perspire;
they quarrel furiously;
they fling convoluted
and incomprehensible arguments
at each other
in this tiny space and the burning sun.
The naked Deceased is lying flat
on the pebbles;
she is pushing them aside, as if trying to creep;
the body of a faint Music Teacher,
exhausted by her hysteric convulsions,
rises from the sea in a Biedermeier armchair;
the candles are burning in the sea;
suddenly,
Diahant Nearly, in black suit,
shoots himself;
the other two lay
    the body
flatly
on the pebble beach.
A Servant, feeling its heavy weight, carries
a huge black candelabra

with a thick burning candle on it;
he walks towards the sea;
he walks straight forward,
holding steadily
this colossal funeral candelabra
in both hands;
    Like automata,
the deceased Anastasia Nearly,
the Bailiff
the Poet,
the Music Teacher
follow him.
The cortege
    slowly
      walks into the sea;
      the candle still burns steadily
      and is visible on the surface;
at this moment, Diahant Nearly—the suicide man—gets up and runs
    hurriedly towards the sea. . . .

The Impossible Theatre
(1969–1973)

The development of art is not a purely formal, linear process, but most of all, within and without, it is a permanent motion and transformation of thoughts and ideas.

The dogma that ideas are fully determined by historical conditions and life situations does not preclude the possibility that, at the same time, they have the autonomous power of creating and molding new historical conditions and life situations, that is, the power of giving birth to new ideas. This, in turn, indicates that they have an autonomous and independent realm of development.

In art, the problem is even more complex because the realms of i m a g i n a t i o n and the "i m p o s s i b l e" are not bounded by historical or present life conditions; rather, they are grounded in dim recesses of the unconscious and in the human condition. These realms have an impact on art, an impact whose intensity is not encountered in any other place.

If we accept the n o t i o n o f d e v e l o p m e n t both in art and artistic creativity as indubitable, we will have to accept all its difficult consequences, which would prevent us from using well-known or sanctioned means and techniques of expression, or those used thoughtlessly for the sake of effect. We will have to take risks, make choices, keep looking for new, unknown, and "i m p o s s i b l e" practices of artistic expression, born from new and leading ideas.

T h e a t r e i s a r t f i r s t o f a l l.

If we are thinking about theatre's development, we cannot enclose ourselves in a small professional realm in order to look for the so-called "pure forms" and for the theatre's particular attributes. This always leads to suspicious practices and dubious experiences.

We have to gather our thoughts and move "beyond" theatre, but not simply in order to create "anti-theatre."

Only when theatre is positioned within the domain of ART and all its problems, may we have a guarantee of theatre's free and vibrant development.

The use of ART as a referent here does not indicate a tendency to formalism or ideological emptiness.

This tendency is one of the major misunderstandings, and one which frequently leads to intellectual misappropriations and dire generalizations. Trends which privilege direct contact with the world's reality reduce their own creative process to the process of "materializing" the world's reflection, to being a document, to providing testimony, or to intervening in the problematics of life's matter. These trends have their unquestionable truths and fascinations, especially in the realm of theatre; however, they become dangerous when they become a program spilling over and beyond the domain of art. This pragmatism is almost unavoidable, because of the unequal balance between the desire to provide immediate, temporal gratification, results, or reactions, and the frequently spent condition of the realm of artistic devices used to accomplish these desires.

This problem notwithstanding, theatre is fascinated by such trends. Today's theatre, not for the first and not for the last time, feels the desire to return to its beginnings and sources.

It wants to find its lineage in primordial rites, rituals, practices, as well as magical arts, holidays, feasts, festivities, gatherings, parades, demonstrations, mass theatre, street theatre, political theatre, agit-prop theatre, in short, in all forms in which art is not a product for consumption, but an integral part of life.

Needless to say this search is also an escape from the dying theatre, and its bureaucratic organization.

These desires and tendencies of the theatre of commitment, as well as audience participation theatre, and in general theatre which aims at identification with life have unfortunately run aground on the shallows of a pretentious passeism, formalistic gimmicks, or the impossibility of freeing themselves from the claws of propaganda. They have assumed and assume, however, an authentic meaning when they cease to function merely as an affected gesture directed into the past, where only vacant forms and façades—empty shells—can be found, and position themselves in the actual problems of art and its avant-garde ideas.

We must stop academic divisions of art into individual and separate disciplines. Such categorizations can only lead to further pseudo-intellectualism, pseudo-professionalism, and pseudo-cognizance.

A theatre person must be an artist, meaning a person who is entirely devoted to artistic ideas, to their development, challenges, risks, and discoveries, and to a desire to explore the "unknown" and the "i m p o s s i b l e."

Up till now, we have referred to such people only as "avant-garde artists."

PSEUDO-AVANTGARDE PROCEEDINGS OF THE PROFESSIONAL THEATRE

Commitment to art means a w a r e n e s s   o f   t h e   a i m s   a n d   f u n c t i o n s   o f   a r t   a n d   i t s   d e v e l o p m e n t.

The mechanism of this commitment and the way it functions are defined in terms of harsh conditions unacceptable to the formalists.

Because of these unacceptable conditions, they prefer a different strategy: a p p l i c a t i o n, in the sense of a superficial application of gimmicks conjured only for the purpose of show, for reaching "temporal" satisfaction and effects (the duration of a play marks the beginning and the end of the process).

Everything [in this theatre] is grounded in false pretense, which is bereft of the sharpness and challenges of authentic artistic endeavors, and therefore, easily palatable.

Since professional theatre, which is still alive thanks to its institutional status, is unable to create an authentic and autonomous idea of development, it tries to modernize itself.

Because such "sudden" processes are never anchored in an in-depth knowledge of the global artistic trends of the twentieth century, the theatre can only try to hold on to that which is on the surface, a temporal measure to survive.

This embarrassing procedure is referred to as a process of "drawing on all the accomplishments of contemporary art."

As a result, the poor remnants or the ghosts of Surrealism are still haunting us onstage today. The professional theatres reduce this grand intellectual tradition to a simplistic veneration, delayed, in any case, for half a century.

Every day, we come across the dead carcasses of these intellectual disasters resulting in stage "guttings," as Witkiewicz would say, or thoughtless a p p l i c a t i o n s of trends. These stagings dominated the art of the 1950s and the 1960s, and attempted to appropriate one of the most fascinating and enigmatic of the arts—that which assumed the name of "n o n - f o r m" art *(l'informel)*.

Informel described a process of reaching the deepest regions of individuality, human existence, ontology, and matter, regions which could not be bound by the rational laws of construction, and which treated the creative process as both a manifestation of spirituality and a c t i o n.

One needs to have knowledge about the vast artistic achievements of this movement to be able to perceive the ignorance and pretense underlying theatrical a p p l i c a t i o n s of its external elements in order to simulate "profound thought," sacrifices, and pathology. A few years after the Happening, a logical consequence of informel art, had exhausted its means, some directors noticed that the happening could be <u>used</u> as form in theatre. They are still using it. Of course, they chose it, appropriately, when it was already safe to do so, when the happening had become almost a museum piece, and, more importantly, when it had become impotent.

Having no knowledge about these phenomena in art, even though volumes have been written on these subjects, theatre professionals do not realize that the essence of the happening was to d e p i c t   r e a l i t y   v i a   r e a l i t y—that the happening excluded the possibility of creating illusion or imitation, and that simultaneous actions created compartmental structures which entirely destroyed all logical networks of reciprocal references.

In order to conceal their "ignorance" and complete lack of commitment to the idea of the happening, they select "taboo" plays, which were supposed to bring them prestige.

Most despicable of all was their lack of concern for the actors, the most important element in theatre, who were left to their own devices and to their traditional means of expression without being given the new methods and forms indispensable for "w i n n i n g   o v e r" a n d a b s o r b i n g new situations.

CURRENT ARTISTIC IDEAS

A n t i – a r t
T h e   d e a t h   o f   a r t

Each and every artistic trend tries to usurp for itself the right to be perceived as the *only* art, as art's e q u a l.

At the stage of a trend's early development and growth, this desire can be explained by a biological and natural vital energy. At the stage of a trend's stultification, this desire can be explained by the survival instinct.

When the latter stage is reached, all possible attempts are made to canonize specific means and methods, which are already dead, as eternal, absolute, and untouchable—simply as the essence of art.

The concept of a r t begins to function as a screen behind which c o n s e r v a t i s m and p r e s t i g e are hidden, and in front of which the banners of aesthetic, humanistic, moral values, etc., are waved. Any protest against this double-standard is branded as an act against a r t.

One should not be surprised, therefore, that all the twentieth-century radical and revolutionary movements, which abolished the centuries-old artistic conventions, thus isolated aesthetic values from activities of life, put forth the ideas of a n t i - a r t and t h e   d e a t h   o f   a r t. These ideas were not a call for destruction or nihilism; on the contrary, they created new directions and new vibrant conditions.

TOTAL CONTROL OVER REALITY

The beginning of the twentieth century, when the most sacred and solid values were eradicated, brought about the most rigid revisions of the "eternal laws," first, in art, then in other domains of life.

It was suddenly noticed that the centuries-old convention of separating so-called aesthetic values, i s o l a t i n g them from the r e a l i t y of life, enclosing them within the boundaries of the so-called w o r k   o f   a r t, was outdated, scholastic and unjustified in its privileging and cultivating of only certain practices.

An arrangement was demanded according to which the so-called aesthetic values would not be isolated from the reality of life, but would be integrated with this reality, and thus, give reality a deeper meaning.
A postulate known as t o t a l   c o n t r o l   o v e r
r e a l i t y was put forward.
It was a ruthless attack and a deadly blow against the art that tried to hide in its dead temples and pantheons.

NOT THE WORK OF ART, THE END PRODUCT OF THE CREATIVE PROCESS, BUT THE P R O C E S S ITSELF:

Consequently, the concept of the w o r k   o f   a r t, as a religious and isolated system, in which aesthetic and formal values were embedded, was fractured.
It is not the purpose of art to produce works or to house the
p r o d u c t s   o f   c r e a t i v i t y. Neither is it its duty to "store" those rare and unique objects it inherits from each epoch.

Art
is foremost
a manifestation and
a s p i r i t u a l activity of a human being;
an expression of his highest
mental and spiritual f a c u l t i e s.
It should be perceived as an
incessant i m p u l s e which stimulates
one's mind and psyche
rather than a symptom.
How ridiculous and obsolete seems the convention in which the a c t   o f
c r e a t i v i t y, this u n i q u e   j o u r n e y of mind and spirit is
merely used to produce an object. How ridiculous and obsolete seems the convention which hides the object behind rigid inter-relationships, only to reveal it to the world, present it to the public, expose it to the
a m b i g u o u s process of r e c e p t i o n (which combines contemplation and admiration with ignorance and contempt), and finally, simply
s e l l it.
There is something immoral in the fact that this "rare" object becomes a "legitimate" sign of the c r e a t i v e
p r o c e s s and as such will have life on its own, will bring fame and glory, recognition and, of course, money to the artist.
The act of rejection of
this p r i v i l e g e
by artists
is a sign of their
non-conformity and
their absolute
dedication to

c r e a t i v i t y.
This act of rejection is more difficult than
any other formal or stylistic
revolution.
It is not the w o r k (the end product),
nor its "eternal"
or its stone-like image
which is important
but
the p r o c e s s of creation,
which u n b l o c k s
mental and spiritual faculties.
This is a significant m o v e m e n t,
whose v i t a l i t y and
l i f e
are not used to produce the work,
but are meaningful in themselves,
for they infiltrate the total
reality and change its constituency.

THE DEFINITION OF THE PROCESS

The place of a depreciated (and to a degree condemned) concept of
"p r o d u c t" (*work* of art), the end result of the creative process, has
been taken by the p r o c e s s itself in its act of creation.
In order to avoid
any misunderstandings,
it should be clearly indicated that
by the p r o c e s s in its act of creation I do not mean
the p r o c e s s of creation
of this "product" ("work of art"),
nor its manifestation in the
extolling of the
process of preparation
nor in the revelation of the "back-stage" details of
the act of creation.
What I mean by the p r o c e s s is the act of creation
which is defined by its inner s t r u c t u r e,
which does not e n d
nor can be ended
with the final touch of a brush.
If such a situation is
i m p o s s i b l e
and i n c o n c e i v a b l e
in life,
this "i m p o s s i b l e"
can be achieved successfully
in art

on the condition that
the elements of this
"p r o c e s s"
are bereft of any other aim
(of any right to be the means
to effective, pragmatic, and specific ends),
than simply
to be perfectly u s e l e s s
and disinterested.

MANIPULATION CONNECTED WITH THE CONCEPT OF THE "WORK OF ART"

The results of this particular way of thinking, which acquire due significance in concrete situations, reveal in full the scope of the changes they introduce and the depth of the dimensions which they permit to be perceived.

Because of the colossal baggage of habitual actions, which may seem to be inborn routines or in compliance with natural laws, an attitude of everlasting contestation, constant control and correction or, more simply, of a highly developed awareness combined with intuition (in art, they are inseparable) are indispensable to preventing one from being sidetracked while following those habitual actions. This is especially necessary when approaching such a complex work as a work of theatre.

Certain characteristics, procedures, circumstances, and manipulations were closely connected with or were an inherent part of the discarded notion of the "work of art." In the past and even today, they seem to have tight bonds and shape the meaning of the concept of art.

The physical rendering of the "work of art" has always been connected with a whole spectrum of activities. These activities embrace the act of creation "o u t   o f   n o t h i n g"—a symptom of extreme sensitivity, artistic fever, hallucinations, visions, shamanic and magic rituals— s h a p i n g,   c o m p o s i n g,   and   c o n s t r u c t i n g.

Creation "o u t   o f   n o t h i n g" meant
juggling with c o n c o c t e d   e l e m e n t s,
which included formal means, methods of arrangement, and various "tricks."

Thus this process has been nothing more than
i m i t a t i o n,
r e - c r e a t i o n
of the model which pre-dated the "work of art,"
the act of p r o c u r i n g   i l l u s i o n,
and its actual r e p r e s e n t a t i o n.

REALNESS

Material, out of which something will be created,
which will be s h a p e d,

with the h e l p of which
some form of r e a l i t y
is e x p r e s s e d
and r e p r e s e n t e d,
ceases to be an
object of creation.
Reality itself
is an object of
creation.
This simple equation
[between reality and creation],
which, today, is an a l l - e m b r a c i n g
symbol of art,
has not yet reached the theatre.
For this reason, it is worth thinking about.
The moment the concept of
the "work of art,"
which was created "o u t o f n o t h i n g,"
out of "c o n c o c t e d" elements,
out of a e s t h e t i c,
r e p r e s e n t a t i o n a l,
i l l u s i o n a r y
value-codes,
is rejected
the artists are left with R e a l i t y,
R e a l n e s s,
which cannot be molded,
because it
"is"
R e a d y - m a d e,
and, consequently, the concepts of
imitation,
representation, and illusion
lose their meaning
(there is no doubt about it).

ANNEXED REALITY

Reality can only be
"u s e d."
"Used" is the only appropriate term.
Making use of reality
in a r t
signifies
an annexation of reality.
The phrase, "in art," demands that
this annexation happen outside of the practice of life;

that it be
c o s t - f r e e,
g r a t u i t o u s,
u s e l e s s, and
p u r p o s e l e s s.
(The term, "absurd," is not
a correct term here, since it signifies
a transfer of meaning from a practice of life
onto an artistic phenomenon.)
These adjectives must not, however,
be associated with a linguistic p l a y,
games, or juggling.
The artistic process of annexing reality
has a deeper meaning.
During this process,
reality
t r a n s g r e s s e s
its own b o u n d a r y
and moves in the direction of the
"i m p o s s i b l e."
The annexed reality contains in itself
real objects,
situations,
and an environment described
by time and place.
Their r e a c t i o n s to each other,
the i n t e r c o n n e c t i o n s between them,
the annexing g e s t u r e
of (as if casting a spell on reality)
r i t u a l
are substituted for
the process of molding
which is out of place here.

THE CLASH BETWEEN REALITY AND REPRESENTATION

I believe that this c o n f l i c t, which takes place in theatre, should be
described in a more detailed manner:
everything that has been said here describes a trend which led to and,
ultimately, found its justification in the Happening.
The Happening, which exerted a paramount influence on the development
of the arts in general, did not alter the formal structure of theatre (this is
yet another proof that theatre is outside of the total domain of ART).
The Happening was theatre's only chance to question the basic value of
the p e r f o r m a n c e,
and its methods of presentation. This aspect of theatre, which has
not been questioned, doubted, or challenged for a long time, is losing

its identity more and more in imitation, wheedling, coquetry, and psychological exhibitionism.
P e r f o r m a n c e
assumes that there exists
absolute and concrete
R e a l i t y
in the past and in the future
which can be
d e p i c t e d,
d e s c r i b e d,
that is,
s h o w n
or
e x p r e s s e d
by imitating it or
creating illusion.

If one, however, accepts the a u t o n o m y of artistic endeavors, that is, that these endeavors constitute a process in which art cannot find its justification in some reality existing outside of art, one will have to either reject reality and its concepts of
p e r f o r m a n c e
and representation
(reality of here and now, which can be m a n i p u l a t e d, as was the case with the happening, will be left),
or,
if, for whatever reason, the existence of this
"p r e - e x i s t i n g"
"r e a d y - m a d e"
reality
is important
(a playtext in theatre or Rembrandt's "Anatomy Lesson" in my 1967 happening under the same title),
ISOLATE IT COMPLETELY FROM OTHER REALITIES AND OTHER ARTISTIC ENDEAVORS (that is, A PERFORMANCE), PREVENT IT FROM OVERLAPPING WITH THEM;
FROM COMPLEMENTING OR EXPLAINING ONE ANOTHER; INSTALL A DIFFERENT REALITY AND MANIPULATE IT, ANNEX IT TO THE FIRST REALITY WITHOUT ANY LOGICAL CONNECTIONS,
and CREATE
TENSIONS
between them.
These processes, realized more and more radically and openly in the works of Cricot 2 Theatre, attempted to target theatre in its most neuralgic organ—Reality.

MANIPULATING REALITY—HAPPENING

R e a l i t y is constituted by the o b j e c t s taken directly from "life"; "real" objects, the simplest, the most neutral—that is—the objects not marked by any formal or aesthetic qualities—
as well as by the a c t i v i t i e s
and the s i t u a t i o n s,
also taken from life; simple, not
d e r i v e d
from any story.
Let us call
such a procedure
a process of "manipulating reality"—
it precludes a possibility of "r e p r e s e n t a t i o n"
because it does not make a reference to any other system.
It would seem then that an a c t o r, who has always been identified with a performance structure, is no longer needed. I still use the word "an actor," because I am fascinated by this "impossibility" of taking away from him this which is believed to be his essential function—to
r e p r e s e n t; and by the possibility of creating a model of a n e w
a c t o r.
In the above-mentioned procedure, which is called a process of "working with reality," the process of r e p r e s e n t i n g cannot exist, because reality is the only thing which is. The events must unfold in such a manner so that they can cross their "life's" boundaries and become a portent of art.
In order for this to happen, one needs to take away their practical and life's function, make them useless, i s o l a t e them.
This is a deciding and fascinating moment—a moment of "placing them on a different trajectory," where other forces begin to be felt: r i s k - t a k i n g d e c i s i o n and
the i m a g i n a t i o n of thought.

NEW ACTOR

This new actor, who got entangled with reality, rejects his traditional ability to represent. It is no longer needed; more than that, it becomes his liability. He must however have the ability to remain focused, be able to concentrate on one activity, know how to "besiege" the object, how to create an action around him; and the most important, be able to leave behind his old skills and talents and move towards
the f e e l i n g
of the "i m p o s s i b l e."

AGAINST THE EXPRESSIVE FORM

To sum up: we are approaching the final moment—
in a place where there no longer is "a work of art" (it was replaced by the concept of

"process")
where form
forming,
representation,
expression
(all of which were replaced by
r e a l i t y)
lost their meaning,
there must disappear the notion of an e x p r e s s i v e form.

Reality,
objects and activities
are a l a n g u a g e,
an a l p h a b e t
a m o d e   o f   t h i n k i n g,
rather than
an e x p r e s s i v e   f o r m.
They are bereft of the expressiveness to which we were accustomed.
The w o r k   o f   c r e a t i o n
g a v e way to
a system of communication, that is,
a p r o c e s s,
a p r a c t i c e,
a r i t u a l,
a g e s t u r e,
and, finally,
an i n t e r v e n t i o n.

THE QUESTIONING OF THE "ARTISTIC" PLACE

It is obvious that, in this new system, those places reserved exclusively for
art and adapted for its reception,
those places where the ambiguous
acts of representation and presentation take place,
those places where everything is justified by fiction,
those sterilized and immunized places (it is difficult to call a museum or
an auditorium a real place)
where everything is readied for the reception of fiction and illusion,
those panopticons,
had to be contested and
abandoned.
It had to be so, because
the above-mentioned systems, which are proposed by art,
do not need and cannot fit into
traditional institutions
of cultural preservation.
Being the very manifestation of life and
a l l - e m b r a c i n g   r e a l i t y,

they have to position and find themselves
in the very essence of this reality.

FROM THE HAPPENING TO THE "IMPOSSIBLE"

The Happening's intervention into reality, which was expressed by and in
the audience's participation, started to empty itself out and lose its power
of action.
The process of sublimating the Happening's physical reality and its
presence in time and space was transferred onto the territory whose
boundaries were expanded and whose landscape of imagination was
shaped by thought, rather than by perception, by the "impossible."
What I regard as important here is the integration of a
great m u l t i t u d e of
s u g g e s t i o n s
so structured that they create in the audience
the i m p r e s s i o n of
the i m p o s s i b i l i t y of
g r a s p i n g
and i n t e r p r e t i n g the whole
from the audience's position.
The audience's p e r c e p t i o n is grounded in
a r e f l e c t i o n
c r e a t e d by a relationship between
objects and actions,
which are not "the work of art,"
or its materialization, but
a point of reference
for cognitive and spiritual processes.
My actions go in two directions: toward the actors and the audience.
I am creating stage actions which are enclosed in themselves, escaping
perceptions, going "nowhere," "impossible."
On the other hand, I refuse to give the audience their rights and privileges.
The situation of the audience is questionable, constantly corrected, and
(physically) altered.

PLAYING

Playing is identified in theatre with the concept of a performance. One
says: "to play a part."
"P l a y i n g," however, means neither reproducing nor reality itself. It
means something "in-between" illusion and reality.
If this notion is taken outside of artistic boundaries, its broader, possibly
more significant, meaning is revealed.
To play chess, to play cards . . .
Its meaning here may be secondary, though, at the same time, it is
essential.

It is a substitute for life's passions, conflicts, and actions; at the same time,
it "purifies" these passions from often dire consequences.
It suggests
commitment,
coincidence,
and the "unknown,"
autonomy,
internal focus,
a break with this "other" reality [of passions, conflicts, and actions],
thus, all the components
of a new theatre.
I do not intend to simplify the matter,
but the notion of a "spectator" keeps emerging here.
A spectator is not an audience member,
but a potential player.
Why then an actor and not a "player"
(*acteur-joueur*)?

THE ACTORS CAN ONLY REPRESENT THEMSELVES

They do not imitate anything,
they do not represent anybody,
they do not express anything,
but themselves,
human façades,
exhibitionists,
con-artists,
who are separated from
and who exhibit their supernatural gifts to the public,
who challenge with their individuality
and their uncommon b e h a v i o r.
They are like
c i r c u s performers,
clowns, jugglers,
fire-eaters,
and acrobats.
They solve all the problems, the dilemma
of autonomy and representation,
with ease.
They meet all the demands
for new actors.

A man with a wooden board on his back,
who is on the verge of insanity,
is
an unusual case of
absurd anatomy:
being completely focused within

the object-like growth
on his body,
he is like a martyr crucified
on himself.

A man with two additional legs
unfolds in front of the dumbfounded crowd
the whole spectrum
of completely new and unknown
benefits, advantages, privileges, and possibilities of
nature's whimsical generosity,
of expanded psychological processes,
and even moral consequences,
side effects, and
surprises.

A man with two bicycle wheels grown into his legs
completely separated from
the reality of a different k i n d
and enclosed in
an inhuman,
but at least for him natural,
feeling for s p e e d
and m o t i o n
that can be realized with the help of his legs
with the consciousness of a vehicle.

A suicide-prestidigitator
commits suicide
systematically
every five minutes
without any harm to his body and mind.
He is dressed in a kind of a white
emballage-bag,
which makes him look like a clown.
This bag, as its details
show clearly,
is a uniform of an army officer,
it is irrelevant in this convention of
which army.
Here, as in a circus, more dangerous actions
are accompanied by music played by
an ever present Gypsy.

A Gypsy and a self-playing violin
A Gypsy plays the violin,
and to be precise,

pretends that he is playing.
The violin is playing itself;
however, since it is a circus-act,
the violin laments and whines
a gypsy song
while the gypsy is lamenting and whining.

A man with a huge piece of luggage,
who never lets it out of his sight,
pulls a human skeleton from it, only
to hide it again with maniacal care.

A man with doors,
who cannot separate himself from them,
aimlessly carries them and performs the only
actions that can be performed with doors—
closing and opening.

A man with two heads
(the second head is between his legs),
who is constantly trying to resolve for himself
two "impossible" consequences of
nature's excess:
two consciousnesses,
two systems of
response and
two apparatuses controlling
one body.

A CLOAKROOM

At all times, one has to question and expose
the false prestige of "the artistic condition,"
which tries to maneuver through sanctioned
critical territory by juggling
expression, performance, presentation,
"pretending," representation
and to prevent the d e l i v e r a n c e of
"r e a l i t y" and truth!
A stage, no matter which one, even the most
dynamic one created with the help of the audience's participation,
is always solid and passive;
it is a place where the actor
wins an artistic status,
prize and glory;
it is an artistic place.
[Our stage] must be bereft of this function.

The place for
"artistic activity"
is taken by
a utilitarian space,
by a C L O A K R O O M,
a real cloakroom.
In the theatre, a cloakroom
is a place and an institution
of the lowest rank;
it is usually an obstacle
one would like to avoid.
If one were to think about it,
a cloakroom is shameless
in its invasion of one's privacy:
we are forced to leave there
an intimate part of us.
It is a terrorist act.
We could push this metaphor even further and say that
during a production
parts of us are hanging there mixed together
with people we do not know;
we are hanging motionlessly
marked by numbers,
violated,
punished,
and so on . . .
. . . this infamous institution has
dominated theatre,
it stands there like a punishing, soulless death squad
led by a group of thugs.
A cloakroom, moving in no direction,
is constantly, aimlessly there,
for its own sake
like art for art's sake.
Cloakroom for cloakroom's sake . . .
A cloakroom works,
expands,
devours more and more spheres of the imagination.
It is continuously working. . . .
It rejects the actors and their rights,
it throws them ruthlessly beyond the boundaries,
or it appropriates, belittles,
deforms,
sterilizes,
tarnishes,
ruthlessly breaks,
and gives false testimonies

to their attempts to "smuggle" in their artistic
activities.

THE PRODUCTION

During the extensive and rigorous theoretical and performance work on a
new production,
there grew and multiplied the layers of the h i s t o r y of the e v e n t s
and
c h a r a c t e r s, all of which found their place in a new performance
reality. Here they are:
A monstrous CLOAKROOM,
ruthlessly destroying the sacred and completely emptied out "artistic
place" and a desired "comfort" of the audience's reception,
brutal CLOAKROOM ATTENDANTS,
one of them, working on the side as a BUTCHER; the other—a
confused TRANSVESTITE with a cherub's face; the action takes place
in a STORAGEROOM, which doubles as a WAITING-ROOM; some
STRANGERS keep moving continuously heavy objects, an actor
with TWO ADDITIONAL LEGS (the Master of the House), an actor
FOLDED like a pancake, a friend of the master of the house WITH TWO
HEADS; a DISTURBED dialogue of a couple, openly MASTURBATING,
an UNKNOWN PERSON—who suddenly conducts a military drill and
other unspecified EXCERCISES WITH THE AUDIENCE, who will soon
invade the stage as 40 MANDELBAUMS,
merciless and primitive BESTIA DOMESTICA with a gigantic MOUSE-
TRAP,
A GANG OF LIBERTINES WITH THE PRINCESS at the head,
AN OFFICER systematically committing suicide,
a barefoot, dirty GYPSY and his self-playing VIOLIN,
a beggar-CARDINAL
grown to the DOORS,
a man with a wooden BOARD on his back,
a man with a SKELETON,
which he endlessly buries and digs out, etc.
The Princess is herded into a HENHOUSE, where she will remain;
she will be exhibited to the public and will become an object of a
shameful practice of the Cloakroom Attendants—PIMPS; this will end
with a parade of the LOVERS.
The master of the house greets his strange guests,
a SHAMELESS ORGY IN A HENHOUSE follows,
everybody leaves for the BATHS—the end of Act I.
Act II begins in the BATHS—the PRINCESS is once again exhibited to the
public; this time as a FREAK WOMAN IN A HENHOUSE;
THE AUDIENCE crowds around the henhouse as around a cage in the
ZOO; the Cloakroom Attendants push around the henhouse-cage with
the freak woman and her lover; the CAGE is covered with a sheet—thus,

it becomes an EROTIC SONOROUS EMBALLAGE—the audience
is eavesdropping; the idea of a duel of the lover, who has been kicked
out from the henhouse-cage, is transformed into an ENIGMATIC
SCENE, a kind of game playing-ritual, going nowhere, completely
unexplainable and gratuitous, almost reaching the zero zones in terms
of its expressiveness and meaning; suddenly, the Cloakroom Attendants
announce the CLOSING OF THE THEATRE, the cloakroom; they
start throwing the audience out; push the actors out; the ACTORS ARE
DEFENDING THEMSELVES; THEY ARE ACTING ON THE SLY,
quickly just to finish their parts;
complete CHAOS;
Bestia Domestica makes use of this pandemonium and REPLACES
the Princess in the chicken coop–cage; she speaks her lines in the love
scene, which ends with a DUEL; she fights against "her" lover using
the MOUSE-TRAP; the lover dies shamefully caught in a mouse-trap;
she STRANGLES the second lover; the guests appear; the Cloakroom
Attendants are trying to prevent the audience from leaving; general
MAYHEM; the Princess is "THROWN INTO THE AUDIENCE" and
drags the body of the strangled lover; she holds him in her arms (a stylized
equivalent of the "Pieta"), and the man with the skeleton, one of the
lovers rejected by the Princess, swallows the pills, which will increase
his sexual prowess but also kill him; he shoots himself; the guests throw
themselves on his body, DEVOUR THE PILLS and dance their last dance,
40 MANDELBAUMS, driven by their desire and jealousy, TRAMPLE
THE PRINCESS TO DEATH and join in the dance of the living and the
dead; the living and the dead, who populate the scene of

THE END OF THE WORLD
and
THE END OF THE PRODUCTION.

There is less and less time left.
So, I need to hurry—
abbreviate, simplify,
and remember the productions of Cricot 2 Theatre.

My "discoveries." In quotes.
Let me use this term, though it does not explain
everything.
It was they (the discoveries) which caused
the i d e a of Cricot Theatre to become
more and more clear and precise.
NEW! Let me emphasize this.
My discoveries were not "ideas."
We know well this phenomenon in theatre.
Ideas serve only to satisfy the most immediate and one-time stage effects
and "success."
My "discoveries" had solid roots.
Maybe the first one was deeply
grounded in my consciousness and in my nature.

One of my first "discoveries":
REAL THEATRICAL PLACE—
not a place constructed with the help of illusion or by
faithfully following the playwright's stage directions.

In *The Return of Odysseus*,
it was not the island of Ithaca,
but a ROOM, destroyed during the war
in Kraków, year 1944!

In the production of *The Country House*,
it was not a country house,
but a WARDROBE, year 1960!,
in which the actors, squeezed impossibly, hung on hangers.

And following this, or rather a simultaneous, "discovery":
PEOPLE-FAÇADES.
An actor achieves the living, human organism
by moving through lifeless and hostile matter.

In the production of *Dainty Shapes and Hairy Apes*,
it was not an open country landscape or an interior of a palace,
but a theatre CLOAKROOM, in which the spectators
left behind them a "piece of themselves," their overcoats.
The scraps of play action, taking place behind the doors leading onto the stage,
were "thrown into" a cloakroom.

The concept of SCRAPS was also a discovery.
We can accept the notion of SCRAPS
(of stage action, speech, movements, objects),
if we believe that w h o l e n e s s
belongs to the PAST, which is enclosed in itself,
and that only SCRAPS reach our
Present.

Following it is the notion of MEMORY,
THE MAIN ENGINE and almost a leading actor of the CRICOT
THEATRE.
It is only the PAST which exists
as real and concrete condition.
The past which is experienced and lived through.
But not the one which is a field where
sentimentality and recollection
graze.
"Bypassing" the present,
we steer clear of narrativity
and the conventional process of
r e f l e c t i o n and
reproduction.
The present is reflected
in the past even more
painfully,
glaringly,
dramatically—
theatrically.

In all those discoveries, described here,
THE REALITY OF THE LOWEST RANK
is deeply grounded.

In *The Emballage Manifesto*
(Year 1963),
I considered the objects
that had lost their use-value
in every-day life
and were "at the threshold of garbage,"
to be an excellent—and the only worth considering—
material for the creation
of a w o r k of art.
The notion of
POVERTY
penetrated right through my Theatre
from the very beginning,
from the time of the Clandestine Underground Theatre.

And one more "discovery":
"THE IDEA OF A JOURNEY."
It left a deep imprint on
the Cricot Theatre;
on everything that I have done
and am still going to do.
Wanderers and their luggage
(The Water-Hen, Year 1967).
A Grand Wanderer.
A Jew—the Eternal Wanderer.
A Fairground Booth—
Life as a Journey
and art as a journey,
which is never ending
and leading into the unknown.

And, finally,
the last "discovery."
The theatre
of DEATH
(Year 1967).
And it is here that a new
c h a p t e r
begins.

Spatial Historiography: *The Dead Class*

I

The image of the Old People in black carrying wax figures of children, also in black, on their backs will forever be associated with *The Dead Class*, which premiered on November 15, 1975, at the Galeria Krzysztofory (Krzysztofory Gallery) in Kraków.[1] *The Dead Class* was hailed both as Tadeusz Kantor's masterpiece and as a seminal production marking a shift in his theatre practice. From that time onward, Kantor's theatre or, to be more precise, Kantor's theatre of death or theatre of essences, confronted and dazzled international audiences and critics.[2] Today, some thirty years later, *The Dead Class* exists only as a memory of those who saw a live performance or of those who viewed a videotape or DVD of the production. For either viewer, *The Dead Class* is as a remote reference point from a bygone era of theatre experimentation, a set of nostalgic and fragmented images—a peculiar form of mnemotechnics—whose presence as well as ocular power are established through the process of representing what can be understood about them. This representation of a present intelligibility locates the Old People in black carrying wax figures of children along the narrative itinerary that steals their presence bit by bit through the "poisonous ingenuity of Time."[3] What is it that fascinates us in *The Dead Class*, whether we do or do not understand the Polish language? Why is it that *The Dead Class* obscured Kantor's previous productions? What is it exactly that Kantor managed to accomplish in this production that differentiates it from his past theatre experiments? How did *The Dead Class* give visibility to Kantor's project of materializing his theatre "from whatever it is it is not"—to paraphrase Herbert Blau?[4] The questions and answers multiply, even in the face of the anguish of verbal hallucinations.

II

As in the past, Kantor was onstage in *The Dead Class*—in the vaulted, low-arched ceiling basement of the Galeria Krzysztofory or another more or less traditional performance space—staring intensely at the audience as they entered the space. In one corner, rather than in the center, four rows of old school desks, pulled as if from the memory of the immemorial past, stood facing the audience. What differentiated this performance environment from other performance environments of the lowest rank used by Kantor between 1944 and 1973—the

197

bombed room, the wardrobe, the theatre cloakroom, and so on—was a rope that separated it from the audience. It was as if an impassable barrier had been raised, rupturing the perspectival order that had, for centuries, constituted the metaphysical and political programs organizing the realms of the visual and the social as well as modern notion of culture, which was born in the public access to the signs of historicopolitical identity and their collective deciphering.[5]

It was this collective deciphering that Kantor challenged with his rope while exposing the technologies for the objectification of a world. It was not, however, the first time he had done this—recall, for example, the moment when he made Penelope sit on a broken kitchen chair in a bombed room to which Odysseus returned from an inglorious military campaign in 1944.[6] In 1975, it was again this collective deciphering that Kantor exposed as a tear in the political field of socialist Poland, annexing reality and its unknown, hidden, or everyday aspects—matter, marginalized objects, degraded objects, everyday realness, self-enclosed actions—all, now, unable to affirm officially sanctioned life. By tearing this fabric, Kantor illuminated the moral conditions created by perturbing the existing order of things. As Theodor Adorno avers in *Minima Moralia*, "it is part of morality not to be at home in one's home."[7]

In *The Dead Class*, however, this rapture over binarism—theatre as an answer to, rather than the representation or affirmation of, reality or life—seemed to position Kantor in a place where he could embark on a new exploit by bringing the spectator's desires for a monocular, perspectival vision and for an instant gratification to an abrupt halt. A rope separated the performance space from the auditorium. It was always there in subsequent stagings or incarnations of *The Dead Class*, an inexhaustible binarism marking an aporia or incommensurability between spaces—the space with the audience, trying to see its reflection in the representations onstage, and the space where Kantor moved among the school desks occupied by the actors, the Old People, staring silently and motionlessly, like wax figures, at the entering audience.

The Dead Class (1975). Photo by J. Dalman courtesy of the Cricoteka Archives.

The monocular vision expressed an infinite emptiness. Unlike Diego Velázquez's *Las Meninas*, the emptiness of *The Dead Class* is not with filled by the image of Philip IV and his wife Mariana arrested in the silver surface of a mirror in the back of the painting—the King (or anyone else) called upon to cruelly restore "what is lacking in every gaze: in the painter's, the model, which his represented double is duplicating over there in the picture; in the king's, his portrait, which is being finished off on the slope of the canvas that he cannot perceive from where he stands; in that of the spectator, the real center of the scene, whose place he himself has taken as though by usurpation."[8] In *The Dead Class*, emptiness remained the center of an anguished perception. In the language of mirrors, reflections, doubles, transferences, and transformations, one heard a distant, murmured, anxious question: "Who is there?"[9]

The audience entered the performance space as a privileged subject, expecting, with narcissistic pleasure, to be projected onto the inaccessible performance surface. This narcissistic pleasure of thought was foiled by a rope and school desks populated by Old People in black exactly in front of the audience. The silhouettes of the Old People were enveloped in a bright and misty light. Caught by this brightness, the spectator's gaze encountered the motionless gaze that leapt out from the space on the other side, cutting straight through the field of representation. Like Clov in Beckett's *Endgame*, the viewers were forced to see their light dying:[10]

In the school desks,
the actors—the Old People,
are sitting or standing,
staring directly at the crowd entering the space,
motionless,
like WAX FIGURES,
masterfully resembling the living. . . .
With the lifeless expressions on their faces of
waiting, curiosity, patience,
they stand until all the audience members enter
and take their seats. . . .
They are exhibited shamefully,
like the condemned at a public execution;
more than that, as if they were DEAD.
From the moment the audience enters,
a separation should be felt—
simultaneously, they should feel repulsed by and attracted to this horrible inhuman
condition.
Like the dead!
"On the other side!"
School desks like catafalques.
THE WAX-FIGURE MUSEUM.[11]

From the very beginning, Kantor served and exploited this binarism. On the one hand, there was a rope separating the performance space from the auditorium, an impassable barrier marking the aporia and incommensurability between the two spaces. On the other hand, there was the inhuman condition of the actors, drastically repositioning traditional relationships between spectators and actors in the theatre:

> FOREIGNNESS. This is a very important and essential characteristic of the actor. From the "Theatre of Death Manifesto": "It is necessary to recover the essential meaning of the relationship: spectator and actor. It is necessary to recover the primeval force of the shock taking place at the moment when, opposite a human (a spectator), there stood for the first time a human (an actor), deceptively similar to us, yet at the same time infinitely foreign, beyond the impassable barrier."
> Foreign . . . the impassable barrier . . . and deceptively similar to us, the spectators. One day, or one night, I found a model for the actor which would fit ideally into these conditions: the dead—I felt afraid and ashamed. . . . It was difficult for me to accept this model. . . . But this difficulty also meant that I was onto something. . . . I continued to write: "If we agree that one of the traits of living people is their ability and the ease with which they enter into various relationships, it is only when encountering the body of a dead person that we realize that this essential trait of the living is possible because of the lack of differentiation between them, because of the sameness and . . . the 'invisibility.' It is only the DEAD who become visible to the living at the price of acquiring their individuality, difference, and their IMAGE. . . ."
> The DEAD and the ACTOR, these two notions started to overlap in my thoughts. More and more, I started to accept these two conditions. Multiple ideas were born in my head. Finally, they all became part of my thinking about theatre. . . . The wax figure became an entity touched by death, fake, existing between a dead person and a living actor. . . .
> I want to achieve a degree of foreignness which would be painfully noticeable by the audience. (*"The Dead Class"*)

Kantor achieved this foreignness by placing the action of *The Dead Class* behind the impassable barrier separating the audience from the actors. But this maneuver was not sufficient. The desired degree of foreignness was attained by placing the school desks and the Old People on the side of the performance space, in a corner of the room. As Kantor contended, an act happening in the center of a room would be given the status of a performance by those watching it. The same act, however, when presented on the side, beyond the circle of spectators, would be perceived as "abnormal behavior, exhibitionism, a shameful act, completely independent and self-sufficient; an act which would not require the spectator's presence."[12]

The space in a corner, separated from the auditorium by a rope and beyond the organizing gaze of the spectator, was where Kantor placed his actors or, to be more precise, his "WAX FIGURES," "infinitely DISTANT, shockingly FOREIGN as if DEAD." This idea seemed to him inexhaustible and, as the production made clear, he could never exploit it enough, as if, liberated from the constraints of linear time and from standards of visibility, Kantor had located his theatre in "the silence at the eye of the scream," where death and his actors escaped the voice of banality.[13] The school desks, like catafalques, "infinitely DISTANT, shockingly FOREIGN," were like *punctum*, a hallucinatory rip, a fissure, cut, hole, or tear, an eruptive detail in the *studium* of forgotten or repressed school days.

Suddenly, the immobilized wax figures at the school desks started to move, as if life had been injected into them. Their returning to life was marked by slow and minute movements of the bodies that "the poisonous ingenuity of Time" denatured and reduced to nothing more than the mechanical rhythms of mannequins, whose stone-frozen faces expressed an infinite emptiness. The torsos were upright, the hands on the desks, the faces looked forward, ready to embark on an unknown journey. Silence. "Grace to breathe that void."[14] After a split second, one of the Old People raised her hand, as if asking for permission to leave. She was joined by other Old People. "Something is taking its course."[15] The hands were in the air, the request to leave becoming more and more pressing. "The meaning of this sign is slowly changing. THE OLD PEOPLE ARE ASKING NOW FOR SOMETHING . . . SOMETHING FINITE."[16] As always, in Kantor's theatre, mundane matters were mixed with everlasting concerns— here, the irrepressible need to go to the toilet was mixed with the desire for eternity. Eschatology and sacrum; there was no escape from the something which tore the fabric of the *studium*. The Old People, one by one, disappeared into the opening, the black hole, the open grave at the back. The school desks were empty. Emptiness and silence provided a momentary relief from the unexpected and somber image. What was going to happen next? "Birth was the death of him. . . . Words are few."[17] Kantor's characters were being born and dying into the thought of a theatre materializing "on the other side," where "life is pushed to its final limits, where all categories and concepts lose their meaning and right to exist" ("Theatrical Place").

The Old People reappeared in the black hole of the opening. Their grand entrance was accompanied by the nostalgic sounds of a waltz, whose opening tune brought back the memory of its title, "If only once again the past could return."[18] But it was not only the past that returned with a melancholy regression into a bygone area. The dreams, desires, hopes, and memories of failure did return, too. The Old People circled the school desks. Their awakening to the dreams and nightmares of history, this Grand Parade of the Circus of Death, as Kantor called it, would have been incomplete without what testified and bore witness to their dying light. The Old People carried with them the wax figures of children—of their own childhood: "The dead children hang over [the Old People], cling to their bodies with strength; others are pulled as if they were a heavy weight, a heavy remorse of the soul, a burden; others 'crept around' the bodies of the ones who grew old, and who killed this childhood with their adulthood in a sanctioned and 'socially acceptable' manner."[19]

The Old People carried with them the tumors of childhood. "The eye will return to the scene of its betrayals."[20] These tumors, like a painful image in the service of violent and bloodied thought, brought forth the possibility that

UMARŁA KLASA

Tadeusz Kantor's drawing to *The Dead Class*. Galerie de France. Photo by Michal Kobialka courtesy of the Kantor Estate.

their childhood past has become a desolate and forgotten storage-room,
where the desiccated memories of and forgotten people, faces, objects, pieces of
clothing, feelings, and images were laid to rest. . . .
. . . This is not sentimentality about getting old;
which desires to bring childhood back to life in one's memory.
This is the condition of complete and TOTAL life,
which cannot continue along the narrow narrative of
the time present! (*"The Dead Class"*)

Unlike the Maeterlinckian or Symbolist ambition to present a *Gesamt-kunstwerk* of evocative images of life before and after the present moment, Kantor's Old People walked onto the stage with the dead bodies of their childhood. Like runaways trying to escape the soul's remorse, they were excited by the possibility of living their past again, to the tune of a familiar waltz, to prove that they were still alive—more, as if to prove that their light reflected the impossible thought of "total, undialectical death."[21]

The idea of undialectical death marked the moment of revelation to the audience, "on the other side," of the meaning of the word *defunctus*.[22] "The place was crawling with them! Use your head, can't you, use your head, you're on earth, there's no cure for that," says Hamm in *Endgame*.[23] Indeed, the place was crawling with them, until they returned to the school desks where they sat down together, with the wax figures of their childhood—another frozen moment, during which the audience had a chance to face the "DISTANT, shockingly FOREIGN" possibility that, as Blau noted, "if you look long enough and hard enough you will really see. What you will see, if you use your head, is that there is no cure for that."[24] There is no cure for a past that is discharged and finished (*defunctus*) yet not dead (defunct). It is an undialectical death that grows in the mind, through Kantor's images and scenes, "grain upon grain, one by one."[25]

Kantor's vision of an infinite emptiness was filled with Old People regressing into the past in their present moment. They could never be dead, for, though deceased, the dead live in our memory of them. The audience could have no memories of these dead, for the Old People were subject to Kantor's desire to make them be what he or his autobiography wanted them to be. Thus, the audience "remembered" only what filled their sight by force. "What do we know about King Solomon?" asked one of the Old People, now a teacher. The other Old People hid under their school desks in panic. The teacher pointed at one of the students, then at another. The pointed finger, like a thunderbolt, hit the students, who fell down dead. The lesson about Solomon continued. The Old Man with His Double successfully answered the question with a list of Solomon's beloved women, an aria of names picked up by the rest of the Old People, whose recitation changed into a sorrowful lament, which grew into a crescendo, then collapsed. The Old People's bodies followed the intensity of the sound, rising in their desks, and then descending into their seats.

The sequence of growth and collapse was repeated once more, during a lesson about King David, a series of non sequiturs picked up and played with by the Old People. These non sequiturs, the shreds of memories of once-memorized lessons, were the banal and everyday recollections engendered by the thoughtless, never-dissipated structures of education. Now the biblical King David was deconstructed phonetically, reduced to a lament expressing loss, pain, and despair, as if coming from another region of memory where history and the everyday wallow together. The lament ceased and, with it, the nightmare of history. Its place was taken by the waltz, its notes, like the voice of singularity in space, penetrated the *studium*. More than that,

> Through this ceaseless repetition,
> which works hypnotically,
> the past, lost and dead,
> is brought back to life.
> On stage, for a split second,
> we witness an unquestionable miracle. . . .
> The Old People rise slowly from their seats
> the further their desks, the higher they rise.
> They create a human wall, which comes to life
> because of the sounds of the waltz;
> their aged backs straighten,
> their heads are raised high,

their eyes are full of life,
their hands are raised as if to a toast.
We are sure that these people
found their time of lost youth again . . .
dead.[26]

The sounds of the waltz disappeared and with them the illusion of new life. The Old People collapsed onto the desks that had given birth to their memories a moment before. This rhythm of birth and collapse was repeated throughout the production. It was used by Kantor to mark the materiality of a newly found reality, even though this new reality would disintegrate and, with it, the Old People, who for a moment were given chance to forget before they awaken into the nightmare of their histories.

The process of reaching deeper and deeper regions of the past, of exploring what had been lost in the process of forgetting or glossed by language and the images through which we remember, became both the mode of operation and the subject of Kantor's "Nocturnal Lesson." Memories "exploded into the nightmares of hell and the nostalgia for Eden; dreams became a precise rendering of reality."[27] In his notes, Kantor observed that actions that once were real and everyday needed to be relocated, put into the "shrunken space" delimited by the rope and occupied by the school desks. There, the actions were out of place and established a tension between them and the space where they were supposed to be executed:

at first, these actions are driven by the logic of life;
gradually this logic disappears and the actions become less and less
comprehensible,
meaningless, bereft of life's rationale,
causing completely UNJUSTIFIED reactions
such as:
ANGER,

**The Dead Class (1975). Photo
courtesy of Jacquie Bablet.**

LAUGHTER,
DISPAIR,
FEAR,
CRUELTY.[28]

In the production, the audience found themselves watching the actors hanging in the Informel wardrobe or reaching zero zones where the space "on the other side," the school desks, stood for the Death Machine in *The Madman and the Nun* (1963). In *The Dead Class*, the Old Man in the WC, seated in the second row of the school desks on the aisle, came to life and began the number-aria running through his head:

8 15 19 21
2 2 2
o
29 34 36 41
o
52 57 59
9 9 9 9!
. . . for 120 percent
o o o o
2
suddenly something catches his attention. . . .
143 . . .
149 . . .
it seems that suddenly he has realized something. . . .
A . . . A . . . scoundrel!
Whaaaat?
Noooo!
Never!!
crescendo of his disbelief; at the height of his disbelief, he calls those around him
to be the witnesses. . . .
Scoundrel!
Son of a bitch!
The Bible will help him in his litany of curses . . . . . .
in the valley of fire . . .
my body . . .
my blood. . . .
o o o o
24 67 97
7 7 7[29]

The number-aria, accompanied by curses and biblical references, brought the audience to the regions of a dream where the past logic of the everyday was ruptured by those events beyond the boundaries of time that revealed its emptiness. The Old Man in the WC was a usurer at one moment and a biblical prophet at another, but also Tumor Brainowicz, the title character from Wit-kacy's play *Tumor Brainowicz*. The Woman behind the Window followed and commented upon the actions the Old Man in the WC executed, while watching the parade of the Old Man with a Bicycle, who, suddenly, as if in a strange dream, spoke the lines of Józef, Tumor Brainowicz's son. The moment the lines were spoken, however, the Old Man with a Bicycle could not remember what he had just said, finding only shreds of thoughts that cut through the remnants of memory. What was left onstage, then, were the unfinished and incomplete images of Old People who repeated memorized words like monuments erupting in the topography of the past and whose memorized questions created a vertigo of unconscious associations. These words and questions woefully underlined the missing articulation between the Old People and a logos that started spinning entropically the moment they leave their school desks—their memory machine—behind.

Complete entropy was prevented by the entry of a Soldier from World War I, yet another apparition from the forgotten regions of memory, who used to be a member of this Dead Class:

> He comes back the way he had died,
> forced out of the trenches, out of the earth, soil,
> mud by a command to attack;
> wearing a tattered overcoat
> with his head in bandages, feverish,
> madness in his eyes;
> he rushes forward to attack.
> He stops.[30]

The sound of the waltz accompanied him and continued as the Soldier led a parade of the Old People around the school desks, where the wax figures of children were left as a reminder of the missing articulation. The memorized phrases of the Nocturnal Lesson punctured the soothing forgetting of the waltz. The parade came to a halt and the Old People retrenched themselves behind the desks to regain their memories. To attempt this, the Old People had to erase that missing articulation; they picked up their tumors—the wax figures of the children—and cast them onto the floor. "The bodies of children are thrown one over the other; they grow into a pile, a horrific pile during this bloody ceremony."[31]

The Old People returned to their desks, yet another reprieve—the silence in the eye of the storm, grace to breathe the void, stirring still. The silence was finally broken by a phoneme-aria resembling a child's language of sounds, an almost antiphonal chant, but bereft of mysterious religious evocations, its "meaning" declaimed by two choruses of the Old People. The phoneme-aria created yet another reality, distant and shockingly different from the silence of a moment ago. Framed as kernel of narration and action from the traditional representational theatre, the phoneme-aria instead destroyed and tore apart a logic of sense and expression, unhousing all those structures and everyday connections that bind language and meaning together:

LEFT SIDE

w y s t r r r	bzyrk	
w y s t r r	brk	
bystry	wyrk	
strk	brk	
. . .		
wyrke	bzyrke	
byrke	wzyrke	
zyrke	wyrke	RIGHT SIDE
		Fumcekaka
		Fumcekaka
		Fum ce ka ka
wyrk	bzyrk	fumcekaka
bystry	wyrk	fumcekaka[32]

The destruction of language as an expression of normative categories was followed by yet another deformation, that of the face, the accepted façade. Making faces was the process of tearing down the official and recognizable demeanors that affirm the structures of belonging and feeling: "Making faces is a strikingly effective weapon of immaturity against the 'seriousness' of adulthood, which often does nothing more than mask its lack of sensitivity, feelings, imagination, or its ruthlessness, duplicity, emptiness. (*"The Dead Class."*)"

The faces were directed at the audience: who were they, when confronted with Old People seated in school desks making faces and deforming their features? "If you look long enough and hard enough you will really see. What you will see, if you use your head, is that there is no cure for that." Kantor knew there was no cure for history—that thing that hurts, or for undialectical death—that thing that escapes the gaze and cannot be interiorized. "Death will come and will have your eyes."[33] Kantor knew that there was no cure for rationalizations that give visibility—that thing that objectifies the world, and for the missing articulation between the living body and those that are "infinitely DISTANT, shockingly FOREIGN, as if DEAD":

THE WORLD OF IMMATURITY.

Through the lessons and school incidents, it is necessary to expose and disclose this reality, to which ADULTS want to introduce children in school. It is necessary to place this world, believed to be mature and responsible, in contrast to the ur-reality, not yet deformed by life's practices, to this *"MATIÈRE PREMIÈRE,"* "RAW MATERIAL" of life.

In this mature world, there are:
History, wars, never-ending wars, battlefields—battlefields of courage and victory, and their equivalents on the other side: infamy, genocides, historical necessity, monuments of glory and death, grand ideologies, pantheons, mausoleums, nightmarish ceremonies, civilizations built on armies, police, prisons, and the laws.

In that other world, there are:
the regions pushed aside by sanctioned consciousness,
ignored with embarrassment,
deeply hidden in bourgeois interiors,
banned, marked by the original sin, fined, constrained and restricted by law and
court verdicts as a menace to and an enemy of the people. (*"The Dead Class"*)

Kantor wanted to find an autonomous structure that would express an
"event strike" in the House of History, in the World of Maturity, as he called it.
The World of Immaturity was an answer. In it, actors could not play the parts of
children; they could only play the parts of Old People who, perversely, returned
to childhood. "It is necessary to recover the primeval force of the shock taking
place at the moment when, opposite a human (a spectator), there stood for the
first time a human (an actor) deceptively similar to us, yet at the same time infinitely foreign, beyond the impassable barrier." Neither the world of the Old
People nor the world of children

can really adapt to the accepted, dominant condition, the officially-sanctioned
reality and its pragmatism.
Both are on the margins, like human reserves.
Both touch upon the condition of nothingness and death. (*"The Dead Class"*)

As Beckett put it, "Birth was the death of him."[34]

The Dead Class (1975). Photo
courtesy of Romano Martinis.

The Old People in *The Dead Class* continued making faces, but, this time, directed at each other, rather than the audience. A perverse battle of fists and kicking ensued, during which the Old People were sucked into the black hole at the rear of the set. Only the carcasses of the wax figures of children in the school desks remained. Silence. A dead class—a strange association with a cemetery. A solemn silence. Kantor walked around the school desks and corrected the postures of the wax figures of children. A figure in a black dress, frozen until now, began to perform her everyday duties, rearranging and introducing order into the world of the classroom—sweeping the floor, placing the wax figures in the school desks, arranging dried-out, moldy books into impossible piles on the front desk, and so on. She was the Cleaning Woman, whose silent presence evoked the figure of Death. "Finished, it's finished, nearly finished, it must be nearly finished. Grain upon grain, one by one."[35] She had almost accomplished the task of organizing the books into a perfectly ordered pile. When she pulled out one page sticking out in the bottom layer, the pile collapsed and, with it, her desire to continue the process. She took a newspaper from Pedel, the custodian, yet another figure, who had sat frozen, in the Dead Classroom. She read the news and advertisements from an old newspaper. "The Archduke Ferdinand was assassinated . . . Wilhelm II has announced a general mobilization in the German Empire." "There will be war," she commented. Animated by the possibility of war, Pedel, an old war veteran declared, once again, his nationalistic sympathies by singing the Austro-Hungarian anthem, after which he slowly disappeared backstage. Kantor and the Cleaning Woman–Death remained. A moment of silence. The silence was broken by the voices of the Old People, repeating memorized phrases from a history lesson. The Cleaning Woman–Death began to scrub the floor as the voices filled the space. She "looks around as if trying to find the source from which these voices, sighs, and complaints are coming. She looks at the school desks and the frozen figures of the dead children. She collects her brooms and runs away."[36]

III

The Old People returned, but they were not the same Old People who had left the Dead Class, though, physically, they looked the same. Now, the Old People, who were still wearing black, funeral suits, spoke the words that no longer belonged to the environment of the Dead Class. As Kantor noted, from this moment on, the reality of the Dead Class was altered by the reality of Witkacy's play *Tumor Brainowicz*. But the play was not to be staged in its entirety with the help of the Old People turned actors. The Old People spoke the lines of the characters from the play not as complete sequences but as a futurist nonrepresentational dialogue—incomplete and illogical, nondevelopmental and nonillustrative, a staccato sentence-aria running through the heads of the Old People, a verbal hallucination out of joint with logic.

Witkacy's play presents a mathematical genius, Tumor, who falls in love with his demonic stepdaughter, Iza, and creates a revolutionary new system of mathematics based on transfinite numbers. A professor, Alfred Green, from the Mathematical Central and General Office in London, kidnaps Iza, hoping this will stop Tumor's creative process and prevent the undermining of the basis of civilization. Tumor follows Iza to the Island of Timor, in the Malay Archipelago where she has been imprisoned. He assassinates the island's chieftain and becomes the King and God of the volcano. Tumor returns to civilization only to drop dead from overcreativity. His life's work and his new lover are stolen from him by Lord Persville, who appears at the end of the play to usurp power.[37]

In *The Dead Class*, Kantor wanted to:

> create the impression that the OLD PEOPLE, characters from the "Dead Class," defined clearly and unequivocally by their past and destiny, were as if "programmed" by the content of *Tumor Brainowicz*. This might have happened by accident, or maybe it was Fate which wanted to make the end of their lives a little bit more exciting. It is possible that this maneuver (a kind of transplant) could have been made successfully and that, under favorable circumstances, all the stage action and the events in the play could have been faithfully and logically repeated—thus represented.
>
> But this would have been a simulacrum bereft of any reality; it would have been nothing more than a stylistic gesture—an improvisation of sorts or just a "dressing-up."
> More important, this would have been against my ideas of theatre.
>
> We have to agree that the reality of the classroom—which is concrete and not ephemeral or illusionary (a playtext)—by absorbing the imaginary, fictitious content and sphere of the play, must, to say it carefully, be altered.
> Of course it is the question of degree.
> One must proceed very carefully (a necessary action even in the most radical transformations), conscious of the hierarchy among the objects: the reality of the classroom is the primary matter, an autonomous reality.
>
> I would like to emphasize the unusual nature of the maneuver which we will be engaged in during the rehearsal process. This must be described with precision, because it is very easy to drift ashore, run aground, go to extremes, and destroy a thin layer of humor and relativism, perversion, disdain and mystification with pedantry and literalness.
> It is those features only that can save us from false seriousness and logic.
> This maneuver is unusual because the rehearsals are not a part of putting a production together. At no stage in the process, is one given the impression that there will ever be an opening night.
> The rehearsal process is a battlefield where two indifferent realities will clash, have a fight whose rules and regulations will make it impossible for either of the two sides to be victorious. ("*The Dead Class*")

These two realities, the autonomous, free, real memory of the Dead Class and the fictitious world of Witkacy's play, encountered each other in the space of *The Dead Class*. Until the end, "the reality of the 'Dead Class' constantly slips into the sphere of the play and vice versa."

The bodies of the characters from the Dead Class were as if invaded by "foreign" entities who would speak through them. The Old Man in the WC was invaded by Tumor Brainowicz; the Old Man with a Bicycle by Józef, Tumor's father; the Woman with a Mechanical Cradle by Gamboline Basilius, Tumor's Wife; the Somnambulistic Whore by Iza, Tumor's stepdaughter; and, finally, the Old Man with his Double and the Double itself by Alfred and Maurice, Tumor's sons. The lines from the play remained recognizable, but, since they were spoken by the Old People, rather than by the fully realized characters from Witkacy's play, they were devoid of any structural logic. They became the ramblings of the Old People who, at that moment, assumed the verbal hallucinatory functions of characters from the play. No longer a playful sequence from a lesson about King Solomon or the making of faces, playing the play was a cruel game without a stable set of rules. Two Old Men dragged the Old Man in the WC to the ever-present outhouse, a banal and crude reality of the lowest rank, and he was kept there by force, shouting out his words and opinions while sitting on the toilet. Suddenly, as if in an attack of epilepsy, the Old Man in the WC was invaded by the alien, ghostly force, who began to speak through him. This foreign ghost, this dybbuk, was Tumor Brainowicz, who screamed,

> . . . banging away full steam ahead . . .
> grips sinking into grips . . .
> Cursed civilization. . . .
> Who is forcing me to pretend . . .
> It simply makes one sick. . . .
> Vomito Negro.[38]

In Witkacy's work, Tumor Brainowicz opens the play by saying, "I am banging away full steam ahead. Grips coming to grips, grips sinking into grips, and the fiery splutter, stirring up a little dust in a storm beyond the grave. Cursed civilization! (*Bangs his fist on the back of the chair.*) Who is forcing me to pretend? Yesterday I read their entire new program. It simply makes one sick to one's stomach. Vomito Negro."[39]

In itself, Witkacy's opening sequence does not follow the structure of traditional expository dialogue. The audience attending Kantor's *Dead Class* witnessed an even further deconstruction of the substance both of Witkacy's the play and of classical dramaturgy. Hearing the lines spoken by the Man in the WC, they entered the domain where Tumor Brainowicz's scattered thoughts were further scattered, repeated, as if sequences accidentally memorized without full comprehension of their intent, sequences easily abandoned or easily delivered with artificial pathos or euphoria.

The opening sequence drew attention to the tension between the concrete reality of the Dead Class "on the other side" and the fictitious reality of the playtext. "Something is taking its course," but that something was not the desire to establish logical connections or interpretations or to build up scenes through textual references. Rather,

the movement [is] in the opposite direction: d o w n w a r d s into the r e a l m
b e l o w, THE ACCEPTED WAY OF LIFE,
which is possible by elimination,
destruction,
misshaping,
reduction of energy,
cooling;
[the movement] in the direction of e m p t i n e s s,
DEFORMITY,
non-form
is an ILLUSION-CRUSHING process
and the only chance to t o u c h u p o n r e a l i t y! ("The Zero Theatre")

Inserting the ghost of Witkacy's *Tumor Brainowicz* created the possibility of touching upon reality "on the other side," a chance to get close to the thought of theatre materializing from whatever it is not: a theatre thinking itself in the corner, separating itself from the audience with a rope, and teasing it with a gesture toward a medium itself, is being reinvented and rearticulated in front of their eyes.

The characters, who invaded the Old People, played out the relationships between Tumor and his sons and Tumor and his wife. Tumor's father, the Old Man with a Bicycle, continued his parade around the school desks without interruption, while the Old Man with a Double and the Double brought in a Family Machine, a strange contraption resembling a gynecological chair. The Woman with a Mechanical Cradle, Tumor's wife Gamboline, was seated on it. Her legs were strapped to the arms of the chair, which opened and closed while she spoke about her desire to give birth to a baby every month so that the world would be populated by Tumor's brilliant offspring, exact copies of him. Before the exchange between Tumor and Gamboline was completed, the Cleaning Woman–Death entered with a mechanical cradle, which was placed between the legs of the Woman with a Mechanical Cradle-Gamboline. The movement of

The Dead Class (1975). Photo by J. Dalman courtesy of the Cricoteka Archives.

the cradle, inside of which were two wooden balls, coincided with the Woman with a Mechanical Cradle-Gamboline's labor. The rhythmical hollow sound of the two wooden balls in the cradle continued throughout the scene, the sound of passing time, of execution, of approaching death—"Birth was the death of him." The Cleaning Woman–Death reentered the space with a broom over her head that, like a scythe, cut through the air to the hollow sound of the wooden balls. The Old People/characters in the play tried to escape this death by running around the school desks, an image bringing to mind a medieval *danse macabre*, imprinted and seeking its place in our memories.

The Cleaning Woman–Death moved systematically forward, the hollow sound of the balls, like *punctum*, marking her every step. The classroom floor became covered with the bodies of the Old People, dropping right and left by the school desks. When they were all dead, the Cleaning Woman–Death left the stage. Silence. As was often the case in Kantor's theatre, the dead came back to life. First, the Pedophile Old Man, having noticed that the Cleaning Woman–Death had left, got up and repeated Maurice's lines from *Tumor Brainowicz*:

But papa only writes poetry to keep his
mental balance when the numbers have gone clean
thorough all of his pores right into
his soul.
Iza is a true poet.
Iza, recite it.[40]

Iza's poem, published in a futuristic children's magazine in Witkacy's play, was recited by the Somnambulistic Whore-Iza, an exhibitionist par excellence, in Kantor's production. In Witkacy's play, the poem was a cabaret spoof of legitimate, "serious" writing. In *The Dead Class*, the poem explored the language used by children, a language that surveyed relationships on the level of a sentence, as children seek their place on the level of emotions, of unconscious conditions, and of inner experiences as yet bereft of the classificatory schemata imposed upon thought by language. Like these children, the Somnambulistic Whore-Iza failed to find her place in the concrete, everyday reality imposed by language. In her recitation, the poem, a verbal hallucination, was the domain of unsuspected associations, new meanings and, since, she was a member of the Dead Class, of mechanical repetitions, linguistic deformations, and Informel decompositions, punctuated by the haunting sound of the wooden balls in the mechanical cradle:

The discovery of the u n k n o w n side of r e a l i t y:
of its elementary state:
MATTER.
And this is how the c o n q u e s t of this mysterious continent begins.
A feverish exploration of the unknown lands.
A New Epoch.
Human sensitivity absorbs all its
attributes and characteristics

which, until now, have not been noticed,
deemed significant,
viewed as suspicious,
warned against,
perceived as abnormal, as deviations,
and as exaggeration. ("The Litany of the Informel Art")

The Cleaning Woman–Death entered again to complete what she had started but obviously failed to finish. This time, she made sure the Somnambulistic Whore-Iza was dead:

> The game is over: not only the absurd imitation of family life, the out-of-hand behavior of the poorly-behaving school children, but also the "Grand Cleaning" of the CLEANING WOMAN. . . .
> The pupils return to their desks.
> As if nothing has happened, they assume proper sitting postures. "As if nothing has happened" . . . this is an excellent way of making sure that any ILLUSION that is being created without our consent,
> is brought down to the "zero condition" of expression.[41]

The "zero condition" of expression signified the process of reaching the matter or the reality—the return to the silence at the eye of the storm. All details and all illusions had been erased, as the scribblings are erased on a blackboard before the next lesson begins. And, indeed, the next lesson was just about to begin.

The reality of the Dead Class returned. The Old People lost all the traits of Witkacy's characters and reincorporated themselves into the school desks— their memory machine. Do they live on in our memory of them or in the memory generated by folding the Old People into the tumors of their childhood? "If you look long enough and hard enough you will really see." The Old Man with a Bicycle, as in previous Dead Class sequences, again assumed the role of the teacher. The lesson, this lesson, was about Prometheus. As before, one of the Old People, this time the Old Man who is Deaf, was singled out to provide a series of answers to impossible questions. His awakening into the nightmare of the lesson was accompanied by a parody, courtesy of the other Old People/circus performers in the classroom. The subject-matter shifted from the length of Cleopatra's nose to Achilles' foot, Adam's rib, and so on. This sequence, which erased the fictitious text of Witkacy's play, replaced it with an absurd memoryscape so filled with the strange, funny, humorous, or incongruous behaviors of the Old People that one's eyes filled with the tears—tears of joy and tears of pain—because "there is no cure for 'that.'" The Dead Class's answers came as a litany-aria, for example, in the declension of "a camel," which turned into a howl, a prayer, a sorrowful song, and a soulful complaint. These were no longer Old People inhabiting the tumors of their playful childhoods. These were Old People facing an open grave, trying to hold onto the minutest shreds of life to stop this *danse macabre*.

The Old Man playing the part of the teacher brought everyone back to the lesson, the moment revealing the wound "on the other side" of the word "defunctus." The declension of "a finger" turned into yet another howl, as if nothing could stop the litany of sounds exposing aporia. The music of the waltz was heard: "If only once again the past could return." The Old People rose up from their school desks—a human wall standing at the verge of an open grave—their hands extended as if making a toast, as if celebrating the return of the past. The waltz ended. The Old People collapsed onto their desks. The escape through space-time-music, the toast to the past, was discharged, finished (*defunctus*).

Suddenly, the fictitious reality of Witkacy's play invaded the classroom. When this happened, it was impossible, however, to reestablish the continuity with the text of the play. The lines spoken by the characters from *Tumor Brainowicz* referred to an action in a different reality—an action that must have taken place outside of this performance space. Similarly, it was impossible to reestablish the continuity of the play's characters, since something must have happened to them while the audience was watching the events unfolding in the Dead Class. Thus, when the "characters" returned to the bodies of the Old People, the audience found themselves in act 1 of Witkacy's play, in the midst of a family quarrel interrupted by the entrance of Alfred Green. He came to arrest Iza, who was charged with being responsible for Brainowicz's attempt to abolish the mathematical status quo. What was shown in Kantor's production were shreds of dialogue from this scene spoken by the Old People. The Old Man with His Double left for the outhouse; he reemerged transformed into the Unknown Man, the articulator of official speech, known to all people living under dictatorships. The Old Man with His Double, empowered by his own language, became the dictator of the absurd universe that had invaded the space of the Dead Class. The nightmare of history unsettled the Dead Class. The Woman behind the Window, playing Balantine from Witkacy's play, tried to send the children off so they would not watch Iza being arrested. The Old People put on their backpacks and prepare to leave, when the speech of the Woman behind the Window turned from a gentle invitation to a walk on a glorious day into a nightmarish invocation of death. The walk became a baton march, and soon the exhausted Old People fell down. This new *danse macabre* around the school desks took place to the tune of the old waltz—"If only once again the past could return"—then silence.

The silence that kept out the void, demonstrated by the Old People, became the theme of the next sequence. Some fatal news was shared in silence, a violence of thought unmitigated by the sound of the waltz or by the recalled word- or sentence-arias from past lessons that, like a ritornello, were supposed to bring solace. One by one, the Old People disappeared into the black hole, but the sequence lasted much longer for the Cleaning Woman–Death. She approached the school desks and, to the rhythm of the two balls rocking in the cradle, started to pull the remaining Old People out of their school desks. The Old Man with His Double was pushed out. When the Cleaning Woman–Death returned, she saw the Double, whom she took for the Old Man with his Double, and furiously pulled him away. Upon her return, she noticed the Old Man with His Double, who had secretly returned. Her anger increased with each consecutive action. The Old Man and His Double and the Double tricked the Cleaning Woman–Death several times, playing with Death, as if it were a hallucinatory ripple across the void. This playing with death drew attention to the possibility that if the dead live in our memory of them, this very sequence, where the Old Man and His Double and the Double managed to trick the Cleaning Woman–Death, proved unequivocally that memory loses its solemn character and contours through repetition. Such is the unsettling substance of the Dead Class.

The memory of the dead returned with the Old People, who emerged from the black hole of the grave into which they had disappeared a moment ago. They came back holding white handkerchiefs. They approached the school desks slowly and with solemnity as if following a funeral cortege. "The school desks become Charon's boat moving along the River Styx toward 'the other side.'"[42] The solemnity was ruptured by their recollections of the dead, a mixture of pathos and humor. These recollections, accompanied by the hollow sound of the two balls in the cradle, were parts of sublime mnemotechnics that, as in the gravediggers' scene in *Hamlet*, lacked any trace of nostalgia for the absent. Instead, the banal statements, everyday gossip, and ruthless comments of the Dead Class defined what was unrepresentable and refused death the consolation of forms and of taste creating a common experience of nostalgia for the impossible. The comments of the Old People could not provide a reality, true or representational, about death, but could allude to what was conceivable in the condition of death:

If we agree that a trait of
living people
is their ease and ability
with which they enter into mutual and manifold
life relationships,
it is only
in the presence of the dead
that there is born in us a sudden and startling
realization of the fact that
this basic trait of the living
is brought forth and made possible by
a complete
lack of difference
between them;
by their
indistinguishability,
by their universal sameness,
mercilessly abolishing all other and opposing delusions,
which is common,
consistent,
all-binding.
Only then when they are dead
that they become
noticeable (to the living);

The Dead Class (1975). Photo
by J. Dalman courtesy of the
Cricoteka Archives.

The Dead Class (1975). Photo
by J. Dalman courtesy of the
Cricoteka Archives.

having paid the highest price,
they gain
their individuality,
distinction,
their IMAGE. ("The Theatre of Death")

The dead became visible in the process of naming them; thus, the names of
the "dead" were read, one by one, by the Old People standing at their school
desks. There were many names, recited in the monotone of an infinite emptiness, measured by the hollow sound of the wooden balls in the cradle:

PELAGIA SITO
BASIA WYPOREK
JÓZEF WRONA
MARCIN POKORNY
SZCZEPAN PALUCH, etc.[43]

As the third name was recited, a Solider from World War I entered with
a pile of death announcements for Józef Wgrzdągiel—a name sounding like a
word in one of the Dead Classes phonetic lessons. The announcements were distributed among the Old People and spread around the floor of the classroom.
As the Old People reached the end of the list and slowly sat down, the naming
turned into a lament. Not for long. The lament was cut short by the Old Man
in the WC, who brought back the fictitious reality of act 2 of Witkacy's play.

IV

From this moment, a total and complete DEBAUCHERY takes over—
the pieces of clothing are stripped off from the bodies—similar to the disrobing
of the dead bodies; a blasphemous robbery of the dead; a shameless practice of
necrophiliacs; an illicit procedures of exhumation of bodies;

from the cemetery to the orgy,
from the grave to the brothel,
"FOREFATHER'S EVE"—a night of touching the dead and death
followed by some kind of ghoulish secretion.
The OLD PEOPLE as if taken down from the catafalques,
exposed to the public view,
Death . . . a cheap shot . . . ersatz . . . shame . . . a rotten smell of the graves . . .
naked bodies . . . not bodies, but their individual parts; individual, shameless, and
in-your-face parts, which are separated and ostentatiously out in the open—
thighs . . . buttocks . . . calves . . . feet . . . breasts . . . groins . . . penises . . .
stomachs . . . underbellies . . .

putrefaction and sex . . . faces painfully serious . . . the eyes attentively following
those ceremonies of nothingness, these celebrations and laborious, pedantic, and
meticulous practices leading NOWHERE, happening here in the ruins of the
school days, among the piles of molding books, at the heap of scattered death
announcements. (*"The Dead Class"*)

With the ruins of their lives in back of them, now the memories of the Old
People were replaced by the events unfolding on the Island of Timor, where
Iza and Tumor Brainowicz found themselves. A decadent and perverse dialogue dominated the current moment. The shreds of Witkacy's fictitious action
ensued—Tumor kills the King of the Island, Patakulo Senior; Patakulo Junior
seduces Iza (yet another phonetic aria or hallucination); Green arrives on the
battleship Prince Arthur. The innocuous unfolding of the dramatic action was
interrupted by the appearance of the Soldier from World War I, the same soldier
who had arrived in the Nocturnal Lesson, out of the forgotten nooks of memory and the real trenches of World War I. His arrival now not only exposed the
fictitious character of the play but also revealed yet another, this time different,
historical narrative about the banality of evil and of war. The soldier, wearing a
tattered overcoat, bandages on his head, advanced to attack. Maybe this is his
time, his minute of glory and fame, his victory and parade, but the moment was
filled with an infinite emptiness:

Hip, hip, hurrah!
We are taking possession
of this country![44]

The Old People/characters in Witkacy's play gathered for a commemorative photograph. Like old photographs whose corners were blunted from having been pasted into an album, the sepia print of history had faded and the picture, working backward through life, revealed an emballage of the dead. The
sound of the waltz was heard—"If only once again the past could return"—but
it could not revive them. The Man with a Bicycle, now the Photographer, took
three shots with his *camera lucida*, the flash powder a reminder that the photograph of an event could only fill the sight with violence through force. The
camera lucida, like many props in Kantor's theatre, beleaguered material body

as well as the imagination as the Old People hid in panic behind their school desks at the flashes of the camera.

Slowly everything seemed to return to normal. The Woman with a Mechanical Cradle–Gamboline, wearing a tattered nightdress, approached the cradle as in a nightmare. She put it in motion. The hollow sound of the balls—the sound of death—filled the space. She, a madwoman, bent over the dead cradle. The Old People ran around the desks, throwing different objects and spitting at her, ritually excluding her from their group or their society. Bent over the cradle, the Woman with a Mechanical Cradle–Gamboline began to sing a Yiddish lullaby to the hollow sound of the wooden balls.

The image evokes concentration camps, transgressing the boundaries both of the Dead Class and Witkacy's play to fill the sonorous space with the possibility that human life was a fatality—a condition that proclaims that men and women were "unwanted intruders on creation . . . destined to undergo unmerited, incomprehensible, arbitrary suffering and defeat." The sin of having been born had acquired a tangible enactment in which, indeed, human presence and identity are crimes.[45] How can one endure the memory of these events, the bloody memory of humans unhoused in being, fallen into the nonplace, the missing articulation, since because there are no speakable words for what is ontologically undesired?

The momentary transgression ended, and the Old People found themselves in Witkacy's last act. In the play, this is the act where all unresolved conflicts need to find a solution, no matter that they cannot be resolved with any adherence to verisimilitude or psychology. In Witkacy's play, the unfolding quarrels and events take place within the four walls of a bourgeois environment. In *The Dead Class*—the space of molding and tattered books, the memories of History, and school lessons—everything happened as if time had accelerated or become compressed. The exchanges between the characters from Witkacy's play were reduced by the Old People/characters to mock-ups of "real" theatrical dialogues about doubts, complaints, and marital quarrels. The very nature of these exchanges implied that, through repetition, they would acquire identity and singular presence, that they would structure their belonging and emotions. But "identity freezes the gesture of thinking," Michel Foucault reminds us. Whereas "to think means to pass through."[46]

Kantor assigned the Cleaning Woman–Death the responsibility of washing away that stabilizing procedure from the bodies of the Old People:

> In their childhood, THE CLASSROOM and THE SCHOOL DESKS brought them [the Old People] together. Then, they all went their separate and individual ways. And now, when they come back for their last performance at the end of their lives, they have nothing in common,
> they are STRANGERS to each other.
> The tiny bodies of children—their childhood—which they carry with them, the only thing that could awaken their memories . . . are lifeless. They, too, are almost dead, touched by death; by a deadly malaise. For the price of being STRANGERS to each other and of DEATH, they win a chance of being art OBJECTS.

This very feeling of ESTRANGEMENT, which brings them closer to the condition of the object, eradicates their biological, organic, and naturalistic live-ness, which has no meaning in art.

They become the elements of the work for having "sacrificed" it.

For having "sacrificed" [live-ness], they became the elements of the work of art.

THE PERFORMANCE gave them their lives.

However, during the performance, new relationships, differences and attachments were created among them.

There began to emerge, like nebulous specters, new figures to be formed by this new life, whose shape and not always noble character are well-known to them.

Slowly, everything started to find its justification in the logic of the unfolding plot, life's cause-and-effect patterns; to leave that place where a perfect, absolute, autonomous and self-contained work of art was to be made—that place, where a godless and lawless creation, rather than god-like reproduction of nature, was to be made.

It is imperative that they be turned into STRANGERS again. It is necessary to take away from them those appearances of normality rationalized by a plot and life itself. It is necessary to expose them to the effects of shame. To strip them bare. To make them all equal as if for the Last Judgment. Worse than that. To bring them to the most discreditable and shameful condition—that of a dead corpse in a mortuary.

It is only THE CLEANING WOMAN–DEATH who can perform this ruthless, but indispensable, maneuver.

THE CLEANING WOMAN performs her duties professionally and ruthlessly. She enters the stage with a bucket of water and a dirty rag. She washes the corpses, wrings the rag; dirty water drops onto the ground.

Stripping the bodies bare, washing their intimate parts, thighs, stomachs, buttocks, feet, faces, fingers; cleaning their noses, ears, groins; a vicious and unceremonious throwing and turning of the bodies.

A continuous and rhythmic rattle of the wooden balls in a cradle.

A poorly-made CRADLE, looking like a tiny coffin, tilts monotonously back and forth; the mechanical movement of the gears of this grim box is completely bereft of tender motherly care; the sounds of a baby are replaced with the rattle of two wooden balls, hitting the walls of the coffin.

A mortuary.

THE CLEANING WOMAN performs the ritual of scrubbing the corpses with appalling disinterest, with precision, and systematically. (*"The Dead Class"*)

While she engaged in a systematic process of scrubbing the bodies of the Old People, the events of Witkacy's played at an accelerated pace. At the end of her marital quarrel with the Old Man in the WC-Tumor, the Woman with a Mechanical Cradle-Gamboline threw the baby out of the window. The two wooden balls were taken out of the cradle and passed from the Old Man in the WC-Tumor to the Old Man with a Bicycle-Józef. The Old Man with a Bicycle-Józef looked into the cradle, as into an open grave, then deposited the balls there.

The Old Man with a Bicycle-Józef returned to the place where he had left his bicycle and began his last journey: "From this moment on, he will endlessly be leaving and saying good-bye,"[47] while the waltz was heard over and over again. The other Old People/characters in the play also endlessly repeated different gestures. The Deaf Old Man announced, and kept repeating, the dire news that Tumor Brainowicz fell victim to his own weakness. The Old Man in WC/Tumor repeated the act of killing the king Patakulo of the Island of Timor. Pedel, the custodian, sang faithfully the Austro-Hungarian anthem, and the Soldier from World War I repeated the act of falling down in front of the Woman with a Mechanical Cradle/Gamboline "as if mortally wounded and [cried] out, while raising a banner in the well-known gesture of the soldiers who had died in the battle of Verdun,"[48] an offer to make the Woman with a Mechanical Cradle-Gamboline the fifth marquise of Nevermoore. The other Old People sat at their school desks and repeated the words to a children's nursery rhyme.

Kantor's theatre of automata was accompanied by the sound of the waltz and the hollow sound of two balls. Every so often, Kantor would raise his hand and the actions would briefly cease while he approached one of the performers and corrected a detail. Upon his sign, the theatre of the automata would resume. After a few repetitions, Kantor would stop the action once again, approach another performer, adjust a detail, and, upon a sign given by him, the theatre of the automata would resume again. The endgame. . . . "Old stancher. You . . . remain."[49]

V

Though Kantor had experimented with parallel actions or spaces as early as the 1961 production of *The Country House*, the parallel actions or spaces used in *The Dead Class* modified his earlier concept:

> When I started to work [on *The Dead Class*], I felt that I was losing my fascination with the method of parallel actions and that I would have to go beyond it. The materials gathered for the production were becoming more substantial . . . the atmosphere of the classroom, attempts to bring back memories, childhood, victories and defeats, more and more clearly defined the idea of the theatre of death, new territories and horizons . . . all of this pointed to the possibility of creating an autonomous production without the need to fall back on drama. . . . I return[ed] to the idea of parallel action. This time, however, its meaning is different. This time, I made use of Witkiewicz's *Tumor Brainowicz*, a creation of pure imagination which, as in Witkiewicz, was grounded in the sphere of our lives. My fondness for literature returned again. This will explain why the conflicts and doubts, at one moment, lean towards drama and, at another moment, towards theatre. *The Dead Class* emerges at the threshold of these indecisions. The characters from *Tumor Brainowicz*, who enter the stage and the classroom, bring with them their fate and destiny. Since they contain in themselves the content of the play, the real action of the "Dead Class" is freed from the play's potent thought. They merge with the figures from the classroom, who also exist at the borderline between life and death. All hell breaks loose. We enter the world of dreams and nightmares. The characters from *Tumor Brainowicz* leave the stage. They disappear. The reality of the classroom begins to exist in its own

environment. After some time they return, but different, as if changed by events about which the audience knows nothing and which must have happened behind the doors. They return in a different moment of the plot.[50]

Kantor's desire to transgress the intellectual and structural boundaries of his productions led to the creation of a new type of performance space. The placement of the action of *The Dead Class* "on the side," in the corner of a room divided into two parts (the world of the living and the world of the dead), allowed Kantor both to focus on the interplay between a dramatic text and those aspects of memory that are usually pushed aside, delegitimized, appropriated, or discredited by adulthood and to destabilize the traditional site for performance.

It was a site beyond the gaze of the spectator. More than that, Kantor placed his actors—his "WAX FIGURES—infinitely DISTANT, shockingly FOREIGN, as if DEAD," in school desks in a corner away from the attention given to the action commanded by actions taking place in the middle of a room. The actors "on the other side" were motionless, like mannequins standing in the corner of a shop window, or like the dead, until the audience members took their seats. Then, the Old People, "individuals built out of various parts, that is, remnants of their childhood, the events of their past lives (not always glorious), their hopes and passions," began to constitute and reconstitute themselves "in this theatrical element, pushing them in the direction of their finite form, which would imprint all their happiness and pain on their masks of death."[51] The actions that ensued created a collage of nocturnal memories of school days, attended lessons, and historical events that, like mirages, appear and disappear in the space of the classroom.

Unlike in his other productions, the audience and the actors of *The Dead Class* did not share the performance space. They were physically separated, as if by an impassable one-way mirror. The audience could see through it and perceive the physical action onstage, which, in turn, engendered their thought processes and cognizance (which, perhaps, explains the fascination the multilingual audiences have had with *The Dead Class*). The Old People, on the other hand, found themselves in a totally different space. The parallel action in the acting space, that is, the memories of school days and the reality of The Dead Class, altered the network of relations on their side of the mirror. The Old People, headed toward death (as Kantor explicitly observes in the notes to the production), encountered a threshold in their space. Since they could not cross it, they could only turn back upon themselves, to give birth to their own image—wax figures of children—in a limitless play of mirrors: "I see myself seeing myself seeing myself," *ad infinitum* in this theatre of reflections and automata:

> the world of the childhood and the world of the old people.
> Neither of them can really adapt to the accepted, dominant condition, the officially-sanctioned reality and its pragmatism.
> Both are on the margins, like human reserves.
> Both touch upon the condition of nothingness and death.

The return of the OLD PEOPLE—at the threshold of death—to the classroom. Birth and death—two extremes which explain each other. (*"The Dead Class"*)

An entirely new set of self-representations was produced in this interplay of mirrors, where the Old People, in their attempts to escape death, found themselves where they had started (their childhood). These self-representations took the form of a new spoken language (the phonetic exercises), a process for constituting and reconstituting historical events (the assassination of Franz Ferdinand in Sarajevo, the announcement of World War I), a method for probing into the concept of how and by whom history has been written (memories of history lessons about Solomon, King David, Cleopatra, Hannibal, Julius Caesar, and Polish and world history), a way to bring to life the forgotten or annihilated history of Galicean Jews, and a way to celebrate traditions (the ceremony of the Polish Forefather's Eve).

The space, in which this interplay repeated and redoubled itself endlessly, was saved from being imprisoned in its own enchanted simulation by "a creation of pure imagination," that is, by the characters from Witkacy's play. Their "fate and destiny" counterbalanced the events in *The Dead Class* by merging the figures from the classroom and the characters from the play. This merger, unlike similar mergers—in *The Water-Hen*, for example—was temporary. The characters from the play would leave and reenter the bodies of the Old People, and the Old People would not be the same, "as if changed by the events . . . which must have happened behind the doors."[52] In a way, the characters from Witkiewicz's play entered from a different dimension, unknown to the Old People. It could be located by a textual reference to the world of Witkacy's play, but that unknown dimension could never fully be classified in the reality of *The Dead Class*. The Old People and the characters in Witkacy's play participated in a reconstruction of the past or history as well as in the world of the play. This process was not a nostalgic reconstruction that would provide spectators "on the other side" with material for consolation and pleasure, but it occasioned an interplay between the Self, memories of school days, historical events, and the staged "Other," repeated over and over again until they disintegrated. The disintegration and disappearance of the fetishized world of appearances was accelerated by the rhythm of birth and collapse triggered by the school desks— the memory machine.

If history and memory produce the murmurs that keep the void out, the void in *The Dead Class* was the void (death) itself. In his "Theatre of Death" manifesto, Kantor articulated his desire to abandon a theatre grounded in physical reality for a theatre that embraced an instant double of the Self—the Other, or the Unthought—a new subject constituted by the mental gaze of the Self. This process needed a "different universe" that would allow the Self to travel through the unremembered space of the past. Being of it, but not in it, provided a unique opportunity to enter this space in order to resingularize it:

It was 1971 or 1972. The seaside. A small village. One street. Small, poor, one-story houses. And one, possibly the poorest of them all: a school building. It was summer. The school was empty and deserted. There was only one classroom in it.

It was possible to peek into it through dirty, dust-covered windows placed very low. They gave the impression that the school had sunk into the ground. My face was glued to the window. For a long time, I peeked into the dark interior of my muddled memory.

Again, I was a little schoolboy in a poor country school; I was sitting at the desk, covered with the graffiti that had been carved into it with a knife, and turning the pages of a book, my fingers covered with ink. The floorboards were deformed by continuous scrubbing; the bare feet of the country boys somehow complemented this floor in a strange way. Whitewashed walls, plaster falling off at the floor level; a black cross on the wall.

Today I know that something important happened at that WINDOW. I made an important discovery. With an incredible clarity, I became aware of the EXISTENCE OF
MEMORY. . . .

Tadeusz Kantor's model/ installation to *The Dead Class*—"A Classroom—A Closed Work of Art" (1983). Photo by Michal Kobialka courtesy of the Kantor Estate.

Suddenly, I discovered its mysterious and inexplicable power. I discovered that it
was a thing that could destroy and create; that it was present at the very moment
of the creative act; at the gates of a work of art. . . .
MEMORY LIVES ON AN EQUAL FOOTING WITH THE REAL EVENTS OF
OUR EVERYDAY LIVES. . . .
MEMORY QUESTIONS
the COMPETENCE
of the OCULAR;
it casts doubt on its arrant power. . . .
Memory lives beyond the reach of our gaze; it is born and grows in the regions of
our feelings and affects.
And tears.[53]

It was not enough for Kantor to bring memory back to the present mo-
ment and make it visible through art. He needed to separate it from the audience with a rope so that the process of exploration became the process of
recovering from the shock "TAKING PLACE AT THE MOMENT WHEN,
OPPOSITE A HUMAN (A SPECTATOR), THERE STOOD FOR THE FIRST
TIME A HUMAN (AN ACTOR), DECEPTIVELY SIMILAR TO US, YET AT
THE SAME TIME INFINITELY FOREIGN, BEYOND THE IMPASSABLE
BARRIER."[54]
Kantor faced the window or mirror of memory—the school desks, the people sitting in them, and the frozen figures of the Cleaning Woman–Death and
the Custodian, the fidgeting semblances of remote memories. It is a mode of
thinking that begins with something existing outside, but then it surpasses the
dialectics of the visible by folding back upon itself in order to explore its own
mode of effectivity and action. Kantor's solitary figure activated the mirror,
turning a flat, fetishized memory into a multidimensional spatial fold on "the
other side." In the performance space, where linear time ceases to function,
this fold perpetually breaks up, curves, and forms itself anew, like "a thought
which . . . curves over upon itself, illuminates its own plenitude, brings its circle
to completion, recognizes itself in all the strange figures of its odyssey, and accepts its disappearance into that same ocean from which it sprang."[55]

A Classroom
(1971 or 1972)

It was 1971 or 1972. The seaside. A small village. One street. Small, poor one-story houses. And one, possibly the poorest of them all: a school building. It was summer. The school was empty and deserted. There was only one classroom in it. It was possible to peek into it through dirty, dust-covered windows placed very low. They gave the impression that the school had sunk into the ground. My face was glued to the window. For a long time, I peeked into the dark interior of my muddled memory.

Again, I was a little schoolboy in a poor country school; I was sitting at the desk, which was covered with the graffiti that had been carved into it with a knife, and turning the pages of a book, my fingers covered with ink. The floorboards were deformed by continuous scrubbing; the bare feet of the country boys somehow complemented this floor in a strange way. Whitewashed walls, plaster falling off at the floor level; a black cross on the wall.

Today I know that something important happened at that WINDOW. I made an important discovery. With an incredible clarity, I became aware of the EXISTENCE OF
MEMORY.

This statement is not, as it may seem to be, colored by exaltation or exaggeration.
In our rational universe, memory, or recollection of the past, has never been given prominence; has never really mattered in cold-blooded dealings with reality.

Suddenly, I discovered its mysterious and inexplicable power. I discovered that it was a thing that could destroy and create; that it was present at the very moment of the creative act; at the gates of a work of art.
Suddenly, everything became clear, as if many doors, leading to remote, infinite space and landscapes, had just been opened.

It was no longer a shameful and sentimental lyrical metaphor, which is attached to the old aged or exalted teenagers.

It came into being in its bitter ephemerality; in its pain of disappearance
and in its sweetness which is born in longing.

Many things became clear.
MEMORY LIVES ON AN EQUAL FOOTING WITH THE REAL
EVENTS OF OUR EVERYDAY LIVES.
It does not separate itself from them; on the contrary, they are necessary
in its strategic planning
and maneuvers
on its path of regressing in to the past, which runs unnamed through the
territory of the everyday, where it brilliantly camouflages
the attack which no power will resist.

And one more discovery and realization:
MEMORY QUESTIONS
the COMPETENCE
of the OCULAR;
it casts doubt on its arrant power.
That moment, when I was standing in front of the school window,
was not a moment of glorious victory for memory, because it was the
time, when art in general, quickly and thoughtlessly,
lost its trust in that which was visible/observable.
But associating this act of mistrust with a thing which,
if I dare to say it, was contemptible, suspected of mysticism and banal or
avuncular sentimentality
was
an ACT of an ENORMOUS DEPARTURE from
MY MUCH-LOVED PRACTICES of
risking the burning at the STAKE and the charges of
the HOLY INQUISITION OF REASON.

Memory lives beyond the reach of our gaze; it is born and grows in the
regions of our feelings and affects.
And tears.
One could not have made a worse choice, at the time, when the
indestructible power of the tribunal of reason was the rule of the land.
One was charged not only with a deviation, but also with looking
backward.
[In order to prevail,] one needed the strong character of a heretic.
I felt like one at that time.

That nostalgia, which for some time now was felt more and more;
that REVELATION, caused by that
something mysterious and demanding attention, standing at
the threshold of the VISIBLE;
that discovery of memory
came to me at the right time, because, in this battle against the forces

of the VISIBLE
and the MATERIAL,
in which I had been engaged,
the strongest arguments of SCIENTISM, infinitely alien to me,
have already been rolled out like canons.

To close this chapter of my life,
it was necessary to make
a REVISION
and to RECUPERATE the meaning
of the notion of the PAST.
I did so.
While traveling through the world, I proclaimed,
the TRIUMPH
of the PAST,
I dared to believe that the past was the only real time
which had any consequence
(in art)
because it has already taken place.

Finally, the memorable moment of decision making
did arrive for me—
MEMORY must be enunciated.
It was necessary to understand how
MEMORY
FUNCTIONS.

And this is how there began a ten-year era
of two of my productions
The Dead Class and
Wielopole, Wielopole,
which were to give testimony to
the true nature of my heretical ideas.
It was the era of my own avant-garde.
The avant-garde of:
the recollection of the past,
memory,
the invisible,
emptiness and death.

Death.
And with it, this is where the innocent looking through
the window ends.
The window contains in itself many dark secrets.
The window arouses fear and premonition of that something which is
"beyond" it.
And the missing children. . . .

A feeling that the children have already lived their lives and are dead now;
and it was only because they are DEAD,
and in their death,
this classroom is filled with the memories;
it is only now that the memories can live
and acquire a mysterious spiritual power.
There is nothing bigger or stronger. . . .

Recently, after ten years, during which
The Dead Class toured the world,
I made one more discovery about this fascination
[of looking] "through the window."
Being visible,
as the condition of perception,
this looking at things "from exteriority,"
this arrogant material "tactility,"
pedantic checking out
made me revolt against them
and go across the THRESHOLD OF VISIBILITY,
this imperious and ruthless condition,
this "barrier," this "partition"
this obligatory condition that will secure
the "SEE-ABILITY."

The idea of *The Dead Class* was born in this
condition of half-seeing, shameful incomplete SEEING.
The idea behind the production was grounded in
the seeing (what is "seeing" after all?)
of that which is tightly covered up with
an impregnable shell,
this well-renown form,
which for centuries has claimed the right
to be the content and the essence of the work of art.
It is considered to be completely tactless
not to stop at this "EXTERIORITY"
and try to walk rudely around it
to see in a different way
as if from "INSIDE,"
as if illegally.
This is not easy.
The price, one pays for it is
a MEETING WITH DEATH.

The Theatre of Death
(1975)

1

Craig's postulate: bring back a marionette. Eliminate a live actor.
A human being—nature's creation—is a foreign intrusion into the abstract
structure of a work of art.

According to Gordon Craig, somewhere on the banks of the Ganges River
two women forced their way into the temple of the Divine Marionette,
which was jealously hiding the secrets of the true THEATRE. They envied
this Perfect Being its ROLE of illuminating human minds with the sacred
feeling of the existence of God; its FAME and GLORY; they secretly
watched and copied its Movements and Gestures, its sumptuous dress;
and began to satisfy the vulgar taste of the mob by offering them their
cheap parody. At the moment when they finally ordered that a similar
monument be built for them, the modern theatre, as we know it only
too well today and as it has lasted to this day, was born. A noisy Public
Service Institution. Together with it, there appeared the ACTOR. In
defense of his theory, Craig quotes the opinion of Eleanora Duse, who, as
he claims, said, "To save the theatre, it must be destroyed; it is necessary
that all actors and actresses die of plague . . . for it is they who render art
impossible."

2

Craig's version: A Human being-actor eliminates a marionette, takes its
place, thereby causing the demise of the theatre.

There is something very impressive in the stand taken by this Grand
Utopian when he says, "I demand in all seriousness the return of the
image of a supermarionette to the theatre, . . . and when it appears,
people will again, as was the case in the past, be able to worship the
happiness of Existence, and render DEATH its due divine and euphoric
homage." Craig, following the Symbolist aesthetics, considered a human
being, driven by unpredictable emotions, passion, and, consequently,
by coincidence, as an element which is completely foreign to the

homogeneous nature and structure of a work of art and which destroys its principal trait: cohesion.

Not only Craig's idea but also the well-developed program of Symbolism, impressive in its own time and its own way, had, in the nineteenth century, the support of isolated and unique phenomena heralding a new era and new art: Heinrich von Kleist, Ernst Theodor Amadeus Hoffman, Edgar Allan Poe. . . . One hundred years earlier, Kleist, for the same reasons as Craig, demanded that a marionette be substituted for an actor, regarded the human organism, which was subject to the laws of NATURE, as a foreign intrusion into Artistic Fiction built according to the principles of Construction and Intellect. He added to this his indictment of the limited physical capabilities of a human being and the charges against consciousness, incessantly controlling and excluding the concepts of refinement and beauty.

3

From the romantic mysticism of mannequins and the artificial creation of a human being in the nineteenth century to the rationalism of abstraction in the twentieth century.

On what seemed to be a safe road traveled by the man of the Enlightenment and Rationalism there appeared out of darkness, suddenly and in increasingly greater number, DOUBLES, MANNEQUINS, AUTOMATONS, HOMUNCULI. Artificial creations, mocking NATURE's creations, bearers of absolute degradation, ALL human dreams, DEATH, Horror and Terror. A faith is born in the unknown powers of MECHANICAL MOVEMENT, a maniacal passion for the invention of a MECHANISM surpassing in perfection and ruthlessness the human organism susceptible to all its weaknesses.

All of this is veiled in the mist of demonism, on the brink of charlatanism, illegal practices, white magic, crime, and nightmares.

This was the SCIENCE FICION of those days, in which the demonic human brain created an ARTIFICAL MAN.

All of this together signified both an abrupt loss of faith in NATURE and in that realm of human activity which was closely connected with nature. Paradoxically, from these extreme romantic and diabolical efforts to take away nature's right of creation there evolved more and more independent from and more and more dangerously distant from NATURE a RATIONALISTIC, and even MATERIALISTIC MOVEMENT of an "OBJECTLESS WORLD," CONSTRUCTIVISM, FUNCTIONALISM, MACHINISM, ABSTRACTION, and finally, PURIST VISUALISM, recognizing only the "physical presence" of a work of art.

This risky hypothesis, whose provenance is none too attractive for the age of technology and science, I take on my conscience and for my personal satisfaction.

4

Dadaism, introducing "ready-made reality," elements of life, destroys the concept of homogeneity and cohesion in a work of art as postulated by symbolism, Art Nouveau, and Craig.

Let us return to Craig's marionette. Craig's idea of replacing a live actor with a mannequin, an artificial and mechanical creation—for the sake of preserving perfect cohesion in a work of art—is today invalid.
Later experiences of destroying the unity of structure in a work of art, introducing "FOREIGN" elements in collages and assemblages, the acceptance of "ready-made reality," full recognition of CHANCE and COINCIDENCE, the placement of a work of art at the sharp edge between REALITY OF LIFE AND ARTISTIC FICTION, made irrelevant those scruples from the beginning of the twentieth century, from the period of Symbolism and Art Nouveau. The two possible solutions— either autonomous art and intellectual structure or naturalism—ceased to be the ONLY ones.
When the theatre, in its moments of weakness, submitted itself to the laws of the human being's live organism, it automatically and logically agreed to follow the laws of imitation of life, its representation and recreation. Under different circumstances, when the theatre was strong and autonomous enough to free itself from the pressure of life and human beings, it created artificial equivalents to life, which turned out to be more alive because they submitted easily to abstraction of time and space and were capable of achieving absolute unity.
Today both of these possibilities have lost their right to exist and their validity as viable alternatives. This is due to the fact that there emerged new situations and new conditions in art. The concept of the "READY-MADE REALITY," wrenched away from life—and the possibility of ANNEXING it, INTEGRATING it into a work of art through DECISION, GESTURE, or RITUAL—has replaced a fascination with (artificially) CONSTRUCTED reality, ABSTRACTION, and a surrealist world, Bréton's "MARVEILLEUX." The Happenings, Events, and Environments with their colossal impetus have achieved the rehabilitation of whole regions of REALITY, disdained until this time, cleansing it of the ballast of life's intentions.
This "DÉCALAGE" of life's reality, its derailment from the tracks of life's practices, moved the human imagination more strongly than the surrealistic reality of dreams. As a result, fears of direct intervention by life and by human beings into the realm of art became irrelevant.

5

From the "Ready-Made Reality" of the Happenings to the dematerialization of the elements of a work of art.

But as with all fascination, so, too, this one after a time became a
convention practiced universally, senselessly and in a vulgar manner.
These almost ritualistic manipulations of Reality, connected with the
contestation of the ARTISTIC CONDITION and the PLACE reserved
for art, gradually started to acquire a different sense and meaning. The
material, physical PRESENCE of an object and the PRESENT TENSE,
in which the activity and action can only happen, turned out to be too
burdensome, had reached their limit. SURPASSING it meant depriving
these conditions of their material and functional IMPORTANCE, that is,
their ability to COMMUNICATE. Because this is the most recent period,
still open and in flux, the following observations derive from and refer to
my own artistic practice.
The object (*The Chair*, Oslo, 1970) became e m p t y, bereft of
e x p r e s s i o n,
c o n n e c t i o n s, r e f e r e n c e s, characteristics of programmed
c o m m u n i c a t i o n, its "m e s s a g e," directed towards
"n o w h e r e," it changed into an empty f a ç a d e.
Situations and activities were enclosed in their own CIRCUMFERENCE;
ENIGMATIC (The Impossible Theatre, 1973); in my own piece,
Cambriolage, an unlawful and illegal BREAK-IN into the place where
tactile reality was extended into its INVISIBLE REALM. The role of
THOUGHT, memory, and TIME becomes increasingly more visible.

6

The rejection of the orthodoxy of conceptual art and the mass "Official
Avant-garde."

The certitude impressed itself on me more and more strongly, that the
concept of LIFE can be vindicated in art only through the ABSENCE
OF LIFE in its conventional sense (again Craig and the Symbolists!);
this process of DEMATERIALIZATION was found on a path, which
circumvented the whole orthodoxy of linguistics (semantics) and
conceptual art. This was partially due to the colossal stampede which
took place on this already official path and which will be remembered
as the last stage of the DADA and its slogans of TOTAL ART,
EVERYTHING IS ART, ALL ARE ARTISTS, and ART IS IN THE
MIND.
I hate crowds. In 1973, I wrote a draft of a new manifesto, which dealt
with this false situation. This is its beginning:

From the time of Verdun, Cabaret Voltaire, Marcel Duchamp's urinal, when the
"artistic conditions" were drowned out by the roar of Fat Bertha, DECISION
became the only remaining human chance; an act of reliance on something that
was or is unthinkable; it functioned as the first stimulant of a creative act as well
as conditioned and defined art. Lately, thousands of mediocre artists have been
making decisions without scruples or any hesitation whatsoever. We are witnesses

of the banalization and conventionalization of decision. This once dangerous path was transformed into a comfortable freeway with improved safety measures and information. Guides, maps, orientation tables, directional signs, signals, Art Centers, Art Co-operatives guarantee the excellence of the functioning of creativity. We are witnesses of the MASS MOVEMENT of artists-commandos, street fighters, artist-mediators, artists-mailmen, epistologs, peddlers, street magicians, proprietors of Offices and Agencies. Movement of this official freeway, which threatens with a deluge of graphomania, and deeds of minimal significance, increases with each passing day. It is necessary to exit it as quickly as possible. This is not easily done. Particularly, at the apogee of the UNIVERSAL AVANT-GARDE, blind and favored with the highest prestige of the INTELLECT, which protects both the wise and the stupid.

7

On the side streets of the official avant-garde. MANNEQUINS appear.

My deliberate rejection of the solutions of the conceptual art, despite the fact that they seemed to be the only way off the path upon which I found myself, led me to place on the side streets the abovementioned facts about the most recent stage in my artistic practice and the attempts to describe them, which provided me with a better chance to encounter the UKNOWN!
I have more confidence in such a solution. Any new era always begins with it actions of little or no importance; actions which happen as if on the sly; which have little in common with the recognized trend; actions which are private, intimate, I could even say, shameful.
Vague. And difficult! These are the most fascinating and essential moments of a creative act.

All of a sudden, I became interested in the nature of *MANNEQUINS.*
The mannequin in my production of *"THE WATER-HEN"* (1967) and the mannequins in *"THE SHOEMAKERS"* (1970 [1972—MK]) had a very specific role: they were as if immaterial extensions, a kind of ADDITIONAL ORGAN of an actor, who was their "proprietor." The mannequins, already widely used in my production of Słowacki's *Balladyna,* were DOUBLES of live characters, endowed as if with a higher CONSCIOUSNESS, attained "after the completion of their lives."
These mannequins were already clearly marked with the sign of DEATH.

8

The mannequin as manifestation of the "REALITY OF THE LOWEST RANK."
The MANNEQUIN as procedure of TRANSGRESSION.
The MANNEQUIN as an EMPTY object. A FAÇADE. Message of DEATH. A model for an actor.

The mannequin which I used in 1967 in Cricot 2 Theatre (*The Water-Hen*) was a successor to *The Eternal Wanderer* and *Human Emballages*; a figure which appeared naturally in my *Collection* as yet another phenomenon, which was consistent with a long-held conviction that it was only the reality of the lowest rank and the poorest and least prestigious objects which are capable of revealing their full objectlessness in a work of art.

Mannequins and Wax Figures have always existed on the periphery of sanctioned Culture. They were not admitted any further; they occupied places in FAIR BOOTHS, suspicious MAGIC CABINETS, far from the splendid temples of art, treated condescendingly as CURIOSITIES destined for the tastes of the masses. For precisely this reason, it was they, and not academic, museum creations that caused the curtain to rise for the blink of an eye.

Mannequins have also their TRANSGRESSIONS. The existence of these creatures, created in the image of a human being, almost "godlessly," illegally, is the result of heretical activities, a manifestation of the Dark, Nocturnal, Rebellious human side. Of Crime and a Trace of Death as the source of cognition. This vague and inexplicable feeling that through this entity, looking almost like a human being but deprived of consciousness and human destiny, a terrifying message of Death and Nothingness is transmitted to us. It is precisely this feeling that is the cause simultaneously of transgression, rejection, and attraction. Of indictment and fascination.

All arguments have been exhausted in indictment. They were all absorbed by the very mechanism of action, which if thoughtlessly defined as the very purpose of action, could easily be relegated to the l o w e r   f o r m s   o f   c r e a t i v i t y. *Imitation and deceptive similarity*, which serve the conjurer in setting his *TRAPS* and deceiving the spectator, the use of "unsophisticated" means, slipping away from the realm of aesthetics, the abuse and fraudulent deception of APPEARANCES, practices from the chest of con-artists!

This indictment completed the accusations directed against a philosophical worldview, which, from the time of Plato to this day, considers the process of revealing Being and a Spiritual Sense of Existence as the purpose of art, rather than the involvement in the Material Shell of the world or in that deception of appearances, which are the lowest stage of existence.

I do not believe that a MANNEQUIN (or a WAX FIGURE) could replace a LIVE ACTOR, as Kleist and Craig wanted. This would be too simple and too naïve. I am trying to describe the motives and the uses of this unusual creature which suddenly appeared in my thoughts and idea. Its appearance complies with my ever-stronger conviction that l i f e can only be expressed in art through the a b s e n c e   o f   l i f e, through an appeal to DEATH, through APPEARANCES, through EMPTINESS, and the lack of MESSAGE.

The MANNEQUIN in my theatre will be a MEDIUM through which passes a strong feeling of DEATH and the condition of the Dead. A model for the Live ACTOR.

9

My elucidation of the situation described by Craig. The appearance of the LIVE ACTOR as a revolutionary moment. The discovery of a HUMAN BEING'S IMAGE.

I derive my observations from the domain of the theatre, but they are relevant to all current art. We can take Craig's suggestively depicted and disastrously incriminating picture of the circumstances surrounding the appearance of the Actor, which he had composed for his own use, a starting point for his idea of the "SUPER-MARIONETTE." Even though I continue to admire Craig's magnificent contempt and passionate accusations (especially since I see before me an absolute demise of today's theatre) and fully accept the first part of his Credo, in which he denies the institution of theatre its reasons for artistic existence, I dissociate myself from his well-known conclusions about the fate of the ACTOR. For the moment of the ACTOR's first appearance before the HOUSE (to use current terminology) seems to me, on the contrary, r e v o l u t i o n a r y and a v a n t - g a r d e. I will even try to construct and "ascribe to History" a completely different picture, in which the course of events will have quite the opposite meaning! The shared circle of tradition and religious rituals, shared ceremonies and shared ludic activities was left by SOMEONE who made a risky decision to BREAK away from the ritualistic Community. He was not driven by pride (as in Craig) to become an object of universal attention. This would have been too simplistic. Rather it must have been a rebellious mind, defiant, skeptical, free, and tragic, daring enough to remain alone with Fate and Destiny. If we also add "with his ROLE," we will have before us the ACTOR. This revolt took place in the realm of art. This described event, or rather manifestation, probably caused much confusion in the minds of others and clashing opinions. This ACT must undoubtedly have been seen as a betrayal of the old ritualistic traditions and practices, as secular arrogance, as atheism, as dangerous subversive tendencies, as scandalous, as amoral, as indecent; it must have been seen as clownery, buffoonery, exhibitionism, and deviation. The actor himself, standing apart from society, made not only fierce enemies, but also fanatical admirers. Simultaneously, condemnation and fame. It would require ludicrous and shallow formalism to explain this act of BREAKING-AWAY (RUPTURING) as egotism, as a lust for fame, or as a manifestation of latent inclinations towards acting. Something much greater must have been at stake—a MESSAGE of extraordinary importance.

Let us try to imagine once again this fascinating situation: OPPOSITE those who remained on this side, there stood a HUMAN DECEPTIVELY SIMILAR to them, yet (by some secret and ingenious "operation") infinitely DISTANT, shockingly FOREIGN, as if DEAD, cut off by an invisible BARRIER—no less horrible and inconceivable, whose real meaning and THREAT appear to us only in DREAMS. As if in the blinding flash of lightning, they suddenly perceived a glaring, tragically circus-like IMAGE OF A HUMAN, as if they had seen him FOR THE FIRST TIME, as if they had seen THEIR VERY SELVES. This must have been a SHOCK—a metaphysical shock. The life image of a HUMAN emerging out of the shadows, as if constantly walking forward—was a moving MESSAGE of its new HUMAN CONDITION, only HUMAN, with its RESPONSIBILITY, with its tragic CONSCIOUSNESS, measuring its FATE on an inexorable and final scale, *the scale of DEATH*. This revelatory MESSAGE, which was transmitted from the realm of DEATH, evoked in the SPECTATORS (let us use our term here) a metaphysical shock. And the craft and the art of this ACTOR (also according to our terminology) revealed that realm of DEATH and its tragic and full-of-DREAD beauty.

It is necessary to redefine the essential meaning of the relationship: SPECTATOR and ACTOR.

IT IS NECESSARY TO RECOVER THE PRIMEVAL FORCE OF THE SHOCK TAKING PLACE AT THE MOMENT WHEN, OPPOSITE A HUMAN (A SPECTATOR), THERE STOOD FOR THE FIRST TIME A HUMAN (AN ACTOR), DECEPTIVELY SIMILAR TO US, YET AT THE SAME TIME INFINITELY FOREIGN, BEYOND THE IMPASSABLE BARRIER.

10

RECAPITULATION:

Despite the fact that we may be suspected and even accused
of scrupulousness, inappropriate under these circumstances,
conquering my own inborn prejudices and fears,
for the sake of a more precise picture
and possible conclusions,
let us establish then the limits of that boundary, which has the name of
THE CONDITION OF DEATH,
for it represents the most extreme point of reference
no longer threatened by the conformity of
the CONDTION OF AN ARTIST AND ART.

. . . this specific relationship,
which is terrifying
and at the same time compelling,
this relationship of the l i v i n g to the d e a d,

the dead, who not so long ago, while still alive, gave not the slightest
reason for this unforeseen spectacle,
for creating unnecessary separation and confusion;
they were not d i f f e r e n t,
did not place themselves above others,
and as a result of this seemingly banal
but, as it would later become evident, rather essential
and valuable characteristic,
they were simply, normally,
in no way transgressing the universal laws,
u n n o t i c e d;
and now suddenly
o n   t h e   o t h e r   s i d e,
o p p o s i t e
they shock us
as if we
w e r e   s e e i n g   t h e m   f o r   t h e   f i r s t   t i m e
placed on display
in an ambiguous ceremony:
venerated
and, at the same time, rejected;
irrevocably different
and infinitely foreign;
and more: somehow deprived of all meaning,
inconsequential,
without the any hope of occupying some position
in our "full" life relationships,
which are only accessible to us, familiar
and comprehensible,
but for them meaningless.

If we agree that a trait of
l i v i n g   p e o p l e
is their ease and ability
with which they enter into mutual and manifold
l i f e   r e l a t i o n s h i p s,
it is only
in the presence of the dead
that there is born in us a sudden and startling
realization of the fact that
this basic trait of the living
is brought forth and made possible by
a complete
l a c k   o f   d i f f e r e n c e
between them;
by their
i n d i s t i n g u i s h a b i l i t y,

by their universal s a m e n e s s,
mercilessly abolishing all other and opposing delusions,
which is common,
consistent,
all-binding.
Only then when they are d e a d
that they become
n o t i c e a b l e (to the living);
having paid the highest price,
they gain
their individuality,
distinction,
their IMAGE,
glaring
and almost
c i r c u s - l i k e.

The Dead Class: Selections from the Partytura
(1974)

FOREIGNNESS. This is a very important and essential characteristic of the actor.

From the "Theatre of Death Manifesto": "It is necessary to recover the essential meaning of the relationship: spectator and actor. It is necessary to recover the primeval force of the shock taking place at the moment when, opposite a human (a spectator), there stood for the first time a human (an actor), deceptively similar to us, yet at the same time infinitely foreign, beyond the impassable barrier."

Foreign . . . the impassable barrier . . . and deceptively similar to us, the spectators.

One day, or one night, I found a model for the actor which would fit ideally into these conditions: the dead—I felt afraid and ashamed. . . . It was difficult for me to accept this model. . . . But this difficulty also meant that I was onto something. . . .

I continued to write: "If we agree that one of the traits of living people is their ability and the ease with which they enter into various relationships, it is only when encountering the body of a dead person that we realize that this essential trait of the living is possible because of the lack of differentiation between them, because of the sameness and . . . the 'invisibility.' It is only the DEAD who become visible to the living at the price of acquiring their individuality, difference, and their IMAGE. . . ."

The DEAD and the ACTOR, these two notions started to overlap in my thoughts. More and more, I started to accept these two conditions. Multiple ideas were born in my head. Finally, they all became part of my thinking about theatre. . . . The wax figure became an entity touched by death, fake, existing between a dead person and a living actor. . . .

I want to achieve a degree of foreignness which would be painfully noticeable by the audience.

Maybe this condition will establish the necessary [impassable] barrier.

For example: a group of people is sitting in a room. They know each other well. The room creates the condition of total isolation and safety.

Suddenly the doors are opened and there appears an unknown person, a stranger, someone dressed differently, or someone who does not belong here.
Such a sudden appearance of a STRANGER is always accompanied by a sensation which feels like fear or trepidation.
In Wyspiański's play, *Warszawianka*, a soldier covered in blood and mud—a messenger of woeful tidings—enters a room where high society women in evening gowns and generals in full regalia are gathered. In Wyspiański's *The Wedding*, ghosts are having conversations with cheerful guests attending the wedding party.

In 1967 [1968—MK], in my Happening, *Hommage à Maria Jarema*, into a gallery filled with opening night guests, I brought a real homeless person in soiled clothing, sticky with sweat, dirty and unshaven, who earned his living on the streets carrying packages and bundles and here was calmly sawing a piece of wood. . . .

Yet another possibility, as if from the regions of deep dreams. In our dreams, we often meet people, who were close to us, but now, without reason, behave towards us as if they had never met or known us. They behave like STRANGERS! The STRENGTH of the feeling of foreignness is very powerful in such a case. Only dead people generate such a feeling in our dreams.

These two examples were for me steeped too much in narrative and psychology, however. I wanted to stay with the real—in the sphere of material things and space.
I discovered a simple method, which had not been used before, to accomplish this.

In 1963, when I was working on the idea of the Zero Theatre, I played with the idea of acting "on the sly," as if "in spite" or "on the side."
Indeed: on the side!
IN THE CORNER! . . .
From the people gathered in a room, let us try to make one of them behave "abnormally" in the middle of that room. Everyone around will see this "abnormal" behavior as performance. Imagine the same action taking place in the corner of the room, on the side. It will be perceived with embarrassment, maybe even with fear. The same action, which in the middle was a performance, a make-believe, a safe event—now, in the corner, was true and real. There appeared a barrier and the condition of being estranged!

The stage has always been and is placed "in the middle"; an extension of the audience's viewing axis; to be seen; to watch a performance!
It is enough to shift the PLACE of the so-called PERFORMANCE to the side, to the corner, skew its axis in order for a strange thing to happen.

From the audience's "natural" field of vision, there disappears that which they have been used to—"a performance." Let us state this clearly: a false-pretence and the idea of showing.

In a corner, it will be seen as an embarrassing exhibitionism, a shameful act, an event which is not for viewing, completely isolated but autonomous and independent: an event which does not rely on the audience's presence. . . .

Kraków 1974

FROM THE DIRECTOR'S NOTEBOOK— 1974

[These are the notes following the Grand Parade of the Circus of Death— i.e., the Old People walking around the school desks.]
This is the MAIN IDEA of the piece.
This is the spine of the piece.
At one stage of the production's development, I have an idea of merging the actors, the Old People, who are returning to their classroom of yesteryear in order to reclaim their childhood, with the wax figures representing children in school uniforms. To integrate them once and for all. I begin to make the first drawings, where the figures of the children "grow out" from (or "grow into") the costumes of the old people.
It looks as if they share the same costume.
Later, I come to the conclusion that the Wax Figures of the children had to be autonomous, because, otherwise the actors could not move freely.
Thus, these wax figures are the mannequins of the boys and girls wearing fresh school uniforms—the boys are wearing long pants; the girls long skirts. They are all in black.
The difference is in how the Wax Figures are carried by the old people.
The Wax Figures are carried on their back, in their hands, across, dragged behind, etc.
. . . as if these were corpses of the children. . . .
. . . The Old People, carry them—their own childhood. . . .
. . . the dead carcasses of children are hanging over or trying to cling to the Old people not to fall off; others are dragged behind, as if they were heavy burdens, bad consciences, "chains around their necks," as if they "crawled" over those who got old, and who killed this childhood of theirs with their sanctioned and "socialized" maturity. . . .

. . . There emerge human CREATURES
with the carcasses of the children grown into them.
In the production notes, it was possible to accurately describe
this ANTHROPOLOGICAL SPECIMEN,
which continues to develop and grow,
beyond the stage of adolescence

as if against all biological laws,
giving birth to new organs,
parasitic "tumors."

On stage, these are humans
who have reached their old age. . . .

Because all of this takes place on stage
(and therefore the costumes should be of interest),
I want to emphasize that the Old People are dressed
in funeral clothing,
as demanded by the old tradition, which still exists in the Polish
countryside,
made ready for them long before their hour of death.

These "tumors" are THEY THEMSELVES, Old People's "LARVAE"
containing inside them the entire memory of their CHILDHOOD,
which was killed by their ADOLESCENCE,
its rationality,
its severe and unforgiving, delinquent laws. . . .

Their childhood past has become a desolate and forgotten storage-room,
where the desiccated memories of and forgotten people, faces, objects,
pieces of clothing, feelings, and images were laid to rest. . . .
. . . This is not sentimentality about getting old;
which desires to bring childhood back to life in one's memory.
This is the condition of complete and TOTAL life,
which cannot continue along the narrow narrative of
the time present!

These CREATURES walk onto the stage
annoyed, irate, ruthless, indifferent, full of themselves. . . .
ANIMAL BEASTS,
with the carcasses of the children.
They walk like the condemned,
stranglers,
child murderers . . .
as if trying to run away from their bad consciences,
enlivened by their long-lost desire . . .
the last waltz—one more time . . .
they jiggle and jerk like mannequins . . .
they shuffle their feet, move their arms, stretch out their heads, puff out
their chests with pride . . .
ostentatiously, as if to prove that they are still alive!
tragic automatons. . . .

Kraków 1974

GRAMMAR

I have always been interested in grammar. At the beginning it was its rules of ordering and construction that fascinated me. Later, I discovered its other possibilities, which I found helpful in my artistic practices.

One of them was a critical analysis of a sentence structure.

A sentence, having an assigned meaning in daily life, is the core of a plot, a narration, which, as it is well known, in a traditional theatre, constitutes the very fabric of a presentational and representational theatre. It was this very life-affirming structure that I blamed for everything that was wrong with theatre and tried to destroy it as often as I could.

This is why I thought that critical sentence structure analysis was an excellent means to destroy life-affirming meaning, life-affirming relations and their consequences.

I found an effective, artistic measure in GRAMMAR. A phrase sentence structure analysis I could easily replace with the notion of deconstruction or decomposition.

I was thinking about the GRAMMAR LESSON already in 1972, when I was working on the idea of the Impossible Theatre and when I had selected Witkiewicz's *Dainty Shapes and Hairy Apes* for the next production. I tried to break down the plot, a literary reality of the dramatic text with this OTHER, SECOND, OR FOREIGN REALITY!

It was supposed to be a school, a class room.

And GRAMMAR!

The mechanism which would accelerate the decomposition of the plot, narration, and the production. I ordered that school desks be built. I placed the actors in them. A strict and terrifying teacher wreaked havoc among those who had been told to be school children despite the fact that they had other plans and intentions.

In *Dainty Shapes and Hairy Apes*, there are 40 Mandelbaums, the essence of manhood, as stipulated by Witkiewicz.

I wanted to title the scene: GRAMMAR LESSON AND 40 MANDELBAUMS. Later I decided against this merger because this particular arrangement did not provide me with a sufficient degree of contradiction.

A cloakroom became a substitute for a classroom.

A school and GRAMMAR returned only in 1975 in *The Dead Class.*

GRAMMAR and its principal function proved to be an effective means of destroying the life-affirming condition of stage action, plot, narration, and production. That is, of ILLUSION! And this is exactly what I am after.

The imperative is to bring down sentences, statements, actor's parts to

different tenses,
modes of declension,
ways of conjugation,
to obliterate their life-affirming meanings and functionality,
to reduce them to etymology,
to phonemes,
morphemes,
verbally,
chorally,
in a linguistic orgy
in a gibberish sing-song
until they become one long groan!

Expose stage actions
situations,
gestures
to similar procedures.
Obliterate their life-affirming meanings,
reduce them to morphemes.
This is difficult and almost impossible.
It requires both theatrical imagination
and the lack of respect for life-affirming processes and procedures.
As a consequence, autonomous forms will emerge—
rather than abstract forms, because they still have the traces of their life-affirming functions.
For example, someone is leaving; but this is a futile act.
That is, s/he will continuously be trying to leave
but shall never leave. . . .

FROM THE DIRECTOR'S NOTEBOOK—
1974

MAKING FACES

Centuries-old schoolboy's pranks: making faces, twisting one's body, contorting one's face. Making faces is a strikingly effective weapon of immaturity against the "seriousness" of adulthood, which often does nothing more than mask its lack of sensitivity, feelings, imagination, or its ruthlessness, duplicity, emptiness. . . .
Making faces, twisting one's body, strips off this official mask of indifference, penetrates into the deep—into the interior, which is guarded cautiously. . . .
None can escape the power of a contorted face. . . .
Making faces contradicts the so-called natural condition and trust-inspiring "truthfulness" of a well-composed face; it deprives it of the exclusive right to represent human kind; it proves beyond any doubt, that this part of a human body believed to express the soul and spirituality, is

also that face which is malleable enough so that it can adapt and adjust to any situation.

These are just its formal attributes.

Contorting one's face is an equivalent here to shattering the academic, indifferent, monotonous, conformist FAÇADE; to preventing the common desire of keeping one's "FACE" at all costs.

MAKING FACES—FACIAL CONTORTIONS is a mirror held up to the adversary, in which s/he needs to see her/his own reflection. Making faces is an expression of all human monstrosities, deviations of nature, brutality, bestiality, debauchery, madness; of all desires and wickedness. It is enough to look at them closely.

There is one more aspect of MAKING FACES—FACIAL CONTORTIONS worth considering:
while making them—and who does not—
we cast aside or cleanse ourselves—
in a witty and clever way—
of all the above-mentioned, none too flattering, characteristics.

MAKING FACES must pierce the audience like an arrow.
It is necessary first to compose the face; only then one can "make" the face,
blasphemously, obscenely, cruelly, loathingly. . . .

**FROM THE DIRECTOR'S NOTEBOOK—
1974**

THE WORLD OF IMMATURITY

Through the lessons and school incidents, it is necessary to expose and disclose this reality, to which ADULTS want to introduce children in school. It is necessary to place this world, believed to be mature and responsible, in contrast to the ur-reality, not yet deformed by life's practices, to this *"MATIÈRE PREMIÈRE,"* "RAW MATERIAL" of life.

In this mature world, there are:
History, wars, never-ending wars, battlefields—battlefields of courage and victory, and their equivalents on the other side: infamy, genocides, historical necessity, monuments of glory and death, grand ideologies, pantheons, mausoleums, nightmarish ceremonies, civilizations built on armies, police, prisons, and the laws.
In that other world, there are:
the regions pushed aside by sanctioned consciousness,
ignored with embarrassment,
deeply hidden in bourgeois interiors,

banned, marked by the original sin, fined, constrained and restricted by law and court verdicts as a menace to and an enemy of the people—if truth be told, exposing only conformism and a hidden secret of the OLD PEOPLE . . .
the regions which are
poor,
forlorn,
naked,
defenseless,
marked by spots,
snot-nosed,
driven by hormones,
pitiable and indecently clothed,
not-yet-fully-developed . . .

ideas-not-fully-flashed-out,
underdeveloped intentions,
impaired. . . .

This is not a happy, sentimental childhood,
but the dark regions, full of fear, anxiety, gone astray,
that is, according to the opinions of the adults,
rather useless
and to be discarded. . . .

The impossibility of linking itself to the world of the ADULTS,
the impossibility of communicating with it. . . .
The awareness that it will always remain on the other side, lonely, and locked upon itself. . . .
What it contains are solidarity, secret initiations, a feeling of belonging to a different species,
like in a reserve. . . .

All these comments can be read easily and without doubt as a literary text.
Our goal however is theatre, not literature.
It is necessary to find a theatrical equivalent for these literary investigations. Theatrical and autonomous. In this literary text, children are the *dramatis personae*. It is necessary to get rid of the presentational style which would show them literally the way it would surely be done in a traditional theatre.
It is necessary to do the opposite—use a method which yields excellent results in art. The actors must not play the parts of the children. They have to be either old people themselves or play the parts of the old people who return perversely to their childhood.

The solution to this problem was found in my unrealized projects, which I had created a few years earlier at the time when Poland was dominated by student and youth theatres—when the admiration for the human body reached the zenith of ritual, initiation, celebration, and, in the end, of counterfeit.

It was at that time that I decided unashamedly to found a group that comprised the old people. Today, this decision naturally coincides with the above-mentioned issues. It became clear to me that the old people must play the parts of children.

Earlier, I wrote the first draft of my "Theatre of Death Manifesto."
The Old People almost dead, standing by their own graves.

The Old People slip into the bodies of the boys (1974)
This "slipping into" is a rather awkward metamorphosis. The Old People slip into the bodies of children as if this metamorphosis was the only (though forbidden) sexual pleasure left to them.

They slip into the bodies of the boys; they brown-nose them. . . . To express this in acting demands a high degree of subtlety and sophistication.

This is one of the ways of imagining oneself experiencing adolescence as if in a dream (and thus also in art). All those symptoms of adolescence or the condition of being an adolescent—clumsy way of expressing oneself, schoolboys' pranks, throwing tantrums, the exhibitionism of basic instincts—should be "shown" as if "on the sly," awkwardly, clumsily, with a painful seriousness of children, as if wallowing in the inner belaborings of trivial problems. . . .

one always needs to remember, to emphasize this condition of the "low rank," embarrassingly naïve, "snotty," bashful (the only concrete reality!)
The Old People, individuals already withdrawn from life,
because of the way they behave now,
because of the shameless return of those "serious and mature" adults to their days of "knee-pants,"
as if they got stuck in their adolescence
and time, without their participation, carved out the faces of the old people,
an embarrassment to their own age
though, this embarrassment and suffering,
return to it human dignity.

and one more encounter:
the world of the childhood and the world of the old people.
Neither of them can really adapt to the accepted, dominant condition, the officially-sanctioned reality and its pragmatism.
Both are on the margins, like human reserves.
Both touch upon the condition of nothingness and death.

The return of the OLD PEOPLE—at the threshold of death—to the classroom.

Birth and death—two extremes which explain each other.

A WAR LESSON.
NAME CALLING.

The entire class goes through the process of making faces, contorting their bodies, making grimaces to A FIST FIGHT.

FROM THE DIRECTOR'S NOTEBOOK— 1974

Every so often, there come to life actions and pranks which are scandalous, embarrassing, and cheap, without any logic or explanation, selfless.
Let us put together a list which will help us in rehearsals and actors' improvisations:
a brawl . . .
pushing,
crowding,
getting squashed,
knocking down,
convulsive motion,
spastic motion,
a group jerk-off,
a crawl around the school desks,
through the school desks,
dispersed motion,
an embrace,
full of suffering,
painfully serious,
with an obsessive/annoying thought on their faces,
engaged in a fist fight,
kicking and screaming.

"THE LOWER FORMS OF LIFE"
"THE FAMILY SCENE"

FROM THE DIRECTOR'S NOTEBOOK— 1974

From this moment on, the imagined, "fictitious" sphere of Witkiewicz's play, *Tumor Brainowicz*, slips into the reality of the classroom, which has already been clearly defined. From the very beginning, it must be obvious that this particular strategy has nothing to do with a representation of or finding a stage equivalent to convey the meaning and content of the play, the way traditional theatres would do.

I want to create the impression that the OLD PEOPLE, characters from the "Dead Class," defined clearly and unequivocally by their past and destiny, were as if "programmed" by the content of *Tumor Brainowicz*. This might have happened by accident, or maybe it was Fate which wanted to make the end of their lives a little bit more exciting. It is possible that this maneuver (a kind of transplant) could have been made successfully and that, under favorable circumstances, all the stage action and the events in the play could have been faithfully and logically repeated—thus represented.

But this would have been a simulacrum bereft of any reality; it would have been nothing more than a stylistic gesture—an improvisation of sorts or just a "dressing-up."
More important, this would have been against my ideas of theatre.

We have to agree that the reality of the classroom—which is concrete and not ephemeral or illusionary (a playtext)—by absorbing the imaginary, fictitious content and sphere of the play, must, to say it carefully, be altered. Of course it is the question of degree.
One must proceed very carefully (a necessary action even in the most radical transformations), conscious of the hierarchy among the objects: the reality of the classroom is the primary matter, an autonomous reality.

I would like to emphasize the unusual nature of the maneuver which we will be engaged in during the rehearsal process. This must be described with precision, because it is very easy to drift ashore, run aground, go to extremes, and destroy a thin layer of humor and relativism, perversion, disdain and mystification with pedantry and literalness.
It is those features only that can save us from false seriousness and logic. This maneuver is unusual because the rehearsals are not a part of putting a production together. At no stage in the process, is one given the impression that there will ever be an opening night.
The rehearsal process is a battlefield where two indifferent realities will clash, have a fight whose rules and regulations will make it impossible for either of the two sides to be victorious.
It is openly stated that a failed scene and defeat may bring about a positive solution to the problem; that one of the conditions which can lead to success is a careless offensive and throwing down of the weapons; that one calls for an interruption of a solid line of attack, for sudden breaks in a front line—all of this looks like a battle fought by children or by a madman.
Observe the encounter between the two realities—one, which is autonomous, free, and concrete ("The Dead Class"), and the other one, which is imagined and a stylistically fictitious literary structure (a play). During those sinful and shady maneuvers; during those crossings over and slippages; during those attempts at creating new characters, often the members of "The Dead Class" would be bigger than life, puff up dangerously, or would become nuanced and more complex.

A reverse could also happen: the events, the play's dramatic personae lose their literary details and circumstances; they become more abstract, general; are filled with disreputable symbolism. . . .
The reality of "The Dead Class" is constantly intertwined with or slips into the sphere of the play and vice versa.

Because the reality of the classroom has already been painted with the broad brush strokes of "hope" and delimited with the horizon of further development (of that I am sure), let us now focus on the dramatic action of *Tumor Brainowicz.*
We will try not to be seduced by the stage action, but to see in it conditions, emotions, and the essence of reality.

"THE MEETINGS BETWEEN THE CHARACTERS"
"TUMOR BRAINOWICZ"

"THE DEAD CLASS"

Tumor Brainowicz, a mathematical genius, the head of a horrid family, a vital force, in a state of exceptional psychological commotion, inner pandemonium, exhibitionism mixing shamelessly knowledge, sex, poetry, and morality or to be more precise the lack thereof.

The Old Man in the WC, an Old Jew, the head of the family, continuously engaged in buying and selling, always counting his profits and losses, quarrelling with his debtors, for sure he is a usurer, bargaining with Jehovah, too; from the time when he was in school, he has indulged in the unhealthy custom of spending long hours in the WC; secretly a sex maniac and exhibitionist.
Caution: it is possible that the schoolboy is modeled after Tumor Brainowicz. But there are sufficient differences between them as well as their respective professions separating them that an interesting individual can be born out of this cross-breeding of characters.

The Old Man in the WC definitely belongs to the world of the "Reality of the Lowest Rank." It is only appropriate that this shabby character play the part of the "genius." This will help us to avoid a literary representation of the Fiction of drama.

Józef
Tumor's father, an old scatterbrain, who understands nothing about the decadent life style of the genius, embarrasses Tumor with his peasant dialect.

The Old Man with a Bicycle
for whom the memory of nighttime bicycle escapades is the only emotion and meaning of life left. . . .

The precision with which he moves this strange-looking and non-functional vehicle can be equated with dysfunctional behavior. . . .

Note well: the bigger the "class" and professional differences, the better results can be achieved. The more scandalous the behavior, the closer it gets to being real.

Gamboline Basilius
from the princely house, wishing she could breed like a rabbit (in her own words) giving birth to Tumor's children, pregnant with a baby already named Ibisa (Iza). Giving birth is the highest sexual pleasure for her.

The Woman with a Mechanical Cradle
A cruel joke played on her by the whole class is imprinted in her memory of schooldays—when caught after a chase, she recalls being forced onto this strange gym equipment, which forced her to spread and close her legs mechanically.
This is how she learned about giving birth.
Now, in this "Dead Class," the Old People bring back this cruel memory using the Family Machine, which could only been dreamed up and executed in a nightmare. . . .
The Somnambulistic Whore's pregnancy is "brought to its logical conclusion" in this nightmare with a precise recitation of the elementary school ABCs.

Ibisa (Iza)
In Witkiewicz's "list of characters," she is the daughter of Gamboline Basilius from her first, aristocratic marriage [to Roman Kretchborski], Tumor's step daughter, "wildly exciting," demonic, and cynical young girl, who torments even the biggest brains with her almost metaphysical organ, in which her intellect and sex were mixed together to create an unpredictably explosive concoction.
Because it is already in the first family quarrel that the family secrets are revealed, we find out that Tumor has betrayed Gamboline with none other than his stepdaughter Iza.

The Somnambulistic Whore
Following the rules of Theatre Cricot 2, she is placed much lower than Witkiewicz's women's intellectual and erotic perversion.
Her exhibitionism revealed itself already when she was at school.
Nobody knows what happened to her later.
She came back unexpectedly for this last lesson of the Dead—now, she plays the part of the Somnambulistic Whore. Tonight she walks around the school desks, rather than the streets, and, with an obscene gesture, shows her breast to the passers-by.

There are also two sons of Tumor:
Alfred and Maurice,

two exemplars well fitting to this dysfunctional family.
They function as foils to other characters.
They are like "exclamation" marks completing the scandalous
undertakings of the main characters.

They can be found in the auras of two Old People:
The Old Man with his Double and The Double.
Sometimes, The Pedophile Old Man speaks their lines referring to some
family secrets.

A FAMILY SCENE

That which is just about to begin is no longer a school lesson,
but a strange game played by the children, which is cruel, full of
incomprehensible shortcuts, references, and secret codes. . . .
The Old People—The Pedophile Old Man, The Deaf Old Man, The
Absent-Minded Old Man from the Last Row—pull unceremoniously,
rather drag, The Old Man in the WC to the place which figures
prominently in his name—that is, to the poor, country, school
outhouse—WC. It is only this vulgar name, an outhouse, which can fully
express the function of this embarrassing object of the lowest rank.
Nobody really knows what is going to happen to the Old Man in the WC.
He is kept there by force. He is standing upright on the toilet, his hair
disheveled, screaming his outrageous views.
This is his moment, which resembles an epilepsy attack, when an
"ALIEN" force "slips into" a human and begins to speak through him.
Here this "alien" is Tumor Brainowicz.
The Old man in the WC is still the same old Jew, a usurer, part-time
Prophet, sitting at the top of the infamous Mount Sinai.

The Old People, whose advanced age adds a touch of madness to this
schoolboy's prank, torture and torment the Old Man in the WC without
purpose.

The Old Man in the WC complies and utters Tumor's lines scattered
throughout the play; he puts them together in a meaningless way;
regurgitates them, possibly not fully understanding their meaning; he
abandons them easily and without scruples; he declaims them with
artificial pathos and euphoria in his voice. . . .

FROM THE DIRECTORS' NOTEBOOK—
1974

CHILDREN'S LANGAUGE—INFORMEL

In Witkiewicz's play, there are digressions which are of a completely
different genre and nature.

These texts are poems, lacking any artistic value, kitschy, cabaret-style, pompous, which are a mockery of the so-called "legitimate" writing. Written and read, the way one reads any book, they can, when perceived as a deliberate travesty, indirectly contribute to generating positive aesthetic responses.

This form of indirect action on stage—and to be more precise, in the autonomous theatre, which operates according to its own "direct" language not making a reference to any other language, and thus loses the quotation marks around the phrase, direct, and acts upon us directly without being screened by the mind—becomes kitsch. More important, it loses the element of mockery, especially in a situation when everything else is almost complete mockery and derision.

A proper declamatory style used to recite these poems, whose punch line is linguistically refined as well as its literary quality, would limit their reception to their linguistic nature, thus, a very particular domain of reception, and would be against my artistic convictions. I am always interested in assigning a universal character to all forms and objects.

For a long time, in my artistic practice, I have been interested in exploring the language used by children; the forms they use when they begin to talk, at the time when a very limited vocabulary can no longer satisfy the newly born and quickly developing consciousness, the expanding emotional sphere or the realm of inner feelings and perceptions, which is still in the subconscious but already demanding a way of verbalizing its presence. This type of language does not yet have a grammar, pauses, comas, periods, question marks—which demarcate, classify, or determine the linguistic structure.

It lacks connecting phrases, prepositions, conjunctions of any kind which give a sentence meaning, direction, rationale. . . .

These overflowing and pouring-in-meanings crowd together, push, press, and bubble—and when stopped with a barrier or a levy constituted by the lack of "legitimate" means of expression, they express themselves spontaneously in a way which, as one may argue, is natural, original, and true!

This is "informel" matter, which acts and moves unfiltered. . . .

Its natural means of expression is a repetition of the same word or cluster of words.

This act of repetition contains in itself the whole spectrum of emotion from hope to regret to despair to stubbornness—it is an act of "clamoring" to the outside world. . . .

The lack of connecting phrases is a sign of another condition of the children's language: the ability to quickly jump into a different and remote sphere of meanings and surprising, strange associations. . . .

What is created is a forlorn lament, litany,

full of sighs, invocations, pleas,
sounding like a prayer. . . .

There exists one more way to recite lessons or poems: school-like,
nonsensical, emotionless, dull, monotonous, memorized, mechanical. . . .
There is a good word describing this: regurgitation; for example, one
regurgitates a prayer or a poem. In this process, there are places where
one "stumbles," forgets, a desperate quest for the forgotten fragment,
hesitates, encounters empty places, which one wants to fill in. . . .
Again, repetition is the best solution is these situations. . . .

Following these rules, The Somnabulistic Whore recites a poem, which Iza
wrote.
Iza, as it should be recalled, is a poetess in this horrendous household.
This is Iza's poem in Witkiewicz's play:
Once there was a little fetus in the dusky by-and-bys,
Someone gave a shove by chance, someone stole a secret glance
And out came pretty toes.
First of all they had to christen, find the name and then to baptize,
Then baptize it Moogle-wise.
Once there was a little kitten, once there was a soft green mitten,
Ate its breakfast in the by-and-bys.
Someone gave a secret glance, someone stole a shove by chance,
They all cried out their eyes.

In the production
THE SOMNABULISTIC WHORE recites the poem:
there was a little fetus in the du . . .
there was a little fe . . .
there was, there was,
there was a little fetus,
was, was, was
in the dusky. . . .
Someone gave a shove, someone gave a shove, someone, someone. . . .

Once there was a little fetus in the dusky by-and-bys . . .
Someone gave a shove by chance, by chance,
someone, someone, and out came pretty . . .
and pretty, someone, someone, someone stole a secret glance . . .
a secret glance and pretty . . .
and, pretty, and pretty. . . .
and out came pretty toes,
and pretty, first, first, first
they had to christen, find the name and then to baptize,
christen, then, then, then to baptize,
then baptize,

then baptize it Moogle-wise
Moogle-wise!!!!!

FROM THE DIRECTOR'S NOTEBOOK—

Different kinds of elocution appropriate for different situations must be
used here.
God forbid: one must not assemble well-known and poor attempts at
offering parody used as a method in bad political cabarets.
One must begin elsewhere.
One must begin with the reality of the classroom;
with the recitation of the poem by a lazy student, who is paralyzed by
dreadful fear.
A great challenge for an actor.
A complete amnesia and paralysis of memory.
Stutter.
A hasty quest for the forgotten fragment in memory.
Repetition to gain time.
Exhausting repetition reaching the limits of abstraction.
A desperate desire to cling to the remnants of meaning.
Simultaneous confirmation and contradiction.
Reaching pure abstraction.
Then, we slowly leave the place of the classroom.
What follows is the process of finding "aesthetic" pleasure and delight in
this condition of absurdity.

FROM THE DIRECTOR'S NOTEBOOK—
1974

From this moment, a total and complete DEBAUCHERY takes over—
the pieces of clothing are stripped off from the bodies—similar to the
disrobing of the dead bodies; a blasphemous robbery of the dead; a
shameless practice of necrophiliacs; an illicit procedures of exhumation of
bodies;
from the cemetery to the orgy,
from the grave to the brothel,
"FOREFATHER'S EVE"—a night of touching the dead and death
followed by some kind of ghoulish secretion.
The OLD PEOPLE as if taken down from the catafalques,
exposed to the public view,
Death . . . a cheap shot . . . ersatz . . . shame . . . a rotten smell of the graves . . .
naked bodies . . . not bodies, but their individual parts; individual,
shameless, and in-your-face parts, which are separated and ostentatiously
out in the open—
thighs . . . buttocks . . . calves . . . feet . . . breasts . . . groins . . .
penises . . . stomachs . . . underbellies . . .

putrefaction and sex . . . faces painfully serious . . . the eyes attentively
following those ceremonies of nothingness, these celebrations and
laborious, pedantic, and meticulous practices leading NOWHERE,
happening here in the ruins of the school days, among the piles of
molding books, at the heap of scattered death announcements. . . .

Remember the faces . . . notes to the actors: our faces do not belong to us,
the face belongs to the audience . . . a defenseless face, exposed to insults
and all other invectives . . . empty and bare, defiant . . .
existing only for itself and in itself—like a sex organ. . . .

Invigorated by the tropics,
the "colonial" luxury of the European
conquistadors,
a decadent and perverse love exchange
between Tumor and his stepdaughter
IZA ends in an uncontrolled outburst of
jealousy and a complete
laxity of moral laws.
This is the apex of surrealist
freedom of expression and action.

Already earlier the waves of the "EVENTS," which seemed to be endless,
began to lose their clarity, their ritual soothing monotony, and began to
swirl up as if a different, new element wanted to come to life—a woeful
resignation changed into a passionate calling, sudden spasmodic cries of
thunderous passions and animal desires. . . .
It was as if DEATH, called for, has finally arrived with her Circus Troupe
of nightmarish carnival revelers wearing contorted masks of Pain, Evil,
Desire, and Sin. . . .

Two Old People—THE WOMAN BEHIND THE WINDOW and THE
SOMNABULISTIC WHORE—throw themselves with fury at THE
PEDOPHILE OLD MAN; they undress him piece by piece.
THE OLD MAN FROM THE LAST ROW meets the same fate—he is
undressed by the Old People next to him.
Now, both are naked.
According to my belief that life in art manifests itself in the lack of
life (the way it is defined in life) and this is why the dead façade is an
equivalent of proper reality in art—
the genitals of the two naked men are replaced with their exact, artificial,
and, of course, dead replicas.
They are standing upright with their new appendages, helpless, not
knowing what will happen to them next.

There are already two characters from Witkiewicz's play, Tumor and Iza, in the classroom.

In the above-mentioned love-dialogue, TUMOR—THE OLD MAN IN THE WC, made furious by a cynical IZA-WHORE, cries out:

THE OLD MAN IN THE WC—TUMOR

Now, I am really mad!
I feel such monstrous insatiability
that my brain is turning to hot mush.
Send for Anak Agong!

FROM THE DIRECTOR'S NOTEBOOK—

. . . Two Malays enter the stage.
The action of the play takes place in the island of Timor ruled by a deity-volcano, Ganong Malapa. In a moment, the rightful ruler of the Island, Patakulo Senior, will die. Iza will cause the death of his son, Patakulo Junior, with her cynicism. In this caricature of Colonial Robinson Crusoe, any desire for a "proper" costume design would be naïve and stupid.
We abandon any idea of having exotic costumes or make-up.
Instead, we have two naked men—relics and victims of a ghoulish and orgiastic ritual. This pair of naked men in a classroom full of Old People dressed in black creates a sharp contrast between the two groups. This contrast is equally drastic and comical as the contrast between the Europeans dressed in tropical outfits and naked Malays wearing their exotic costumes.

FROM THE DIRECTOR'S NOTEBOOK—

In this production, where the action takes place at the threshold between life and death and where we are exploring matters far more important than the fictitious adventures of the play's characters—it would be stupid and naïve to pay attention to such unimportant questions as, for example, why did Professor Green come to the Island, or, for this matter, to the sensational episode of arresting Professor Tumor for the second time. Not to mention that paying attention to the happy ending, that is, the fact that, having removed his rival, Professor Green is finally free to conquer debauched Iza, would be nothing more than the stuff of Harlequin romance novels.
Let us then allow Professor Green to be that secretive and ambiguous character; that STRANGER, that NEW ARRIVAL, that political, government FUNCTIONARY.
We had already met him once before.
Now, he is arriving with a black pirate flag.
The augur of death, terror, and theatrical finale.

In order that the final, closing victory not belong to him, he is turned into an operatic Don Juan. This victory, in its much simplified version, is brought instead by A SOLDIER FROM WORLD WAR I.

A SOLDER FROM WORLD WAR I

He is the same one who suddenly appeared during the Night Lesson—an uninvited guest, who came to the last meeting of the class before death; a ghost from the trenches or from the common grave, his tattered uniform splattered with mud, still moving forward in an attack formation. All signs indicate that these are his final moments. The hour of the empty victory. And of the empty parade. Just for show.
He leads this platoon in funeral suits for the last parade.
He raises his black standard high in the air in front of the school desks; in front of his class.

A SOLDER FROM WORLD WAR I

Hip! Hip! Hurrah!
We are taking possession
of this country!

HISTORICAL DAGUERREOTYPE

Everybody spontaneously takes their place for a commemorative photograph. The dead, too. As if in the old photographs, their placement is arranged; they are ready to "enter into history." Above them, there is a black flag.
All of this, like the sepia photographs in the family albums, looks too straight, too conventional, and . . . too banal.
To complete this picture all one needs is an old camera.
THE OLD MAN WITH A BICYCLE is the one who has one.
He places it in front.
The sounds of the waltz, "François-Waltz," as always in important moments, accompanies this historical scene.
But the camera is not the usual camera.
It reveals surprising possibilities in its black box. The eye of the camera can be extended into infinity. It moves like a snake and grows like some kind of a mechanical phallic organ.
The operating secrets of this mysterious box are shamefully simple.
Technology should not obscure the allure of Mr. Daguerre's happy times.
At the end of the camera's bellows, there is a sufficiently long rope which runs behind the stage—its length is the length of the stage. The rope is in the hand of a helper who is waiting for the sign from the photographer.
When the sign is given, the rope is pulled, thus, causing camera's eye to telescope, which will be extended three times.
The bellows are getting longer and longer.
Once the photograph is taken, the rope is released.

The rest will be done by the photographer.
The helper is THE CLEANING WOMAN–DEATH. She must be strangely attracted to this box; feel kinship; perceive common destiny of serving the same purpose.

THE OLD MAN WITH A BICYCLE—

a photographer—
places the camera, corrects its location; he is very precise and demanding; pulls out an old gun and cries out excited:
"Attention!"
and shoots.
At the same time the bellows of the camera are extended forward.
The Old People posing for the photograph, deafened by the scream and the shot, step back.
The photographer shoots again.
He cries out:
"Attention!"
With visible trepidation, with the faces obediently turned towards the camera and the demonic photographer, hypnotized by the attack of the "organ" from the magic box, the Old People posing for the photograph run into the school desks, fall down, stumble.

The Photographer shoots one more time. His triumphant scream:
"Attention!"
If one is to abandon the phallic metaphor, the bellows of the camera can be compared to an elephant's trunk, used to attack its victims.
In panic and fear, the "models" of the victorious photographer withdraw into the back of the classroom, behind the school desks.

FROM THE DIRECTOR'S NOTEBOOK—
1974

That which moved me the most and excited me about working on the production—beyond and above the idea of "the Dead Class"—was the need to move forward; to go beyond the existing experiences; to find a new structure for a theatre, in which the relationship between a preexisting playtext and the content of the production would enhance the notion of the autonomous art work.

I have to admit that my attachment to a literary text and to my recognition of its existence in a production were very strong.
The method of parallel actions—the playtext and the stage action—used by me until now was no longer sufficiently productive. It was no longer good enough, even though it eliminated well-known and approved methods of professional theatre practice, starting with the lowest degree

of being "faithful" to the text, via the process of "decoding" the playtext, and finishing with the loftiest realm of "interpreting" the playtext.
I viewed these actions as the pretentious posturing of professional con-artists and the main reason why the theatre was in crisis.
Even though—let me repeat this—I thought that I had exposed those emptied-out methods in my theatre practice (unfortunately, or maybe fortunately, this was rarely noticed), *The Dead Class* was to be a more radical step towards achieving a complete autonomy of theatre.

Let me elaborate here on my definition of the above-mentioned methods of parallel action:
the playtext and the stage action.
This method is deeply grounded in my desire to fulfill my own creative process without looking for support in a text, which has already been formed by someone else.
The idea of fulfilling my own creative process means an act of expressing the ideas, which were born or are still being born in the realm of visual arts; my poetic musings; philosophical or aesthetic!
I want to express these ideas in theatre, in the stage action.
When asked why I do not write a play myself, I respond:
(And this is the second point I would like to make.) One should not write plays. For me, this is an outmoded literary genre, which hinders the theatre's potential for attaining its autonomy. And it is this autonomy that I have been interested in from the very beginning. A written play must be repeated on stage with the help of theatrical means. This justifies the employment of the idea of reproduction, illustration, and even worse, of interpretation. I say, even worse, because every second-rate theatre director claims rights to offer an interpretation when his/her knowledge is not sufficient to faithfully realize a playtext.
I create the stage action out of events, activities, situations, accidents, characters.
The stage action consists of a chain of sequences, which do not form a logical plot, are not logically connected; each one of them is its own beginning; from the beginning, they are isolated and exist for themselves. Moreover, the fact that they are "close to each other" is shocking and absurd.
These are the activities, situations, objects, which are separated from life and no longer in relation to its other elements.
Bereft of life's use-value and service-value, they become autonomous, real, and, more important, they are freed from the tired desire to use them to illustrate and symbolize something else.
They are REAL. This word expresses their radical status.
What joins them is the common idea. For example, in the production of *The Water-Hen* the common idea was the idea of a journey.
As mentioned above—this chain of sequences is outside of the logic of life. The strategy of generating provocative and surprising (this is very important!) encounters is the expression of FREEDOM!

The sequence of events in a production is an equivalent of the drama's plot, but it does not illustrate or symbolize it.

The sequence of events of the free and autonomous realm of the stage action is born (this is the correct phrase here) in the process of distancing and alienating itself from the plot; by rejecting and setting up contradictions, which are an insult to all legitimate customs; which are the threshold of the "impossible"; which are shameless and shocking.

That which conjoins them is TENSION.

The power and strength of this tension is a barometer of success for this creative act; the creative act, when it is impossible to define which was first: the chicken or the egg.

This suggests that the attempt to find an equivalent of the autonomous stage action for the drama's plot is nothing more than a naïve and academic investigation. Such an investigation would only reduce the process to interpreting or illustrating—the idea of autonomy would thus be lost.

This is simply an act of creation which is impossible to define—it can only be described by phrases such as: a flash of inspiration, a fluke, a coincidence. . . .

1974

A small digression and explanation: I have mentioned that we should stop writing plays and, at the same time, I indicated that I am very much attached to this literary genre. I would like to explain these two conflicting statements.

I believe that a dramatic text is a very significant element of theatre. I am far from restructuring the literary genre called theatre. I am fully convinced that it will exist for a long time. This is beyond the point, however.

I do believe that drama should exist as one of the possibilities in theatre, which could be as revolutionary as the idea of the autonomous theatre, rather than only as a text "to be performed."

There are also other possibilities. When I am faced with my favorite plays by Maeterlinck, Wyspiański, or Ibsen, I am very much aware of the importance of this literary genre. It may be so because we were brought up respecting centuries-long tradition of drama.

Their theatre is a grand theatre of imagination. It does not require a material form. I am convinced of this!

There is one more thing that needs to be mentioned—the choice of a playwright. (In Cricot 2 Theatre, Witkiewicz is the author of choice.) This is an important consideration. By choosing only one playwright, I negated

the idea of a professed "formal richness" which is revealed in a vast
selection of playwrights.
Such a phrase only covers up the poverty of ideas, or even lack of them,
and the possibility for a development.
The choice of one playwright in Cricot 2 Theatre created a unity;
a necessity of a singular solution—these are the most profound
characteristics of an autonomous and authentically creative process.

The discovery of the idea of the parallel action (1961), which I described
above, was my argument for coining the phrase that "we do not play
Witkiewicz's texts, but we play with Witkiewicz."
This is the end of this much too long, though necessary, digression.

1974

When I started to work [on *The Dead Class*], I felt that I was losing my
fascination with the method of parallel actions and that I would have to
go beyond it.
The materials gathered for the production were becoming more
substantial . . . the atmosphere of the classroom, attempts to bring back
memories, childhood, victories and defeats, more and more clearly defined
the idea of the theatre of death, new territories and horizons . . . all of this
pointed to the possibility of creating an autonomous production without
the need to fall back on drama.
In the process of building and multiplying new images, situations, and
characters, there emerges a real threat that this new and original matter
of the production, just emerging, which is becoming more dense, may
unwittingly become a self-enclosed production, which folds back upon
itself, points to its own content—thus, that it can become a plot, which
will demand that it be presented according to the rules that I had banned.

I am fully aware that a uniform, logical expansion of the matter of the
production will give birth to the elements of the plot.
I return to the idea of parallel action. This time, however, its meaning
is different. This time, I made use of Witkiewicz's *Tumor Brainowicz*, a
creation of pure imagination which, as in Witkiewicz, was grounded in
the sphere of our lives. My fondness for literature returned again. This
will explain why my conflicts and doubts, at one moment, lean towards
drama and, at another moment, towards theatre.
The Dead Class emerges at the threshold of these indecisions.
The characters from *Tumor Brainowicz*, who enter the stage, which is the
classroom, or the classroom, which is the stage, bring with them their fate
and destiny. Since they contain in themselves the content of the play, the
real action of "The Dead Class" is freed from the play's potent thought.
They merge with the figures from the classroom, who also exist at the

borderline between life and death. All hell breaks loose. We enter the world of dreams and nightmares. The characters from *Tumor Brainowicz* leave the stage. They disappear. The reality of the classroom begins to exist on its own. After some time they return, but different, as if changed by events about which the audience knows nothing and which must have happened behind the doors. They return in a different moment of the plot. This is how the plot functions in this poetic rendering; at the same time, because of the lack of logical explanation for the gaps in its unfolding, the plot itself is invalidated and not taken too seriously.

Above all, these gaps play yet another function, which was already described.

This programmatic ignoring of the plot; the act of diminishing its value and significance—that significance, which is used to help carry the burden of the idea—is partially justified by the fact that it was Witkiewicz himself who placed this lofty idea in the fabric of the plot, which had a dubious rank and status, almost equal to that of kitsch, of Harlequin romance novels, lacking any artistic value, an operetta.
By so doing, he successfully avoided falling into the trap of pathos, thoughtless procreation, or other plagues.
In my vocabulary, I use the term:
REALITY OF THE LOWEST RANK
to describe similar practices.

FROM THE DIRECTOR'S NOTEBOOK—
1974

In Witkiewicz's play, it is already the third act. The plot is becoming more and more complex and difficult to decipher. From this moment on, everything is rushing helter-skelter towards the end. The pace accelerates like a film in fast forward. The author does not hide the fact that he must bring all the conflict to swift resolution. He is doing this hurriedly and—it must be noted—carelessly pays little or no attention to verisimilitude or psychological motivations. The feeling of an impending catastrophe and panic drives these actions. Everything rushes headlong recklessly. It is only natural that little attention is paid to the aesthetic values and the logic of the plot, both of which are closer to glitziness of operetta than to those of legitimate drama. The cause-and-effect logic of hope and the unfolding of plot, which have existed until now, disappears. It seems that a new kind of plot is constructed, as if, in this rush of insanity, we were to start again from the beginning.
Even the most diligent and patient audience member hastily gives up on the idea of following events and moods, which change with a maddening speed, and surrenders to the power of the whirlwind within the four walls of this HORRENDOUS BOURGEOIS ROOM.

On stage, all of this matters very little.
In this poor classroom, DEATH takes its heavy toll.
No one even attempts to consider a proper denouement.
The characters of *Tumor Brainowicz* will drop dead one by one and their
bodies will be massed with other nameless bodies!

Continued:

A DIALOGUE—EMPTY SHELL

Tumor is at home again.
It seems that everything is back to normal. There is no trace of the past
adventures and escapades.
As if they had never taken place.
Isidore, with whom Gamboline was pregnant
during the first two acts, was finally born.
A tempestuous and, as always, shocking
dialogue between Tumor and Gamboline.
Tumor announces that he is definitely
leaving Gamboline and
getting a divorce.

FROM THE DIRECTOR'S NOTEBOOK—

It would be simply naïve to partake in this bourgeois conflict. There are
more important things that we need to attend to.
We will focus only on the intensity of this marital scene. A comic aspect
of this affair, which is always lurking at the bottom of such a quarrel, will
control the increasingly tragic sentiment and will make it seem starker
without the pathos, which also accompanies such events and makes the
scene lose its sharpness and realness.

In order to remove the narrative [plot] structure from this quarrel, let us
reduce its "semantic" layer to a pattern, which is almost abstract and
which does not lead to any resolution, but which retains the "thickness"
of its language—its everyday expressions bordering on mental decrepitude
bereft of any logic or sense. Circumventing all analytical speculations, let
us say that it resembles an endless chatter.
In my vocabulary, such a dialogue will be called "a dialogue—empty
shell."
Bereft of real aim and left without knowing what a resolution might be,
THE OLD MAN IN THE WC—TUMOR, who is its receiver, responds
making faces and with meaningless murmurs under his breath.
A Dialogue—Empty Shell.
A string of words and phrases, whose intonation only is heard and which
help decipher the meanings.

Someone is quarrelling; someone is being chastised; someone is bitterly complaining, etc.
Each phrase and each line end categorically and unquestionably,
that is, it is directed towards some kind of a definitive conclusion,
which closes the matter once and for all.
On stage, there is no sign of reaching a conclusion, an end, or a goal.
Intonation, which, full of meaning and determinate sonic value,
hovers over the complete nothingness.
Each phrase and line must have its clear sonorous meaning:
reproach, rebuke, admonishment, complaint;
excuses, threats, curses,
persistent questioning, boring enumerations. . . .

. . . Actually, we should forget about the play's plot, which is becoming more and more complex.
However, this mutual interplay
between the dramatic plot and the fate
of the Dead Class—becomes as equally fascinating a game as the dramatic plot proper.
I call it: NEGOTIATIONS WITH DEATH.
This is why we will follow Tumor's fate a bit longer.

THE WASHING OF THE CORPSES
FROM THE DIRECTOR'S NOTEBOOK—

In their childhood, THE CLASSROOM and THE SCHOOL DESKS brought them [the Old People] together. Then, they all went their separate and individual ways. And now, when they come back for their last performance at the end of their lives, they have nothing in common, they are STRANGERS to each other.
The tiny bodies of children—their childhood—which they carry with them, the only thing that could awaken their memories . . . are lifeless. They, too, are almost dead, touched by death; by a deadly malaise. For the price of being STRANGERS to each other and of DEATH, they win a chance of being art OBJECTS.
This very feeling of ESTRANGEMENT, which brings them closer to the condition of the object, eradicates their biological, organic, and naturalistic live-ness, which has no meaning in art.
They become the elements of the work for having "sacrificed" it.
For having "sacrificed" [live-ness], they became the elements of the work of art.
THE PERFORMANCE gave them their lives.
However, during the performance, new relationships, differences and attachments were created among them.
There began to emerge, like nebulous specters, new figures to be formed by this new life, whose shape and not always noble character are well-known to them.

Slowly, everything started to find its justification in the logic of the unfolding plot, life's cause-and-effect patterns; to leave that place where a perfect, absolute, autonomous and self-contained work of art was to be made—that place, where a godless and lawless creation, rather than god-like reproduction of nature, was to be made.

It is imperative that they be turned into STRANGERS again. It is necessary to take away from them those appearances of normality rationalized by a plot and life itself. It is necessary to expose them to the effects of shame. To strip them bare. To make them all equal as if for the Last Judgment. Worse than that. To bring them to the most discreditable and shameful condition—that of a dead corpse in a mortuary.

It is only THE CLEANING WOMAN–DEATH who can perform this ruthless, but indispensable, maneuver.

THE CLEANING WOMAN performs her duties professionally and ruthlessly. She enters the stage with a bucket of water and a dirty rag. She washes the corpses, wrings the rag; dirty water drops onto the ground. Stripping the bodies bare, washing their intimate parts, thighs, stomachs, buttocks, feet, faces, fingers; cleaning their noses, ears, groins; a vicious and unceremonious throwing and turning of the bodies.

A continuous and rhythmic rattle of the wooden balls in a cradle.

A poorly-made CRADLE, looking like a tiny coffin, tilts monotonously back and forth; the mechanical movement of the gears of this grim box is completely bereft of tender motherly care; the sounds of a baby are replaced with the rattle of two wooden balls, hitting the walls of the coffin. A mortuary.

THE CLEANING WOMAN performs the ritual of scrubbing the corpses with appalling disinterest, with precision, and systematically.

in the play:
a family disagreement
ends up with Tumor's
final decision
and also with curses:

in the performance:
At the end of the DIALOGUE—EMPTY SHELL, THE CLEANING WOMAN forces THE OLD MAN IN THE WC–TUMOR to lay down on the school desks and pulls off his pants, socks, and shoes. She lifts his legs one by one and wipes them with a dirty rag.

While stretched out like a dead corpse, THE OLD MAN IN THE WC–TUMOR listens to the arguments of the dejected WOMAN WITH A MECHANICAL CRADLE–GAMBOLINE.

Driven to the limits by her endless and tedious litany, he sits enraged on the top of the school desk with his feet dangling; he straightens his glasses and, at the very moment when the unhappy madwoman finally stops a long list of her accusations, he screams at her:

THE OLD MAN IN THE WC-TUMOR

Today, I am divorcing you!
Out of my sight, you damned slut!
I am the lord of the world!

These are the same lines, which Tumor speaks in the play.
They have a clear meaning now in the context of the earlier
explanations. . . .

FROM THE DIRECTOR'S NOTEBOOK—

At this moment, in Witkacy's play, an extremely dramatic and shocking
event takes place: Gamboline, with a look of total madness and despair,
dashes to the window and throws the still-diapered baby out of it. While
reading the playtext, this action may impress a poorly educated reader.
While presented on stage of the most traditional theatre, this action will
be nothing more than a pitiful trick.
This is why, as well as because I reject the idea of the presentational or
representational aspect of drama, we will pay no attention to this action
in the play.

Using this as an example, my very basic conviction can be explained: no
stage action which is to illustrate the text, can equal the power contained
in a given action expressed through the dramatic structure of the play.
The idea of stage acting based on this old convention and belief is today
naïve and simplistic.
Let us return to the incident with the still-diapered baby, who was thrown
out the window by his own mother.
Let me emphasize that we respect all life categories and conditions, since
the dramatic text makes direct references to life's experiences. This is
the law of the dramatic structure of the play. The shock caused by this
monstrous act cannot be adequately expressed by any presentational or
representational (most *trompe-l'œil*) strategy or technique.
This is why I abandon this naïve practice.

A MAD ACTION OF THE WOMAN WITH A MECHANICAL CRADLE

in the play:
Gamboline
responds to
Tumor's insults:

in the performance:

THE WOMAN WITH A MECHANICAL CRADLE-GAMBOLINE
reaches an inner decision in response to the insults of THE OLD MAN IN
THE WC-TUMOR. She says:

THE WOMAN WITH A MECHANICAL CRADLE-GAMBOLINE

So, this is it?
Everything I have done for you means nothing to you now?
I am to be treated like a dog for my attachment to you?
You dare to insult
what is most precious and holy in me?
Deal with this, you double-trickster!

Gamboline throws the baby out the window.
    Everyone freezes; and full of expectations, stares at the mad woman.
She walks steadily, as if on stilts, toward the cradle.
At this tense moment, the rattle of the wooden balls becomes impossible
to bare.
The barefoot mad woman, wearing her torn and dirty night-shirt, bends
over the cradle and wraps the wooden balls in dirty rags. She holds them
in stretched-out hands; and, holding them as if something precious and
holy, she slowly approaches THE OLD MAN-TUMOR.

FROM THE DIRECTOR'S NOTEBOOK—

It all should have the atmosphere of a dream.
The wooden dry balls, which during the course of the performance,
became a sign of a mystical image or a symbol of a child—because of their
low and shameful object-ness or condition of being an object—somehow
reduce this child into being a dead object; they deaden and lessen him.
The wooden balls became holy and,
at the same time, sacrilegious;
this which is untouchable and,
at the same time, cursed.
Invisible inside of the CRADLE-COFFIN, they seemed to be
intimately connected with it.
Taking them out became an act which was forbidden and prohibited.

    in the performance:

    THE OLD MAN-TUMOR, in the grip of fear, stares wide-eyed at the
cradle and at that something that THE WOMAN-GAMBOLINE carries
in her hands while she approaches him; he covers his face with hands in a
defensive gesture.
THE WOMAN-GAMBOLINE stands in front of him; throws the bundle
at him; he tries to catch it; the rest makes a loud groan.
Suddenly, OLD MAN-TUMOR, as if nothing has happened, takes the
bundle and puts it into his pocket.

in the play:
Green is appalled by
Gamboline's crime:

At this moment, THE OLD MAN WITH HIS DOUBLE-GREEN comes up and horror-struck shouts:

THE OLD MAN-GREEN

But Mrs. Tumor Brainowicz!
People do not do things like that!
This is sheer barbarity!

A SCANDALOUS BEHAVIOR OF THE OLD MAN COMING OUT FROM THE WC

in the performance:
THE OLD MAN WITH A BICYCLE-JÓZEF comes out at the most inopportune moment.
The old scatterbrain has no idea what is going on around him. While pushing his bicycle, he is reading a newspaper; he is pointing at something in it; but nobody pays any attention to him.

in the play:
Józef, Tumor's father,
as Pilate, unwittingly "falls" into the "Crucifixion-story":

THE OLD MAN WITH A BICYCLE-JÓZEF

shoves the newspaper in THE OLD MAN-TUMOR's face, his son, and speaks through clenched teeth:
Begging your humble pardon. But they have
written up my boy here in the paper!
A hero! A thinker! A genius at ideas!
But where is that island? And is it true that
he claimed to be the son of a fiery mountain?
Oh, my boy, that was not nice of you to disown
your legitimate father and you will be punished. . . .

Tumor
at the brink of exploding:
THE OLD MAN-TUMOR stammers; irritated, he grabs the newspaper from THE OLD MAN WITH A BICYCLE-JÓZEF and flings it to the floor. . . .

THE OLD MAN-TUMOR
Damn it all to hell,
get rid of that trashpaper.

He stares at the old man, his father, no matter what; pulls out two wooden balls from his pocket and gives them to him as a "gratuity" ["*pour-boire*"].

He corrects his glasses. Despite the fact that he is still without his pants and his feet are dangling, he is sitting aloof.

The porters carry in
a "dead corpse"
of the child.

   The Old Józef takes the two wooden balls into his hands with tenderness and very carefully.

THE OLD MAN WITH A BICYCLE-JÓZEF

They did not even spare the child, sons and daughters of a bitch!

   Holding the wooden balls in his hands, as if there the relics, he marches forward towards the cradle; he stops in front of it; with all his focus directed at them, he raises them up, as if wanting everybody to see them; then, suddenly and unceremoniously, he drops them into the cradle, as if into an open grave.
He stares at them a bit longer. . . .
Then, resolutely, he returns to where he left his BICYCLE and embarks on his last journey.
However, before he departs forever, he turns towards the audience, smiles, and, with a solemn gesture, pulls a big folded handkerchief out of his pocket; he unfolds it very carefully and in stages; he grabs one of its corners and waves it as if saying good-bye.
He must be saying farewell to the audience and everyone else.
Then, he folds the handkerchief equally carefully—first into halves; then, into quarters—and puts it back into his pocket.
And so, he will keep repeating this sequence of folding and unfolding until the very end.

This sequence is called:
THE DUMBSTRUCK OLD MAN WITH A BICYCLE LEAVES
SAYING GOOD-BYE TO THOSE PRESENT
From this moment on, he will endlessly be leaving and saying good-bye.

THE WASHING OF THE CORPSES—CONTINUED

During these events, THE CLEANING WOMAN continues "washing the corpses." THE WOMAN WITH A MECHANICAL CRADLE-GAMBOLINE is the next one in line for this cruel and shameless ritual. After her tumultuous row and her horrendous action, she is sitting, completely exhausted, barefoot and almost naked in her dirty nightgown shirt, on a pile of dirt and garbage. She does not resist.
THE CLEANING WOMAN begins to hurry. With a basket and a dirty rag, she rushes towards THE SOMNABULISTIC WHORE-IZA. She pulls off her high-laced shoes; she knocks her over and pulls up her dress; she

takes her time to wash her carefully: the thighs, the knees, the calves, and the feet; unceremoniously, she pulls out her breast—the one that THE SOMNABULISTIC WHORE shamelessly exposed—and washes it with zeal. This is too close to necrophilia.

GREEN AGAIN. DISGUSTING BROWN-NOSING.

in the performance:

Having seen THE OLD MAN WITH A BICYCLE-JÓZEF, who is saying good-bye to everyone waving his big, white handkerchief, THE WOMAN WITH A MECHANICAL CRADLE-GAMBOLINE says:

Your own Papa-Anthropoid
has evaporated into thin air!

Having said this, she sits on the toilet of the already well-known outhouse and gets ready for her last appearance in this show.

Even though nothing should surprise us in this apocalyptic circus, something unexpected and embarrassing happens, however.

in the play:
Green, who is cunning and obsequious,
flatters
Tumor:

THE OLD MAN WITH HIS DOUBLE-GREEN, this despicable and sleazy character, runs up to Tumor and lies down at the bare feet of THE OLD MAN IN THE WC-TUMOR. He begins to feel them up, lick them, and almost makes love to them as if to satisfy his perverted, erotic fetish. . . .

THE OLD MAN-GREEN

I am still here,
I will stay with him.

This disgusting moment is compounded by THE CLEANING WOMAN, who, with passion and fierceness pulls down the pervert's pants, strips him naked, knocks him down and begins to scrub one by one: his legs, thighs, buttocks; ruthlessly, not paying any attention to the screams and shouts coming from every corner, she whips his body with a dirty rag.

Tumor
calls him unspeakable
names:

THE OLD MAN IN THE WC-TUMOR

indifferent to THE OLD MAN-GREEN's flattery, calls him names:
You miserable crab, you eavesdropper on
unthinkable thoughts,
you psychic kept-man of a degenerate adolescent,
you blockheaded intellectual rag-picker,
you birdcage for colored feathers,
you powderpuff, you lackey of
strumpeted infinity. . . .

THE DEAF OLD MAN BRINGS AN AWFUL PIECE OF NEWS. ETERNITY OR CLEANING OF THE EARS.

in the play:
Tumor's son brings
an awful piece of news, spread around
by his enemies—
Professor Brainowicz,
in his new theory, has renounced
the concept of infinity. . . .

in the performance:
THE CLEANING WOMAN enters trotting. She carries THE DEAF
OLD MAN on her back. THE DEAF OLD MAN, a newspaper crier,
announces the sensational news:
THE DEAF OLD MAN (Tumor's son)
Listen to me! Listen to me!
Only I beg you, be brave,
do not let this news upset you!
Tumor Brainowicz has fallen victim
to his own weakness. . . .
(he repeats this news endlessly. . . .)

The entire class is getting ready for the last adolescent prank, whose
victim is of course a stone deaf OLD MAN, as if brought in for that
purpose by THE CLEANING WOMAN.
This circus-like trick requires a special mechanism.
THE OLD MAN WITH HIS DOUBLE and THE DOUBLE drag the OLD
DEAF OLD MAN away from THE CLEANING WOMAN. They stand
him upright and pull a long rope through a tube attached to the back of
THE OLD MAN'S old-fashioned hat.
The tube's ends are just above the ears. From a distance, one has an
impression that a rope was threaded through the ears and head of THE
DEAF OLD MAN.
Now, all that needs to be done is to pull the rope.
And, indeed, the two doubles, who positioned themselves on either side,
pull the rope in one direction and next in the opposite one.

THE DEAF OLD MAN, standing in the middle, seems to be strung on a thread.
And this is how the cleaning of his ears is done.
The old man never stops repeating the news.

INEXCUSABLE RUN OF THE OLD DEAF MAN.

And he, too, from now on, will run endlessly in circles without purpose.

It is quite possible that THE DEAF OLD MAN, on his own initiative, became eager to continue with this circus-like exercise.
He pulls the rope right and left with both of his hands.
His movements are mechanical.
He rushes forward. Stops. Cleans his ears.
Cries out: Tumor Brainowicz has fallen victim. . . .
Freezes, as if the mechanism stops operating.
Pause. The mechanism is in motion again. Its springs must be working.
The old man, as if unexpectedly, reaches a decision. He rushes forward.
Stops. Cleans his ears by pulling the rope right and left. Cries out: Tumor Brainowicz has fallen victim. . . . Freezes. Pause.
And so this will endlessly continue.

TWO NAKED CORPSES—THE VICTIMS OF THE OLD MAN IN THE WC—
DRIVE HIM TO DESTRUCTION.
THE OLD MAN IN THE WC DROPS DEAD TOGETHER WITH HIS TWO CORPSES.

And so, this is how they will endlessly continue dropping dead and getting up, one by one.

THE OLD MAN IN THE WC-TUMOR continues with a strange activity, which he began some time ago, of standing at the top of the desk and of washing the WINDOW, mechanically, monotonously, and tirelessly as if he were in a dream. THE WOMAN BEHIND THE WINDOW stands on her toes in order to better observe the final death throes of the entire CLASS.
THE SOLDIER FROM WORLD WAR I must have some devilish plan for one more and last prank. He drags THE ABSENT-MINDED OLD MAN FROM THE LAST ROW-PATAKULO SENIOR, who was inexcusably shot dead by THE OLD MAN-TUMOR and is now lying in the CORNER. THE SOLDIER FROM WORLD WAR I places him next to THE OLD MAN-TUMOR, who keeps washing the dirty WINDOW; and on the other side, he places THE PEDOPHILE OLD MAN-PATAKULO JUNIOR. He whispers something to the two of them and leaves.
Both, Patakulo Senior and Junior are stark naked as at the Last Judgment.
Both, as dead corpses should, stand stiff upright, facing the audience.

Now, THE DEAD-JUNIOR slowly turns his naked upper body around, as if on an axis, towards THE OLD MAN-TUMOR. He lifts his face up towards him and makes a face of a "dead person." Then, he drops dead. THE OLD MAN-TUMOR screams in panic and turns his face away from this dreadful DEAD mask.

An even more terrifying image is he going to see on the other side. THE DEAD-SENIOR, old Patakulo exactly repeats his "unhappy" son's mask of a "dead person." He regains composure (still as if on an axis) facing the audience. He drops dead with his face down.

Only the naked back and the back of his head are visible.

(It is necessary to keep the precision and mechanical nature of the movements, which are to imitate the mechanism of a clock.)

THE OLD MAN-TUMOR, the way it happens in the play, suddenly clutches at his heart in pain and cries out: . . . Patakulo! . . . and, as if thunderstruck, falls onto the bodies of his victims.

And so they will endlessly continue to drop dead and get up until boredom strikes. . . .

PEDEL'S PARTICIPATION

When "Patakulo!" is heard, Pedel, as if on somebody's command, gets up, salutes, and sings a servile Austro-Hungarian anthem:
Gott erhalte,
Gott beschütze,
Unsern Kaiser,
Unser Land. . . .

A WOEFUL COURTSHIP OF THE SOLDIER FROM WORLD WAR I.
HESITATION OF THE WOMAN WITH A MECHANICAL CRADLE.

THE SOLDIER FROM WORLD WAR I takes upon himself the responsibility of completing the play's plot, even though he is not mentioned among the dramatis personae.

He adds this duty to the responsibilities of a soldier in the trenches, getting ready for the attack. In order to stay close to the atmosphere of the Dead Class, he holds a black funeral banner in his hand. He leaps forward to attack bearing the funeral banner; falls down in front of THE WOMAN WITH A MECHANICAL CRADLE-GAMBOLINE, as if mortally wounded, and cries out, while raising a banner in the well-known gesture of the soldiers who died in the battle of Verdun, which can be seen on a post-card:
"Will you, Madam,
become the fifth marquise of Nevermoore?"

Attacked in such a prosaic manner, THE WOMAN WITH A MECHANICAL CRADLE-GAMBOLINE, answers coyly:
"But, Mr. Alfred
it is much too early!"

And they, too, will endlessly continue repeating their gestures and words, which become more and more empty and meaningless. . . .

THE PUPILS PLAY A CARDGAME WITH DEATH ANNOUNCEMENTS

THE ABSENT-MINDED OLD MAN FROM THE FIRST ROW, THE OLD MAN WITH THE DOUBLE, THE DOUBLE, THE SOMNABULISTIC WHORE, AND THE WOMAN BEHIND THE WINDOW sit down in the first row and begin to do that which is always done when there is nothing else to do, that is play cards.
Moreover, this activity is banned at school and, therefore, is inseparably connected with the atmosphere of the classroom.
And because this is the Dead Class, the pupils play with DEATH ANNOUNCEMENTS.
They become more and more involved, taking many risks. THE DEATH ANNOUNCEMENTS are passed back and forth from one person to another, are thrown down and trumped; the clatter of the wooden balls in the cradle-coffin is mixed with the sounds of the "François-Waltz."
The players chant a well-known choosing game:
EENIE, MEENIE, MINEY MO.
CATCH A MONKEY BY THE TOE.
IF HE HOLLERS, LET HIM GO.
EENIE, MEENIE, MINEY, MO!
and so they will eternally play this game.

THE CLEANING WOMAN–DEATH ACTS OUT HER NEW PART SHAMLESSLY.

THE CLEANING WOMAN, who, at one moment, disappeared unnoticed, returns to play her new part.
The successive stages of the metamorphosis of this class janitor from an odious and menacing CLEANING WOMAN, progressively revealing the sharp traits of DEATH, lead to the only possible final metamorphosis in this theatre of death—to a vulgar OWNER OF THE BROTHEL.
Now, with her arse and huge breast protruding provocatively and her lips painted with a perverse lipstick, she is smoking a cigarette—
a vulgar and sensuous face;
an arrogant, but confident, walk;
her entire figure makes one forget
about nostalgia and a woeful mourning for this performance. . . .
There is no more time to contemplate this character
because the wild and mad
THEATRE OF THE AUTOMATONS CONTINUES—
Everyone keeps repeating their halting gestures and words, which will never be completed, as if shackled and imprisoned by them forever. . . .

Theatre of Similitude

I

According to legend mentioned in Cicero's *De oratore* and Quintilian's *Insitutio oratoria*, the art of memory came into being with Simonides.[1] The story goes that when Simonides had left an evening banquet, the entire building collapsed, burying the remaining guests. The relatives of the dead, who came to seek the bodies for burial, were unable to identify the bodies, for they had been mutilated to the point of being unrecognizable. Simonides, the sole survivor, was summoned because he remembered the order in which the guests had been sitting and, thus, could identify the dead. But to locate and to name the dead, Simonides needed not only to recall the images of the banquet and of the guests, but also, using a specific mnemonic lexicon (language and narrative), to give these memories an intelligible shape.

Even if he did not know about Simonides, Horatio, too, understood the power of recollecting and narrating the past. The moment he uttered the first words, standing in front of Fortinbras, the subjectivity of the dead, constructed out of the sediment of his memory of the recent events, permanently marked his and our present:

> And let me speak to th'yet unknowing world
> How these things came about. So shall you hear
> Of carnal, bloody, and unnatural acts,
> Of accidental judgments, casual slaughters,
> Of deaths put on by cunning and forced cause,
> And, in this upshot, purposes mistook
> Fall'n on th'inventors' heads. All this can I
> Truly deliver. . . .[2]

Simonides and Horatio draw attention to mnemotechnics, which was born of accidental violence to bodies and of a cultural or political need to answer that violence with an act of commemoration and of burying the dead. At the same time, Simonides and Horatio mark the fracture between the living and the dead, or between the Self and the Other, whose presence and identity are established in the process of representing what can be understood about it. This representation of a necessarily present intelligibility locates the dead along the narrative itinerary (spoken and written words) that steals their presence and autonomy bit by bit until there is nothing left but a memory of them. Mnemotechnics, to paraphrase Jean-François Lyotard, is thus "the esthetic of the sublime. But it is nostalgic; it allows the unpresentable to be invoked only as an absent content, while form, thanks to its recognizable consistency, continues to offer the reader or spectator material for consolation and pleasure."[3]

Such a practice, however, is no longer acceptable, as evidenced by Kantor's *The Dead Class*, where a nostalgic reconstruction of the traces of Kantor's memories of school days and historical events was constantly challenged and prevented from acquiring solid framing or from offering the spectators material for consolation and pleasure either by other events happening in the performance space (a parallel reality introduced by Witkacy's *Tumor Brainowicz*) or by Kantor himself. The desire of the Self to subjugate his memory and his autobiography to being what Kantor wanted them to be could never be fulfilled. A complete reconstruction of memory, and hence history, was impossible, because the rhythm of remembering and forgetting, thus of birth and collapse, could only accelerate the process of memory's and the Self's (dis)appearance.

The process of memory's and the Self's disappearance is not a progressive movement on a historical trajectory but a procedure that elaborates an initial forgetting of the actions and words that are older than memory and the language used to describe it. It draws attention to the historicity of a present moment and expresses the tension between its different enunciations rather than establishing a singular presence and identity, which Simonides and Horatio "would truly deliver." This procedure of recalling to mind (anamnesis) defines the very aporia of knowledge: "a non-coincidence between facts and truth, between verification and comprehension" or between the Self and the Other.[4]

This may be why when the process of memory's and the Self's disappearance is articulated, the accompanying performative act will always be fragmentary. The fragments, like the shards of a broken mirror that cut through the remnants of the metaphysics of technical efficiency, are the components of a dynamic process of arrangement and rearrangement, construction and reconstruction, as well as time and space, curving and folding back upon themselves. This process, as *The Dead Class* made painfully clear, calls for the strenuous search for the memory of the Other that coincides with the Self, who, like an artistic Emballage, preserves and protects these fragments:

> Emballage—
> when we want to shelter
> and protect,
> to preserve,
> to escape the passage of time.
> Emballage—
> when we want to
> hide something
> deeply.
> EMBALLAGE—
> must be isolated,
> protected from trespassing,

ignorance,
and vulgarity.
Emballage.
Emballage.
Emballage.[5]

II

Kantor's strenuous search for the memory of the Other received a new treatment in *Wielopole, Wielopole* (1980), *Let the Artists Die* (1985), and *I Shall Never Return* (1988). Each one of these productions dealt with different dimensions of the dialectical relationship between the artist and the text he desires to reveal or between the idea (the self's memory) and the image (a ready-made haunting the invisible fragments of his life), controlled by resemblance or similitude.

An image endowed with resemblance is an image that is controlled, measured, and modeled after; it merits the quality because it is regulated and possessed by something (a dramatic text) or someone (a playwright, director, actor) who bestows upon it a privileged position. As suggested in the previous two chapters, Kantor questioned resemblance-oriented systems and illusion, which they generated. He did so by introducing the notions of real place and real objects, which replaced artistic place and artistic objects, as evidenced by his arguments in the manifestos of the Autonomous Theatre, the Informel Theatre, the Zero Theatre, the Theatre-Happening, and the Impossible Theatre. What was significant in these manifestos was Kantor's belief that a radical rejection of illusion was possible only in the process of penetrating the very foundations of reification obscured by the seductions of everyday life and by traditional theatre and its accepted, normative structures.

In 1944, the world of drama (its illusion and its constructed plot) was "thrown" into life (real life). *The Return of Odysseus* did really take place in the reality in which he (Kantor) lived in 1944. He encountered the characters from the play in his life and on the streets. As he noted, there was no difference between them and the people around them:

> It was obvious that these "returning" dramatis personae cannot be coming from the world of the "SHADOWS" (though, as it became clear in *The Dead Class*, they had a lot in common with the dead); that they had to be LIVING people. LIVING people not only in a biological sense of this world, but also in its "social" one—this meant that they belonged to our time and our life,
> to our everyday,
> to our condition
> to our PLACE, a place existing in our life and our time. . . .
> It was important that a fictitious character of drama cease to be fiction;
> that it establish some secret relationship with the reality of life, with our everyday life;
> that it find in life its own e x t e n s i o n .[6]

Beginning in 1944, Kantor employed different places, a destroyed room, a poorhouse, a café, a post office, a launderette, a railway station, and a theatre cloakroom, which belonged to his reality of the lowest rank. The discovery that everyday reality could be a subject and an object of art and that art could employ real actions and real objects (later known as bio-objects—a wardrobe, a funeral machine, an annihilation machine, and school desks) delimited the boundaries of Kantor's topography of representational practices between 1944 and 1973.

Even though *The Dead Class* (1975) did make use of a bio-object (the school desks in a classroom), this classroom, however, was not a reality of the lowest rank. Rather, "it was a black hole, in front of which the whole auditorium stopped."[7] Separated by the impassable barrier, the audience watched the Old People seated in school desks, a bio-object par excellence, which was intimately connected to them and generated their emotions of fear, happiness, love, friendship, suffering, and freedom. Every time the Old People left their school desks and disappeared into the black hole of death, of the unknown, or of the unconscious, they returned to them to sustain their presence. Moreover, the performance space in *The Dead Class* was no longer defined in terms of the real place. By 1975, the materiality of the real place was replaced by "a pensum that reveals the meaning of the word 'defunctus'"[8]—a thought that was separated from the audience, inaccessible to them, and that made them perceive the anguish of Kantor's explorations of the structures of memory generated by the Old People. Real place was replaced by thought that belonged to the order of similitude that does not represent but affirms the existence of the holder of discourse. This affirmation is

> an atavistic g e s t u r e of human beings, who at the beginning of their own
> history needed to affirm their identity.
> Create something as if for the second time,
> out of that which already exists,
> "that is their own"—their human "own";
> repeat that which had already been created—by the gods,
> open themselves to god's jealousy and revenge,
> take a risk,
> be prepared to face the impending defeat,
> know that theirs will be futile endeavors,
> bereft of future,
> having only this one chance,
> bereft of their glamorous life's meaning and final end,
> *papier-mâché* façades.[9]

This atavistic gesture of repetition creates papier-mâché façades, which exist only to be seen and are a substitute for real objects, because real objects can spoil, break down, or deteriorate due to their continuous use. Papier-mâché façades do not. Neither do they have a use-value or function assigned to them. Understandably, such objects attracted Kantor's attention and emerged in his postreal place and post-bio-object artistic explorations.

Having gone through the period of challenging representation, Kantor focused on the act of repetition—thus, the act of creating something as if for the second time. This process of repetition was, for him, a metaphysical aspect of illusion—the same illusion that he had fought against for decades. Now, illusion provided Kantor with the opportunity to move reality and the real or realness into a different space and a different time. They acquired different names in different productions: a room of imagination in *Wielopole, Wielopole*, a storage room of memory in *Let the Artists Die*, or the inn of memory in *I Shall Never Return*.

Wielopole, Wielopole (1980) was a record of this transformation and of the process of multiplying different affirmations through repetition. Wielopole is the name of the town where Kantor was born in 1915. It is a real place, described by Kantor as a "small and typical town in the Eastern part of Poland with a big market square and a few dilapidated streets. In the square stood a little shrine dedicated to one of the saints where faithful Catholics gathered. There was a well there too, next to which at full moon Jewish weddings took place. On one side of the square were a church, refectory, and cemetery. On the other side, a synagogue, a few narrow Jewish streets with their own cemetery. Both sides lived in an agreeable symbiosis."[10]

The production was not, however, a reconstruction of Kantor's childhood memories of Wielopole. He had already accomplished this in *The Dead Class*. Wielopole existed for him in memory. Now, through the process of repetition, signaled already by the title of the production itself, Kantor decided to materialize onstage not a representation of reality (a mirror image of the real place), but another Wielopole created as if for the second time, in order to recuperate what could have been lost in the mnemonic process of placing the dead along the narrative itinerary. The repetition of Kantor's memories of Wielopole as papier-mâché façades materialized in this other space and this other time wherein the illusion of the past events was a portent of this other universe. This other universe, this other life's reality, could only be sensed now, in a different way, affirming the atavistic gestures of human beings, who came into a space liberated from the seductions of everyday life and its fetishized, enchanted simulacra.

The performance space in *Wielopole, Wielopole*, a simple wooden platform, was almost empty except for a few pieces of furniture—a bed, a wardrobe, a window, and a few chairs.[11] Kantor moved around them. He opened and closed a wardrobe, changed the position of chairs, and pushed a bed to a new location onstage. Once these introductory procedures were completed, on a signal given by Kantor, the doors, upstage center, opened, and the actors appeared onstage. They were divided into two groups. One group, the actors who were the family members, lay down on the stage floor, their bodies scattered around. The other group, the actors in soldiers' uniforms, sat or stood in a corner in two rows, posing as if for a commemorative photograph. Kantor closed the doors:

This is my Grandmother,
my mother's mother—Katarzyna.
And this is her brother, the Priest.
We used to call him uncle.

He will die shortly.
Over there, there sits my Father.
The first one from the left.
On the reverse side of this photograph,
he sends his greetings.
The date is: September 12, 1914.
In a moment, my Mother-Helka will enter.
The rest are the Uncles and the Aunts.
They all had already met their end somewhere in this world.
Now, they are lying scattered around in this room, imprinted as memories:
Uncle Karol, Uncle Olek, Aunt Mańka, Aunt Józka.
From this moment on, their "fates and fortunes" begin to change going through
radical changes, often quite embarrassing, such as they would have not been able
to face, had they been still alive.[12]

Kantor remained onstage. Unlike, in, for example, *The Dead Class*, where
Kantor could be seen staring intensely at the memory machine, the school desks,
or the audience on the other side of the impassable barrier, here, he moved the
objects onstage as if trying to establish the contours and the content of the room
of his childhood. But,

It is difficult to define the spatial dimension of memory.
Here, this is a room of my childhood
with all its inhabitants.
This is the room which I keep reconstructing over and over again
and which is destroyed over and over again.
Its inhabitants are the members of my family. ("The Room. Maybe a New Phase")

The room of his childhood on this stage was of course a repetition of that
other room that only existed in his memory:

The room of my childhood
is a dark WHOLE, which is full of junk.
It is not true that a childhood room in our memory
is always sunny and bright.
It is turned into such by
a literary convention.
It is a DEAD room,
as well as a room of the DEAD.
Recalled,
it dies.
If, however, we take small pieces out from it one by one,
for example, a piece of a carpet,
a window, and outside of it, a street going nowhere,
a ray of sunshine which hit the floor,
father's yellow leggings,
mother's lament,
a face behind the window—

maybe, we will begin to put together a real
ROOM of our childhood
and, by so doing, put together
this production.[13]

A room of Kantor's childhood was not a literary metaphor or a set design. Nor was it a place where he explored the interplay between the universe of memory and the world of literature. Neither had any use for Kantor any longer. As he stated,

> After many speculations and transformations, the ROOM in *Wielopole, Wielopole* acquired a final form which neither corresponded to a meticulously described concept of the REAL PLACE nor to this of the BIO-OBJECT. The concept of the BIO-OBJECT has become too physical and too much of a burden. . . .
> THE ROOM cannot be a REAL PLACE. It cannot be a r e a l   r o o m . If we take to consideration the audience, the room could not possibly be perceived as a intimate room of childhood but as a public forum.
> There is also another reason: the room cannot be real, i. e., exist in our time, because this room is in our MEMORY, in our RECOLLECTION OF THE PAST. This is the room which we keep constructing over and over again and which is destroyed over and over again. This pulsating rhythm must be maintained, because it delineates the real structure of our memory.
> At the same time the ROOM cannot be "furnished"; cannot be the place beyond which the auditorium begins; cannot be the stage. If it were, the room would be nothing more than a scene design, which would irrevocably crush our hopes for achieving r e a l n e s s .
> All those speculations force us to abandon logical analysis and rational thinking. Probably we will have to expand the meaning of r e a l n e s s onto the plane of immaterial MEMORY.
> We will have to accept m e m o r y as the only r e a l n e s s . This means that we will have to build a rational model of m e m o r y and define its sphere of activities as well as means of expression. This means that we will have to transfer the concept of r e a l n e s s onto the platform of EVENTS, ACTION, and ACTING. . . . ("The Room. Maybe a New Phase")

Not only was it difficult to define the spatial dimension of memory, "the only realness," but, since the process of recalling memory is questionable in itself for it is always connected with making a choice of what will and will not be remembered and made visible, Kantor suggested that this process either onstage, in writing, or in one's recollections of the past events, was nothing more than a process of "renting" or "leasing" memories to be shown. Kantor's recollection of the past made use of "hired" people who played parts of the characters in or inhabitants of his room of memory:

> In recollection of the past,
> real or noble characters do not exist.
> Let us admit openly, that the process of the recollection of the past
> is always suspicious and does not leave one clean.

It is nothing more that a process of renting memories.
Recollection of the past makes use of "hired" people.
These are shady, mediocre, suspicious characters,
who are waiting to be "hired" like seasonal help.
They look unfresh, unwashed, poorly dressed, weak,
eaten up by life, badly made up for the people, who are often close to us.
This suspicious character dresses up like a recruit to play the part of my father
My mother is played by a street walker,
the uncles by the homeless.
The widow of a highly-esteemed town's photographer,
who works hard to maintain the reputation of the Photography Shop
"Memory" is played by a frightful cleaning woman
who works in a church's morgue.
Let us not even mention the Priest.
His sister is nothing more than a simple kitchen help.
And one more character—Uncle Stasio, a mournful wreck of a Siberian exile—
a traveling peddler with a hurdy-gurdy.[14]

This was indeed a memorable collection of characters who were used by
Kantor to construct his room of memory. Once the sign was given by Kantor,
they entered the performance space. The first episode was entitled, "A childhood room, which I keep reconstructing over and over again and which is destroyed over and over again." In order to articulate Kantor's understanding of
the functioning of memory, the difficulty of defining its spatial dimension, the
ambiguity coded into the process of recalling memories, as well as the process
of "hiring" the actors, the shady characters—not to be the members of Kantor's family but merely to bring them back to life—consider a passage describing Uncle Karol's and Uncle Olek's futile attempts to furnish the room and to
arrange the bodies of the family members: [15]

UNCLE KAROL   looks around the room; recognizing
                                     the place, he grins at himself and his
                                     memories. It seems that there is some-
                                     thing wrong. A black suitcase attracts
                                     his attention.

A suitcase . . .

A suitcase was on the table . . .

Yes!

                                     He comes up to the table, touches
                                     a suitcase as if he wanted to check
                                     something. The suitcase brings back a
                                     sudden association. He looks at Uncle
                                     Olek sitting motionless in a chair.

Uncle Olek!

Uncle Olek was not sitting down then . . .

He was standing or walking . . .

> Uncle Olek gets up. He looks at the suitcase intently.

UNCLE OLEK

A suitcase was on the wardrobe . . .

> While carefully carrying a suitcase, he bumps into a chair.

And this chair?

> UNCLE KAROL notices the body of Grandfather Priest. The dead the Priest is sitting in a chair.

Grandfather?

Grandfather was not sitting down either!

Nor was he standing up.

> He is very surprised with his discovery. Both Uncles are engulfed in the solitude of their indecisions and memories.

UNCLE OLEK   stubbornly

And this chair?

A chair by the table!

And where was a table?

A table was in front of the chair.

Next to the chair

a table. . . .

And the doors?

> UNCLE KAROL   He lifts the Priest's body from the chair. He seems not to remember—

Grandfather was not sitting!

                Now, he seems to remember.

He was lying down!

Yes. He was.

His head was at the bedhead.

                He lays the Priest on the bed.

And the doors were opposite the window.

UNCLE OLEK   Trying to be systematic.

The window close to the table . . .

The wardrobe in the corner . . .

And the table?

Was there a table?

                He is besieged by doubts.

UNCLE KAROL

When Grandfather was opening the doors to come in,

the window was opposite the . . .

UNCLE OLEK   He recounts the actions like a child who is trying to solve a math problem.

If the suitcase was on the wardrobe,

the chair next to the table,

and the window was closed

what was Uncle Olek doing?

                Suddenly everything is absurdly mixed up.

And Józka was lying down,

no! There was no chair!

And the table?

He pulls the table towards the doors without paying any attention to the bodies of Aunt Józka and the Grandmother.

UNCLE KAROL

He is deep in his thoughts.

The Grandmother was standing next to the Grandfather.

The Grandfather was lying down.

But there was not Aunt Józka here!

UNCLE OLEK

There was no table either!

He holds the table above Aunt Józka.

The Grandfather was lying down, but Aunt Józka was not here.

UNCLE KAROL

He seems to agree.

No, it was not here.

Aunt Józka was not here.

Uncle Olek puts down the table. Together, they carry out Aunt Józka's body.

And Aunt Mańka?

She was not here either.

They carry out Aunt Mańka.

UNCLE OLEK

He is still trying to figure out the mystery of the table.

And this table?

And this table?

He pulls the table towards the doors.

And the table. . . .

Uncle Olek and Uncle Karol continued changing the location of the objects and removing the people who should or should not have been in the room of memory. This game could continue *ad absurdum*, but it was suddenly interrupted by the uncles' negation of their own presence onstage. If indeed, Uncle Karol was not there, his twin, Uncle Olek, was not there either. In other words, the uncles, who were the agents of the construction, deconstruction, and reconstruction of the room of memory, left or died in front of the audience. The room of memory, which had been called into being by Kantor's opening of the doors a moment ago, was empty now. However,

In front of us,
in this poor and dusky room,
behind the doors,
a storm and a inferno rage,
and the waters of the flood rise.
The weak walls of our ROOM;
of our everyday or
linear time
will not save us. . . .
Important events stand behind the doors
it is enough to open them. ("The Room. Maybe a New Phase")

Once the doors were opened, important events and people entered the room and dispersed in all directions in the process of constituting and, later, reconstituting its shape. As Kantor observed, memory can be equated with the interior of a room, that is, space. Space, as he suggested in "Lesson 3" of *The Milano Lessons*, was energy

which does not have an exit, or a boundary;
which is receding, disappearing,
or approaching omni-directionally with changing velocity;
it is dispersed in all directions: to the sides, to the middle;
it ascends, caves in,
spins on the vertical, horizontal, diagonal axis. . . .
It is not afraid to burst into an enclosed shape,
defuse it with its sudden jerking movement,
deform its shape. . . .[16]

Thus, memory, energy in a different universe, which could be sensed through art, burst into an enclosed room from behind the closed doors and altered the existing network of relationships inside it. Kantor, the holder of discourse or memory, watched the process of materialization and dematerialization of the most intimate aspects of the Self. They were defused and reconstituted anew the way papier-mâché objects are when external forces hit them. The opening sequence visualized this process onstage. The audience entering the performance space saw Kantor, who was organizing the room of memory onstage. Once his actions were completed, he gave a sign, and the family members entered. Uncle Karol and Uncle Olek began to move or remove the objects and the people in the room. The destruction and reconstruction of the room were performed according to what Uncle Karol and Uncle Olek remembered about its spatial arrangement. Their actions were unsuccessful not only because they could not agree about the location of the objects or the people, or whether they should or should not be present in the room, but, more importantly, because the room could never be fully organized. Giving it a final form would signify a process of giving a memory a fixed contour as well as of stabilizing a dynamic practice of recalling to mind, both of which were contrary to Kantor's intentions of exploring spatial dimensions of memory. In his introductory statement to *Wielopole, Wielopole*, Kantor noted,

> These introductory remarks raise my doubts about the nature of my endeavor, because we are not supposed to see it as "art," or "a spectacle." Instead, it will be a "rehearsal," that is, an attempt to bring back the time which is gone and people, who lived in it and who are gone too. As any "rehearsal," it will be an exploration of intentions and dreams which, by their nature, can never be fully complete or logical. It will not present us with well-known people and events, whose significance and functions are dutifully described in family memories or history books. It will not be a presentation of "memorized" people and events, but an attempt to "apply" the actors to those people and events. . . . One should not, therefore, be surprised when crucified Christ will not be shown. His place will be taken by Adaś, who just happened to be there, or the Priest, around whom the whole FAMILY is gathered. One should not be surprised when war's absurdity will not have a true or historical representation. This little room and the old photograph of the soldiers, who were just about to leave for the war, should be enough.[17]

When the Uncles left the stage, the Grandmother entered. Bent over the bed with the body of the Priest—Uncle Józef-Priest—on it, she intoned, together with the choir heard from afar, a psalm usually sung during the last rites. Her singing was interrupted by the Local Photographer's Widow, who attempted to enter with a bizarre tin camera resembling a machine gun. The opening of the doors disclosed a new space, an antechamber to the room of Kantor's childhood, an open interior of imagination where "the threats of memory are woven."[18] The body of a woman, who seemed to be dead, clothed in a white, tattered wedding dress, was lying there. The Grandmother kept saying, "Not yet. Not yet," to the Local Photographer's Widow signaling that Uncle Józef-Priest was still alive. Finally, the Local Photographer's Widow, despite the Grandmother's anxious "Not yet," entered with her odd-looking camera, expelled the Grandmother, and stood in front of the body of the now-dead Uncle Józef-Priest. She paused to contemplate the scene for a moment and, like the Cleaning Woman–Death from *The Dead Class*, embarked on a somber duty of scrubbing and preparing the body for the funeral rites and the final photograph. Once these tasks were completed, the Local Photographer's Widow opened the doors to let the family members in. The family entered, with jittery and jerky movements, slowly advancing toward the head of the bed. The Local Photographer's Widow took the family portrait with the deceased. Once it was taken, the family was unceremoniously thrown out.

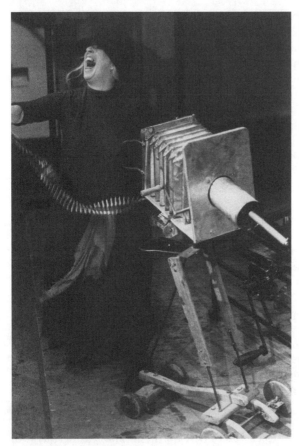

Wielopole, Wielopole (1980).
Photo courtesy of Romano
Martinis.

With the family gone, a forgotten group of men in military uniforms, thus far squeezed into a corner on the side, came to life. These were the young recruits just about to leave for the battlefront. Their faces were pale white, as if they were already dead in the Kantorian time warp—as if the impending future event of their death had already marked them in the present moment. These pathetic, nondescript figures in full regalia, seen by Kantor as illegal tenants of his room of childhood memories, arrived from the past only to "perform" a single pose that was to be registered by the Local Photographer's Widow's infernal *camera lucida*.

And, indeed, the Local Photographer's Widow moved a few steps away from the gray infantry—this spectral platoon—and pointed the camera at them. She laughed. While checking the camera, she adjusted the mechanism, revealing a thin gun barrel aimed straight at the soldiers. The camera was a machine gun. Every shot taken sounded like a volley of a machine gun fire. The soldiers froze. The Local Photographer's Widow, pleased with herself, exited, laughing hideously.

Was the presence of the platoon of recruits an accidental entry from behind the doors of the room of imagination? Or were they there from the very beginning, hovering as if between life and memory? As Kantor asserted in his production notes, while thinking about *Wielopole, Wielopole,* he discovered a new model for an actor, one that provided the actors with new possibilities as well as new performative gestures and actions. Until *The Dead Class,* Kantor's theory of an actor, who could only play himself or herself rather than a character from a fictitious world of drama, adhered to what Artaud called a performance on a nontheological stage. In *The Dead Class,* the actors were placed behind the impassable barrier that would make them look infinitely distant, shockingly foreign, as if dead, to the audience on the other side. While working on *Wielopole, Wielopole,* Kantor came across an old souvenir photograph of recruits who were probably waiting to be sent to the battlefront. For him, the images on the photograph were associated with gray, pitiful figures that were already transfixed by their encounter with death—death that had already come and singled them out, already had a look for everyone, and which had already dressed them in its horrific, "ceremonial" uniforms. Kantor observed,

> Two deeply-grounded characteristics of their condition could be identified with this one, which for centuries, has stigmatized the condition of an actor:
> one—the IRREVERSIBLE and FUNDAMENTAL DIFFERENCE (like with the dead) between them and us, CIVILIANS-SPECTATORS, sensed to such a degree that it erects a barrier; evokes a feeling of the IMPOSSIBILITY of crossing it; a feeling experienced only in a nightmare.
> Two—a horrifying awareness, which is also only experienced in a nightmare, that this DIFFERENCE applies to beings belonging to the same species as we do—thus, this difference applies to US,
> that, it is we who are these ALIENS, the DEAD,
> that we are confronted with our own image, with which we must become REUNITED.
> AN ARMY (it is difficult to say: a soldier)
> and
> AN ACTOR.[19]

The triad, the army-actor-spectator, merits a further explanation. The following two passages may elucidate this relationship:

> On stage, we have an ARMY, inhabiting the corner of the ROOM.
> Soldiers, walking towards us from the past, "d e a d,"
> reduced to a single grimace and a single moment,
> "resurrected" (I shall have to find a character who will perform this "miracle")
> acting without conviction, as if separated from or parallel to life and memory.
> Of course, there is nothing mysterious about these symptoms,
> which describe the condition of being in the ARMY.
> But in the ROOM, alongside the ARMY performing as if on the sly,
> there are also CIVILIAN-ACTORS,
> whose appearance, behavior, and mentality

are close to—blood-relations of—the SPECTATORS.
The SPECTATORS identify with the CIVILIAN-ACTORS
in their degree "zero" of expressivity,
and, thanks to them, discover within themselves little by little
condition of being, which is similar, if not identical, to that of the ARMY,
THEY EXPERIENCE ALL THOSE EMOTIONS AND FEELINGS, which
arise when one is confronted with oneself, stripped down to
the empty shell, to being a thing/an object, the DEAD.
A tide of thoughts is set in motion; its ebb and flow
disclose always more and more shockingly but clearly
the FACE of a HUMAN.[20]

Now, the second passage:

This collective organism looks like some kind of nightmarish machine,
whose moving parts are the people
deprived of their free will,
whose individual freedom is violated,
tortured,
dehumanized.
We see before our eyes a reified abstract of that special, artificially produced
Human Species, which is called
THE ARMY. . . .
These are the soldiers,
whose condition in this production and in this room is clearly defined already in
scene one:
they belong to the world, which has been "repeated," are a product of practices,
which I would describe as dubious and suspicious, performed in the dark recesses
and warehouses of life.
They have been r e p e a t e d; are a replica, therefore, fraudulent, the living dead
from birth.
They are caught into the trap.
They are bereft of their past and future life.
They have forgotten everything. They have settled for a life of a single moment.
They live parallel to life.[21]

The soldiers, the abject inhabitants of Kantor's room of memory, became a model for an actor in this theatre exploring the spatial dimensions of the recollection of the past. The audience, while watching their mechanized movements, their dehumanized shouts, and their tortured faces, was faced with this artificially engineered human species. There was nothing glorious or patriotic about the actions of this army of soldiers. From the time the photograph was taken, they belonged to death, which would come to claim their bodies. In Kantor's theatre, this act was repeated over and over again. Repetition, as he noted, was an atavistic gesture of creating a human again, but as if for the first time—a papier-mâché façade, ready to serve the audience that primeval force of a shock, Kantor talked about in the "Theatre of Death" manifesto. This time, however, there was no rope separating the audience from the actors on the other side. There was no impassable barrier, offering rapture over binarism, that marked the condition of the living and the condition of the dead. There was no metaphysical shock of the theatre of the automata. Here, in *Wielopole, Wielopole*, the family members, the other inhabitants of this room of memory, which Kantor kept constructing, deconstructing, and reconstructing, were a mirror, one may say, on whose surface the face of the soldier from that other side and the face of the spectator on this side were simultaneously reflected and cojoined. While watching the heap of broken images and people repeating their actions *ad infinitum*, Kantor provided us with an intimation of the world in which an actor offered to the audience a difficult lesson about memory as the necessary condition for constructing the structures of belonging and emotions:

> These DEAD FAÇADES
> come to life, become real and important
> through this stubborn REPETITION OF ACTION.
> Maybe this stubborn repetition of action,
> this pulsating rhythm
> which lasts as long as life;
> which ends in n o t h i n g n e s s;
> which is futile;
> is an inherent part of MEMORY. ("The Room. Maybe a New Phase")

This could explain why Uncle Józef-Priest, who was already laid out and clad for the last resting place, came to life. He looked around the room, directed his gaze at the doors, which had closed behind the Local Photographer's Widow, who had taken his last photograph, and, finally, concentrated on the soldiers in the corner. "Marian Kantor" were the only two words he uttered. There was no response. Uncle Józef-Priest approached the platoon and lifted a soldier in the front row. He tried to make him stand upright, but the soldier, Marian Kantor, fell down. Uncle Józef-Priest tried again. Finally, Marian Kantor remained standing. The sound of a military march, "The Gray Infantry" was heard. Uncle Józef-Priest disappeared behind the doors only to come back carrying a huge wooden cross on his shoulders. He encouraged the soldier to march. Marian Kantor's feet began to move. He tripped over. Stopped. Tried again. Uncle Józef-Priest, with the cross, marched on his own in front of the audience. Suddenly, as if remembering something important, he took the cross off his shoulders, placed it against a chair, and walked toward the doors. From behind the doors—from the antechamber between the room and the open interior of imagination, as noted by Kantor— Uncle Józef-Priest dragged the body of the Bride and placed her next to Marian Kantor.

This was the opening of the "posthumous nuptials." Uncle Józef-Priest conducted the ceremony. While he read the marriage vows, Marian Kantor, the Father, remained silent. His face was completely lifeless. The Priest prompted the answer—"I do." Something like a gobble came out of Marian Kantor, accompanied by rattling of his teeth. Uncle Józef-Priest moved to the other side and read the vows to Helena Berger, Mother-Helka. She responded in a weak voice, "I do." He returned to Marian Kantor and urged him to repeat the vows. Marian Kantor, the lifeless façade, could only produce nondescript noise in his effort to recall the sound of a human voice. Kantor observed,

> Keeping in mind
> that this ARMY
> is d e a d,
> has lost both its blood and its memory
> lived through some obscure cataclysm,
> as a direct consequence of the procedure of
> "r e p e t i t i o n"
> (the photograph).
> All that is left of them is only this papier-mâché surface;
> all that is left of them is only this gesture
> and some shreds of life, dead film negatives.
> Should one attempt to revive some fragment of their life (only on stage, of course),
> they will cry out in the idiom of the barracks, having lost forever their faculty of
> language and memory—they will jerk, charge, kill, walk off in any direction, fight
> to death with who knows whom, collapse and die.[22]

Uncle Józef-Priest moved to Helena Berger's side. She repeated the words of the vow. Finally, Uncle Józef-Priest placed the stole on their hands and, thus, completed the ceremony. Marian Kantor took hold of Helena Berger's body and walked away toward the doors dragging her, as if to an open grave. The white veil trailed behind. The black stole fell onto the ground. Uncle Józef-Priest led the other soldiers away. All these actions were to the tone of "The Gray Infantry." Finally, Kantor approached the doors and closed them. End of act 1.

These memory events were followed by exits and reentries of different characters emerging from "an open interior of our imagination . . . where the threats of our memory are woven."[23] Memory came to life in the form of the "dead," the members of Kantor's family, who populated the world of the stage through a

**Wielopole, Wielopole (1980).
Photo courtesy of Romano
Martinis.**

repetition of events and actions. "They continuously repeat all their movements as if they were imprinted on a film-negative shown interminably."[24]

The audience, thus, witnessed in act 2, "Vilification," the Family's return to the room clutching their belongings; their procession from the doors and the other end of the room as if it were a long journey filled with ambushes, perils, evacuations, and endless returns; Uncle Olek's and Uncle Karol's repetitive actions expressing their inability to stabilize memory; the troubles with repetition as evidenced by the ambiguous relationship between real Uncle Józef-Priest and the mannequin of Uncle Józef-Priest; the return of the Father-on-leave; the return of yet another shred of memory—Uncle Stasio, a Siberian exile; the family's vilification of the Father-on-leave; the family's vilification of Mother-Helka— Mother-Helka's Golgotha; the return of the dead soldiers; Mother-Helka's victimization by the soldiers; and the second wedding.

In act 3, the audience saw "Crucifixion," the return of the family to the room; yet another repetition of Uncle Olek's and Uncle Karol's actions—this time, the sequence consisted of dressing and undressing in a reversed order; Aunt Mańka's religious crisis—Gospel story of Christ's crucifixion told as a sinister counting of hours before an impending tragedy; the appearance of Aunt Mańka wearing a military (Himmler's) uniform; the unmasking of the repetition of and the ambiguous relationship between real Uncle Józef-Priest and the mannequin of Uncle Józef-Priest; the court martial of Uncle Józef-Priest administered by the Uncles to the sound of the wooden rattles; the entrance of the soldiers, who bury their bayonets in Uncle Józef-Priest's body; the return of the soldiers with the cross; Uncle Józef-Priest's collapse under the weight of the cross; the soldiers' hunting down of Adaś as a new victim; Adaś's crucifixion to the sound of the wooden bells of death; and the retreat of all the inhabitants.

In act 4, the audience watched Adaś's mobilization and departure to the front; the return of Uncle Józef-Priest with a suitcase and a rifle—all that remained of Adaś; the appearance of Uncle Stasio and his music in the moment of need, the showing of the infernal cattle car used to transport the soldiers to the front; the display of the jumbled bodies dead and alive; the Requiem for Adaś performed by Uncle Józef-Priest; the return of the Local Photographer's

Widow/Death, who swept the floor behind the doors where a split second ago the bodies of the soldiers were buried during Uncle Józef-Priest's Requiem.

Finally, in act 5, the audience witnessed "the Last Supper," the moral havoc among the Family caused by the death-bed machine rotating indiscriminately the body of Uncle Józef Priest and his mannequin; the consequences of this havoc: Uncle Józef Priest inexplicably left alone onstage; the return of all the "actors," the Family and the Soldiers, to perform yet another funeral for Uncle Józef-Priest (the mannequin nailed to the cross and the funeral procession) the dance of death; an unexpected intrusion of Aunt Mańka, now playing a part of a Rabbi; her desperate song; the multiple deaths of the Rabbi executed by a firing squad; the final preparations for the last gathering of the "Family" before the final "departure"—the Last Supper; and the final moment—the participants frantically organizing themselves around the makeshift table, with the family in front; the soldiers and the wax figures of the dead soldiers behind; the Local Photographer's Widow, of course, also a part of this moment before the departure, placing her infernal *camera lucida* in front to take the photograph; and the salvo of the machine gun. Silence. They all froze for a moment around the table, covered with the white cloth, caught in their emotive gesture; then, while Uncle Stasio played his melody wrought with nostalgia, they slowly retreated behind the doors.

When they all had finally left the stage, Kantor came up to the table, carefully folded the white cloth, and with a gesture punctuated the last chord of Uncle Stasio's song: "In the end everybody must leave."[25]

The music (Chopin's Scherzo in B-minor mixed with a Polish Christmas carol for Uncle Stasio, Psalm 110 sung during the ceremony of the last rites for Uncle Józef-Priest, a Polish military march, "The Gray Infantry," for the soldiers, the Rabbi's Jewish song) and Kantor's memory (presented by "hired" actors) destabilized the possibility of constructing a single memory. The music and the repeated gestures challenged such process by showing that the mnemotechnics used by Simonides and Horatio to truly deliver their stories was nothing more than a dubious and suspicious process of the recollection of the past. By exploring spatial dimensions of memory, Kantor remained faithful to

Wielopole, Wielopole (1980). Photo courtesy of Romano Martinis.

not being at home in one's home—and to be more precise, to not being at home in one's room of memory. Indeed, as *Wielopole, Wielopole* struggled to intimate, it was difficult to define spatial dimensions of memory. Here onstage, Kantor constructed, as if for the first time, a room of his childhood, which he kept reconstructing over and over again. While so doing, he kept reconstructing its inhabitant over and over again—the members of his Family and the Soldiers, who were squeezed into a corner. The Family members kept repeating their banal gestures and

> will keep repeating those banal,
> elementary, and aimless activities
> with the same expression on their faces;
> concentrating on the same gesture
> until boredom strikes.
> Those trivial activities,
> which stubbornly and oppressively preoccupy us,
> fill up our lives. ("The Room. Maybe a New Phase")

This repetition of actions, like the folding of representation back upon itself, transformed the linear sequence of life into frozen-in-time negatives. In *Wielopole, Wielopole*, those stored negatives were presented as incomplete fragments that appeared and disappeared, leaving additional traces before they dissipated into nothingness. The negatives onstage produced an intricate collage that allowed the Self to integrate the pieces lifted out of memory into a new creation. *Wielopole, Wielopole* presented the following negatives: act 1—Family (the room of the dead), three dead photographs (Uncle Józef-Priest, Family, Soldiers); Marian's and Mother-Helka's wedding/funeral ceremony; act 2—Family (the room of eternal family quarrels), Mother-Helka's Golgotha (the secrets of family life mixed with the Passion of Christ), Marian's and Mother-Helka's second wedding/funeral ceremony; act 3—Family (repetition of everyday actions), the judgment of Uncle Józef-Priest, the crucifixion of Adaś (the second

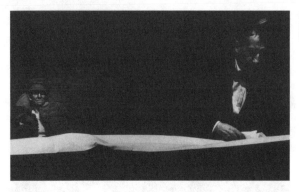

Wielopole, Wielopole (1980).
Photo courtesy of Romano
Martinis.

Golgotha); act 4—Family (the fear about Adaś is mixed with the fear of Apocalypse), Adaś's death and funeral; act 5—Family (the collapse of the image),
Uncle Józef-Priest's funeral (the third Golgotha), the Rabbi's funeral song and
his multiple deaths, the Last Supper. All sequences were constantly disrupted
by the entrances and exits of ur-matter from behind the doors. This ur-matter
could be the family members or the soldiers who burst in and interrupted the
slow development of the negative and forced it to assume a different shape.
For example, Uncle Józef-Priest's funeral cortege in act 5 was interrupted by
the sudden appearance of the Rabbi from behind the doors. A Jewish song was
heard. The chant was broken by a death squad, formed out of the soldiers,
who killed the Rabbi. Uncle Józef-Priest helped the Rabbi get up. The song was
heard again. The Rabbi was killed again. The action was repeated three times.
Finally, the Rabbi got up and left the stage.

Kantor made clear in *Wielopole, Wielopole* that what was being watched
were his intimate commentaries about life and death, about his family and historical events, and about Christianity and Judaism. These commentaries materialized in a different, second space, defined by repetition and its variants:

> The most profound [variant] is e c h o
> the same as the one that exists here, but immaterial,
> a sudden conscious realization of passing
> and d e a t h.
>   Another variant:
> a kind of l e a r n i n g process (to drill something into one's memory),
> Indeed: m e m o r y, which transfers the real into the past, which is constantly
> dying
> Yet another variant:
> if t i m e could shrink—
> then, we would have r e p e t i t i o n *par excellence*; never ending, frightful, and
> inhuman repetition,
> because our "calendar time," the time used to regulate and describe our bodies
> would not be able to save us from experiencing both
> eternity and n o t h i n g n e s s at the same time,
> that is, to save us from death. ("Illusion and Repetition")

Repetition, echo, memory, time, and mockery dominated this second space of *Wielopole, Wielopole*. As the production indicated, the process of constructing and reconstructing the room, the entrances and exits of characters, and the repetition of events and gestures constituted a complex network of relationships that created a space that was "other," another real space. Inside it, the multiple deaths of Uncle Józef-Priest acquired significance in the process of the composition and recomposition of the act. The echo, an immaterial equivalent of an aspect of the real, redefined traditional (religious) icons and their cultural functions. The act of putting a thorn crown on Mother-Helka's head before she is raped by the soldiers, Aunt Mańka's quoting of the Gospels and the Book of Revelation, the crucifixion of Adaś, the funeral cortege that follows a cross with Uncle Józef-Priest's mannequin on it, and the "Last Supper" of the family members before their final departure are just a few examples of this juxtaposition. Memory, which is constantly dying, was visualized by Uncle Olek and Uncle Karol, who moderated the number of people or objects present in the room. Finally, since linear time was abandoned, past, present, and future were coexistent. Thus, the Father in the wedding ceremony was simultaneously the Bridegroom, a soldier from the photograph mentioned by Kantor, and a soldier who had died during the war.

An interpretation of *Wielopole, Wielopole* can be derived from the tension between Kantor and the memories presented onstage. The room of imagination was positioned within the space visualized by the Self. Once activated, the room of Kantor's memory was transferred to the three-dimensional space of the stage, a heterotopia, a countersite to the real site in which the rules of the real site are recognized, questioned, and contested, in which the rules of real space were discarded by Kantor's rejection of traditional concepts of illusion and time.[26] Instead, this new space was defined by repetition and its three powerful components: echo, memory, and nonlinear time. In his treatment of heterotopia, Michel Foucault provides an example that illustrates this "other space" with the help of a mirror metaphor, that is, a mirror that exists between real sites and heterotopias: "In the mirror, I see myself there where I am not, in an unreal, virtual space that opens up behind the surface; I am over there, there where I am not, a sort of shadow that gives my own visibility to myself, that enables me to see myself there where I am absent."[27]

In this process of transfer, Kantor saw himself where he was not, in an unreal space, though real for him, that allowed him to experience life's reality in a different manner—through an opening of this other, inner space, as if behind the surface of a mirror. Within this space, his actors were put into motion or stopped by him. Kantor made the invisible visible by locating his immaterial memories in a three-dimensional heterotopic performance space. What spectators saw was the decomposition and recomposition of parts of his life. At the same time, the images on the other side of the mirror in the imaginary, heterotopic space, were negatives of Kantor's memory. Significantly, for the viewer, whose gaze was positioned between Kantor and his room of memory, both spaces were real, even though they functioned in different dimensions:

The weak walls of our ROOM;
of our everyday or
linear time
will not save us. . . .
Important events stand behind the doors
it is enough to open them. ("The Room. Maybe a New Phase")

III

The opening of the doors so that different, almost accidental, illogical, or even useless objects and people could enter his room of imagination described Kantor's creative process. Indeed, this is how he wrote about his process while working on the next production, *Let the Artists Die*, which premiered in Nürnberg on June 2, 1985.[28] Sometime in March of 1982, Kantor heard a story told to him by a gallery owner in Paris. Apparently, the gallery owner had wanted to expand the exhibition space, which required permission from the inhabitants of the building where the gallery was located. The neighbors protested and were unwilling to accept the argument that the works of the exhibited artists could bring recognition to the district. On the contrary, one of the neighbors loudly announced, "Let the artists die." Soon after Kantor had heard this story, he discussed the possibility of creating a new production in Nürnberg. It occurred to him that

> the only piece that I could create in Nürnberg and nowhere else is the story
> about a nail—a nail that was driven into and punctured Veit Stoss's cheeks as
> punishment for his debts. This took place when the Master, now an old man
> driven by yearning for his hometown, left Kraków, where he had built his life's
> masterpiece, an altar to the Virgin Mary, to return to Nürnberg.
> "LET THE ARTISTS DIE," I said excited by the coincidence and the similarity
> between the two stories. And this is the title of the new production.[29]

Let the Artists Die was not about the building of the altar, however. Kantor was trying to find a way that would allow him to discuss the problem of torture, martyrdom, brutality, and human bestiality rather than the nature of a work of art. He was interested in exploring the condition of being oppressed and the representation of torture onstage:

> If one were to show torture as one of the scenes of a play or as a performance
> piece, one would generate emotion by the very act of s e e i n g a brutal and
> bloody scene.
> In the production, the scene of creating a work of art—the building of an
> altar—is transformed into a torture scene. When the ALTAR—a WORK OF
> ART—is transformed into a TORTURE CHAMBER, an emotion is felt as a
> consequence of this unexpected TRANSFORMATION. The torture scene ceases to
> be a theatrical spectacle. It acquires a different depth.
> I never tried to find a stage equivalent for the process of creating a work of

art—an altar. From the very beginning, this scene was associated in my mind with
b e s t i a l i t y and m a r t y r d o m .[30]

When dealing with bestiality and martyrdom in the 1944 production of *The
Return of Odysseus*, Kantor annexed the war reality and refused to provide it
with the right to define the function of objects or people. He showed the incommensurability between the artistic object, whose function was assigned to it by
a convention, and the degraded object, which was reduced to a useless shell by
war. The same process was equally true for objects and people. "I am Odysseus.
I have returned from Troy" was a sonorous signification marking the mergence
of another world, wherein "objectness" or "subjectness" was established in a
manual process of signification and establishing a network of relationships between objects and people, who found themselves in the destroyed room balancing on the threshold between uselessness and eternity. Now, some forty years
later, this condition was given a new shape, which was prompted by the phrase
"let the artists die" and a nail driven through Veit Stoss's cheek, as well as the
discovery of the bodies of Polish soldiers killed by the NKVD in Katyń during
World War II. Indeed, "it is difficult to define spatial dimensions of memory."

While preparing *Let the Artists Die*, Kantor further elaborated on the distinction between the artistic object, which was a part of a work of art defined
as a cultural product, and the artistic object, which was a part of an autonomous work or a gesture of space-time-matter. Kantor's was not a nostalgic call
for the sublime, or transcendental, quality in a work of art, which had been
so forcefully inscribed and overdetermined since Immanuel Kant's *Critique of
Judgment* (1790). On the contrary, as noted in previous chapters, because of his
experience with constructivism as well as in Dada and surrealism, Kantor attempted to bring to the fore that quality of a work of art that was autonomous,
that is, nonrepresentational, nonillustrative, and existing-in-a-medium, as well
as "real" in itself, that is, it was not a stage equivalent, but it was reality that
exists nowhere else:

> This unusual language is not well received by the authorities because
> it escapes censorship,
> regulatory moral,
> social,
> and rational categories;
> the opinions generated by
> sanctioned ideologies, practical situations, existing conditions,
> assumptions or goals.
> It cannot be judged by known criteria.
> All criticism leveled against it is naïve and embarrassing
> revealing and unmasking
> stupidity and small-mindedness.
> Like thunderbolts, there travel
> the most intimate,
> shockingly awkward,
> strictly forbidden,

criminal,
blasphemous,
nefarious,
offensive thoughts, concepts,
images, circumventing logic and the laws of probability, crisscrossing, falling into
nothingness without a trace—
the whole inferno of all of that which is called
"IN THE MIND."[31]

This "in the mind" was, for Kantor, a condition that can be visualized as
Informel matter, which does not have a limit or a boundary, or as the mind's
vast interior, that gives birth to irony and protest, as well as provides the creative process with the power to circumvent nostalgia for the sublime or regula-
tory norm and categories.

With the first opening of the doors by the caretaker, who in the past was
known as Charon, the ferryman of the dead, the actors, wearing black dresses
and suits, entered and started to place wooden crosses in what looked like an
ordinary room with a few chairs and a bed. The One Who Is Being Seen Off
joined them onstage. The actors dressed him in travel clothes. The physician,
Aesculapius, who "wandered in from my school days, when the Olympians
gods often used to sit with us in the poor wooden school desks,"[32] came and
checked the pulse of the One Who Is Being Seen Off, who was departing. The
sounds of the funeral march were heard and the One Who Is Being Seen Off"
started to leave. And thus began his journey. The actors stood in the back, holding hats in their hands. The music stopped; the actors left the stage. The over-
ture was over and the performance proper was just about to begin.

Let the Artists Die presented us with new space for the exploration of "an
activity that occurs if life is pushed to its final limits where all categories and
concepts lose their meaning and right to exist; where madness, fever, hysteria, and hallucinations are the last barricades of life before the approaching
TROUPES OF DEATH and death's GRAND THEATRE."[33] In his commentaries on *Let the Artists Die*, Kantor indicated that

Let the Artists Die (1985).
Photo courtesy of Romano
Martinis.

one will find neither the setting
nor the action on this stage.
In their stead, there will be a journey
into the past, into the abyss of memory
into the past time that is gone irrevocably,
but which still attracts us,
into the past time, which floats into
the regions of DREAMS, INFERNUM,
THE WORLD OF THE DEAD,
AND ETERNITY. . . .[34]

The space that was entered was neither a classroom with school desks in the corner nor a room constructed and reconstructed by Kantor, but a room of memory, where everything was happening at once, whose shape was altered by the characters and forces invading it from behind the doors. For this reason, the old name, "the room of memory," was abandoned and a new name "the storeroom of memory," a place where characters from all different past events would meet, was introduced. The "wayfarers" appearing in the storeroom of memory would bring their individual and different memories with them. These memories, as *Wielopole, Wielopole* unequivocally asserted, could never be presented in a chronological order; rather, as Kantor insisted in this production, they were put together, as if they were the frames of a film negative stacked one atop another. In the program notes to the production, he defined these negatives in the following manner:

Negatives
do not describe the place of action,
but are the NEGATIVES OF MEMORY that are interimposed
that are re-called from the PAST,
that "slip" into the present moment,
that appear "out of the blue,"
that place objects, people, and events together . . .
that discard patterns of logic, which are binding in everyday life.[35]

Unlike *The Dead Class*, where the negatives were produced by the memory machine, or *Wielopole, Wielopole*, where they were acted out by the "hired" characters who created and re-created the room of memory, *Let the Artists Die* presented the negatives that were interimposed in space. Once memory was called forth, it folded back upon itself, generated new images that crashed into each other. Onstage, these memories were shown simultaneously as a cluster of negatives. Since, as Kantor pointed out, they were transparent, the Self, or the audience, could only see one frame, which contained the imprints and traces of all other frames recalled from the storeroom of memory. For example, the space in act 1 was both a childhood room and a cemetery storeroom. A bed, a night table, a door, and chairs shared the space with wooden cemetery crosses. There was no division between them. The space in act 2 was a childhood room, *teatrum historiae*, and an asylum for beggars and artists "*maudits*" of François

Let the Artists Die (1985).
Photo courtesy of Leszek
Dziedzic.

Villon; in act 3, a childhood room, an altar or work of art, and a torture chamber; in act 4, both an asylum and a prison cell.

The childhood room or cemetery could be transformed in any direction. It
waited for something or somebody (a negative or a set of negatives) to appear
from behind the doors of the room. In act 1, the process was initiated by the
owner of a cemetery storeroom, who entered to open his business at midnight.
He was joined by the mother, who would not stop talking, and the twins in
search of their individual identities—the "tenants" of the cemetery storeroom
returning from their nocturnal walks. Once they entered the stage, it seemed
that both space and time started simultaneously to recede into the past and to
fast forward into the future. This double transformation of bringing the past
(life) and the future (death) together was acted out onstage by the twins. One
of the twins was in bed dying; the other one sat at the bed observing the last
moments of his twin. One of them, I—the Dying One, was the stage character; the other one was the Author describing his incurable illness and his own
dying. Both of them were observed by Kantor, "I—the Real One," who was
seated in a chair on the side. In the hour of death, the image of a little pram was
evoked. The pram conjured up the time of childhood and the image of a little
soldier who, while the funeral march was played, entered the space with his
little wooden pram or cart. Kantor noted,

> I consist of a multiple series of characters embracing all possibilities from
> childhood up to the present moment—all marching from the DEPTHS OF TIME.
> They are all me.
> I am sitting on stage: I—THE REAL ONE
> On the bed lies one of the twins:
> I—THE DYING ONE . . .
> In a moment A LITTLE SOLDIER will show up—
> I—AT THE AGE OF SIX
> IN A PRAM.[36]

All of these different negatives of Kantor were simultaneously present onstage. These various images of Kantor evoked different memories, which assumed physical shapes and generated their own memories. Thus, "the happy Little Soldier [was] followed by his entourage and his dreams, THE THEATRE OF DEATH, THE COFFIN GLORY OF THE MAN WHOSE NAME WILL NOT BE MENTIONED HERE, A MISERABLE FIGURE WALKING ONE STEP BEHIND THE LITTLE SOLDIER, HIS LOYAL GENERALS, TIN SOLDIERS, DEAD, just their uniforms. Silver ones. For the first time my little room of memory is exposed to suffering and mutilation."[37]

Kantor's room of memory was invaded by characters from history and by his theatre of death. The parade of the ghosts of soldiers, accompanying a historical figure of the leader in a military dress on a skeleton of a horse, to the tune of a military march, "The First Brigade," brought back the historical negative from the World War I—or it could be World War II? The ghosts of the past slowly withdrew, leaving the little soldier and the leader on a horse. The theatre of death was replaced by another theatre of death—a story of agony and death of the Dying One as told by the Author—the author of this exact imagination of the delirious time past and time future. The Doctor was called for the dying man. He pronounced the verdict: "*Tethneksei met oligas horas* [He will die in a few hours]. Death has spoken in a classical tongue."[38] However, unlike similar death sequences in *Wielopole, Wielopole*, this one exemplified not the spatial dimensions of memory or time warp, as was the case with Adaś's death, for example, but the theory of negatives in the multidimensional performance space. While the story of death was told, Aesculapius became a victim of the theory of negatives—in this world pieced from shreds of memory simultaneously present, he was trapped in the impossibility of leaving linear time. He failed to pronounce the death of the Dying One, confused by the presence of different images of Kantor onstage: I—the Real One, I—the Author, I—the Dying One, and I—at the Age of Six. To save himself, Aesculapius withdrew toward the exit: "The impossibility of bringing life and death together is fulfilled. Of course, this can only happen in the world of illusion and at play. The feeling of touching eternity while being still alive. I want to restore to the word reflection its essen-tial meaning and implications, which are tragic, dangerous, much deeper than those which we were taught to believe in by the false con-missionaries of the truth-to-nature dogma. Something far more important is. The extension of our reality beyond its boundaries so that we can better cope with it in our lives."[39]

In act 2, "the COMPANY OF WANDERING COMEDIANS entered from nowhere, pulled into the room, as if by some secret power. The Little Room of my Imagination turns into a Nocturnal Asylum which gives shelter to beggars, Bohemian artists, cutthroats as if François Villon has arrived with his troupe having traveled from the depths of time."[40] These were not accidental, wander-ing actors. They had accompanied Kantor for decades. They had always lived behind the doors ready to enter when he was ready for them to enter. He knew them well:

I love
the poetry inside you,
your *poetry*,
your own,
but *DIFFERENT* for each and every one of you;
this poetry which is devoured by
l i f e,
this everyday life,
day after day,
month after month,
year after year,
everyday life with no end;
this poetry
which one hides inside
to save it from life;
this poetry
which is so often forgotten
and which gloriously erupts
on s t a g e .[41]

The parade of comedians, who mixed with the characters in Kantor's room of imagination, ensued. When the parade ended, everyone seemed to return to his or her routine activities. They were dictated by the objects they carried with themselves: thus, a Hanged Man with his gallows were grown into one, a Pimp addicted to card playing was with his card table, a character washing his dirty feet was with his basin, a Bigot was with her kneeling-desk, a Prostitute was with her overcoat, which when opened, revealed her black lingerie; and a Dishwasher was with her sink. These people with their objects, these *bio-ob-jects*, as Kantor called them, were not simply props or the elements of set design but were closely associated with the actors and the functions they performed.[42] These objects had their own life, independent of the action onstage. The ac-tors were their living parts, rather than vice versa. These bio-objects brought the functions of the characters to a higher pitch—thus, the gallows made the Hanged Man sing his arrogant song, the card table made the Pimp continue

playing cards, the kneeling-desk made the Bigot mutter her prayers, and the sink made the Dishwasher clean the dishes without a break, etc. While the Hanged Man with his gallows, the Pimp at his table, the Bigot with her kneeling-desk, and the Dishwasher with her sink tried desperately to execute their words, gestures, and actions, the Author attempted to describe the last moments of I—the Dying One. In this theatre of the everyday, which dominated the room of imagination now turned into an asylum for the different characters, everything was mixed together—vulgar songs and patriotic military ballads, prayers and the shouts of a card-player, and the agony of death and the ecstasy of life.

The inferno of everyday life mixed with the *theatrum mortis et gloriae* was interrupted by the appearance of a guest "from the other side," Veit Stoss, a fifteenth-century sculptor. Now, however, he was dressed in the costume of a Bohemian artist from Montmartre. In the room of memory, Kantor created for Veit Stoss, an asylum where Stoss would build an Altar that resembled his Kraków masterpiece. In a world governed by the Theory of Negatives, the altar was, however, transformed into a prison cell and a torture chamber. The parts of the Apostles were executed by the inhabitants of the Asylum, with the Bigot playing the part of the Mother of God. From behind the doors, the two helpers brought in the wooden objects, which had been inspired by those on the Altar. Here, however, these objects were turned into the infernal objects of torture. The wandering comedians were squeezed into them; the wheels and ropes were tightened so that they could not escape. Thus, the mysterious objects from the Altar were turned into the machines of torture that shackled the Hanged Man, the Pimp, the Bigot, the Dishwasher, and the Author. Now, they were convicted artists left to die. Their bodies, contorted by the machines of torture, were removed from the stage. But not for a long time. A moment later, the doors opened only to reveal the mutiny of the martyrs. They returned with their machines of torture on their backs to perform the dance of freedom. When finished, they disappeared behind the doors again. Only the machine or the pillars of their martyrdom remained onstage. Silence. The wandering comedians returned. Now, they found themselves in a prison cell:

Prison.
It is both a concept
and a perfect,
meticulously and thoughtfully structured model of man's history. It is undeniably a
"product" of man and civilization.
The fact that "prison" is set up against man; that it is a brutal mechanism
established to crush man's free thoughts happens to be one of the grimmest
absurdities. However, similar absurdities can be found in abundance in history
and in the illustrious *"magister vitae."*
Let us leave it then for history
to determine innocence or
guilt.
Let us consider
the ontological aspect of prison and its . . .
eschatology.
Prison . . .
A word which sticks in the throat . . .
There is something final about it; a feeling that something has happened that
cannot be undone or revoked. . . . The gates of prison close behind a man, as
the gates of an open grave close over the dead who "walk" through them. In a
moment the grave-diggers will be through with their work. The living are standing
yet for a long while . . . as if they could not accept the idea that he is to be left
"there"
alone! ("Prison")

But they were not alone: the inmates heard the faint knocking, to which
they responded by tapping on the objects of their everyday lives—such as the
gallows, the table, and the kneeling-table. Veit Stoss joined them in this prison
from which the artist tapped his "message" out to the world. Silence. Suddenly,
a response was heard.

Let the Artists Die (1985).
Photo courtesy of Leszek
Dziedzic.

In the final moments, the inmates of the apocalyptic theatre built the last barricade out of the objects of their torture and oppression. Kantor's room of imagination or cemetery storeroom from act I was now a barricade built by Veit Stoss:

> Once again I see
> this apparition,
> outlawed and
> tainted with madness;
> which is able to
> convey
> by means of violence and change
> the most dramatic manifestation of
> ART and *FREEDOM*! ("Prison")

All the inhabitants of the room of imagination or cemetery storeroom or asylum, including the historical figure and the soldiers, were on the barricade. At the top, a prostitute or angel of death, like the symbol of the French Revolution in Delacroix's painting, was on the top. The shots were fired. Silence.

Let the Artists Die offered a commentary on memory and reflection. The characters that appeared in the space were generated by Kantor's memory. The characters who shared the room of memory built three-dimensional pictures out of frequently repeated gestures of everyday reality (the washing of feet, card playing, lovemaking, praying, traveling, dying, etc.). The images were in a constant process of transformation bereft of any logical, causal, or continuous patterns. These transformations were instigated by the appearance and disappearance of characters from behind the doors. The audience could know what was hidden behind the doors. The doors were the partition behind which a different space existed. This other space had the power of destabilizing the room of memory by revealing the forces and shadows that had been rendered invisible, erased, or killed.

Let the Artists Die (1985).
Photo courtesy of Leszek
Dziedzic.

The multiple and variable dimensionality of the space of memory, of the Other, was also characterized by the process of the superimposition of negatives from different times. As Kantor indicated, the negatives of memory that were recalled from the past slipped into the present moment. This coexistence of past, present, and future moments was clarified by Kantor's discussion of the figures of the Self (I—the Real One) and the Other(s) (I—at the Age of Six and I—the Dying One). The Self posited in front of the mirror surface was observing its relation to the Other(s) located on the other side. The emergence of this relationship in Kantor's theatre prompted a set of questions. Did Kantor, who was approaching a mirror, leave behind three-dimensional, absolute space and time in order to reveal a multidimensional image? Did Kantor project onto the mirror that fragment of the Self that used to disappear with him as image-maker? Is it possible that the moment the Self turned to look at the mirror, he saw himself as a distant ghost, an instant double, the Other(s)? Did the Other acquire its own, autonomous identity, and could it now approach the Self from an unknown direction, from the past (I— the Age of Six) and the future (I—the Dying One)?

Kantor's essay "Reflection" provided an answer: "I am walking forward. There is a mirror in front of me; the invisible boundary of a mirror which marks the beginning of an extension of reality and the time of poetry. I am walking forward. Someone, who is another I, is walking up to me. In a moment, we will pass each other or bump into each other. I am thinking about this moment with growing uneasiness. However, it does not escape my perception that I am not walking forward but in the direction of the depth where I started a moment ago. I am walking forward back."[43]

By being onstage throughout the performance, Kantor positioned himself within the boundaries of the visible world, organized according to the idea of the permanence of objects. This reality was questioned, however, because it excluded the space of the Other generated by the Self "on the other side." The other space was an extension of present reality into the regions of both the past and the future, all of which, as the Theory of Negatives pointed out, were coexistent. The Self, therefore, could encounter all of his own creations at the same time: I—a Naked Baby, I—at the Age of Six, I—a Barefoot Boy in Shorts, I—in a School Uniform, and, finally, I—the Dying One.

In *Let the Artists Die*, the images of I—at the Age of Six and I—the Dying One can be seen as a spatial representation of the image of the Self who, while moving in the direction of the mirror, perceived its silvered boundary. Faced with the boundary, the Self projected its own image upon it. This image, however, was not a reflection of the Self, but was created by the "I-Over-There," the Other (the twin brother) who could not be silenced or appropriated by the Self. The Other was the Self in "a different universe which exists and can only be sensed through art." In the "Theory of Negatives," the Other-in-a-different-universe contained all possible past, present, and future variants that were generated by the Self. Kantor, the Self in a room of memory or cemetery storeroom, could then see himself seeing himself at the age of six seeing himself dying seeing himself, *ad infinitum*.

The process of the Self playing the memories of the Other over and over in order to constitute and reconstitute itself, was enriched by the imposition of the negatives of different historical, moral, and ethical codes upon it. In act 2, the room of memory was turned into an asylum where the company of traveling artists presented a performance of "*Let the Artists Die.*" "Things are happening that are possible only in a dream. The only DOOR in this place, which is said to have some great secret meaning, begins to move in our direction."[44] Veit Stoss, a *personage trouvé*, "a found figure," from "the other side," built an Altar. But here, in a world governed by the Theory of Negatives, the altar was transformed into a prison cell. The concept of an art work born in prison expressed Kantor's fascination with the ambiguity contained in different types of the means of coercion. On the one hand, prison was, for him, a mechanism of discipline creating docile bodies. Therefore, the closing of gates behind a prisoner was like the closing of the grave over the dead body. In both cases, the person was "shut off" from exerting any impact on the world of the living. On the other hand, prison was "an idea separated from life by an ALIEN impenetrable barrier," space freed from the external order of things, from social observation, from normalizing judgment, whose powers stopped at the threshold of prison. At the same time,

> The man who is already "on the other side" is setting off on his journey. He is
> going to travel
> alone, left to himself,
> destitute
> with nobody but himself to rely on.
> He walks aimlessly and hopelessly
> along a deserted and eerie path. . . .
> Nothing but marching on . . .
> from the height of,
> I daresay,
> imagination's wild wanderings and madness
> I saw this apparition
> in front of my eyes
> in a ghostly landscape of horror.
> [This apparition] was like an idea, which against all reason and all logic, hovers at
> the doorway of my new
> THEATRE. ("Prison")

Although *Let the Artists Die* contained all the elements of Kantor's theories of theatre, emphasis was laid on the perception of theatre as an autonomous space in which the Self acknowledged the power of and the desire to be with the image(s) in the mirror. The mirror surface was the site where two simultaneous dimensions converged: the dimension of the mind (Kantor's memory) and the dimension of a theatre space (Kantor's memory enacted). Even though Kantor was always present onstage during every performance to correct or erase the actors' work, he broke the pattern of reflective space by rejecting any deterministic, reproductive mirroring of real space. Instead, his room of memory was ready to be transformed in any direction by energy from behind the doors of the room. In Kantor's theatre, the doors functioned as an opening through which the unknown would burst in and irrevocably alter the network of relations. "It is enough to open them."[45]

In Kantor's theatre, the characters who appeared onstage were the shadows that were made invisible when they were first conceived in Kantor's memory. During the performance, however, the shadows leapt aside into the space "on the other side," a space not bound by linear temporal progressions. In *Let the Artists Die*, the characters that unfolded themselves in the room of memory weaved three-dimensional pictures by using gestures from everyday reality. The relationship between Kantor's space and the space of his characters was never stable. During this process the past and the future traces were made visible because of the forces existing behind the doors and of the laws of reversibility functioning in that space. Consequently, as Kantor asserted in his essay "Reflection," "If we take a step further on this road, it might happen that a smile will turn into a grimace; virtue to a crime; and a whore will become a virgin."[46] If we take a step further, the characters on the barricade became the inmates of an apocalyptic theatre of death ready to defend themselves against all-powerful consumption, all-powerful production, all-powerful communication, and all-powerful holy technology that commodify both a human being and his or her works of art.[47]

IV

In 1988, Kantor presented *I Shall Never Return*, which, indeed, was a step further in his thinking about the function and the nature of theatre that he called the theatre of personal confessions:

> Personal confession . . .
> an unusual and rare technique today.
> In our epoch
> of an increasingly collective life,
> a terrifying growth of collectivism, [personal confessions]
> a rather awkward and inconvenient technique.
>
> Today, I want to find the reason
> for my maniacal passion
> for this technique.
>
> I feel it is important.
> There is something ultimate about it,
> something that is manifested only when one is faced with
> the E N D.
> I feel that realizing
> the reasons for this manifestation
> can

perhaps
still save us from
complete despondency. ("To Save From Oblivion")

In *The Dead Class,* Kantor explored his obsessions—World War I, World War II, Nazi power, the banality of evil, his own memories of the past. In *Wielopole, Wielopole,* the inhabitants of his room of memory allowed Kantor to explore his thoughts about life and death, abut his family and historical events, and about Christianity and Judaism. *Let the Artists Die* addressed the condition of an artist in contemporary society. The negatives of his private life, history, and art diverged, converged, or coalesced in order to reveal the active terrain on which Kantor staged his battle against

history,
the history of
mass Movements,
mass ideologies,
passing terms of Governments,
terror by power,
mass wars,
mass crimes. ("To Save From Oblivion")

His individual human life was to be set against the "consumerism of the world" even at the price of "pain, suffering, despair, and then shame, humiliation, derision."[48] Kantor's life was already projected onto the stage in his theatre of similitude. While the memories belonged to Kantor and his mnemonic stage techniques, the spectators were deprived by Kantor of the narcissistic pleasure of being reflected in the gaze of the actors. Instead, they watched the interplay between the observing subject functioning in a three-dimensional space and the object(s) positioned in a multidimensional space "on the other side." This relationship was visualized as a clash between the Self (Kantor) and the Other (his memories). The Self and the Other(s) lived in different dimensions. Though linked and existing in another and for another, it was the Self who was an instigator of the action, never fully a participant, and only the spectral figures, which were affirming his existence by staging what he wanted to remember, reminded us of Kantor's omnipresence in the picture. The Self continued to live in a real place, the Other(s) in an autonomous room controlled by the Self monitoring the (dis)appearance of memory traces, which existed for a split second before they were given to the infinity of space. A new maneuver was to take place in *I Shall Never Return,* which was to secure that Kantor's memories be taken literally as a gesture recounting death, destruction, humiliation, torture, massacres, and the piles of corpses:

I am . . . onstage
I will not be a performer.
Instead, poor fragments of my

own life
will become
"ready-made objects." ("To Save From Oblivion")

What does it mean for one's life to become a ready-made object? Kantor wrestled with this question in "The Real 'I,'" a text written in 1988 while he was working on *I Shall Never Return*:

Everything I have done in art so far,
has been the reflection of my attitude
toward the events
that surrounded me,
toward the situation
in which I have lived;
of my fears;
of my faith in this and not something else;
of my distrust in what was to be trusted;
of my skepticism;
my hope. ("The Real 'I'")

Such an attitude, however, was not necessarily novel, since, as it could be argued many artists whose work is driven by Aristotelian aesthetics, Brechtian epic theatre, Artaud's theatre of cruelty, or Augusto Boal's theatre of the oppressed could make a similar claim. Kantor, however,

to express all this
and for [his] own use,
[he] created
the Idea of Reality
which renounced
the idea of illusion,
that is,
a procedure recognized as elemental
for the theatre . . .
of PERFORMING,
of representing,
of "reproducing"
what had been written
as drama (a "play"). ("The Real 'i'")

The very praxis used by Kantor to accomplish this marked the subsequent stages of the transformation of the Cricot 2 Theatre—the Autonomous Theatre, the Informel Theatre, the Zero Theatre, the Theatre-Happening, the Impossible Theatre, and the Theatre of Intimate Commentaries. Every single one of them introduced a set of techniques that were employed in order to radically reposition the functioning of Kantor's theatre in the historical and cultural milieu. Finally, noted Kantor,

The moment has finally arrived
in my artistic life,
which I begin to consider
as a *résumé*,
the ultimate moment—
I should say—
when one makes a self-examination.
How was it really
with that reality?
Have I really done for it all that I could?
I began to be a harsh
judge of myself. ("The Real 'I'")

These three passages, which refer to Kantor's understanding of the function of his artistic praxis, his processes deterritorializing representation by annexing reality, and his desire for reflexivity, were brought together when he was ready to make self-examination and to turn his own individual life into a ready-made object. But could this self-examination happen in the space behind the invisible, impassable barrier where Kantor, the holder of discourse, initiated the actions by organizing the space of his room of memory, controlled how the memories would unfold in this space, and observed how they would disappear into the infinity of the space behind the doors? Could this happen in Kantor's room of memory or cemetery storeroom known from *Wielopole, Wielopole* and *I Shall Never Return*? Possibly not, since, as Kantor declared,

When I wanted to be a child,
someone else was a child,
not the real "I"
(this can still be excused).

When I wanted to die,
someone else was dying for me.
He was playing the part of me dying.
And that "playing,"
which I had excommunicated,
functioned perfectly well.

When with persistence, longing,
and stubbornness,
I kept returning to the memories
of my School Class,
it was not I, but the others (the actors)
who returned to school desks—
returned, "performed,"
and "pretended." ("The Real 'i'")

Kantor made clear that he desired to destroy the dichotomy between the Self and the Other, which had existed in his praxis until now; between him reflecting on the events surrounding him and the actors projecting these attitudes on the multidimensional space of the room of memory; between the spaces here and there; and, finally, between the body and memory. This could only happen in a new space he was ready to enter:

> In a moment I shall enter with my "luggage"
> a shabby and suspicious
> i n n.
> I have traveled to it for a long time.
> At nights.
> Sleepless nights.
> I have traveled here to meet,
> I am not sure what, with apparitions or people.
> To say that I have been c r e a t i n g them
> for a many, many years
> would be an overstatement.
> I gave them life, but they gave me theirs.
> They were not easy to deal with; nor were they obedient.
> They have traveled with me for a long time
> and gradually left me at various crossroads and stops.
> Now, we are to meet here.
> Maybe for the last time.
> Just as at the time of the Polish "All Saints' Day."
> I we see them again.
> After all those years. ("The Real 'I'")

Unlike in the past, where Kantor would be onstage organizing his room of memory while the audience was entering the performance space, this performance space—the inn "like all inns and bistros, exists somewhere in a forgotten Street of Dreams. All the events that take place there happen at the threshold of time. One more step and we can find ourselves beyond it. The everyday passes almost imperceptibly into eternity. Everything loses its meaning."[49] It was here in the space beyond time and beyond all the rules that Kantor was to encounter the "ready-mades" of his life in order to stage the battle against his end of the century.

The inn, a simple space with many doors at the back, was filled with "vulgar inn tables as if rented from an ice-cold mortuary."[50] The dripping of water marked the passage of time. The Innkeeper, with precision and logic, organized the tables, which must have been left in disarray by other guests. His staccato movements were occasionally interrupted by simple statements, which sounded vaguely familiar—a title of Tumor Brainowicz's book, comments about order and pure mathematical forms.

There were two other guests at the Inn: a Priest, possibly a priest from *Wielopole, Wielopole*, who sat asleep at one of the shabby tables, and the barefoot Dishwasher in a tattered sack, who squatted at another table. As an

I Shall Never Return (1988). Photo courtesy of Romano Martinis.

Argentine tango, "*Tiempos viejos*," was played, the Market-Place Speaker or Orator, a drunkard, entered to deliver one of his fine speeches for the Bride and the Groom. His words were drowned by the music. Suddenly, obtrusive banging and knocking at the inn's doors were heard. The doors opened and a troupe of wandering actors burst into the space. They were "the apparitions from the past," characters from Kantor's previous productions—the "ready-made" objects. Some of them were wearing the black uniforms of the Old People from *The Dead Class*, some were in traveling costumes from *The Water-Hen*, and some others in costumes from *Wielopole, Wielopole* and *Let the Artists Die*. They brought in with them objects from those productions. They looked confused; they were not sure if indeed they were supposed to meet "him" here. Some of them were sure that "he" would come late as always. Not having met "him," the wandering actors left the stage.

They returned. They refused to continue their journey. Some of them remembered that they were supposed to say something at this very moment. The actors hurriedly "acted out" fragments from their "plays." Those fragments and characters were all mixed up; for example, a figure from *The Dead Class* used an object from *Wielopole, Wielopole*; the Hanged Man from *Let the Artists Die* sang his song while holding a mannequin of the boy from *The Dead Class*, who was dressed in the costume from *The Water-Hen*. The impression given by this traveling troupe of actors was that both the characters and the events onstage were the negatives of a film negative, which were imposed one atop another. This could explain the lack of correspondence between a character and costume as well as an object carried. These apparitions from the past were the participants in the battles staged by the Cricot 2 Theatre—the battles for reality that could no longer be appropriated by the prevailing conventions or having an assigned use-value; the battles for depreciating the value of reality by exploring its unknown, thus-far-hidden or everyday aspect of life; matter, marginalized object, degraded objects, everyday realness; the battles against a thoughtless procreation of forms; battles for the "impossible"; and the battles for a mode of thinking that begins with the exteriority but then folds back

I Shall Never Return (1988).
Photo courtesy of Jerzy
Borowski.

upon itself in order to explore its own effectivity and action. These battles were brought back by the Water-Hen with her bathtub, two Hasidic Jews, the English Lady, the Pimp, the Grand Gymnast, the Woman with a Rat-trap, the Princess of Kremlin in a henhouse-cage, the Hanged Man, and Adaś, who later would be the Gambler.

The negatives unfolding onstage were suddenly interrupted by Kantor's indecisive entrance. Wearing a black suit, he was accompanied by the Bride in tattered wedding dress, reminiscent of Mother-Helka's wedding dress in *Wielopole, Wielopole*. He led her gently to a table. The Bride's mannequin-like movements were slow. Finally, both sat down. First, nobody paid any attention to him. Once recognized by the actors, Kantor's recorded voice was heard:

> Ladies and Gentlemen! Where did I come from? I have always stood by the doors and . . . waited. And now I am sitting! In the middle! An important person. And others are waiting for me to leave. I stood by the doors. The doors . . . and this waiting "molto importante!" I have to go . . . I have to follow this road to the end. Ladies and gentlemen, you will watch this. And afterwards you can forget about me! Will we fall asleep tonight? Will we awake in the middle? Will we stare at the ceiling with sightless eyes? Ladies and Gentlemen, a toast![51]

While the monologue was delivered, the actors provided a running commentary mocking and deriding Kantor, introducing their own cynical remarks, and asserting their individuality and independence. These were not Kantor's memories (the inside) that shaped the outside (Kantor's memory enacted by the actors, who interiorized the mnemonic projections). These, indeed, were "ready-mades" that, now, could explore their own mediality with specificity provided by characters they used to play modified by the individuality of the actor.

The last words of the monologue were drowned in the sounds of "*Tiempos viejos.*" The toast was followed by Kantor's second monologue—his will to create the "Last Emballage":

Dear Actors, Colleagues. . . . Yes, in order to create something, create this world in which you will soundly ascend to applause, I have to fall down—and—I am falling. Our paths are reversed. When one is very unhappy, then suddenly some hellish power is born in this trash called man. One should nourish it. First unhappiness, then this power. I have virtually nothing else to say. Ladies and Gentlemen forgive me my evil and be happy. One has to endure it somehow. Stay with me at the bottom for awhile—An artist must always be at the bottom, because only from the bottom can one shout in order to be heard. There, at the bottom, we can understand one another. But later, just do not go down into hell. Perhaps. . . .[52]

The "apparitions from the past" interrupted his monologue—"I face them abused, mocked and accused. The machine gun from my *Wielopole, Wielopole* fires a burst of shots, without result. It is always like this in illusions and dreams. Untouched, I go out carrying my 'graveyard' luggage."[53] The sounds of the tango. Screaming and shouting, all the characters or actors, except for the Innkeeper and the Dishwasher, left the stage. A momentary auditory relief.

Kantor appeared a second time as if expecting something important, this time, however, without the Bride. So did the Priest, who was to perform some kind of a ceremony. For the time being, while "*Tiempos viejos*" was played, the Priest danced around the stage, as if the sound of the tango made him remember a different past, place, and time. As "Salve Regina" was heard, the doors opened. A Young-Kantor Mannequin, dressed up for either a wedding or a funeral, and the Bride, who stood next to him, emerged in the opening. Now, it was clear that a wedding ceremony was to be performed here. The Priest, however, kept dancing neglecting his duty. The wedding vows were celebrated by the Innkeeper, who spoke words, which had been prompted to him by the Priest.

The wedding ceremony was reminiscent of another wedding ceremony that had taken place many years before and was repeated in *Wielopole, Wielopole*. The repetition, echo, and time warp—well-known devices in Kantor's theatre—were given here a new performative function, which transformed the theory of negatives from *I Shall Never Return*. While working with the students in Milano in 1986, Kantor wrote,

> Behind the PHRASE, a WEDDING CEREMONY,
> we have discovered an entire world of thoughts and commentaries which is loaded with ambiguous meanings, almost symbolic and metaphorical. . . .
> The concept of a WEDDING CEREMONY has expanded to allow us to express our anxieties, fears, doubts, questions, accusations, hopes.[54]

Similarly, in *I Shall Never Return*, the wedding ceremony explored anxieties, fears, doubts, questions, accusations, and hopes about love and death—Eros and Thanatos:

> Death and love. . . .
> The moment came
> when I could not tell
> one from the other.
> I was enchanted by both.
> Nights came,
> because nights were my time of creation,
> the nights came when death
> carefully guarded the entrance
> to my Poor
> Little Room of Imagination. ("The Real 'I'")

In the theory of negatives, different frames are interimposed—thus, the names of the Bride and Bridegroom were omitted, a ceremonial stole was a kitchen rag used by the Innkeeper to wipe off the tables, and the ceremony itself was performed not by a priest in a church but by the Innkeeper at the Inn existing somewhere in a forgotten street of dreams at the edge of time. Love and death were intertwined in this ceremony observed by Kantor, who was watching his mannequin standing silently by the doors next to the Bride in a tattered white dress, who, too, was standing there silently. Kantor watched this ceremony, which, in turn, allowed him to watch his own intimate thoughts, anxieties, and hopes. He watched silently the jittery movements of the Bride in the tattered wedding dress, the dancing priest, the vacant expression on the faces of the actors as he stood at the threshold between his room of imagination and the space behind the doors. This time, however, there was no impassable barrier that would separate Kantor from the objects of his creation. He and the specters found themselves in a space that, like the performance space in *The Return of Odysseus*, was no longer governed by preestablished rules and conventions. It was a room, Kantor's inferno of thoughts and images reflecting his attitude toward the events surrounding him.

When the ceremony was over, it was followed by "a few surprises" prepared by the Innkeeper: the dance of the two Bishops from *Where Are the Snows of Yesteryear*, the dance of the Rabbi from *Wielopole, Wielopole*, and the wedding greeting of two Hassidic Jews from *The Water-Hen*. However, even the

Innkeeper could not control what would appear in this Inn-Inferno. When the side doors opened, Shmul from *Wielopole, Wielopole,* a poor and terrified rabbi, who must have been dragged out from his synagogue, was seen trying to escape his executioners, the Violinists in the uniforms of Nazi soldiers. The rabbi, running and falling, conducted the violinists, who "played" while goose-stepping the anonymous Hebrew prayer song "*Anì maanim* [I do believe]," known as the lament of the Jews marching into gas chambers. When the parade was over, the lament was picked up by the Dishwasher, "who became the symbol of the Promised Land."[55]

At the end, the Bride and the Bridegroom withdrew and the doors were closed behind them "as the gates of an open grave close over the dead who 'walk' through them."[56]

When all apparitions from the past disappeared, "most clearly, in [their] journey into the more and more distant past, [they] approached the time of war."[57] The Dishwasher carried two more forgotten pieces from behind the doors: Odysseus's shabby military uniform, in which he returned to Kraków in 1944—"I am Odysseus. I have returned from Troy"—and "a mournful piece of junk the apparition of my FATHER." Kantor's recorded voice announced, "I died on January 24, 1944."[58] These indeed were "the apparitions of the past—cruel and merciless."[59]

The wandering actors returned, dragging with them the school desks from *The Dead Class.* While placing the desks in a row, they spoke the names of the people, which had been used in the memorial roll in *The Dead Class.* The scene, reminiscent of that particular sequence in *The Dead Class,* culminated in the transformation of the memorial roll into the lament. The lament ended, and with it the wandering actors collapsed into their seats and fell asleep at the top of the luggage that they had brought with them. A moment of silence. It was interrupted by the entrance of the soldiers, who approached the Innkeeper and forced him into Odysseus's uniform. "*Anì maanim*" accompanied this transformation.

The story of Odysseus's return was shown not as the restaging of scenes from the 1944 production but as a collage of scenes played by the characters

I Shall Never Return (1988).
Photo courtesy of Romano
Martinis.

from *Wielopole, Wielopole, Dainty Shapes and Hairy Apes,* and *The Dead Class,* "directed" by the Priest. The entrance of Uncle Stasio with his violin or hurdy-gurdy marked the beginning of the reconstruction of Odysseus's return. Uncle Stasio, now Femios—the bard—played a ballad, his Christmas Carol from *Wielopole, Wielopole,* which evoked the legendary story of Odysseus' return to Kraków, his Ithaca during the war. First, there was an encounter between Odysseus and the Beggar; then, an encounter with Telemachus, followed by the scene with the Lovers fighting for Penelope, played by the Bride; finally, a contest between the Lovers for Penelope. The machine gun/photo camera from *Wielopole, Wielopole* was rolled in. It was a bow this time. The Lovers were unsuccessful in using it. It was on Odysseus who could make it work. Having killed all the lovers, who in their last gasp for life played the children's game from *The Dead Class* like a ritornello, Odysseus approached Kantor and sat down with him at the table.

Odysseus showed him where to read in a script that Kantor had written in 1944 while working on Wyspiański's *Return of Odysseus*: "In my own homeland, I have uncovered hell. I walked into a graveyard. I killed everything. Everything—I pushed away. The past's false happiness has fled. There is nothing before me. . . . The coast of Ithaca. . . . Seagull fly there. The wild birds of my youth. There—is my homeland. There the song of my life has ended. Nobody can return to the world of their youth. I had my homeland in my heart. Now, it is in my desires. A shadow. I yearn for a shadow. A boat full of people. . . . Who are they? The waves separate me from their voices. The waves separate me from a boat of the dead. Wait! Stop! Stand still!"[60] The boat of the dead with Charon/ The Water-Hen at the helm led the apparitions across the Styx River. Odysseus stood up and joined the spectral crowd.

The Innkeeper came back and tried to reconstruct the Inn. The Bride slowly entered and approached Kantor's table. Finally, the actors returned and, while "acting out" their parts, tempted Kantor to embark on yet another journey with them. It seemed that everything returned to normal. However, such a condition was no longer a viable possibility—the gravediggers, accompanied by the lady in black, Death herself, came onstage and started to cover all the props of Kantor's grand theatre with black dust-sheets or shrouds. Appropriately, Berlioz's march from *The Damnation of Faust* was played while they were performing their task. Finally, when all was done, the gravediggers left the stage. This was the Grand Emballage par excellence:

Emballage, Emballage—
. . . exists
beyond the boundaries of reality. . . .
Emballage—
. . . balances at the threshold—
Emballage, Emballage—
between eternity
and
garbage. . . .
EMBALLAGE—

Must be isolated,
protected from trespassing,
ignorance,
and vulgarity.
Emballage.
Emballage.
Emballage. ("The Emballage")

The Dishwasher, the symbol of the Promised Land, while singing "*Anì maanim*," "dug out" the actors. Solemnly, they disappeared behind the doors. So did the Bride. Kantor looked around the stage and followed the Bride:

My "intimate epilogue"
I lead away my
LAST EMBALLAGE.[61]

By entering the performance space in *I Shall Never Return*, Kantor irrevocably altered the parameters of the room of memory or imagination he had created in *Wielopole, Wielopole* and *Let the Artists Die*. The room of memory or imagination was a heterotopia. It was a counter site to the normative real in which the rules of the real site were recognized but questioned and contested, in which absolute time and space were discarded by Kantor's rejection of traditional concepts of illusion and representation, and in which Kantor saw himself there where he was not. He saw himself there where the shadows gave him visibility and enabled him to see himself where he was absent. The room of memory or imagination was no longer activated in the real place and then transferred into the "imaginary space." The room of memory became a space that contained in itself a multitude of intersections of which Kantor was no longer a primary creator. Indeed, that space existed somewhere in a forgotten street of dreams at the edge of time, which in itself was nothing more than a mode of thinking, as Einstein declared at the beginning of the twentieth century. As

**I Shall Never Return (1988).
Photo courtesy of Romano
Martinis.**

I Shall Never Return suggested, any attempts at policing it would be frustrated by its more underground or clandestine aspects—that is, something would enter through the doors: Kantor himself, the actors, the spectral objects and people, or the shreds and shards of intimate and historical memories that mercilessly cut through all senses and all bodies.

This multitude of intersections was increased because the characters, apparitions, or wandering actors existed simultaneously within the spaces of their "plays" and could be transformed and acquired a new dimension by assuming a function of characters from a different "play." For example, two Hasidic Jews from *The Water-Hen* danced the tango from *Where Are the Snows of Yesteryear*, and the Innkeeper became Odysseus from *The Return of Odysseus*. This coexistence and reinvention or rearticulation of a new function was not, however, limited to the characters or actors but was also used in the formation of the "acting" space (the Inn was a café, a cloak-room, a classroom, a room, an asylum) and of the text (*The Return of Odysseus* presented as a collage from all other productions). As the Theory of Negatives suggested, all of those characters, images, lines, and objects created individual negatives that were interimposed and created a single negative, containing the elements of all other negatives.

This was why, as *I Shall Never Return* showed, the space of the overlapping negatives was not a stable space that could have been controlled by Kantor, as he had done in all prior productions. The space in this production was altered by each accidental entrance or exit of Kantor or characters from different dimensions—perhaps from the dimension of a classroom in *The Dead Class*, a room in *Wielopole, Wielopole*, or from the cemetery storeroom or asylum in *Let the Artists Die*. Since the apparatus of control ceased to exist and the act of transfer (from life to art) could no longer take place, the space in *I Shall Never Return* did not have its counterpart in any other real or imaginary space. Instead, this space existed for itself and could fold back only upon itself to reveal its inside. This self-reflexivity of the space was further emphasized by the presence of Kantor in it, functioning alongside other elements from the dimension of art. In this manner, the space of life and the space of art were not parallel, or binary, opposites, but they coalesced to share their fate and destiny.

I Shall Never Return was an appropriate title for the production. Having crossed the threshold separating him from his previous theatre experiments, Kantor could never return to playing the part of himself controlling, erasing, and correcting the execution of his memories onstage. In the process of transgressing boundaries, Kantor considerably changed the discourse about memory in *I Shall Never Return*. Now memory was a spatial fold through which the immanent outside came into being as a form to disrupt the history of forms. It existed as an overlap of two dimensions: the dimension of life (Kantor's memory or "inside") and the dimension of art (Kantor's memory enacted onstage or "outside"). The emergence of this new formation transformed the praxis of the redoubling of spaces, the formation of inside and outside, and the folding of spaces in Kantor's theatre.

By entering and participating in the events unfolding in the inn, Kantor altered the relationships between the inside and outside. Until this production, "the inside" shaped and molded "the outside" of Kantor's "intimate commentary."

A memory trace was first identified, second retained, third materialized, and fourth dispersed. The process of interiorization of "the outside" was limited to the exploration of those elements that constituted it for a split second within the boundaries of "the inside." The constitution and reconstitution of the Old People in *The Dead Class*, of the family members' repetitive gestures in *Wielopole, Wielopole*, and of the multiple spaces (a room, a cemetery storeroom, an asylum, and a prison) in *Let the Artists Die* exemplified this process. These productions, their adherence to the theatre of similitude notwithstanding, still made use of a traditional binary in which the Self created the Other(s) in the reassuring world in which Kantor's consciousness could not be really distinguished. The family members in *Wielopole, Wielopole* or the fragmented Selfs generating their own history in *Let the Artists Die* were reduced to a particular object or a double whose function was to affirm Kantor's presence via the exploration of spatial dimensions of memory or via the confrontation between the Self and the Others. The reason for this gesture and maneuver was poignantly expressed by Kantor, who insisted on the need to extend "reality beyond its boundaries so that we could better cope with it in our lives. An extension which will give us an intimation of another world in the metaphysical and cosmic sense, the feeling of touching other realities."[62]

I Shall Never Return showed, however, that the relationship between the inside and outside, between the Self and the Other(s), could no longer be formulated in terms of the interiorization of the outside by Kantor projecting his memories onto the performance space "on the other side" or in terms of reducing the Other(s) to a particular object or subject, but they had to be treated in terms of the coexistence of inside and outside. This coexistence of inside and outside in the space of the inn signaled a departure from the world without Others, since until now they had been viewed only as the objects constructed by the Self—thus, as otherwise Other or doubled Self—and an arrival in a world where the Other was neither an object nor a subject but "a structure of the perceptual field, without which the entire field could not function as it does."[63]

In short, the Other was a structure that could be actualized by characters appearing from behind the doors and by so doing establishing the relativity of the others already present in the performative or mnemonic space in the process of entering into possible relationships with them. Recall, for example, the sequence dealing with the return of Odysseus. The Other, Odysseus, then, was the expression not of a form or shape but of what could be visualized in the perceptual field—his return to Ithaca, to Kraków (1944), and to the Inn of *I Shall Never Return*, each one of them expressing a different possible structure: a return of Odysseus to a mythological homeland; a return of Odysseus to a city occupied by the Nazis during World War II, where the fiction of Wyspiański's drama merged with the reality of life; and a return of Odysseus to the inn of memory to give evidence "of our fate, our hopes, our desires at the ruins of our Inferno, our end of the century."[64]

If such a proposition is tangible, the expressed possible world existed, but it could not exist outside of what expressed it. The Other was "the expression of a possible world . . . it is the structure which conditions the entire field and its functioning."[65] Consider, to continue with the Odysseus sequence, the execution of

Odysseus's return in *I Shall Never Return*. The possible world of his return was presented by the traveling troupes of actors seated in their school desks, the memory machine from *The Dead Class*. The very presence of Odysseus conditioned not only what could be seen onstage but also the functioning of that bio-object. The apparitions from the past, whose new parts were assigned by the Priest from *Wielopole, Wielopole*, were a possible world having its own coherence at that very moment. Each of these possible worlds, which could generate its own memory and history, as exemplified by *Let the Artists Die*, shared now a vision of the *Return of Odysseus*. They assumed the functions of Femios, the Beggar, Telemachus, the Pedagogue, the Lovers, and Penelope. But this acting "together" was only temporary. Once they "acted out" the parts assigned to them by the Priest, they returned to their school desks—their limbo of dreams and nightmares, where they were waiting for something or someone to arrive from behind the doors.

Whereas Kantor's presence suggested the existence in a physical and visible, three-dimensional universe, the presence of apparitions implied the existence of a mental, multidimensional universe created as an expression of a possible world. This multidimensional universe could not be shaped by the certainties of absolute time and absolute space but was informed by structures that had no correspondence in the world of the body. The space in which Kantor found himself, the inn, was a site where two universes converged in a conjunction between Kantor onstage and poor fragments of his life—the ready-made objects.

Having found himself in the space of the manifold, Kantor, unlike Simonides or Horatio, presented us with a room of memory, or what is left of it, that would always be the site of unregulated relationships. It was in this site that memory traits or narratives—the "ready-made objects"—would escape intelligibility that locates the dead along the narrative. At the end of *I Shall Never Return*, Kantor, in the intimate epilogue after his self-examination, entered the "empty night"—the world of simulacrum. His was not, however Baudrillard's order of things or fatal strategies, which are more real than the real,[66] but Deleuze's image, which is no longer endowed with resemblance. "The catechism, so much inspired by Platonism, has familiarized us with this notion. God made man in his image and resemblance. Through sin, however, man lost the resemblance while maintaining the image."[67] Maybe, now, the impassable barrier had finally disappeared. Nothing separated Kantor from his "ready-made objects." Nothing separated Kantor from "their voices." Nothing protected his consciousness from doubt.

V

"The Twelfth Lesson" of *The Milano Lessons* (1986) describes clearly the role Kantor had played in *Wielopole, Wielopole*, *Let the Artists Die*, and *I Shall Never Return*. He assumed the function of the chronicler narrating the events of the twentieth century:

World War I.
Millions of corpses
in the absurd hecatomb.

After the War,
old powers were abolished. . . .
World War II.
Genocide,
Concentration Camps,
Crematories,
Human Beasts, Death,
Torture,
Humankind turned into mud
soap, and ashes,
Debasement,
The time of contempt. . . .
The 1940s, 1950s, 1960s, 1970s have passed.
All the time . . .
I have been perceiving warning signals that ordered me and dictated that I choose
one action of the other—
PROTEST,
REVOLT
AGAINST THE OFFICIALLY RECOGNIZED SACRED SITES,
AGAINST EVERYTHING THAT HAD A STAMP OF "APPROVAL,"
FOR REALNESS,
FOR "POVERTY."[68]

While watching a heap of broken images and objects representing a self-representation onstage, and while listening to the words describing the fragments of life finding their fate and destiny in the school desks, the room of memory, and the room of memory or cemetery, we listen to the Self listening to the people from his immemorial past and watch the Self watching the wars, the events, and the people parade in front of his and our eyes. We listen to the Self listening to their protests against being accepted by bourgeois aesthetics, absorbed by the artistic trends, and systematized into orders. Do we have the courage to see through the masks and to realize that "to speak is to do something—something other than to express what one thinks; to translate what one knows, and something other than to play with the structures of a language; to show that to add a statement to a pre-existing series of statements is to perform a complicated and costly gesture?"[69]

Maybe, this is why Kantor so frequently talked about constructivism, Dada, and surrealism and their techniques of protest, mutiny, and negation—despite the fact that these movements failed to provide a successful model for oppositional representational praxis that would challenge the orthodoxy of state capitalism—or about *l'Art Informel* of Wols, Fautrier, Mathieu, and Pollock manifesting forms that were freed from the strict laws of construction and were instead always changing and fluid, negating, decomposing, dissolving, deconstructing, or destroying a promise of representation:

TODAY, IN THE DILAPIDATED WORLD DOMINATED BY THE
CIVILIZATION OF UNIVERSAL CONSUMERISM,

THIS REVOLUTIONARY SPIRIT OF CONSTRUCTIVISM, THE FIGHT FOR
THE VICTORY OVER REALISM AND MINDLESS WORLD OF PRACTICAL
LIFE, HAS EITHER BEEN APPROPRIATED BY THE ART MARKETS OR
DEEMED TO BE PASSÉ.
IN THE TIMES WHEN THE SPIRIT OF BOURGEOIS PRAGMATISM
REEMERGES IN OUR CIVILIZATION,
IT IS IMPERATIVE THAT THE CONSTRUCTIVISTS' LESSON BE
REMEMBERED,
AND THAT THEIR GOALS, WHICH THEY MIGHT NOT HAVE FULLY
REALIZED, BE FINALLY PERCEIVED.
ONE NEEDS ALWAYS TO DISCREDIT, BRAND, AND DISTURB
THIS PETTY, LOW QUALITY MATERIALISM, THIS RIDICULOUS
FORMALITY, THOSE GLITTERING LIGHTS OF HIGH-LIFE
WITH DERISION, IRONY, AND VEXATION
[ONE NEEDS TO IRRITATE THEM WITH] THE MYSTICAL,
APOCALYPTICAL VISION OF THE CIRCUS OF OUR EPOCH.[70]

Do we have the courage to listen to those voices in that other world, in Kantor's world of similitude, in which Kantor's room of memories was beyond the confines of time and space?

Will we fall asleep tonight?
Will we wake in the middle?
Will we stare at the ceiling
with sightless eyes?[71]

Pace Kantor and his theatre of similitude.

Theatrical Place
(1970s–1980s)

FROM THINKING ABOUT THE FORM AND THE FUNCTION OF THEATRE TO THINKING ABOUT A PRODUCTION AND NOT VICE VERSA

Conventional and professional theatrical "mode of operation" is grounded in a common belief that art (drama) is the modus operandi and the reason for the existence of theatre. This is why so much attention is paid to the selection and the creation of a repertoire. The rehearsal process as well as all other activities connected with the "staging" of a play constitute the very content of a theatrical work. There is little time left for the exploration of the function and form of theatre.

My work on the staging of *The Return of Odysseus* (1943–44) was not due to my "philological interests" in the text. It was driven by a long process of development of theoretical investigation into the nature of theatrical problems and a rejection of my own inclinations and attitudes, whose appeal needed to be contested, because they were nothing more than stylistic solutions. Old and fake! I was more and more aware of the fact that the quest for truth implied the acceptance of radicalism in art— and this was my grand private discovery at the time.

These thoughts, full of doubts, uncertainty, anxiety, and finally, revealing a solution, marked, in an accelerated time, the stages of my development. It was a process of the d e v e l o p m e n t of thought within the boundaries of art. A difficult process. It was to lead to a p r o d u c t i o n. Not to the staging of a play—the play was only matter of the production. The process was reversed, unlike the process in a conventional theatre. And this has remained with me until now.

THE "ODYSSEUS" ADVENTURES

FIRST STAGE: A BOX SET

—I was attracted to the ominous subject-matter of *The Return of Odysseus*, or should I say, the despair and tragic impossibility of return to one's homeland, already during my university years before the war—
—This was when everything began—and it is worth noting this moment to see how things would change later on.

—I was particularly sensitive to the problem of fate and death. These were the traces left by the symbolist tradition of Maeterlinck and Wyspiański. This was why, despite the fact that I admired it greatly, the cold scaffolds of pure constructivism were alien to me. M O O D was more important—my own, inner, dramatic, tragic mood with all of its formalistic consequences, which were not always in agreement with the radicalism of an abstract construction—an abstract construction which was at that time the only one that could express that truth I was after. But this was not abstraction in its pure sense.

Rather, it was the world of objects, deeply buried but felt in abstract forms and in remote allusions: a column-to be, wall fragments-to-be, a rock-to be, a plank or a wooden beam, a sea wave shown as an object, a sky cut out from cardboard—some pieces of a forgotten land.

This first stage of my Odysseus, and theatre, adventures in the period between 1938 and 1939, was formed with a b o x   s t a g e in mind—an opening enclosed by a backstage.

It was also enclosed within the limits of ILLUSION for two reasons: first, pictorial elements located the action not in a real place where the audience was, but on the island of Ithaca, in Odysseus's place or inside of the palace, and, finally, at the seaside—thus, in an illusionary place; second, these different "illusory places" were positioned in an equally illusory "o t h e r" space, different from the one where the audience was seated. By giving them illusory depth, the lights turned them into an I M A G E, I L L U S I O N.

THE ODYSSEUS ADVENTURES (CONTINUED)

IN THE EMPTY ROOM
SYMBOLIC FORMS

The war broke out in 1939.
I stopped thinking about a box set or about "normal" theatre.
Only an e m p t y   r o o m was at my disposal.
This made me rethink drastically the concept of space and stage place.
The design drawings from that period (I was not thinking yet about executing them) clearly show this change. However, the traditional and sharp division into the stage and the auditorium was visible. One side of the room was for the stage—the other, for the audience.
The change was that there were no a r c h i t e c t u r a l   e l e m e n t s that localized the action.
The reality of the room, possibly because of its size, was so palpable and strong that any architectural elements that were supposed to create illusion (an artificial wall, column, or doors) lost their right to exist because they would never evoke it; they looked funny and naïve.
—What was left were
s y m b o l i c   f o r m s,
a kind of a sculpture (which could be in a room), or a screen, or a curtain.

In *Balladyna*, this s y m b o l i c form-sculpture was a flat form made
out of metal sheet, whose shape resembled a profile of a face with an
eye socket and a "mouth"; a primordial fetish "playing" the part of the
nymph, Goplana.
The costumes were the forms, too. Of course, they were movable forms.
At this "symbolic" stage of thinking about *The Return of Odysseus*, I
drafted three design variants with a similar symbolic form-sculpture. The
mass of a pyramid with a semicircle of a bow. Of course, this the famous
bow of Odysseus.
I am not ready yet to add the reality of "life"—of the room into the
i m a g i n a r y (not illusionary) sphere of a production. I c o v e r up
the real wall of a room with a screen—
with the last shred of illusion, or, should I say, of the imaginary sphere.
If I am still attracted to the charm of a column,
I destroy it with an ordinary ladder.
Finally, I make a decision to accept the empty and colorless whitewashed
walls of the room as part of "artistic work."
The walls are bare, naked.
They cordon off the room.
The room is a site of imagination.
The room is the world.
An awfully e m p t y world.
And in this emptiness—USELESS WRECKS.
Under the wall-heaven,
there lies a long and heavy gun barrel.
Odysseus sits on it.
Somewhere on the other end of
this world-room,
there is a piece of poor, simple wooden plank—
remains of a shipwreck. A Wreck.
Maybe, at the very end,
"on the horizon,"
under the wall,
the audience will be seated.
But still the reality of this room—
these walls—heaven
produce imaginary illusion.
I would like to paint them myself—using grays and whites—
an empty canvas.
Maybe, it will never happen,
or it can never happen,
that a real, living space of a room, a room in which we live,
becomes part of the domain of imagination;
that this real room
becomes a site of events, situations, objects, and people,
belonging to imagination;
that life is mixed with illusion;

reality with art.
Maybe, illusion and art will always deprive the real of its practical side,
that is,
de-real the real;
making it s y m b o l i c!

Screens-backstage,
wooden platforms—ship decks
ship masts,
ladders,
WRECKS.
Still a ROOM.

I introduce such real objects which do not have any use-value and
therefore can become the objects of imagination belonging to this other
domain of not-life.

A SCREEN-BACKSTAGE
can imply a wall,
but not the wall in this room,
and simultaneously imply backstage.
To avoid confusion,
I turn it around.
One can see wooden frames,
strange signs and scribbles.

WOODEN TILTED PLATFORMS
can be an extension of the floor,
that makes one walk in a different way.
They can also be a deck of a shipwreck.

A LADDER
is a real object;
it also implies
that the room has been emptied out of life;
that it has been renovated, transformed.
A ladder is an empty shell, too.

On the platform, which is also a deck,
a MAST can be placed.
All that needs to happen is that an old beam be found in a demolished
house.
Odysseus's Bard can also be an object.
It is enough to fasten a wooden h a n d holding a LYRE (without strings,
of course)
and a r a g, classically draped,
to the beam.

A KITCHEN CHAIR
IN PLACE OF A FAKE ANTIQUE

Here comes the penultimate chapter of my thinking about *The Return of Odysseus*. Wishing to give it life, drag it out of memory after all these years, I need to reconstruct that moment of inspiration, that enthrallment felt when one discovers something new in oneself and for oneself. I will have something more to say about this "discovery" soon, because it will resurface many a time in the future out of the unconscious rather than be an obsession.

An object finds its way into the unconscious when, despite its trivial nature, outward appearance, or quotidian quality, it performs in art more complex functions than initially perceived. It can happen that, after many years of being forgotten, it returns,

appears suddenly to signal new hope and new life.

This "discovery" was, for me,

a c h a i r,

and to be more precise, many chairs.

Simple, poor, kitchen chairs, freed from the pretension of chairs, in which we sit to rest after a day's work, which beckon us with their simplicity. Simply

f u n c t i o n a l chairs. Today! For us!

Later I named them—

objects of the Lowest Rank.

An OBJECT.

Art always takes up subjects which, for many people, are not worth its attention. Banal subjects; subjects which are held in contempt.

A C H A I R

made me think about an elemental condition of a human,

the act of s i t t i n g.

It can be said that the act of sitting is the next stage of human development after this "revolutionary" moment when a human being assumed

a s t a n d i n g position.

To be different.

Possibly, a human became a laughing stock at that moment.

Vertical?!

I wrote a short essay about "sitting" in 1944. Many years later, after many new experiences with a CHAIR, I wrote a kind of "résumé" entitled *A Chair*. If I perceive this as a discovery, I do so for significant reasons. It was so, because an o b j e c t, wrenched from life's reality was put into an artificial aesthetic structure. At that time such a process was unheard of. Much later I discovered a dada term for it—*"l'objet prêt."*

This explanation refers to art in general. In theatre, this poor CHAIR also played its "revolutionary" part.

A kitchen chair

replaced a striking, but conventional, ILLUSION of fake antiques, columns, false waves of the Aegean Sea; the grandiose myth of the Antiquity.

What a "scandal"; what "poor" taste.

But here it is—the audience members, people like we, are sitting in those chairs.

People as "simple" as those chairs!

It seems that they do not have a chance to reach the heights of Mount Olympus. But, maybe this is the point. Maybe it is necessary to expose that false "ascension."

It is important that they be simple; authentic, us—today!

Maybe then, after this difficult maneuver, a Greek profile, or a Greek dress, or Nike's Wing will be seen again. . . .

This kitchen CHAIR was far more controversial than placing a g u n b a r r e l next to it. It was resting on a trestle smeared with mud and cement.

It was symbol of our epoch or, in the Time of Odysseus, an object unearthed from the p a s t!

THE LAST STAGE OF ODYSSEUS'S JOURNEY: THEATRE. 1944

The last stage.
Excerpts from my essays from 1944.

. . . It is only in the place and time when it is the least expected, something can happen that we will a c c e p t without reservation.

This is why theatre, a place which has been completely anesthetized and deadened by century-long traditions and conventions, is the least suitable site for the b e c o m i n g of drama.

. . . It is necessary to create such atmosphere and such conditions so that the illusory reality which is placed in them, b e c o m e s s o m e t h i n g t h a t c a n b e b e l i e v e d i n; something real and concrete.

So that Odysseus, returning to his Ithaca, does not appear in the domain of i l l u s i o n, but in the dimension of o u r r e a l i t y.

[So that Odysseus, returning to his Ithaca, appears] among real objects, that is, the objects whose everyday function is well known to us; and among real people, that is, the people who are in the audience.

A PLAY-A WORK OF LITERATURE
THE BEGINNING OF EVERYTHING

It was a p l a y *(la pièce—das Stück*—a play) after all which became the p o i n t o f d e p a r t u r e. Literature was for me much more real than life's reality. It belonged to the sphere of imagination, which I was accustomed to and knew how to navigate through. It was a process that led to madness, in which there was no difference between life and fiction; where hallucinations are as real as the real itself.

There was nothing peculiar in this fascination of mine with literature; it is, I would say, a necessary condition for the work in theatre. What was strange was that a chosen play, or should I say a "found" play, was not one of many but was the only one. Nothing existed beyond it; it was becoming a concrete r e a l i t y; t o d a y's reality; o u r reality; l i f e's reality (literally).

I wish to describe in detail that i n n e r condition of mine; that *"l'état d'âme"* and the entire process that took place at the threshold between imagination and life; a process that revealed my proclivities and the reasons for my artistic actions.

In my consciousness, the past, written into the work of art, the novel, or a play, existed as a highly compressed reality.

Those "chronicles" of events, those notes and descriptions constitute our inner existence in subsequent epochs.

Here: Odysseus's life

There have been many Odysseuses through history.

But only this one life exists and is of importance—

because it was turned into a w o r k o f a r t.

Homer

and

Wyspiański.

It was thanks to them that this life of Odysseus, full of many sensational details, has remained in our m e m o r y.

A particular fragment of life (usually the life of the main character) was pressed into a play; a work of art. From the life's perspective, it was becoming fiction, illusion. It was gaining however a higher sense of reality: art

and a material quality (as I believed then) which was much more significant than the one our life's reality is so proud of: the sphere of imagination.

FICTION'S (PLAY'S) EXTENSION INTO LIFE
AN UNKNOWN EPILOGUE

It was deeply rooted in me that
this f i c t i o n (a play) can,
because of the high degree of compression of its own matter,
be c o n j o i n e d with l i f e,
our e v e r y d a y l i f e,
and that this j o i n i n g
can create a completely NEW ARRANGEMENT,
new, thus an almost impossible (as a normative category)
shock,
explosion,
something that is INCOMPREHENSIBLE,

UNREACHABLE:
A PRODUCTION.

I believed that this sphere of fiction (drama) could be e x t e n d e d into
the sphere of l i f e. The possibility of being extended into life implied that
fiction would have to succumb to the changes and unforeseen turns of fate
which dominate life.
And because it found itself in a foreign system—in l i f e—this life will
deform and sublimate this new life, "making it strange" and making it
thrive.
It is as if this new life "entered" life—into today's people, into the places
of everyday living, into our activities, our conditions, our holidays, our
wars, and our catastrophes;
it did so, the way a demon, as it was believed in the past, could "enter"
the body of a living being and started to speak and act through him/her.

NEW THEATRICAL S P A C E
WHERE F I C T I O N APPEARS (1980)

The process of extending the sphere of Fiction and Imagination into the
sphere of our life's reality was colored by metaphysics which, in fact,
was an inherent part of this process. This process of extension changed
entirely the perception of theatre. The first perception to be modified was
that of the concept of theatrical space, which ought to be conditioned by
the sphere of life.
However, the stage, the auditorium, theatre—thus the traditional and
conventional space which was equipped to "receive" drama or Fiction
(neutral, "abstract," sterile, uncontaminated by life)—cannot possibly be
the plane in which fiction could be elevated, and then reach the plateau of
life. Theatre was thus the least suitable place for this process to take place,
and there arose a need to find a space outside of it—in reality.

DIGRESSION. CORRECTION AND EXPLANATION

I would like to stop here to explain some things and provide some
definitions that may enhance the understanding of my thought.
Both the majority of critics and those others, who have been "inspired"
by my method, have often oversimplified the nature of my thought
process and thus have never understood its essentials which were too
radical for them.

DIGRESSION CONTINUED.
STAGE I L L U S I O N AND ITS UR-MATTER

The theatre is probably one of the most anomalous of institutions.
The actual auditorium made of balconies, loges, and stalls—filled with
seats—finds its parallel in a completely different space. This "s e c o n d"

"lurking" space is the space in which everything that happens is
FICTION, illusion,
artificial, and produced only to m i s l e a d or "c h e a t" a spectator.
All the devices which are used to achieve this deception are skillfully
hidden and imperceptible to the spectator.
What he sees are only mirages of landscapes, streets, houses, and interiors.
They are mirages because this world, when seen from backstage, is
artificial, cheap, disposable, and of *"papier-mâché."*
Penetrating behind this "magnificent" imitation and "façade" we reach
the "BACK"—a True Stage.
This stage is huge, awe-inspiring, and as if lying in wait. It is ALIEN.
PRIMORDIAL, but seemingly tamed by those glittering, ornamented
balconies, caryatids, loges, and seats.
A plain wall extends behind the blue sky. Ropes, cables, lights, lifts, and
iron platforms "operate" above the green crown of trees and behind
the marble walls of the palaces. The whole of this inferno of machinery,
worked by the hands of the theatrical proletariat, moves the wheels
of the stage which creates the thin veil of illusion that is cast upon the
audience's eyes.

DESTRUCTION OF "THE WINTER PALACE" OF ILLUSION

It seems to me that this double metaphor could explain the appearance
of constructivism at the time of the Revolution. Constructivism exposed
fissures in the glittering surface of illusion. It cast a piercing light on the
"BACK"[stage], showed it in full light without shame. Constructivism
divorced itself from the "aristocratic" circles which turned out to be
nothing more than weak and empty constructs. This act of revolution was
positive, at least as far as social changes were concerned.
However, such an explanation is neither necessary nor sufficient, as will
soon be shown.

FROM THE OTHER SIDE OF ILLUSION, OR THE FAIRGROUND BOOTH STAGE, SYMBOLISM

Before the mansion of i l l u s i o n was torn to pieces, charm,
atmosphere and the poetry of the b a c k s t a g e had been noticed.
There is a moment in the theatre when malicious and poisonous charms
operate. It is when the lights go out, and the audience leaves; when the
auditorium is empty and gray mist descends upon the objects on the
deserted stage; when the magnificent scenery and costumes, which a
moment ago were glittering in the lights of the ramp, are reduced to
common materials; when the gestures and emotions, which were full of
life and passion, have faded. Maybe then we will desire to walk across
the stage to find the remnants of life, which moved us a moment ago, as
we would walk through a cemetery. Was it only fiction? That was why
symbolists were fascinated by the poetry of poor scenery and costumes

which were made of paper, by the pathos of melancholic Pierrots and jugglers, who concealed their wrinkles, defeats, and the tragedy of human existence behind their masks. The stage, the FAIRGROUND BOOTH STAGE, this empty world, is like life's final burst of energy before it dissipates into eternity; it is like an illusion.

At the doorway of a poor shack, there stands an old Pierrot who searched for his Colombine in vain. His make-up is smudged by tears.

RETURN TO THE FAIRGROUND-BOOTH STAGE

Before this image disappears from our memory and poor Pierrot leaves forever, I would like to say something that may simply and explicitly describe my journey towards Theatre.

Even though in different periods and at the different "stages" of my journey I used to label all the places I had visited (the Zero Theatre, the Informel, the Impossible Theatre, the Theatre of the Lowest Rank, the Theatre-Happening, the Theatre of Death), this FAIRGROUND-BOOTH STAGE has always existed at the back of my mind. All those other names have only preserved it from official and academic stultification. They were like the titles of consecutive chapters which described my struggle and victory over the forces lurking to trap me throughout my journey into the UNKNOWN and the IMPOSSIBLE.

For the last half of the century, the poor Fairground-Booth Stage has been nearly forgotten. It has been suppressed from memory by purist ideas, constructivist revolutions, surrealist manifestations, metaphysics of abstraction, happenings, environmental art, the ideas of open or conceptual theatre, anti-theatre, big battles, hopes, and illusions as well as defeats, disappointments, and pseudoscientific degenerations.

Today, after having fought many battles, I see clearly the journey which I have accomplished. I understand why I have stubbornly refused to accept both official and institutional status, in other words, why my theatre and I have been stubbornly refused any privileges bestowed upon us with the achievement of a certain social position. The only tangible answer to this is that my theatre has always been recognized as the Fairground-Booth Stage.

THE ONLY TRUE THEATRE OF EMOTIONS.

CONSTRUCTIVISM ONCE AGAIN, ITS UTOPIA AND SCHOLASTICISM

In order to finish this lengthy digression, to get to my own conclusions, and what is more important, in order to define clearly my theatrical personality, which has frequently been simplistically associated with either the noble past of constructivism or the inanity of the post-war avant-garde, I feel the need to elaborate on the great reform of theatre in the Revolution. The constructivists, who perceived a social revolution paralleling that in art, believed that art and its formal means would infiltrate life to such a degree that the two would become one; that, in the near future, art as such would disappear and would be identified with the perfect arrangement of life.

THE DISAPPEARANCE OF THE DEMARCATION LINE BETWEEN THE STAGE AND THE AUDITORIUM

This concept of the material infiltration of art into life caused the barrier, which had separated them, to be eliminated.

Art ceased to be a reflection of life and its illusion.

In its relationship with life, art functioned as a project, a proposal, a manifesto, and an analogous structure. It did not require contemplation but cognizance. In theatre, the barrier was created by both a ramp and a curtain. When these were abolished, the shouts and screams that were heard evoked the image of the destruction of the Bastille.

The ILLUSION of the stage was torn to pieces. So was the belief in its magnificence and power. The crude BACK[stage] and its mechanism were brought to the fore. The walls of Elsinore crumbled to pieces on stage. In their stead, "working" constructions, platforms, ladders, and ropes were raised enthusiastically.

ILLUSION was replaced by less radical forms, by "light" information, and by an autonomous image of cubist forms. In the jargon of theatre historians, this process of changes was called

t h e   d i s a p p e a r a n c e   o f   t h e   d e m a r c a t i o n   l i n e
b e t w e e n   t h e   s t a g e   a n d   t h e   a u d i t o r i u m. This "disappearance" was demanded by the revolution which, on the one hand, foresaw the necessity of activating the passive audience, and, on the other hand, the necessity and the possibility of immediate contact between the actors and the audience. There was a need to destroy the distance that separated the auditorium and the stage. That was done. Thus illusion, which required this distance and which was based on the existence of this demarcation line, had to disappear.

It was replaced by an arrangement, which I would call an "installation," that is a construct, the aim of which was to transmit a text, a plot, and actor's performance.

A MATERIALIST REVOLUTION REVEALS ITS METAPHYSICAL SIDE

There was a moment during this disappearance of the demarcation line between the stage and the auditorium and the destruction of illusion in which I felt particularly strongly—a moment of d i s c l o s i n g the BACK of the stage, which had an almost metaphysical and sacred quality; a moment of revealing the UR-MATTER of the stage.

This hidden and carefully guarded reality which initially was filled with illusion; this enclosed in itself WORLD—dark and empty, wooden planks, an abandoned spotlight, the backs of the panels, canvases with mysterious numbers and letters on them, a ladder resting on a cement wall, a wooden platform, a kitchen chair, a piece of a wall or a fence, a column—foreign objects which lost their power of illusion. . . .

This is precisely the environment where a miracle can happen, where imagination can materialize as reality, where ghosts, beings from another dimension, appear for a split second in order for us to see them at the threshold between the shadow of death and life. This was where, at a certain stage of my work in 1944, I was waiting anxiously and faithfully for the return of Odysseus.

WHEN THE CURTAIN NEITHER GOES UP NOR FALLS DOWN, OR THE DIFFICULTIES WITH ILLUSION AND FICTION

Total i l l u s i o n and f i c t i o n existed in the naturalistic set up. A spectator could remain a witness to the events on stage, because he was aware that everything that was happening on it and within the frames of the box stage was only fiction. His role was limited to that of spectator and witness.

This passive reception of the naturalistic i l l u s i o n on stage could not bring full satisfaction.

There arose the need for a more active perception of the work on stage and of a work of art in general.

It was apparent that the work itself had to be modified in the process of activating the senses. Its structure and function had to be changed.

The work ceased to be a r e f l e c t i o n of life which connoted a safe perception and a comfortable condition for the spectator. It became a challenge, a provocation, an indictment, which demanded that the spectator express opinion and answer the questions that were posed. The work was directed at him. The spectator could not remain passive.

Illusion, which used to stand between these events and the audience, had to disappear.

Therefore, the distance established by the ramp and the proscenium, which like a moat in the zoo guarded spectators from the attacks of wild animals, was demolished.

The acting space was detached from an illusory horizon and pushed forward towards the audience.

This having been done, there was no place for deceptive scenery and palaces.

A stage floor, bridges, stairs, and platforms were enough.

Acting, which was limited by the fourth wall in the past, was now directed at the audience; it had all the elements of a frontal a t t a c k!

On the one hand, the purpose of this revolution in theatre was to make the audience participate actively in what was happening on stage and in the performance. To be more precise, the aim was to make them participate actively in f i c t i o n and i l l u s i o n.

On the other hand, its purpose was to bring f i c t i o n closer to life's reality, to create the illusion (sic!) that we were observing life's events.

The former goal was achieved by the rejection of all the devices which were used by i l l u s i o n; by mixing up the place of stage action with that reserved for the spectators; by placing the actors among the audience and the audience among the actors. In the hospital, the audience was sitting at the beds of the patients; in the prison, they shared the cell with the inmates; in the street fights, they were so close to the fighting that it should have been required of them to participate in them. But, of course, that never happened. In yet other settings, the audience was placed among the furniture in the living room which was described in the stage notes. However, the living room was not a real one, as it was a representation of a living room whose description could be found in drama, and thus in the sphere of fiction. Therefore, a spectator was only a spectator and perceived as such, he was placed there illegally, falsely, or even untactfully. The placement of the spectator and the actor at the same "level," giving them (more or less) equal rights, the hope that the f i c t i o n of drama and of acting would lose their undesirable characteristics and get closer to truth and reality, were a result of the naive new faith of the constructivist revolution, which firmly believed in the possibility of creating a magnificent world in which the perfect integration of life and art could take place. Later (that is nowadays) the same concepts when enunciated by our "false" avant-garde, which is bereft of knowledge and scruples, sound flat and stupid.

The latter goal, whose purpose was to depose i l l u s i o n, was even more difficult to achieve. A lot has been done to reduce the power of f i c t i o n, to bring it closer to life, and to make it a part of life's reality. The stage action was placed not in the theatre but in an authentic place which was analogous to that of the play. Kaiser's *Gas* was played in a gas chamber. But this radical solution was nothing more than a naive and false attempt.

Even though the FICTION of drama was transferred to the plane of reality, it did not cease to exist. Moreover, this exact tautology, this parallel existence of the text of the place and the real space was often a naturalistic device which could easily have been used by Stanislavsky. The FICTION of the drama was still treated in a conventional way—it was p e r f o r m e d! The place was forgotten . . . after a few brief moments. One could assert that the spectator was placed in the centre of the action. But it might as well have been said that the degree of ILLUSION was multiplied. The spectator was placed in a centre which was full of illusion and, of course, of fiction. But this multiplication of illusion was only discovered after the spectator had left the theatre—or I should rather say, a gas chamber—when illusion dissolved.

All these devices, methods, and struggles, which were undertaken during that heroic time of the Revolution and avant-garde in art, had their unquestionable right and a colossal power of convincing anyone by their radical character. Therefore, it should not come as a surprise that they helped mold my imagination when I was young. Only later, during the war, did I discover the numerous inconsistencies and shortcomings of this approach.

That was when I made my own discovery.

THE CRITIQUE OF CONSTRUCTIVISM AND MY OWN SETTLING OF ACCOUNTS WITH ILLUSION AND FICTION

Now, having reached the end of this long digression, I am returning (with satisfaction) to my final Odysseus-like adventures, to the beginning of my theatrical endeavors, and my concept of theatre.

All the above-mentioned battles between constructivism and illusion and fiction, all the attempts to destroy the latter were only formal.

This was because the meaning of the concept, which stood in opposition to reality, had not been precisely defined.

REALITY "IS." IT IS IN LIFE, IN THE REALITY OF OUR LIVES.

ILLUSION and FICTION (of drama and of acting) have not been destroyed because they were not set against the true REALITY.

FICTION has not come in contact with REALITY; it has found its extension in REALITY.

There was no REALNESS. There was only a place, THEATRE, which, like a sanctuary, was separated from life and was dedicated to aesthetic experiences.

Therefore, the spectator still found himself in the space which was reserved for theatre, in the institution whose job was to s m u g g l e in and manipulate with f i c t i o n.

The spectators were coaxed into believing that they experienced fiction as if they were experiencing "reality of life."

MY CONTEMPT FOR
THE "HOLY" STAGING

I think that I had an inborn aversion to
the idea of "staging"
to: IMITATING,
PRETENDING,
SIMULATING of
characters, parts, situations, plots, place, and action.

All that which was believed to be the essence and a natural condition of theatre and acting; that which was never to be questioned; that which was beyond a shadow of a doubt; that which was absolute—
all that sounded f a l s e and dubious to me.

This aversion of mine must have been perceived by the professionals as my lack of any theatre training. If, of course, they noticed it at all. For me, this aversion of mine had far reaching consequences. It was a principal characteristic of my attitude toward and my understanding of theatre; a characteristic which differentiated my artistic activities from those of

other avant-garde artists of the 1920s, who feverishly were looking for
new ways of staging and performing.
My theatre, grounded in the idea of the rejection of the notion and
practice of STAGING,
finds itself o u t s i d e of theatre;
an active process of contestation of theatre and its structures.
But these terms came much, much later and had a mixed impact on it.
LET ME REMIND YOU OF THE DATE: 1944!
I should add here that my transgressions against the universal code of
theatrical behavior—not fully defined even today—separate me from the
contemporary professional theatre as well as this theatre, which calls itself
avant-garde, dominated by the power of s t a g i n g and the growing
power of i l l u s i o n and f i c t i o n, which, like an avalanche, crushes
everything coming down.

A SMALL DIGRESSION

In this anti-theatrical activity, which could be defined as
dissent,
heresy,
protest,
I needed to find a different path and a different a c c e s s to theatre.
And a completely different way of manifesting and fulfilling my passion;
my passion (despite all that I have written) for t h e a t r e.

SO THAT FICTION OF A DRAMA COULD "ENTER" OUR LIFE

I passionately and strongly believed in the world of d r a m a, its sphere
of imagination and its
f i c t i o n, and its secret powers.
I thought that what happens in a play, does really happen in life, today, all
around me.
I blamed theatre for turning this true reality into a poor-quality copy and
illusion.
I considered it pedestrian to reduce the grandeur and the truth of drama
to those doubtful procedures of imitating the heroes, of attaching to them
the gestures and the words, which did not belong to them, forcing them to
p r e t e n d. . . .
In my feverish "inner" condition (*l'état d'âme*), I gradually stopped
making a distinction between fiction and life in my creative process.
Everything happens at the threshold between imagination and life.
I started to believe that the characters from a play would appear in my
(our) life; that they would return and, maybe, would remain with us
for some time. Such a belief was prompted by a call from the past—by
the memory of "All Saints' Day," known also as the Day of the Dead; a
ritual.
Maybe, all that needed to happen were just a few "magic" adjustments. . . .

I saw those characters everywhere—around the corner, in a dark dive, on the stairs, in the corner of a yard . . .; they were busy doing something; they were visible; they did not know that I was following them. . . .
They were like us. . . .
It was obvious to me that these "returning" characters from a play could not belong to the world of the "SHADOWS" (though as *The Dead Class* showed, they had a lot in common with the dead); that they have to be the LIVING BEINGS.
ALIVE not only in a biological sense, but also alive in "social" terms— thus, belonging to our life and our time,
our every day,
our situations and our conditions;
and to PLACE, a PLACE in our life and our time.
A PLACE!
This is a correct word, which could contain in itself a solution to this almost impossible situation.
I was aware of the fact that despite my "metaphysical" attitude to a p l a y,
its content was FICTION.
It was necessary that f i c t i o n o f a p l a y cease being fiction.
That it establish some secret relationship with life's reality; with our everyday life.
That it be e x t e n d e d into the sphere of life.
That it "enter," like a demon, as it was believed in the past, the body of a living being and start to speak and act through him/her.

THE QUESTIONING OF THE ARTISTIC PLACE
THE PLACE OF THEATRE IN LIFE'S REALITY

It was an extremely important d i s c o v e r y in the development of my idea of theatre.
Let us remember the date: 1944!
This discovery destroyed the illusion of the art's sacred altar and its mystery.
It was not easy to say this simple sentence:
. . . theatre is the least suitable place for the materialization of drama . . .
Theatre, a place separated from the sphere of practice of everyday life, a place-reservation, like a museum, intended and reserved for the presentation and reception of FICTION, cannot be a site of the desired mutual penetration and c o n j o i n i n g of
FICTION and LIFE.
It was clear to me that this act, which was almost like a sexual penetration, could not take place in the theatre but o u t s i d e of it; in the very centre of life.
Of course, this did not mean a well-known process of transferring stage action into site-specific locations:
gothic cathedrals where religious mysteries were to be linked to ecclesiastical celebrations;

inner-courtyards of castles, where the ghosts looked more real;
public squares so that ludic carnivals would be more alive.
The attempts to locate stage action in a mysterious or bizarre environment
are of the same kind since, except for the mood, they do not change
anything in the structure of stage fiction.
These attempts are aesthetic, pretentious, and false.
I spend all this time discussing these phenomena, because they are easy
and seductive stylizations, which are treated seriously and their surface
appearance is often confused with an authentic discovery.

A SCANDALOUS CLASH BETWEEN THE FICTION OF DRAMA AND A PLACE

If I found a place for drama and its imaginary structure outside of theatre,
in the very center of life, I did so for a reason.
By "accepting" a place existing in the reality of life, the fiction of drama
TOOK ON ITS FORMS, SITUATIONS, and CHARACTERS; IT
"SLIPPED" INTO THEM AND THROUGH THEM REACHED US AS
TRUTH-REALITY.
A PLACE was a FILTER.
Fiction was becoming reality of the same kind as the reality of the
audience—their world and their time.
This being the case, it was impossible to suggest that there was a parallel
or analogous relationship between drama and place.
THIS WAS ALSO MY DISOVERY.
A chosen place has to be in conflict with the content of drama.
The fiction of drama must be out of place.
It must be scandalously and shockingly out of place.
This conjoining of drama and a place must take the form of a c l a s h;
It must be surprising; alogical; in which one system cannot explain the
other;
Two a l i e n and h o s t i l e systems.
It is only now that a real relationship can be established
as a consequence of this penetration!

THE DESCRIPTION OF PLACES FROM 1944 UNTIL TODAY

These are the p l a c e s which I used for my theatre or about which I
used to dream. I cannot really fully explain what it was in them that made
me chose them and why I did so.
Their "elementary" everyday quality. . . .
mundanity . . .
their state of neglect . . .
nostalgia, melancholy, sadness . . .
their passing . . . poetry,
maybe, their miserable condition, their "poverty" . . .
I might have chosen them because of my proclivity and my attitude,
manifesting itself from the beginning, towards THE REALITY OF

THE LOWEST RANK, which, as I described it in my EMBALLAGE MANIFESTO, shows the object that reveals its essence balancing at the threshold between GARBAGE and ETERNITY.

A RAILWAY STATION — People waiting for their trains the way they wait for their destiny; people saying good-byes, people waiting—the audience; people who are all waiting for—the actors.

During the war, at nights, I was waiting for Odysseus, returning to his homeland; for Odysseus getting off the train.

A POST-OFFICE — with piles of bags with letters, parcels, boxes, and packages; with anonymous information; suspended in a vacuum between the sender and the addressee. . . .

A DEMOLISHED, BOMBED ROOM — there were many of them during the war; walls with plaster falling off; lose floor planks; bullet holes; abandoned parcels covered with plaster and cement (the audience seated on them); a molded board hanging from the ceiling; a metal cable stretched across the room; attached to it, a Nazi loudspeaker, called "a yapper" by the people; in the corner, a cart wheel smeared with mud; a gun-barrel resting on a trestle—the remnant of a lost civilization—was laid across the room. . . . Odysseus returned to this ghastly room of 1944, rather than to his Ithaca.

A POORHOUSE — almost a garbage dump . . . with broken pieces of beds; abandoned machines from the workshops of slave laborers; in parts an asylum, in parts a prison; debris; crumbling walls. It is here that the events of S. I. Witkiewicz's The Water-Hen took place. A troupe of VAGRANTS, Travelers, Eternal Wanderers assumed the parts of decadent Noblemen, Cardinals, Bank Officials, Blasé Artists, Dandies, Lackeys, English Ladies, Libertines, and Lechers.

The idea of "environment" (a work of art defined as "environment") and "poor art" was fully developed in 1961 in my INFORMEL

THEATRE (S. I. Witkiewicz's *The Country House*)

A LAUNDERETTE

a place where dirty clothes are washed; a ritual of everyday life; cleaning; cleansing; almost an antique catharsis mixed with washtubs and soap. . . .

piles of newspapers, which are washed and dried; vulgar washer-women screaming the announcements, titles of articles—the war, accidents, funerals, weddings, birthdays— clouds of steam. . . .

A CAFÉ

tables put together—similar tables can be found in morgues; a macabre feats of beggars and vagrants, who carry their earthly belongings with them, thus giving testimony to the saying—

"omnia mea mecum porta" (all I have, I carry with me). I named these creatures created by me—"The Wanderers and their Luggage." Their luggage were their flaws, crimes, lovers, eccentricities, obsessions (for example, the Gigolo was forever joined with his lover, whom she continuously stabbed to death; two Hassidic Jews were joined with "the Plank of the Last Resort"), the real and well-trained waiters serve the audience and the actors; later, in this café-dive, the scenes from Witkacy's world of the nouveau riche, aristocracy, and church officials were played out.

A CLOAKROOM

a cloakroom was a huge iron cage with hooks and hangers similar to those used in slaughterhouses where pieces of meat are hung on the walls. It was a rather "gruesome" installation.

The audience who needs to go through this installation was forced to leave their coats. They were guarded by two cloakroom attendants—executioners, who imposed the rules of a slaughterhouse on the artistic domain of drama.

The plot of *Dainty Shapes and Hairy Apes*
(because this is the play by Witkiewicz I
am talking about), takes place in the palace
populated by high society, the select elite, and
in the atmosphere of refined and sophisticated
conversations, was presented in a THEATRE
CLOAKROOM, and not on STAGE—a place
of holy illusion—but in its antechamber, a
place of the lowest rank in theatre.

A CLOAKROOM

At all times, one has to question and expose
the false prestige of "the artistic condition,"
which tries to maneuver through sanctioned
critical territory by juggling
expression, performance, presentation,
"pretending," representation
and to prevent the d e l i v e r a n c e of
"r e a l i t y" and truth!
A stage, no matter which one, even the most
dynamic one created with the help of the audience's participation,
is always solid and passive;
it is a place where the actor
wins an artistic status,
prize and glory;
it is an artistic place.
[Our stage] must be bereft of this function.
The place for
"artistic activity"
is taken by
a utilitarian space,
by a C L O A K R O O M,
a real cloakroom.
In the theatre, a cloakroom
is a place and an institution
of the lowest rank;
it is usually an obstacle
one would like to avoid.
If one were to think about it,
a cloakroom is shameless
in its invasion of one's privacy:
we are forced to leave there
an intimate part of us.
It is a terrorist act.
We could push this metaphor even further and say that
during a production
parts of us are hanging there mixed together

Theatrical Place   **349**

with people we do not know;
we are hanging motionlessly
marked by numbers,
violated,
punished,
and so on . . .
. . . this infamous institution has
dominated theatre,
it stands there like a punishing, soulless death squad
led by a group of thugs.
A cloakroom, moving in no direction,
is constantly, aimlessly there,
for its own sake
like art for art's sake.
Cloakroom for cloakroom's sake. . . .
A cloakroom works,
expands,
devours more and more spheres of the imagination.
It is continuously working. . . .
It rejects the actors and their rights,
it throws them ruthlessly beyond the boundaries,
or it appropriates, belittles,
deforms,
sterilizes,
tarnishes,
ruthlessly breaks,
and gives false testimonies
to their attempts to "smuggle" in their artistic
activities.

Theatrical Place (1970s–1980s):

THE INFAMOUS TRANSITION FROM THE WORLD OF THE DEAD INTO THE WORLD OF THE LIVING. FICTION AND REALITY (1980)

When I was working on the production of Stanisław Wyspiański's play *The Return of Odysseus* at the Underground Theatre in 1944, I jotted down the following short sentence in my director's book: "Odysseus must really return." Ever since that day, I have remained faithful to the meaning of this sentence. It signified the need to find a t r a n s i t i o n from the world of "beyond" to the world "here," from the condition of being dead into that of being alive. That was the outcome of my long meditations and difficult decisions; meditations on the concept of the theatre—my theatre. This idea of transition could have been a tangible solution in a mystical system. However, in theatre, [in order to achieve this transition], one had to take into account the need to use completely unconventional and unusual devices.

One had to d i s c o v e r the method. It was not merely the war and Troy from which Odysseus returned. More importantly, he returned from "out of the grave," from the realm of the dead, from the "other world" into the sphere of life, into the realm of the living; he appeared among us. The return of Odysseus established a p r e c e d e n t and a p r o t o t y p e for all the later characters of my theatre. There were many of them. The whole procession that came out many productions and dramas—from the realm of FICTION. All were "dead," all were returning into the world of the living, into our world, into the present. This contradiction of d e a t h - l i f e perfectly corresponded to the opposition between f i c t i o n - r e a l i t y. From this moment on, one had to be consistent and draw radical conclusions about acting; one had to resist the temptation of psychological, questionable, and well-known methods of demonstrating mystical states and of the situations from the verge of "this" and "that" world.

If the system of death (eternity) is absolute and pure, the sphere of life is the reality is of a lower rank. The matter of life is seriously "contaminated." This "contamination" is largely responsible for the creation of art and theatre. A "dead" character (from a drama), who is ennobled by the fact that he is dead and placed as if in a "mausoleum of eternity," finds his "double" . . . a living double. But the fact that he is alive is very suspicious. The character is brutally reduced to a common, indeterminate, "low" personage, a poor imitation through which we can only discern traces of the greatness possessed by the "prototype" and eternity as well. A dead greatness can only be perceived through live reality which is commonplace and of the lower rank. Death can only be perceived through the misery of everyday routine; fiction (of drama) through a real place of the lowest rank.

THE ESSENTIAL MEANING OF THEATRE

Reincarnation is an extreme and ultimate concept which exists at the borders of human reasoning. It is a concept which was born out of human faith, rebellion, and the myth of immortality; out of a primordial sense of the union with the transcendental sphere. It was conceived in the deepest stratum of our existence. It is an echo of "paradise lost"; of an absolute and perfect balance that is unattainable for our culture and a mentality which has gone through the inferno of the skeptical and critical mind several times over. What we are left with is the state of nostalgia and a sense of failure. They can be found at the roots of ancient tragedy (the concept of irreversibility of human fate) and the intellectual pessimism of our epoch. These states, I am convinced, are also our only c h a n c e and r e a s o n f o r g e n u i n e c r e a t i v i t y.

I would state further that t h e a t r e i s t h e p l a c e t h a t r e v e a l s—l i k e s o m e f o r d s i n a r i v e r d o—t h e

traces of "transition" "from that other side"
into our life.
An ACTOR, who assumes the condition of A DEAD MAN, stands
in front of the audience. A performance, whose form is closely
connected with that of a ritual or a ceremony, could be equated with
a treatment which makes use of a s h o c k. I would gladly call it a
m e t a p h y s i c a l one.

LIFE—REALITY OF THE LOWEST RANK

Warning: let us beware and not place easily our trust in individuals who,
misusing those metaphysical reasons, offer us gloomy and blunt pathos or
the pretentious and empty gestures of shamans. A feeling of a tight-rope
dance, irony, sarcasm, and a sense of humor are a h u m a n
a s p e c t of metaphysics. They are also a manifestation of human
intelligence. This is a positive part of our inheritance from the age of
REASON.
One more thing which is seldom taken into consideration: all forms (in
art), whose highest goal is to affirm life in the world known as "the other
side," are OPPOSED to life, as well as to the status and code of life. They
are ANTITHETICAL to life and that is why they are
s c a n d a l o u s and shocking when defined in terms of its categories.
This is the reason why my "Zero Theatre" (1963) was a theatre of
phenomena and states which exist "below zero," and were directed
towards emptiness, indistinctness, and "low" values. This was the reason
why I proclaimed the realness of the lowest MATERIALISTIC regions
and, horrors!, of moral ones. This was the reason why, in theatre, I
substituted the archaic, pathetic, and "divine" concept of
r e i n c a r n a t i o n for the human act of i m p o s t u r e, which
admitted to the stage s w i n d l e r s and c r o o k s; for s n e a k i n g
in, which reflected the obscure methods of "impure forces"; for
t r a n s f o r m a t i o n, which denoted a psychological process that was
colored by mysticism. However, I always felt this mysterious tremor and
awe-inspiring sensation of "the other world" in all those real processes
of the lower rank. . . . I felt this tremor while waiting at the station for
Odysseus's return from Troy.

THE ITHACA OF 1944

. . . The room was destroyed. There was war and there were thousands
of such rooms. They all looked alike: bare bricks stared from behind a
coat of paint, plaster was hanging from the ceiling, boards were missing
in the floor, abandoned parcels were covered with dust (they would be
used as the auditorium), debris was scattered around; a plain platform
reminiscent of the deck of a ship, were discarded at the horizon of this
decayed decor; a gun barrel was resting on a heap of iron scrap; a military
loudspeaker was hanging from a rusty metal rope. The bent figure of a

helmeted soldier wearing a faded overcoat stood against the wall. On this day, June 6, 1944, he became a part of this room. He came there and sat down to rest. Despite his poor condition, he carried a menacing air. When everything returned to normal after the intrusion from the outside, when the date was established, and when all the elements of the room seemed to become indispensable elements of this composition, the soldier turned his head to the audience and said this one sentence: "I am Odysseus, I have returned from Troy." This everyday REALNESS, which was firmly rooted in both place and time, immediately permitted the audience to perceive this mysterious current flowing from the depth of time when the soldier, whose presence could not have been questioned, called himself by the name of the man who had died centuries ago. A split second was needed to see this return, but the emotion raised by it stayed much longer . . . in memory!

REALITY AS MEDIUM. THE MAGIC OF REALITY

. . . FICTION of drama was, in my deep conviction, the sphere of death . . . the dead characters . . . the past for me. REALNESS, into which this F i c t i o n entered, had to be extremely prosaic, mundane, and of a low rank. It had to be a part of our time and our lives. This particular use of a "stage device" had nothing to do with the avant-garde trend of the twenties to dissolve the borders between f i c t i o n and life and to turn the spectators into the witnesses of a true event.
My attitude toward the realness of life was not particularly specified. Neither did I maintain that this realness should have been consolidated. It was only an extremely important and necessary condition and medium of "rendering" f i c t i o n or the world of the dead. In our perception we have two images, one that comes from our reality and the other from the world "beyond," which are imposed on each other. This process of achieving a total picture was almost a mysterious ritual which was celebrated as if illegally in a secret place or in deep corners of our consciousness; on a deserted plane of life or an eerie cemetery where the living build houses for the dead.
On the other hand, this method had nothing in common with the "mystery" of Surrealism. I did not find it necessary to c o n s o l i d a t e (this is the term which I use to refer to the process of blocking a production) strangeness, pure elements of the absurd, illogical associations which can be found in art. These elements, called "mystery" in literature, turned into bizarre elements once transferred onto the stage. The plays of Witkiewicz as staged in the professional theatre could serve as a prime example here. No one has realized, or maybe no one has understood, that this "surrealistic" mystery which is contained in the literary structure of the plays cannot textually be transferred into another structure either theatrical or any other. Moreover, the time of the heroic battles of surrealism has long passed away and faded from memory. This mystery must be found somewhere else.

THE REALITY OF THE PLACE

The fiction of drama becomes "r e a l i t y" through
a PLACE,
its characteristics and action.
During the performance, the actors do not s h o w a fictitious action of
the drama nor its fictitious characters (what could be perceived as their
natural function) but perform activities and behave in a way imposed
upon them by the REALITY OF THE PLACE and its characteristics.
A LAUNDERETTE was once such a space.
Washerwomen,
washtubs,
hot water,
steam,
hanging laundry,
the act of washing and hanging, etc.,
acquired, however, a new significance and meaning while going through
various stages of euphoria, excitement, and unruliness.
Thus, this nearly naturalistic REALITY has suddenly gained new,
somewhat suspect, characteristics. It swelled and began to "speak"
in a foreign tongue as if it were "possessed." It identified itself with
something that is alien or dead to us. This process of change is the
process of "slipping" of the F i c t i o n of drama, which I labeled THE
WORLD OF THE DEAD, into reality. Of course, the PLACE cannot be a
background only; it ought to be closely connected with its activities,
situations,
actions,
characters,
with its psychological and emotional states. . . .

THE DEFINITION OF THEATRE ONCE AGAIN

Theatre is an activity that occurs if life is pushed to its final limits where
all categories and concepts lose their meaning and right to exist;
where
madness, fever, hysteria, and hallucinations are the last barricades of life
before the approaching TROUPES OF DEATH and death's GRAND
THEATRE.
This is my definition of theatre which is poetic and mystical.
But this is the only way one can think and talk about theatre. This is why
my theatrical activities cannot be classified according to any rational or
pragmatic categories that used to describe naive and academic exercises in
theatre activities.
True theatre activity is the process of c r e a t i o n
which is deeply rooted
in the "w o r l d b e y o n d."

PATTERNS OF ACTION

Two predispositions influenced my thinking about theatre. First—it was my deep conviction that
a d r a m a was not a literary structure, but, first of all, an arrangement of f i c t i o n; an imaginary reality.
Second—it was my profound aversion to the idea of "s t a g i n g" and my decision to reject and eliminate this method in my theatre work.

A DRAMA-FICTION IS THE WORLD OF THE DEAD

I used to have two versions of interpreting a d r a m a.
One: A f i c t i o n (of a drama) was an arrangement which is conceived in the mind (and later written down), which did not exist in life's reality. This was a definition in the spirit of rationalism.
The other definition was highly mystical.
It still fascinates me today.
F i c t i o n does not live in life; and in this lacking of life—in this nothingness—it is closer to death and its infinite domain.
This may be why I have always perceived a d r a m a - f i c t i o n as the DEAD WORLD AND THE WORLD OF THE DEAD.
Strange was that theatre "o n t h e o t h e r s i d e." Without the audience. The stage, like a cemetery, was full of the abandoned "stage pieces"—pitiful ruins with names similar to those on the tombstones: "the castle," "the woods," "the square," "the drawing-room," "the port." The Dead kept r e p e a t i n g interminably, as if "for eternity" (time does not exist there), the words, the parts, the plot's events, which did take place sometime ago in real life. They really did take place!
Now, it is possible to imagine, that the "text," which had been written later by a living playwright, Shakespeare or Wyspiański, is a transfer from that THEATRUM MORTIS.

THE REJECTION OF "STAGING"

The second thing, which was influential in my thinking about theatre, was my aversion to the idea of "staging" believed to be an innate characteristic of a theatre practice (I may add: of a traditional theatre practice). It is commonly maintained that the idea of "staging" is a process of materializing and realizing of a d r a m a - f i c t i o n. In reality, however, the contrary is the case. The process of staging is the process of multiplying the illusion of a drama-fiction. Let me be more obvious: the process of staging is the process of false pretense, simulation (of emotions), and replica (of places).
From the very beginning, all these procedures were for me ridiculous, mundane, and shameful. I could not accept them; nor could I use them.
The rejection of the idea of the "staging" a drama-fiction was a defining and distinct quality of my theatre practice.
This was unacceptable to theatre professionals.

WORKING WITH LIFE'S MATTER

A radical negation of the idea of "s t a g i n g" led to the questioning of the "artistic" condition and by extension of the idea of a work of "art" and of an "artistic" place.

Having rejected these sanctioned and fully endorsed values, what was left was the idea of WORKING WITHIN EVERYDAY LIFE'S REALITY, in life itself, in the present tense, and in a place, where everyday activities are performed.

These ideas were discovered and used in the visual arts in the 1960s.

I made use of them in 1944.

CONTESTATION OF AN ARTISTIC PLACE
A REAL PLACE

This working within reality, and not illusion and fiction, led to:

—the rejection of the institution of theatre and its stage as well as the auditorium, as well as the places taken out of the reality of everyday life and reserved only for fiction and illusion—and

—the necessity to find a REAL PLACE within the reality of everyday life, which is clearly defined and has specific attributes.

CHARACTERISTSTICS OF A REAL PLACE

We must not forget that, in this REALITY we need to find a reference to
a d r a m a
the world of FICTION,
"the W o r l d   o f   t h e   D e a d,"
which the starting point of these risky decisions and hazardous definitions.

This is why the following conditions should be taken into consideration:

—a chosen place in life cannot be similar to the place of Fiction; it cannot be analogous. On the contrary, the further removed, the more different, the more contradictory it is, the better chances that this lack of similarity
will produce
its difference;
the better chance to perceive, on the one hand
the (REAL) MATERIALITY OF A PLACE,
and on the other hand, the feeling of THAT "OTHER" WORLD OF THE DEAD.

PARTYTURA OF A REAL PLACE

—It is necessary to create a "p a r t y t u r a" of a PLACE—a blue-print of its activities, atmosphere, and features that can be felt and are manifested. It will be almost a "plot" of a PLACE and
a primary m a t t e r of a production, which is autonomous and real.

A TRANSITION FROM "THAT OTHER WORLD"
TO THE WORLD "HERE"

Now, what follows is the most perilous activity, which takes place, at the
border between "that other world" and the lowest regions of life.
It is necessary to cause a d r a m a - f i c t i o n, the "W o r l d   o f
t h e   D e a d" to accept its second life;
that its Characters—their fate and destiny—and its Place be "transferred"
into the real, our everyday life during a procedure marked by the traces of
this mystical ritual when the dead finds its sacrificial victim.
A fascinating ambiguity: a live actor is "inhabited" by the dead.
A place, which is domesticated, yet "FOREIGN."
Because art does not recognize and does not make use of the miracles
of the everyday life, it is necessary to induce a "s i m u l a t e d
m i r a c l e," employ a procedure which is forbidden by the laws of
nature; a procedure of the lowest rank; almost a fraud. It is necessary to
provide these wandering and ephemeral dead with
an ALIVE DOUBLE;
a double from our world and our time;
to "inject" the spectral matter of the dead into a live human being.
And one more (last) piece of advice:
The more the DOUBLE is connected with life and its l o w (by
comparison with "eternity") desire for living, the further it is from the
O R I G I N A L (the Dead)—
the more distinct and glaring this fascinating ritual of
GRAFTING,
DOUBLING, and
REPETITION,
the truer the essence of theatre
will be.

Two aspects, with two corresponding stages, are connected with my
notion of the REAL PLACE, which I devised in 1944.
The first one was the discovery that life's reality can be the very matter
of a work of art—this can be accomplished without the use of imitation,
representation, or interpretation.
This simple sentence led to the decisions which had major revolutionary
consequences:
questioning of a w o r k   o f   a r t, understood as an artificial
arrangement which was "artistically" constructed,
and replacing it with a   r e a l   o b j e c t, "brut," taken out directly
from life;
further, to the questioning of the a r t i s t i c   p l a c e—theatre,
museum—and replacing it with a   r e a l   p l a c e, which was planted
firmly in life.
It should be clearly stated that whereas the decisions and the postulates
of the 1960s, which were the driving force behind the developments in

painting, the same decisions and postulates had no impact on theatre, which despite its seemingly revolutionary proclamations remained grounded in its professionalism and provincialism. This is why the post-war avant-garde in theatre was short lived.

To continue my deliberations:

the third component of this new thinking was a c t i o n, a c t i v i t y, f u n c t i o n, which imitated nothing, represented nothing, was not a form of "acting" or showed something—but it was an action taken out of the practice of everyday life; a process of working with and manipulating a REAL OBJECT; a process of annexing a REAL PLACE,

an isolated activity, which had no aim in life; which was ineffective. Almost an activity in and for itself.

This is the first aspect of REALITY and the REAL PLACE, which was written down in my biography under the rubric: 1944.

Much later, in the 1960s, similar activities were labeled the happenings. These analyses and retrospective statements are my attempt to reclaim these concepts, which I had devised much earlier.

This first aspect and phase of the above-described procedure could be seen as finished and enclosed in itself.

But I was only halfway through. It was only now that the second phase, which was much more important and more fascinating, was just about to begin; a phase when FICTION (of a drama) slipped into the found REALITY OF LIFE during an almost mystical act. I have already described this act as the Grand Entrée of the Theatre of Death. And it was exactly this REALITY of life, this prosaic reality of life whose quality and characteristics were limited by life's practical and utilitarian side, that caused anything, which was not it, that came into contact with it was so foreign and unbelievable that it could only be seen as a sign of intrusion from "the other side" and from the other world.

CRISIS OF THE REAL PLACE

The fact that I found the idea of the REAL PLACE to be too restrictive and empty was prompted by a well-known phenomenon of reducing reception to something that is commonplace, familiar, and conventional. These adjectives refer to what I would call a happening activity. Let us look more closely at this.

The REAL PLACE, a sphere of life delimited by its utilitarian function (for example, a launderette) (real or organized in a specific way, as if "fabricated") had a homogeneous set of characteristics: environment, objects, machines—all of which pointed to the fact that it was a launderette. The actors, who performed functions and roles connected to and determined by this place (a launderette), also belonged to it.

The question was about those who in the past had been called the audience. Who was the audience (in this launderette)?

They could be the clients (of this launderette), tourists, curious onlookers, accidental passers-by, or those who were lured into this place, fell into a trap. Victims! Yes! Maybe this is the most appropriate way of describing them.

The privilege of a firmly established condition of being an audience member, which allowed them to maintain a distance between them and the actions unfolding on stage; to be able to pass judgments; to feel superior to the actors and the stage itself; and, in some sense, to perform the function of the judges, was taken away from them.

They were deprived of the independent, according to them, sacred reception of sensation of the
h i g h e r   k i n d. Because, is it not true—they said with conviction— that the function of art was to supply s e n s a t i o n s only; those ephemeral—luckily—feasts of illusion; those sublimated extracts of life.

They were lured into and abandoned in this REAL PLACE without defenses which are provided by ILLUSION AND DISTANCE.

They were thrown into situations in which they were forced to deal with the raw and rough matter of life that—according to the sacred laws of aesthetics—had nothing to do with a work of art.

Bereft of the privileges, they had the same status as the PLACE and its FUNCTIONS; they were unceremoniously stirred into the matter of life; they were expected even to participate in the actions taking place around them. Their response at first was that of disappointment and indignation—until they got used to their new roles.

After some time, this violent encounter between ILLUSION and the rough matter of real life was reduced to a sanctioned practice, a convention, and, finally, a pretentious f a d.

The feeling of a constant threat, even surprise, or danger gave birth to some kind of masochism, which became more and more intolerable, especially since this new kind of pleasure, which had in it the thrill of something forbidden and risky, was false, more and more driven by the experience that this constant threat was nothing more than fiction and the danger was staged and fake.

And that was the end of this adventure. It was necessary to embark on a quest for new lands. Nobody believed in the REALITY OF A PLACE any longer. Once again, it was nothing more than FICTION. The entire project lost its purpose and reason to exist.

FURTHER DEVELOPMENT: THE O B J E C T

With the turn of the wheel of fortune and with the passing of time eroding it, the PLACE, which up till now had been a real placenta for drama's FICTION, became, in its life's matter, too burdensome, too inert, and too . . . literal.

The laws of art, distorted by human logic and human idiocy turned maliciously the realness of a place into . . . FICTION.

ILLUSION, a reflex of "that other" world and "other" theatre, which was a breeding ground for all metaphors, transformations, and poetry, called for a more luminous and independent m e d i u m. For the time being, this medium was still viewed as a binary to ILLUSION and FICTION. It was still in favor of the real.

But this real and realness no longer revealed themselves through a PLACE which imposed its laws upon all elements of theatre.

This m e d i u m now was the OBJECT.

Autonomous, enclosed in itself. *L'OBJET D'ART.*

It had one peculiar characteristic: its own live o r g a n s: the ACTORS.

This is why I called it a BIO-OBJECT.

BIO-OBJECTS were not props which would be used by actors.

They were not "stage pieces" among which the "action" takes place.

They created an indivisible totality with the actors.

They exuded their own autonomous "life" which had nothing to do with the FICTION (plot) of a drama.

This "life" and its signs were the building blocks of the essential content of a production. This was not a   p l o t; it was the production's m a t t e r.

The presentation and manifestation of the "life" of this BIO-OBJECT was not a representation of that which existed beyond and outside of it.

It was autonomous—thus, r e a l!

BIO-OBJECT—a work of art.

THE LIFE OF THE OBJECT—A MATTER OF A PRODUCTION

The matter of a production was constituted by the "inner life" of the OBJECT, its characteristics, its destiny, its sphere of the imaginary. The actors became its l i v e parts, organs. They were as if g e n e t i c a l l y connected with that object. They produced a live and moving BIO-OBJECT which secreted the elements of a stage action. It could have been an amorphous (I called it "*informelle*") or a mechanical stage action. Without the actors, this object was a hollow façade, unable to perform any action.

On the other hand, the actors were conditioned by it; their functions and activities were generated by it.

DRAMA—THE WORLD OF FICTION,
ITS PLACE IN A BIO-OBJECT

The FICTION (plot) of a drama, continuously disappearing and reappearing, "shone through" the "life" of these b i o - o b j e c t s. A term "to shine through"—seems to be the most adequate to describe the process.

Equally significant is this characteristic of the disappearance and reappearance of a dramatic plot, FICTION. At times, it suddenly disappeared inexplicably; at times, it appeared unexpectedly.

The actors would pick up its course of events and its characters, but they did so without enthusiasm, as if "under pressure," since they seemed to be preoccupied with their inner existence.

This exerting of pressure (one of my favorite means of expression) was the responsibility of the Footman, the Music Teacher, and the Bailiff—all in one person—in *The Country House*.

In *Dainty Shapes and Hairy Apes*, a similar responsibility was shared by a pair of Cloakroom-Attendants; in *The Madman and the Nun*, by two sad Torturers.

THE SO-CALLED DEVELOPMENT IN ART AND CHRONOLOGY

In art, the logic of a phenomenon's successful development does not often coincide with a linear chronology.

Often, I have the impression, which fascinates me, that TIME in art, in its course of events, encroaches upon the notion of eternity.

As if past and future did not exist in it.

As if the phenomenon of succession or progression did not exist in it.

It is only later, after it is already over, we arrange the facts and events according to the logic of our time, following our cause and effect.

All these explanations of the relationships between the ideas, my attempts at locating, defining, and analyzing them, help me identify for myself my expanding past, discover its transformations, which may lead me to new solutions.

With the passing of time, we realize that everything, however, always remains in this infinite
i n t e r i o r.

Everything is intertwined—one could say: exists simultaneously.

The idea of the OBJECT, which, in my analysis, is derived from the notion of the REAL PLACE, and after its demise, became its substitute—emerged much too early, in the 1961 production of *The Country House*, and a bit later, in the 1963 production of *The Madman and the Nun*—despite the fact the notion of the REAL PLACE had not exhausted its potential and was quite "effective" even later—in the 1967 production of *The Water-Hen* and the 1972 [1973—MK] production of *Dainty Shapes and Hairy Apes*.

The idea of the OBJECT, which emerged in the 1961 production of *The Country House*, could be seen as premonition, if I were to use our notion of time sequence.

It may be appropriate then to acquaint oneself with this OBJECT.

Here it is:

A WARDROBE
An authentic old wardrobe.
A WARDROBE was not a stage piece or a stage.

When it was open, it revealed live human beings: the actors. The wardrobe was not a bizarre-looking scenic background for the actors playing in *The Country House.*
The wardrobe was itself—nothing else.
It was an autonomous REALITY.
The actors were part of this wardrobe, as if they live inside of it.
Existed in it.
A wardrobe was imagination's privileged space,
The wardrobe's interior had its secrets, murky nooks, recesses pushed beyond official consciousness, clandestine practices, and "corrupt" behaviors.
The action of "h i d i n g" is associated with it. This hiding, this putting out of sight, and this covering up abound with the most bizarre possibilities.
Pieces of clothing, which are part of us and have a secret power of transformation, metamorphosis, and "d r e s s i n g   u p," are hung on the hangers. Our possessions, souvenirs, past, memories, letters, and secrets are laid to rest there.
In the wardrobe, the people, looking like pieces of clothing or dried-up little creatures. Once the wardrobe is open, they fall out or, because unaccustomed to light, they hide in the murky recesses.
Within this structured and well-organized "l i f e" of a wardrobe, the actors, who are hanging and swinging like pieces of clothing on hangers, have their de-eroticized dialogues.
Or mixed together with packages and sacks, they begin to resemble these objects of the lowest rank, lose their individual dignity, fall through the limits of common sense, and behave in a childish way. . . .

THE FUNERAL MACHINE
The second OBJECT in this production was a "Funeral Machine" in the shape of an enormous coffee grinder (or rather—as the events on stage made it clear—a meat grinder).
The machine was wrapped in a thick, dirty tarpaulin fastened securely with rope. On the top, it had a visible opening for loading; at the bottom, a movable drawer on wheels covered with a metal sheet. A human body could be fit into it.
A tube connected the top opening with the drawer. This inner mechanism, which was invisible to the audience, had a dreadful bolt and a crank at the end. The implausible dimensions of the "grinder" gave an impression of "inner" life and the function of this monstrous and grim-looking object.
The object took the form of a M A C H I N E.
It was my first THEATRICAL MACHINE.
Autonomous and metaphoric.
There were many others later.
A peculiar "*objet d'art.*"

A JUNK-PRAM
There was one more OBJECT in *The Country House*: a heavy, iron
JUNK-PRAM from the City Utility Department.
This atrocious chariot was used as a pram for two babies.
This was my first MOVABLE PLACE.

I am writing this after many tears. Maybe today these elements arrange
themselves in my consciousness with the logic of sense. It can be so
because later experiences were superimposed upon them. This is why,
in order to remain faithful to history, below is the description of the
WARDROBE from 1961 from the times of the Informel Theatre.

A WARDROBE (notes from 1961)
A wardrobe was my *"objet trouvé."* When placed on stage (in 1957,
Cricot 2 Theatre) as the only object, it functioned as a catalyst of many
human matters and secrets. In 1961, in S. I. Witkiewicz's *The Country
House*, it was the only stage space. Thus, the whole world. This had
serious consequences.
In our analysis, let us not pay too much attention
to statements, which could be seen as naïve.
Let us allow our imagination to cross the boundary delimited
by a simple self-evident nature of phenomena;
a boundary illegally placed by
small and petty minds.
Beyond it begins our activity!
A wardrobe is, if carefully thought about, an object
whose characteristics are ambiguous and unclear.
Let me draw attention to the fact that
it only acquires its full and proper meaning
when it is . . . closed!
It is only then that it becomes "solid."
We have just crossed the limits of being ridiculous;
freed from all possible accusations,
we act at our own risk.
We change the scale of our imagination.
Here an object (a wardrobe), which is discussed by us,
is suddenly and inexplicably altered:
it separates itself from its surroundings, closes itself, isolates itself.
And this is when it begins to simulate for good!
Usually, it pretends to be a façade of an ornamental building;
it easily and quickly adopts
appropriate styles,
which are dictated by the occasion;
and in this quickly assimilated and dubious
compilation of styles,
it tries to fool us!
When this charade becomes more and more deceitful—

its existence expands further
in our imagination,
beyond its familiar
and disciplined meanings
and domestic functions.
It expands
on that other side.
Its wings,
like backstage, suddenly open up
to the deeper and murkier regions of
this, one could say domestic, INTERIOR.
Now, in this oppressive and stifling climate,
dreams unfold,
the nightmares of the night are born,
the practices escaping the light of the day,
corrupt behaviors,
shameless and cruel,
are carried out.
Now—
and not in some mystical misty space—
but here, separated from the everyday reality
by this thin and weak wall,
we feel that we touch upon the condition of non-existence
and Death.

All this took place
in Cricot 2 Theatre,
in 1961.
It was enough to open the doors of the WARDROBE.

Kraków, 1961

Also to remain faithful to "history," I am providing the original 1963 text describing another BIO-OBJECT, which I named THE ANNIHILATION MACHINE. It was an object which was
b u i l t (rather than transferred from the reality of life).
Only the parts of the machine we real:
poor, old, folding chairs!
It was the chairs which connected it to the REAL—of course, to the Reality of the Lowest Rank, which turned this MACHINE into something that was useless and ridiculous.
However, on stage it acquired extraordinary and all-powerful characteristics.
This is its description:

THE ANNIHILATION MACHINE
A small platform
is the stage.

Almost all of it
is taken up by a huge pile of
folding chairs,
which look alike—
faded, bitten by rain and time,
"seated-out,"
folded and arranged as in a storage-room,
functionless,
linked together with rusty wires,
ropes,
that is put into motion.
Its movement acquires psychological characteristics:
it is sudden,
furious,
nervous,
bouncing up and down,
interrupted,
dying out,
jittery,
ridiculous,
monotonous,
ominous.
The sound is:
blunt, dry, clattery,
repetitive.
This huge object performs many functions:
it eliminates,
pushes out,
acts mercilessly,
thoughtlessly,
automatically,
bluntly,
makes one feel anxious,
it is ridiculous and tragic,
fascinating,
it draws to itself and rejects.
I used an object,
whose exceptional
utilitarian quality
provides it with realness,
which is nagging
and brutal,
whose motion
and function,
absurd in itself,
allowed me to transfer it
to the sphere of multiple meanings—

poetry.
The space which
is left for the actors
has nothing to do with that space
which fascinated theatre until now.
Actually, there is little left of it.
Reduced to the zero zones,
this space is so small
that the actors need
to fight
if they want to
stay on it.

SCHOOL DESKS IN THE DEAD CLASS
School desks are always in a CLASSROOM. But it was not a
CLASSROOM—REAL PLACE.
It was a black hole, a void, in front of which
the whole auditorium
s t o p p e d.
To make it worse, a rope functioned as a barrier.
It must be that there existed a d i f f e r e n t barrier, which is more
powerful and terrifying.
In this black, hopeless space of the void, the SCHOOL DESKS were a
stark example of a BIO-OBJECT.
In the s c h o o l   d e s k s, one could sit, stand; all human conditions
and emotions—suffering, fear, love, first signs of friendship, coercion, and
freedom could be found there, too.
The s c h o o l   d e s k s bracketed the live, natural human organism,
which has always had an inclination to "use" space freely, so that it is
rigorous and ordered.
They were like a womb that gives birth to something new and
unexpected—
something that, every so often, attempted to leave the s c h o o l
d e s k s for that black and empty space; that something that would
return to them (the s c h o o l   d e s k s) every time the way one returns
home-womb!

ROOM. MAYBE A NEW PHASE
After many speculations and transformations, the ROOM in *Wielopole,
Wielopole* acquired a final form which neither corresponded to a
meticulously described concept of the REAL SPACE nor to that of
the BIO-OBJECT. The concept of the BIO-OBJECT has become too
physical and too much of a burden. What I aimed to achieve in this new
production was a further development of the idea of r e c o l l e c t i o n
and m e m o r y which first surfaced in *The Dead Class*.

The following are the notes I took during the rehearsals of *Wielopole,*
Wielopole. They describe content rather than physical space, since the
s p a c e was simultaneously the content and the
t h o u g h t of this production.

It is difficult to define the spatial dimension of memory.
Here, this is a room of my childhood
with all its inhabitants.
This is the room which I keep reconstructing over and over again
and which is destroyed over and over again.
Its inhabitants are the members of my family.
They continuously repeat all their movements and activities
as if they were imprinted on a film-negative shown interminably.
They will keep repeating those banal,
elementary, and aimless activities
with the same expression on their faces;
with the concentration on the same gesture
until boredom strikes.
Those trivial activities,
which stubbornly and oppressively preoccupy us,
fill up our lives. . . .
These DEAD FAÇADES
come to life, become real and important
through this stubborn REPETITION OF ACTION.
Maybe this stubborn repetition of action,
this pulsating rhythm
which lasts as long as life;
which ends in n o t h i n g n e s s;
which is futile;
is an inherent part of MEMORY. . . .

There is also a place "BEHIND THE DOORS,"
a place which is somewhere at the back of the ROOM;
a DIFFERENT space;
—an open interior of our imagination—
which exists in a different dimension.
This is where the threats of our memory are woven;
where our freedom is born. . . .
We are standing at the door giving a long farewell to our childhood;
we are standing helpless
at the threshold of eternity and death.
In front of us,
in this poor and dusky room,
behind the doors,
a storm and a inferno rage,
and the waters of the flood rise.
The weak walls of our ROOM;

of our everyday or
linear time
will not save us. . . .
Important events stand behind the doors
it is enough to open them. . . .

THE ROOM cannot be a REAL SPACE. It cannot be a r e a l   r o o m.
If we take into consideration the audience, the room could not possibly be
perceived as an intimate room of childhood but as a public forum.
There is also another reason: the room cannot be real, i.e., exist in our
time, because this room is in our MEMORY, in our RECOLLECTION
OF THE PAST. This is the room which we keep constructing over and
over again and which is destroyed over and over again. This pulsating
rhythm must be maintained, because it delineates the real structure of our
memory.
At the same time the ROOM cannot be "furnished"; cannot be the place
beyond which the auditorium begins; cannot be the stage. If it were,
the room would be nothing more than a scene design, which would
irrevocably crush our hopes for achieving r e a l n e s s.
All those speculations force us to abandon logical analysis and rational
thinking. Probably we will have to expand the meaning of r e a l n e s s
onto the plane of immaterial MEMORY.
We will have to accept m e m o r y as the only r e a l n e s s. This means
that we will have to build a rational model of m e m o r y and define its
sphere of activities as well as its means of expression. This means that
we will have to transfer the concept of r e a l n e s s [the real] onto the
platform of EVENTS, ACTION, and ACTING. . . .

This process is explained in *Wielopole, Wielopole* by the fact that the
spectacle lacks the element of FICTION (drama), which would call forth
and procreate illusion. Therefore,
r e a l n e s s [the real] is the only element that ought to exist. And this is
it! EVENTS, ACTION—on stage—are this n e w
r e a l n e s s! Recollections of the past, functioning of MEMORY are
real, because they are . . .
f u t i l e!

Postscriptum:
Wielopole, Wielopole has just seen the light. Maybe, many of its secrets
and mysteries will be explained in the near future.

The Room: Maybe a New Phase
(1980)

After many speculations and transformations, the ROOM in *Wielopole,
Wielopole* acquired a final form which neither corresponded to a
meticulously described concept of the REAL SPACE nor to that of
the BIO-OBJECT. The concept of the BIO-OBJECT has become too
physical and too much of a burden. What I aimed to achieve in this new
production was a further development of the idea of r e c o l l e c t i o n
and m e m o r y which first surfaced in *The Dead Class*.

The following are the notes I took during the rehearsals of *Wielopole,
Wielopole*. They describe content rather than physical space, since the
s p a c e was simultaneously the content and the
t h o u g h t of this production.

It is difficult to define the spatial dimension of memory.
Here, this is a room of my childhood
with all its inhabitants.
This is the room which I keep reconstructing over and over again
and which is destroyed over and over again.
Its inhabitants are the members of my family.
They continuously repeat all their movements and activities
as if they were imprinted on a film-negative shown interminably.
They will keep repeating those banal,
elementary, and aimless activities
with the same expression on their faces;
with the concentration on the same gesture
until boredom strikes.
Those trivial activities,
which stubbornly and oppressively preoccupy us,
fill up our lives. . . .
These DEAD FAÇADES
come to life, become real and important
through this stubborn REPETITION OF ACTION.
Maybe this stubborn repetition of action,
this pulsating rhythm
which lasts as long as life;

which ends in n o t h i n g n e s s;
which is futile;
is an inherent part of MEMORY. . . .

There is also a place "BEHIND THE DOORS,"
a place which is somewhere at the back of the ROOM;
a DIFFERENT space;
—an open interior of our imagination—
which exists in a different dimension.
This is where the threats of our memory are woven;
where our freedom is born. . . .
We are standing at the door giving a long farewell to our childhood;
we are standing helpless
at the threshold of eternity and death.
In front of us,
in this poor and dusky room,
behind the doors,
a storm and a inferno rage,
and the waters of the flood rise.
The weak walls of our ROOM;
of our everyday or
linear time
will not save us. . . .
Important events stand behind the doors
it is enough to open them. . . .

THE ROOM cannot be a REAL SPACE. It cannot be a r e a l   r o o m.
If we take into consideration the audience, the room could not possibly be
perceived as an intimate room of childhood but as a public forum.
There is also another reason: the room cannot be real, i.e., exist in our
time, because this room is in our MEMORY, in our RECOLLECTION
OF THE PAST. This is the room which we keep constructing over and
over again and which is destroyed over and over again. This pulsating
rhythm must be maintained, because it delineates the real structure of our
memory.
At the same time the ROOM cannot be "furnished"; cannot be the place
beyond which the auditorium begins; cannot be the stage. If it were,
the room would be nothing more than a scene design, which would
irrevocably crush our hopes for achieving r e a l n e s s.
All those speculations force us to abandon logical analysis and rational
thinking. Probably we will have to expand the meaning of r e a l n e s s
onto the plane of immaterial MEMORY.
We will have to accept m e m o r y as the only r e a l n e s s. This means
that we will have to build a rational model of m e m o r y and define its
sphere of activities as well as its means of expression. This means that
we will have to transfer the concept of r e a l n e s s [the real] onto the
platform of EVENTS, ACTION, and ACTING. . . .

This process is explained in *Wielopole, Wielopole* by the fact that the spectacle lacks the element of FICTION (drama), which would call forth and procreate illusion. Therefore,
r e a l n e s s [the real] is the only element that ought to exist. And this is it! EVENTS, ACTION—on stage—are this n e w
r e a l n e s s! Recollections of the past, functioning of MEMORY are real, because they are . . .
f u t i l e!

Postscriptum:
Wielopole, Wielopole has just seen the light. Maybe, many of its secrets and mysteries will be explained in the near future.

Etudes—Sketches of a Scenario

. . . I am thinking about ways I may create on stage
the environment and situations in which the condition of an ARMY
could be identified with the condition of an ACTOR.
On stage, we have an ARMY, inhabiting the corner of the ROOM.
Soldiers, walking towards us from the past, "d e a d,"
reduced to a single grimace and a single moment,
"resurrected" (I shall have to find a character who will perform this
"miracle")
acting without conviction, as if separated from or parallel to life and
memory.
Of course, there is nothing mysterious about these symptoms,
which describe the condition of being in the ARMY.
But in the ROOM, alongside the ARMY performing as if on the sly,
there are also CIVILIAN-ACTORS,
whose appearance, behavior, and mentality
are close to—blood relations of—the SPECTATORS.
The SPECTATORS identify with the CIVILIAN-ACTORS
in their "zero" degree of expressivity,
and, thanks to them, discover within themselves little by little
a condition of being, which is similar, if not identical, to that of the
ARMY;
THEY EXPERIENCE ALL THOSE EMOTIONS AND FEELINGS,
which
arise when one is confronted with oneself, stripped down to
the empty shell, to the point of being an object, the DEAD.
A tide of thoughts is set in motion; its ebb and flow
disclose always more and more shockingly but clearly
the FACE of a HUMAN.
The ARMY—individuals of this human species—
thus constitute the MODEL of the actor.
As the action on stage unfolds, so emerge their characters.

–n.d.

"The Last Supper" Sequence of Rehearsals

MARCH 12, 1980:

The scene of the Last Supper must take place "behind the doors," on the sly, "in a corner" following the rules of a children's game and their secret, enigmatic code, which is incomprehensible to adults. It needs to look pathetic and poor.

The doors to the room are open, but they can close at any moment.

Uncle Karol, Uncle Olek, Aunt Mańka, Aunt Józka, the Grandmother, and Adaś play in The Last Supper.

Why are the adults, "the inhabitants of the room" playing the game?

The Crucifixion scene was set up and acted out by the soldiers who, after changing their clothes and putting on priests' birettas, regressed into the time of their childhood. I started to think that these "gospel" games played by children on the sly, away from the adults who do not interrupt them—gradually invade the "official" stage and burst into the imagination of the adults.

MARCH 17, 1980 (A LATER NOTE WAS INSERTED HERE):

Of course, the "gospel" scenes are not really acted out by "children." This would be too naïve and too literal.

Simply, a place "BEHIND THE DOORS"; a place reserved for imagination, conjures up a special aura, it is a magic place, which brings about a profound metamorphosis in the actors transforming them into children.

It is, as if, another space—a dimension of imagination.

It is necessary however first to discover this "o t h e r s p a c e" so that it can be used.

In order to do so, we will engage in activities,

which are conventional,

performed "on the quiet,"

hastily,

in trepidation,

even to use known terms—

INEFFECTUALLY, that is,

only acted out
without—of course—any practical results;
thus,
pathetic,
poor,
contemptible—
lacking expressive gestures, which at least might have made them
p l a u s i b l e and reminiscent of the a c t u a l   e v e n t—
and in response to some enigmatic code.
This metamorphosis cannot start from any ready-made image in the
imagination—(the more so, since these are adult actors—the inhabitants
of the ROOM),
but rather from preparatory scenarios, which will have the character of
conspiracy, the hatching of a plot, and of an arrangement (maybe even: of
recollection).

MARCH 12, 1980 (CONTINUED):

The rear walls are pushed back. The doors remain open. The entire
antechamber "box" is visible.
A table is inclined diagonally towards the front of the stage.
(where did it come from?)
Cramped and crowded round the table is the family, the inhabitants of the
ROOM.
Their movements are exaggerated and convulsive.
They are quarrelling about some inheritance.
For the time being, the actors are improvising.
On the floor of the ROOM lies the body of the Priest—the mannequin.

This family scene, scandalous as it is, is soon to be transformed into "The
Last Supper." It is supposed to happen in a way that looks as if a slide of
Leonardo's famous painting has been superimposed upon it.
Because Judas is the antihero of this scene, I call to mind the Rabbi from
Wielopole.
The Rabbi must be present. It is quite possible that he will play a vital
part later on.
Aunt Mańka—the Lunatic must dress up as the Rabbi. . . .
Mańka-Rabbi sings the Rebecca song—
not an imposing psalm, but, in the tradition of Cricot 2 Theatre, as is
often the case, there is included a vulgar song from a cabaret of ill repute.
The quarrel about the inheritance continues. (Can this be in Polish,
German, or Yiddish?)

The quarrel about inheritance slowly transforms into the scene depicted
in "The Last Supper." The actors shout and wave their arms. A psalm is
heard. It gets louder and louder and then is suddenly cut off.

At the same moment, the movement of one actor stops and the voice is cut off. What remains in motion is Leonardo's painting.
Finally, the Priest, seated in the middle,
opens his arms in a well-known gesture.
And thus, gradually, with precision, an image is formed out of the geometry of shoulders, hands, faces, and bent bodies reacting to that one single statement: "One of you will betray me."

APRIL 2, 1980:

Having watched the former version of "The Last Supper," it looks to me, on second thought, too one-dimensional and flat. Some changes are essential—the images need to clash more violently; sharp and sudden associations need to be created; a surprising superimposition of the "negatives" should be more striking.

The ghoulish-looking army, the platoon of living corpses, there in the corner of the room, a disgusting impression of a pile of squirming MAGGOTS.
The FAMILY, moving out, resembles a panic-driven EVACUATION in time of war.
The next transformation is of Aunt Mańka into a nightmarish puppet, a Nazi general.
The Circus of the Apocalypse.
A march of CRIPPLED-DEAD soldiers, mixed up with NAKED BODIES and GRAVEYARD CROSSES.
A NURSE with a corpse in a pram.
The return of Uncle Stasio—a Siberian exile, now a mixture of BEGGAR and PEDDLER, of a JUGGLER FROM THE FAIRBOOTH and a PHONEY FIDDLE VIRTUOSO, with a sham fiddle–hurdy-gurdy.
The long table of the Last Supper is covered with a MILITARY MAP.
This Last Supper is celebrated on battle-fields and in WAR cemeteries.

Below is the transcript from the rehearsal:
As usual, I know nothing at the beginning. Then, something begins to take shape, and suddenly an idea is born. . . .

The family is at the table, as usual as if "glued" to it.
Pitiful snatches of everyday quarrels, reproaches, rebukes, fears. . . .
The soldiers are in the corner; the pose they strike is almost the same as in the first scene, but, now, it is more relaxed; they are sitting in the corner and nothing or no one is going to move them.
In the middle of the room, the body of the Priest lies on the floor, arrayed for the coffin.
The family quarrels shamelessly about the inheritance.
The Little Rabbi bursts in. He is in despair. He sings his lamentations, the vulgar song from a cabaret of ill-repute.

The soldiers take aim.

A volley of shots.

The Rabbi falls to the ground.

The dead Priest slowly gets up. He must have heard in this world on the other side the shots fired at the Rabbi and has come back to help him in his hour of need; he lifts him carefully with great care.

The Rabbi "comes to" and the Priest returns to "resting in peace."

The Rabbi, delighted, starts to sing his lament—his lugubrious song.

The soldiers take aim.

A volley of shots.

The Rabbi falls to the ground.

The dead Priest, i n d e f a t i g a b l e, rises and lifts the body of the Rabbi.

The third times this happens, when the Priest has yet again performed his gesture of devotion to his little friend—
the Rabbi abruptly l e a v e s the stage.

The soldiers begin to move,
crawling like maggots,
a sort of palpitation,
or spasm,
as if they are experiencing a surge of electricity passing through them.
Their faces gradually come to life,
their mouths open,
their eyes turn,
then, their hands, feet.
Each limb moves separately,
like a part of a overwound mechanism.
They totter,
they lift their legs stiffly,
they carefully place one leg in front of the other,
as if trying to remember how to do so,
tormenting themselves,
awfully serious.
Looking at them creates an unpleasant impression of
something tragic,
of children or paralytics
or the dead.

The family with d i s g u s t shuts them from view in a wardrobe. But they crawl out from behind the wardrobe.
Threatened, the FAMILY leaves.
It is like an EVACUATION.
The Uncles push the Aunts out;
dragging the table and chairs
hastily.

Uncle Olek stays behind, weighed down with chairs;
he shouts: Karol, Józka—
they call each other names,
in disarray, they go into the antechamber behind the doors,
where immediately,
they begin their quarrels and loud discussions all over again.

At the same time, Mańka-Rabbi has undergone a new transformation
behind the wardrobe—now, swaggering like a mannequin, she appears
as Mańka-Himmler.
Still swaggering, she marches on
and leads the wretched soldiers out
from behind the wardrobe.
She is at the head.
Their march is carried out—of course—with difficulty,
with many falls, knocking each other down, and collisions.

But the family can no longer remain behind the doors—
slowly, they squeeze back into the room

And in this general commotion of
the SOLDIERS dragging along their carcasses, legs, and feet—
in their tragic-comic agony of recalling the details from their lives, and
the INHABITANTS of the ROOM, the FAMILY, which even in the
upheaval and chaos of this—what seems to be—wartime evacuation, does
not forget about their shameful habits,
there forms a semicircle gradually
at the back of the stage.
They are all mixed together,
now absurdly made equal,
as at the LAST JUDGMENT,
the pimping uncles,
the prostitutes,
the possessed,
the comedians and the clowns,
the deserters,
the soldiers-on-leave,
the recruits,
the naked corpses of the condemned,
the Priest and his double,
the Nurse with the Corpse (formerly the photographer's widow) . . .
Finally,
there emerges
one more spectral corpse—
the Siberian exile—the fiddler—the invalid with a crutch.
He is getting ready for a concert to be performed for such a large
auditorium.

But the old violin case is empty.
The fraudulent gestures of this
wretched con-artist—the Siberian exile—
will do no good here.
There is nothing left for him but to pull out the shamefully hidden
crank and
turn it.
A Christmas carol—
Chopin's Scherzo in *h-moll*
heavily deformed by
his *"orgue de Barbarie"*—his hurdy-gurdy.
Everyone is waiting and waiting. . . .
Maybe this is not the Last Supper
but instead
Christmas Eve
with carols.
They all begin to move forward,
very slowly,
The Uncles unfold the military map
like a long tablecloth;
they are all crowding around this
military table,
The Priest, in the middle, opens his arms in a familiar gesture.
There can longer be any doubt
that this will be
the Last Supper,
La Ultima Cena.
The laymen act out the gestures of the Apostles,
the soldiers,
caught in some final
deadly thrust,
fall down one after the other—
and then
the tablecloth falls—the military map.
They all stop and remain with their frozen gestures
in this emptiness,
the soldiers are lifeless,
shriveled,
dead—
The Nurse with the Corpse laughs hideously.

MAY 8, 1980 (I):

I am still not pleased with this scene, which was put together during the
last few rehearsals.
Just before the rehearsal, I am drawing a new plan.
Leonardo's painting, which I have always deeply admired,

arouses in me some perverse desire to "desecrate"
its superhuman order and its stillness;
and by this act of violence
make it a part of the real.

The FAMILY's shameful quarrel OVER the inheritance
turns into a hellish nightmare.
A CIRCUS-BROTHEL.
THE BED-DEATH MACHINE reveals all its secrets.
They turn it faster and faster.
Now the mannequin of the Priest appears;
now the PRIEST—THE LIVE ACTOR appears.
The family is divided into two groups.
One accepts the Mannequin;
the other the Live Actor.
They take their turns in turning the machine faster and faster.
The quarrel becomes more and more violent.
They throw the Live Priest to the floor.
They arrange his body.
Fake lament.
The family stands at the open grave.
They carefully erect the cross.
The FUNERAL ceremony.
The LITTLE RABBI's intervention.
The LITTLE RABBI's despair.
The CABARET song about REBECCA.
The sequence with the FIRING SQUAD.
The LITTLE RABBI falls to the floor.
The PRIEST rises from the dead to help the LITTLE RABBI.
The LITTLE RABBI departs forever.
Suddenly everything begins to go wrong in this world,
in this ROOM,
a general malfunctioning,
the ARMY starts crawling like maggots
in their tragic-comic agony,
The FAMILY with disgust tries to hide
these ALIEN INHABITANTS of the room behind the WARDROBE.
(A WARDROBE is an important object in the CHILDHOOD ROOM.)
Aunt Mańka has undergone a new transformation—
there emerges a monstrous PUPPET OF A NAZI GENERAL,
MAŃKA-HIMMLER. She swaggers like a child in a fancy dress.
She is at the head of the ARMY
of the lead soldiers,
dead,
screaming,
in their death throes,
mixed together with THE DEAD CORPSES OF THE CONDEMNED,

with the CROSSES dug out of the graves,
a march of the CRIPPLES,
of the DEAD.
PANIC.
a wartime EVACUATION in terror.
FLIGHT.
A CATASTROPHE,
the cries of the family,
a complete disintegration,
d i s s o l u t i o n,
e x p o s u r e,
now we can truly see who these dignified members of the FAMILY really
are,
hired bodies
from the STAGE ACTORS' EMPLOYMENT OFFICE,
and not the relatives at all,
they do not know each other,
the Uncles—the dirty pimps,
Helka—the prostitute,
Józka—a run-away from the home for the perverted,
Mańka—a run-away from a lunatic asylum,
The Father-on-Leave—a deserter,
The Grandmother—kitchen help,
the Recruits,
the Naked Corpses.
Every one of them tries to be somebody else.
Everyone of them advertises his/her wares "for sale,"
a monstrous CIRCUS,
Bad acting of bad actors
posturing like JUMPING JACKS,
HELL, BROTHEL,
THE LAST JUDGMENT,
THE APOCALYPSE,
utter licentiousness.
On the bed, Aunt Józka and the naked condemned,
Helka with her legs apart lies on the object called "Golgotha,"
Aunt Mańka with the Mannequin of the Priest experiences a religious
rapture,
Helka—the MANNEQUIN is raped by the SOLDIERS,
the actors in the chairs
in spastic movements,
plenty of CROSSES
as in a cemetery.
Into all of this, the PRIEST slowly walks in.
There appears also a spectral image of the EXILE—
the FIDDLER with his CAROL.
Slowly in this hellish circus,

in this utter LEVELING of everything,
there emerges a remote image and r e p e t i t i o n
of a well-known picture of the Last Supper.
The soldiers hold their GUNS above the long table,
The "Civilians—the Family" repeat vainly the gestures of the apostles.
And this is how possibly the LAST supper will be fulfilled,
while a CAROL makes it seem like Christmas Eve. . . .

MAY 8, 1980 (II):

I read aloud to the actors the text of the *Partytura* of the Last Supper
before the rehearsal.
We begin to rehearse it and to shape the stage action.
All that which was shocking and provocative in the written text, did not
achieve the desired tension in acting.
Simply, in order to achieve this tension, a different technique and acting
method needed to be employed—one that uses narrative and illustrative.
And this was the reason why nothing happened on stage.
Narrative techniques, or story-telling, and even more so illustrative
techniques are alien to Cricot 2.
I radically changed the plan of stage action during the course of the
rehearsal.
Yet again, I am learning that the nature of my work precludes the
possibility of writing a *"Partytura"* before a rehearsal. It is exactly the
rehearsal, with its spontaneous and unexpected decisions, thoughts, and
actions that are writing the *"partytura."* All that needs to be done is to
transcribe the rehearsal at the end.

. . . If the image of the *Last Supper* is to be "violated," it needs to begin
to exist in its pure form. That means: a table must be covered with a
pristinely white starched tablecloth, with the traces of folds clearly visible.
And indeed, such a table, covered with a white cloth, is placed downstage.
Now, compose the image without the actors.
Right at the back, tightly pressed together, there are four naked
mannequins.
I have noticed that placing them in one regular row gives them a rhythmic
and expressive power. If scattered around the stage, they created an image
which was realistic. The same is true for the crosses. There are a dozen of
them or so.
They are churchyard crosses. I place them in front of the mannequins as a
part of the cemetery military unit. Then, the MANNEQUINS of the Priest
and Helka are seated on chairs. And the live Helka, too. Next comes a
row of chairs for the FAMILY.
Finally, the TABLE.
And this is how it is supposed to look at the end.
At the beginning, none of this exists.
It is the FAMILY who solemnly sets up the stage, concentrating hard as if
following some mysterious DESIGN, whose purpose is not fully known,

but the precision of its execution is crucial for the outcome. This goes on for a long time—this preparation for something that must HAPPEN, something that is IMMINENT; they even use the soldiers, moving them around like graveyard monuments, correcting their gestures . . .
It seems that everything is almost finished;
that this order of things will last forever.
Now everything is almost ready.
The FAMILY sits down at the TABLE.
Their gestures are more and more reminiscent of those in the *Last Supper*.
But not fully yet.
It is so because the Family continues with its violent and scandalous quarrels about the inheritance, about the deep resentments of the time past, about the past events, and about the memories of things past.
The Father-on-Leave keeps swearing;
the mad Helka repeats over and over again the vows of her unhappy marriage;
The Little Rabbi-Judas (this time)—whistles something indistinctly, possibly his Rebecca song.
Suddenly, the UNCLE STASIO—the EXILE—the beggar and the black sheep of the FAMILY, enters.
They all recognize him.
Despite the fact that he has already appeared under different circumstances and in different scenes, but in this world, where TIME presents itself to the SPECTATORS as ETERNITY—this film negative of the recollection of the past, which shows up at the end—is the FIRST FRAME.
Uncle Stasio begins to play; it is his last performance.
A CHRISTMAS CAROL.
Maybe, this *Last Supper* is Christmas Eve after all?
This melody has evidently some fatal power,
for suddenly the soldiers at the back of the stage begin stirring precariously, coming to life.
The ORDER, which was established with such care and precision, begins abruptly to fall apart, to break to pieces—
a horrifying seething mass of naked bodies, SOLDIERS, rifles, CROSSES.
Everything collapses at the back of the stage—into one huge cemetery.
In front, the *Last Supper* takes place.
THE CAROL continues.
At first, the FAMILY calmly clears the table,
removes the chairs, withdraws backstage.
But their departure gradually turns into an escape, evacuation, catastrophe, the end of the world.
They push, fall, crawl, pull the dead corpses, wounded, crosses, all their earthly possessions. . . .
On the EMPTY STAGE, only the PRIEST remains—the SORROWFUL POLISH CHRIST.

MAY 30 (1980):

Even though I have already decided that the final version of "The Last
Supper" was indeed final, I still want to give free play to my imagination.
I do not intend to rehearse "The Last Supper." I simply want to test the
functioning of the table and light collapsible metal legs. A table was to
become the table only at the end. It was supposed to be brought onto the
stage in the form of two very long, dirty, and rough-hewn planks, the kind
the bricklayers use as scaffolding. The soldiers bring in the planks. Maybe
they will use them to shore up the trenches. They put the planks down. It
is only at the end that the FAMILY suddenly picks them up, quickly opens
out the metal legs hidden under them, and lays an immaculately white
tablecloth on the table they have just made.
But now I do not like these metal stumps. They are removed. We are left
with only two bare planks. I am thinking about what to do with them.
For now, they are taken away. Their time will come.
But this does not set my mind at rest. I am anxious to come up with
a different solution to the problem of the TABLE. This is an essential
o b j e c t in *The Last Supper*.
I am placing the chair, as in the last version, in the front of the stage;
behind them, the naked corpses of the soldiers, like naked convicts;
behind them, the cemetery crosses; and, at the end, the ARMY.
Their rifles, with fixed bayonets, stick out.
Now, having arranged these, I need to work out the rest.
The FAMILY, in its entirety, sits downstage on the chairs.
The whole world is as if WAITING for something to happen.
Suddenly, the two UNCLES run off.
A moment later, they reappear staggering under the weight of an awfully
long PLANK.
They force their way through the wall of people, chairs, and the soldiers'
naked corpses. They do not pay any attention to anything around them.
They push aside or overturn everything in their path. The Priest falls to
the ground; naked mannequins, chairs, and people fall into disarray.
Right behind the two Uncles, two soldiers appear with a similar PLANK.
The two planks wobble dangerously over the heads of the actors.
It seems that, in a moment, these two heavy, dirty, and mud-stained
objects, God knows where they were found and why they are brought in
here, will fall onto the stage, killing the actors and smashing everything
else with their weight.
The planks are finally placed downstage, resting on whatever can be
found, or perhaps the actors will hold them.
Everything shakes and wobbles. Complete chaos.
The choir's mighty voices, intoning the PSALM, lend a religious air to the
events.
Amid the growing disquiet, the FAMILY continues in an accelerated
tempo, as if SOMETHING threatened to cut off their quarrels, the
resentments of time past, and their recollection of memories of things

past. Vivid gestures accompany this disgraceful quarrel, but their
deliberate form foreshadows *The Last Supper.*
Suddenly, the naked corpses of the soldiers are shamelessly pushed
forward.
Evidently, the Army in the back is becoming more and more impudent—
the malfunctioning organisms begin to run autonomously and
destructively.
They push the WARDROBE to the front of the stage, paying no attention
to the actors, thrusting it over the edge of the stage platform right in front
of the AUDIENCE;
from the other side, A WINDOW, A TABLE, CHAIRS, and a BED are
pushed; the soldiers turn the crank of the bed.
The Exile-Peddler, taking advantage of the confusion, elbows his way
through to the front, just right behind the window and gets ready for his
tacky concert.
The PHOTOGRAPHER wheels in her CAMERA; then, a PRAM WITH
THE CORPSE.
The WARDROBE, in front of the audience, opens from the front and
from the back, letting the soldier rush through it, as in some diabolical
cabaret;
shameless, naked mannequins are dragged around and wallow on the
floor;
The PRIEST and his MANNEQUIN-DOUBLE lie on the floor debased.
The words of the PSALM are drowned by the MILITARY MARCH.
Those around the table assume the definitive gestures and postures of *The
Last Supper.*
The EXILE-PEDDLER begins his last concert.
A CHRISTMAS CAROL.
The actors slowly leave the stage, moving towards the back of the stage,
looking around, and gradually disappearing one after another.
The PRIEST remains on stage.
I take him by the hand and slowly lead him away.
Then I return, fold up the tablecloth with care and precision,
put it under my arm
and exit.

                                                    –n.d.

Prison
(1985)

Prison.
It is both a concept
and a perfect,
meticulously and thoughtfully structured model of man's history. It is
undeniably a "product" of man and civilization.
The fact that "prison" is set up against man; that it is a brutal mechanism
established to crush man's free thoughts happens to be one of the
grimmest absurdities. However, similar absurdities can be found in
abundance in history
and in the illustrious *"magister vitae."*
Let us leave it then for history
to determine innocence or
guilt.
Let us consider
the ontological aspect of prison and its . . .
eschatology.
Prison . . .
A word which sticks in the throat . . .
There is something final about it; a feeling that something has happened
that cannot be undone or revoked. . . . The gates of prison close behind
a man, as the gates of an open grave close over the dead who "walk"
through them. In a moment the grave-diggers will be through with their
work. The living are standing yet for a long while . . . as if they could not
accept the idea that he is to be left
"there"
alone!
Painfully alone. . . .
They are standing
helpless and powerless
at the verge of
something that
they can neither touch nor name. . . .
The man who is already "on the other side" is setting off on his journey.
He is going to travel
alone, left to himself,

destitute
with nobody but himself to rely on.
He walks aimlessly and hopelessly
along a deserted and eerie path. . . .
Nothing but marching on . . .
from the height of,
I daresay,
imagination's wild wanderings and madness
I saw this apparition
in front of my eyes
in a ghostly landscape of horror.
[This apparition] was like an idea, which against all reason and all logic,
hovers at the doorway of my new
THEATRE.
Once again I see
this apparition,
outlawed and
tainted with madness;
which is able to
convey
by means of violence and change
the most dramatic manifestation of
ART and *FREEDOM*!
. . . Prison . . .
is an idea
separated from life by an *ALIEN*, impenetrable
barrier.
It is so separate [from the world of the living] that
if this blasphemous likeness is permitted—it will be able to shape THE
WORK OF ART.
. . . The metaphoric use of this obscure image
for the creative process may be revolting or immoral.
So much the better!
This would surely mean
that we are on the right track!

Reflection
(1985)

Against the background of a dark and dirty earth, I saw a bright spot the size of a saucer.

It was shining too brightly to be a part of that earthly matter out of which everything else has been created.

When I raised my eyes above the rooftops, I saw the sky, which was shining as brightly as the spot, and which did not belong to this Earth either.

That "something" which was shining was the sky reflected in a piece of a broken mirror.

Reflection.

A phenomenon abused by art which defies naturalism.

A man who, for the first time, saw his reflection in the still waters must have experienced an illumination. Against the advice of surrealists one must not step into, God forbid, must not walk through the surface of the mirror.

Remain in front of it.

The reflection itself is a wonder. A mystery of the universe is enclosed in it. [This reflection shows] reality which is as if split into two, moved away from itself, caught and locked away

as if in a prison

or as if lowered into the grave and thus no longer belongs to this world.

The impossibility of bringing life and death together is fulfilled.

Of course, this can only happen in the world of illusion and at play. The feeling of touching eternity while being still alive.

I want to restore to the word reflection its essential meaning and implications which are tragic, dangerous, much deeper than those which we were taught to believe in by the false con-missionaries of the truth-to-nature dogma.

Something far more important is: The extension of our reality beyond its boundaries so that we can better cope with it in our lives.

An extension which will give us an intimation of another world in the metaphysical and cosmic sense, the feeling of touching other realities.

Let us call it art,

or even better,

poetry, which I perceive as a daring expedition into the unknown
and the impossible.
Do not identify poetry
with fiction,
illusion or
deception.

Poetry is an extension of reality;
its roots are in reality which is mundane,
banal,
gray,
and despised by mediocre poets.
Despised.
I want to define this process which eludes all conventions and norms, and
is practically banned.
But first, one poetic condition must be fulfilled:
the reflection of reality is its extension which is as real and substantial as
the reality. Anyway, maybe everything is but a reflection. . . .
I am walking from the depths of infinity, which I have left behind. I am
walking forward. There is a mirror in front of me; the invisible boundary
of the mirror which marks the beginning of an extension of reality and the
time of poetry. From this moment on let us repeat the warning: everything
is reality, illusion does not exist. Maybe it will be easier for us to enter
the world of poetry. I am walking forward. Someone, who is another I,
is walking up to me. In a moment we will pass each other or bump into
each other. I am thinking about this moment with growing uneasiness.
However, it does not escape my perception that I am not walking forward
but in the direction of the depth where I started a moment ago. I am
walking forward back.
And then I realize that the other person, the I-Over-There, is not walking
forward but in the direction of the depth which I left behind me. I lift my
hat with my right hand.
The raised hat is on the right-hand side of my body. He, the other I,
makes the same motion. Even though he does it on the same side of the
body, he uses his left hand. I tell him to use his right hand as I did, he
obeys, but then his raised hat is

ON THE OPPOSITE SIDE of my body
and of my hat.
I have noticed that this correction of reversibility gives the right
impression of

REFLECTION on stage in real space. . . .
If we take a step further on this road, it might happen that a smile will
turn into a grimace, virtue—a crime, and a whore will become a virgin.

Due to those mysterious laws of reversibility, the imperative of contemptible death in the title refers to the artists. Fame and glory touch down the hell of the bottomless social pit;
the world of bums, pimps, artists, whores.
Art, the noblest of man's ideals, turns into a despicable chamber of torture,
out of which the artist's appeal to the world is tapped in a prison code.

To Save from Oblivion
(March 1988)

My productions
The Dead Class,
Wielopole, Wielopole,
Let the Artists Die,
and this last one,
I Shall Never Return,
all of them
a r e   p e r s o n a l   c o n f e s s i o n s.

Personal confession . . .
an unusual and rare technique today.
In our epoch
of an increasingly collective life,
a terrifying growth of collectivism, [personal confessions]
a rather awkward and inconvenient technique.

Today, I want to find the reason
for my maniacal passion
for this technique.

I feel it is important.
There is something ultimate about it,
something that is manifested only when one is faced with
the E N D.
I feel that realizing
the reasons for this manifestation
can
perhaps
still save us from
complete despondency.

Personal confession . . .
A suspicion of narcissism,
so effective at other times,

becomes at this moment
childishly naive.

This game of confession is far more serious.
Ominous and dangerous.
Almost like a struggle for life or death.

And here is the map of this battle:
in the front, there is
the contempt (mine)
for "general"
and o f f i c i a l
History,
the history of
mass Movements,
mass ideologies,
passing terms of Governments,
terror by power,
mass wars,
mass crimes. . . .
Against
these "powers"
stands the
S m a l l,
P o o r,
D e f e n s e l e s s,
but magnificent
History of
i n d i v i d u a l
h u m a n
l i f e.

Against
half-human creatures
stands
a h u m a n b e i n g
the one, who centuries ago,
at the beginning of our culture
was identified by two words:
"Ecce Homo,"
a domain of spiritual life
of the most precious
and the most delicate matter.
It is only in
this "individual human life" that
TRUTH,
DIVINITY, and

GRANDEUR
were preserved.

They should be saved
from destruction and oblivion;
saved from all
"powers" of the world;
despite the awareness
of impending failure.

I was born during
The First World War.
During
The Second World War
came my youth.
Some words from its (war's) vocabulary
have always remained with me:
a struggle, a failure, a victory.
I cannot deny that
there was also the word
a leader,
which reverberated frequently
in my childhood dreams.
I have played the part of a leader up till now.
A Poor Troupe of Actors
of a Wandering Theatre
is my headquarters and my army.
Wonderful artists.
We fight together.
I wanted to say:
we create.

So let's return to my
"war" map.
In this theatre of a formidable
and ruthless war,
I make
(onstage)
the most risky and desperate
maneuver
of my life.

I am almost certain
that it should ensure
victory.
I believe it will be so,
though I know that this victory cannot happen here,

here in this world,
I SHALL BE A VICTIM.
Just as before a battle, I conduct
a rigorous "inspection" of my combat unit
called
"individual human life."
Too weak!
In need of reinforcement.
It has been infiltrated by
too many alien elements
from the turbid sea of collective life:
Deserters,
Even spies.
It has lost its identity;
and, therefore, its power.
It must be reinforced
at any price.

And here starts
my maneuver
(and another language).

During sleepless nights
of suffering and despair
(allow me to keep their content
to myself)
loneliness is
gradually born.
Great.
Infinite
and ready for
the *entrée* of death.
Individual life,
its contours and features,
its "matter"
come into sharp and harsh
focus.
At last,
"an integrated combat unit"
is cut off
from collective life.
Its power is enormous.
At last, I have
what I needed:
I N D I V I D U A L   L I F E!
M I N E!
And, that is why, its strength is increased hundredfold!

Now, it will be victorious in the battle with
the c o n s u m e r i s m
of the world.

I can bring it now
onto the s t a g e.
Show it to the public.

And pay the price of
pain,
suffering,
despair,
and then
shame,
humiliation,
derision.

I am . . . onstage
I will not be a performer.
Instead, poor fragments of my
own life
will become
"ready-made objects."

Every night
RITUAL
and SACRIFICE
will be performed here.

The Real "I"
(April 1988)

Everything I have done in art so far,
has been the reflection of my attitude
toward the events
that surrounded me,
toward the situation
in which I have lived;
of my fears;
of my faith in this and not something else;
of my distrust in what was to be trusted;
of my skepticism;
my hope.

To express all this
and for my own use,
I created
the Idea of Reality
which renounced
the idea of illusion,
that is,
a procedure recognized as elemental
for the theatre . . .
of PERFORMING,
of representing,
of "reproducing"
what had been written
as drama (a "play").
The word "reproducing"
had a false ring—
something in it would contradict autonomy,
the autonomy of the theatre.
I was proud of my radical thoughts.
I was not, however, orthodox enough
to believe in them to the end.

In practice
I would indulge myself
in doubts "on the side,"
and probably this was what saved
my productions from being boring and dry.

It does not mean that I am going to
abandon this idea today.
With its help, I did
increase the autonomy of the theatre,
and denounce the commonly used
and pretentious
method
of "pretending" for real,
of "experiencing emotions" for real,
etc., etc.

The moment has finally arrived
in my artistic life,
which I begin to consider
as a *résumé*,
the ultimate moment—
I should say—
when one makes a self-examination.
How was it really
with that reality?
Have I really done for it all that I could?
I began to be a harsh
judge of myself.

When I wanted to be a child,
someone else was a child,
not the real "I"
(this can still be excused).

When I wanted to die,
someone else was dying for me.
He was playing the part of me dying.
And that "playing,"
which I had excommunicated,
functioned perfectly well.

When with persistence, longing,
and stubbornness,
I kept returning to the memories

of my School Class,
it was not I, but the others (the actors)
who returned to school desks—
returned, "performed,"
and "pretended."
If the truth be told,
I must say that what I achieved was the ability
to show
with passion and satisfaction
that they were "pretending."
My presence onstage
was supposed to cover up
the failure of my idea of the "impossible":
of "non-acting,"
and to rescue at least
its last proof and argument:
"p r e t e n d i n g."

But deep in my soul
I did not give up.
Life itself
gave me a hand. . . .

I understand
this last journey in my life
as well as in my art
as a never-ending journey
b e y o n d   t i m e
and b e y o n d   a l l
r u l e s. . . .

I felt it was a fulfillment
of my unrelenting thought of returning
to the time of youth,
the time of "boyhood."
(How many paintings did I make
with always that image
of a "boy.")

There was my home.
The real one.
I shall be dying,
but, I will not admit
that I am old.

Death and love. . . .
The moment came

when I could not tell
one from the other.
I was enchanted by both.
Nights came,
because nights were my time of creation,
the nights came when death
carefully guarded the entrance
to my Poor
Little Room of Imagination.

I understood
that the time of victory had come.
This victory, however, was won in my Room of Imagination.
To enter the stage,
not as a "guardian" of a fortress,
which I defended against "performing,"
but as a real "I"
which does not need
performance,
pretending, etc. . . .

I needed two methods.
The first:
not to say a word,
to remain as mute and empty
as a grave.
So death advised me.

The second was grounded
in my conviction
that I should not expect anything more than
derision and
and mockery
from the audience,
the public,
generally speaking,
the so-called world,
whose cynicism
is unparalleled.

It was necessary to forestall their reaction.
I have all I need.
Indifference,
derision,
malice,
of the world
I give to . . . the actors;

those miserable characters of the past.
They will do it better
and more pointedly.

To make public
what in the life of an individual
has been most intimate,

and what contains
the highest value,
what to the "world"
seems to be
ridiculous,
something small,
"poverty."

Art brings this "poverty"
into daylight.
Let it grow.
And let it reign.

This is the role of Art.

Illusion

THE FUNDAMENTAL MEANING OF ILLUSION

I am interested in capturing a fundamental meaning of illusion. If it simply signified a process of d o u b l i n g, r e f l e c t i o n of reality—for example, a wardrobe, why is it not sufficient to make A SECOND IDENTICAL WARDROBE?
Of course the answer is simple: it is not sufficient to do so because it is necessary to "double" a wardrobe in an a r t i f i c i a l manner; to t a k e a w a y from it its f u n c t i o n it performs in reality. This can only be achieved if it be placed in the domain of i l l u s i o n.

Its reason for being, its essential reason, that it was once discovered and that still, even today, fascinates us is that it allows us to e x p e r i e n c e reality of life in a d i f f e r e n t way; a way that has nothing to do with l i f e, that is not marred by a p h y s i c a l e f f o r t nor a necessity of practical use; a way which is completely free, pure—a cerebral, spiritual i n n e r perception.

TOTAL ILLUSION

Illusion belongs to the domain of the arts. But it also exists outside of it.
Illusion has different degrees of amplitude.
Total illusion is not a criterion for the meaning of a work of art.
The meaning of a work of art is defined by something else.
Total illusion can be an attribute of a work of art, which at the price of committing a kind of deception of the viewer—provides para-aesthetic experience.
This is why it can be of significance in some trends of anti-art.
Total illusion can exist in painting, and in its phenomena such as *trompe l'œil*, panoramic landscapes, or hyperrealism.
It can be found in sculpture—in the wax figures at the Madame Tussaud and in hyperrealistic sculptures. Of course, it can be found in film and in theatre: in illusionary naturalism—in illusionary landscapes, interiors, and architecture—in acting.

ILLUSION

Illusion, even when viewed from the perspective of reality, has a meaning that should be taken into account.

First of all, one may consider the possibility of classifying it as a phenomenon of a "l o w e r   r a n k."

Born in fraud, deception, with a miraculous glamour for the masses, it has always been pushed to the margins of noble, fine arts.

Second, one may consider its lack of function and functioning in l i f e, which has been taken away from the object it shows.

In that, illusion is similar to the happening; its annexing of reality by depriving it of its purpose and life's function. The difference is however that an object and reality remain intact in the happening.

An object is created through deception in i l l u s i o n.

Which one is worse?

Maybe this is worth thinking about.

ILLUSION—A NEGATIVE TERM

The term illusion contains in itself a part that is negative and which wreaks havoc in the arts.

In order to reach these dangerous regions, let us consider illusion in its general terms.

As such, it presents itself as a   d o u b l e, r e f l e c t i o n, r e p r o d u c t i o n of reality, which exists outside of the work of art. This simple understanding of illusion undercuts its ambiguity and its "metaphysics."

What is left are mere practices, which more and more often are perceived as its only raison d'être and which at the end are turned into a thoughtless c o n v e n t i o n; practices which only lead to most immediate effects and gratification.

A r t i f i c i a l i t y is turned into pretentiousness; d o u b l i n g into simpering.

FILM'S ILLUSION

Film gives the experience of t o t a l   i l l u s i o n.

I l l u s i o n   i s   t h e   e s s e n t i a l   e l e m e n t   o f   t h e   s t r u c t u r e   o f   a   f i l m.

The discovery of film was the discovery of this marvelous possibility.

The possibility of an i l l u s i o n a r y   i m a g e (a dream of baroque painters) was fully realized in the i l l u s i o n   o f   m o v e m e n t.

A triumphant development of film proves that this ability of an artificial production of i l l u s i o n is needed by the people.

And this development seems not to have an end.

Stereoscopic film is hyper-illusion.

. . . horses are galloping at the audience. . . .

wheels of a train are rattling over their heads . . . bullets are flying . . . grenades are exploding in the auditorium . . . even smells surround us . . .

the images are created among the audience . . . a flat screen is no longer big enough.

Total i l l u s i o n disappears when a film projector is turned off.

This is when one becomes aware of the meaning of i l l u s i o n.

of its LACK OF MATERIALITY

of its fraudulent nature,

of its essence: REFLECTION OF

REALITY.

ARTIFICIALITY.

−n.d.

Illusion and Repetition

For many years, I used to proclaim REALNESS for different reasons. No matter which one, they were all grounded in an almost sacred, absolute reason, which common language could not describe. It was all about truth. In the name of REALNESS, I rejected the term ILLUSION (or fiction). Maybe I did so because I was afraid to succumb to it. Simply, I was too attracted to it.
But I will discuss this later.
For the time being, I am still its radical adversary.
This general statement here will help us to describe the course of events. There are already too many imprecise statements, mixed terms, and simplistic comments. It is necessary to provide digressions, explanations, and correction.
Let us begin with the most essential one:
the act of rejecting i l l u s i o n is not important in itself; w h a t i s
i m p o r t a n t a r e t h e r e a s o n s w h y i t i s r e j e c t e d.
Forgetting about this leads to superficial comments, which can be harmful in the long run.
This may lead to bringing together what may look like similar phenomena, disregarding their differences and the fact that such an equation will be completely false and lead to disinformation.
For example:
the opponents of i l l u s i o n associated with the Great Reform
in theatre and with the Avant-gardes of the twentieth century,
rejected i l l u s i o n as a consequence of their condemnation of realism
and naturalism.
However, in my theatre, I reject i l l u s i o n in the name of r e a l n e s s,
which I bring to the fore and strengthen—
that REALNESS, which, for centuries, was the unyielding convention
barred from becoming a valid feature of a work of art, letting in only its
FICTION and REFLECTION;
that raw reality, which is
unprocessed "artistically"
and wrenched away from life;
that REAL OBJECT, which has replaced
an "artistic object."

The difference—as shown by this comparison—is quite insurmountable!
History and its events unfolded in an unpredictable way. The Avant-garde
of the 1920s set INTERPRETATION (this was a name used in theatre)
against realism, naturalism (and, of course, illusion).
No one will challenge the fact that, at that time, it was the only viable
solution.
There were many of those "i n t e r p r e t a t i o n s" in art of the first
half of the twentieth century. But this is beyond the point here.
The idea of "i n t e r p r e t a t i o n" slowly became the common law in
the arts.
Everyone was using it.
It was unscrupulously used.
The more this once-radical proposition and its supplementary
practices revealed their disintegration, the more strengthened was my
FASCINATION with REALNESS, an alien idea to INTERPRETATION,
ABSTRACTION, and CONSTRUCTION.
And again, the history and its events unfolded in an unpredictable way.
So did my encounters and relationship with REALNESS and ILLUSION
continue:
After many years and experiences of a n n e x i n g   r e a l i t y (of life),
recognizing its radical intervention into the very structure of a work
of art, in the happenings, actions, and manifestations—REALNESS
started to weigh me down with its materiality. I do admit that en masse
exploration of these once-dangerous and unconquered lands had an
impact on me too.
Truth became common fashion, which was unbearable.
It was necessary to find it elsewhere.
At that time, in an unorthodox way, I used to declare that realness cannot
exist on its own and that it must confront its foe:
i l l u s i o n.
Now, I noticed something new—that ILLUSION next to its conventional
side has also a m e t a p h y s i c a l side;
that a primitive function, which is derived from and prescribed by
servitude to nature and life's reality, is not its essence.
This m e t a p h y s i c a l side of i l l u s i o n,
which has not been noticed thus far,
is R E P E T I T I O N—
almost a ritual;
an atavistic g e s t u r e of human beings, who at the beginning of their
own history needed to affirm their identity.
Create something as if for the second time,
out of that which already exists,
"that is their own"—their human "own";
repeat that which had already been created—by the gods,
open themselves to god's jealousy and revenge,
take a risk,
be prepared to face the impending defeat,

404 *Illusion and Repetition*

know that theirs will be futile endeavors,
bereft of future,
having only this one chance,
bereft of their glamorous life's meaning and final end,
papier-mâché façades.

A ritual,
as if on the other side of life,
entangled in its arrangement with d e a t h.
One must say loudly and clearly:
this "dubious" procedure of REPETITION
is both a protest and a challenge.
It can also be added easily now:
it is the e s s e n c e of a r t!
as well as an idea that has penetrated this production
entitled tellingly:
"W I E L O P O L E, W I E L O P O L E."
And as everything else in theatre,
a production will surrender to its charm and poetry.
Maybe this is why the following addition
and theatre commentary will not be out of place.

ILLUSION c a r r i e s realness onto a different path
Poets would claim—a path of poetry.
Maybe, this is a d i f f e r e n t, o t h e r s p a c e.
And absolute time, not our absolute time.
Maybe poetry is a signal of this o t h e r world,
which moves along a different path
beyond the walls of our r o o m.
This C A R R Y I N G onto a different path happens in a special way;
a way well known to children in their world:
through REPETITION.
Repetition has different shapes and forms.
The most profound [variant] is e c h o
the same as the one that exists here, but immaterial,
a sudden conscious realization of passing
and d e a t h.
Another variant:
a kind of l e a r n i n g process (to drill something into one's memory),
Indeed: m e m o r y, which transfers the real into the past, which is
constantly dying
Yet another variant:
if t i m e could shrink—
then, we would have r e p e t i t i o n *par excellence*; never ending,
frightful, and inhuman repetition,
because our "calendar time," the time used to regulate and describe our
bodies

would not be able to save us from experiencing both
eternity and n o t h i n g n e s s at the same time,
that is, to save us from death.

I can multiply the examples of this repetition because they give us
unlimited possibilities for actors' creativity, acting.

One more variant (not the last one yet):
repetition-mockery. Children's game.
Unfinished games, full of profound meaning.
The best weapon against dull, dangerous pseudo-seriousness.
Dangerous to life. I have already learned that lesson from history.
A child defends life; conditions it. And an artist does the same!

Repetition erases from realness its life's function, meaning, and the power
of its practical action.
As a consequence of this procedure (which, when it was performed for the
first time, must have been ingenious)—
realness becomes powerless, useless,
but this is the only way it can acquire a immense power
in the domain of thought and imagination—that is, in the domain that
decides about the dynamic quality of human life and DEVELOPMENT.

                                                              –n.d.

My Meetings with Death
(1987)

I was six.
I touched the face of the old priest.
He had always talked to me.
Now, he did not say a word.
His face was ice cold.

I walked with others
up the sandy road.
Nobody talked.
They were walking and
staring forward
as if they wanted to
get somewhere very quickly . . .
The old priest
was lying on a wooden cart.
I had never seen him in this position—
he had always sat with his back straight.

When I was very sick,
in the eyes of my mother who
was bent over me,
I saw a shadow
that reflected something more than
her distress or her love
as if she could
see beyond . . .
beyond me.
When I was sick,
in the fever-driven imagination,
I saw a slow-moving funeral procession—
mine.
Carried on the shoulders of my friends,
I felt that I was ennobled, different than others,
magnificent.
Later, I understood that

this was a portent of Art.
From the very beginning,
I equated Art with Magnificence.
But, already in this childhood dream,
Art was joined with Her.
With death.
When I am gone, magnificence will remain.

. . . During the war, I saw Her standing behind the figures of the soldiers. . . .
. . . I recognized Her in the voices of zealous speakers . . .
. . . in the flare of hand grenades and candles . . .
. . . in the triumphant sounds of the military marches. . . .

The years have passed.
Seduced by youth,
I forgot about Her.

. . . The time of THEATRE has come.

My theatre . . .
She suddenly appeared and then disappeared backstage.
She left behind her prop on stage, a COFFIN.
The Artist, his two Dead Wives,
the Tyrant, Pope Julius II sat at it.
A SESSION about the art started.
SHE was the moderator.
Invisible.

. . . Ever since that time, she regularly showed up on stage to perform her
"parts."
She would show up more and more often.
Tragic Death—she would elevate her wretched remnants onto the plane of
pathos.
Mocking Death—she would scorn everything that was mediocre and
banal with her clownish laughter.
Slowly, she had become my "partner."
She guided me through her steep and dangerous roads.

Her face was beautiful, still like a stone, and silent
like eternity.
She stood quietly backstage
sure of her charm and allure. . . .
I watched mesmerized
how, on stage, life in some kind of
maddening,
indignant,
and magnificent

disintegration of its everyday
was shamelessly disclosing
its T R U T H
that had been hidden at the bottom. . . .
But it was HER truth,
Magnificent,
Difficult to bear,
seen through tears, tears of grief, of euphoria,
and through LAUGHTER!

The Bridegroom stood next to the d e a d Bride.
Abandoned ruthlessly in a corner,
dragged into the ritual site by the Priest,
she vowed love, faithfulness, and obedience . . .
for better or worse. . . .
And then
when the moving ceremony ended,
the Bridegroom, in a soldier's uniform,
embraced the dead body
and dragged it to life,
for better or worse. . . .

The Priest died m a n y t i m e s
on his death bed
as if for the public.
He died in shame and disgrace,
because the death bed prepared for him was a spit
rotated by the Cleaning-woman from the Cemetery storeroom.
She rotated the devout body. . . .
H u m i l i a t i o n
and m o c k e r y
were HER public demonstration,
the same way as the Golgotha and
the CROSS, a holy cross today,
were the instrument of shame.

The soldiers walked into the battle,
into her open arms. . . .
Mr. Daguerre's invention, a camera,
she altered into her own instrument,
a deadly machine-gun,
that registered for eternity the images
of the soldiers marching to the front. . . .
She was without shame.
She was magnificent in her shamelessness.
She did not fear the most damning comparisons.

At her wish and command, a "FUNERAL MACHINE"
resembled dangerously closely
a GRINDER with a handle that was turned
by the Servant-Gravedigger. . . .
She was never contemptuous of the object of the lowest rank . . .
Old FOLDING CHAIRS pulled together with a rope
gave birth to a dreadful DEATH MACHINE.
HER machine!
She did not even spare herself.
She became a vulgar Cleaning Woman
sweeping the floors in a poor Classroom
A BROOM was substituted for her
medieval scythe.
She could do so, because she was sure of her victory.
The Old People returning to the Classroom
carried the carcasses of children: their childhood.
Dead.
A vicious BIRTH MACHINE, unambiguously
used in the act of labor
and an accompanying cradle, in which two wooden
balls, like human bones, gave a dry sound. . . .
When I was returning to my Wielopole,
I used to leave her in the room of my childhood. . . .
She had always correctly placed in it all the family members. . . .
When the Grand Marshal
rode
his favorite HORSE,
whose skeleton is only left now,
surrounded by his GENERALS,
who had risen out of their graves at his command,
I saw her ride madly and triumphantly
on a different horse.
And the time did arrive,
when,
convinced of her penultimate triumph,
she dared to stage the ultimate blasphemy:
I saw HER backstage.
There was no triumphant aura around her.
She stood straight up and tense
as if she were to pronounce the truth
that was difficult to bear but that was the most profound.

On stage,
a w o r k   o f   a r t
was born
in PRISON!

In HER cell, the cell of death!
Is it possible that I have touched upon the grand mystery of art
that was trying to hide the tragic condition of the CREATIVE act?

I had a feeling that she was preparing yet another surprise for me.
That there is something important that was left out; something that does
not allow her to rest.
She left her place backstage.
She appeared in the stage's spotlight . . .
in all her glory . . .
as if getting ready for her last battle.
I looked with fear and despair . . .
She was standing opposite her biggest rival,
L O V E.

Capricious LOVE . . .
this love which dies when lost
and that love which remains
and stays by you
in defeat
until the end.
Then SHE came,
powerful and all-mighty,
able to turn defeat into VICTORY.
I watched BOTH of them
entwined in the eternal bond.
The storm of applause.
The performance has ended.
The auditorium is empty.
I am alone.
SHE is standing
backstage.

Memory

(1988)

MEMORY,
memory of the past,
held in contempt
by the S O B E R - M I N D E D—
highly valued members of human kind
(I have always suspected them of being slow minded)—
and by those "gluttons" of the everyday
devouring voraciously the present
to reach speedily the future and its promises.
MEMORY
ruthlessly pushed aside
by those troupes marching
f o r w a r d, toward the f u t u r e. . . .

MEMORY . . .
worth thinking about!
I was d i s c o v e r i n g it
gradually, with enthusiasm, and often with despair.
I felt THEATRE was the right place for it.
I was not mistaken!
THE STAGE
became its
A L T A R!

Now, I feel as if
I committed a theft,
a theft of a sacred relic
(this is an imprint from my childhood spent in "the shadows of the
Church").
Later, [I was possessed] by the profound and blasphemous idea that ART
was a threshold between HEAVEN AND EARTH,
between the TEMPLE and (excusez le mot) the BROTHEL,
between the TEMPLE and the PRISON.

After this secular explanation,
let us approach the ALTAR again.
[Altar] is the only appropriate word,
because all the activities of this "MASS," which has just started, parallel
another u n - r e a l, almost mystical
process.
T I M E was u n - r e a l.
TIME PAST
and everything that was real in life
were bereft of their life's function and life's effectiveness
in this un-real TIME.
[The past and everything that was real] were P U R I F I E D;
purified artistically.
All that is good and all that is bad [was purified].

It was my DISCOVERY.
It was mine.
I did not treat MEMORY as a well-known device
used to describe the past or travel back in the depths of time.
I DISCOVERED ITS TRUTH!
In order to make this momentous (at least for me) discovery, two things
were needed:
a child's naïveté
and the ability to see unique spatial possibilities on the stage
I had both of them.
Let one of my commentaries to *Wielopole, Wielopole*
speak for my "DISCOVERY":

It is difficult to define the spatial dimension of memory.
Here is a room of my childhood,
which I keep reconstructing over and over again
and which is destroyed over and over again.
It is destroyed with all its inhabitants.
Its inhabitants are the members of my family.
They continuously repeat all their movements and activities
as if they were recorded on a film negative shown interminably.
They will keep repeating those banal,
elementary, and aimless activities
with the same expression on their faces;
concentrating on the same gesture
until boredom strikes.
Those trivial activities,
which stubbornly and oppressively preoccupy us,
fill up our lives. . . .

These D E A D F A Ç A D E S
come to life, become real and important
through this stubborn R E P E T I T I O N of actions.

Maybe this pulsating rhythm,
which ends in
NOTHINGNESS
which is FUTILE
is an inherent part of M E M O R Y. . . .

My "DISCOVERY" (made already in *The Dead Class*)
introduces new psychological elements into stage acting
and a new type of "SPACE," a non-physical space.
The CONDITION OF DEATH—of the DEAD,
[was] RE-CREATED IN THE LIVING,
TIME-PAST MYSTERIOUSLY SLIPPED INTO
TIME-PRESENT.

The past exists in
memory.
D E A D!
Its inhabitants are
D E A D, too.

They are dead, but, at the same time,
alive,
that is, they can
move, and they can even
talk. These p o o r
symptoms of life have, however, no
purpose or
consequence.
Pulled out of a three-dimensional,
surprisingly flat
practice of life,
they fall into the hole of—
allow me to say this word—
E T E R N I T Y.
They lose their life's functions
and all their privileges
acquired during their earthly passage
(one should not, however, belittle the value of this passage).
to become E T E R N A L.
Let me make this ominous sounding word
more human
and say:
they become *art*.
They become a W O R K   O F   A R T.

Having reached familiar grounds,
it is worth, and even necessary,
to record—

for the sake of historical memory—
those important devices of expression,
almost "commandments,"
that accompanied [me]
during this "D I S C O V E R Y."
Here they are:
Memory,
makes us of N E G A T I V E S
which are still-frozen—
almost like metaphors,
but unlike narratives—
which pulsate,
which appear and disappear,
which appear and disappear again
until the image fades away;
until . . . the tears fill the eyes.
And one more word or commandment:

R E P E T I T I O N,
almost like a prayer,
or like a litany,
is a signal of S H R I N K I N G
T I M E.

Having and knowing how to use
these means of expression,
which are so precisely defined,
I could create
a M E T H O D,
a S C H O O L . . .
But,
why should I?

4

Spatial Historiography: *Silent Night*

I

In July 1990, Tadeusz Kantor presented *Silent Night* in Avignon with the students of the Institut Supérieur des Techniques du Spectacle.[1] Before it started, Kantor remarked that what the audience was just about to experience was not a Cricot 2 production. Nor was it a play, a stage design, or an annexed theatre space. What they were about to see was a room in his house, which had burned down. There was only a chimney left—a chimney that Kantor had painted many times. It used to be his room—his room of imagination or memory. Now all that had remained of it was rented to Stefano (Nino), a musician, and Hélène (Helka), his friend.

The audience was asked to "think otherwise" about Kantor's theatre.

This was no longer Kantor's room of memory, where he could explore spatial dimensions of memory and of historical time, a childhood room or storeroom where Kantor encountered the fragmented selves generating their own memories and recollections of the past, or the inn of memory that engendered the relationship between Kantor and his artistic creation. This was no longer a space, organized by the holder of discourse, where, while maneuvering between a window, the doors, a bed, a table, and chairs, the hired actors, the dubious characters of a Wandering Troupe of Actors, or the material shards of his artistic résumé, presented the images that have

been the reflection of [his] attitude
towards the events
that surrounded [him],
towards the situation
in which [he has] lived;
of [his] fears;
of [his] faith in this and not something else;
of [his] distrust in what was to be trusted;
of [his] skepticism;
[his] hope. ("To Save from Oblivion")

This was no longer a site where he made the audience face the wars and the political events of the twentieth century.[2]

Finally, this was no longer a place where his creative process, defined as a conscious act of molding the memories with the techniques of absurdity, protest, blasphemy, or transgression, was viewed by the audience.

The room—Kantor's room of memory—was rented out.

Silent Night, however, not only marked a shift in Kantor's artistic practice but, and maybe more importantly, redefined the notions of memory and of archiving myth or history. It did so by suggesting that memory—that memory that he explored in his intimate theatre of *The Dead Class* (1975), *Wielopole, Wielopole* (1980), *Let the Artists Die* (1985), and *I Shall Never Return* (1988)—invoked the unpresentable in presentation itself; that it "[refused] the consolation of correct forms, [refused] the consensus of taste permitting a common experience of nostalgia for the impossible";[3] and that a myth or history could no longer produce a cultural, ideological, or political image that was authorized by the ideological apparatus of state power. Neither could they express a sentiment preserved in a radical, albeit utopian, memory.

In *Silent Night*, Kantor constructed a space of representation where myths and current historical events coalesced to show the fissures in a traditional construction of meanings and symbols associated with culture or history and staged as a utopian, or dystopian, figuration in theatre.

In order to accomplish this, Kantor presented us with a space that had lost its signifying, recognizable features:

A long time ago, I was fascinated by
the Atlantis
disaster;
by that "world" before our world,
by the only known "R e p o r t" about it by Plato,
and by Plato's opening words:
"that night."
Then everything started anew and out of nothing. (*"Silent Night* [Circotage]")

The stage, a simple platform, was filled with objects and people. Up center, there was a chimney of a burned-down house. Stage right, there was a wooden wall containing a set of doors and a window. Between the wall and the chimney, there was an opening through which the backstage was seen. A single beam of a white light was reflected on the back wall. Stage left, there were a table and a few chairs. An Emballage, human figures shrouded in white sheets, was on the floor down center. Nino, a figure in black holding a cello, was seated stage left. "Now then, here on this stage, / the end of the world, / after a disaster, / a heap of dead bodies / (there are many of them) / a heap of broken Objects— / this is all that is left."[4]

When the doors opened, Helka, a woman in a tattered white dress, entered and came up to the window. Nino began to play the cello. Helka beckoned him to stop playing and come up to the window. Judging by her words, there was nothing outside. There was only gray light illuminating the endgame landscape reminiscent of Samuel Beckett's *Endgame*. It was quite possible that there was only death outside; that everything was in ruins. Nothing stirred. If indeed that

was the case, there was no reason for Nino to change his course of action—he continued to play the cello. Angered by his indifference, Helka started to collect and wash the dishes that must have been thrown around by the guests, who had been here "that night," the night of the disaster. Her complaints and shouts were drowned by the sounds of a tango that must have been played "that night" and whose remanences, like echo, kept ricocheting around the room. The music stopped.

> Then—according to the principles of my theatre—
> the dead "come alive" and play their parts as if nothing happened.[5]

The figures tried to tell their stories. However, it was quite obvious that their recollection of the past was sketchy and fragmentary. The stories were their intimate confessions about things they had retained in memory after the disaster. It was as if the process of recalling to mind elaborated the forgetting, provoked by the disaster "that night." Their attempts to organize the memory shreds into coherent narratives came to naught. Only individual words and phrases, or disconnected prayers and songs, were all they remembered. Thus, Hana retained the memory of a small bird that had fallen into a hole; Manuel of a trip to Badajoz where he, a six year-old boy, had been left alone in a hotel room; Stefano of his father who, like the devil, would make circles with fire; Paul of a pain in his lung and his tears of disbelief that nobody would console him; Renaud of his encounter with his mother, whom he had never met before; Carmelo of an accident with firecrackers; Lucie of being locked up in a room with three little Teddy bears; Béatrice of driving away after hitting a bicyclist; Bruno of his jump with an umbrella into nothingness; Sophie of the unnerving death rattle; Franck of a telegram from July 1939 he had found in an old barn, containing a desperate plea for a quick return; Philippe of the death of his grandmother; Marc of a song about life and death; Eugé of a situation in Europe; Lina of civil war and the police repressions against the Muslim women; Emmanuel of the day when Mitterand won the elections in 1981; and, finally,

Natasha the memory of history, which she believed was not her own but was part of the multitude of histories.

Nor were their attempts at deciphering the function of the objects they carried with them successful. A cross, a mailbag, a chair, a broom, an umbrella, and a newspaper roll, like Penelope's chair from *The Return of* Odysseus (1944), were nothing more now than only empty reminders of their past.

The sounds of the tango returned. The figures began to dance in a rhythm that brought about the distant echoes of their individual pasts, now, expressed through a singular motion—a slow movement, a quick movement, a jerky movement, or a circular movement—as if music, a gesture of time-space-sound, entered them and gave birth to new forms and movements:

> It is not afraid to burst into an enclosed shape,
> defuse it with its sudden jerking movement,
> deform its shape. . . .[6]

In the meantime, Helka and Nino continued to clean up the room.

The sounds of the tango were muffled by the opening notes of "*Silent Night.*" A man on his knees entered the room. In his arms he carried a baby. He left the baby in the middle of the stage. All, except for Helka and Nino, left the stage. One of the figures returned and offered the baby to Helka. Not fully convinced, Helka accepted the baby. The music increased to provide a background for this Nativity scene—Nino with his cello stood next to Helka holding a baby in her arms. The scene was observed and commented upon by the figures, now called the neighbors, whose heads could be seen through the doors and the window:

> In this poor room of imagination,
> the Holy Night of Nativity
> is fulfilled for the second time.
> The recollection of that other night which took place two thousand years earlier
> causes that Nino accepts the part of Joseph
> and Helka that of Mary.
> But everything is nothing more than
> a recollection
> full of bitterness and
> tears
> because all was in vain.
> This futility;
> this impossibility
> can be seen
> in the act of repetition.
> Nino and Helka
> act as if they played a difficult scene
> from the everyday life situation
> which suddenly becomes that "holy night"
> two thousand years earlier.

We are almost convinced
that a miracle has happened.
That, indeed, it is that night
that Joseph,
and that Mary.[7]

But, suddenly, the music died and with it the illusion of a perfect harmony. Helka left the baby on the floor and returned to her domestic chores. A sigh of disappointment from the onlookers. The music returned and with it the "story" that circumvented the everyday reality—Helka was offered the baby once more, and the Nativity scene was repeated. The music died again and so did the harmony, the story, and the recollection of that "other" space and the "other" night. The sequence was repeated once more. Finally, to end this unsuccessful "staging" of the event, a soldier with a gun entered the room and forced Helka and Nino offstage.

The Kneeling Man, who brought in the baby and observed the stage events from stage right, was accosted by three figures in black, one of whom was referred to by Kantor as the "Undesirable." While "*Silent Night*" was sung in German, the Kneeling Man was turned into a living sculpture by the three "suspicious characters." His body was wrapped in reels of white paper carried by the Undesirable.[8] The Kneeling Man became an emballage, a human sculpture, produced by the Undesirable as if to mark the fact that a person who caused the Nativity sequence could not be a part of the everyday of the stage and needed to be sublimated into being an abstract notion of the higher, not to say, religious, order. This violent act was accompanied by the sinister tones of "*Silent Night.*"

Nino and Helka with the baby returned from their journey. They looked around. Everything seemed to look familiar. Consequently, they proceeded with their everyday activities—Helka returned to washing the dishes and Nino was reading New Testament's story of Pontius Pilate. The words "crucifixion of Christ" were spoken by Nino. Helka kept correcting Nino's pronunciation.

Silent Night (1990). Photo by Monique Rubinel courtesy of the Cricoteka Archives.

"This lasts for some time / long enough to comfort and reassure the audience."[9] Once this was achieved, a requiem was heard from the speakers. Nino took the cello and played along. The doors opened and a procession, led by a man carrying a wooden cross on his shoulders, entered. The stage—this room of the everyday—became Golgotha. The procession stopped. Nino watched how the cross was erected. He looked around for a person who could play the part of the Crucified One. Carmelo, a factotum, advised him. First, Nino pointed a finger at a poor seminary student. The student was placed against the Cross. Carmelo was not, however, fully satisfied with the choice. Then a volunteer raised his fingers, but he was dismissed. Finally, Carmelo suggested a new person. This time, a Hasidic Jew was chosen to play the part. Nino approved the choice. And so did the rest of the people gathered around the Cross. The Hasidic Jew fit the Cross perfectly. The onlookers slowly and with indifference left the stage. A soldier came up to the Cross. A single shot ruptured the solemn tones of the requiem. For a split second Helka and Nino remained standing under the Cross. Then, even they, having collected their belongings, left the stage. Two men in the black suits of gravediggers brought in a wooden coffin or box. The priest, who followed them, ordered the body to be put in it. The Emballage, the primary cause of this series of events, or recollections, rather than the crucified Hasidic Jew, was put inside the box and carried away.

The crucified Hasidic Jew remained alone onstage. After some time, he looked around and decided to get down from the cross. He sat on a chair at the doors and waited. Helka, Nino, Carmelo, and the Undesirable entered the room and greeted him. They all seemed to be bored and as if waiting for something to happen. Nino, out of boredom, began to practice playing the cello. Suddenly, from behind the doors, voices singing a revolutionary *Ça ira* indicated that time must have passed. The crowd, led by a woman seated on a guillotine and a priest, wanted to enter through the doors, but Helka pushed Nino to close it to keep them out. Despite his action, the crowd burst onto the stage through all possible openings in this burned-down room. The guillotine was placed next to the Cross. Its blade cut through the air. While the woman (known as a Woman—Commissar—Hangman) operated the guillotine, the crowd, blessed by the priest, continued the revolutionary song. For the time being, the guillotine kept cutting through the empty air. The heads had not fallen yet. The monotony was broken by one of the women who put her head on the guillotine.

> She must have always dreamt to be
> Marie Antoinette,
> will soon change all of this
> using her head made of plaster.
> And this is how history fulfilled its destiny
> according to the possibilities existing in my poor room (*"Silent Night*—Partytura [Circotage]")

A head fell into the basket. The singing continued. The woman, Marie Antoinette, put her head on the guillotine again. A sudden confusion. The priest ordered that she be taken away. The woman was seated at the table next to a copy of her severed head. Nino and Carmelo started the post mortem comparisons, that is, Carmelo placed the makeup on the face of the woman so there was no discrepancy between her and the copy, here seen as the original. Helka became jealous and started an argument with Nino. The revolutionary tune drowned her complaint.

Silence. But not for long. In this room, "time loses all its attributes and characteristics. A true Inferno."[10] Bereft of its linear and absolute quality, time ceased to function as the condition by which to live and a measure of progress. Rather, past, present, and future coexisted in this space after "that night." The music returned. However, unlike in the earlier sequences, the melodies used in the cricotage, that is, the tango, *"Silent Night,"* the requiem, and the *Ça ira*, were mixed together. So were the events—Bethlehem, Golgotha, Bastille, a poor room of imagination—situations, and figures who were associated with a particular event. First, there was the tango. A woman in black danced the tango from the opening sequence. Her dance was interrupted by *"Silent Night."* Helka, who was sitting at the steps of the Cross, picked up and lulled the baby. The requiem called forth the Hasidic Jew, who assumed his function

Silent Night (1990). Photo by
Monique Rubinel courtesy of
the Cricoteka Archives.

as the Crucified One. Then, the revolutionary tune and the actions of the guillotine were presented. The sequence was repeated: the tango and the dance of the woman in black, *"Silent Night"* and Helka with the baby, the requiem and the Hasidic Jew, and the *Ça ira* and the guillotine. The sequence was started again—the tango and the woman in black followed the music until it emptied itself out and the dance stopped. All other actions collapsed, too. Exhausted, the inhabitants of the room and history sat down on the floor and remained silent. "There is nothing more left. . . . All, with the empty expression on their faces, stare at the audience."[11] *"Silent Night"* returned. A gun barrel was wheeled in. A shot. Everybody was killed. The shot was repeated. The dead bodies could be seen scattered around the Cross, the guillotine, and the chimney. "The world begins anew."[12]

II

In the *partytura* as well as at the beginning of a performance, Kantor observed that, in order to prevent a misrepresentation of his theoretical ideas, it was necessary to indicate that the chimney in the middle of the stage was his:

> A chimney from one of my paintings.
> Every one of my paintings is my home.
> This is a chimney from my home
> after it burnt down.
> This is not a set design. (*"Silent Night*—Partytura [Circotage]")

This statement regarding the presence of a chimney of a burned-down house onstage merits further consideration. Ever since the 1944 production of *The Return of Odysseus*, Kantor desired to create a space for his theatrical experiments that could no longer be appropriated by artistic conventions or commodified into an object with an assigned use-value. A chair that appeared in a performance space in 1944, in a bombed room, was a decrepit object nearly obliterated by war activities that, now, "was void of any life function. . . . And when its function was imposed on it [during a performance], this act was seen as it were happening for the first time since the moment of creation."[13]

The same could be said now about the room after "that night." To continue: the 963 objects of the 1963 Anti-Exhibition, letters, newspapers, maps, and used bus tickets, for example, were

> THINGS THAT HAVE NOT YET BECOME WORKS OF ART,
> THAT HAVE NOT YET BEEN IMMOBILIZED. ("My Work—My Journey")

Later, Kantor's Informel (1961), Zero (1963), and Happening (1973) theatres attempted to depreciate the value of traditional theatrical space by exploring its unknown, hidden, or everyday aspects. By 1975, these experiments were perceived by Kantor as engendering their own existence through the processes of assigning meaning and function to the objects that were theoretically pulled out from conventional theatrical reality.

The house I moved into was . . . too solid.
I often went outside to look for my old
Poor Room.
When back in the house, I lived, rather I "squatted," in different rooms.
I did not feel at home there.
I looked through the windows
into alien places and foreign court-yards.
Finally, I deserted
this "solid" house. ("A Short History of My Life")

In the 1975 production of *The Dead Class*, Kantor created a "house" behind a rope that separated it from the auditorium. In the 1980 production of
Wielopole, Wielopole, that "house" was replaced by the room of memory. In
the 1985 production of *Let the Artists Die*, Kantor's new "house" was framed
by the theory of negatives, where Kantor, the Self, watched the parade of the
broken images of the Self. Finally, the 1988 production of *I Shall Never Return*,
Kantor walked into a new "house," where he was a visitor who arrived there
to meet with his artistic creations.

Thus, the definition or perception of a performance space was never stable
in Kantor's theatre. Not only its shape but also its function was in a continuous
motion. A performance space could be a real place of the lowest rank, an Emballage, a Happening, a room of memory, a space in between, a multi-space, or
a found room. Its parameters altered with the changes in Kantor's temporary
positioning of his ways of seeing and thinking about representation of objects
or memories onstage:

I moved into a new house.
In it, I discovered my "pit."
I felt comfortable there.
Then came the journey through the world.
At any cost, I tried to squeeze this wonderful and glittering outside world
inside the walls of the Poor Room.
Sometimes, I managed to do so.
But even this desire died.
The Poor Room became too solid.
It was not mine any longer.
One night, it burnt down.
There was only a chimney left
as is often the case. ("A Short History of My Life")

The performance space, viewed by Kantor as his "home," his poor room
of imagination, belonged thus to him and only to him. Now, in *Silent Night*,
the room of imagination was leased to Nino and Helka, who, as proprietors,
had the right to let other people in with or without Kantor's knowledge or
understanding:

From the dim recesses,
as if from the abyss of Hell,

there started to emerge
people, who had died a long time ago,
and memories of events,
which, as in a dream,
had no explanation,
no beginning, no end,
no cause, or effect. . . .
The i m p r i n t s
impressed deeply
in the immemorial past. (*"Silent Night* [Cricotage]")

In the past, as Kantor observed, the people, phenomena, and events that emerged as images in his room of memory were often altered or camouflaged, even rendered invisible, in order to fit the demands of an avant-garde praxis.

First, I found an intellectual
justification for their
p r e s e n c e,
sudden appearances,
stubborn returns.

I believed that I needed to build pure, autonomous structures
representing c o n s c i o u s n e s s over them. (*"Silent Night* [Cricotage]")

Now, a simple image, not modified by conventions, stylistic ornamentations of metaphors and symbols, moral codes or idealizing procedures, was admitted to the room of memory, a burned-down house, where there was only a chimney left. But a chimney was not the only marker of the "event" that had taken place:

Now then: here—on this stage:
the end of the world,
after a disaster,
a heap of dead bodies
(there were many of them)
and a heap of broken Objects—
this is all that is left. (*"Silent Night* [Cricotage]")

The dead, according to the principles in Kantor's theatre, came "alive." "Then everything started anew and out of nothing." As the actions onstage indicated, the room of memory became their only space, rather than a point, of reference. This space, however, did not have a solid framing that could provide the informatic or optical system of reference. Consider, for example, the figures' futile attempts to reconstruct the past events or their attempts at deciphering the functions of the objects. As in the 1944 production of *The Return of Odysseus*, when Penelope was sitting on a chair, for example, the act of sitting in *Silent Night* was also an act happening for the first time in this new reality.

"The [physical] object acquired its historical, philosophical, and a r t i s t i c function!"[14]

The erasure of memories of the figures and of functions of the objects opened up the space of representation. This space of representation was not defined by the sovereignty of a speaking or viewing subject or a group identity. It was not yet striated, that is, ordered by "constancy of orientation, invariance of distance through an interchange of inertial points of reference, interlinkage by immersion in an ambient milieu, constitution of a central perspective."[15] It was entirely oriented toward experimentation in contact with objects or people appearing from behind the doors. As such, it fostered connections between people and objects that were not previously established. The object

> had to justify its being to itself rather than to the surroundings that were foreign to it.
> [By so doing, the object] revealed its own existence.[16]

So did the figures.

Once their world of everyday was reborn, the world of the transcendental phenomena was born. The Nativity scene can serve as an example of this practice here. It is noteworthy that Kantor's rendering of that sequence, though a relative unfolding of the event synchronized with the tempo and rhythm of "*Silent Night*," was not a nostalgic reconstruction of the biblical story. The sounds of "*Silent Night*" made Helka and Nino assume the traditional functions of the Virgin Mary and Joseph; however, the illusion of scriptural harmony was ruptured when the music disappeared. Having repeated unsuccessfully the sequence a few times, a soldier with a gun interrupted Helka's and Nino's desire to construct an event through a repetition of actions and gestures in order to orient themselves in Kantor's unstriated space.

The following scene, the Emballage scene, provided an even more penetrating commentary. Emballage, according to Kantor's 1964 essay, on the one hand, performs functions that are utilitarian and prosaic. It is enslaved to the content that it covers. Once the content is removed, the wrapping, that is, the Emballage, is a pitiful sign of its past glory and importance. In Kantor's art an umbrella, a human body, and a coffin are examples of poetic Emballages that conceal and protect the content from trespassing, ignorance, and vulgarity.[17] Here, the Kneeling Man, who brought in the baby, performed a nonnarrative function in a well-known sequence. He was, however, instrumental in constructing an event in Kantor's room of memory. Consequently, the three "suspicious characters" were used to turn him into a monumental living sculpture—an Emballage. Only as an Emballage could he participate in an abstract recreation of a phantasmagoric event. But this recreation came to naught. The function of the Emballage could not thus be fulfilled. There was nothing to be concealed or protected. "*Silent Night*," sung in German, was a blasphemous and cynical comment on the desire to construct or determine a center or order.

The world of miracles was not the only world that was constructed by the figures onstage. The crucifixion and the revolution sequences were the two sequences that received particular treatment. Although the events were recognizable in terms of either religious or historical reference, the images on-stage challenged one's desire to reduce them to a particular cognitive or histori-cal object or another collective subject or memory. Neither of them adhered to a biblical or historical representation, deconstruction, or collage of events. Their orientation references were in a continuous variation. Nino, who assumed the function of Joseph in a previous sequence, was elected to choose the Crucified One. A woman, who was one of the dead, became Marie Antoinette. Since the orientation in a performance space was changing according to the functions as-sumed, the people and the objects established a complex network of relation-ships between themselves and the events while they were staging these events in a performance space. *Silent Night* made clear that the image was neither an ob-ject in the field of one's perception that could have been identified nor a subject altering one's perception. Instead, the image was the structure that conditioned the entire perceptual field of and the mnemonic practices in Kantor's room of memory. As such, the image's shape could never be fully stabilized, striated, or complete.

Nothing encapsulates this notion better than the closing moments of the cricotage. The room of memory, or what was left of it, was the space of un-regulated relationships. There was nothing stable in the field of perception that would delineate its scope and boundaries. There was no foreground or back-ground, no past or future, no perspective or center—just different pieces of mu-sic—the tango, "*Silent Night*," the requiem, and *Ça ira*, which produced events that connected randomly with other events and objects in space. Their traits or narratives were not necessarily linked to traits or narratives of the same nature. Instead, they brought into play very different regimes of signs, codification, and practices. There could not be a closure to this cricotage but simply, a sugges-tion that, after the gun shot, the Atlantis disaster, everything started anew and out of nothing:

> Surprisingly enough, all of this
> is nothing more than a
> r e p e t i t i o n.
> Therefore, everything and anything
> can happen (onstage):
> a d i f f e r e n t   a c t   o f   c r e a t i o n,
> deformation,
> blasphemy,
> correction. . . .
>
> Maybe
> this repetition
> and its creation, which is different from the "original,"
> will allow us to see our world,
> this "original,"
> as if we saw it for the first time.
> We, the spectators from the time
> before "that night," that memorable and dreadful night,

look at this second
"e d i t i o n"
of the world
with assurance,
because we know all that there is to know,
we have known all that there is to know for so long
that reality became for us so
d e t e r m i n a t e,
it was not worth a question. (*"Silent Night—*Partytura [Cricotage]")

III

Taking a cue from Gilles Deleuze, it can be said that Kantor visualized onstage what postmodern theory included in its narrative: a tactic of exposing the dominant representational practices that desire to "freeze the gesture of thinking" in order to gloss over what escapes us in the commemorative procedures of history—that history that brings everything into the present in its pursuit of truth through the analysis of empirical data or of documentary evidence. As Kantor's treatment of the French Revolution, for example, made it clear, he was not interested in a trustworthy reconstruction of the past based on the exploration of different types of evidence; nor was he interested in introducing new theories that would provide yet another site for an interpretation and add to a Western thesaurus of historical motifs explaining distortions or misrepresentation of the emblematic events authorizing the Enlightenment. Rather, as the repetitive nature of the event suggested, the aporia of decision, the illusion of progress, and incredulity toward metanarratives defined this history that is never present to us in anything but in a discursive form. That is to say, what is at stake in our reconstruction of history after "that night" is not the existence of the real but, given that the real is apprehended through cultural categories, the awareness of the versions of the real that dominate spatial practices, which embrace production and reproduction of social formations, representations of space, which are tied to the production of codes and signs, and representational spaces, which form all senses and all bodies.[18] As in the past theatre experiments, which explored the characteristics of the real place, Kantor, incapable of staging surfaces, created reality onstage that renounced a singular, "official," smooth reality as it was constructed and defined by the dominant ideology serving the illusion of truth. Recall, for example, his places of the reality of the lowest rank—a railway station, a bombed room, a poorhouse, a launderette, a café, a cloakroom—contesting traditional concepts of representation affirming life and those conventions, which as an act of senseless procreations of forms and illusion, participated in appropriating reality. In *Silent Night*, the sequence with the Emballage explored how the event, initiated by the Kneeling Man, could be monumentalized as a singular representation Nativity. The external narratives and retelling of the story, accompanied by the soothing sounds of the Christmas carol, almost suppressed other possible renderings of that sequence onstage had it not been for the three unsuccessful attempts at staging the scene.

The Emballage itself could be seen as a visual metaphor for Michel de Certeau's observation in *The Writing of History* that "in history everything begins with the gesture of *setting aside*, of putting together, of transforming certain classified objects into 'documents.' This new cultural distribution is the first task. In reality it consists in *producing* such documents by dint of copying, transcribing, or photographic these objects, simultaneously changing their locus and their status. This gesture consists in 'isolating' a body—as in physics—and 'denaturing' things in order to turn them into parts which will fill the lacunae inside an a priori reality. It forms the 'collection' of documents."[19]

In other words, as Michel Foucault asserted in his *Archaeology of Knowledge*, history, "in its traditional forms, undertook to 'memorize' the *monuments* of the past, transform them into *documents*, and lend speech to those traces, which, in themselves, are often not verbal, or which say in silence something other than what they actually say; in our time, history is what transforms *documents* into *monuments*."[20] In order to accomplish this, it deploys a mass of elements, which are to be grouped, made relevant, and placed in relations to one another in order to form totalities. Foucault reminds us not just that the archive is "that whole mass of texts that belong to a single discursive formation" but "the archive is first the law of what can be said, the system that governs the appearance of statements as unique events."[21] His references to "the law of what can be said" and to "the appearance of statements as unique events" within the archive propel his argument that objects housed in the archive do not accumulate endlessly, nor do they disappear at the mercy of chance, "but they are grouped together in distinct figures, composed together in accordance with multiple relations, maintained or blurred in accordance with specific regularities."[22] The archive, Foucault notes, is not what participates in epistemic violence perpetrated by and through the ideological state apparatuses defining how archival objects and subjects are or can be thinkable, identified, or contrived, but it is what "differentiates discourses in their multiple existence specified by the law of what can be said and enunciated about the functioning of these discourses in their own duration."[23] Thus, the archive is "the general system of formation and transformation of statements."[24]

In *Silent Night*, Kantor constructed a field of formation and transformation in which objects (both mythical and historical) were wrestled from their "proper" meanings assigned to them by tradition or ideology. By so doing, he drew attention to the aporia of historical knowledge: a noncoincidence between history, which is written so that time cannot erase human undertakings (Herodotus) or a privilege of being, and history, which bears witness to the missing articulation between the sayable and the unsayable in every event.

This aporia is also the site of the tension between the living body and Logos, as evidenced by the fragmented stories of the dead people who came to life after "that night." This tension, this difficulty in passing through or passing over, is invariably accompanied by an enunciation of their becoming, rather than being; of something that is trying to establish its identity once it is liberated from the bondage of utility so that, dissociated from its previous function, it can enter into new relationships with other objects and people to reinvent and rearticulate itself. At the same time, the existence of what is becoming or taking its course in the nonplace—a burned-down room with only a chimney left—is a process of recalling to mind what expresses the tension between different enunciations taking place in a dynamic space that makes room for the absence, rather than establishes a singular presence and identity. The procedure expresses, thus, the tension between the events and the representation of knowledge (modes of scientific viewing, analysis, and education), between the events and culture (modes of belonging and social or political interaction), between the events and memory (software as message, commercial representation), or between the materiality of the Self and the immateriality of the Other.

This may be the reason why when the postulate of the missing articulation, or the aporia of historical knowledge, is articulated, the accompanying performative act will always be fragmentary. The fragments, like the shards of a broken mirror, cut through the remnants of the metaphysics that inhabit the structures of thought. The performative mode of fragments is a dynamic process of rearrangement that calls for the strenuous search for the memory of the Other that coincides with the Self, who will always remain beyond it and preserves and protects these fragments from becoming a material for consolation and pleasure.

Consequently, it is no longer a matter of determinate forms, which would be defined by knowledge, or of constraining rules, which would be defined by the power of the absolute time and space, but a matter of practices or modes of a perpetual movement of reorganization and realignment—the Kantorian repetition. If it is possible to fathom such a perpetual movement of reorganization and realignment, our function is not only to face, but also, and maybe more importantly, to acknowledge the past and present rationalizations that established the visibility of and gave life to the object of inquiry. If this suggestion can compel consideration about history, it may be that the focus of a historical investigation will be on the manner in which history's objects are or can be thinkable, identified, or contrived—thus, represented—on the idea of a historical event that is produced as a specific narrative according to this representational mode and, ultimately, on the challenges these present to a historian moving through the "archive." That is to say, taking a cue from de Certeau and Kantor, there is no question that the events occurred and that the documents were written. What is emphasized here is how these events—the Nativity, the Crucifixion, the French Revolution—are described, how they made meaningful, and how they become worthy of record or notice by the past and the present. Thus, an event, or a document, as their repetitive stagings in *Silent Night* makes painfully clear, cannot be governed by preestablished rules and categories that archive or simulate its presence or materiality as the object of a historical investigation. An event, or a document, enunciates the taking place of fragments every time it is presented.

Maybe, to paraphrase Kantor, this repetition will force us to abandon our pious vision of the events that protect our consciousness from doubt. Maybe this repetition is a procedure of anamnesis—of recalling to mind—that elaborates an initial forgetting, prompted by the words delimiting the contours of silence.[25] Maybe, while writing history, we will be able to acknowledge the presence of the Other who makes us enunciate our historicity in the moment of utterance.

Thus, rather than being absorbed into an epistemological unit, the Other, as the events onstage indicate, makes us perceive "It" as the structure that conditions the entire field and its functioning, rather than as an object in the field or another subject of the field to be deciphered and "named" by our language of intelligibility. If indeed, as Deleuze would have it, the Other is an expression of a possible world, then, the procedure of recalling to mind elaborates an initial forgetting.[26] "It is like the emergence of another world."[27] It allows for the intrusion of another world into the visual world of figurative narratives (or normative texts) and draws attention to the possibility that traditional practices, though they still abound, are no longer conceivable—we have already witnessed how they acquired their own historicity in the dynamic process of folding.

In *Silent Night*, Kantor presents us with a heap of broken images and objects that could never be fully identified or transformed into a readable place and manifest themselves as a series of effects that are indefinitely reproducible, or as Jean Baudrillard suggests in *The Illusion of the End*, are indefinitely recyclable.[28] This is why, at the end of *Silent Night*, Kantor's room of memory, or what was left of it, was the space of unregulated relationships. There was nothing stable in the field of perception that would delineate its scope and boundaries. There was no foreground or background, no past or future, no perspective or center. Different pieces of music (the tango, "*Silent Night*," the requiem, and *Ça ira*) produced events that connected randomly with other events and objects in the space (the dance, the Nativity scene, the Crucifixion, and the revolution). Their traits or narratives were not necessarily linked to traits or narratives of the same nature. Instead, they brought into play very different regimes of signs, codification, and practices:

> Maybe
> this repetition
> and its creation, which is different from the "original,"
> will allow us to see our world,
> this "original,"
> as if we saw it for the first time. ("*Silent Night* [Cricotage]")

If indeed repetition creates a better possibility for us to approach what cannot be grasped or understood, Kantor provided us with an artistic creation that responds to Adorno's call for an autonomous work of art and Lyotard's unpresentable in presentation itself. *Silent Night*, as a performative mode of fragments, gives us the opportunity to experience what needs to remain nonconceptual and unstriated, even when its exteriority is molded by the selection of materials and an explanation.

The remainders left aside articulate the search for the memory that is no longer a part of mnemotechnics but "the extension of our reality beyond its boundaries so that we can better cope with it in our lives."[29] Kantor voided the history caught in the act of inventing forms of presentation of the events in absolute space and absolute time.

The written, the striated, and the conceptual represent the sonorous, the optical, and the linguistic surface of an event. It is only a representational practice, bereft of a soothing *ritornello*, doubling, or imitation, that establishes the moment of breaking away from history and its already consumed image. To eliminate the "sensational" means to recognize that the "event strike" in the House of History is a permanent condition that pursues the tactics of resistance—a radical operation against being enucleated by the ideology of the past and the theory of the present moment. The theoretical formulations, often practiced indiscriminately under the banner of postmodern commitment to pluralizing and fragmentation, entrap the events. The events, framed by narrative and visual forms, by which we experience history to protect our consciousness from doubt, can be consumed, demand the ownership of representation through symbolic gestures, and eliminate the anxiety caused by seeing knowledge as nonconceptual (as Adorno avers). As such, the events leave us at a loss for ethical or committed actions. They acquire the status of trophies from a tour through the simulated images of history, which need not even be accurate, as long as their effects allow us to establish the nostalgic desire for the real—the Nativity, the Crucifixion, the French Revolution.

Consequently, maybe, there is only the "event strike" left that sends a shock wave across a smooth surface of visibility. Maybe, there is only the "event strike" left that refuses to accept the act of reducing the depth of the event into its sonorous or logocentric effects. In *Silent Night*, this smooth surface is broken by a never-ending repetition—a strike in the House of History. It forces us to acknowledge its conditions of existence rather than the politics of gain or loss, its movement and position *vis-à-vis* the acquired rationalizations of the past and present imaginations rather than its fixed position in the landscape of order, its challenge to what we would like to make visible through its corporeality and materiality in order to reconcile ourselves with life and death, and its function in problematizing our language of intelligibility and field of visibility in which events are made meaningful, worthy of record or notice, and visible. Maybe there is only the "event strike" left, since "we no longer make history. We have become reconciled with it and protect it like and endangered masterpiece. Times have changed. We have today a perfectly pious *vision* of the Revolution cast in terms of the Rights of Man. Not even a nostalgic vision, but one recycled in the terms of postmodern intellectual comfort."[30] Maybe there is only the "event strike" left, since, when the strike is crushed, there will only remain "appearance, and then again, appearance: for the rest take up the bodies, what else is there to say? Except that not to say it *then* is to start thinking about power."[31]

While watching the performance, one is aware that "it is sometimes necessary to turn against our own instincts and to renounce our experience" to resist erasure of and by history.[32] While watching *Silent Night*, one is remained of memories of that night and of Kantor, who was always unhoused in his own house. The house that

> one night . . . burnt down.
> There was only a chimney left
> as is often the case. ("A Short History of My Life")

A Short History of My Life

I live in the middle of my country and in the centre of my town.
But I have always been "outside."
I have lived through different times—bad times and good times.
Bad—when I was persecuted, called names, and ignored.
"Good"—when false pretense of praise and respect were painted on the
tormented faces of those whose expression stayed always the same.
But I was never admitted to the ranks of the elite.
The elite believed that my understanding of the service to my country and
to my town would be too sober-minded.

Today, all the stages of my life, when I look at them from a distance
today, look like different homes.
A house.

Before the war—when I was young—
the whole world was my home. A future world.
In the times of World War II,
My Poor Room of Imagination
was found.
A ravaged pit.
In it, I begun the hard work of a slow process of raising the walls
of my world.
I had a feeling that it would be spacious.
I was raising the walls relentlessly and stubbornly.

Then, after the war,
the house I moved into was . . . too solid.
I often went outside to look for my old
Poor Room.
When back in the house, I lived, rather I "squatted," in different rooms.
I did not feel at home there.
I looked through the windows
into alien places and foreign court-yards.
Finally, I deserted
this "solid" house.

I moved into a new house.
In it, I discovered my "pit."
I felt comfortable there.
Then came the journey through the world.
At any cost, I tried to squeeze this wonderful and glittering outside world
inside the walls of the Poor Room.
Sometimes, I managed to do so.
But even this desire died.
The Poor Room became too solid.
It was not mine any longer.
One night, it burnt down.
There was only a chimney left
as is often the case.

And again, one night
I cried in excitement:
I have found my
Poor Room of Imagination,
and of my childhood.
I filled it with wonderful objects
and palatial love.
I was not embarrassed by its poverty,
I felt rich and Complete.
But it burnt down, too!
There was only a chimney left
as is often the case.

And now—
I do not know if the roof still exists,
Because darkness
has veiled everything around and above me.
But, even in this darkness
I keep building my walls, my windows, and my doors
Anew
In the growing space of my imagination—
But only in the space of my imagination,
and in my solitude.
What perseverance!!!
The chimney stands still—
the dead carcass of a house! . . .
It is getting dark.
It is probably the time to close
the doors of my Poor Room of Imagination.

–n.d.

Silent Night (Cricotage)
(1990)

Lost somewhere in a calendar.
There were many of those
h o l y   n i g h t s in my life.
However, I only remember
this one:
Wintertime.
A deep, dark, starlit night.
Everything [was] veiled in snow.
Holding our hands
and searching for that one
Bethlehem star,
my sister and I
were standing under the sky with
our heads up.
We were only a few years old.

At home, a Christmas tree; the family,
the old Priest,
Santa Claus, who looked like
our Sacristan, gathered for the
Christmas Eve Supper.

We ran out into
the dark night,
only the two of us,
we were waiting for something to happen. . . .
For something to happen . . .
Then we ran down to
the stable
to listen to the animals
talk in human voices.
Suddenly, a sleigh arrived
with a sleigh-man carrying a torch.
We got into the sleigh
and were waiting curled up. . . .

Children always wait for something important to happen. . . .
Anything can happen in such a night.

The night,
a tender
and long-awaited
lover.
During one such night,
my theatre was found,
P o v e r t y,
happiness and T E A R S,
and love. . . .
Slowly a m i r a c l e,
a r t,
revealed itself.

Children always wait for something.
I have been waiting all my life
for something that I believed
would happen.

I

THE END OF THE WORLD.
It all started
earlier, much earlier
than the production discussed here.
An image of the e n d,
of the e n d o f l i f e,
of death,
of calamity,
of the end of the world,
has always been deeply present
in my imagination,
or maybe, it has always been a part of me.

And not without a reason!

A long time ago, I was fascinated by
the Atlantis
disaster;
by that "world" before our world,
by the only known "R e p o r t" about it by Plato,
and by Plato's opening words:
"that night."
Then everything started anew and out of nothing.

Now then: here—on this stage:
the end of the world,
after a disaster,
a heap of dead bodies
(there were many of them)
and a heap of broken Objects—
this is all that is left.
Then—
according to the principles of my theatre—
the dead "come alive"
and play their parts
as if nothing happened.

There is more.
The figures,
which begin their lives again,
do not have any recollection of the past.
Their attempts at putting
the memory shreds together
are futile and desperate.

So are their attempts at putting
the objects together.
They try to put them correctly
together
to decipher their functions.
A bed, a chair, a table, a window, doors,
and those which are more complex,
a c r o s s, a g u i l l o t i n e,
and finally, the tools of
war. . . .

What an incredible collection of
different creative behaviors, despair,
surprises, mistakes. . . .

First and
gradually,
the world of the everyday,
the lowest possible form of mundane existence,
is born.
Then, the world of
the transcendental phenomena,
miracles, and sacred symbols
are born.
Finally, the world of
collective actions,

the whole civilization. . . .
Surprisingly enough, all of this
is nothing more than a
r e p e t i t i o n.
Therefore, everything and anything
can happen (onstage):
a d i f f e r e n t   a c t   o f   c r e a t i o n,
deformation,
blasphemy,
correction. . . .

Maybe
this repetition
and its creation, which is different from the "original,"
will allow us to see our world,
this "original,"
as if we saw it for the first time.
We, the spectators from the time
before "that night," that memorable and dreadful night,
look at this second
"e d i t i o n"
of the world
with assurance,
because we know all that there is to know,
we have known all that there is to know for so long
that reality became for us so
d e t e r m i n a t e,
it was not worth a question.

We watch this primeval,
awkward wrestling
and, suddenly, discover,
as if for the first time,
the essence of their elemental activities,
of objects,
of functions.
For example,
a chair . . .
sitting . . .
a state of being seated. . . .

This will more or less be the action of
of this ground-rending story.
We are getting to its end.

Out of the debris
of the lost civilization,

the people will create something
completely unknown,
the object-monster.
The object-monster explodes.
We have already seen this!
The End!
The End of the World!

This is a simplified
image of a production
which was hanging
together with others
on the walls of my Poor
Room of Imagination
and Memory.
(August 1990)

II

MY HOME
The End of the World
has always reentered the minds and imaginations of people
in the time of disasters
of nature
as well as human madness.

There has not been an age in the history of human kind
which fits the image of
Apocalypse, the end of human kind, and
the end of l i f e on our p l a n e t so perfectly
as the twentieth century.

Since the beginning of my artistic life
this i m a g e
has always lived in me,
deep inside of me.
All the images from my room of Imagination and Memory
have been, and still are, grounded in "it."

Now, I want to pull it out,
the way one pulls out an image from one's childhood.
One must not be ashamed of its naive features.
Throughout the whole of my life, I have ignored its presence
"down there," in the dark depths.
I believed that I needed to build pure, autonomous structures
representing c o n s c i o u s n e s s over them.

Wrong.
Today, I realize that this u n-c o n s c i o u s   i m a g e
has always been rupturing
those conscious activities.
Today, I want to show it adorned,
without the stylistic ornamentations
of metaphors and symbols.

I do not know why.
Maybe it is high time I did it.

But I do know that I have to be careful
and stay faithful to my principles
and methods.

When our "sober-minded" r e a l i t y
(be it on stage or on the canvas)
begins to transfer onto the image,
which is pulled out from the dark recesses of the unconscious,
where a nightmare is nothing more than a misty premonition,
well-known
"everyday" shapes,
the image suddenly transgresses
all the boundaries of the human imagination.
Its "realization"
(be it on stage or on the canvas) and
an attempt to d e s c r i b e it
are submerged in pretentious
pathos and in the shapeless mass of
the used material devices and tools, whose
volume, often shocking, is dictated as if by
the specific gravity of the i m a g e itself.
We know such practices only too well.

This long statement
was necessary in order to
contrast the image with
my m e t h o d.
I must admit that I also
wanted to show its m a g n i t u d e (value)
and p a t h o s, which I have just discarded
in my work of art.

However, I am perfectly aware that
the image can never be represented
by a literal or a "quantitative"
representation or description.

Only the stupid or the conceited could think that.
Neither can it be represented,
especially today,
by symbolic maneuvers or
metaphoric structures.

My "method," or should I rather say,
my strategy
is simple.

I show
its magnitude
via "the Reality of the Lowest
Rank."
I am not afraid to show it
in its lowest possible condition,
its poverty,
its ridiculousness, its irony,
its blasphemy, its shame—
in my Poor
Little Room of Imagination
and Memory—
in "my Home."
Finally, I have returned to
where I started,
to the title:
"My Home."

In the middle of the stage,
I put a c h i m n e y
of a burnt down house.
Poor.
Very poor.
It was a chimney from
one of my p a i n t i n g s.
The painting was entitled:
"My Home"
after a fire,
after a disaster.
Will it be able to "contain"
the "magnitude" of
the End of the World?
I was sure that it would.
I strongly believed in the
power of its "p o v e r t y."
I wanted it to be
my home,

at any price.
Every one of my paintings was
my home.
I did not have any other.
They burned down one by one.
Only a chimney left each time.
A chimney from my painting.
This is a chimney from my
home.
This is my home.
Here, on this stage.
(June 1990)

III

IMPRINTS
I have recently discovered
their existence.
I have suddenly noticed that
certain events,
people, phenomena
keep r e t u r n i n g to me
as if d r a w n by some unknown force in me.
They return intrusively,
even though I keep throwing them out;
I was ashamed of their "unsatisfactory q u a l i t y."

These events, phenomena, and people
were of
h i g h   r a n k;
they represented
the highest,
commonly accepted
values,
which were full of pathos
and historical, religious, and moral prestige.

At the same time,
my memory
would bring me their image which was
becoming poorer and poorer,
less serious,
more ashamed,
more intimate.
They would not leave me in peace.
They would force their way onto my stage,
and onto my canvas.

I needed to do something about them.
I needed to discover my own "method"
to show their
m a g n i t u d e.

First, I found an intellectual
justification for their
p r e s e n c e,
sudden appearances,
stubborn returns.

In the past,
I thought a creative process to be
an act of a conscious
d e c i s i o n,
an acceptance of the
i m p o s s i b l e,
an attack conducted with the help of
a b s u r d i t y,
p r o t e s t,
b l a s p h e m y,
t r a n s g r e s s i o n,
a d i s c o v e r y,
a j o u r n e y into the unknown,
into the p a s t.

I was self-confident,
proud of myself,
and "avant-garde."
But there appeared suddenly
other
"p o w e r s"
with no cries, or war slogans.
They brought with them
s i l e n c e,
and the taste of
e t e r n i t y,
d e a t h,
the abyss of memory,
desperate cries of the past,
worry-free days of childhood.

My artistic process underwent a change.
Those acts and decisions,
which were conscious and autonomous,
were given the function of
artistic d e v i c e s.
I did not discard them.

From the dim recesses,
as if from the abyss of Hell,
there started to emerge
people, who had died a long time ago,
and memories of events,
which, as in a dream,
had no explanation,
no beginning, no end,
no cause, or effect.
They would emerge
and would keep returning stubbornly
as if waiting for my permission to let them enter.
I gave them my consent.
I understood their nature.
I understood where they were coming from.
The i m p r i n t s
impressed deeply
in the immemorial past.

The most important thing is to accept them.
Then, not to be afraid of discovering
their image, which is getting
simpler and simpler,
which departs from all sacred conventions,
moral codes,
and idealizing procedures.
One should not be ashamed of
i m m a t u r i t y,
c h i l d i s h n e s s.

I understood that if
I probed deeper into "shame,"
an act which in itself is courageous,
I would find
t r u t h
and
m a g n i t u d e
cleansed of morality
and pathos
down there.

F A T H E R
His imprint.
My eyes could not look high enough,
so, there are only his
b o o t s
which are knee-high.
My sensitive ear would catch

incomprehensible
curses of the father and
his strange walking pattern:
one two, one two. . . .
Nobody else walked like this.
Then, I learned a word to describe it:
to march, marching.

C R O S S
As a child I lived
at the presbytery,
at the house of the priest, my grandmother's brother.
A Cross.
Its imprint was deeply engraved upon me. It was different.
Unusual.
It was not used in everyday practice.
It evidently belonged to the priest—
a figure as mysterious as the cross—
my "grandfather."
He introduced me to the cross.
I could see it everywhere I went:
in the church, at the cemetery.

C E M E T E R Y
I would visit it frequently;
an un-usual place.
Its imprint is also deeply engraved upon me.
I would believe in what I was told,
that is, that people live there u n d e r g r o u n d.
Now, they live in p e a c e.
I remember that I liked to
go there.
While there, I would be in the grip of a
mood . . . only much later
would I have names for it,
m e l a n c h o l y,
pensiveness.
A child does not need them.
I would forget about
running and playing
with other children. . . .

The Crosses on the cross-roads.
C R O S S - R O A D S
also worth remembering.
Having a walk with my Mother,
I would always pretend that

I could not decide
which road to take.
I have been drawn to
the cross-roads.
When I saw one from the distance,
I would rush in its direction.

A Cross above the bed;
above the place where I would fall asleep.

D R E A M
The child's world.
His natural environment.
One does not create it.
One does not need to make any effort to make it.
One i s it.
We are not in it.
We are this world.
Almost like eternity.
I did not know what it meant
to dream.
I could feel the dream's presence,
or I should rather say,
I could sense it while
still at its t h r e s h o l d,
when my mother was putting me to bed.
To bed.
A bed—the door
to the world of dreams.

A Cross above the bed.
It was this Cross that
made me
"k n e e l"
before I went to sleep, at the bed,
and repeat,
after my Mother,
some words
spoken to this Cross.

K N E E L I N G
It was an activity which was foreign to me.
My mother's reprimands. . . .
And I, I do not know why,
whether I did not know how,
[or] I did not want to,
or I was ashamed. . . .

While kneeling,
I would say words which I did not understand.
What is more,
I would say them to
someone who was
i n v i s i b l e.

Today, when I think about this,
I am sure, that this condition of
i n v i s i b i l i t y
had a profound meaning to me then
and also later.

K n e e l i n g
was, I thought,
a form expressing one's attitude toward this
i n v i s i b i l i t y.
I must have been
particularly s e n s i t i v e
to its presence.
I felt it.
I was convinced that
there existed m o r e
than everything here that I could t o u c h
or see around me.
This child's desire for the
"invisible"
was not a result of a dislike or a fear
of the R e a l world,
in which I lived, and which
was around me.
(In the words of adults,
this desire would be labeled the desire
for melancholy or mysticism.)

On the contrary.
Despite my innate shyness
and poor health,
I felt a great need for
this world,
for the figure of my mother,
for her deep solicitude for my health,
for her love for me,
for the familiar faces,
for the familiar smiles,
for running in the woods, meadows,
dirt-roads

with the village boys,
for the shops on the market square. . . .
I want to say that I
really clung to
this world of the everyday.

This was the very reason why
I sensed strongly
the "presence of the
i n v i s i b l e"
world, which existed
beyond the boundaries of the "r e a l";
which was
d i f f e r e n t,
I n e x p l i c a b l e,
And at the same time,
i n e x o r a b l e,
p o w e r f u l and
all-embracing,
higher. . . .
It was only later that
I understood its attributes.
And it was even later that
I pulled this "invisible"
down into the real world.
That was
m y   a r t.

I need to describe this
world of my c h i l d h o o d
in the utmost detail.
It was the only world
which contained
the w h o l e   t r u t h
in its incredibly fragile
matter.
This is the reason why I am
constantly returning to it.

In childhood,
this "higher" invisible world
would indiscriminately be intertwined
with the everyday reality.

It was only later that
I was taught
the attributes of the invisible

world
and their superiority over
the mundanity of the everyday
by the sciences, religion, and morality.
There came a time, however,
in which I made decisions about my life,
my fate and my art,
when I made a momentous
discovery.
Actually, it was not
a discovery;
rather, it was a decision.
All those grand,
solemn, "sacred,"
inviolable concepts, words,
figures, and phenomena
were dragged by me down
to "earth."
As in childhood, once again,
they were mixed together
with the Poor Reality
of the everyday.
They were no longer
p o m p o u s,
trimmed with honors,
unreachable,
rigid, stilted, or stagnant.
They came to life.
Nobody venerated them any longer,
but many shed tears. . . .

To return to my
childhood
and to this "sacred"
i n v i s i b i l i t y.
I would look for it
everywhere.
I would strain my eyes in search of it. . . .
I would look into the sky—
the clouds like angels,
a M a n with a white beard,
a guardian A n g e l
behind me,
and my f a t h e r,
who, as my mother had told me,
went to the war,
I n v i s i b l e,

soon, I would see
the P r i e s t, who
disappeared.

A Cross above the bed.
It was this Cross that
made me
"k n e e l"
before I went to sleep, at the bed,
and repeat,
after my Mother,
some words
spoken to this Cross.

A R M Y
When I was seven, in 1922,
two regiments of the Polish Army
"marched"
across the market square of
a little village
lost somewhere in the middle of nowhere.
Mother:
These are soldiers.
The child did not understand
this simple sentence.
Child:
All the people around me wear
different clothes—
they all wear
the s a m e
g r a y clothes.
Mother:
They wear
u n i f o r m s.
G R A Y.
Child:
they all carry something
on their shoulders.
Mother:
Those are
G U N S.
The guns kill
our enemies.
Child:
They all raise their legs up
together!
(the child shows signs of enthusiasm)

Mother:
This is a soldier's walk.
They are m a r c h i n g.
Child:
People walk the way they want to,
in different directions.
They all walk next to each other,
one behind the other,
at the same pace,
in one
direction.
Mother:
They walk in . . .
P A T T E R N S.
The child, however, feels that this
order (almost geometrical)
is alien to human nature.

This is how
the A R M Y
in line
marched into my Poor
Room of Imagination and Memory.
Gray Infantry.

Silent Night—Partytura (Cricotage)
(1990)

After a catastrophe.
In order to prevent a misrepresentation of
my ideas,
let me explain that a chimney
in the middle of the stage is
my chimney—
a chimney from one of my paintings.
Every one of my paintings is my home.
This is a chimney from my home
after it burnt down.
This is not a set design.
This is my "home."
Now, I can do in this home
whatever I desire.
I can even rent it.
As it will soon become clear,
I have rented this room to Nino, a musician playing the cello,
and to his friend, Helka.
He, as well as everyone else that he let into
this room "that night" is dead;
after the catastrophe.
If we can accept this end of the world
in this poor room
during that sleepless night
when everything can happen,
let us stay awhile
with those who are
lying down there covered
with the shroud of. . . .
Let us begin:

1.   After the Catastrophe.
Nino and Helka
He, inseparable from his cello, wears a long, black shirt.
She, too, wears a shirt, which must have been white some time ago.

She cleans the windows; she screams at poor Nino.
"That night" there must have been a big party here.
The guests, like the people of Pompeii,
lie on the floor the way death found them there—
covered with her shroud.
Helka's screams and shouts.
"Come here, Nino. Look through the window. Nothing but ruins!"
Nino continues to play. The sounds of the tango.
Helka's screams.

2.   The World is Created Once Again.
The people come back to life.
But they forgot everything.
All that is left are the intimate shreds of their lives.
Now, the sounds of the tango are clearly heard.
They dance.
Everybody dances.
The man on his knees carries a baby
bundled up in sheets.
Behind him, a woman with straw.
But nothing is happening yet.

3.   The Night of the Second Nativity.
Suddenly the sounds of the tango disappear.
Everything comes to a standstill.
As if the world stopped for a moment.
In this pause, one can hear, as if from far away,
the sounds of "Silent Night."
Now we know what is going to happen.
A man with a baby in his arms
moves towards the centre.
A girl with straw places it on the floor.
The baby is laid down on it.
The melody of "Silent Night"
in its full glory.
In this poor room of imagination,
the Holy Night of Nativity
is fulfilled for the second time.
The recollection of that other night which took place two thousand years
earlier
causes Nino to accept the part of Joseph
and Helka that of Mary.
But everything is nothing more than
a recollection
full of bitterness and
tears
because all was in vain.

This futility;
this impossibility
can be seen
in the act of repetition.
Nino and Helka
act as if they played a difficult scene
from the everyday life situation
which suddenly becomes that "holy night"
two thousand years earlier.
We are almost convinced
that a miracle has happened.
That, indeed, it is that night,
that Joseph,
and that Mary.
But the Christmas carol "Silent Night"
ends abruptly.
So does the illusion.
And again—there is only Nino, an unhappy musician;
and Helka, who keeps yelling.
The defeat and loss of memory
is repeated
a few times.
It should be added that
the curious flock of the neighbors
watches these futile
and pitiful efforts
through the doors and windows.
To end this unsuccessful
scene,
Herod's soldier
with a rifle
rushes in.
And, as it is written in the Bible,
Nino-Joseph and Helka-Virgin Mary,
with all their belongings and the inseparable cello,
fulfill their written destiny—
they escape to Egypt,
here, the backstage.
During this entire scene,
a strange "Kneeling-man"
waits in the corner.
"A Guest from the Other Side."
The one who carried the newborn baby in his arms.
There is also the other one, whose
function is defined by the adjective
"undesirable."
Clearly, the "Undesirable"

believes that the "Kneeling-man,"
the cause
of the nativity,
is so banal and everyday
that he needs to be transformed into an abstraction.
He accomplishes this
by turning him into an
Emballage—
a well-known genre of an act of creation.
The "Kneeling-man"
becomes a ghastly
sculpture.
To complete this blasphemy,
the "Undesirable" sings "Silent Night"
in the sinister fashion of a vagabond actor
of François Villon.

4.   Crucifixion.
There is nobody on stage.
Silence.
Slowly, the doors open ajar.
A piece of a cello can be seen in the opening;
then, Nino's head;
behind Nino, there is Helka with her belongings.
The return from the journey.
They look around their old place.
They look into the nooks and crannies.
Everything seems to be the way it was before.
They will continue their everyday life activities
here in this room.
This lasts for some time;
long enough to comfort and reassure the audience.
Unfortunately,
Nino begins to play the cello.
The melody that is heard
is not a portent of anything good.
The funeral psalm
of that Grand Night.
The doors are open.
And everything that
occurred a few centuries ago
staggers through them.
A Man with a cross
and the entire procession of
the familiar faces of the neighbors—
we know them well by now.
And suddenly, this

room of Everyday Life
becomes Golgotha with a Cross.
Nino—the host looks
in the crowd for the one, who
will play the part of
the "Crucified One."
Carmelo—the factotum—advises him.
First, they choose
an innocent seminary student.
A cry from the crowd.
The victim is placed against the cross.
Carmelo-Factotum, not satisfied,
points to another—
a shy Hasidic Jew
hiding in the crowds.
It is he who will perfectly
play the part of the "Crucified One."
A cry from the crowd.
The end.
The crowd has satisfied its desire for a spectacle.

5.   The Time of the Heads Cut Off.
An empty stage.
There is only an innocent Hasidic Jew hanging on the cross.
After a while, he decides to get down.
He sits in the chair under the window.
He is discouraged.
The "Undesirable" enters.
He looks around the empty room
as if he were here for the first time.
He carefully inspects the cross.
He sits down at the base of the cross
without conviction.
Again, the doors open.
Helka enters
as if coming back from shopping.
Behind her, there is Nino with his cello.
Ça va?
Ça va?
Everyone looks bored.
Nino begins to play the cello.
He plays the scales.
He starts and stops.
Everyone is waiting for something to happen.
It seems that nothing will happen again.
But the time is not frozen.
It carries with it a new melody—

one can recognize—
Ça ira, ça ira.
A horde of neighbors
with a guillotine.
At the head, a "Woman-Commissar-Hangman"
and a Priest with a cross;
he is possibly a radical liberal.
One more moment and
the guillotine and the horde invade the room.
The guillotine's blade begins to cut through the air.
the "Woman-Commissar-Hangman" and
the Priest with the cross
carefully perform their functions.
She drops the blade of the guillotine;
he blesses the crowd with the cross.
All of this happens in the void—
the heads have not fallen yet.
But, this is no longer the case—
one of the neighbors—
she must have always dreamt to be
Marie Antoinette,
will soon change all of this
using her head made of plaster.
And this is how history fulfilled its destiny
according to the possibilities existing in my poor room.
Also, time loses all its attributes and characteristics.
A true Inferno.
Everything is mixed together—
music,
events, situations, and
people;
Tango, "Silent Night," a requiem for Holy Week,
and a revolutionary *Ça ira*;
Bethlehem, Golgotha, Bastille, and my Poor Room. . . .
In the end, everything calms down—
a return to the everyday,
which is also Hell.
Immobilized and lifeless,
the people, not knowing what to do next,
stare blankly at the audience.
Herod's soldier wheels in a cannon.
The "Undesirable,"
makes his last effort and,
while singing "Silent Night" with a hoarse voice,
lights the fuse.
A loud explosion.
The people fall down.

The end of the world.
It is difficult to say which one.
The "Undesirable" continues to sing
"Silent Night."
Silence.
Nothingness.
Hana raises her head.
She looks around and
says—
"The world is being created anew."

5

The Space of *Khora*

I

Throughout his entire artistic life, Tadeusz Kantor was engaged in a systematic exploration of a theatrical space that revealed *"the traces of transition from 'that other side' into our life"*[1]—a space where we could watch a parade of the remanences of events, memories, and people that wove an intricate fabric of Kantor's reality, history, and autobiography:

My "credo":
The only complete truth in art is
a representation of one's own life,
a disclosure of all its details without shame,
a discovery of one's F A T E
and D E S T I N Y. ("My Room")

Trying to save from oblivion his individual life from being absorbed by "official / History, / the history of / mass Movements, / mass ideologies, / passing terms of Governments, / terror by power, / mass wars, / mass crimes,"[2] Kantor was engaged in the process of defining and redefining representation and, thus, problematizing current discussions about the relationship between the artist and his revelatory text, between auto and biography, and between self and its representation in postmodern theatre, culture, and politics. Kantor's discourse flowed and folded back upon itself and engendered, saturated, destroyed, and opened up the entire space of artistic representation, as he implied in a statement made shortly before his death:

My life and my destiny
have always identified themselves with
my works of art. A Work of Art.
They have always realized themselves in my work.
They have always found their solutions in it.
My HOME has always been and is
my Work.
A Painting, a production, a theatre, a stage. ("My Room")

These four elements could never, however, be treated as stable reference points mapping out the landscape of his life, because they were given different shapes and meanings depending on the pressures of the historical, cultural, and ideological networks of relations within which he found himself positioned. A painting could be a metamorphosis, a collage, a décollage, an emballage, Informel art, an abstraction, figurative art, or an object or abstraction. A performance could be a reality of the lowest rank, an Emballage, an Informel, a Happening, Impossible theatre, a memory negative, or a found reality. A theatre and a stage could be a real place, a room of memory, a cemetery storeroom, a room of imagination, or a room in a burned-down house.

At the same time, ever since he had abandoned the project of first treating traditional representation as juxtaposed to his artistic experiments with painterly techniques and theatre, as he called it, wrenched from the order of things in the 1950s and the 1960s and second of sublimating the space of his autonomous Theatre-Happening by enclosing it within its own systems of representation and producing its own commentary, Kantor focused entirely on his need to "[freeze] the historical momentum and [to oblige] the mind to go where it need not degrade itself"[3] and to record the traces of (his)story.

I am . . . onstage
I will not be a performer.
Instead, poor fragments of my
own life
will become
"ready-made objects."

Every night
RITUAL
and SACRIFICE
will be performed here. ("To Save From Oblivion")

What does it mean to be onstage and to watch fragments of one's life become "ready-made" objects, *l'objet prêt*, common, insignificant, manufactured and "possessed" objects?

Kantor's theatre of personal confessions provided an answer. This answer, however, a complex performative palimpsest, like the theory of the negatives showed, was a rich fabric of interwoven thought and memories. In *The Dead Class* (1975), the memory machine, the school desks, gave life to the Old People, the dead façades, who were woken up as if from a somnambulistic dream to accommodate what it had brought forth from the deep recesses of Kantor's mind. His biography was objectified by the aesthetic codes that represented some form of reality by giving autonomy, independence, and a privileged position to the traces of Kantor's memories of schooldays and historical events. This process was, however, constantly challenged and prevented from acquiring a solid framing or an acknowledged autonomous status by either other events (a parallel reality introduced by Witkacy's *Tumor Brainowicz*) or by Kantor himself, who enforced the disintegration of this "enchanted simulation."[4]

This space that fetishized the world of appearances was further explored in *Wielopole, Wielopole* (1980), *Let the Artists Die* (1985), and *I Shall Never Return* (1988). *Wielopole, Wielopole* established an imaginary horizon within which history and thought would be contained. A coherent and sustainable image was supposed to be projected by the actors who were "hired" by Kantor to construct and represent what he wanted to self-represent: his childhood, World War I, World War II, his father, his mother, his uncles, his aunts. All of them appeared and disappeared, confirmed and negated, revealed and concealed the elements of a conscious fantasy of repeated gestures and words until tears fill the eyes.[5] In *Let the Artists Die*, the different fractal bodies of Kantor, which were simultaneously present onstage, evoked different memories that assumed physical shapes and generated their own memories and biographies. Kantor's room of memory from *Wielopole, Wielopole*, now invaded, collapsed into a prison cell and a torture chamber. The characters became the inmates of an apocalyptic theatre of death, defending themselves against all-powerful consumption, all-powerful production, all-powerful communication, and all-powerful holy technology that commodify both human beings and their works of art.[6] Finally, in *I Shall Never Return*, Kantor had irreversibly erased the boundary between the three-dimensional world of the Self and the multidimensional world of the stage of Abstraction (the Other—the characters from his productions) by refusing to reestablish their and his own identity:

> The fate of the most important matters of life and art
> was decided in the inn—
> in the c l a s h between two alien systems
> which would never explain or complement each other. ("A Painting")

In the closing scene, Kantor sat at the table with an ultimate simulacrum—an Emballage par excellence, "a fragile and 'poetic' / Emballage of / the skeleton and death, / and of hope that it will last / until Doomsday"—whose identity, as the production made clear, was only the desired desire of the Self.[7]

From that moment on, it was impossible to locate Kantor and his self-representation, because both of them dissolved in a way that escaped us. In the past, at least, we could position the world of resemblance and similitude behind the ropes or within the walls of the room. Now, Kantor entered the "empty night," where darkness veiled everything around and above him and where the events unfolding in a theatre space were of a different order—no longer created, projected, or fetishized as the world of appearances. Rather,

> From the dim recesses,
> as if from the abyss of Hell,
> there started to emerge
> people, who had died a long time ago,
> and memories of events,
> which, as in a dream,
> had no explanation,
> no beginning, no end,
> no cause, or effect. ("*Silent Night* [Cricotage]")

The Figures from within the frames of Kantor's theatre of personal and intimate confession were finally liberated.

II

Today Is My Birthday is a repetition of the last rehearsal that took place on December 7, 1990.[8] Kantor died that night.

> But there is a certain ambiguity here.
> We cannot be sure whether
> the play depicts the environment and the ensemble of actors in a theatre who are
> preparing [*Today Is My Birthday*] . . .
> or
> whether the play plunges us into the realm of "illusion"[9]

to prepare us for the "real" "birthday ceremony" that would take place later.
In a split second, such a scenario seemed to be possible:

> Engulfed within this gnawing turbulence of
> reflections, feelings, doubts, and hopes,
> I need to set my past in order,
> I need to review my ideas in the context of here and now,
> I need to put old ideas aside into the chest of memory—
> simply, I need to clear the field of action
> for my new production.
>
> *My room onstage and*
> *the plot*
>
> The action takes place onstage.
> A real action. Let us assume so.
> I have decided to move in and live onstage—
> I have here my bed, my table, my chair, and, of course, my paintings.
> I have often imagined my room in a theatre,
> inside of the theatre,
> onstage, rather than in a hotel.
> So, my—as I call it—Poor Room of Imagination
> is placed onstage.
> I have to arrange it.
> It should not look like a stage room.
> I will assemble onstage, in this room of mine, all the objects
> as though I really decided to *live* here.
> A bed, a table, a chair,
> doors (important),
> an oven with a chimney, and
> "canvases" on easels.

A ROOM
Mine.
Private. ("My Room")

The memory of Kantor's presence onstage emphasized his physical absence now, however. The folding chair, where he was supposed to sit, stood empty. Unlike the people (the Cleaning Woman, a human Emballage, Pedel, Doctor Klein, the Soldiers, the Generals, the Politicians, the Dignitaries, the Gravediggers) or the objects (a molded book, an oven with a chimney, Kantor's paintings, a family photograph, the machines of power, crosses, a family table) that performed different functions in Kantor's theatre experiments, the chair was one of very few objects onstage that did not have its own immediate stage history. Multiple questions came consequently to mind. Was it possible that the chair was an object-actor from the 1944 production of *The Return of Odysseus*? Was it here to remind us about that distant act of sitting that was happening for the first time in a new reality—a reality that was a countersite to that reality legitimized and legitimating the prewar systems of power and orders of things? And to continue this thought, was *Today Is My Birthday* an act happening for the first time in Kantor's artistic journey that was meandering between the landscape of debris within and without the seductive and seducing spaces of twentieth-century history?[10]

But Kantor was no longer onstage to provide answers. His body had long been

at the threshold—
Emballage, Emballage—
between eternity
and
garbage. ("The Emballage")

"FURTHER ON, NOTHING."[11] As many times in the past, Kantor, the "Grand Scoffer," contradicted himself. Further on, there was everything—yet another theatre experiment, which marked the next transformation in Kantor's theatre positioned at the threshold between the world of illusion and the world of reality. That is,

in the process of falling out from the world of illusion
and falling into the real world,
elements, illusion,
people
provoke the
DISINTEGRATION OF
ILLUSION. ("A Painting")

Further on, there was Kantor's voice that gave intelligibility to his spectral image and haunting words: "Again, I am on stage. I will probably never fully explain this phenomenon either to you or to myself. To be precise, I am not on stage, but at the threshold. In front of me, there is the audience—you, Ladies and Gentlemen—that is, according to my vocabulary, REALITY. Behind me, there is the stage, that is, ILLUSION, FICTION. I do not lean towards either of the two sides. I turn my head in one direction, then in the other direction. A splendid *résumé* of my theory."

The words activated and gave life to a motionless figure seated in one of three frames onstage. The figure, the Self-Portrait, began to imitate Kantor and his gestures while repeating the words from the recorded monologue. Even though the words referred to the action that was presented onstage, they could not silence the cry that Kantor attempted to hide in his private diaries:

> Late in the night.
> I am alone;
> alone in the studio.
> I am alone.
> Alone.
> From the paintings
> the people and the figures
> that I created
> are staring at me.
> They cannot help me.
> They are imprisoned.[12]

Indeed, a perfect résumé of his theory. Its traces can be found in yet another note from August 1989:

> A painter is in his studio,
> there is only a frame of his painting . . .
> a painting . . . and what to do with reality, the reality with a capital R?
> I will need to change my attitude toward reality. . . .—
> and at the drawing—
> a painting showing something hanging,
> in front of it, there is a painter, who is energetically manipulating a long brush
> around the hanged body,
> the painter's bed is in the corner. . . .
> At the bottom of the page, there is
> a sequence of scenes and situations—
> situations that haunted me
> situations that could easily be created onstage
> with the help of a mechanism such as a painting:
> execution, war,
> genocide,
> war victims,
> whores, brothels, masters,
> ministers, generals,
> policemen, spies. ("A Painting")

The stage, a simple platform, was occupied by three wooden frames representing paintings. "The space within the frame would be empty; / its depth would be filled by the actors / and the proprietor's imagination."[13] Up center there was an empty frame. The frame stage right was occupied by Kantor's double, the Self-Portrait, who sat on a chair. The frame stage left was also empty for the time being. An Emballage (human figures wrapped in sacks) was on the floor between the three frames. Down left there were a chair, a table with an old lamp, a molding book, an old photograph, a loose piece of paper, and an iron bed with the Shadow of the Proprietor on it. An old oven with a chimney and a washbowl with dishes were down right. All these objects had their particular artistic and production history in Kantor's theatre of memory:

> The space of Reality must be expanded in order for it to embrace
> such non-physical territories as
> MEMORY.
> One needs to place an equation mark between Memory and Reality.
> This means that one needs to create
> a real structure of m e m o r y,
> of its activities. ("A Painting")

The silence onstage was interrupted by Kantor's distinct voice coming from a loudspeaker. "Again, I am on stage. I will probably never fully explain this phenomenon either to you or to myself. To be precise, I am not on stage, but at the threshold. In front of me, there is the audience." While the monologue was spoken, a figure resembling Velázquez's Infanta Margarita in a black lace dress entered the frame stage left through the doors in the backdrop. At the same time, the double came to life and began to repeat the words of the monologue and to imitate Kantor's gestures. The voice from the loudspeaker stopped abruptly. The double suddenly lost his balance and fell out of the framed space into the performance space:

Today Is My Birthday
(1990–91). Photo courtesy of
Romano Martinis.

The people from the world of fiction
enter my room.
I would meet them at the stairway, at the street corner;
they do not differ from us,
but they behave in a strange way;
they avoid me;
they pretend they are preoccupied with something;
they run away.
Fiction penetrates my life.[14]

A threshold between the world of illusion and reality was crossed over. The double approached the table, touched Kantor's chair (now empty), lit the lamp, took a piece of paper from the table, and began to read: "Again, I am on stage. I will probably never fully explain this phenomenon either to you or to myself. To be precise, I am not on stage, but at the threshold. In front of me, there is the audience—you, Ladies and Gentlemen—that is, according to my vocabulary, REALITY. Behind me, there is the stage, that is, ILLUSION, FICTION. I do not lean towards either of the two sides. I turn my head in one direction, then in the other direction. A splendid résumé of my theory." "Let me tell you about the event that has happened to me. It happened one Saturday." Kantor's recorded voice interrupted, repeated the last sentence spoken by the Self-Portrait, as if trying to establish a dialogue with the living or fetishized object, and continued the story of his encounter with a poor girl at the Cricoteka in Kraków.

While the voice was retelling the events of Kantor's meeting with a poor girl, the doors behind the center frame opened and the Poor Girl, wearing a gray overcoat and holding a big gray canvas bag, slowly entered. She looked around and repeated Kantor's words: "Why is everything so sad?" Kantor continued the story while the Poor Girl commented on his recollection of the event:

I came!
I will stay here until the end;
I shall never leave again.

Having said this, the Poor Girl stepped over the frame and moved toward the table. She kept repeating, "Why is everything so sad?" She was followed by other actors—the Mother, the Father, the Priest, and Uncle Stasio:

From the dim recesses,
as if from the abyss of Hell,
there started to emerge
people, who had died a long time ago,
and memories of events,
which, as in a dream,
had no explanation. (*"Silent Night* [Cricotage]")

Like the Poor Girl, the Family, the Absent Ones, crossed over the threshold marked by the frame and moved toward the table, where Kantor was supposed to be seated. Now their words of complaint or concern were directed to the empty chair. They were mixed with the sounds of "*Tango delle rose*," whose rhythm was punctuated by Poor Girl's "refrain"—"Why is everything so sad? What sadness." Finally, the Poor Girl, unnoticed by the Absent Ones, came up to Infanta's frame and forced her out. The Poor Girl took Infanta's place and tried to imitate her pose—she pulled up the wings of her overcoat, stood upright on her toes, and tried to look regal. A miserable copy of the Infanta in a black lace dress. A general laughter of the Absent Ones. It was only the Mother, who, feeling compassion for the Poor Girl, led her away. The Self-Portrait took Infanta by her hand and placed her inside of the frame—"My Infanta."

> The Poor Girl returned:
> Yes, but it is always the same;
> could not we do anything. . . .
> Is it going to continue for a long time?
> What are you doing here?
> Still it is always the same thing,
> the same story,
> the same misery,
> the same sadness,
> the same old thing . . .
> It cannot go like this forever. . . .[15]

The Poor Girl forced the Absent One into the space between the central frame and the doors in the backdrop—the Doors of Death. They sat down on the chairs standing there:

> It was supposed to be my story.
> But what do you want me to do with this old junk?
> Always the same story:
> Your father,

Today Is My Birthday
(1990–91). Photo courtesy of
Caroline Rose.

your mother,
your Uncle Stasio,
the Priest from Wielopole.
I do not know what to do with this.
But there is no table?[16]

At this moment, the Cleaning Woman entered the space with an old plank and handled it over to the Poor Girl, who was within the frame of the central painting:

They hold the plank in their arms,
they talk to each other—
as if they wanted to stress
the distinct nature
of the threshold between illusion
and reality;
more than that,
between Death and life.[17]

Once the table was in place, the Poor Girl withdrew through the Doors of Death. "Why is everything so sad? What sadness" were her last words.

The Cleaning Woman approached the family seated within the central frame and placed a bottle of wine and glasses on the table. Once this task was accomplished, she came up first to the empty chair and then to the Self-Portrait and said, "Today is your Birthday. It is your anniversary today. You are 75." The Self-Portrait left his frame stage right and approached the photograph on the table. It was his family photograph. He looked at it carefully; and, in order to complete the image represented on it, he joined the group seated at the table behind the central frame. "*Tango delle rose.*" The old photograph came to life. But its life was not the one that had been registered on the flat surface of the photograph standing on the table; rather, it was self-created. As if from the other side, a voice of Priest Śmietana from Wielopole was heard. The Priest/actor listened to the voice of the real Priest delivering a toast at Kantor's birthday celebration in Wielopole in 1983 and repeated some of the phrases. The Cleaning Woman prompted the missing words

of the voice of the real Priest
Śmietana, the parish priest of Wielopole;
The ILLUSION of a character:
The real Priest Śmietana is
played by an illusory and not-real
Priest Śmietana
and not even on stage
but inside of a painting.
ILLUSION
to the second degree.
But the acting of the not-real

is REAL to a great degree:
The not-real Priest listens to the words
of the real Priest
and conveys his words to
the guests at the table;
he does not do this faithfully,
but sloppily, using his own words,
because he does not hear well.[18]

The birthday celebration within the space of the painting resumed. The old photograph came to life. The Mother and the Father repeated the gestures frozen on the family photograph: he held a glass; she poured the wine. This time, however, these gestures happened as if beyond the confines of time caught still on the photograph. While these actions were repeated interminably, the Self-Portrait broke out of a frozen posture. Suddenly, the Father, who "every so often used to experience psychological crises," seemed to have an identity crisis at that very moment—he started to chase after his double and twin, who had stolen his face.

The "birthday" ceremony was interrupted by the entrance of a newspaper boy, who announced the outbreak of World War I. The hands stretched out from the Emballage to catch the newspapers flying in the air. "The Poor Room of Imagination becomes a battlefield."[19] The Self-Portrait returned to his frame stage right. Before the soldiers disappeared behind the Doors of Death, they posed for a commemorative photograph framed by the frame center stage reminiscent of the photograph of the soldiers from *Wielopole, Wielopole*.

The war destroyed the family portrait *vivant* and the illusion. Once the soldiers disappeared, Kantor's room was reassembled to accommodate other "images" (the Emballages as well as Maria Jarema and Jonasz Stern, Polish avant-garde artists), only to be invaded and destroyed once again by politicians, generals, soldiers, and their machines of power or war. The Emballages, as the Self-Portrait reminded us reading the excerpts from the Emballage Manifesto,

Today Is My Birthday (1990–91). Photo courtesy of Caroline Rose.

were a symbol of what needed to be protected from senseless actions, ignorance, and vulgarity. The Emballages, now dead after the invasion by the organs of war, were removed from the space between the frames and pushed behind the central frame by the Cleaning Women and the Shadow. A pile of bodies. Doctor Klein (Jehovah) appeared from behind the Doors of Death. "It is quite possible that s/he has arrived here to help those human creature—the Emballages."[20] Doctor Klein sneaked by the dead bodies and entered the space between the frames. It was here that, having encountered a Water Carrier from *Wielopole, Wielopole,* she or he, having forgotten about the function to be performed here, engaged in a dance accompanied by Jewish folk music. Now, "he is no longer a doctor; he could be or maybe he is Jehovah."[21] Then a kind a biblical ritual took place—it could have been the day of creation of humankind performed anew after a catastrophe, which happened "that day."[22] The Emballages were given a new lease on life. Today was their birthday, too.

The desire to protect the traces or people from disappearance within a mnemonic apparatus that placed them as intelligible signs on a narrative itinerary continued in the next sequence. This time, it was Maria Jarema and Jonasz Stern who entered Kantor's room of imagination. Kantor's voice was heard reading his homage to Jarema:

> I am writing to you
> on the last page.
> A place of honor.
> The order has been reversed here.
> You made the last page,
> the page of truth.
> The officials of our
> "h i s t o r y"
> had placed you on the last page.
> They did so without scruples;
> afraid of your G R E A T N E S S.
> While the front pages were covered with
> the mediocre
> "H e r o e s" of the day.[23]

Jarema, with whom Kantor created Cricot 2 Theatre in 1956, delivered a lecture on the aesthetics of abstract art using the Infanta, who had just returned to her frame, as an example of misuse of space, artistic thought, and a missed opportunity to transform the matter of reality. Jonasz Stern, who emerged out from the mysterious luggage brought in by Jarema, told the story of his survival of a Nazi pogrom in Lvov. His story was a collage of the text spoken by the actor playing Stern and Stern's prerecorded testimony. The spoken text was never precisely aligned with a prerecorded voice, which carried it in different directions simultaneously. This lack of correspondence between a spoken and prerecorded texts brought to mind a passage from Giorgio Agamben's *The Remnants of Auschwitz,* where he makes the following observation: "The human being can survive the human being, the human being is what remains after the destruction of the human being, not because somewhere there is a human essence to be destroyed or saved, but because the place of the human is divided, because the human being exists in the fracture between the living being and the speaking being, the inhuman and the human. That is: *the human being exists in the human being's non-place, in the missing articulation between the living being and logos.*"[24]

If such a thought is tangible, the imprint from the immemorial past, which entered Kantor's room of imagination unadorned and unaltered, was a materialization par excellence of this idea. At the end of the monologue, Jarema and Stern disappeared into the mysterious luggage or black box or coffin.

The poor room of imagination—Kantor's HOME—was ready to receive other imprints from the past that would enter through the Doors of Death: the Infanta, whom the Shadow tried to seduce; the Poor Girl, whom the Priest tried to seduce; and the Family holding desperately to a table top as if it could save them or provide semblance of stability. The Absent Ones repeated interminably their old gestures and words that had already been heard many times in this room. Then,

THE NOISE OF THE MOB IS HEARD
BEHIND THE DOORS. . . .
The noise gets closer and closer. . . .
THE MOB ENTERS!
The Room is invaded by the
"MECHANISMS OF POWER":
a tank, a gun barrel, a "squad car";
machine-guns,
party secretaries, policemen, murderers.[25]

The poor room was again a battlefield. Rape and plunder. The universal chaos was accompanied by Haydn's *String Quartet in D*, opus 76. The Self-Portrait, who attempted to control the situation, failed, and the war destroyed

Today Is My Birthday (1990–91). Photo courtesy of Bruno Wagner.

the room and its inhabitants, who continuously kept reliving their deaths, rapes, and misery. "*Quelle barbarie*," screamed the Poor Girl, leaning against the frame of the Infanta's frame. Pause. While the "*Tango delle rose*" was played, all the characters left the stage. The Self-Portrait looked around: "My Poor Room of Imagination. My home. My home on stage, which, like a fort, defends itself against the attacks of the mob, against the governments, against politics, against all unlawful trespassing, against ignorance, against vulgarity and stupidity. My weapon is *my imagination, childhood memories, my poverty, my solitude, and Death waiting over there*, and a grand actress and her rival: *Love*."[26]

After the nightmare, the Shadow and the Cleaning Woman tried to put the Room or Inn of Imagination or Memory back together. Their effort was interrupted by the entrance of three NKVD soldiers, who pulled the Self-Portrait out of his frame and thrust him into the central frame: "The floor in the central frame has risen as if to absorb the body destined for death. The central frame is turned into a Death Chamber."[27] The image of torture and death was pushed toward the audience. While the Self-Portrait was tortured by the NKVD soldiers, Vsevolod Meyerhold's words from his letter to Molotov, in which Meyerhold retracted all his confessions because they had been beaten out of him, punctuated their blows. Meyerhold's plea for life and freedom remained unanswered, even here in this room. If the politicians could not or chose not to save him, the only response can be an homage to Meyerhold performed by the actors of the Poor Theatre of François Villon, who had emerged from the dim corners of Kantor's room of imagination.

The Cleaning Woman pushed the frame into its backdrop, then she and the Shadow pushed the frame aside. Once the frame of the central painting was removed, a different space containing a wooden door was disclosed. Offenbach's "*La belle Hélène*" filled the space. The door opened and the gravediggers from *I Shall Never Return* brought in the crosses from *Let the Artists Die*. They put the crosses all over the room. The Poor Girl emerged. Behind her were bio-objects (a dignitary stuck to his chair and a man with a pulpit), monuments of war and death, circus cages with generals in them, a monument-tank with

Today Is My Birthday (1990–91). Photo courtesy of Caroline Rose.

a human body, and the machines of power and war. The second movement of Beethoven's *Eroica* symphony charged the atmosphere. A funeral cortege appeared from behind the doors, led by the Priest with a cross. The Self-Portrait, the Father, his Double, and Uncle Stasio carried a wooden board/table/coffin on their shoulders. The Mother followed. The board was put on trestles in front of the audience. The Family sat at it as if they were sitting at the Last Supper table. The Self-Portrait stood up: "Again, I am on stage. I will probably never fully explain this phenomenon either to you or to myself. To be precise, I am not on stage, but at the threshold." His words were drowned by Haydn's music. Universal disorder and chaos erupted. Suddenly, the music died. Everything and everybody was frozen in a final gesture.

III

Seen in the context of his post-1975 experiments, *Today Is My Birthday* indicates a shift in Kantor's treatment of the relationship between immaterial memories and the processes of representing them. Whereas *The Dead Class, Wielopole, Wielopole, Let the Artists Die,* and *I Shall Never Return* introduced performance spaces that existed beyond time, were countersites to real spaces, transformed in any direction, or were self-consistent and existed for themselves, the last production dismantles these spaces and takes apart their stylistic forms. This is achieved by positioning four frames onstage, which organize and decompose transcendental as well as sensory illusion.

The first frame is between the auditorium and the performance space that is organized by a fixed place assigned to Kantor himself. Had he been alive, he would have walked around or sat on a chair, as he used to, and would have assumed the function of the holder of discourse projecting the invisible traces of his memories onto and participating in the events unfolding in the performance space. Now, only his ghost or memory is hovering within this frame about whose boundaries the audience is reminded by Kantor's voice from a loudspeaker: "Again, I am on stage. . . . To be precise, I am not on stage, but at the threshold."

The memory of Kantor's presence onstage emphasized his physical absence now. Instead of the body, there are his statements about life, death, memory, the room of imagination, and theatre. Maybe, indeed, Carlos Fuentes was right when he announced in *Terra Nostra,* "You are one in your memory. You are another in the time you cannot remember."[28] Now, these statements begin to give solid contours to what always wanted to stay ephemeral and "not too solid" but begins to emerge as "Tadeusz Kantor."[29] It is difficult not to make these statements, because many of us still have our recollections of Kantor's presence and of that bleak December day in 1990. These recollections are a painful reminder that the person who generated our creative energy is no longer with us. Even though Kantor and we belong to different dimensions, writing or reading about his artistic endeavors may create a site, or an illusion of a site, where there exists a possibility for all of us to function "as if past and future ceased to exist. . . . Everything is intertwined, one could say: everything exists simultaneously."[30] Kantor, who, even when alive, hovered like a ghost around the stage, allows us to see ourselves in his exteriority and to reexamine our own thoughts about life, death, memory, history, and theatre.

By so doing, Kantor makes us realize that Michel de Certeau's argument in *The Writing of History* that "a fact that has been recorded and is today assumed to be historically valid is shaped from conflicting imaginations, at once past and present."[31] De Certeau never disputes that certain events may have occurred or, I may add, that certain people existed. Rather, he emphasizes the ephemerality of events or existence and how the uncertainties are transformed into permanent texts belonging to the dominant representational and normalizing structures. In order to avoid this and similar appropriations, de Certeau argues for the process of writing of history in which the focus would be on how events or people are described, how they are considered meaningful or important, and how they become worthy of record or notice. Accordingly, the function of a historian is to walk around acquired rationalizations of the past and the present in order to destabilize the representation of the event or a person solidified by a system of the past and present structures of belonging. His or her function is to expose them "to question that order, to marvel that it exists, to wonder what made it possible, to seek, in passing over its landscape, traces of the movement that formed it, to discover in these histories supposedly laid to rest 'how and to what extent it would be possible to think otherwise.'"[32]

One of the consequences of this process is that we realize that, while destabilizing the representation of the event or a person, we disturb the language of intelligibility that had been established through a relation with the other by the past and present structures of belonging. The event's ephemerality must have been given surface permanence in the process of establishing its visibility. In order to obtain this visibility, the language of intelligibility delineates what will be remembered, what will be understood, and what must be forgotten. At the same time, as Michel de Certeau reminds us, the language of intelligibility promotes a selection between what can be understood, accepted, and aesthetically palpable and what must be forgotten in order to obtain the representation of the event. However, "whatever this new understanding of the past holds to be irrelevant—shards created by the selection of materials, remainders left aside by an explanation—comes back, despite everything, on the edges of discourse or in its rifts and crannies: 'resistances,' 'survivals,' or delays discreetly perturb the pretty order of a line of 'progress' or a system of interpretation."[33]

This resistance to representational effects bring to mind Samuel Beckett's *Endgame,* Joseph Beuys's paintings or reminiscences of World War II, Francis Bacon's "A Study of Velázquez's Portrait of Innocent X," Robert Wilson's installation, *Memory/Loss,* Meredith Monk's *Volcano Songs,* Peter Handke's *Die Stunde da wir nichts voneinander wußten,* and Daniel Libeskind's architectural designs for the Jewish Museum in Berlin. All these works are stark examples of representational practices that challenge traditional representation by exposing the fissures in its surface permanence and the crisis of all referential systems anchoring it at the end of the twentieth century. There is no linear progression toward some resolution or intellectual comfort waiting at the end. "Me—me to play. . . . Old stancher. You remain," says Hamm in *Endgame,*[34] a play where contemplation of the post–Auschwitz and post-Hiroshima world needs to happen in a place where mind can go without the fear of degrading itself. "I see my light dying," responds Clov.[35] This is also the response of Innocent X (Bacon), of a captive tortured by the sun and by man, so his memories would disappear within five days (Wilson), of a body whose image fades away after the explosion (Monk), of characters silently crossing the stage transversely (Handke), or of people staring at the voids cutting through the exhibition spaces creating an irregular set of spatial displacements and discontinuities (Libeskind).[36] Beckett, Beuys, Bacon, Wilson, Monk, Handke, and Libeskind produce knowledge and representational practices that are governed not by the totality of their effects but their inherent structure. "They are knowledge as nonconceptual objects. This is the source of their greatness. It is not something of which they have to persuade men, because it should be given to them."[37] As nonconceptual objects, these works of art destabilize the constancy of distance between the points of reference, show "nothing" that screams in the presence of the invisible, turn against our instincts, and force us to renounce our experience. As nonconceptual objects, these works create nomad art of close vision in which all orientations, landmarks, and linkages are in a continuous variation.[38] "No line separates earth from sky, which are of the same substance; there is neither horizon nor background nor perspective nor limit nor outline nor form nor center; there is no intermediary distance, or all distance is intermediary."[39] Similarly, the events unfolding within the space of the first frame and Kantor's recorded voice commenting upon those events are a reminder of the nonconceptual quality of objects and people onstage.

The second, third, and fourth frames are concrete and visible. Stage right, there is a frame containing the Self-Portrait; up center, a frame with the Doors of Death, from behind which different characters will emerge; and stage left, a frame with the Infanta. Each of these frames has its own history.

Always present onstage during his productions, the Self-Portrait is a singular mirror in which Kantor's image, like the image of Philip IV in Velázquez's *Las Meninas*, usurps the position of the privileged subject of representation by erasing the objects positioned within the performance space. It is only by so doing that Kantor could restore what was lacking in the formation of a stage image. For the audience, he justified the reasons why they could not find their own reflection in the character onstage or why they were not invited to participate in the formation of this representation—the performance stage, wrenched from the conventional, everyday reality, was Kantor's storeroom of objects, independent of the conventional order of things. Consequently, those structures, which could mold the real by simulating verisimilitude and affirming life, were erased by Kantor's singular presence onstage. For the actors, he made this practice intelligible, explaining it in terms of the condition of death: "The moment of the ACTOR's first appearance before the HOUSE (to use current terminology) seems to me, on the contrary: revolutionary and avant-garde. I will even try to compile and 'ascribe to HISTORY' a completely different picture, in which the course of events will have a meaning quite the opposite. . . . IT IS NECESSARY TO RECOVER THE PRIMEVAL FORCE OF THE SHOCK TAKING PLACE AT THE MOMENT WHEN, OPPOSITE A HUMAN (A SPECTATOR), THERE STOOD FOR THE FIRST TIME A HUMAN (AN

ACTOR), DECEPTIVELY SIMILAR TO US, YET AT THE SAME TIME IN-
FINITELY FOREIGN, BEYOND THE IMPASSABLE BARRIER."[40]

Reflections and doubles silently mutter an almost inaudible question: "Who
is there?"

The frame with the Doors of Death (or, to be more precise, the gap between
the frame and the door) is a place where the exchange between the Self and the
Others had taken place since *The Dead Class*:

> In front of us,
> in this poor and dusky room,
> behind the doors,
> a storm and a inferno rage,
> and the waters of the flood rise.
> The weak walls of our ROOM;
> of our everyday or
> linear time
> will not save us. . . .
> Important events stand behind the doors
> it is enough to open them. ("A Room. Maybe a New Phase")

Once the doors were open, Kantor's room of imagination was filled with
objects and people who kept emerging, disappearing, and reemerging in different shapes or which performed varying functions in Kantor's life as a visual
artist: a molded book from the "Emballage Manifesto" and *The Dead Class*,
an oven with a chimney from *Silent Night*, a series of his paintings from the
different stages of Kantor's artistic journey, a family photograph and a family
portrait from *Wielopole, Wielopole*; his recent paintings, *I Am Leaving This
Painting* and *Infanta Margarita Came to My Room that Night*; the Cleaning
Woman from *The Dead Class*, *Let the Artists Die*, and *I Shall Never Return*;
a human Emballage; the janitor; Pedel from *The Dead Class*, a figure who assumed a posture of Doctor Klein in this production but was already present in
The Water-Hen and *The Dead Class*, *Wielopole, Wielopole*, and *I Shall Never
Return*; the soldiers, generals, politicians, and dignitaries as well as their monuments and machines of power from *Wielopole, Wielopole*, *Let the Artists Die*,
and *I Shall Never Return*; the gravediggers and their crosses from *Wielopole,
Wielopole*, *Let the Artists Die*, and *I Shall Never Return*; and, finally, a family
table from *Wielopole, Wielopole*.

The frame with the Infanta, in her black lace dress covering a construction
made of whalebone, is a visual representation of Kantor's 1962 essay about two
versions of his painting *Infanta Margarita*:

> Velázquez's Infantas
> like relics . . .
> are dressed in real and ornate coats. . . .
> wearing these stately garments . . .
> [they] shamelessly exhibit their complete indifference
> to the public.

The facades of death
enclosed in paper boxes. . . .
s e c o n d   v e r s i o n
. . .
a gray, second-rate canvas . . .
a portrait itself consists of two separate parts which were later joined together with
iron hinges.
The painting can be folded like a suitcase. It seems that nobody cared that the
Infanta looks as if broken into two halves. . . .
Maybe, it was done for practical reasons in order to make easier the transport and
the showing of the Infanta, the curiosity of the Wandering Panopticum. . . .
An old postman's mail-bag was a substitute for Infanta's famous dress which, like
a chasuble, was spread over the frame, made of whalebones.
It was believed to be an adequate imitation.[41]

In *Today Is My Birthday*, both Infantas existed in the space of the room or
found reality. Infanta (version I) represented a work of art which, for Kantor,

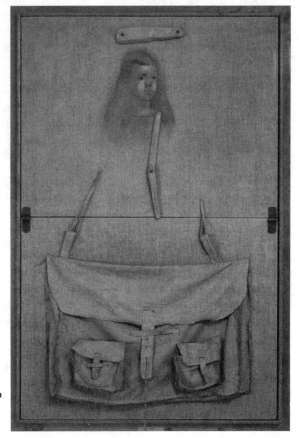

Tadeusz Kantor's painting,
"Infanta According to
Velázquez" (1966–70). Muzeum
Sztuki in Iódź; (Poland). Photo
by Michal Kobialka courtesy of
the Kantor Estate.

was a "closed system" positioned within its own reality and historicity (the time of Velázquez). Infanta (version II) was Kantor's creation. The two Infantas revealed their characteristics by displaying the tensions between them, their incompatible systems of representation, and between them and other characters who tried to resolve the conflict. For example, the Self-Portrait defended the Infanta (version I). The Priest tried to seduce the Poor Girl/Infanta (version II). Jarema criticized the traditional features of the Infanta (version I). The Poor Girl/Infanta (version II) provided a commentary on the war events that burst into the room. The Infanta (version I) left the room when the war erupted. The Poor Girl/Infanta (version II) entered the dimension of the room or found reality from the space behind the Doors of Death.

As the events onstage indicate, however, these frames are not fully stable and enclosed in themselves. Neither do they produce their own representations and commentaries as envisioned in Artaud's closure of representation in a nontheological space. Rather, they can be seen as openings into a discourse that exists as an open field positioned outside of and beyond stage history, an autonomous theatre, or Kantor's autobiography. Recall, for example, the moments when the Self-Portrait can no longer contain himself within his frame and falls into the performance space, or when the Infanta, ridiculed by the Poor Girl and Maria Jarema, leaves her frame and participates in the actions onstage, or when "people, who had died a long time ago, memories of events which, as if in a dream, had no explanation," intrude from behind the Doors of Death. Once the characters and the events emerge in the space of this "other" discourse, the frames, though still present, stand empty. Together with the temporary erasure of the content of the frames, the narratives represented by them cease to be binding and, consequently, the "characters" can engage in exchanges that are not determined by the traces of their past representations. More importantly, "The explanation of 'illusion' is being offered to you in the present, in the sense of the 'illusion' thus reflected; and it is always a partial explanation that must forever be started anew, prolonged, tied together; its importance arises more from the pressures it exerts on the general text than from any 'truth' it is supposed to reveal, its conveying of information or deformation."[42]

The Self-Portrait, the Infanta, and the people or memories do not simply tell their individual stories, nor is there "any truth [they are] supposed to reveal"; rather, they disclose and map out the topography of this "other" discourse.

This "other" discourse in Kantor's theatre is a space of representation that, unlike Artaud's nontheological space, produces itself and its own commentary without ever sublimating its form and shape, as the opening exchange between Kantor's recorded voiced and the Self-Portrait, evidenced. The "other" discourse is similar to Plato's definition of the spaces involved in the construction of an object:

> It must be agreed that there exists, first, the unchanging form, uncreated
> and indestructible, admitting no modification and entering no combination,
> imperceptible to sight or the other senses, the object of thought: second, that
> which bears the same name as the form it resembles it, but is sensible, has come
> into existence, is in constant motion, comes into existence and vanishes from a

particular place, and is apprehended with the aid of sensation: third, space which is eternal and indestructible, which provides a position for everything that comes to be, and which is apprehended without the senses by a sort of spurious reasoning and so is hard to believe in—we look at it indeed in a kind of a dream and say that everything that exists must be somewhere and occupy some space, and that what is nowhere in heaven or earth is nothing at all. And because of this dream state we are not awake to the distinctions we have drawn and others akin to them, and fail to state the truth about the true and unsleeping reality: namely, that whereas an image, the terms of whose existence are outside its control in that it is always a moving shadow of something else, needs to come into existence in something else if its to claim some degree of reality, or else be nothing at all, an exact and true account of what is ultimately real supports the view that so long as two things are different neither will come to be in the other and so become at once both one and two.[43]

The "other" discourse, the third space—the Platonic *khora*—is neither the space of the holder of discourse nor the space of a sensible or physical representation; that is, it belongs neither to Kantor nor to the objects of his creation (the framed narratives). At the same time, it "contains it all," and it makes the formation of representation possible. It is not a mediator between dialectical oppositions. It is not a passive receptacle into which Kantor could throw forms and objects, nor is it a spatial interior molded by its objects.

As Peter Eisenman notes, this space, Plato's third space, is "like the sand on the beach: it is not an object or a place, but merely the record of the movement of water, which leaves traces of high-tide lines and scores imprints—erosions— with each successive wave receding to the water."[44] In Kantor's *Today Is My Birthday*, the space between the four frames records the four faces or frames of representation. Being neither the place nor the nonplace, it creates and produces nothing, not even an event, since an act would establish an order, consolidate a form, or make a promise. Rather, an order, a form, or a promise can only be introduced, shaped, or made within the boundaries of the "frames." Thus, for example, the two-dimensional space of the Self-Portrait is activated by Kantor's voice, the Poor Girl pushes out and takes the place of the Infanta; the Infanta, when criticized by the Poor Girl and the Family, is led back to her frame by the Self-Portrait before he returns to his own; and the Self-Portrait joins the group seated behind the central frame for the "birthday ceremony" only to return to his picture when the room of imagination is invaded by war and its mechanisms of destruction.

During *Today Is My Birthday*, however, the space between the frames became the focal point of the discourse where diverse traces of representation were gathered together before they were dispersed back into their frames to prevent the temporal articulation of the operation that could be appropriated by the eye. Every time this happened, an image, the terms of whose existence were suddenly outside of and beyond the control of "framed" representation, came to life to claim some degree of reality, as did the Self-Portrait in the opening scene when he could no longer contain himself within the frame of a painting and fell out into the space of *khora*. So did the other characters in the closing scene. The space between the frames was filled with the objects and characters from Kantor's past productions. All intermingled, they repeated the words and the phrases from those other pieces. The irrepressible chaos of the moment was beyond becoming a "framed" narrative. This *negative vivant* could only be a record of the imprints and the erosions of "successive wave[s] receding to the water"—a discourse about the disintegration of monocular representation, defined either in Aristotelian or Platonic terms, modified by Alberti's 1435 rules of a single-point perspective ordering a transfer of objects from a real to an imaginary space.

Artaud's nontheological space of representation, in which life is doubled and emptied by negation and Kantor's double move of wrenching objects or spaces from everyday reality and separating them from the appropriating gaze of the audience, dissolved radically the traditional notion of representation. Rather than speaking of a representation, these theatre artists speak within a representation. To speak within a representation is to acknowledge that it is neither a process of transfer (Aristotle) or doubling (Plato), but a practice of the formation of an object that, as it emerges within a particular index of reality and as it is coded into practices, is assigned a status. This status legitimizes its movement into various other networks and fields of use. Once the locus is established, the identity of representation can be maintained, disseminated, or challenged. Such a practice can lead to the establishment or replacement of the boundaries, evaluation, or reevaluation of agent and agency, and establishment or reestablishment of the mode of functioning of the subject. Each in his own way, Artaud and Kantor dealt with representation not by opposing it but by providing strategies and tactics from within to articulate the practices that alter the mode of functioning and topography of representation. In *Theatre and Its Double*, Artaud contributed a strategy that produces a space of representation that no external authority or hierarchy can appropriate. In his artistic work, Kantor drew attention to a strategy and a maneuver that problematized the postulate of reality by transgressing the boundary between the world of illusion and the world of reality, the particularity of the subject position by showing its heterogeneous moments, and, ultimately, a tactic of nomadic thought that, while traveling through the landscape of representation, recorded the erosions in the idea of permanence in representational performance and visual arts.

IV

Today, almost two decades after his death, faced with his *ouvre* defined by the phantoms, the historian, the spectator, and the art critic are confronted with unstable eclectic historical and intellectual records that are quickly becoming nostalgic traces of Kantor's presence onstage. What is left out however is the specificity and singularity of Kantor's practice that was always a reflection of his attitude toward the events and the situation in which he worked. His theatre was, as he so forcefully contended, not a representation of, but an answer to reality.[45] This answer was shaped by the objects of the reality of the lowest rank, which ruptured a utopian dream by exploring the fissures and cracks in national mnemotechnics. *Today Is My Birthday* presents us with the unsettling substance of Kantor, who no matter how hard we try, can never be reduced to one of the elements on a smooth surface. To think about Kantor's theatre practice is not only to approach the condition of blooded thought but also, and maybe more importantly, to think about a radical theatrical practice that interrogates the ontology of theatre that takes exception to the normative order of things in order to think "otherwise." Having been awakened to the nightmare of history, Kantor never cut himself off from the world but staged a battle for life or death in his poor room of imagination:

And here is the map of this battle:
in the front, there is
the contempt (mine)
for "general"
and o f f i c i a l
History,
the history of
mass Movements,
mass ideologies,
passing terms of Governments,
terror by power,
mass wars,
mass crimes. . . .
Against
these "powers"
stands the
S m a l l,
P o o r,
D e f e n s e l e s s,
but magnificent
History of
i n d i v i d u a l
h u m a n
l i f e.

Against
half-human creatures
stands
a h u m a n b e i n g
the one, who centuries ago,
at the beginning of our culture
was identified by two words:
"Ecce Homo,"
a domain of spiritual life
of the most precious
and the most delicate matter.
It is only in
this "individual human life" that
TRUTH,

DIVINITY, and
GRANDEUR
were preserved.

They should be saved
from destruction and oblivion;
saved from all
"powers" of the world;
despite the awareness
of impending failure. ("To Save from Oblivion")

Maybe this last thought—a call for action "despite the awareness of impending failure"—is also a call for ethics and historiography not only in Kantor's room of imagination or memory but also in the practices of our everyday
life. Kantor's theatre and its poor or real objects, reality of the lowest rank, autonomous works of art, zero zones, impossible condition, complex mnemotechnics, and emballages visualized onstage an anamnesis that elaborates initial
forgetting induced by the languages of intelligibility; a heterotopia that offers
a countersite to the real site, cairological time that liberates a human from the
constraints of linear and progressive time, a challenge to what Kantor had perceived as official art or mass culture in a socialist Poland, and the process of
deterritorializing representation by the objects that can no longer be or are not
yet appropriated by the artistic convention or commodified into an assigned
use-value.

These material forms, articulated and rearticulated by Kantor and the Cricot 2 Theatre, give testimony to his practice of enunciating his own historicity
in the encounter with the Other, which he defined not as a subject or an object
but as a historically and ideologically structured field of perception. Kantor's
artistic gesture of time-space-matter took shape of an ethical maneuver or battle
that was always *in* reality but necessarily not *of* it:

1914
World War I.
Millions of corpses
in the absurd hecatomb.
After the War:
old powers were abolished;
generals' ranks, medals, and epaulets
monarchs' crowns
were thrown into the garbage cans;
Fatherlands went bankrupt;
nationalism turned out to be nothing more than a base primitive instinct.
In the context of such a colossal ignominy in the world, which up till that time
forced us to acknowledge its existence as the only judicially permissible one, the
attitude of the Dadaists was a healthy action and reaction:
DERISION,
DISREGARD,

MUTINY,
PROTEST,
NEGATION,
BLASPHEMY,
SACRILEGE of all the SHRINES,
QUESTIONING of all social values.
A holy concept of art was mocked.
CONSCIENCE, which according to the old order should have conditioned the
work of art,
was replaced by COINCIDENCE.
FORM and its perfection, which ought to have EXPRESSED important content,
was replaced by crude REALNESS which expresses nothing and simply IS.
A quarter of a century passed.
World War II.
Genocide,
Concentration Camps,
Crematories,
Human Beasts,
Death,
Tortures,
Human kind turned into mud, soap, and ashes,
Debasement,
The time of contempt. . . .
And this is my (and our) answer:
THERE IS NO WORK OF ART
        (later this statement would get a more intellectual label: disavowal of the
work of art).
THERE IS NO "HOLY" ILLUSION,
THERE IS NO "HOLY" PERFORMANCE.
THERE IS ONLY AN OBJECT WHICH IS TORN OUT OF
LIFE AND REALITY
        (the history of art has given it a more sophisticated name: *l'objet prêt*).
A CART WHEEL SMEARED WITH MUD became a work of art.
THERE IS NO ARTISTIC PLACE
        (such as the museum or the theatre)
THERE IS ONLY REAL PLACE
(Odysseus returns from Troy to a room destroyed by the war, a railway station,
staircase).
SUBLIME AESTHETIC VALUES ARE REPLACED WITH
POVERTY!
POOR OBJECT
(a cart wheel smeared with mud, decayed wooden board, a kitchen chair on which
Penelope would sit).
ARTISTIC ATTITUDE IS DESCRIBED BY:
PROTEST,
MUTINY,
BLASPHEMY AND SACRILEGE OF SANCTIONED

SHRINES,

SLOGAN: AGAINST PATHOS, FESTIVITIES, AND CELEBRATION!

Today, I will revise my ATTITUDE from 1944.

In the 1960s, having come across dadaism, which had already then been a museum piece, I realized that my protest of 1944 was the protest of Dada in 1914.

I felt that I was Dada's son and it was only then that I learned the name of my "father."

To make a distinction between a theatre EVENT and performance of *The Return of Odysseus*, I will refer to my artistic ATTITUDE as: THE TIME OF ODYSSEUS.

A feeling of an inescapable death, which was the mark of the war

and a premonition in my THEATRE OF DEATH thirty years later,

covered my attitude and that time with a veil of metaphysics which was alien to the spirit of DADA.

The concept of POOR-NESS, which was fully explored in my IDEA OF REALITY OF THE LOWEST RANK, contained in itself a dose of LYRICAL tone and (heaven forbid!) EMOTIONS,

which were foreign to Dada.

These are the differences that make THE TIME OF ODYSSEUS mine.

1944 to the present.

This attitude, whose shocking, but precious to me, symptoms I have just enumerated, ought to have disappeared at the end of the war.

The 1940s . . . 50s . . . 60s . . . 70s . . . have passed.

Artistic ideas have been breaking the surface,

however, all the time, as if from far beyond, maybe, it was my inner voice, I have been perceiving warning signals that ordered me and dictated that I choose one action over the other—

PROTEST,

REVOLT

AGAINST THE OFFICIALLY RECOGNIZED SACRED SITES,

AGAINST EVERYTHING THAT HAD A STAMP OF "APPROVAL,"

FOR REALNESS,

FOR "POVERTY. . . ."

Is it possible that the time of contempt,

of bloody and wild instincts,

of absurd actions by authorities who refuse to become "civilized"

has never left us since the dawn of history?

The answer to this question is indubitably given by the art of the discussed decades.

"Listen" carefully and you will hear the answer.

In 1948, the authority in power

attempts to put an end to the freedom of art.

In my little and confined room of imagination

I begin to hear clearly in my art the liberating

"ORDERS" of those times.

They become a part of me, my own.

The only true ones.

Fascinating.

I begin to realize that I have to make them clearer, increase their energy level, and give them the power of aggression!

At the same time, I have to make quite an important "REVISION" in order for the spirit of DADA and the TIME OF ODYSSEUS to stay alive.

With the passing of time, other perilous symptoms of our epoch emerged and grew in strength. Those were:

NARROW-MINDED BUREAUCRACY,

OMNI-PRESENT TECHNOLOGY,

CANNIBALISTIC CONSUMPTION,

COMMON AND MANDATORY MATERIALISM OF LIFE THAT DEVOURS HUMAN MIND AND SPIRIT.

Nightmarish malls have become the temples of a new deity of consumption and materialism.

I am listening carefully to that "Inner Voice":

ONE HAS TO STAY UNFAITHFUL TO THIS NEW TEMPLE AND THIS NEW GOD AT ALL COSTS!

My creative work, whose roots are grounded in the subconscious, "understood" this inner voice and command much earlier and quicker. The Intellect goes through and becomes aware of a different and NEW STAGE of cognizance:

SPIRITUALISM,

SPIRITUAL IMPERATIVE,

PREMONITION OF THE OTHER WORLD,

THE MEANING OF DEATH,

THE MEANING OF THE "IMPOSSIBLE,"

"AN IMPATIENT WAITING AT THE DOORS," BEHIND WHICH THERE ARE REGIONS THAT ARE INACCESSIBLE TO OUR MINDS AND CONCEPTS. . . .

I do not have the time to speculate whether or not this mysterious "assemblage" has been rooted in my subconscious and my character for a long time.

This "revision" seems to be anti-Dada. However, it seems so only at the first glance. The Dadaists were against their time and their world. This "revision" is also done to our present time. A big one! It is a correction of our world, whose strength has grown to an uncontrollable degree.

At the same time, the madness of the material world leads to other types of madness: hyper-baroque conventions in art, an unrestrained spread of ILLUSION, and a delirium of eccentricity. Surrealism and its means are used indiscriminately in impotent actions void of any intellectual power. The only purpose in art is to show and demonstrate their eccentricity.

Imagination, that dangerous and blasphemous region of human psyche excavated by the Surrealists, is turned into a mechanism producing fireworks.

Charlatans and mediocrity pretend to be the high priests of MAGNIFICENCE.

In a period of terror by the trend for MAKING EVERYTHING STRANGE (which has nothing to do with "magnificence" in surrealism)

one needs courage to suggest:

EVERYDAY,

BANAL,

POOR,

AND UNADORNED
REALITY.
Today, it is only REALITY that can give birth to true
MAGNIFICENCE,
"IMPOSSIBLE,"
SUPERSENSUOUS.
IT IS ENOUGH TO TAKE CAUSE-AND-EFFECT FROM IT!
REALITY WILL BE AUTONOMOUS AND NAKED.
AND THIS IS ALSO A KIND OF "REVISION."
After many years, the war slogans of Dada and surrealism are mixed together.
New forms emerge.
New forces appear which threaten human freedom.
If we want to stay faithful to the spirit of nonconformity, we must find in ourselves
a NEW SPIRIT OF REVOLT, even if it is foreign to the old slogans.
This is the reason why we have to "revise" constantly.
The Surrealists differed from the Dadaists in that they added positive, scientific,
and cognitive values to the destructive slogans of Dada.
They believed that the function of art is not only to provide intellectual and
aesthetic stimulation, but also to REVOLUTIONIZE human awareness, which
was in the grip of stereotypes and the patterns of a practical mind, to destroy a
pragmatic, practical experience of the real world, to expand awareness to include
new regions of the psyche previously dismissed,
and, finally, to reach a higher level of human existence.
In the context of this logical argument and this perfect train of thought, today
we are distrustful, almost feeling guilty: we do not believe anymore in rational
arguments.
THE EXPERIENCES OF THE XXTH CENTURY HAVE TAUGHT US THAT
LIFE DOES NOT RECOGNIZE RATIONAL
ARGUMENTS.
By so saying, we are more irrational than
irrational surrealism.
And this is the first revision.
Today, we also know how PERILOUS ARE SOCIETY'S MOTIVATIONS FOR
THE ARTS.
And this is the second revision.
Art's didactic purpose and its utilitarian tendencies no longer provide a convincing
argument.
Utilitarian arguments concerning the accessibility of art, and creativity based on
the principle that "and you too can be an artist," advocate MEDIOCRITY!
And this is the third revision:
It is only one's world which is of any importance, that is,
the world which is created in isolation and separation,
the world which is so strong and suggestive,
that it has enough power to occupy and maintain
a predominant part of the space
within the space of life!
In this sense,

THE SPACE OF LIFE, AND EVERYTHING THAT IS CONTAINED IN THIS
PHRASE,
EXISTS PARALLEL TO
THIS OTHER SPACE,
THE SPACE OF ART.
THE TWO OF THEM CONVERGE, OVERLAP,
AND COALESCE
SHARING THEIR FATE AND DESTINY. . . .
AND THIS IS ENOUGH![46]

My Room
(1990)

The following are a few additional explanations and comments:
engulfed within this gnawing turbulence of
reflections, feelings, doubts, and hopes,
I need to set my past in order,
I need to review my ideas in the context of here and now,
I need to put old ideas aside into the chest of memory—
simply, I need to clear the field of action
for my new production.
My room onstage andthe plot
The action takes place onstage.
A real action. Let us assume so.
I have decided to move in and live onstage—
I have here my bed, my table, my chair, and, of course, my paintings.
I have often imagined my room in a theatre,
inside of the theatre,
onstage, rather than in a hotel.
So, my—as I call it—Poor Room of Imagination
is placed onstage.
I have to arrange it.
It should not look like a stage room.
I will assemble onstage, in this room of mine, all the objects
as though I really decided to *live* here.
A bed, a table, a chair,
doors (important),
an oven with a chimney, and
"canvases" on easels.
A ROOM
Mine.
Private.
The only place
in this w o r l d,
the world ruled by the ruthless laws of
collectivism,
banality,
and society;

the only place
in this world,
where the individual,
policed by society,
can hide,
be a master of his fate and destiny.
A Poor place,
whose existence is constantly endangered by
the "public mechanisms" [of power]
Is this the reason why
this "sacred place"
this "HOME of mine"
is exposed onstage to the public?
These statements are not empty phrases or metaphors.
They are TRUTH.
My life and my destiny
have always identified themselves with
my works of art. A Work of Art.
They have always realized themselves in my work.
They have always found their solutions in it.
My HOME has always been and is
my Work.
A Painting, a production, a theatre, a stage.
My "credo": The only complete truth in art is
a representation of one's own life,
a disclosure of all its details without shame,
a discovery of one's F A T E
and D E S T I N Y.
I have often explained that the reasons for these processes
are grounded neither in exhibitionism nor in narcissism,
but in the desire to strengthen
the "individual life,"
in order to help it escape the imminent death
and the destruction by inhuman "c o l l e c t i v i s m."
This can be done by adding
one little word, "m y,"
to the "individual life."
The boundary between
the stage and the auditorium
is the victory line,
not to be crossed over,
not to be conquered.
This world of collective
and public life
has been irreversibly stopped
at this Maginot line.

A Painting
(1990)

Before I made a decision to
place my Poor Room of Imagination
onstage,
I placed a painting there;
an idea born contrary to all my principles.
In addition, the painting was standing on an easel.
The painting would be represented by a frame.
The presence of the easel would be marked at the bottom and at the top
[of the frame];
the space within the frame would be empty;
its depth would be filled by the actors
and the room-proprietor's imagination.
I am looking at a piece of paper with this idea on it—
. . . August, Thursday, 1989—
at the notes—
A painter is in his studio,
there is only a frame of his painting . . .
a painting . . . and what to do with reality, the reality with a capital R?
I will need to change my attitude toward reality. . . .—
and at the drawing—
a painting showing something hanging,
in front of it, there is a painter, who is energetically manipulating a long
brush around the hanged body,
the painter's bed is in the corner. . . .
At the bottom of the page, there is
a sequence of scenes and situations—
situations that haunted me
situations that could easily be created onstage
with the help of a mechanism such as a painting:
execution, war,
genocide,
war victims,
whores, brothels, masters,
ministers, generals,
policemen, spies. . . .—

and one more short
but telling note—
no one has ever done this before. . . .

The "p a i n t i n g" continued.

If I place my home onstage,
my Little Room of Imagination—
I am doing this for the first time—
if I place the painter's room onstage,
I have to show his paintings too.
At the beginning, I had my doubts about this idea.
I am against illusion;
however, mine is not the limited mind
of an orthodox person.
I know only too well that theatre cannot exist
without illusion.
I accept illusion,
because by accepting its existence,
I can keep destroying it interminably.
Each and every act of destruction in art
is always . . . positive!
I would like here to make a
correction of some of my ideas,
which I had fully presented in my
essay "Theatrical Space."
It was the 1970s.
A correction was necessary,
because the nature and the matter of a performance
had been altered.
At that time I wrote:
". . . After the war, I encountered
Surrealism.
I felt that my roots were firmly grounded
in Surrealism.
There was a reason why I spent my formative years in Kraków,
in this Polish Necropolis
and the Polish capitol of Symbolism.
However, from the very beginning, something essential
separated me from that artistic trend.
From the very beginning, I was suspicious about
illusion,
this principle element
which would give birth to
the surrealistic 'm a r v e l'
('*le marveilleux*').
From the very beginning, I was close

to R E A L I T Y.
1944,
The Return of Odysseus.
I announced proudly that Reality,
the reality of life,
should be
the matter of the work of art.
I gave it the name
P O O R   R E A L I T Y.
Later, I named it
the F O U N D   R E A L I T Y
('*realité trouvée*')
Dada—which had created this term—
had been forgotten by that time.
But, while gradually discovering its past history,
I found myself more attracted to it than to Surrealism.
This is the reason why I labeled my 1944 discovery with
a term that was accepted by history."

In that memorable year of 1944,
I pronounced another important word:
real p l a c e.
A theatrical place;
however, not the official place
reserved for the presentation of a drama,
but a place which was wrenched from the reality of life,
a place which belonged to life's practice
and to the everyday.
It is here that my correction can be seen.
The FICTION of drama enters
life's ("found") p l a c e
during some mystical act.
A Grand Entree of the Theatre of Death.
It was this banal Reality of life—
whose qualities were limited by life's
practical and utilitarian functions—
which allowed us to see any act of probing it
with anything that was not a part of it
as a *transgression*
so alien and unbelievable it
could be perceived as
THE IMPRINT OF AN ACTIVITY
FROM THE "OTHER SIDE,"
from the other world!
(I believe that an artistic activity,
which can neither be fully explained
nor agree with the logic of life,
is an imprint of the activity from "the other side"

[*de l'au-delà*].)
. . . The Fiction of drama enters the Reality of life. . . .
With the passing of time, this dictum was changed
because drama (dramatic fiction) was no longer used
in my theatre.
Action and stage *personae*
were born onstage
during the "creative process,"
during the rehearsals.
While working on *Wielopole, Wielopole*
I made a correction.
I wrote then: ". . . it must be a
MEMORY Room
which I keep reconstructing over and over again and which is destroyed
over and over again;
a room which is pulsating.
The space of Reality must be expanded in order for it to embrace
such non-physical territories as
MEMORY.
One needs to place an equation mark between Memory and Reality.
This means that one needs to create
a real structure of m e m o r y,
of its activities.
This structure will be constituted by the ACTION of
recalling memories.
The action of memory."

Those few notions from the past,
like commandments, are still protecting
my act of creation.

The "Found Reality,"
the "real (found) place,"
became in time nothing more than a convention,
having lost its power to oppose FICTION,
all because of imitation and due to a gradual
acceptance by the audience.
Radical actions were pushed aside into different territories.

What was left were the REALITY postulate
and the adjective POOR (reality).

Today, I will add another element:
to construct
without illustrative ILLUSION.
A kind of a construction site or a storage-room
of objects which are its inherent parts.

Such a site is presented in
my current production,
Today Is My Birthday.
Onstage (sic!),
I am putting together (CONSTRUCTING) my home,
my POOR room of imagination.

The method of
p l a c i n g
a c t i o n s and s i t u a t i o n s,
which are shockingly and scandalously out of place,
has acquired a particular significance.
For example, in *I Shall Never Return*,
the fate of the most important matters of life and art
was decided in the inn—
in the c l a s h between two alien systems
which would never explain or complement each other.
The action, which was neither supported
nor "illustrated" by the environment,
became sharp and shriekingly
r e a l.

If suddenly we stopped making a distinction between
f i c t i o n and l i f e,
we would be placed at the threshold of schizophrenia.
The people from the world of f i c t i o n
enter my room.
I would meet them at the stairway,
at the street corner;
they do not differ from us,
but they behave in a strange way;
they avoid me;
they pretend that they are preoccupied with something;
they run away.
Fiction penetrates my real life.

And again:
in *Today Is My Birthday*,
this CLASH
between two a l i e n systems
is an act of VIOLENCE.
My Poor Room
is invaded by the "ORGANS" of war—
a tank, a gun-barrel, a "squad car";
my poor room is turned into a
battlefield.
It is more than just "out of place."

There is also a different quality of this "clash"
void of any logic:
". . . the mob is pushing forward . . ."
No commentary . . .

The functioning of ILLUSION
and IMITATION
in a theatrical process and activity
became accepted to such a degree
that they were no longer questioned.
REPRESENTATION:
in the era of all-embracing avant-gardes,
I rejected this notion,
I called it names—
"reproduction," "pretense," etc.
Of course, what was rejected was the "representation"
employed in conventional theatres,
defined by the whole baggage or system of
l i f e's n a r r a t i v e
plot development,
life's c a u s e s and e f f e c t s,
life's purpose.
From the very beginning, I made use of
procedures which extirpated
life's c a u s e s and e f f e c t s
from s i t u a t i o n s, f i g u r e s, o b j e c t s,
a c t i o n s.
What was left was r e a l n e s s itself.
"Representing" as such lost its reason for being.

The epithet:
p r e t e n c e,
its pejorative meaning was
consciously and unequivocally
expressed through PLAYING in my theatre.
It successfully destroyed
illusion
sustained by the psychology of life.
[Playing] ran efficiently on NOTHINGNESS.
The notion of "nothingness" was very
important in my work.
This type of r e p r e s e n t a t i o n,
this "p r e t e n c e,"
this playing on n o t h i n g n e s s,
are very effective during
the process of recalling
m e m o r i e s,

or the functioning of m e m o r y,
during which we are faced with
a phenomenon,
which is derivative,
repetitive,
bereft of concrete or solid grounding.
This is exactly what happens in
Today Is My Birthday.
(This is also what happened in past productions.)
The existence of the P A I N T I N G and its interior
in this production create the illusion of the SECOND DEGREE,
in the presence of which my Poor Room
onstage
(which could be seen as illusion)
becomes r e a l i t y.

In *Today Is My Birthday,*
a threshold between
the world of ILLUSION
and our world of REALITY
is crossed.
This has already been discussed.
I want to emphasize that this
method of action is an important characteristic of this production.

And one more observation:
in the process of falling out of the world of illusion
and falling into the real world
elements, illusions, people
provoke the DISINTEGRATION OF ILLUSION ITSELF.

From the Beginning My Credo Was . . .
(1990)

From the beginning, my
c r e d o was that art has never been and can never be a
representation of,
or a **mirror** held up to the reality of
life.
This primitive creed
was upheld only by the dogmas of naturalism
and materialism.
Art is
an **answer**
to reality.
This imperative **need** to
provide an **answer** is probably
the very essence of the creative process.
The more tragic this reality is,
the stronger the "inner" dictate to
provide an answer,
to create
a "different" reality which is
f r e e, autonomous,
able to win a moral victory over
the other one,
and bring
spiritual dignity back into our time.

I was true to my
nature,
my need to question and
protest.

This situation, whose
inhuman conditions
would compel me
to provide an a n s w e r,
gave me

s t r e n g t h and s e l f - d e t e r m i n a t i o n
indispensable in the process of
creating a g r e a t work of art.
this quality was of great importance to me.

I hope that I have explained
sufficiently
the function of reality in my art,
reality, in which
I had to live,
and to which I would constantly return
against the laws of logic and
against common sense.

There was, thus, the reality of life,
which has already been sufficiently described and
positioned,
and in it, or against it,
my theatre,
my paintings,
my works of art—
the Other reality—
which was autonomous and free.

As I have already stated,
the Other [reality] was not and was not supposed to be
a representation or
a reflection of reality.
Nor was it
a narrative or a document
whose function would be to brand,
to indict and
call for questioning before the jury
and history.
This method of
putting together a performance,
which is used so frequently today
when there is unlimited freedom of speech,
was a l i e n to me.
I wanted something more.
I wanted to reach "deeper."
What does this mean?
This means that the plans
for my "maneuvers" were not restricted to
the Polish theatre of reality, but
would penetrate the
world theatre of thought,

expressed through art.
(I was often accused of lacking
patriotism in my own country.)
From the very beginning,
I was absorbed by the ideas
of the radical avant-garde.
Radical art charmed me
with the risks it was taking;
the ideas of the avant-garde were
universal, worldly; they
**transgressed the boundaries between countries,
and transcended the destinies of motherlands.**
The precise ideas of the avant-garde
were not limited to only one discipline; they
infiltrated the whole of art:
poetry, visual arts,
music, and theatre.
As I was trained to be able to feel
the logic of art,
I paid attention to and valued:
deep knowledge
about art:
thinking,
definitions and
methods.
This is the reason why
I have always been critical about
theatres, or to be more precise,
those theatre groups that
have mushroomed all over in the last few decades,
which exploited the great "discoveries" of
Surrealism and the Happening
in a superficial manner, for mere effect,
without any commitment to the ideas
or . . . knowledge about them.
I am disclosing the details concerning
my attitudes toward art, which cannot be
contained in commonly accepted opinions.
Anyway, the commonly accepted opinions frequently
turn out to be nothing more than **misconceptions**.

Let me proceed further.
In the post-war reality
(already described in detail)
the situation and the status of
the rebel,
the dissident,

the political emigrant
was almost a cause for veneration.
I was among those who contributed [to this attitude],
even though those situations and statuses
were a l i e n to me.
It seemed ridiculous to me to
position my ideas
within and against the intellectual vacuum
of all those policemen of cultural
and human lives.
The notion of being an emigrant was
in conflict with my need to
question and protest;
my need for the "w a l l"
to hit my head against—
this signified a creative process for me.
Let me continue.
Underground.
Clandestine activities.
A traditional, romantic evaluation of those activities
seemed to me, God forbid,
somewhat
s u p e r f i c i a l.
A natural human desire is to
be in **contact** with the world,
the d e s i r e to be in c o n t a c t
at any price.
In the 1950s, I used to paint a lot,
even though I knew that
I would not be allowed to exhibit
my works.
Although I painted solely "for myself,"
I needed to do so,
I did not consider my work
a "c l a n d e s t i n e" activity.
On the contrary. My paintings were
a window to the world, to the free world
as well as its thoughts and ideas.
I did believe that there would come a time
when my paintings would be l o o k e d a t.
I did not know
what function they could
perform then. It was enough for me, however,
that, when I was painting them in
the enclosed space of my studio,
I was f r e e.

I want to reach t r u t h,
I want to reach this deepest and rawest layer
by stripping and leaving behind
all those
"o r n a m e n t a t i o n s"
used to dress, trim, and adorn it . . .

I want to state openly that
this need to create theatre
and visual arts,
which would be d i f f e r e n t
from the reality of political terror and
of police vigilance,
was grounded neither
in a moral obligation
to create
a R e s i s t a n c e   M o v e m e n t,
nor in feelings of p a t r i o t i s m,
nor in the h e r o i s m of the underground movement.
I do believe that this process of
creating a d i f f e r e n t,
o t h e r
reality, whose freedom is not
bound by the laws of any system of life,
or the act itself, which is like a Demiurge's act
or a dream,
is the aim of art.
I keep stubbornly repeating this thought,
because I am suspicious that,
in the epoch of "the Spring of the Masses,"
and of the fight for political and economic freedom,
this notion of
the highest freedom
which is demanded by
art
will not be understood,
or even deemed unnecessary. . . .
Freedom in art
is a gift neither from
the politicians
nor the authorities.
Freedom is not bestowed
upon art by the authorities.
Freedom exists inside of us.
We have to fight for freedom
within ourselves,
in our most intimate interior,

in our solitude,
in our suffering.
It is the most delicate domain,
the domain of soul and spirit.
This is the reason why I am
suspicious about those theatres,
and artistic activities in general,
which have emerged recently
during the "dictatorship of the Proletariat"
with (*a priori*) programs
of the fight for political freedom
for religious freedom,
for patriotism.
The situation was worsened when
avant-gardish ideologies
were also mixed into these programs.

Notes

PREFACE

1 *Kantor, A Journey through Other Spaces: Essays and Manifestos, 1944–1990,* trans. and critical comm. Michal Kobialka (Berkeley: University of California Press, 1993); "Forget Kantor," *Performing Arts Journal* 47 (May 1994): 1–17.
2 See "The Emballage."
3 Alain Badiou, *Ethics: An Essay on Understanding of Evil* (London: Verso, 2001), 42–43.
4 Tadeusz Kantor, "The Milano Lessons: Lesson 12," in *Journey*, 258–59.
5 Hans-Thies Lehmann, *Postdramatic Theatre*, trans. Karen Jürs-Munby (New York: Routledge, 2006).
6 Jean-François Lyotard, *The Postmodern Explained*, trans. Don Barry, Bernadette Maher, Julian Pefanis, Virginia Spate, and Morgan Thomas (Minneapolis: University of Minnesota Press, 1993), 80.
7 Henri Lefebvre, *The Production of Space*, trans. Donald Nicholson-Smith (Oxford: Blackwell, 1991), 33.
8 Kantor, "The Milano Lessons: Lesson 12," in *Journey*, 260.
9 See Fredric Jameson, *A Singular Modernity: Essay on the Ontology of the Present* (London: Verso, 2002).
10 Gilles Deleuze, *The Deleuze Reader*, ed. Constantin V. Boundas (New York: Columbia University Press, 1993), 194.
11 Antonin Artaud, *Theatre and Its Double*, trans. Victor Corti (London: John Calder, 1970), 17.
12 See "My Work—My Journey."
13 See Kantor, "The Milano Lessons: Lesson 12," in *Journey*, 246–65.
14 Michel Foucault, quoted in Gilles Deleuze *Foucault*, trans. and ed. Seán Hand (Minneapolis: University of Minnesota Press, 1988), 119.
15 Theodor Adorno, *Minima Moralia* (London: Verso, 2002), 39.
16 See "The Room. Maybe a New Phase."

1. TOPOGRAPHY OF REPRESENTATION

1 Plato, *Phaedo*, trans. and ed. David Gallop (Oxford: Oxford University Press, 1993)
2 Aristotle, *Physics*, trans. Robin Waterfield (Oxford: Oxford University Press, 1996), 194a; 199a
3 Jean-François Lyotard, "Representation, Presentation, Unpresentable," in *The Inhuman: Reflections on Time*, trans. Geoffrey Bennington and Rachel Bowlby (Stanford: Stanford University Press, 1991), 119–20.
4 Gustave Courbet, "Art Cannot be Taught," in *Realism and Tradition in Art: 1848–1900*, ed. Linda Nochlin (Englewood Cliffs, NJ: Prentice-Hall, 1966), 35.
5 A. Forsee, *Albert Einstein: Theoretical Physicist* (New York: Macmillan, 1963), 81. For discussion of these theories and experiments, see, e.g., Max Jammer, *Concepts of Space* (Cambridge, MA: Harvard University Press, 1969); Milič Čapek, *The Philosophical Impact of Contemporary Physics* (New York: Van Nostrand Reinhold, 1961); Stephen Kern, *The Culture of Time and Space* (Cambridge, MA: Harvard University Press, 1983).

6 See Michal Kobialka, "Vulnerable Space: The Symbolist Desire/Practice of Thinking the Other," *Yearbook of Interdisciplinary Studies in the Fine Arts* (1991): 277–98.

7 Vasilii Kandinsky, "Reminiscences," in *Complete Writings on Art*, 2 vols. (Boston: G. K. Hall, 1982), 1:364.

8 See, e.g., Linda Dalrymple Henderson, *The Fourth Dimension and Non-Euclidean Geometry in Modern Art* (Princeton: Princeton University Press, 1983); J. H. Matthews, *Theatre in Dada and Surrealism* (Syracuse, NY: Syracuse University Press, 1974); Christiana J. Taylor, *Futurism: Politics, Painting and Performance* (Ann Arbor, MI: UMI Press, 1979); Annabelle Melzer, *Latest Rage and Big Drum* (Ann Arbor, MI: UMI Press, 1980).

9 George Steiner, *No Passion Spent* (New Haven, CN: Yale University Press, 1996), 129.

10 Theodor Adorno, "Commitment," in *The Essential Frankfurt Reader*, ed. Andrew Arato and Eike Gebhart (Oxford: Basil Blackwell, 1978), 300–318.

11 Adorno, "Commitment," 312–13.

12 Ibid., 317.

13 While talking about the relationship between the authority and nonautonomous forms, Adorno observes that "newspapers and magazines of the radical Right constantly stir up indignation against what is unnatural, over-intellectual, morbid and decadent: they know their readers. The insights of social psychology into the authoritarian personality confirm them. The basic features of this type include conformism, respect for a petrified facade of opinion and society, and resistance to impulses that disturb its order or evoke inner elements of the unconscious that cannot be admitted" (ibid., 303).

14 Jacques Derrida, "The Theatre of Cruelty and the Closure of Representation," in *Writing and Difference* (London: Routledge & Kegan Paul, 1978), 232–50.

15 Ibid., 232.

16 Ibid., 233–34.

17 Ibid., 233.

18 Ibid., 234.

19 Ibid., 235.

20 Ibid., 237.

21 Ibid., 235.

22 Ibid., 238.

23 Ibid., 243–46.

24 Ibid., 249.

25 C. Wright Mills, *Power, Politics, and the People*, ed. Irving Louis Horowitz (New York: Ballantine, 1963), 299.

26 Kantor, "The Milano Lessons: Lesson 12," in *A Journey through Other Spaces: Essays and Manifestos, 1944–1990*, trans. and critical comm. Michal Kobialka (Berkeley: University of California Press, 1993), 258.

27 Kantor, "Annexed Reality," in *Journey*, 71.

28 Kantor, "Teatr Niezależny," in *Tadeusz Kantor—Metamorfozy*, ed. Krzysztof Pleśniarowicz (Kraków: Wydawnictwo Naukowe, 2000), 72–74.

29 Ibid., 74–76.

30 Ibid., 77.

31 Ibid., 77–78.

32 Artaud, quoted in Derrida, "Theatre of Cruelty," 237.

33 The cast of *Balladyna* included Maria Krasicka (Balladyna), Ewa Siedlecka (Widow), Jerzy Turowicz (Kirkor), Henryk Jasiecki (Hermit), Tadeusz Brzozowski (Grabiec), Franciszek Puget (Councilor), Janina Kraupe (Goplana's voice), Marta Stebnicka (Skierka), Anna Chwalibożanka (Chochlik), Marcin Wenzel (Filon), and Mieczysław Porębski (Commentator).

34 Kantor, quoted in Krzysztof Pleśniarowicz, *Kantor* (Wrocław: Wydawnictwo Dolnośląskie, 1997), 49.

35 See Oskar Schlemmer, "Man and Art Figure," in *The Theater of the Bauhaus*, ed. Walter Gropius and Arthur S. Wensinger (Middletown, CN: Wesleyan University Press, 1961); V. Kandinsky, *Concerning the Spiritual in Art* (New York: Wittenborn, Schultz, 1947).

36 The cast of *The Return of Odysseus* included Nana Lauowa (Penelope), Tadeusz Brzozowski (Odysseus), Marta Stebnicka (Telemachus), Anna Chwalibożanka (Melantho), Marcin Wenzel (Phemius), Ali Bunsch (The Suitor, The Servant), Andrzej

Cybulski (The Suitor, The Shepherd), Franciszek Puget (The Suitor).

37 Kantor, "Ulisses," in *Metamorfozy*, 94–95.

38 Kantor, "Powrót Odysa," in *Metamorfozy*, 99–100.

39 Kantor, "The Milano Lessons: Lesson 1," in *Journey*, 211.

40 Kantor, "Teatr Niezależny," in *Metamorfozy*, 66.

41 See "From the Beginning My Credo Was . . . "

42 Walter Benjamin, *Illuminations*, ed. and intro. Hannah Arendt (New York: Schocken Books, 1968), 257.

43 See "Theatrical Place."

44 Kantor, "The Milano Lessons: Lesson 1," in *Journey*, 211–12.

45 Giorgio Agamben, *Infancy and History: Essays on the Destruction of Experience*, trans. Liz Heron (London: Verso, 1993), 101.

46 Adorno, 318.

47 Kantor, "Teatr Cricot 2," in *Metamorfozy*, 144.

48 Kantor, "Klisze przyszłości," in *Metamorfozy*, 109.

49 Christina Lodder, *Russian Constructivism* (New Haven, CN: Yale University Press, 1983), 61.

50 Mieczysław Porębski, "Pierwszy rok," in *W kręgu lat czterdziestych*, ed. Józef Chrobak (Kraków: Galeria Krzysztofory, 1992), IV: 68.

51 Tadeusz Kantor and Mieczysław Porębski, "Grupa Młodych Plastyków po raz drugi," in *Deska*, ed. and comm. Mieczysław Porębski (Warszawa: Murator, 1997), 31–36

52 Kantor, "The Milano Lessons: Lesson 1," in *Journey*, 208.

53 Kantor, quoted in Wiesław Borowski, *Kantor* (Warszawa: Wydawnictwo Artystyczne i Filmowe, 1982), 31. See also Tadeusz Kantor, "Surrealizm," in *Stowarzyszenie Artystyczne—Grupa Krakowska: W kręgu lat czterdziestych* (Kraków: Galeria Krzysztofory, 1990), 27–28.

54 Borowski, "Rozmowa z Tadeuszem Kantorem," in *Kantor*, 32–33; *Metamorfozy*, 111–12.

55 Malevich quoted in Charlotte Douglas, *Swans of Other Worlds: Kazimir Malevich and the Origins of Abstraction in Russia* (Ann Arbor, MI: UMI Research Press, 1980), 107.

56 Kantor, "The Milano Lessons: Lesson 3," in *Journey*, 217–18; "Po wojnie," in *Metamorfozy*, 123–24.

57 Kantor, "Komentarze intymne do rysunków okresu metaforycznego," in *Metamorfozy*, 130.

58 Ibid.

59 For a detailed discussion of these two meetings, see Klaudiusz święcicki, *Historia w teatrze Tadeusza Kantora* (Poznań: Wydawnictwo Poznańskie, 2007), chap. 2.

60 Kantor, "O sztuce (O marzeniu)," in *Tadeusz Kantor: Wędrówka* (Kraków: Cricoteka, 2000), 166–67.

61 See the chronology in *Journey*, 3–14 or http://www.cricoteka.com.pl/en for productions designed by Kantor in the period between 1950 and 1955

62 Kantor, "Teatr Artystyczny," *Życie Literackie* 173 (1955): 5.

63 Ibid., 5.

64 See "The Informel Theatre."

65 Kantor, "Warunki teatru autonomicznego," in *Metamorfozy*, 169. In 1955, together with Maria Jarema, Kantor organized Cricot 2 at the Dom Plastyków (The House of the Visual Artists) in Kraków. (From 1956 until 1990, the Cricot 2 Theatre was housed at the Krzysztofory Gallery in Kraków, a Renaissance building that belonged to the Catholic Church. The Kraków authorities gave Kantor the first floor and the basement. Nearly all the performances and exhibits of Kantor's works were presented in the rectangular low-vaulted ceiling rooms of the basement.) The founding manifesto, "Powstanie Cricot 2" (unpublished ms., 1955), stated that "the Theatre assumes the name of Cricot 2, thereby perceiving itself as a continuator of the tradition of the pre-war theatre bearing the same name. Cricot 2 is the actors' theatre, theatre which seeks its new and radical methods of acting in contact with the avant-garde artists. Cricot 2 Theatre puts forward the idea of theatre defined as a work of art, governed by its own autonomous existence, and opposed to a traditional theatre of thoughtless procreation of forms, which has irrevocably lost the freedom to create and the power of action." The first Cricot was founded by Józef Jarema in Kraków in the spring of 1933. It was the experimental theatre of avant-garde visual artists (Henryk Gotlieb, Maria Jarema, Włodzimierz Marczyński, Piotr Potworowski, Andrzej Pronaszko, Ludwik Puget, Czesław Rzepiński, Jonasz Stern, Zygmunt Waliszewski, and Henryk Wiciński), musicians (Jan Ekier, Artur Maławski, Alojzy Kluczniok, and Leon Goldfuss-Arten), actors-directors (Wojciech Woźnik and Władysław Krzemiński), and of people who were not directly associated with the arts. Among the actors, e.g., were a teacher of Polish literature (Stanisław Żytyński), doctors (Gustaw Nowotny, Kazimierz Makoś), a lawyer (Ludwik Gołąb), an amateur dancer (Jacek Puget), and future actresses (Elżbieta Osterwianka, Zula Dywińska). The performances of plays were accompanied by a variety of other events, including mime and dance recitals, formalistic recitations of poetry, recitations of the works of the Polish futurists (Peiper), presentation of the old French-style cabaret ballads, and satires about Kraków's cultural and artistic life. Cricot was deeply rooted in European avant-garde artistic movements of the time and in Polish modernism. See Stanisław Marczak-Oborski, *Teatr w Polsce: 1918–1939* (Warszawa: Państwowy Instytut Wydawniczy, 1984), 288–94.

66 Borowski, "Rozmowa z Tadeuszem Kantorem," 51–52.

67 Kantor, "Teatr Cricot 2," in *Metamorfozy*, 145.

68 The cast of *The Cuttlefish* included Jadwiga Marso (Alice d'Or), Kazimierz Mikulski (Paul Rockoffer), Krzysztof Pankiewicz (The Head on the Column), Stefania Górniak (Rockoffer's Deceased Wife I), Zofia Bielawska (Rockoffer's Deceased Wife II), Stanisław Nowak (The

Uncle I), Andrzej Pawłowski (The Uncle II), Marian Słojkowski (Pope Julius II), Maria Jarema (The Old Woman I), Krystyna Łukasiewicz (The Old Woman II), Maria Ciesielska (Ella), Jerzy Nowak (Hyrcan IV), Stanisław Gronkowski (The Servant).

69 Borowski, "Rozmowa z Tadeuszem Kantorem," 52.

70 Ibid., 52.

71 Stanisław Ignacy Witkiewicz (Witkacy), *The Cuttlefish*, trans. D. Gerould, in *A Treasury of the Theatre*, ed. J. Gassner and B. Dukore (New York: Simon & Schuster, 1970), 626–37.

72 Zbigniew Herbert, "Cricot 2," *Twórczość* 7 (1957): 160.

73 Kantor, "Partytura 'Mątwy' S. I. Witkiewicza, 1956," in *Metamorfozy*, 158–60.

74 *The Cuttlefish*, in *A Treasury of the Theatre*, 626–28.

75 Kantor, "Abstrakcja umarła, niech żyje abstrakcja," in *Metamorfozy*, 179.

76 Kantor, "Notatnik," in *Metamorfozy*, 182.

77 Kantor, quoted in Pleśniarowicz, *Kantor* (1997), 103.

78 Kantor, "Notatnik," in *Metamorfozy*, 184.

79 *The Deleuze Reader*, ed. and intro. Constantin V. Boundas (New York: Columbia University Press, 1993), 165.

80 *Deleuze Reader*, 167.

81 Kantor, "Litania sztuki informel—1955," in *Metamorfozy*, 190.

82 The cast of *The Country House* included Maria Zającówna (The Mother), Leszek Kubanek (The Steward of the Estate), Hanna Szymańska (The Governess), Stanisław Rychlicki (Nibek), Jan Güntner (The Poet), Tadeusz Walczak (The Factotum), Bogdan Schmidt and Stefania Górniak (The Orphans).

83 Stanisław Ignacy Witkiewicz (Witkacy), *The Country House*, trans. Daniel Gerould (unpublished ms.).

84 Tadeusz Kantor, "Szafa," in *Ambalaże* (Warszawa: Galeria Foksal, 1976), 13.

85 Kantor, "W małym dworku—Partytura," in *Metamorfozy*, 210.

86 Ibid., 224.

87   Kantor, "Odczyt w Budapeszcie," in *Tadeusz Kantor: Wędrówka*, 180.

88   Jean-François Lyotard, *Postmodern Fables*, trans. Georges van den Abbeele (Minneapolis: University of Minnesota Press, 1993), 217.

89   Bertolt Brecht, "On Gestic Music," in *Brecht on Brecht*, trans. John Willett (New York: Hill and Wang, 1986), 104.

90   Kantor, "Czy możliwy jest powrót Orfeusza!" in *Metamorfozy*, 193.

91   Kantor, "Okolice zera," in *Metamorfozy*, 245.

92   See "The Emballage."

93   Ibid.

94   Kantor, "Ubranie—Emballage," in *Metamorfozy*, 346.

95   Stanisław Ignacy Witkiewicz (Witkacy), *The Madman and the Nun*, in *The Madman and the Nun*, ed. and trans. Daniel Gerould and C. S. Durer (Seattle: University of Washington Press, 1968). The cast of *The Madman and the Nun* included Jan Güntner (Alexander Walpurg), Hanna Szymańska (Sister Anna), Maria Stangret (Mother Superior), Stanisław Rychlicki (Dr. Jan Bidello), Tadeusz Korlatowicz (Dr. Ephraim Grün), Bogdan Śmigielski (Professor Ernest Walldorff), Zbigniew Bednarczyk, Tadeusz Kwinta, Józef Wieczorek (The Attendants).

96   In Witkacy's play, the hero, Walpurg, a decadent poet and drug addict, is confined in a straitjacket in the insane asylum, where an enthusiastic Freudian psychoanalyst, Dr. Grün, tries to discover his hidden complex. After seducing Sister Anna and murdering one of his doctors, Walpurg hangs himself in order to escape from further psychiatric persecution at the hands of his keepers. As his body lies on the floor of the madhouse, a cured and elegantly dressed Walpurg saunters through the door with the doctor he has recently killed. He takes the now-liberated nun to buy her clothes in town. The bewildered psychoanalyst Grün, feeling that he is the one who has gone mad, is left trapped in the asylum to battle the enraged guards and Walpurg's corpse.

97   See "The Zero Theatre."

98   Ibid.

99   See "Cricot 2 Theatre."

100   Jean-François Lyotard, *The Postmodern Explained*, trans. Don Barry, Bernadette Maher, Julian Pefanis, Virginia Spate, and Morgan Thomas (Minneapolis: University of Minnesota Press, 1993), 14.

101   Walter Benjamin, cited in Douglas Crimp, "This Is Not a Museum of Art," in *Marcel Broodthaers* (Minneapolis: Walker Art Center, 1989), 72.

102   Giorgio Agamben, *Means without End: Notes on Politics*, trans. Vicenzo Binetti and Cesare Casarino (Minneapolis: University of Minnesota Press, 2000), 57.

103   Mike Sell, "Bad Memory: Text, Commodity, Happenings," in *Contours of the Theatrical Avant-Garde: Performance and Textuality*, ed. James M. Harding (Ann Arbor, MI: University of Michigan Press, 2000), 160.

104   See *Happenings and Other Acts*, ed. Marielle R. Sandford (New York: Routledge, 1995).

105   The participants included Wiesław Borowski, Zbigniew Gostomski, Edward Krasiński, Anka Ptaszkowska, Erna Rosenstein, Mariusz Tchorek, Agnieszka Żółkiewska, Maria Stangret, Alfred Lenica, Krystyn Jarnuszkiewicz, and Tadeusz Kantor.

106   Borowski, 85.

107   Kantor "Happening-Cricotage," in *Metamorfozy*, 363–69.

108   Borowski, 85.

109   Jean Baudrillard, "The Murder of the Real," in *The Vital Illusion*, ed. Julia Witwer (New York: Columbia University Press, 2000), 61–83.

110   See "The Emballage."

111   The cast of *The Water-Hen* included Tadeusz Walczak (The Father), Jan Güntner (Edgar), Maria Stangret (Tadzio), Zbigniew Bednarczyk (Duchess Alice of Nevermore), Mira Rychlicka (The Water-Hen), Stanisław Rychlicki (The Scoundrel, Korbowa-Korbowski), Barbara Kober (The Girl I), Zofia Kalińska (The Girl II), Tadeusz Kwinta, Jan Krzyżanowski (Ephemer Typowicz), Lesław Janicki (Isaak Specter), Wacław Janicki (Alfred Evader), Jacek Stokłosa (The Soldier I), Adam Marszalik (The Soldier II), Franciszek Boczkajn (The

Waiter I), Jakub Kupiec (The Waiter II), Wojciech Wyrwa (The Waiter III), Maria Południak (The Woman), Piotr Pałamasz (The Legs).

112 Kantor, "Theatre-Happening," in *Journey*, 85–86.

113 Kantor, "Linia podziału," in *Metamorfozy*, 370.

114 Jean Baudrillard, *The System of Objects*, trans. James Benedict (London, New York: Verso, 1996), 16.

115 Kantor, "The Milano Lessons: Lesson 3," in *Journey*, 217.

116 *Deleuze Reader*, 194.

117 The participants included Zbigniew Gostomski, Edward Krasiński, Wiesław Borowski, Anka Ptaszkowska, Erna Rosenstein, Mariusz Tchorek, Maria Stangret, Tadeusz Kantor, and seven postmen.

118 Kantor, "List. Partytura," in *Metamorfozy*, 384–89.

119 Borowski, 93.

120 See, e.g., *Out of Action: Between Performance and the Object, 1949–1979*, a catalogue of an exhibition organized by Paul Schimmel (Los Angeles: Museum of Contemporary Art and New York: Thames and Hudson, 1998), 311.

121 Kantor, "Panoramiczny happening morski," in *Metamorfozy*, 393–402.

122 The bibliography on the subject is too extensive to be quoted here. For information about the Happenings see Allan Kaprow, *Assemblage, Environments, and Happenings* (New York: Harry N. Abrams, 1966), as well as Sell and Sandford.

123 Kantor, "Panoramiczny happening morski," in *Metamorfozy*, 400.

124 Ibid., 401.

125 Witkiewicz, *The Water-Hen*, in *The Madman and the Nun & The Crazy Locomotive: Three Plays, Including The Water-Hen*, ed., trans., and intro. Daniel Gerould and C. S. Durer; foreword by Jan Kott (New York: Applause Theatre, 1989), 37–79.

126 Kantor, "Kurka wodna. Partytura," in *Metamorfozy*, 425–28.

127 Ibid., 429–30.

128 Kantor, "Kryzys realnego miejsca," in *Teatr śmierci: teksty z lat 1975–1984*, ed. Krzysztof Pleśniarowicz (Wrocław: Ossolineum, 2004), 396.

129 Kantor, "Odczyt w Budapeszcie," in *Tadeusz Kantor: Wędrówka*, 181.

130 See "The 'i' Theatre."

131 Kantor, "Miejsce Teatralne," in *Wielopole, Wielopole* (Kraków: Wydawnictwo Literackie, 1986), 124. The cast of *Dainty Shapes and Hairy Apes* included Lesław Janicki, Wacław Janicki (The Cloakroom Attendants), Maria Stangret (Bestia Domestica), Zofia Kalińska (Princess Sophia), The Audience (40 Mandelbaums), Zbigniew Bednarczyk (Pandeus Clavercourse), Jan Güntner (Tarquinius Flirtius-Umbilicus), Stanisław Gronkowski (Sir Grant Blaguewell-Padlock), Bogdan Grzybowicz (Sir Thomas Blaso de Liza), Jacek Stokłosa (Dr. Don Nino de Gevach), Kazimierz Mikulski (Graf Andre Vladimirovich Tchurnin-Koketayev), Stanisław Rychlicki (The Gypsy), Wiesław Borowski (Oliphant Beedle), Zbigniew Gostomski (The Leader of the Mandelbaums, Goldmann Baruch Teerbroom).

132 Stanislaw Ignacy Witkiewicz (Witkacy), *Dainty Shapes and Hairy Apes*, in *The Belzebub Sonata*, trans. Daniel Gerould and Jadwiga Kosicka (New York: PAJ Publications, 1980).

133 Kantor, "Teatr niemożliwy," in *Metamorfozy*, 609.

134 *Deleuze Reader*, 194.

2. SPATIAL HISTORIOGRAPHY

1 It should be noted here that there were three versions of *The Dead Class*—version I: 1975–77, version II: 1977–86 (after 1500 performances, Kantor made the decision to no longer show *The Dead Class*), and version III, recreated by Kantor for a 1989 production filmed by Nat Lilenstein. The references in this chapter are to Kantor's notes to *The Dead Class* (the so-called "Partytura") as well as to Lilenstein's film version of *The Dead Class*. This cast of *The Dead Class* included Maria Stangret-Kantor

(The Woman with a Mechanical Cradle), Celina Niedźwiedzka (The Somnambulistic Whore), Andrzej Wełmiński (The Old Man with a Bicycle), Zbigniew Gostomski (The Woman behind the Window), Mira Rychlicka (The Old Man in the WC), Roman Siwulak (The Pedophile Old Man), Wacław Janicki (The Old Man with his Double), Lesław Janicki (The Double), Maria Krasicka (The Absent-Minded Old Man from the First Row), Jan Książek (The Absent-Minded Old Man from the Last Row), Jacek Stokłosa (A Soldier from World War I), Michał Krzysztofek (The Deaf Old Man), Teresa Wełmińska (The Dead Girl), Krzysztof Miklaszewski (Pedel), Stanisław Rychlicki (The Cleaning Woman–Death), Lech Stangret (Puer Aeternus). For a detailed analysis of the literary sources for *The Dead Class* and a performance analysis see Krzysztof Pleśniarowicz, *The Dead Memory Machine: Tadeusz Kantor's Theatre of Death* (Aberystwyth, Wales: Black Mountain Press, 2000).

2   The term "theatre of essence" comes from Jan Kott, *Kadysz: Strony o Tadeuszu Kantorze* (Gdańsk: Wydawnictwo słowo/ obraz teoria, 1997), 14.

3   The phrase "poisonous ingenuity of Time" can be found in Samuel Beckett, *Proust* (London: Chatto and Windus, 1931), 4.

4   Herbert Blau, *The Dubious Spectacle: Extremities of Theatre, 1976–2000* (Minneapolis: University of Minnesota Press, 2002), 2.

5   Jean-François Lyotard, *Inhuman Condition*, trans. Geoffrey Bennington and Rachel Bowlby (Stanford: Stanford University Press, 1991), 119–20.

6   See "Topography of Representation," for details.

7   Theodor Adorno, *Minima Moralia* (London: Verso, 1974), 39.

8   Foucault, *The Order of Things: An Archaeology of Human Sciences* (New York: Random House, 1973), 15.

9   William Shakespeare, *Hamlet* in *Shakespeare: Complete Works* (London: Oxford University Press, 1974), 1.1.

10   Samuel Beckett, *Edgame*, in *Stages of Drama*, ed. Carl H. Klaus, Miriam Gilbert,

and Bradford S. Field (Glenview, IL: Scott, Foresman & Co., 1981), 929.

11   Tadeusz Kantor, "Umarła klasa— Partytura," in *Pisma: Teatr śmierci— Teksty z lat 1975–1984*, ed. Krzysztof Pleśniarowicz (Wrocław: Ossolineum, 2005), 48–49.

12   Kantor, in *Pisma*, 48.

13   Samuel Beckett, *Ill Seen Ill Said* (London: John Calder, 1982), 29.

14   Ibid., 59.

15   Beckett, *Endgame*, 935.

16   Kantor, in *Pisma*, 50.

17   Samuel Beckett, *A Piece of Monologue*, in *The Collected Shorter Plays of Samuel Beckett* (New York: Gove Weidenfeld, 1984), 265.

18   This particular waltz, composed by Adam Karasiński with words by Andrzej Własta, is also know in Poland as "François-Waltz." Kantor used an instrumental version of the waltz in the production.

19   Kantor, in *Pisma*, 51–2

20   Beckett, *Ill Seen Ill Said*, 27.

21   The phrase "undialectical death" is taken from Roland Barthes, *Camera Lucida: Reflections on Photography*, trans. Richard Howard (New York: Hill and Wang, 1982), 72.

22   Beckett, *Proust*, 72.

23   Beckett, *Endgame*, 941.

24   Herbert Blau, *Sails of the Herring Fleet* (Ann Arbor, MI: Michigan University Press, 2000), 104.

25   Beckett, *Endgame*, 926.

26   Kantor, in *Pisma*, 62.

27   Ibid., 65.

28   Ibid., 63.

29   Ibid., 63–64.

30   Ibid., 72–73.

31   Ibid., 77.

32   Ibid., 78.

33   Cesare Pavese, "Death will come and will have your eyes," in *Disaffections: Complete Poems 1930–1950*, trans. Geoffrey Brock (Port Townsend, WA: Copper Canyon Press, 2002), 347.

34   Beckett, *A Piece of Monologue*, 265.

35   Beckett, *Endgame*, 926.

36   Kantor, in *Pisma*, 91–92.

37 Stanisław Witkiewicz (Witkacy), *Tumor Brainowicz*, in *Belzebub Sonata*, trans. and ed. Daniel Gerould (New York: Performing Arts Journal Publications, 1980).
38 Kantor, in *Pisma*, 96–97.
39 *Belzebub Sonata*, 72.
40 Kantor, in *Pisma*, 103.
41 Ibid., 108.
42 Ibid., 139.
43 Ibid., 142.
44 Ibid., 156.
45 George Steiner, "Absolute Tragedy," in *No Passion Spent* (New Haven: Yale University Press, 1996), 129.
46 Michel Foucault, quoted in Michel de Certeau, *Heterologies: Discourse on the Other*, trans. Brian Massumi (Minneapolis: University of Minnesota Press, 1986), 194.
47 Kantor, in *Pisma*, 175.
48 Kantor, in *Pisma*, 182.
49 Beckett, *Endgame*, 951.
50 Kantor, in *Pisma*, 92–93. See "The Dead Class."
51 Kantor, "Umarła klasa—Objaśnienia" (unpublished ms.), 1.
52 See "The Dead Class."
53 Kantor, *Klasa szkolna. Dzieło zamknięte*, exhibition catalogue, ed. Krzysztof Pleśniarowicz (Krakow: Cricoteka, 1995), 6; also, in Kantor, *Pisma*, 24–26.
54 See "The Theatre of Death."
55 Foucault, *The Order of Things*, 334.

3. THEATRE OF SIMILITUDE

1 Cicero, *De oratore*, ed. and trans. H. Rackham (Cambridge: Harvard University Press, 1976), 2:351–55; Quintilian, *Institutio oratoria*, ed. and trans. H. E. Butler (Cambridge: Harvard University Press, 1980).
2 William Shakespeare, *Hamlet*, 5.2, 368–75.
3 Jean-François Lyotard, *The Postmodern Explained*, trans. Don Barry, Bernadette Maher, Julian Pefanis, Virginia Spate, and Morgan Thomas (Minneapolis: University of Minnesota Press, 1992), 14.
4 Giorgio Agamben, *Remnants of Auschwitz: The Witness and the Archive*, trans. Daniel Heller-Roazen (New York: Zone Books, 1999), 12.
5 Tadeusz Kantor, "Emballage Manifesto," in *A Journey through Other Spaces: Essays and Manifestos, 1944–1990*, trans. Michal Kobialka (Berkeley: University of California Press, 1993), 81.
6 Kantor, "Miejsce Teatralne," in *Pisma: Teatr śmierci. Teksty z lat 1975–1984*, ed. Krzysztof Pleśniarowicz (Wrocław: Zakład Narodowy im. Ossolińskich, 2004), 329–30.
7 Kantor, "Miejsce Teatralne," in *Pisma*, 404.
8 Samuel Beckett, *Proust* (London: Chatto and Windus, 1931), 72.
9 Kantor, "Miejsce Teatralne," 340–41.
10 Kantor, quoted in Wiesław Borowski, *Tadeusz Kantor* (Warszawa: Wydawnictwo Artystyczne i Filmowe, 1982), 18.
11 The cast of *Wielopole, Wielopole* included Tadeusz Kantor, Stanisław Rychlicki (Uncle Józef-Priest), Jan Książek (Grandmother Katarzyna), Teresa Wełmińska/Ludmiła Ryba (Mother-Helka), Andrzej Wełmiński (Father Marian), Maria Kantor (Aunt Mańka, That Fellow, Rabbi), Ewa Janicka (Aunt Józka), Wacław Janicki (Uncle Karol), Lesław Janicki (Uncle Olek), Maria Krasicka (Uncle Stasio), Lech Stangret (Adaś), Maria Rychlicka (The Local Photographer's Widow), Marzia Loriga, Giovanni Battista Storti, Loriano della Rocca, Luigi Arpini, Jean-Marie Barotte, Roman Siwulak, and Anna Halczak (Soldiers).
12 Kantor, "Wielopole, Wielopole—Partytura," in *Pisma*, 206.
13 Ibid., 207.
14 Ibid., 209.
15 Ibid., 209–14.
16 Kantor, "The Milano Lessons: Lesson 3," in *Journey*, 217.
17 *Wielopole, Wielopole* (Kraków: Wydawnictwo Literackie, 1984), 34.
18 See "The Room. Maybe a New Phase."
19 Kantor, "Wielopole, Wielopole—Partytura," in *Pisma*, 217.
20 Kantor, "Etiudy—Szkice sceniczne," in *Pisma*, 273.
21 Kantor, "Sceny z wojskeim," in *Pisma*, 285–86.

22 Kantor, "Notatki "Wojsko," in *Pisma*, 284.

23 See "The Room. Maybe a New Phase."

24 Ibid.

25 Kantor, "Wielopole, Wielopole—Partytura," in *Pisma*, 267.

26 For a detailed analysis of the notion of heterotopia see Michel Foucault, "Of Other Spaces," *Diacritics* (Spring, 1986): 22–27.

27 Foucault, "Of Other Spaces," 24.

28 The cast of *Let the Artists Die* included Tadeusz Kantor (I—the Prime Mover), Lesław Janicki (I—the Dying One), Wacław Janicki (The Author of the *Dramatic Persona*), Michał Gorczyca (I—at the Age of Six), Maria Kantor (We Know who this Character is), Maria Krasicka (The Mother), Mira Rychlicka (Aesculapius), Zbigniew Bednarczyk (The Caretaker, The Cleaning Woman), Stanisław Rychlicki (The Guard), Lech Stangret (The Pimp/Gambler), Roman Siwulak (The Hanged Man), Jan Książek (The Bum), Teresa Wełmińska (The Cabaret Whore, The Angel of Death), Ewa Janicka (The Bigot), Andrzej Wełmiński (Veit Stoss), Marzia Loriga, Giovanni Battista Storti, Eros Doni, Loriano della Rocca, Luigi Arpini, Jean-Marie Barotte, Andrzej Kowalczyk, Wojciech Węgrzyn (Generals).

29 Kantor, "Historia tytułu," in *Niech sczezną artyści* (Kraków: Cricoteka, 1988).

30 Kantor, "Trzeba użyć nieba by pokazć ziemię," in *Niech sczezną artyści*, n.p.

31 Kantor, "Prawda całkowita," in *Niech sczezną artyści*, n.p.

32 Kantor, *Przewodnik po spektaklu, Niech sczezną artyści* (Kraków: Cricoteka, 1988), n.p.

33 See "Theatrical Place."

34 Kantor, *Przewodnik po spektaklu, Niech sczezną artyści*, n.p.

35 Ibid.

36 Ibid.

37 Ibid.

38 Ibid.

39 See "Reflection."

40 *Przewodnik po spektaklu, Niech sczezną artyści*, n.p.

41 Kantor, "To the Actors of Cricot 2 in the Moment of Doubt," *Performing Arts Journal* 47 (May 1994): 34.

42 Kantor, "Dalszy rozwój: przedmiot," in *Pisma*, 397.

43 See "Reflection."

44 Kantor, *Przewodnik po spektaklu, Niech sczezną artyści*, n.p.

45 See "The Room. Maybe a New Phase."

46 See "Reflection."

47 Kantor, "The Milano Lessons: Lesson 12," in *Journey*, 251–56.

48 See "To Save From Oblivion."

49 Kantor, *Nigdy tu już nie powrócę—Przewodnik* (ms.), n.p.

50 Ibid. The cast of *I Shall Never Return* included Tadeusz Kantor (I—in person), Marie Vayssiére (She—the Bride; joined the Company in the Fall of 1988), Ludmiła Ryba (the Dishwasher), Lesław Janicki and Wacław Janicki (Hasidic Jews from *The Water-Hen*; the Bishops from *Where are the Snows of Yesteryear*), Maria Krasicka (the Siberian Exile from *Wielopole, Wielopole*), Mira Rychlicka (the Water-Hen), Zbigniew Bednarczyk (the English Lady from *The Water-Hen*), Stanisław Michno (the Market-Place Speaker), Zbigniew Gostomski (the Priest from *Wielopole, Wielopole*), Lech Stangret (the Gambler from *Let the Artists Die*), Roman Siwulak (the Gigolo from *The Water-Hen*), Jan Książek (the Grand Gymnast from *The Water-Hen*), Teresa Wełmińska (the Princess from *Dainty Shapes and Hairy Apes*), Ewa Janicka (the Woman with a Rat-Trap from *Dainty Shapes and Hairy Apes*), Andrzej Wełmiński (the Inn Keeper), Stanisław Dudzicki (the Rat), Loriano della Rocca (Shmul from *Wielopole, Wielopole*), Luigi Arpini, Jean-Marie Barotte, Eros Doni, Włodzimierz Górski, Janusz Jarecki, Andrzej Kowalczyk, Luigi Mattiazzi (the Violinists; These Serious Gentlemen), Anna Halczak (This Lady).

51 Kantor, *Nigdy tu już nie powrócę—Przewodnik* (ms.), np.

52 Ibid.

53 See "The Emballage."

54 Kantor, "The Milano Lessons: Lesson 6," in *Journey*, 233.

55 Kantor, *Nigdy tu już nie powrócę—Przewodnik* (ms.), np.

56 See "Prison."

57 Kantor, *Nigdy tu już nie powrócę*—Przewodnik (ms.), np.

58 Ibid.

59 Kantor quoted in *Nigdy tu już nie powrócę*, a film by Andrzej Sapija produced in 1988.

60 Kantor, *Nigdy tu już nie powrócę*—Przewodnik (ms.), np.

61 Ibid.

62 See "Reflection."

63 See Gilles Deleuze, "A Theory of the Other," in *The Deleuze Reader*, ed. Constantin V. Boundas (New York: Columbia University Press, 1993), 59.

64 Kantor, *Nigdy tu już nie powrócę*—Przewodnik (ms.), np.

65 Deleuze, "A Theory of the Other," 61–62.

66 *Jean Baudrillard: Selected Writings*, ed. Mark Poster (Stanford: Stanford University Press, 1988), 166–206.

67 Gilles Deleuze, *The Logic of Sense*, ed. Constantin V. Bounds (London: Athlone Press, 1990), 257.

68 Kantor, "The Milano Lessons: Lesson 12," in *Journey*, 258–60.

69 Michel Foucault, *The Archaeology of Knowledge* (New York: Pantheon Books, 1972), 209.

70 Kantor, "The Milano Lessons: Lesson 6," in *Journey*, 228–29.

71 Kantor, *Nigdy tu już nie powrócę*—Przewodnik (ms.), np.

4. SPATIAL HISTORIOGRAPHY

1 *Silent Night* was presented on July 8–11, 1990 at the Chapelle des Pénitents Blanc in Avignon. The cast included Hana Zavadilova, Manuel Serrano, Stefano Fogher, Paul Bourdin, Renaud Lille, Carmelo Carpenito, Lucie Le Touze, Béatrice Ollinger, Bruno Levy, Philippe Cal, Sophie Ducrez, Franck Nadal, Philippe Avril, Marc Baylet, Eugé Nil, Lina Nassar, Emmanuelle Demors, Natasha Megard, Hélène Famin, Patrick Marchand; Music: Emmanuel Gouvello, Costumes: Fabienne Varoutsikos; Advisor: Tadeusz Kantor; His assistants: Anna Halczak, Marie Vayssiere, and Ludmiła Ryba.

2 See Chapter 1, "Topography of Representation," and Kantor's comments in "My Work—My Journey" as well as in "The Milano Lessons: Lesson 12," in *A Journey through Other Spaces: Essays and Manifestos, 1944–1990*, trans. Michal Kobialka (Berkeley: University of California Press, 1993), 258–60.

3 Jean-François Lyotard, *The Postmodern Explained*, trans. Don Barry, Bernadette Maher, Julian Pefanis, Virginia Spate, and Morgan Thomas; afterword Wlad Godzich (University of Minnesota Press, 1993), 15.

4 See "*Silent Night* (Cricotage)."

5 See "*Silent Night* (Cricotage)."

6 Kantor, "The Milano Lessons: Lesson 3," in *Journey*, 217.

7 Kantor, "*Silent Night*—Partytura" (unpublished ms.), 6–6a. While working on his productions, Kantor wrote *partyturas*. A *partytura* can be understood here as a collage of various texts, notes, and descriptions of terms and concepts that were created by him during the process of developing a production.

8 This sequence is reminiscent of Kantor's "Living Emballage," which was executed as a part of Happenings done in Warszawa in 1965, Kraków in 1966, and Nürnberg in 1968. See Wiesław Borowski, *Kantor* (Warszawa: Wydawnictwo Artystyczne i Filmowe, 1982), 68–76.

9 See "*Silent Night*—Partytura (Cricotage)."

10 Ibid.

11 Ibid.

12 Ibid.

13 Kantor, "The Milano Lessons: Lesson 1," in *Journey*, 211.

14 Ibid.

15 Gilles Deleuze, "Nomad Art: Space," in *The Deleuze Reader*, ed. Constantin V. Boundas (New York: Columbia University Press, 1993), 166–67.

16 Kantor, "The Milano Lessons: Lesson 1," in *Journey*, 211.

17 See "The Emballage."

18 Henri Lefebvre, *The Production of Space*, trans. Donald Nicholson-Smith (Oxford: Blackwell, 1991), 33.

19 Michel de Certeau, *The Writing of History*, trans. Tom Conley (New York: Columbia University Press, 1988), 72–73.

20 Michel Foucault, *The Archaeology of Knowledge and the Discourse on Language*, trans. A. M. Sheridan Smith (New York: Pantheon Books, 1972), 7.

21 Ibid., 126, 129.

22 Ibid., 129.

23 Ibid.

24 Ibid., 130.

25 Lyotard, *Postmodern Explained,* 80.

26 Deleuze, "A Theory of the Other," in *Deleuze Reader*, 61.

27 Deleuze, "Minor Languages and Nomad Art," in *Deleuze Reader*, 194.

28 Jean Baudrillard, *The Illusion of the End*, trans. Chris Turner (Stanford: Stanford University Press, 1994), 23.

29 See "Reflection."

30 Baudrillard, *Illusion of the End*, 23–24.

31 Herbert Blau, "Afterthought from the Vanishing Point: Theatre at the End of the Real," in *The Theatrical Gamut*, ed. Enoch Brater (Ann Arbor: University of Michigan Press, 1995), 297.

32 Deleuze, "Painting and Sensation," in *Deleuze Reader*, 189.

5. THE SPACE OF *KHORA*

1 See "Theatrical Place."

2 See "To Save from Oblivion."

3 Theodor Adorno, "Commitment," in *The Essential Frankfurt Reader*, ed. Andrew Arato and Eike Gebhardt (Oxford: Basil Blackwell, 1978), 318.

4 The term "enchanted simulation" is borrowed from Arthur Kroker, *The Possessed Individual: Technology and the French Postmodern* (New York: St. Martin's Press, 1992), 76.

5 See "The Room. Maybe a New Phase."

6 Kantor, "The Milano Lessons: Lesson 12," in *A Journey through Other Spaces: Essays and Manifestos, 1944–1990*, trans. Michal Kobialka (Berkeley: University of California Press, 1993).

7 See "My Work—My Journey."

8 In January 1991, *Today Is My Birthday* premiered in Toulouse and in Paris. The cast included Andrzej Wełmiński (The Self-Portrait, Vsevolod Meyerhold), Marie Vayssiére (The Poor Girl), Loriano della Rocca (The Shadow), Ludmiła Ryba (The Cleaning Woman), Wacław Janicki (The Father), Lesław Janicki (The Individual Who Has Appropriated Father's Face), Maria Krasicka (The Mother), Roman Siwulak (Uncle Stasio), Zbigniew Bednarczyk (The Priest Śmietana from Wielopole, Ewa Janicka (Maria Jarema), Zbigniew Gostomski (Jonasz Stern), Mira Rychlicka (Dr. Klein-Jehova), Jan Książek (The Water-Carrier from Wielopole, Gravedigger), Teresa Wełmińska (The Infanta), Lech Stangret (The Newspaper-Boy from 1914, Gravedigger), Stanisław Michno (Pedel from *The Dead Class*, NKVD Soldier, Gravedigger), Eros Doni, Jean-Marie Barotte (Emballages, NKVD Soldiers, The Power People), Janusz Jarecki, Andrzej Kowalczyk, Bogdan Renczyński, Włodzimierz Górski, Piotr Chybiński (Emballages, The Power People), Eugeniusz Bakałarz (The Power People, Gravedigger), Stanisław Dudzicki (Gravedigger).

9 Kantor, "The Milano Lessons: Lessons 8, 9, 10, and 11," in *Journey*, 243–45.

10 See "From the Beginning My Credo Was, . . ."

11 See "My Work—My Journey."

12 Unless otherwise noted, all the quotes come from Tadeusz Kantor's private diaries, parts of which were made available to me by Anna Halczak.

13 See "A Painting."

14 Kantor, "Dziś są moje urodziny—Partytura," *Tadeusz Kantor: Pisma z lat 1985–1990*, ed. Krzysztof Pleśniarowicz (Wrocław: Ossolineum, 2005), 260.

15 Ibid., 266.

16 Ibid., 268.

17 Ibid., 269.

18 Ibid., 271.

19 Ibid., 276.

20 Ibid., 281.

21 Ibid.

22 See Kantor's notes to *Silent Night* in Chapter 4.

23 *Aujourd'hui c'est mon anniversaire* (Milano: Cappelletti & Riscassi Arti Grafiche—Corsico, 1991), 20.

24 Giorgio Agamben, *Remnants of Auschwitz: The Witness and the Archive*, trans. Daniel Heller-Roazen (New York: Zone Books, 1999), 135.

25 *Aujourd'hui c'est mon anniversaire*, 16.

26 Ibid.

27 Ibid.

28 Carlos Funetes, *Terra Nostra*, trans. Margaret Sayers Peden (New York: Farrar, Straus, and Giroux, 1989), 445.

29 See "A Short History of My Life."

30 Kantor, "Notes to a Film Script, *Powrót Odysa*" (unpublished ms., 1990), 5.

31 Michel de Certeau, *The Writing of History*, trans. Tom Conley (New York: Columbia University Press, 1988), xv.

32 Michel de Certeau, *Heterologies: Discourse on the Other*, trans. Brian Massumi (Minneapolis: University of Minnesota Press, 1989), 194.

33 de Certeau, *Writing of History*, 4.

34 Samuel Beckett, *Endgame* (New York: Grove Press, 1958), 2.

35 Ibid., 12.

36 For a description of Wilson's installation, "Memory/Loss," see "Of Lost Memories and Nomadic Representational Practices," *Journal of Dramatic Theory and Criticism* 9 (Fall 1994): 179–93; for a description of Libeskind's Jewish Museum in Berlin, see "Of the Memory of the Human Unhoused in Being," *Performance Research* 5, no. 3 (Winter 2000): 41–55.

37 Adorno, "Commitment," 317.

38 See *The Deleuze Reader*, ed. Constantin V. Boundas (New York: Columbia University Press, 1993), ch. 19, for definitions of nomad art and haptic space.

49 Gilles Deleuze, "Nomad Art: Space," in *Deleuze Reader*, 167.

40 See "Theatre of Death."

41 Kantor, "Infantka Margarita," (unpublished, ms., 1962).

42 Jacques Derrida, "The Apparatus or Frame," in *Dissemination* (Chicago: University of Chicago Press, 1981), 299.

43 Plato, *Timaeus and Critias* (Harmondsworth, England: Penguin Books, 1971), 70–71.

44 Peter Eisenman, "Guardiola House, Santa Maria del Mar," in *Deconstruction*, ed. Andreas Papadakis, Catherine Cooke, and Andrew Benjamin (London: Academy Group, 1989), 163–66, 163. For a critical analysis of Plato's *khora* see Jacques Derrida, "How to Avoid Speaking," *Languages of the Unsayable*, ed. Sanford Budick and Wolfgang Iser (New York: Columbia University Press, 1989), 3–70.

45 See "To Save from Oblivion."

46 Kantor, "The Milano Lessons: Lesson 12," *Journey*, 258–63.

Selected Bibliography

(A bibliography of works pertaining to Kantor is available on the CRICOTEKA Web page, http://www.cricoteka.com.pl/en.)

BOOKS, ARTICLES, INTERVIEWS, REVIEWS, AND SPECIAL ISSUES

Alexander, C. "Du jamais v à Nancy." *L'Express* (international edition), May 9–15, 1977.

Alternatives Théâtrales. "Kantor, homme de théâtre." December 1995.

Amey, C. *Tadeusz Kantor. Theatrum Litteralis.* Paris: L'Harmattan, 2002.

Amort, A. "Weise Anarchie der Bilder." *Kurier,* May 6, 1987.

Andersen, S. "Avantgarde pa Hovikodden." *Arbeiderbladet,* January 21, 1976.

Armino, M. "Kantor, el prodigio." *Cambio,* August 16, 1987.

Arpini, L., ed. *L'illusione vissuta. Viaggi e teatro con Tadeusz Kantor.* Florence: Biblioteca Spadoni & Titivillus Edizioni, 2002.

Art Press. Special issue, *Art* 6 (1985).

Ascherson, N. "The Artist as Traitor." *Scotsman,* August 28, 1976.

Ashton, D. "Paintings by Tadeusz Kantor Leader of Movement, at Seidenberg Gallery." *New York Times,* October 6, 1960.

Bablet, D. "Entretien avec Tadeusz Kantor." *Travail Théâtral* 6 (1972).

———. *Les Revolutions Scéniques du XX siécle.* Paris: Société Internationale d'Art, 1975.

———. *Le Théâtre de la Mort.* Lausanne: Editions L'Age d'Homme, 1977.

———. *Il Teatro della Morte.* Milan: Ubulibri, 1979.

———. "Ulysse et Kantor sont de retour." *Théâtre/Public* 11–12 (1988).

———. "Ulysse est en France." *L'Express* 1976 (1989): 74.

———. *Tadeusz Kantor.* Paris: Editions du CNRS, 1983, 1990, 1993.

Baigneres, C. "Tadeusz Kantor, un franc-tireur polonais." *Le Figaro,* May 20–21, 1974.

Balicka, B. "Idę na poszukiwanie samego siebie." *Wieczór Wrocławia,* February 23, 1987.

Bandettini, A. "A scuola di Kantor." *Tutto Milano,* April 1988.

Banu, G., ed. *Kantor, l'artiste à la fin du XXe siécle.* Paris: Actes Sud-Papiers, 1990.

Baran, Z., ed. *Pierścień "Balladyny." Gra z Teatrem Podziemnym Tadeusza Kantora.* Kraków: Cricoteka, 2003.

Barber, J. "An Inchoate Vision of the World." *Daily Telegraph,* August 25, 1972.

———. "Riches from the Poorhouse." *Daily Telegraph,* September 11, 1972.

———. "Digging up our Buried Years." *Daily Telegraph,* September 6, 1976.

La Bardonnie, M. "La Mort, La Peur, Le Mensonge." *Le Monde*, May 12, 1977.

Barea, P. "Tadeusz Kantor: La memoria visible." *Deia*, May 14, 1987.

Barroso, M. "Tadeusz Kantor y su grupo Cricot 2." *El Correo Espanol*, May 12, 1987.

Bartoli, F. "Kantor: Bal Rond per Tintagiles." *Il castello di Elsinore* 1 (1988).

Bellingeri, E. *Cricot 2: Immagini di un teatro*. Rome: Le Parole Gelate, 1981.

Benach, J.-A. "La lugubre y furiosa memoria de Kantor." *La Vanguardia*, March 20, 1987.

Bercoff, A. "Les polonaise de Cricot II. Une Cour des Miracles Polonaise à Paris: la campagnie T. Kantor." *L'Express*, April 15–21, 1974.

Berrutti, R. "Los cautivantes rituales de Kantor." *Clarin*, August 22, 1987.

Billington, M. "*The Dead Class*." *Arts Guardian*, March 13, 1976.

———. "Fringe on Top." *Guardian*, August 30, 1976.

Blonski, J. "Powrót Witkacego." *Dialog* 9 (1963).

Blum, H. "Wystawa Młodych Plastyków." *Twórczość* 12 (1946).

———. "Teatr Tadeusza Kantora." *Odrodzenie* 35 (1946).

Bogucki, J. *Szkice Krakowskie: Od Stwosza do Kantora*. Kraków: Wydawnictwo Literackie, 1956.

Borowska, B., ed. *Wielopole, Wielopole*. Warszawa: Wydawnictwo Literackie, 1984.

Borowski, W. "Ambalaże." *ITD*, May 23, 1965.

———. "Teatr Kantora Cricot 2." *Współczesność* 9 (1970).

———. "Malarstwo Kantora: Ambalaże i Multipart." *Współczesność* 28 (1970).

———. "Happeningi Tadeusza Kantora." *Dialog* 9 (1972).

———. "Funkcja tekstu w teatrze Cricot 2." *Dialog* 8 (1973).

———. "Les happenings de Tadeusz Kantor." *Theatre in Poland* 4–5 (1973).

———. "*Dainty Shapes and Hairy Apes*: Mis en scène by Tadeusz Kantor." *Theatre in Poland* 1 (1974).

———. "Tadeusz Kantor and his Cricot 2 Theatre." *Studio: International Journal of Modern Art* 5 (1974).

———. "'Cricotage' Tadeusza Kantora." *Kierunki* 50 (1975).

———. "*Umarła Klasa*." *Literatura*, May 17, 1976.

———. "Tadeusz Kantor." *Scena* 5 (1977).

———. *Tadeusz Kantor*. Warszawa: Wydawnictwo Artystyczne i Filmowe, 1982.

Brion, M. *Art since 1945*. New York: Abrams, 1958.

Broch, A. "El angel de la muerte." *La Vanguardia*, March 27, 1987.

Brunelli, V. "Con i sogni di Kantor aperto a Firenze un nuovo teatro." *Corriere della Sera*, May 22, 1987.

Buscarino, M. *La classe morta di Tadeusz Kantor*. Milan: Universale Economica Feltrinelli, 1981.

———. *Kantor: Cyrk śmierci*. Edited by R. Valtorta. Bozen: Edition Sturzfluge, 1997.

Burzawa, E. "Kantor w Norymberdze." *Życie Literackie* 27 (1985).

Calandra, D. "Experimental Performance at Edinburgh." *The Drama Review* T60 (December 1973): 53–68.

Calvocoressi, R. "Tadeusz Kantor: Cricot 2 Theatre." *Studio International* 1–2 (1977).

Caplan, L., and K. Rabińska. "Metoda klisz." *Dialog* 12 (1980).

Cassou, J. "Le degel artistique en Pologne." *Prosme des arts* 4 (1956).

Catalóquio Artes. Special issue, *Catalóquio Artes* 89 (June 1991).

Chambers, C. "Experiments in the Polish Experience." *Morning Star*, September 20, 1976.

Chernel, L. "Groteskspiele um den Tod." *Wiener Zeitung*, May 6, 1987.

Chevalier, D. "Kantor, Aujourd'hui." *Art et Architecture* 3–4 (1959).

Chrobak, J., ed. *Memorie del teatro: Il viaggio di Tadeusz Kantor*. Florence: Biblioteca Spadoni & Titivillus Edizioni, 2002.

———, ed. *"Powrót Odysa" i Podziemny Teatr Niezależny Tadeusza Kantora w latach 1942–1944*. Kraków: Cricoteka, 2004.

———, ed. *Wielopole Skrzyńskie di Tadeusz Kantor*. Kraków: Cricoteka, 2005.

Chrobak J., K. Ramut, T. Tomaszewski, and M. Wilk. *Kunstgewerbeschule, 1939-1943 i Podziemny Teatr Niezależny Tadeusza Kantora w latach 1942–1944*. Kraków: Cricoteka, 2007.

Chrobak J., M. Rogalski, and M. Wilk, eds. *Panoramiczny happening morski*. Kraków: Cricoteka, 2008.

Chrobak J., L. Stangret, and M. świca, eds. *Tadeusz Kantor. Wędrówka*. Kraków: Cricoteka, 2000.

Chrobak, J., and N. Zarzecka, eds. *Kantor dossier: Wielopole, Wielopole*. Kraków: Cricoteka, 2007.

Compagnion, N. "Tadeusz Kantor. Qu'ils crevent les artistes!" *Paris Match*, April 17, 1987.

Cork, R. "Enter the Hollow Man." *Evening Standard*, September 23, 1987.

Coveney, M. "Edinburgh Festival, Cricot 2." *Financial Times*, August 24, 1973.

Cournot, M. "Kantor, le peintre." *Le Monde* 12592 (1985).

Craipeau, M. "Tadeusz Kantor: En Pologne l'art abstrait n'est plus clandestin." *Observateur*, March 12, 1976.

Creación. Special issue, *Creación* (May 1995).

Critique. Special issue, *Critique* (January–February 1984).

Czartoryska, U. *Od pop-artu do sztuki konceptualnej*. Warszawa, 1973.

———. "Teatr śmierci Tadeusza Kantora." *Dialog* 5 (1976).

———. "Kantor: nowe propozycje." *Projekt* 4 (1976).

Czas kultury. Special issue, *Czas kultury* 6 (2000).

Davis, Y. "La classe morte." *Théâtre/Public* (March 1978).

de Ita, F. "La solution al arte es la obra cerrada porque la abieta es facil y propiciatoria al consumismo." *uno más uno*, March 10, 1979.

Dialog. Special issue, *Dialog* 8 (1973).

Dialog. Special issue, *Dialog* 2 (1977).

Didaskalia. Special issue, *Didaskalia* (December 2000).

Didaskalia. Special issue, *Didaskalia* (February 2006).

Dirico, J.-M. "Tadeusz Kantor. Entre la marge et la glorie." *Liberte*, April 3, 1987.

Done, K. "Around the Festival Fringe." *Scotsman*, August 27, 1973.

Doplicher, F. "Tadeusz Kantor: Il regista non esiste." *Sipario* 339–40 (1974).

Drossart, A. "Un evenement considerable: *La Classe Morte* par le Cricot 2 du Polonais Tadeusz Kantor." *Le Soir de Brussels*, May 5, 1977.

Dultz, M. "Freiluft-Emballage in Nürnberg." *Abendzeitung*, May 9, 1968.

Dursi, M. "La commedia di Witkiewicz alla ribalta *Una gallinella* spennata." *Il Rest del Carlino*, May 7, 1977.

du Vignal, P. "Tadeusz Kantor." *L'art vivant* 50 (1974).

———. "Tadeusz Kantor. La classe morte." *Art Press International* (April 1977).

———. "Qu'ils crevent, les artistes!" *Art Press International* (September 1985).

Duvignaud, J., and F. Gründ. "Tadeusz Kantor. Résponses a onze questions." *Internationale de l'Imaginaire* (Spring 1989).

Dzieduszycki, A. "O taszyzmie, filmie abstrakcyjnym i nowoczesnej scenografii." *Odra* 1 (1958).

Dziewulska, M. "Kantor, czyli pamięć." *Przegląd Katolicki* 18 (1986).

Eide, H. "Poetiske paraplayer med forpliktelser." *Dagbladet*, October 12, 1971.

Ekman, M. "Doden pa scenen." *Huvudstadsbladet*, June 4, 1988.

Ekwinski, A. "Totalna Realność: Rozmowa z Tadeuszem Kantorem." *Argumenty* 29 (1972).

Elsom, J. "Decor by Babel." *Listener*, September 2, 1976.

Eruli, B. "Tadeusz Kantor: imagine del corpo e manichini ne *La classe morta*." *Quaderini di Teatro* (May 1980).

———. "Wielopole, Wielopole." In *Tadeusz Kantor*. Paris: Editions CNRS, 1983, 1990.

———. "Tadeusz Kantor." *Scenes* 2 (April 1986).

———, ed. *Tadeusz Kantor. Entretiens*. Paris: Editions Carré Arts&estétique, 1996.

Espinoza, P. "La esencial tristeza del arte." *Pagina*, August 22, 1987.

Esslin, M. "*The Dead Class*." *Plays and Players* 10 (1976).

Eyre, R. "Inside the Human Corral." *Scotsman*, August 21, 1972.

Feltrinelli, G., ed. *La classe morta di Tadeusz Kantor*. Mialno: Feltrinelli Editore, 1981.

Fenn, W. "Am Rand der Vernichtung Bilder einer degradierten Realitat: die Embellagen des Polen Tadeusz Kantor." *Nürnberger Nachrichten*, November 26, 1976.

———. "In der Holle des Lebens." *Nürnberger Nachrichten*, March 17, 1977.

Fergombe, A. *Tadeusz Kantor: de l'écriture scénique de la mort à l'instauration de la mémoire*. Valenciennes: Presses Universitaires de Valenciennes, 1997.

Fik, M. *Trzydzieści pięć sezonów*. Warszawa: Wydawnictwo Artystyczne i Filmowe, 1981.

Flor, H. "Vart Liv som embalasje." *Dogbladet*, January 24, 1976.

Le Fort, P. "Le Théâtre Zéro de Tadeusz Kantor." *Quotidien de Paris*, April 11, 1974.

Freitag, W. "Veit Stoss tanzt mit der Dirne Tango." *Die Presse*, May 6, 1987.

Gabanch, P. "Nits de mort i de guerra." *Diari de Barcelona*, March 20, 1987.

Gerould, D. "A Visual Artist Works Magic on the Polish Stage." *Performing Arts Journal* 4 (1980).

———. "Kantor at Home." *American Theatre* 11 (1986).

Gieraczyński, B. "Kantora przekraczanie doskonałości." *Odra* 6 (1983).

Giroud, M. "Kantor, un autre vision de l'art et du theater." *Kanal*, October 1984.

Godard, C. "*Les Mignons et les Guenons*." *Le Monde*, April 20, 1974.

———. "Desordres de mémoire." *Le Monde*, September 30, 1988.

———. "Teatrologie de la mort et de la dersion." *Le Monde*, May 18, 1989.

Granath, O. "Teater i Amsterdam: Var inte pessimist!" *Dagens Nyheter*, March 22, 1977.

Grodzicki, A. "Kantor." *Życie Warszawy* 307 (1974).

———. *Les metteurs en scenes en Pologne*. Warszawa: Państwowe Wydawnictwo Artystyczne i Filmowe, 1975.

———. "Tadeusz Kantor and His Cricot 2." *Theatre in Poland* 8 (1977): 9–14.

Grund, F. "Responses a onze questions." *Internationale de l'Imaginaire* 12 (1989): 5–19.

Gryglewicz, T., ed. *W cieniu krzesła. Malarstwo i sztuka przedmiotu Tadeusza Kantora*. Kraków: Universitas, 1997.

Grzegorzewski, J. "Scenografia Tadeusza Kantora." *Współczesność* 8 (1963).

Grzejewska, A. "Dzieło sztuki jest zamknięte." *Miesięcznik Literacki* 10 (1978).

Gutowski, M. "W pracowni Tadeusza Kantora." *Współczesność* 7 (1968).

Halczak, A., ed. *Cricot 2 Theatre: Information Guide: 1986*. Kraków: Cricoteka, 1988.

———. *Cricot 2 Theatre: Information Guide: 1987–1988*. Kraków: Cricoteka, 1989.

———. *Cricot 2 Theatre: Information Guide: 1989–1990*. Kraków: Cricoteka, 2003.

———. *Tadeusz Kantor. Zbiory publiczne*. Kraków: Cricoteka, 2003.

Halczak, A., and B. Renczyński, eds. *Tadeusz Kantor. Obiekty/przedmioty. Zbiory Cricoteki. Katalog prac*. Kraków: Cricoteka, 2007.

Hartung, K. "Kantor bringt es zu Ende." *taz*, May 27, 1988.

Heijer, J. "Dodenklas van Tadeusz Kantor: emotioneel en uniek Pools theater." *Handelsbald*, March 2, 1977.

Heliot, A. "Tadeusz Kantor de retour." *Le Quotidien*, June 7, 1989.

Hertz, U. "An Interview with the Director of Cricot 2 Tadeusz Kantor." *Third Rail* 7 (1985–86).

Hirschmann, Ch. "Gegen den Tod anspielen." *Neue AZ*, May 6, 1987.

Hniedziewicz, M. "Nowa propozycja artystyczna: Manifest 70 Kantora." *Kierunki* 43 (1970).

———. "Czas przeszły, czas żywy teatru Kantora." *Kultura*, March 21, 1976.

Hontanton, R. "El alucinante Tadeusz." *El Diario*, August 14, 1987.

Hystrio. "Dossier T. Kantor." Special issue, *Hystrio* 4 (2000).

Jablonkówna, L. "Szatniarze i widzowie w teatrze Niemożliwym." *Teatr* 9 (1973).

Jenkins, R. "Ring Master in a Circus of Dreams." *American Theatre* 11 (March 1986).

Jodłowski, M. "O gwoździu co przebija twarz." *Odra* 5 (1987).

Johnsrud, E. H. "Det Skjedde pa Hovikodden." *Aftenposten*, October 18, 1971.

———. "Nar det utenpa er selve innholdet." *Aftenposten*, January 20, 1976.

Journal of Dramatic Theory and Criticism. Special issue, *Journal of Dramatic Theory and Criticism* 10 (Fall 2005).

Jurkiewicz, M., J. Mytkowska, and A. Przywara, eds. *Tadeusz Kantor. Z Archiwum Galerii Foksal*. Warszawa: Fundacja Galerii Foksal, 1998.

Kelera, J. "Postać jaskrawa i niemal cyrkowa." *Odra* 9 (1976).

Kemp-Welch, K. "Excursions in Communist Reality: Tadeusz Kantor's Impossible Happenings." *Object* 8 (2005–6).

Kiraly, N. "Ars poetica Tadeusza Kantora." *Konteksty* 1 (2005).

Kłossowicz, J. "Cricot 2." *Współczesność* 21 (1969).

———. "Scenariusz przedstawienia: *Umarła Klasa*." *Dialog* 2 (1977).

———. "Tadeusz Kantor's Theatre of Emotions." *Theatre in Poland* 3 (1981).

———. "Był absolutnym heretykiem. . . . O Stanisławie Ignacym Witkiewiczu mówi Tadeusz Kantor." *Literatura* 8 (1985).

———. "Tadeusz Kantor's Journey." *The Drama Review* T111 (Fall 1986).

———. "Cricot 2: *Nigdy tu już nie powrócę*." *Dialog* 1 (1989).

———. *Tadeusz Kantor: Teatr*. Warszawa: Państwowy Instytut Wydawniczy, 1991.

———. *Tadeusz Kantors Theatre*. Edited by H. Xander and A. Francke. Basel: Verlag Tübingen, 1995.

Kobialka, M. "Kantor—Candor: An Interview with Tadeusz Kantor." *Stages* 6 (1986).

———. "Let the Artists Die?: An Interview with Tadeusz Kantor." *The Drama Review* T111 (Fall 1986).

————. "Tadeusz Kantor's Labyrinths of Memory." *Soviet and East European Performance* 11, no. 1 (1991).

————. "Theater der Gefundenen Wirklichkeit: Die Räume bei Kantor." In *Hommage à Tadeusz Kantor*. Nürnberg: Institut für Moderne Kunst, 1991.

————. "The Milano Lessons: Introduction." *The Drama Review* T132 (Winter 1991).

————. "Spatial Representation: Tadeusz Kantor's Theatre of Found Reality." *Theatre Journal* (1992).

————. "Forget Kantor." *Performing Arts Journal* 47 (May 1994).

————. "Topography of Representation." *Theatre Research International* 19, no. 2 (1994).

————. "Of Lost Memories and Nomadic Representational Practices." *Journal of Dramatic Theory and Criticism* 9 (Fall 1994).

————. "Theatre Space and Fictional Place: Tadeusz Kantor's Representational Practices in *The Machine of Love and Death*." *ASSAPH* 10 (1994).

————. "Cisza, wieczność i śmierć." In *Kantor: Cyrk śmierci*. Bozen: Edition Sturzflüge, 1997.

————. "Od poczatku w jego credo . . ." In *Hommage à Tadeusz Kantor*, edited by Krzysztof Pleśniarowicz. Kraków: Księgarnia Akademicka, 1999.

————. "Tadeusz Kantor's Happenings: Reality, Mediality, and History." *Theatre Survey* 43, 1 (May 2002).

————. "Tadeusz Kantor's Odysseus: Imagined Myths and Chronicled Histories." In *Le Maschere di Proteo*, edited by Rosalba Gasparo Messina, Italy: Edizioni di Nicolo, 2003.

————. "Tadeusz Kantor's Practice: A Postmodern Notebook." *Performing Arts Journal* 28, no. 1 (2006).

Koch-Butrym M. "Sobowtóry, manekiny i bio-obiekty w twórczości Tadeusza Kantora." *Kwartalnik Teatralny* 1 (2002).

Kostołowski, A. "Tadeusz Kantor: artysta jako krytyk." *Jeden* 1 (1972).

Kott, J. "The Theatre of Essence; Kantor and Brook." *Theatre* 3 (1983).

————. *The Theatre of Essence*. Evanston: Northwestern University Press, 1984.

————. *Kadysz. Strony o Tadeuszu Kantorze*. Gdańsk: słowo/obraz terytoria, 1997.

————. *Kaddish. Pages sur Tadeusz Kantor*, Nantes: Cecofop, 2000.

————. *Kaddish. Pagine su Tadeusz Kantor*. Milan: Libri Scheiwiller, 2001.

————. *Kaddish. Pages about Tadeusz Kantor*. Tokyo: Michitani, 2000.

Kotuła, A., and P. Krakówski. *Kronika nowej sztuki*. Kraków: Wydawnictwo Literackie, 1966.

————. *Malarstwo-Rzeźba-Architektura*. Warszawa: PWN, 1972.

Kowalska, B. *Polska awangarda malarska, 1945–1970*. Warszawa: PWN, 1975.

Kozień-Świca, M. "Kantorowski mit Paryża." *Pamiętnk Sztuk Pięknych* 1, no. 4 (2003).

Krakówski, P. "Malarstwo Tadeusza Kantora." *Format* 1–4 (1994).

Krzemień, T. "Przedmiot staje się aktorem: Rozmowa z Tadeuszem Kantorem." *Kultura* 37 (1974).

————. "An Object Becomes an Actor: An Interview with Tadeusz Kantor." *Theatre in Poland* 4–5 (1975).

————. "*Wielopole, Wielopole*." *Kultura*, December 14, 1980.

————. "List Artysty." *Odrodzenie* 3 (1987).

Kudo, Y. "Tadeusz Kantor." *OZ* 4 (1990).

Kustov, M. "Le happening de Kantor." *International Theatre Information* (1972).

Kwiatkowski, T. "Krakówski teatr konspiracyjny." *Pamiętnik Teatralny* 1–4 (1963).

Kydryński, J. "Krakowski teatr konspiracyjny." *Twórczość* 3 (1946).

Lamont, R. C. "Builder of Bridges Between the Living and the Dead." *New York Times*, October 5, 1985.

Langsner, J. "Modern Art in Poland." *Art Internatinal*, September 20, 1961.

Lattes, J. "Adventurer in Poland." *Time* (international edition), April 6, 1959.

Van Leeuven, K. "Dodenklas blijft lang op je netvilies stan." *Harlems Dagblad*, March 2, 1977.

Lewsen, Ch. "Actors' Series of Living Sculptures." *The Times*, August 29, 1972.

Liardon, P. H. "Théâtre d'avant-garde en Pologne." *Feuille d'avis de Lausanne*, March 9, 1964.

———. "Interview d'un peintre polonais: Tadeusz Kantor." *Feuille d'avis de Lausanne*, March 11, 1964.

Lido, G. *Kantor. Protagonismo registico e spazio memoriale.* Florence: Liberoscambio editrice s.r.l., 1984.

Lionetti, J. "Que vivan los aristas." *Expreso*, August 28, 1987.

Madeyski, J. "Czy nowa awangarda?" *Życie Literackie* 4 (1959).

Marcabru, P. "Trois visages du théâtre contemporain." *Le Figaro*, May 4, 1976.

Marioni, T. "Tadeusz Kantor." *Vision* 2 (1976).

Martinis, R. *Cricot 2, Immagine di un teatro.* Rome: Le parole Gelate, 1982.

———. *Tadeusz Kantor—Cricot 2.* Milan: Oedipus edizioni, 2001.

Maślińska, I. "Przede wszystkim nie chcę sądzić: Rozmowa z Tadeuszem Kantorem." *Teatr* 6 (1991).

———. "Sztuka jest przestępstwem." *Polityka* 35 (1990).

Massie, A. "Theatre of Death." *Scotsman*, August 20, 1976.

Matuszewska, J. "To nie inżynierowie tworzą postęp ale artyści." *Kierunki* 22 (1973).

Matynia, A. "Konferencja w Cricotece." *Tu i Teraz* 10 (1984).

———. "O fotografii z Tadeuszem Kantorem." *Projekt* 3 (1987).

———. "Biedny pokoik wyobraźni Tadeusza Kantora." *Odrodzenie* 16 (1988).

Maugis, M. T. "Kantor." *Les Lettres Françaises*, December 14, 1961.

Mazzanti, G. "A che servono gli aritisti?" *La Gazzetta di Rimini*, January 20, 1988.

Michelet, J. F. "Kunsten a si det med pakker." *VG*, January 25, 1976.

Michener, J. A. "The Nobel Prize in Painting." *Art International*, December 12, 1962.

Miklaszewska, A. "Kantora Teatr Informel." *Dialog* 7 (1978).

Miklaszewski, K. "Le théâtre autonome de Tadeusz Kantor." *Theatre in Poland* 1 (1973).

———. "Teatr 'i': Rozmowa z Tadeuszem Kantorem." *Kultura*, August 12, 1973.

———. "Une interview de Tadeusz Kantor." *Théâtre Revue Culturelle de L'V.I.E.* 3 (1974).

———. "*Umarła klasa* Tadeusza Kantora." *Magazyn Kulturalny* 1 (1976).

———. "Przejmujący seans Tadeusza Kantora." *Teatr* 9 (1976).

———. "*The Dead Class* by Tadeusz Kantor, or a New Treatise on the Use of the Dummies by Cracow's Cricot 2." *Theatre in Poland* 4–5 (1976).

———. "Cricot 2 i jego historia." *Życie Literackie* 19 (1986).

———. "Konteksty Kantora." *Dialog* 9 (1987).

————. *Spotkania z Tadeuszem Kantorem.* Kraków: Krajowa Agencja Wydawnicza, 1989.

————. *Encounters with Tadeusz Kantor.* Translated by George Hyde. New York: Routledge, 2005.

Monticelli, R. de. "Sulla scena passano fantasmi d'avanguardia." *Corriere della Serra*, January 29, 1978.

Morawiec, E. "Apokalipsa Tadeusza Kantora." *Życie Literackie* 51–52 (1975).

————. "Nowa sytuacja w sztuce." *Życie Literackie* 2 (1979).

————. "Wyspiański i 'teatr śmierci' Kantora." *Dialog* 2 (1979).

Morawski, S. "Happening." *Dialog* 9 (1971).

————. "Happening." *Dialog* 10 (1971).

Moscati, I. "Rissa corale per Witkacy: non raccontate la trama!" *Settegiorni*, January 2, 1974.

Moulin, R. J. "Tadeusz Kantor et les artistes de Cricot 2." *Les Lettres Françaises* 46 (1972).

Nawrocki, P., and H. Neidel. *Kantor; Ein Reisender—Seine Texte und Manifeste.* Nürnberg: Institut für Moderne Kunst, 1989.

————. *Hommage à Tadeusz Kantor.* Nürnberg: Institut für Moderne Kunst, 1991.

Nawrocki, P. "Spuren der Sehnsucht." *Deutsches Allegemeines Sonntagsblatt* 47 (1985).

————. "Tadeusz Kantor: 'Die Künstler sollen krepieren.'" *Apex* 1 (1988).

Neidel, H. "Fundustücke aus dem Jenseits." *Deutsches Allgemeines Sonntagsblatt* 22 (1985).

————. "Kantor war da!" *Mitteilungen des Instituts für Moderne Kunst* 15–16 (1977).

Nelsen, D. "'I Shall never Return' is a Mighty Interesting Trip." *Village Voice*, June 28, 1988.

Nores, D. "*Les Mignons et les Guenons*: Mis en scène de Tadeusz Kantor." *Combat*, April 23, 1974.

Olaguer, G. "El Polaco Kantor estrena hoy su reflexion sobre la muerte." *El Periodico de Catlunya*, March 18, 1987.

Olivier, C. "Une magistral provocation." *Les Lettres Françaises*, May 19, 1971.

————. "Edinburgh—2." *Plays and Players* 1 (1972).

————. "Kantor at Full Gallop: Talk with Tadeusz Kantor." *Guardian* 258 (1972).

————. "Faut-il bruler Kantor?" *Les Lettres Françaises* 11 (1972).

————. "Edinburgh 1." *Plays and Players* (1973).

————. "L'attitude dans l'art." *Travail Théâtral* 16 (1974).

————. "Edinburgh Festival: Cricot Theatre." *Guardian*, August 23, 1976.

Osęka, A. "Jaremianka, taszyzm, Kantor." *Przegląd Kulturalny* 51–52 (1956).

Osiński, Z. "Tadeusz Kantor wobec Leona Schillera w kontekście Andrzeja Pronaszki." *Pamiętnik Teatralny* 1–2 (2005).

Overy, P. "Surrealism without Surfeit." *The Times*, August 31, 1976.

————. "The Bandaged Nude." *The Times*, September 28, 1976.

Ordan, L. "Autonomia teatru." *Fakty*, February 28, 1976.

Paluch-Cybulska, M., ed. *Tadeusz Kantor. Scenografie dla teatrów oficjalnych.* Kraków: Cricoteka, 2006.

Pawłas, J. "Od malarstwa informel do teatru śmierci." *Tygodnik Kulturalny* 5 (1977).

Pagliarani, E. "La Polonia con il 'Teato Cricot 2' alla Rassegna della arti dello spectacolo *Gallinella*." *Paese sera*, March 4, 1969.

————. "Il teatro 'Cricot 2' al Premio Roma." *Paese sera*, March 11, 1974.

Pieniążek, M. *Akt twórczy jako mimesis. "Dziś są moje urodziny"*. Kraków: Universitas, 2005.

Piergiacomi, E. "Kantor profeta dell'avanguardia." *Sipario* 383 (1978).

Pipirijaina. "*Wielopole* de Tadeusz Kantor." Special issue, *Pipirijaina* 19-20 (October 1981).

Pleśniarowicz, K. "Na krawędzi pustki." *Teksty* 4 (1974).

———. "Trafić do swiatowego muzeum." *Kultura* 30 (1978).

———. "Teatr konstruktywnego wzruszenia." *Profile* 5 (1986).

———. "Labirynt Kantora." *Dialog* 9 (1987).

———. *Teatr Śmierci Tadeusza Kantora*. Chotomów, Poland: VERBA, 1990.

———. *Teatr nie-ludzkiej formy*. Kraków: Universitas, 1994.

———. *Kantor. Artysta końca wieku*. Wrocław: Wydawnictwo Dolnośląskie, 1997.

———, ed. *Hommage à Tadeusz Kantor*. Kraków: Cricoteka, 1999.

———. *The Dead Memory Machine. Tadeusz Kantor's Theatre of Death*. Kraków: Cricoteka, 1994; Reprint, Aberystwyth, Wales: Black Mountain Press, 2000.

Porębski, M. "Wystawa Młodych Plastyków w Krakówskim Pałacu Sztuki." *Przegląd Artystyczny* 1–2 (1946).

———. "Nowe rysunki Tadeusza Kantora." *Przegląd Artystyczny* 2 (1954).

———. "Maria Jarema i Tadeusz Kantor w salonie 'Po Prostu.'" *Po Prostu* 52–53 (1956).

———. *Sztuka naszego czasu*. Warszawa: Sztuka, 1956.

———. "Iluzja. Przypadek. Struktura." *Współczesność* 1 (1957).

———. "Tadeusz Kantor," *Współczesność*, August 3, 1963.

———. "Tadeusz Kantor, Ekspozycja Popularna." *Współczesność* 1 (1964).

———. *Deska*. Warszawa: Murator, 1997.

Ptaszkowska, A. "O wystawie Tadeusza Kantora." *Kamena* 4 (1957).

———. "Wielka wystawa Tadeusza Kantora." *Projekt* 1 (1964).

———. "Ambalaże." *ITD* 23 (1965).

———. "Cricot 2 Tadeusza Kantora." *Współczesność* 13 (1967).

———. "Kim jest Tadeusz Kantor." *Twórczość* 7 (1967).

———. "Happeningi w Polsce." *Współczesność* 9–10 (1969).

Puck. Special issue, *Puck* 2 (1989).

Puzyna, K. "Rozmowa o *Umarłej klasie*." *Dialog* 2 (1977).

Raboni, G. "Ulisse nella barca di Caronte." *Corriere della Sera*, April 25, 1988.

Raczek, T. "Misterium umierania. Teatr Kantora." *Polityka* 33 (1982).

Radice, R. "*Da Gallinella D'Aqua* Teatro polacco—La Campagnia Cricot 2 di Cracovia alla Galleria d'arte moderne di Roma con l'opera di Witkiewicz." *Corriere della Sera* 3–4 (1969).

Rangon, M. "Kantor, Cimaise." *Revue de l'art actuel* 3–4 (1959).

Reichardt, J. "Kantor." *Arts Review*, October 1, 1976.

———. "Kantor's Tragic Theatre." *Architectural Design* 11 (1976).

Resenzvaig, M. *El teatro de Tadeusz Kantor*. Buenos Aires: Leviatan, 1995.

Ricard, J. *Tadeusz Kantor, Emballages 1960–1976*. Nürnberg: Galerie Johanna Ricard, 1976.

Rich, F. "Stage: Kantor's 'Let the Artists Die.'" *New York Times*, October 15, 1985.

———. "Auteur Directors Bring New Life to Theatre." *New York Times*, November 24, 1985.

————. "Tadeusz Kantor's Intimations of God and Death." *New York Times*, June 16, 1988.

Rigotti, D. "Kantor, resta la memoria." *Avvenire*, April 26, 1988.

Rocca, G. "Ecco il mio teatro." *Paese Sera*, January 27, 1988.

Roeder, G. "Poetisches Trippeln uber Abgrunden." *NZ*, March 17, 1977.

Rose, C. *Tadeusz Kantor*. Maubeuge: Miroirs, 1991.

Rosenzvaig, M. *El teatro de Tadeusz Kantor*. Buenos Aires: Leviatan, 1995.

Rozanski, R. "Wielki mistrz teatru." *Słowo Polskie*, February 23, 1987.

Rumler, F. "Trip in die Katakomben der Angst." *Der Spiegel*, March 10, 1971.

Rutten, A. "Dodenklas: een beangstigende bezetenheid." *Trouw* 3 (1977).

Ruhle, G. "Die schweren Träume des Tadeusz Kantor." *Frankfurter Allgemeine Zeitung*, March 18, 1977.

Ryba, L., ed. *Oggetti e macchine del teatro di Tadeusz Kantor*. Palermo: Museo Internazionale delle Marionette, 1987.

Sagarra, J. "El minucioso trabajo de Kantor." *El País*, March 15, 1987.

————. "El constructor de emociones." *El País*, March 18, 1987.

Sandauer, A. "'Awangarda' i awangarda." *Kultura* 20 (1973).

Savioli, A. "Una gallinella troppo condita; Nello spettacolo del Cricot 2 di Tadeusz Kantor hanno spicco i valori visuali." *L'Unità*, March 4, 1969.

————. "Al Premio Roma il Cricot 2 di Cracovia con 'la pillola verde.'" *L'Unità*, March 11, 1974.

————. "Kantor e i suoi fantasmi." *L'Unità*, April 25, 1988.

Scarpetta, G. "Pour. . . ." *Art Press* 5 (1983).

————. "Portrait de l'artiste en revenant." *Tadeusz Kantor, Plus Loin, Rien*. Paris: Galerie de France, 1989.

————. "Tadeusz Kantor. Le retour de Maitre Kantor." *Globe* 37 (1989).

————. "Ce qu'ils appellant la liberté." *La Regle du jeu* 1 (May 1990).

————. *Kantor au présent*. Paris: Actes Sud, 2000.

Schorlemmer, U. *Tadeusz Kantor. Er War Sein Theater*. Nürnberg: Verlag für Moderne Kunst, 2005.

————, ed. *Sztuka jest przestępstwem: Tadeusz Kantor a Niemcy i Szwajcaria*. Kraków: Cricoteka 2007.

Schlagheck, I. "Grosse Ausstellung des polnischen Theatermanns und bildenden Kunstlers Tadeusz Kantor; Verpackung ist alles." *Nürnberger Zeitung*, November 25, 1976.

————. "Das irrationale als bestandteil der Wirklichkeit." *Nürnberger Zeitung*, November 27, 1976.

Schneider, H. "Zerstorung der Illusion." *Die Zeit*, March 25, 1977.

Schulze-Vellinghausen, A. "Witkiewicz und Kantor kommen an." *Theater Heute*, April 4, 1966.

Skiba-Lickel, A. *Aktor według Kantora*. Wrocław: Zakład Narodowy im. Ossolińskich, 1995.

Sculatti, M. "Lezioni di teatro firmate Kantor." *La Repubblica*, March 22, 1988.

Seelmann-Eggebert, U. "Witkacy: eine Entdeckung. Tadeusz Kantor inszenierte den *Schrank* in Baden-Baden." *Echo*, March 12, 1966.

————. "Theater des 'Katastrophismus.'" *Echo der Zeit*, April 3, 1966.

Sergi, S. "Avanguardia al 'Roma.'" *La Nazione*, March 11, 1974.

Shepherd, M. "Scottish International." *Sunday Telegraph*, August 20, 1972.

Sienkiewicz, M. "Świadomość sztuki: Rozmowa z Tadeuszem Kantorem." *Literatura* 48 (1974).

————. "Seans Tadeusza Kantora." *Przekrój*, December 14, 1975.

Silvestri, F. "Amore e morte nel mondo di Kantor." *Burattini* (December 1987).

Stachelhaus, H. "Auf der Suche nach dem Unmoglichen Spektakel." *NRZ am Sonntag* 47 (1974).

Stangret, L. *Tadeusz Kantor. Malarski ambalaż totalnego dzieła.* Kraków: Art + Edition, 2006.

Staniszewska, W. "Konstruktywizm w twórczości teatralnej Tadeusza Kantora." *Format* 1–4 (1994).

Stoll, D. "Oma schneidet Grimassen zur Toten-Sinfonie." *AZ*, March 17, 1977.

———. "Die Schone in Hasenstall." *Abendzeitung Nürnberg*, May 24, 1988.

Suchan, J., ed. *Tadeusz Kantor. Niemożliwe/ Impossible.* Kraków: Bunkier Sztuki, 2000.

Święcicki, K. *Małe ojczyzny Europy w teatrze Tadeusza Kantora.* Kraków: Cricoteka, 2002.

———. *Historia w teatrze Tadeusza Kantora.* Poznań: Wydawnictwo Poznańskie, 2007.

Szczawiński, J. "Tadeusz Kantor: epitafium dla epoki." *Słowo Powszechne*, March 11, 1976.

Szpakowska, M. "Tekst Witkiewicza a scenariusz Kantora." *Dialog* 8 (1973).

Szydłowski, R. "Tadeusza Kantora teatr życia i śmierci." *Fakty* 15 (1982).

Taborski, B. "'Umarła Klasa.' Tadeuszowi Kantorowi." *Scena* 5 (1977).

Taranienko, Z. "Teatr 'i': Rozmowa z Tadeuszem Kantorem." *Kultura* 30 (1973).

———. "Materia, czas, człowiek." *Sztuka* 4 (1976).

Tchorek, M., and G. M. Hyde. *Wielopole, Wielopole.* London: Marion Boyars, 1983. Reprint, 1990.

Teatr. Special issue, *Teatr* 7 (1990).

Teatr. Special issue, *Teatr* 10 (2006).

Teatralnaja Žizn. Special issue, *Teatralnaja Žizn* 9 (1993).

Tei, F. "Il palcoscenico della morte." *Corriere di Firenze*, May 22, 1987.

Temkine, R. "Un entretien avec . . . Du Théâtre clandestin au Théâtre Zéro." *Comédie-Française* 12 (1980).

Thibaudat, J.-P. "Kantor ne reviendra jamais à Wielopole." *Liberation* 2488 (1989).

Thieringen, T. "Ratsel ohne Erklarung." *Suddeutsche Zeitung*, March 17, 1977.

Tian, R. "Il Cricot 2 di Cracovia al 'Premio Roma.' In uno spettacolo polacco l'avanguardia deglianni 30. Una nuova versione dell'idea di 'teatro totale.'" *Il Messaggero*, March 4, 1969.

Theatre in Poland. "Kantor: Wielopole, Wielopole." Special issue, *Theatre in Poland* 1 (1996).

Theatre in Poland. Special issue, *Theatre in Poland* 1 (1981).

Théâtre/Public. Special issue, *Théâtre/Public* 166–67 (2003).

Tisdall, C. "Kantor at the Whitechapel." *Guardian*, September 29, 1976.

Tomassucci, G. "Cricotage, Ou sont les neiges d'antan di Tadeusz Kantor." *Rivista di literature moderne e comparate* 37, no. 3 (1984).

Torres, R. "Tadeusz Kantor. Una protesta permanente." *El Europeo* 10 (March 1989).

Torresin, B. "Crepino gli artisti." *La Repubblica*, January 21, 1988.

Toshimitsu, T. "A Conversation with Tadeusz Kantor." *Theatre* (June 1990; Japan).

Travail théâtral. Special issue, *Travail théâtral* (Winter 1972).

Trezzini, L. "La riconquista della vita con Cricot 2." *Sipario* 277 (1969).

Turowski, A. "Cricot 2." In *Jeden.* Warszawa: Galeria Foksal, 1972.

Ubersfeld, A. "Kantor a present." *Théâtre/ Public* 39 (1981).

Vaizey, M. "Kantor's Package Tour of Life." *Observer*, October 17, 1976.

Valoriani, V., ed. *Kantor a Firenze.*Florence: Biblioteca Spadoni & Titivillus Edizioni, 2002.

Vidal, J. C. "Conversacion con Tadeusz Kantor." *Los Cuadernos del Norte* May–June (1983).

Volkoff, A. "Shiraz Arts Festival: Kantor's Negative Theatre." *Teheran Journal*, August 21, 1974.

———. "Kantor is Arbitrary, Gimmicky." *Teheran Journal*, August 22, 1974.

———. "Neither Fish nor Fowl, but Lots of Surrealism." *Teheran Journal*, August 26, 1974.

von Drathen, D. "Die Metamprphosen eines Odysseus der Kunst." *Künstler* 3 (1999).

Wallach, A. "Personal Confessions of a Polish Director." *New York Newsday*, June 14, 1988.

Wardle, I. "*The Dead Class*: Collage of Art." *The Times*, August 30, 1976.

Weisenburger, H. "Tadeusz Kantor in Baden-Baden." *Badische Zeitung* 12, March 13, 1966.

———. *Three: Facts 1966–1972*. Warszawa: Galeria Foksal, 1973.

Wiegenstein, R. "Zug der Schatten." *Frankfurter Allegemeine Zeitung*, May 31, 1988.

Wiewiora, D. *Materie, kollektive Erinnerung und individuelle Existenz im Theater von Tadeusz Kantor (1938–1991)*. Kraków: Universitas, 1998.

Winer, L. "Travellers Amid the Debris of Trails and Joys of Life." *New York Newsday*, June 16, 1988.

Wirsing, S. "Kein Abschied." *Frankfurter Allegemeine Zeitung*, May 30, 1988.

Yomota, I. "To Leave and to Return. A Conversation with Tadeusz Kantor." *Bungakukai* (July 1990).

Zirndorf, ed. *Tadeusz Kantor: Theater des Todes*. Nürnberg: Institut für Moderne Kunst, 1983.

Żmudzka, E. "Kantor—realność najniższej rangi." *Teatr* 1 (1984).

Żurowski, A. "Pulling Faces at the Audience: The Lonely Theatre of Tadeusz Kantor." *New Theatre Quarterly* 4 (1985).

EXHIBITION CATALOGUES (IN CHRONOLOGICAL ORDER)

Tadeusz Kantor. Düsseldorf: Kunsthalle Grabbeplatz, 1959.

Kantor. Lausanne: Galerie Alice Pauli, 1964.

Tadeusz Kantor. Baden-Baden: Staatliche Kunsthalle, 1966.

Kantor, peintures récentes. Paris: Galerie de L'Université A.G., 1966.

Panoramiczny happening morski T. Kantor. Koszalin: Koszalińskie Towrzystwo Społeczno- Kulturalne, 1967.

Happening "List." Warszawa: Galeria Foksal, 1967.

Happening "Hommage à Maria Jarema." Kraków: Galeria Krzysztofory, 1968.

La Chaise. Stolen. Tadeusz Kantor. Oslo Henie-Onstad Kunstsenter, 1971.

Umbrella. Edinburgh: Richard Demarco Gallery, 1972.

Wszystko wisi na włosku. Tadeusz Kantor. Warszawa: Galeria Foksal, 1973.

t.kantor REZERWAT LUDZKI. Kraków: Galeria Desa, 1975.

Tadeusz Kantor. Ambalaże. Warszawa: Galeria Foksal, 1976.

Tadeusz Kantor. Emballages 1960–76. London: Whitechapel Art Gallery, 1976.

Rembrandt-Preis 1978 an Tadeusz Kantor. Kraków: Johan Wolfgang von Goethe-Stiftung, 1978.

Le opere di Tadeusz Kantor i pittori di Cricot 2. Milan: Palazzo Reale, 1979.

La Troupe Cricot 2 et son Avant-garde. Paris: Centre Georges Pompidou, 1983.

Oggetti e macchine del teatro di Tadeusz Kantor. Palermo: Museo Internazionale delle Marionette, 1987.

Tadeusz Kantor. Plus Loin, Rien! Paris: Galerie de France, 1989.

Tadeusz Kantor. Przedmioty, klisze pamięci. Wrocław: BWA, 1990.

Kantor, peintures, dessins. Orlean: Centre d'Arts Contemporains; Grande Galerie, Petite Galerie, 1990.

Tadeusz Kantor. Nimes: Musée d'Art Contemporain de Nîmes, 1991.

Tadeusz Kantor. Malarstwo i rzeźba. Kraków: Muzeum Narodowe 1992.

Grupa Krakówska 1932-1994. Warszawa: Zachęta, 1994.

Labirynt zwany Teatr/The Labyrinth Called Theatre. Kraków: BWA, 1994.

Tadeusz Kantor: My Creation, My Journey. Tokyo: Sezon Museum of Art, 1994.

Tadeusz Kantor. Rysunki z lat 1947–1990. łódź: Galeria 86, 1994.

Tadeusz Kantor: "Powrót Odysa" Podziemny Teatr Niezalezny/"The Return of Odysseus" The Clandestine Independant Theatre 1944. Kraków: Cricoteka, 1994.

Kantor. Fantomy Realności. Katowice: Centrum Scenografii Polskiej, 1995.

Tańczyli na moście wiek cały. Kraków: Arsenał, 1995.

Tadeusz Kantor. Klasa Szkolna—Dzieło Zamknięte. Kraków: Cricoteka, 1995.

Tadeusz Kantor 1915–1990: Leben im Werk. Nürnberg: Kunsthalle Nürnberg, 1996.

Tadeusz Kantor: La scena de la memoria. Madrid and Barcelona 1997.

Wystawa Sztuki Nowoczesnej. Pięćdziesiąt lat później. Kraków: Starmach Gallery, 1998.

Tadeusz Kantor Informel. Kraków: Starmach Gallery, 1999.

Kantor. Motywy hiszpańskie. Kraków: Muzeum Narodowe, 1999.

Tadeusz Kantor. Klisze pamięci. Copenhagen: Rundetaarn, 1999.

Nowocześni a socrealizm. Kraków: Starmach Gallery, 2000.

Verteidigung der Moderne Positionen der Polnischen Kunst nach 1945. Künzeslau: Museum Würth, 2000.

Mam wam coś do powiedzenia. Tadeusz Kantor—autoportrety. Kraków: Muzeum Narodowe, 2000.

Tadeusz Kantor. Dipinti, disegni, teatro. Firenze: Palazzo Pitti, 2002.

Tadeusz Kantor. La clase muerta. Murcia: Iglesia de Veronicas, 2002.

Balladyna według Kantora. Kraków: Cricoteka, 2002.

Tadeusz Kantor. Umení a pamet. Prague: Czech Museum of Fine Arts, 2003.

Gdzie są niegdysiejsze śniegi—Cricotage Tadeusza Kantora. 25 lat później. Kraków: Galeria Krzysztofory, 2003.

Tadeusz Kantor z Wielopola, Wielopola. Warszawa: Galeria Foksal, 2003.

Tadeusz Kantor. Kolekcja "A." Kraków: Cricoteka, 2003.

Fin des temps! L'histoire n'est plus—L'art polonais du 20e siècle. Tulon: Hôtel des Arts, 2004.

Święci rewolucji, Maria Jarema, Tadeusz Kantor. Poznań: Galeria Fizek, 2004.

Tadeusz Kantor. Njegovo gledalisce in slokarstvo. Ljubljana: Mestna galerija, 2004.

Interior imaginacji/Interior of Imagination. Warszawa: Zachęta, 2005.

Ośrodek Teatru Cricot 2—Cricoteka. Warszawa: Biblioteka Narodowa, 2005.

Pejzaż w twórczości mlarskiej i rysunkowej Tadeusza Kantora. Kraków: Cricoteka, 2005.

Teatr niemożliwy. Performatywność w sztuce Pawła Althamera, Tadeusza Kantora, Katarzyny Kozyry, Roberta Kuśmirowskiego i Artura Żmijewskiego/The Impossible Theatre. Performativity in the Works of Paweł Althamer, Tadeusz Kantor, Katarzyna Kozyra, Robert Kuśmirowski i Artur Żmijewski. Vienna: Kunsthalle, 2005;

London: Barbican Centre, 2006; Warszawa: Zachęta, 2006.

Kantor en Rhône-Alpes. Lyon, 2006.

Tadeusz Kantor. Między kościołem a synagogą. Kielce: Galeria Współczesnej Sztuki Sakralnej, 2007.

Tadeusz Kantor i WSSP w Krakówie 1947–1950, Kraków: Galeria Krzysztofory, 2007.

Wojtek Sperl. Fotografie z seansu Tadeusza Kantora, Umarła klasa" 1975-1976. Kraków: Cricoteka, 2007.

FILM AND VIDEOGRAPHY

INDVIDUAL PRODUCTIONS

Umarła klasa, dir. Andrzej Wajda, TVP, 1976, 75 min.

Umarła klasa, dir. Nat Lilenstein, La Sept, Paris, 1989, 92 min.

Wielopole, Wielopole, dir. Andrzej Sapija, W.F.O. łódź, 1984, 70 min.

Wielopole, Wielopole, dir. Andrzej Zajączkowski, OTV Kraków, 1983, 70 min.

Niech sczezną artyści, dir. Andrzej Zajączkowski, OTV Kraków, 1986, 77 min.

Niech sczezną artyści, dir. Nat Lilenstein, La Sept FR 3 Paris, 1987, 80 min.

Nigdy tu już nie powrócę, dir. Andrzej Sapija, TVP S.A. 1990, 81 min.

Dziś są moje urodziny, dir. Andrzej Zajączkowski, OTV Kraków, 1991, 77 min.

Aujourd'hui c'est mon annivesaire. La dernière répétition du spectacle de T. Kantor, dir. Jacquie Bablet, J. Sirot, CNRS Audiovisuel, Paris 1991, 75 min.

CRICOTAGE

Gdzie są niegdysiejsze śniegi, dir. Andrzej Sapija, W.F.O. łódź, 1984, 33 min.

Gdzie są niegdysiejsze śniegi, dir. Tadeusz Kraśko, TVP 1984, 40 min.

Un matrimonio, Centro di formazione professionale per le techniche cinetelevisive, Milan, 1986, 60 min.

La macchina dell'amore e della morte, CRT Milano, Teatro Litta 1987, 42 min.

Une dernière courte leçon, dir. Jacquie Bablet, Institut International de la Marionette de Charleville-Mézières, CNRS Audiovisuel, Paris, 1988, 40 min.

Ô douce nuit, dir. L. Champonnois, Institut Supérieur des Techniques du Spectacle et Equipage, Avignon, 1990, 40 min.

DOCUMENTARIES

By Krzysztof Miklaszewski

Szatnia Tadeusza Kantora czyli Nadobnisie i koczkodany w Teatrze Cricot 2, OTV Kraków, 1973, 33 min.

Ostatnia wieczerza, OTV Kraków, 1983, 16 min.

Powrót do Wielopola, OTV Kraków, 1983, 25 min.

Moja historia sztuki—Według Malczewskiego, OTV Kraków, [1984–86], 25 min.

Moja historia sztuki—Lekcja Wojtkiewicza, OTV Kraków, [1984–86], 34 min.

Ja mistrz, 1985.

Niech sczezną artyści, Interpress, Warszawa, 1985, 43 min.

O powinnościach artysty, OTV Kraków, 1985, 35 min.

By Andrzej Sapija

Manekiny Tadeusza Kantora, W.F.O. łódź, 1983, 23 min.

Kantor, TVP S.A., W.F.O. łódź, 1985, 75 min.

Powrót OdysaTadeusza Kantora. Notatki z prób, TVP S.A., W.F.O. łódź, 1988, 60 min.

OTHER FILM WORKS

Somnambulicy, dir. Mieczysław Waśkowski, Antoni Nużyński, Państwowa Wyższa Szkoła Filmowa w łodzi 1957, 9 min.

Multipart, dir. Krzysztof Kubicki, M. Młodecki, Warszawa, 1971.

Istnieje tylko to co się widzi, dir. Andrzej Sapija, Camerovid, 1991, 22 min.

Próby, tylko próby . . ., dir. A. Sapija, Cricoteka, Kraków, 1992, 74 min.

Marek Rostworowski. Lekcje z Kantorem, dir. Małgorzata Skiba, Kraków, 1997, 23 min.

Wit Stwosz to ja—Tadeusz Kantor, dir. Andrzej Białko, Kraków, 1996, 40 min.

Tadeusz Kantor, dir. Andrzej Sapija, Cricoteka, Kraków, 1999, 16 min.

FOREIGN FILMS (BY COUNTRY)

ENGLAND

Kantor, dir. D. Ward, G. Cardazzo, Filmakers, London, 1987, 35 min.

FRANCE

Tadeusz Kantor, Peintre, dir. Denis Bablet CNRS Audiovisuel, Paris, 1984, 100 min.

Le théâtre de Tadeusz Kantor, dir. Denis Bablet, CNRS Audiovisuel, Paris, 1985, 144 min.

Geneza Umarłej klasy, dir. Nat Lilenstein. La Sept FR 3, Paris, 1989, 15 min.

Les Classes d'Avignon—Tadeusz Kantor, dir. L. Champonnois, Institut Supérieur des Techniques du Spectacle et Equipage, Awignon, 1990, 59 min.

GERMANY

Kantor ist da. Der Künstler und seine Welt. dir. Dietrich Mahlow, Saarlandischer Rundfunk, 1969, 60 min.

Sacke, Schrank und Schirm, dir. D. Mahlow, Saarlandischer Rundfunk, 1972, 85 min.

Kantor, dir. Engelbrecht, Nuremberg, 1977, 45 min.

Die familie aus Wielopole, dir. Michael Kluth, Westdeutscher Rundfunk, 1980, 45 min.

Tadeusz Kantor, dir. M. Lange, NDR, 1990 45 min.

Das Theater des Todes. Tadeusz Kantor—Künstler, Katzer, Provokateur der Welt, dir. Michael Kluth, MDR RFN 1997, 58 min.

SWITZERLAND

Hommage à Tadeusz Kantor, TV Suisse Romande, Geneva, 1991, 44 min.

ITALY

Kantor racconta Kantor, dir. M. Bosio, Nico Garrone, Rome, 1980, 50 min.

Candid Kantor, dir. Giancarlo Soldi, CRT Milan, 1985, 42 min.

La macchina dell'amore e della morte di Tadeusz Kantor, dir. Ariel Genovese, Milan, 1987, 35 min.

Writings by Tadeusz Kantor

1946

"Grupa Młodych Plastyków po raz drugi [Young Visual Artists Once Again]." *Twórczość* 9.

"Sugestie plastyki scenicznej [Some Suggestions on a Visual Aspect of Stage Design]." *Przegląd Artystyczny* 1.

1948

"Po prostu sztuka [Simply Art]." *Życie Literackie* 22.

1950

"Abstrakcja umarła—niech żyje abstrakcja [Abstraction is Dead—Long Live Abstraction]." *Życie Literackie* 50.

1955

"O aktualnym malarstwie francuskim [Contemporary French Visual Art]." *Życie Literackie* 47.

"Teatr artystyczny [Art Theatre]." *Życie Literackie* 173.

1956

"Cricot 2." *Życie Literackie* 27.

1957

"Tadeusz Kantor odpowiada na 8 pytań [Tadeusz Kantor Answers 8 Questions]." *Przegląd Kulturalny* 18.

1961

Ob die Rückkehr von Orpheus möglich ist? [Is the Return of Orpheus Possible?].

Hamburg: Staatliche Hochschule für Bildende Kunste.

1963

Teatr autonomiczny [The Autonomous Theatre]. Kraków: Galeria Krzysztofory.

"Teatr Niezależny w latach 1942–1945 [The Independent Theatre, 1942–1945]." *Pamiętnik Teatralny* 1–4.

1965

"*Ambalaże—manifest* [Emballages Manifesto]." *ITD* 23.

1966

Komplexes Theater [Complex Theatre]. Baden-Baden: Theater der Stadt Baden-Baden und Staatliche Kunsthalle.

1967

List [A Letter]. Warszawa: Galeria Foksal.

"Refleksje o muzeum nowoczesnym [Some Thoughts About a Structure of a Modern Museum]." *Współczesność* 3.

Teatr Happening. Teatr wydarzeń [The Theatre-Happening. The Theatre of Events]. Kraków: Galeria Krzysztofory.

1968

"La Lettre: Partition de happening [A Letter: The Text of the Happening]."

"Emballage Manifeste [Emballage Manifesto]." *Opus International* 2.

1969

À propos de La Poule d'eau [Concerning *The Water-Hen*]. Kraków: Galeria Krzysztofory.

La nascita del teatro Cricot 2 [The Birth of the Cricot 2 Theatre]. Kraków: Galeria Krzysztofory. (Published in French, 1971; Polish, 1982).

Le premier emballage [The First Emballage]. Kraków: Galeria Krzysztofory. (Published in Polish, 1976.)

Teatro Informel [The Informel Theatre]. Kraków: Galeria Krzysztofory. (Published in French, 1971; Polish, 1982.)

Le Théâtre Zero [The Zero Theatre]. Kraków: Galeria Krzysztofory. (Published in Italian, 1969; Polish, 1982.)

"Le Théâtre Zero [The Zero Theatre]"; "Emballages Manifeste [The Emballage Manifesto]"; "Le premier emballage [The First Emballage]"; "Lettre; partition-happening [A Letter: The Text of the Happening]"; "À propos de *La Poule d'eau* [Concerning *The Water-Hen*]"; "Leçon de l'anatomie d'après Rembrandt: partition-happening [Anatomy Lesson According to Rembrandt: The Text of the Happening]." *Grammatica* 3.

1970

Manifesto 1970. Warszawa: Galeria Foksal. (Published in Polish, 1971.)

Multipart. Warszawa: Galeria Foksal.

1971

La condition d'acteur [The Situation of an Artist]. Kraków: Galeria Krzysztofory.

Méthode de l'art d'être acteur [The Acting Method]. Kraków: Galeria Krzysztofory.

Préexistence scénique [Scenic Preexistence]. Kraków: Galeria Krzysztofory.

"Préface du programme de *La Poule d'eau* [An Introduction to *The Water-Hen*]"; "Préexistence scénique [Scenic Preexistence]"; "Methode de l'art d'être acteur [The Acting Method]"; "La condition d'acteur [The Situation of an Artist]."

Théâtre Cricot 2, Textes de Tadeusz Kantor. Nancy: The World Theatre Festival.

1972

"*Les Cordonniers* de Witkiewicz [*The Shoemakers* by Witkiewicz]." *Les Lettres Françaises* 11.

"Happeningi [Happenings]." *Dialog* 9.

"Naissance du Cricot 2 [The Birth of Cricot 2]"; "Théâtre Informel [The Informel Theatre]"; "Manifeste du Théâtre Zéro [The Zero Theatre Manifesto]"; "La condition d'acteur [The Situation of an Artist]." *Travail Théâtral* 6.

"Le Théâtre Impossible [The Impossible Theatre]." *Les Lettres Françaises* 12.

1973

"*Kurka wodna* [The Water-Hen]." *Dialog* 8.

Wszystko wisi na włosku [Everything is Hanging by a Thread]. Warszawa: Galeria Foksal.

1974

Les acteurs ne représentant qu'eux-memes [Actors Only Represent Themselves]. Kraków: Galeria Krzysztofory.

Anti-exhibition. Kraków: Galeria Krzysztofory. (Published in Polish in 1975).

L'art informel—Théâtre Informel [Informel Art—the Informel Theatre]. Kraków: Galeria Krzysztofory.

Cambriolage. Kraków: Galeria Krzysztofory.

Controverse entre la realite et le concept de la représentation [The Controversy about Reality and the Concept of Representation]. Kraków: Galeria Krzysztofory. (Published in German, 1974.)

Du Happening et l'Impossible [Of the Happening and the Impossible]. Kraków: Galeria Krzysztofory.

Forty Mandelbaums. Kraków: Galeria Krzysztofory. (Published in German, 1974.)

Kleiderablage [Cloakroom]. Warszawa: Galeria Foksal.

Manipulation de la realité: Happening
[Manipulation of Reality: Happening].
Kraków: Galeria Krzysztofory.

Teatr Niemożliwy [The Impossible Theatre].
Gniezno: Galeria B.

Vom Happening zum Unmöglichen
[From the Happening to the Impossible].
Warszawa: Galeria Foksal.

1975

Rezerwat ludzki [Human Reservation].
Kraków: Galeria Desa.

Teatr śmierci [The Theatre of Death].
Warszawa: Galeria Foksal. (Published in
French, 1976; in English, 1977.)

*Theoretical Essays and Program Notes
to "The Dead Class."* Kraków: Galeria
Krzysztofory. (Published in French, German,
Italian, Polish, and Spanish.)

1976

Ambalaże [Emballages]. Warszawa: Galeria
Foksal.

1977

"Klasa szkolna. Postacie Umarłej klasy [A
Classroom. Dramatic Personae of *The Dead
Class*]." *Dialog* 2.

Le Théâtre de la Mort [The Theatre of
Death]. Lausanne: L'Age d'homme.

1978

Cricotage. Kraków: Galeria Krzysztofory.

1979

Il teatro della morte [The Theatre of Death].
Milano: Ubulibri.

1980

*Theoretical Essays and Program Notes to
"Wielopole, Wielopole."* Kraków: Cricoteka.
(Published in French, German, Italian,
Polish, and Spanish.)

1981

La classe morta di Tadeusz Kantor [*The
Dead Class* of Tadeusz Kantor]. Milano:
Feltrinelli Economica.

Wielopole, Wielopole. Milano: Ubulibri.

1982

Métamorphoses [Metamorphoses]. Paris:
Edition du Chêne/Hachette-Galerie de
France.

1983

Tadeusz Kantor: The Theatre of Death.
Tokyo: Parco Picture Books.

*Tadeusz Kantor: Theater des Todes. Die
Tote Klasse. Wielopole, Wielopole* [Tadeusz
Kantor: *The Theatre of Death. The Dead
Class. Wielopole, Wielopole*]. Zirndorf:
Verlag für moderne Kunst.

Tadeusz Kantor. Paris: Editions du CNRS.

1984

El teatro de la muerte [The Theatre of
Death]. Buenos Aires: Ediciones de la Flor.

Wielopole, Wielopole. Kraków-Wrocław:
Wydawnictwo Literackie.

1985

*Theoretical Essays and Program Notes to
"Let the Artists Die."* Kraków: Cricoteka.
(Published in Italian, German, French,
Polish, and Spanish.)

1986

"The Autonomous Theatre"; "The Informel
Theatre"; "The Zero Theatre"; "Theatre
Happening"; "The Theatre of Death";
"The Work of Art and the Process"; "The
Situation of an Artist"; "New Theatrical
Space. Where Fiction Appears"; "The
Infamous Transition from the World of the
Dead into the World of the Living. Fiction
and Reality"; "Room: Maybe a New Phase";
"Prison"; "Reflection." *The Drama Review*
T111.

1988

"Che cos'è la poesia e la pittura? [What are
Poetry and Painting?]." *Poesia* 2.

Lezioni milanesi [The Milano Lessons].
Milano: Ubulibri.

Tadeusz Kantor. Ein Reisender—seine Texte und Manifeste [Tadeusz Kantor. A Traveler—His Texts and Manifestos]. Nürnberg: Institut für moderne Kunst.

Theoretical Essays and Program Notes to "I Shall Never Return." Milano: Cappelletti and Riscassi, s.r.l. (Also published in Italian, German, French, Polish, and Spanish).

1989

List do Marii Jaremy [A Letter to Maria Jarema]. Kraków: Galeria Krzysztofory.

"Moje spotkania ze śmiercią [My Meetings with Death]." *Życie Literackie* 10.

1990

"Café Europe." Spichi dell'Est: Galleria D'Arte.

Leçons de Milan [The Milano Lessons]. Paris: Actes Sud.

Let the Artists Die. Tokyo: Sakuhinsha.

O Douce Nuit [Silent Night]. Paris: Actes Sud-Papiers.

"Od początku w moim credo . . . [From the Beginning in my Credo was . . .]." *Teatr* 7.

"Sąd idzie [The Day of Judgement is Coming]." *Teatr* 4.

Wielopole/Wielopole. London: Marion Boyars.

1991

Het Circus van de Dood [The Circus of the Dead], a collection of Tadeusz Kantor's writings edited by Johan de Boose. Amsterdam: International Theatre & Film Books.

Lekcje mediolańskie [The Milano Lessons]. Kraków: Cricoteka & Biuro Kongresowe Urzędu Miasta Krakowa.

"Memory." *Soviet and East European Performance* 11.

Ma création, Mon voyage. Commentaires intimes [My Work. My Journey. My Intimate Commentaries]. Paris: Editions Plume.

La mia opera. Il mio viaggio. Commento intimo [My Work. My Journey. My Intimate Commentaries]. Milano: Federico Motta Editore.

"The Milano Lessons: Lesson 12, "Before the End of the XXth Century." *The Drama Review* T132.

"The Real 'I'"; "To Save from Oblivion." *Performing Arts Journal* 38.

Theoretical Essays and Program Notes to "Today Is My Birthday." Milano: Cappelletti and Riscassi, s.r.l. (Published in Italian, German, French, and Polish.)

"To wszystko jest prawda" [All this is True]!" *Teatr* 9.

1992

"My Room"; "A Painting." *Theatre Journal* 44.

1993

A Journey through Other Spaces: Essays and Manifestos, 1944—1990. Berkeley: University of California Press.

1994

"Texts, Essays, and Intimate Commentaries." *Performing Arts Journal* 47 (May).

2000

Metamorfozy, Teksty o latach 1938-1974 [Metamorphoses. Texts: 1938-1974]. Kraków: Cricoteka & Księgarnia akademicka.

2003

La classe morta de Tadeusz Kantor [The Dead Class of Tadeusz Kantor]. Milano: Libri Scheiwiller.

2005

Metamorfozy, Teksty o latach 1938-1974 [Metamorphoses. Texts: 1938-1974]; *Teatr* śmierci. Teksty z lat 1975-1984 [Theatre of Death. Text: 1975-1984]; *Dalej już nic.* Teksty z lat 1985-1990 [Further on, Nothing. Texts: 1985-1990]. Wrocław: Zakład Narodowy im. Ossolińskich; Kraków: Cricoteka.

Michal Kobialka is Professor of Theatre in the Department of Theatre Arts and Dance at University of Minnesota. His published works include *Medieval Practices of Space and Of Borders* and *Thresholds: Theatre History, Practice and Theory*, both published by University of Minnesota Press, and a book-length study of Kantor's work, *A Journey through Other Spaces: Essays and Manifestos: 1944–1990* (University of California Press, 1993).